AF608040

Reading William Gilmore Simms

William Gilmore Simms Initiatives: Texts and Studies Series
David Moltke-Hansen and Todd Hagstette, Series Editors

Reading William Gilmore Simms

Essays of Introduction to the Author's Canon

Edited by Todd Hagstette

THE UNIVERSITY OF SOUTH CAROLINA PRESS

Published by the University of South Carolina Press
Columbia, South Carolina 29208

www.sc.edu/uscpress

Manufactured in the United States of America

26 25 24 23 22 21 20 19
10 9 8 7 6 5 4 3 2

Library of Congress Cataloging-in-Publication Data can be found at http://catalog.loc.gov/.

ISBN: 978-1-61117-772-5 (cloth)
ISBN: 978-1-61117-773-2 (ebook)

Publication of this book is made possible in part by the generous support of the Watson-Brown Foundation, together with the Caroline McKissick Dial Publication Fund of the South Caroliniana Library and the University Libraries of the University of South Carolina.

Contents

Preface

William Gilmore Simms deserves his reputation as perhaps the best known and certainly the most accomplished writer of the mid-nineteenth-century South. Born in Charleston in 1806, he lived all of his life in South Carolina; he was no mere provincial, though. With lifelong connections in the publishing industries of New York and Philadelphia, multiple travels into the American western frontier, and encyclopedic knowledge of the nation's history, Simms earned the status of a literary citizen of the country as a whole, as well as of his region. His literary ascent began early, with his first book publication appearing when he was nineteen years old and his reputation as a literary genius secured before he turned thirty. Over a career that spanned nearly forty-five years, he established himself as the American South's premier man of letters—an accomplished poet, novelist, short fiction writer, essayist, historian, dramatist, cultural journalist, biographer, and editor. None was more prolific than he. Sadly, as the political separation of the country intensified in the course of the nineteenth century, Simms was forced more regularly to choose his allegiance, to America or to the South. The two were not as compatible as once imagined, and Simms the southerner won out. At the end of his life with his career and status tied securely to his region, Simms found himself on the losing side. When he died on a summer day in 1870, his literary reputation was already beginning its long decline.

Flash forward to a summer day in 2011 in the offices of the *Simms Initiatives*, the massive digital humanities project sponsored jointly by the Watson-Brown Foundation and the University of South Carolina Libraries and designed to promote and disseminate Simms's legacy and work. I sat in our office that afternoon listening to two prominent Simms scholars, David Moltke-Hansen and Jim Kibler, banter about the author's views on progress. At the risk of over-simplifying their positions, the former tended to see Simms as cautiously optimistic about society's ongoing development into newer forms of itself, whereas the latter saw the author as a traditionalist suspicious of progress. Moltke-Hansen at the time was the director of the *Simms Initiatives*, a post he would soon bequeath to me, and Kibler was the Simms Visiting Research Professor at the South Caroliniana Library that summer. The debate they were having was an old one—I had heard versions of it periodically throughout Kibler's residence at the library—one of the reasons for which was that both scholars were able to cite a vast amount of support from Simms's extensive published works. Seeking a temporary truce by taking a moment to marvel at the complexity of thought available in Simms's work, Kibler remarked that, really, before one could write on Simms with confidence, one had to read everything the author had written. Immediately, all three of us laughed.

It was not exactly that Kibler was trying to make a joke; he was at least half serious in his declaration. Rather, it was that the mere suggestion that any one person could (much less, would) ever read *everything* Simms wrote was somewhat preposterous. The collection is just too big. Even the most learned nineteenth-century and southern cultural scholars, even those who have read dozens of Simms works, have only scratched the surface of Simms's canon. Two of the most well-read Simms scholars on the planet were the ones having that summer argument, and even they cackled at the suggestion of reading all of his work.

To offer some context, the *Simms Initiatives* digital collection of the author's works, which features more or less all of his book publications, his scrapbooks, and some secondary material, contains nearly 45,000 pages by Simms. That would be an astounding number on its own, but even it does not represent the full collection of Simms's writing. The number, after all, only accounts for his book publishing and a portion of his manuscripts. Because of his lifelong involvement in the periodical industry of the nation, Simms is reckoned to have produced an amount of uncollected work in the pages of journals and newspapers at least equal to his book publishing throughout his life. In fact, Moltke-Hansen and Kibler agree that Simms wrote on average one poem and one review per week for every week of his working life, a span of over forty years. Add the fugitive periodical material to the books, throw in the unpublished manuscripts, and the page count becomes staggering. No wonder readers can find a sufficient array of perspectives in those pages to sustain a debate all summer long.

That volume of writing is impressive, certainly, but it also marks one of the single largest barriers to the study of William Gilmore Simms. To even dabble in his ideology is a rather significant commitment. Complicating things is the popular and critical disregard that Simms has suffered for most of his posthumous existence. An unfortunate fate for the man Edgar Allan Poe famously declared to be the nation's finest writer. The ebbing of Simms's reputation has received various explanations. Some argue it results from progressive William Peterfield Trent's largely dismissive 1892 biography of the author; others that it stems from the changing tastes of the American reading public which no longer cotton to verbose and ornate Romantic writing; some claim the identity-based jettisoning of white male authors in the wake of the canon revisions of the modern academy accounts for Simms's decline; others suggest it has been primarily due to a lingering distaste for the proslavery and pro-confederate values Simms held and that became wildly outdated in the postbellum world. These contentions all contain some truth, but even in aggregate they do not justify Simms's erasure.

Happily, the tide has turned. Scholars view Trent with some suspicion, critics have recognized that Simms's style is more nuanced and complex than simple genre assignation suggests, and whatever the political zeitgeist, then or now, students of southern and American culture now recognize the significance of the author in the larger arc of that history. Yet the problem of access persists. The breadth of Simms's output, coupled with his late obscurity, still make him a difficult author to approach in scholarship, in the classroom, and in casual reading. Helping to overcome this difficulty is the purpose of the present collection. Seeking simultaneously to respond to and drive forward Simms's recent change in reputational fortune, this volume provides an easy access point into the author's sizable canon.

This book is an outgrowth of the publishing arm of the *Simms Initiatives*. Early in the development of that digital project, as we contemplated the resource we would be providing, the decision to scan all of our Simms materials to print-quality standards seemed to permit the most future uses as an augment to the online collection. But, why wait for the future? Why not offer new textual issues of these books as well as digital surrogates? After all, few Simms works were then in print, nor had they been for most of the previous century. Thanks to a partnership with the University of South Carolina Press and the rise of inexpensive print-on-demand publishing technology, we ultimately developed a fifty-eight-volume print collection of the selected works of the author. Most of these were stand-alone texts, while many of the shorter works were combined into omnibus volumes. These books were produced to be affordable enough for student use, thereby potentially opening up Simms to a greater classroom presence. In the end, through this selected edition, more of Simms's work became simultaneously available in print than at any time in the past, including in the author's own lifetime.

As most of the versions included in the print edition were appearing in that form for the first time in a long time—some had not been available since their first printing—a scholarly presence within them seemed needed. The goal of this series was not just to reprint the majority of Simms's books, but to reignite interest in them. So, we contracted with a number of Simms, nineteenth-century American, and southern cultural scholars to produce new critical introductions for each book in the series. These would function as guide texts to readers. They would summarize the known research on each work or collection of works and introduce readers to the larger contexts of the texts included. While useful as a resource for serious scholars, these introductions were designed to speak to the neophyte. At some level, all readers of Simms find themselves in this position, given how many texts have not received significant critical attention. Indeed, in the case of some of the lesser-known works, these introductions marked the first serious scholarship ever produced.

What does this have to do with the present volume? Well, this fifty-eight-volume collection of selected works offers a number of positive steps forward in Simms studies: access to the majority of the author's published works, classroom editions of his books for teaching and traditional reading, and an academic contextualization of individual works or series by knowledgeable scholars. But, this multi-volume collection only incrementally alleviates the enduring barrier represented by the magnitude of Simms's corpus. An individual volume in the collection provides adequate entry into a text, but a reader has to come to the work somehow—either because of prior knowledge or from a willingness to consume something new. The former of those reasons does little to open the Simms canon beyond its current known commodities, and the latter is unlikely due to lack of institutional awareness of the author. How do we expose, in full, the scope of Simms's work?

Enter the present book. Consisting of new introductory essays commissioned for many of the fifty-eight volumes in the selected works collection, it provides current information and judgments about most of Simms's major works (other volumes included are posthumous publications, such as the collected letters; these do not feature new introductions and thus are not represented here). The thirty-eight essays in this collection, together with the biographical overview of Simms following this preface, are the work of twenty-four individual scholars, a number of whom have contributed multiple pieces or treated multiple works in single essays. Covering nearly Simms's entire separately published *oeuvre*, the critical introductions are an offering exclusively of the publishing aims of the *Simms Initiatives*; these essays are not part of the online collection of resources. They, and the biographical overview, represent the most up-to-date and comprehensive considerations of Simms's literary production and world. Building on the capstone 1992 literary biography of Simms by John Caldwell Guilds, this book stands as the only single-volume collection of scholarship whose primary function is to provide compendious critical access to Simms texts of all kinds, popular and well-known as well as obscure and largely unstudied. One has here a guide and a primary point of entry into the expansive landscape of Simms's imagination and thought and their study. As such, this book should serve as a springboard to increased notice and broadened consideration of the antebellum South's most prolific writer.

Though not necessarily intended to be read cover-to-cover, when this book is considered in full, many of the hidden or forgotten potentials in Simms's work come into focus. There is great diversity of thought in his writing, of course, and yet great consistencies also emerge. Written by two dozen different scholars of various backgrounds and experience levels, these essays nonetheless reveal a portrait of Simms's thought that moves in identifiable trends and coherent patterns. In considering Simms's frontier writing, John Miller, David Moltke-Hansen, Jillian Weber, and I all find common themes at play, so that his border fiction offers a distinct vision of America's westward expansion that the author maintained over the span of more than half a dozen books. Conversely, the full complexity of Simms's views on the Revolutionary period in American history come to light in the evaluations of Sean Busick, Jim Kibler, Jason Johnson, Moltke-Hansen, Jeff Rogers, and Steve Smith, considering another dozen titles. Joining the influences of fiction, history, biography, and epistolary editing, Simms developed a multifaceted understanding of the nation's founding.

Familiar outposts of Simms's literary expression are given more substantial attention here than one typically has found. Ehren Foley, Nick Meriwether, Alex Moore, and Carey Roberts join Busick and Rogers in discussing the at-times overlooked importance of Simms as an historian, journalist, and political writer. Longtime advocates of Simms's poetry Matt Brennan and Johnson offer an enthusiastic exploration of the full scope of the author's work in this genre; complementing and complicating this picture is Cole Hutchison's historically based analysis of Simms's poetic proclivities in late life. Simms's efforts to grapple with America's colonial past are evaluated here by Kevin Collins, Meriwether, Mike Odom, and Moltke-Hansen. These essays find in this portion of Simms's corpus a full gamut of literary expression, from the steadfastly successful to the ambitiously failed to the newly classic, the heavily experimental to the surprisingly modern. Sam Lackey, John McCardell, Brian Fennessy, Matt Simmons, and I all urge recognition of Simms as one of our country's founding and foremost gothicists. Agreeing with Edgar Allan Poe's assessment of Simms's strengths, all of us see these shorter works in the Gothic mode as forsaken glories in the literary history of the nineteenth century.

In the course of these essays, many scholars have also turned their critical eye to works that have received almost no scholarly attention before, even in Simms's lifetime. Simmons takes an in-depth look at the frustrating inconsistency of the author's Spanish romances, ultimately challenging the notion from the biographers that these works were a complete waste of Simms's literary talent. Both Nan Morrison and Abigail Smith bring to light the author's lifelong, though largely unrealized, fascination with the dramatic arts. As an unsuccessful dramatist himself, and as a sophisticated appreciator and naively enthusiastic compiler, Simms had a tormented relationship with the stage that makes for a fascinating study. Finally, David Shields presents Simms's varied efforts at composing in the epigrammatic and idiomatic forms within the larger framework of laconics in American literary history.

To be sure, not every work in the Simms *oeuvre* is a hidden gem, but lost diamonds are to be found here. When considering an author whose total output is as large as that of Simms, it is unsurprising that some titles might come up short of masterpiece standards; equally surprising, though, would be if all of them did. In fact, one recurring claim that unifies nearly all the essays in this collection is that Simms is deserving of more readership and greater scholarly attention. His finest works were, of course, instrumental in defining the tropes and trends of southern and nineteenth-century American letters; they are thus deserving of sustained academic attention. But even his failed efforts should be reexamined.

According to nearly every contributor in this volume, something noteworthy can be found in each of Simms's works. This collection offers the opportunity for readers to find out for themselves. I hope it is a chance some will take.

At one point in time, the major obstacle to approaching Simms was finding his work in print; then it was navigating the uncharted immensity of his collection to discover relevant texts; now the only impediment is the reader's willingness to experience the range of that work. This book is your roadmap and your field-guide. As the contributors inside repeatedly suggest, there is beautiful and sometimes foreign territory to be found in the far-flung worlds of William Gilmore Simms's fecund imagination. It can be a trip well worth taking. It might still be laughable to imagine reading *every* book, but thanks to the essays included here, readers can now at least be knowledgeable about Simms as if they had.

Acknowledgments

This book has been a massive undertaking and represents the culmination of years of development. As such, the debts have really piled up. I'm not sure I can repay them, but I at least want to offer a word of gratitude and recognition. First, my sincerest thanks to David Moltke-Hansen. From the time we worked together on the *Simms Initiatives* until the present, my academic development and career have been fundamentally changed. The present volume is the most recent outgrowth of David's influence. My thanks to him not only for first suggesting this project to me and for being a constant advocate, but also for the generosity he always shows with his time and knowledge. Sharing the top spot is Tad Brown and the Watson-Brown Foundation. Without their generous support—financial and moral—this project would not have come to be. I will be forever grateful for the opportunities their largesse has provided me personally and the academic world in general. Also part of this illustrious group is Tom McNally, dean of libraries at the University of South Carolina, whose vision and academic ambition helped lead to the funding and housing of the *Simms Initiatives*, which ultimately enabled the current collection.

The two dozen scholars whose work appears in this collection also deserve thanks. Some were asked to distill their vast knowledge of a text to a short, digestible introductory piece; others were asked to forge brand new work on an utterly unfamiliar text and have it make sense. All rose to the challenge. The folks at the University of South Carolina Press have worked steadily on the series that enabled this collection over the years; I want to thank Jonathan Haupt, Linda Fogle, Pat Callahan, Ashley Mathias, Suzanne Axland, Bill Adams, and especially Alex Moore. My effusive gratitude too to the members of the *Simms Initiatives*, who helped establish the texts in the selected edition, proof contributions, and generally "guy Friday" many aspects of this project. They include Jessica Hemphill, Bella Wenum, Kate Boyd, Ashley Knox, Jillian Weber, Sam Lackey, Mike Odom, Matt Simmons, and Ehren Foley.

Institutional support for this project came from various departments at the Universiy of South Carolina, including the excellent folks at the Institute for Southern Studies, the staff of the Thomas Cooper Library, and my former colleagues at the South Caroliniana Library. For more than 20 years the Simms Society has worked tirelessly to promote the work evaluated in this collection. We all owe them for their efforts; without the groundwork they laid, this volume would never have been envisioned, much less produced.

Finally, I want to thank my family, my wife, Elise, and my son, Davis. True, they didn't really *do* anything per se. And, in fact, they were more likely to distract me from, rather than contribute to, this project. But, those distractions had their own value. Plus, they stood silently, but steadfastly, by me as I all but killed my prospects for future employment by returning to school to pursue a PhD . . . in English . . . in southern literature . . . in the nineteenth century. I applaud their faith and generosity, even as I question their wisdom.

William Gilmore Simms

A Biographical Overview

DAVID MOLTKE-HANSEN

Harper's Weekly put it succinctly in its 2 July 1870, issue: "In the death of Mr. Simms, on the 11th of June, at Charleston, the country has lost one more of its time-honored band of authors, and the South the most consistent and devoted of her literary sons" (qtd. in Butterworth and Kibler 125–26). Indeed no mid-nineteenth-century writer and editor did more than William Gilmore Simms to frame white southern self-identity and nationalism, shape southern historical consciousness, or foster the South's participation and recognition in the broader American literary culture. No southern writer enjoyed more contemporary esteem and attention, at least after Edgar Allan Poe moved north. Among American romancers (or writers of prose epics), only New Yorker James Fenimore Cooper was as successful by the 1840s. In those same years, Simms became the South's most influential editor of cultural journals. He also became the region's most prolific cultural journalist and poet, publishing an average of one book review and one poem per week for forty-five years.

Before his death Simms saw his national reputation fall along with the Confederacy he had vigorously supported and with the slave regime that many in the North had come to despise. Nevertheless reprints of most of the twenty titles in the selected edition of his works, first published between 1853 and 1860, appeared up until World War I. Thereafter only *The Yemassee*, an early romance about an Indian war in colonial South Carolina, continued in print. The tide began to turn in the 1950s, when five volumes of Simms's letters appeared and a growing number of his works came out in new editions. Publication in 1992 of the first literary biography, by John C. Guilds, and establishment of the William Gilmore Simms Society and *The Simms Review* the next year at once reflected and fostered this revived interest. Yet not until the 2010 launch of the digital Simms edition of the South Caroliniana Library of the University of South Carolina did scholars of southern, American, and nineteenth-century culture begin to have digital access to all of Simms's separately published works. Through the University of South Carolina Press, readers may also now obtain more of Simms's works in book format than the author ever saw in print at one time.

Clearly the decline in the critical standing of, and historical attention to, Simms and his oeuvre in the century after his death has reversed in the years since. The last three decades of the twentieth century saw more published on Simms than the previous hundred years (Butterworth and Kibler 126–200; *MLA International*). The last decade of the twentieth and first decade of the twenty-first centuries saw more dissertations and theses on him (41) than had appeared in all the years before. This is not to say that Simms is yet given the attention directed to some of his contemporaries. For the first decade of the twenty-first century, the *Modern Language Association International Bibliography* lists roughly four times as many scholarly publications on James Fenimore Cooper, more than ten times as many on Nathaniel Hawthorne, and sixteen times as many on Edgar Allan Poe. Not surprisingly, therefore, Simms is not yet included in most anthologies of American literature, although he is a subject or a source in an expanding and ever more diverse body of scholarship.

To prepare to read Simms, it is important to see his writings in multiple contexts. He rarely wrote about himself outside of his more personal poems and his letters (some 1500 of the many thousands of which survive). Yet he systematically drew on his background, personal experience, and relationships in his work. He also shaped that work through a progressively developed poetics and philosophy of life, history, and art. He did so in the context of his very broad reading of both contemporary and earlier western literature and in the midst of multiple professional engagements and responsibilities. The richness and variety of these writings and involvements make Simms a key figure for future understanding of the literary culture, issues, and networks in mid-nineteenth-century America.

Background

Simms's family history reflected the dynamics that fueled the spread southward and westward of the populations, plantation economy, and society of the South Atlantic states. Simms's ancestry also reflected the Scots-Irish and English roots of what became identified by the 1830s as southern culture, a generation after the end of most immigration to the region. Two of Simms's grandparents, William and Elisabeth Sims, were Scots-Irish and migrated to South Carolina from Ulster. One, John Singleton, was an American-born son of putatively English immigrants, who had come to South Carolina from Virginia. The fourth, Jane Miller, was daughter of two Scots-Irish and Irish descended people—John Miller, of North and then South Carolina, and Jane Ross. Ross's family also migrated to South Carolina from western Virginia, where members lived cheek by jowl with other Scots-Irish families, who migrated to the Carolinas (White). Simms's father and Uncle James migrated in 1808 from Charleston to Tennessee, then to Mississippi. This was after the bankruptcy of the elder William's business and the deaths of his wife and their other two sons. Following the last of these losses, the elder Simms's hair turned white in a week. To his anguished eyes, Charleston appeared "a place of tombs" (qtd. in Guilds, *Literary Life* 6, 12).

For the son, however, Charleston was home—so much so that he refused to leave his maternal grandmother and move to Mississippi when his uncle came to get him in 1816. Then the fifth largest and by far the wealthiest city, as well as one of the greatest ports, in America, Charleston was at the peak of its influence (Moltke-Hansen, "Expansion" 25–31; G. Rogers, *Charleston*). Cotton culture on the sea islands to the south, begun in 1790, and rice culture in impounded lowcountry tidal marshes meant that the port was filled not only with sailors of many lands and languages, but also with enslaved people of many African and Creole cultures and speech ways (slaves continued to be imported legally in large numbers until 1808). This street life made vivid the transnational nature of plantation agriculture and the fact that the developing region's dramatically expanding borders "were not just geographic; they also were human, historical, and intellectual" (Moltke-Hansen, "Horizons" 19).

Even more important for the future author, the expanding region's borders and nature were taking imaginative shape. The West of the senior William Gilmore Simms and the first Creek War in which he fought, the Revolutionary War of the young Simms's maternal grandfather, and the backcountry of many related Scots-Irish settlers all became grist for a lonely, energetic boy who spent as much time with books as he could (Simms, *Letters* 1: 161). The possibilities of such settings, incidents, and characters were not confined to history alone. Simms reported that he "used to glow and shiver in turn over 'The Pilgrim's Progress,'" while "Moses' adventures in 'The Vicar of Wakefield' threw [him] into paroxysms of laughter" (Hayne, "Ante-Bellum" 261–62). Sir Walter Scott's Border and medieval romances and James Fenimore Cooper's Leather-stocking tales also deeply colored his imagination (Simms, *Views* 1: 248; and Moltke-Hansen, "Horizons" 6–15). As affecting were the ghost stories and Revolutionary War tales of his grandmother and the verses sent, and tales told, by his father.

These diverse tales became reasons to explore—in books, but also on the ground. As a boy, Simms ranged through the city and along the banks of the Ashley River, which fed into Charleston Harbor. He did so in search of scenes of colonial and Revolutionary battles and incidents (*Letters* 1: lxii). He first heard his uncle's and father's many Irish and frontier stories when they visited in Charleston in 1816 and 1818, respectively. He heard more on his trips to Mississippi during the winter of 1824 through the spring of 1825 and again in 1826. The first trip took him through Georgia and Alabama, where he saw elements of the Creek and Cherokee nations. At the time, Simms later reported, he was a boy "cumbered with fragmentary materials of thought, . . . choked by the tangled vines of erroneous speculation, and haunted by passions, which, like so many wolves, lurked, in ready waiting, for their unsuspecting prey" (*Social* 6). When he first got to Mississippi, traveling partly by stage, partly by riverboat, and partly by horse,

Simms learned that his father had just come back from "a trip of three hundred miles into the heart of the Indian country" (Trent 15). Later father and son "rode together on horseback to various settlements on the frontier of Alabama and Mississippi" (Guilds, *Literary Life* 10–11, 17–18). Simms recalled "having traveled 150 miles beyond the Mississippi" (M. Shillingsburg, "Literary" 120). The next year he returned to the Southwest by ship. "During this [second] trip he carried a 'note book.'" There he jotted episodes, encounters, stories heard, characters seen, and descriptions of the landscapes unfolding around him. He also wrote "at least sixteen poems" (Kibler, "First"; M. Shillingsburg, "Literary" 123).

Simms took a third western trip five years later, writing letters back to the newspaper that by then he was editing (*Letters* 1: 10–38). Together these three trips provided materials for his writings over more than forty years. "The first . . . produced mainly short fiction; the second inspired much poetry; . . . the first and third . . . yielded three novels written in the 1830s" (M. Shillingsburg, "Literary" 119). This was, in part, because of the trips' timing. Sixteen years after the first trip, Simms told students at the University of Alabama that in the interval their world had changed from a howling wilderness into a place of growing civilization (Simms, *Social* 5–6). Had he not gone when he did, he would have been too late to see the frontier. Later travels took him to many other places and also provided much grist for his writing. Never again, however, did he experience the frontier firsthand. Furthermore, on these later trips Simms was a practiced professional writer, no longer that boy haunted by passions.

Personal Life

After the ten-year-old boy's momentous refusal to leave Charleston, his grandmother sent Simms for two years to the grammar school taught on the campus and by the faculty of the nearly moribund College of Charleston. By then Simms was already "versifying the events of the war [of 1812]" that had just concluded, publishing "doggerel" in the local papers, and learning to read in several languages (*Letters* 1: 285). His trip west a decade later helped him decide to pursue both literature and a career in law, but back in Charleston—despite his father's urging that he stay in Mississippi. Upon his return home, he began to read law and also launched a literary weekly, the *Album*, which ran for a year. He became engaged to Anna Malcolm Giles, daughter of a grocer and former state coroner.

A year later the young couple married. This was six months before Simms was admitted to the South Carolina bar, on his twenty-first birthday, and not long before he was appointed as a city magistrate. Although living up the Ashley River in the more healthful, less expensive village of Summerville, Simms kept a law office in the city. Shortly after using his maternal inheritance to buy the *City Gazette* at the end of 1829 and moving down to Charleston Neck, just north of the city limits where he had lived as a boy, Simms lost both his father and his maternal grandmother. He also found himself attacked because of his Unionist stance in the Nullification crisis, which resulted from South Carolina's rejection of a federal tariff. Then, in early 1832, Simms's wife died. Soon after, he took his four-year-old daughter back to Summerville and determined to sell his newspaper and leave the state for a literary life in the North.

Fueling his ambition was the correspondence Simms had begun several years earlier with an accountant—Scots immigrant James Lawson—whose work Simms had published in his *City Gazette* but not yet met. At the time Lawson, seven years Simms's senior, edited a New York City newspaper and, in addition to writing plays and poetry, was a friend to a wide literary circle, as well as Simms's informal literary agent (McHaney, "Early"). Simms's trip north in the summer of 1832 saw the two begin a lifelong friendship, cemented as they squired ladies about and interacted with Lawson's literary circle. In subsequent years Simms multiplied the number of his friendships in both the North and the South, making them in some measure a replacement for the family he had lost. Lawson remained the closest of his northern friends, while James Henry Hammond, a future governor and U.S. senator, became his closest friend in South Carolina.

Late in 1833, after his Summerville house burned down, Simms wrote Lawson to say that he was enamored of "a certain fair one" (*Letters* 1: 73). Seventeen-year-old Chevillette Eliza Roach was the daughter of "a literary-minded aristocrat of English descent" with two plantations on the banks of the Edisto River in Barnwell District (later Bamberg County) (Guilds, *Literary Life* 70). The courtship was protracted, as Simms felt it necessary to clear first debts that friends had bought up on his behalf. He also was determined "to marry no woman" before he was "perfectly independent of her resources, and her friends" (*Letters* 1: 78). Therefore he did not propose until the spring of 1836. The nuptials took place seven months later, and as a result, Simms came to call the four thousand acres of Woodlands Plantation, with its seventy slaves, home. It was twenty years, however, before he took over management of the plantation and, then, only in the wake of his father-in-law's sickness and death. Five years after that, he lost his second wife, the mother of fourteen of his fifteen children. Nine of the children Chevillette bore him had already died, devastating Simms repeatedly. Five were still living (three sons and two daughters), as was Simms's daughter by his first marriage, who helped raise the youngest of her siblings. Those remaining children—even Gilly, who fought in the Confederate army—all outlived their father. Gilly and a brother-in-law ran Woodlands after the war, when Simms, though dying of cancer, was earning what he could by writing again for publications in the North and editing one or another South Carolina newspaper.

Career

The trip north in 1832 did not result in Simms moving there. Except during the Civil War, however, he returned almost every year. This was because the contacts he made, and the exposure to literary culture that he enjoyed, helped him define his future as an author. Earlier he had written fiction and criticism as well as journalism, filling the pages of several short-lived cultural journals and his newspaper, but between the ages of nine and twenty-six Simms had focused his literary efforts primarily on poetry. Beginning with his first book of verse in 1825, he had published five small volumes in Charleston. A couple had received positive notice in New York, and in the fall of 1832, J. & J. Harper issued the sixth volume anonymously as *Atalantis: A Story of the Sea*. Coming back the following summer, Simms had in hand for the Harpers a Gothic novella, *Martin Faber*, and after his return south, he also would send the manuscript of his first two-volume border romance, *Guy Rivers: A Tale of Georgia*.

The reception of these and the romances and short stories that followed quickly made Simms one of the nation's most successful fictionists. He continued to issue poetry as well—roughly a collection every three years over the thirty-seven years that he worked as a professional author. But this output was dwarfed by the fiction—on average a title every year (counting several serialized works but not counting the many revised editions). Then there were the two dozen separately published orations, histories, and biographies, as well as edited collections of documents and dramas, and a geography of South Carolina. Add to these the revised editions and the further printings and issues of his own works and it appears that Simms saw a title coming off the presses at the rate of one every three months or so. Making that figure all the more astounding is the fact that, during more than a dozen of those years (the early-to-mid 1840s, the late 1840s-to-early 1850s, and the mid-to-late 1860s), he also was editing a cultural journal or newspaper. Furthermore he contributed reams of reviews and poems, hundreds of op-ed pieces and columns, and dozens of short stories and public addresses, which were never collected and published in volume form.

His career mapped an arc. It ascended meteorically in the 1830s and peaked in the early-to-mid 1840s, before beginning to descend. One reason was the popularity of the historical fiction that Simms began to write. When he left behind the law, his first newspaper, and the Nullification controversy, as well as his sadness, historical fiction was all the rage. Sir Walter Scott had fueled the craze, beginning with the publication of his first Border romance in 1814. He died in September 1832. Seventeen years Simms's senior, James Fenimore Cooper, the closest America had to a Scott at the time, was at the peak of his reputation and success, having started publishing his romances in 1820. Thus the way had been prepared for a writer of Simms's historical imagination and preoccupations. Within five years of his first trip north, moreover, Lawson's (and now his) circle became loosely affiliated with a nationalistic and Democratic group, self-styled Young America, after Young Italy and similar ethnic, nationalist, European, cultural and political movements (Moltke-Hansen, "Horizons"). Edgar Allan Poe and other members gave Simms's first fictions positive, if not uncritical, attention.

By the end of the 1830s, paradoxically, Simms, like Cooper, found his success attracting unauthorized editions of his works, as Britain and America did not have an international copyright agreement. Further, in the wake of the panic of 1837, Americans bought fewer books. Simms's response was to diversify his portfolio. He turned to biography and history, including his hugely successful *Life of Francis Marion* (1844). He also returned to the editor's chair, overseeing one and then another cultural journal. These were unlike the ones he had edited in the 1820s: they included contributions by numerous authors, not just those from Charleston, but from the larger region and also the North. The ambition motivating the journals was to connect and promote Charleston intellectually. Consequently the journals more closely resembled metropolitan quarterly reviews in their offerings.

The mid-1840s saw Simms involved in politics, even serving a term in the South Carolina legislature. By the middle of the Mexican-American War in 1847, he had concluded that the South needed to become an independent nation. Thereafter, although he maintained ties with many in the Young America circle, he no longer promoted his writings as fostering Americanism in literature (*Views*). Instead he increasingly emphasized the ways in which his three romance series—the colonial, the Revolutionary, and the border—were making tangible and meaningful the origins and development of the future southern nation and the sad but inevitable consequences for Native Americans (Watson, *Nationalism*; compare Nakamura). Sectional politics colored more and more of Simms's perceptions, speeches, and private communications. The rising tide of abolitionism had him aghast. It also fed his growing sense that his position in American letters was slipping. He returned to editing and his poetry, which was more often explicitly about the South, became increasingly patriotic in tone. Although his first biographer, William Peterfield Trent, insisted that Simms's declining standing reflected the change in literary fashion from historical romances to realistic novels, Simms in fact wrote more and more as a social realist in the 1850s (Wimsatt, "Realism").

The Civil War consumed Simms. As he wrote Lawson, "Literature, especially poetry, is effectually overwhelmed by the drums, & the cavalry, and the shouting" (*Letters* 4: 369–70). He did manage to editorialize often and to rework and finish things long on his desk, including poems, a novel, and a dramatic treatment of Benedict Arnold, the northern traitor in the Revolutionary War. Then, in the wake of the Confederacy's loss and the failure of his vision for the South, he found himself recording the loss in a new newspaper, dealing with the trauma in his poetry, and becoming more existential and psychological in his fictional treatments. Simms's old New York friends tried to help. He did edit and see through publication a volume of Confederate war poetry. Yet it is a measure of his reduced stature that the several new romances he published appeared only in serial form. In part this may have been because he was in a sense competing with himself. Publishers were beginning to reprint volumes out of the selected edition of his writings. Many of Simms's works were available in book form, just not his new works.

Associations

As the *Letters* testify, Simms had complex, overlapping networks of friends and colleagues. As a boy and young man, he received the friendship, patronage, and commendation of a variety of well-placed people in Charleston, including Charles Rivers Carroll. It was Carroll with whom he read law, to whom he dedicated his first romance, and after whom he named a son. Both men were Unionists during the Nullification controversy. So were Hugh Swinton Legare (later U.S. attorney general) and the considerably older William Drayton, as well as lawyer and editor Richard Yeadon and Greenville, South Carolina, newspaper editor Benjamin Franklin Perry. Also considerably older than Simms was James Wright Simmons, who had joined with Simms to launch the *Southern Literary Gazette* in 1828, when Simms was twenty-two. Through him Simms had direct contact with such British literary figures as Leigh Hunt and Lord Byron (Kibler, *Poetry* 15).

The next group of influential friends and collaborators that Simms acquired were members of the Lawson circle and included such figures as Edwin Forrest, the Shakespearean actor, and Evert Duyckinck, who published several of Simms's volumes in Wiley and Putnam's series, Library of American Books, which he edited. Among the many others were poets and editors William Cullen Bryant and Fitz-Greene Halleck. Simms also made nonliterary friends in New York and Philadelphia, such as John Jacob Bockee and William Hawkins Ferris, the cashier at the U.S. Treasury office in New York who, after the war, helped Simms, Henry Timrod (poet laureate of the Confederacy), and others.

As a Barnwell planter, Simms met a widening circle of South Carolina's leaders and literati. For instance, his acquaintance with James Henry Hammond began in the late 1830s and deepened into a friendship in the early 1840s. It was in the early 1840s, too, when he again was editing cultural journals, that Simms became friends with many southern writers. He regarded several of them, including Virginians George Frederick Holmes, Edmund Ruffin, and Nathaniel Beverley Tucker, as members, together with Hammond and himself, of a "sacred circle." Uniting the circle was members' devotion to the South and a shared sense of the marginal status and critical importance of the life of the mind in a largely rural and unintellectual region (Faust, *Sacred*). Others of Simms's wide connections in the region did not interact as much with each other, but Simms often corresponded with Maryland novelist and lawyer John Pendleton Kennedy, Irish-born Georgia poet Richard Henry Wilde, Alabama lawyer and writer Alexander Beaufort Meek, and Louisiana historian and assistant attorney general Charles Gayarré, among others. By the 1850s, when Simms once more returned to editing a cultural journal, many of the writers whom he recruited were members of a younger generation. Poets Paul Hamilton Hayne and Henry Timrod were two.

Often they and a half dozen others of Simms's and their generations met in Russell's Book Shop in Charleston and adjourned to dinner at Simms's Smith Street home, "dubbed 'The Wigwam'" (*Letters* 1: cxxxvi). Shortly before his death fifteen or so years later, Simms wrote Hayne, "I am rapidly passing from the stage, where you young men are to succeed me" (*Letters* 5: 287).

Thought

The welter of Simms's works disguises unities and dynamics of the thought underlying them. From early on Simms was convinced that art ennobles or transforms, as well as gives voice to individuals and societies; therefore it must be cultivated assiduously. Without the potential for high artistic attainment, he insisted, societies are not ready for the independence and regard of free peoples. This is where Simms the historian joined Simms the poet. Societies develop, he argued (using the stadialism of the Scottish historical school), from imitation through self-assertion to achievement and also from savagery through strife to settled agricultural communities and, ultimately, to a hierarchical civilization supporting a rich artistic life. It was the job of the artist to help envision the goal, inspire the pursuit, and inform the process. That process was at once progressive and dialectical. Order, without dynamism, stifled development, as did the obverse—the dominance by ungoverned impulses or uncontrolled license. This was true in the individual, but also in societies as a whole. War was necessary for civilization, but its success was measured in the securities of the home, the center of cultural production and reproduction.

Whether in the public or in the domestic arena, "the true governor, as [Thomas] Carlyle call[ed] him—the king man—"guided rather than impeded the forces of change and progress (Simms, "Guizot's" 122). There were few such men with the capacity to lead. The same was true of nations. Neither all people nor all peoples were equal in either capacity or attainment. That was why Native Americans were overrun and Africans had been enslaved by European peoples in the New World. Indeed, Simms argued, "slavery in all ages has been found the greatest and most admirable agent of Civilization," giving education and examples to less evolved peoples (*Letters* 3: 174). The degree to which a people had evolved mattered. That was why, he held, Americans had won independence from the most powerful empire in the world. They had done so through their Revolution, led by an elite that felt correctly its time had come (Simms, "Ellet's" 328). By mid-1847 that also was Simms's judgment for the South: the region had evolved enough to become independent (*Letters* 2: 332). The hope inspired and then failed him and the people he sought to lead.

While not all men could rise to the highest rank, they all had the same responsibility at home. There the father was patriarch, protector, and head, while the mother was nurturer, moral instructor, and heart. There, too, children's characters and minds were formed by age twelve (Simms, "Ellet's"). Children's upbringing was critical to citizenship, and it was through her sons and the support of her husband, father, and brothers that a woman shaped the public sphere. The culture and character instilled in the child expressed and informed not just the household, but the larger society—the people.

"The history of peoples and their embodiments in institutions, states, and artistic productions—these were the great subjects" in Simms's view (Moltke-Hansen, "Horizons" 12). Yet "poets were the only class of philosophers who had recognized" this until his own day, when at last "we now read human histories. We now ask after the affections as well as the ceremonies of society" (Simms, "Ellet's" 319–20). Peoples or races—that is, ethnic groups—were not unchanging any more than were their politics and their cultures. They either advanced or were overrun by history. Further, new peoples emerged, and old identities were submerged. The Spanish conquistadors were the creation of centuries of conflict with the Moors: their motivation was the glory of conquest, not the routine of trade or the plow. On the other hand, the English settlements in North America reflected the impulse to transform the wilderness into verdant farms and build society (Simms, *Views* 64, 178–85; Simms, *Social* 8). The same impulse drove Americans westward in Simms's own day and gave Americans their manifest destiny.

To explore these facts of the South's settlement and its place in international conflicts, Simms wrote all together, between 1833 and 1863, two romances set in eighth-century Spain, two set during the Spanish exploration and conquest of the Americas and two during the later English colonization of South Carolina, seven set during the American Revolution, and—depending on how one counts—perhaps eight set on the borders of the nineteenth-century South. After the war he published one more Revolutionary romance and two more that, like it, were set beyond the boundaries of civilization. He left as well two unfinished romances, also set beyond society's normal reach. These works, however, no longer had as their framing justification the cultivation of the South's future and civilization.

White southerners had their independence foreclosed by the war. In his last works, therefore, Simms found himself exploring the psychological, philosophical, and historical impulses that led to the Confederacy's demise and what, in the aftermath, it meant to be a good man and to build for the future, however impoverished. On the first score, he argued that the impulse to idealism behind abolitionism ignored historical realities, becoming inhuman in its consequences. On the latter score, he affirmed responsibility for one's dependents and the virtues of stoicism, as well as a continued commitment to the beauty and truth of art and the impulses to the cultivated life and fields. Therefore, in the face of the burning of his Woodlands home and library in February 1865—during the march of General William Tecumseh Sherman's U. S. army through the Carolinas and in the midst of desperate circumstances—he insisted that home, or the ideals and past characterizing its potential, still was at the center of true civilization, but only if elevated by art (Simms, *Sense* 8, 17). It was wrong to measure civilization by the getting, spending, and mad dashing, or material progress and utilitarianism, characteristic of both a capitalistic North and also many southerners. He had often attacked these traits even before the war, insisting that "the work of the Imagination, which is the Genius of a race, is only begun when its material progress is supposed to be complete" (Simms, *Poetry* 12).

Writings

Simms expressed many of his ideas most personally in letters and most cogently in essays, speeches, and occasional introductions to his books. But he illustrated them most fully in his fiction and poetry. By the time he arrived in New York in 1832, he had formed many of the core ideals and beliefs that would shape his work. His application of them, however, modified his understanding over time. Growing as a writer and growing in knowledge and experience, he also grew as a thinker.

In his hierarchy of values, poetry came first. It was a prophetic calling as well as evocative of the deeply felt (or, sometimes, the fleeting) and thus testimony to the perdurance and transcendence of the beautiful and the human spirit. Yet, as Simms often ruefully reflected, prose spoke to many more people. That was a principal reason why he turned to writing prose epics or romances. He gave his most concerted consideration of poetry's value and roles in three lectures in Charleston in 1854. Over the prior three years he had given portions of them in Augusta, Georgia, Washington, D.C., and Richmond and Petersburg, Virginia. Entitled *Poetry and the Practical*, they did not see print until 1996, as Simms never found the time to expand them as he wanted. On the other hand, his last address on the same themes, *The Sense of the Beautiful*, was issued soon after he delivered it, also in Charleston.

Many of his important reviews have not yet been gathered. A recent collection of *William Gilmore Simms's Selected Reviews on Literature and Civilization* appeared in 2014, and Simms collected some of his *Views and Reviews in American Literature, History and Fiction*, which came out in 1846 and 1847 in two "series." Beginning with a consideration of "Americanism" in literature, the first series explored the themes and periods of American history for treatment by the novelist. Simms argued there, and in forewords to several of his romances, that fiction rendered the past more truthfully, interestingly, and tellingly than histories and biographies could because fiction—like poetry—required imagination to look beyond what is not known or expressed. The second series examined additional American writers and what distinguished them.

Despite their early success, Simms's romances, novellas, and stories provoked mixed reviews. Poe eventually concluded that Simms had become "the best novelist which this country has, on the whole, produced" but also insisted that "he should never have written 'The Partisan,' nor 'The Yemassee.'" This was in a review of *Confession*. That novel, like the Gothic *Martin Faber*, demonstrated, Poe contended, that Simms's "genius [did] not lie in the outward so much as in the inner world." Yet he nevertheless wrote of Simms's short-story collection *The Wigwam and the Cabin* that "in invention, in vigor, in movement, in the power of exciting interest, and in the artistical management of his themes, he has surpassed, we think, any of his countrymen." Other critics, especially in the genteel and Whiggish Knickerbocker circle, joined Poe in condemning what they considered to be the excessively graphic and vulgar qualities of many characters and scenes, and Simms's prolixity and sententiousness, in his romances (Butterworth and Kibler 64, 50).

The violent realism and earthiness of the romances did not result in realistic novels. Although Simms received early praise for his characterizations (particularly those of women), he used the romance formula, with its stereotypic heroes and heroines, predictable themes, and conventional polarities. People were on quests, had lost their way, were fighting long odds, were carrying forward the banner of (and modeling) civilization, were mired in the slough of despond, were resisting all the claims of civilized society and behavior, or were pursuing love interests. Deceitfulness, selfishness, and greed opposed honor, high-mindedness, and honesty against the backdrop of the South's development from the earliest days of Spanish exploration to the westward movement in Simms's own youth.

It was only gradually that Simms married the psychological acuity of some of his portraits of the interior struggles of his Gothic characters and fiction to the historical romance. Helping him think through how to do so were the biographies he wrote in the mid-1840s, but also the incidents on which he focused particular fictions, such as the murder in *Beauchampe; or, The Kentucky Tragedy* (1842). However incomplete the blending of realism and romanticism or of stereotypical and socially individuated renderings through the 1840s, by the 1850s Simms fundamentally had made the transition to social realism in such works as *Woodcraft* and *The Cassique of Kiawah*. Indeed some scholars have considered *Woodcraft* the first realistic novel in America (Bakker, "Literary Frontier"; Wimsatt, "Realism").

In some sense disguising the transition is the fact that Simms also increasingly wrote as a humorist and, in so doing, often rendered his late narratives fabulistically, when not writing social comedy or stories of manners. This dimension of Simms's work was largely hidden, however, until the 1974 publication of *Stories and Tales*, volume 5, in the Centennial Simms edition, edited by John C. Guilds. There, for the first time, readers had access in print to "Bald-Head Bill Bauldy." There, too, for the first time one could read together "Legend of the Hunter's Camp," and "How Sharp Snaffles Got His Capital and Wife," which was published posthumously in *Harper's Magazine* in October 1870. These and other stories and tales made it clear that Simms was a fecund contributor to southern and American humor.

Humor let Simms take up issues that he could not otherwise address in print and still expect to be well received. He did so both during and after the war. The war also pushed Simms past the emerging fashion of social realism. Having destroyed the familiar, the preoccupation of much realistic fiction, the war made the liminal central (M. Shillingsburg, "Cub"). While his romances and tales had often explored life on the edge or in extreme circumstances, whether in war, on the frontier, on the verge of madness, or in fanciful realms, it had done so against a backdrop of, and with the goal of affirming, social norms and development. In the war's wake that goal seemed absurd. Mythologized memories of a healthy past might nurture a sense of the beautiful but could not help one deal with the present. Thus Simms's conclusion, in a March 1869 letter to Paul Hamilton Hayne: "Let us bury the Past lest it buries us!" (*Letters* 5: 214). Fifteen months later he lay dead in the 13 Society Street, Charleston, home of his oldest daughter, with shell holes in the walls of the bedroom he had shared with several children.

Posthumous Reputation

The twenty years after Simms's death saw him often respectfully treated, first in obituaries, later in memoirs and columns, and also in literary dictionaries and encyclopedias. Yet Charles Richardson's 1887 *American Literature: 1607–1885* proved a harbinger of a shift: Simms, Richardson observed, was "more respected than read," having "won considerable note because he was so sectional" and then having "lost it because he was not sectional enough," although he showed "silly contempt for his Northern betters" (qtd. in Butterworth and Kibler 130). Five years later Trent's biography of Simms appeared. It was the first full-length, scholarly treatment. Its central thesis was that Simms's environment frustrated his abilities: the South was inimical to art and the life of the mind, and Charleston high society's hauteur marginalized Simms despite his talent and character. Trent's second thesis was that Simms's commitment to the romance and his romanticism meant that his works had become largely unreadable in an age of literary realism. Although Vernon Parrington and later scholars recognized Simms's impulses to realism, the two theses long shaped Simms criticism and, indeed, also helped frame study of antebellum southern literature and intellectual life (Parrington 2: 119–30).

A Virginian born in 1862, Trent was a progressive who wanted a New South radically different from the old. He saw his pioneering study of Simms as an opportunity to criticize what the Civil War had made untenable. From his perspective the Old South was not the expanding and rapidly developing environment, with a deep history, that Simms portrayed, but a place where slavery stultified and stunted the growth and progress displayed by the North. Southern—especially South Carolinian—writers occasionally challenged Trent's agenda and conclusions, but those critiques had little impact. Not until after publication of the Simms letters in the 1950s did scholars begin to consider the author in the historical and contemporary contexts that he had rendered in his poetry and fiction. And not until after the centennial of his death did a growing number of scholars, having concluded that southern intellectual history was not an oxymoron, begin to study in detail the culture in which Simms participated and to which he contributed so voluminously and variously.

Some of these scholars also have had agendas: they wanted to see Simms included in the American literary canon, for instance, or they wanted to defend the heritage that in their view Trent, and so many others, inappropriately belittled or ignorantly dismissed. More fruitfully, other scholars have begun to reframe the understanding of nineteenth-century American intellectual life by stripping away preconceptions that characterized earlier evaluations of Simms and his contemporaries. They are closely examining the historical record and transatlantic and other contemporary contexts and developments in the process. Although the pursuit of canonical status in a post-canonical age seems quixotic at this point, the explosion of the canon is leading to more varied fare being offered and may, therefore, mean that Simms, now that his work is widely available, will be more often anthologized as well as studied. Defensiveness about Simms and the antebellum South may warm the hearts of like-minded people, just as critics of the Old South have been encouraged by shared presuppositions and disdain. Yet dueling cultural ideologies do not advance comity and may only reinforce mutual incomprehensions. Continued, deep research in original sources and the theoretical reframing that Atlantic history, the history of the book, and other perspectives offer—these approaches promise most for further study of Simms, his works, and his world.

The Army Correspondence of Colonel John Laurens

JEFFERY J. ROGERS

William Gilmore Simms had a passionate, life-long fascination with history. It was the inspiration for so much of what he wrote. It is most clearly evident in his series of novels set in his native South Carolina during the American Revolution, but it can be found throughout his large and diverse body of work. Of all nineteenth-century American authors, he thought more often, and thought more deeply, about the uses of history for the purposes of fiction than any other, and he excelled at making his literary efforts successful artistically while also remaining true to the historical settings and circumstances they portrayed. This remarkable achievement has long been recognized by literary scholars. Historians too have complimented Simms's work. For example, respected historian George C. Rogers, Jr. described Simms's Revolutionary War romances as actually giving, "a better picture of the times than do the history books" (*Charleston* 48). Among those nineteenth-century American litterateurs who longed for a distinct American literature, Simms envisioned a national literary epic which would chronicle, through the media of fiction, the founding, maturation, and independence of American society and the American people. With literary depictions of American history from exploration and its colonial beginnings through to the age of manifest destiny, and beyond, he largely succeeded. Although several of his mid-nineteenth-century peers also wrote historical fiction or historically-themed poetry, the scale and scope of Simms's vision and his attention to detail and accuracy distinguish his *oeuvre* as a unique accomplishment in nineteenth-century American literature and thereby separates Simms from his contemporaries.

It was not simply for the purposes of fiction, however, that Simms was drawn to history. Although he is best remembered as a novelist and poet, Simms was also an important early American historian and biographer. Indeed, of all the writers working in the South prior to the Civil War, Simms is now recognized as "the central figure in historical studies" (Busick, *Sober* xi). In addition to numerous historical and biographical sketches, essays, and articles published in a variety of journals, Simms wrote and saw published eight works of history and biography in book form during the course of his life. These included *The History of South Carolina*, published in 1840 with a revised edition in 1860, and biographies of Revolutionary War generals Francis Marion (1844) and Nathanael Greene (1849), the famed savior of the Virginia colony John Smith (1846), and the legendary French knight the Chevalier Bayard (1847). As expansive as his interest in history was, however, it was clearly the American Revolution, particularly the southern experience of the Revolution, to which Simms was especially dedicated. The presence of *The Army Correspondence of Colonel John Laurens, in the Years 1777–8, Now First Printed from Original Letters Addressed to His Father, Henry Laurens, President of Congress, with a Memoir* among his historical works is a consequence of that dedication.

Like other historians of his generation, Simms saw great value, as well as intrinsic appeal, in the collecting of manuscripts and other materials useful to historical scholarship. He began collecting manuscripts around the age of 29 and by the time of the Civil War had amassed a large and valuable collection. Writing to William J. Rivers in 1862 he estimated that his personal library at Woodlands, his Barnwell District, South Carolina plantation, was close to, and probably exceeded, "10,000 volumes" and that the manuscripts alone were equal to 50 bound and printed volumes (*Letters* 6: 233). Building such a collection over the years had cost Simms "great painstaking and research, and some money" (*Letters* 5: 44). Among those represented in the collection were George Washington, John Jay, Richard Henry Lee, John Adams, Thomas Paine, Francis Marion, John Rutledge, Horatio Gates, Baron de Kalb, William Moultrie, Baron von Steuben and Patrick Henry. Simms was no mere antiquarian autograph collector. His was a serious collection rich in material relating to and from the hands of various individuals who had been pivotal figures in the era of the American Revolution. As might be expected from his particular interests, the collection was especially strong with respect to the Revolution in the South.

Subject: John Laurens

One of the more substantial parts of the collection consisted of approximately 1,200 items of papers relating to the Laurens family of South Carolina, chiefly Henry Laurens and his son John. Of French Huguenot ancestry, Henry Laurens was born in Charleston in 1724 and became wealthy as a merchant and rice planter. A prominent businessman and political figure, he was elected a delegate for South Carolina to the Second Continental Congress on 10 January 1777 and later that year was made that body's president. During Laurens's term as president, the Continental Congress transmitted the Articles of Confederation to the states for ratification, and he was one of South Carolina's signers of the Articles. Henry Laurens was also a delegate at the negotiations that produced the Treaty of Paris in 1783 which ended the War for American Independence.

According to Alexander Hamilton, a man who knew him well, John Laurens was, "a citizen whose heart realized that patriotism of which others only talk" (G. Massey 230). He was born in 1754 and spent his childhood in Charleston and at Mepkin, his father's plantation located on high bluffs overlooking the Cooper River. He entered the University of Geneva in 1772 and, despite conflicted feelings on it as the choice of a profession, began the study of law in London in 1774. When not studying or attending the Inns of Court, the young John Laurens became absorbed with the growing crisis between Britain and her American colonies. He attended sessions of Parliament, personally witnessed King George III address the House of Lords, and, through family and friends, conveyed news of events in England back to South Carolina. While in England, his devotion to republicanism and the American cause grew in fervor, and he returned to Charleston in April of 1777 determined to join the fight.

He journeyed with his father to Philadelphia in July of 1777 where Henry Laurens took his seat in the Second Continental Congress. Soon afterward, John Laurens applied to join General George Washington's staff as an aide-de-camp, a position also held by his friend Alexander Hamilton. The educated and polished young man made a strong impression on Washington, who asked Laurens to "become a Member of my Family" and serve as a volunteer aid (G. Massey 73). Laurens saw combat in the battles of Brandywine Creek (11 September 1777), Germantown (4 October 1777), and Monmouth (28 June 1778). He was wounded at Germantown and, at Monmouth, had a horse shot from under him. During these battles Laurens repeatedly displayed a courage and zeal which bordered on, and by some accounts crossed into, recklessness. His actions on the battlefield won Laurens the renown he craved but also a reputation as a man who, "went out of his way to encounter danger and even seemed to court death" (G. Massey 167). This was a perception shared by Washington, Hamilton, and the Marquis de Lafayette.

On 29 December 1778 the British captured Savannah, Georgia, the first step in their 'Southern Strategy' to roll up the American colonies from the south, isolate New England, and thereby end the colonial rebellion. With Charleston now threatened, Laurens made the proposal for which he is perhaps best remembered today. He argued that to stop the British advance in the South slaves should be armed and granted freedom in exchange for their service. On 25 March 1779 a congressional committee to address the military crisis in the South, proposed by and including Henry Laurens, took up the proposal and four days later the Continental Congress resolved that Georgia and South Carolina should raise a regiment of 3,000 African American slaves to be commanded by white officers. It then commissioned John Laurens a Lieutenant Colonel in the Continental Army.

John Laurens returned home and was elected to the South Carolina House of Representatives into which he introduced his plan for a black regiment. It was rejected twice, once in 1779 and again in 1780. When British General Augustine Prevost threatened Charleston in May of 1779, Governor John Rutledge and the Privy Council offered to surrender on the condition that the state be considered neutral for the duration of the war. Laurens strongly opposed this offer believing the city should be defended. When it was rejected Laurens rejoiced exclaiming, "thank God! we are upon our legs again!" (G. Massey 138). In the fall of 1779 Laurens commanded an infantry column in General Benjamin Lincoln's failed effort to evict the British from Savannah, and he was captured and became a prisoner of war when Charleston fell to Charles Cornwallis on 12 May 1780. He was exchanged later that year.

Aware of his intimate knowledge of the dire condition of the Continental Army, in December of 1780 the Continental Congress appointed Laurens a special minister to France in the hope that he could impress upon the French the urgent need for more aid. Arriving in March of 1781, and putting his cultivated social graces and command of the French language to good use, John Laurens secured a loan from the Netherlands, military supplies, and a commitment of French naval support in a mere two months. He returned to America in time to join Washington's army at Yorktown and was chosen by Washington to represent the American side during the negotiation of Cornwallis's surrender.

After Yorktown, Laurens returned to South Carolina where he tried yet again to induce his fellow South Carolina legislators to back his plan for a black regiment. Again, the effort failed. He then joined General Nathanael Greene's army, in command of light troops, but spent most of the remainder of his life at the head of a network of spies who gathered information on British activities in Charleston. As they prepared to evacuate Charleston, the British launched foraging raids into the interior of the state to obtain supplies. One of these raids was up the Combahee River. Laurens joined in the effort to oppose it. Shortly before dawn on 27 August 1782 Laurens and his small detachment encountered a force of about 150 Redcoats near Chehaw Neck. Although outnumbered and outmaneuvered, Laurens determined to attack the British. At the commencement of the American charge the British opened fire and Laurens was killed.

Origin of the Work

Precisely when and how Simms acquired the Laurens papers is not known, but on 11 February 1845 Simms expressed an interest in producing, "a series of papers made up of brief biographies of distinguished men of the Revolution in the South, interspersed with their original Letters" (*Letters* 2: 29). In addition to John and Henry Laurens, Simms named John Rutledge, Horatio Gates, William Heath, Arthur Lee, and Patrick Henry in connection with this proposed series. He had written earlier to Henry G. Langley of the New York *Democratic Review* and publisher of his 1844 biography *The Life of Francis Marion*, about the prospect of publishing this series. In early April of 1845 Evert Augustus Duyckinck, one of his close New York literary friends wrote to Simms that he had mentioned the proposed series to John L. O'Sullivan, editor of the *Democratic Review* and that O'Sullivan had consented to their publication.

Simms apparently began the research necessary to produce a volume on John Laurens soon after the exchange of these letters, and that research continued into 1846. On December 21 of that year he wrote to editor and critic Rufus W. Griswold inquiring about an article touching upon John Laurens which had appeared in the 2 December 1784 issue of the *Independent Chronicle* of Boston (Simms thought at the time that the newspaper had been published in Philadelphia). Despite this brief engagement with the project, however, no series of papers such as he had proposed to Langley and Duyckinck came forth from Simms. Doubtless, other projects and demands crowded them off his desk. During the period from 1845 to the start of the Civil War Simms saw ten major novels, two biographies, a collection of short stories and numerous other works published. Nonetheless, Simms never abandoned the idea of doing something worthy of publication with his manuscript collection. He drew on it extensively to publish a two-part article on John Rutledge for the *American Whig Review* in 1847 and one on the Baron de Kalb for the *Southern Quarterly Review* in 1852. He also published a series of articles titled "Revolutionary Letters" for *The Historical Magazine* from 1857 to 1859. These articles were essentially transcribed letters from his collection with brief introductions to the documents.

The Civil War and its aftermath would do much to determine the fate of Simms's collection of John Laurens papers. In his 31 May 1862 letter to William J. Rivers, Simms expressed his anxiety that the war would threaten his plantation with its large library and manuscript collection. "I wish to save my library," he told Rivers, "but my first regard is for these valuable old documents," a collection of "very rich" material. Simms had good reason to be anxious. In October of the previous year Union forces began their conquest of the South Carolina coast, and Simms feared that if Charleston should fall, his property, a mere 70 miles inland, would soon afterward be exposed. He therefore implored Rivers, a professor of Greek literature at South Carolina College in Columbia, to receive his Revolutionary War manuscripts and be "the custodian of these treasures." Simms told Rivers that, "I had proposed Lives of Henry and John Laurens," with "selections from their correspondence & a running commentary." Noting further that he had "made notes of them, & examined them carefully" but had nonetheless, "made few draughts upon their contents," Simms suggested Rivers could assist him in preparing them for publication (*Letters* 6: 233).

Simms may have been particularly nervous about losing his library and manuscripts at this time because on 29 March 1862, only two months before writing to Rivers, his house had caught fire. The blaze was subdued but not before substantial damage occurred. Simms had only recently added a separate wing to the house to serve as his library. Probably completed no more than a month before the fire, this timely addition may very well have saved the manuscripts found in *The Army Correspondence of Colonel John Laurens* from destruction. Writing to close friend William P. Miles afterwards Simms said, "I have saved all my MS.S and nearly all my library. The wing was saved" (*Letters* 4: 400). Forebodings of a Union Army threat, however, began to be realized on 30 December 1864 when General William T. Sherman's army, fresh from its capture of Savannah, Georgia, began to cross the Savannah River into South Carolina. That same day, Simms was at Woodlands preparing to evacuate, packing up his manuscript collection and other selected items for shipment to Columbia. He hoped to save his entire library, but the manuscripts were his priority. He was unable to return to Woodlands before the Union army appeared in Barnwell District. In Columbia, Simms and his family were not present at Woodlands when it was burned by stragglers from Sherman's army. The library was totally destroyed but, the manuscripts had been saved.

Sources and Composition

Following the war, Simms renewed his efforts to publish the Laurens papers. He spent the summer of 1866 in New York City and the surrounding boroughs trying to establish new and reestablish old connections with publishers and friends, disrupted as they had been by the Civil War. This included seeking a publisher for the Laurens papers as well as other pieces he had written or planned to write. With the help of Duyckinck, an agreement was reached with The Bradford Club to publish a portion of the John Laurens papers. Founded in 1859 by John B. Moreau in New York City, The Bradford Club, named after William Bradford the first printer in the colony of New York, met periodically and published volumes on topics related to American history. These volumes were printed in a limited quantity and distributed to the club's members and subscribers. It published seven numbered volumes from 1859 to 1867 before the club dissolved. A non-numbered volume by Duyckinck titled *Memorial for John Allen* was published by the club in 1864. It was probably his previous connection that accounts for Duyckinck's apparent ease in arranging for The Bradford Club to publish Simms's *The Army Correspondence of Colonel John Laurens* which was the seventh and last volume published. Furthermore it was, in Simms's words, a "plan proposed by" Duyckinck which determined the form the volume would take (*Letters* 4: 584).

In New York with the Laurens papers at hand, Simms began work immediately after the agreement had been reached. He asked Duyckinck for materials which would assist him in preparing a memoir of Laurens which would precede the selection of letters to be included in the volume. Specifically, he requested a copy of the volume of D. Appleton and Company's *The New American Cyclopedia* which Duyckinck had co-edited and which contained biographical sketches of Henry and John Laurens, both authored previously by Simms. Additionally, he asked for the volume of George Bancroft's *History of the United States* which covered the period in which the letters to be included were written. References to other sources can be found in the "Memoir" included in *The Army Correspondence of Colonel John Laurens*. Therein Simms quotes from the *Memoirs of Arthur Lee* and from letters written by George Washington and John Adams to Henry Laurens (*Letters* 4: 587–88). It is possible he used other sources in writing the "Memoir" but these are not identified. Certainly some of the historical background for the "Memoir" could simply have come from Simms's extensive, lifetime of reading in the history of the American Revolution.

On 28 September 1866 Simms reported to Duyckinck that he had finished, "in a rough penciled draft, the memoir of Laurens," and would begin revising and copying the next day (*Letters* 4: 605). The contents he outlined in this letter would be the final contents of the volume. In addition to the "Memoir" is an 1824 letter from John Church Hamilton, an historian and the fourth son of Alexander Hamilton, which described Laurens's military and diplomatic career. Hamilton had been supportive of an 1823 petition to Congress from John Laurens's son-in-law, Francis Henderson, and his grandson, Francis Henderson, Jr., to obtain, "reimbursement for the out-of-pocket expenses [John Laurens] incurred in his military and diplomatic service and payment of the interest due on the balance of his diplomatic salary" (G. Massey 236). When the petition reached the floor of the U.S. Senate it was supported by an eloquent speech from South Carolina senator Robert Y. Hayne who defended Laurens's character against the charge of recklessness. Despite the support of Hamilton and Hayne, the petition failed. Doubtless because including the letter and speech, both laudatory in tone, one from a descendant of Laurens's close friend and famed Founding Father and the other from a U.S. Senator, added luster to and further details about Laurens's life to the volume, Simms placed them at the end of the "Memoir." Finally, he included a poem, "Lines on the Death of Colonel Laurens" by Philip Freneau, whom Simms described as, "the poet *par excellence* of the American Revolution" (*Laurens* 40).

Evaluation

The memoir which preceded these additions, as might be expected, is highly adulatory. Given its brevity, it does not offer a comprehensive biography of Laurens, but it does provide sufficient context for the letters which follow it. Those letters, what Simms called "Laurens' camp letters," span the period from 13 August 1777 to 18 October 1778 and are all addressed to his father. While he possessed other Laurens letters from outside this time-frame, some of which he quotes in the "Memoir," Simms never directly addressed his decision to set these particular letters apart in the finished volume. It is only speculation, but perhaps he thought that because these letters were addressed to Laurens's father during the period he served as president of the Continental Congress and they were written by the son from roughly the time he began his service with Washington to before he transferred to South Carolina, Simms believed they comprised a set with a loose but coherent narrative. This was, after all, the period during which

Laurens first experienced the war and began to demonstrate those qualities which would win him lasting fame.

Although not a full biography, the "Memoir of Laurens" which precedes the letters can be read in the context of Simms's other biographical works. All of the men about whom Simms wrote biographies were military men, men of action, whom Simms judged to be both outstanding solders as well as men of exceptional virtue, worthy of praise and, where and when possible, emulation. They were also men who, by the exercise of that virtue and through their actions on the battlefield, directed the course of history in ways Simms considered transformative and progressive. John Smith, for example, is credited with saving the Virginia colony, and thereby the English project of colonization in the New World, thus making the American experiment in republican government possible. Speaking of Smith in his 1846 biography, Simms said of such men: "They seem to conceive and to think more justly while in action than in repose. It is the necessity which provokes the thought." It was men like Smith, Marion, Greene, and Bayard who "commonly appear to shape and regulate the transition periods in society; to time and to direct its enterprises; to infuse its spirit with eagerness and enthusiasm, and to meet, with the happiest resources and the most unfailing intrepidity, the frequent exigencies which hang about the footsteps of adventure" (2). This sentiment is similarly expressed by Simms in describing Laurens as "one of those leaders who never know when they are beaten—a characteristic which in war is very much like a virtue" (*Laurens* 27).

It is unsurprising, then, that Simms used a significant amount of space in the "Memoir" establishing the virtuous character of John Laurens. He describes an honorable young man, serious and inquisitive, who faced the difficult dilemma of choosing a profession with introspection and self-honesty. His natural intelligence and personal graces made him a valued member of Washington's staff and a successful diplomat. His ferocious courage, of the sort demonstrated by the other military figures about which Simms chose to write at length, made him an excellent warrior. Such courage (Simms never called it recklessness) won Laurens "the title of the Bayard of America" (*Laurens* 39). In all, when *The Army Correspondence of Colonel John Laurens* was published in 1867 it encompassed 250 total pages, including a highly detailed index. The image of Laurens preceding the title page is from a brooch miniature.

Following the Civil War, Simms's personal finances were in a dire condition. With a house to rebuild and a family to care for he was eager to establish sources of income wherever they could be found. While in New York during the summer of 1866 he sold some of his Washington papers for $250 to an unknown buyer. In May of 1867, having finished editing *The Army Correspondence of Colonel John Laurens*, but not yet seeing the printed volume, he began to consider selling the Laurens papers. With assistance coming again from Duyckinck, as well as John Jacob Bockee, the papers were sold, probably sometime before July of 1867, for

$1,500 to the Long Island Historical Society which, in 1985, changed its name to the Brooklyn Historical Society. Those papers were transcribed and microfilmed and sold some time in the 1960s, and today Simms's collection of Laurens papers is located at The South Caroliniana Library of the University of South Carolina in Columbia. With the funds from this initial sale, Simms partially rebuilt his house at Woodlands.

In his *John Laurens and the American Revolution*, Gregory D. Massey claims that antebellum South Carolinians were keen to praise "their Revolutionary forebears" such as John Laurens so that their example could inspire resistance as their slavery-based society was increasingly being challenged from without (2). Just as those Revolutionary ancestors stood against British tyranny, so would antebellum South Carolinians oppose the tyranny of antislavery forces seeking to undermine their society. Holding up Laurens, a man who opposed slavery, as a model of the virtue South Carolina slaveholders should emulate was a deep irony of history. While Massey makes no mention of Simms's treatment of Laurens's life, the fact that John Laurens was a native of the Palmetto State was doubtless a source of pride for Antebellum South Carolina's premiere literary figure. Simms was also not ignorant of the use of history for polemical purposes in the sectional rivalry which was the single greatest theme of American history during his lifetime. And, like some other South Carolinians who addressed the life of Laurens, Simms said nothing of Laurens's plan to recruit slaves as soldiers in the "Memoir," although he certainly knew about it. Coming immediately in the wake of the Civil War, Simms's *The Army Correspondence of Colonel John Laurens* might be viewed as yet another salvo in the historiographical contest between North and South for the greater claim of contribution to the founding and independence of the United States.

As ardent a southerner as he was, Simms's engagement with history, however, was never cynical or narrowly utilitarian. He thought of his historical scholarship as a genuine effort to understand the past and to propagate that understanding to others. His passion for history was obviously linked to his identity as a South Carolinian, a southerner, and a nineteenth-century American. He certainly believed that to be of value, history should be written to inform and instruct the present, but all who seriously study the past believe so. All historians interpret the past and write history from a contingent, historically-formed vantage point. In this Simms was anything but unique. Still, there is in his body of historical writing an earnest desire to know the past as it was and to divine its meaning for the edification of the present. This is the very *raison d'être* of the historian. To do this, the historian must respect the sources which afford us a window into the past, our only hope at anything approaching an objective standard on which historical knowledge can be based. In the preparation and publication of *The Army Correspondence of Colonel John Laurens* we see Simms's profound respect for those sources and a clear demonstration of his belief that in making those sources publically available he was advancing historical understanding. This volume is not the only example of Simms's efforts at documentary editing, but it is arguably his most important. In his "Memoir of Laurens" and the selection and arrangement of Laurens's letters we find a dedicated, thoughtful editor and historian at work, and our knowledge of the past, of Laurens, and of Simms, is greater because of it.

Border Beagles: A Tale of Mississippi

JOHN D. MILLER

Prior to the publication of *Border Beagles: A Tale of Mississippi* in 1840, the last time the American reading public saw the character Clement Foster was when the outlaw was escaping justice in the final pages of *Richard Hurdis: A Tale of Alabama* (1838) by floating down the Black Warrior River on a cotton bale. Foster was taunting his pursuers, suggesting they may meet again in Arkansas. One of that novel's heroes discourages a marksman from shooting Foster, claiming that the outlaw "may one day become an honest man" (402).

Instead, antebellum readers next encountered Foster in rural Mississippi, using the alias Ellis Saxon and leading the organized crime ring whose name supplies the title for William Gilmore Simms's *Border Beagles*. Ostensibly a sequel to *Richard Hurdis*, *Border Beagles* shares only this single character with its predecessor. Consequently, *Border Beagles* can be read independent of *Richard Hurdis*. There is value in doing so. *Border Beagles* represents the first time humor is a leitmotif in Simms's long fiction, and the author analyzes competing paradigms of legal justice more thoroughly than he had in preceding novels. However, as part of the Border Romance series, to which *Richard Hurdis* belongs as well, *Border Beagles* can also profitably be read as another iteration of Simms's narrative about the evolution of the Old Southwest into a stable extension of the American South.

Like *Richard Hurdis*, the temporal setting of *Border Beagles* is some time in the early 1830s, following the Choctaw Cession. However, *Border Beagles* takes place in the small towns that sprung up in Mississippi following Removal and in the surrounding woodlands and swamps. The conclusions of both novels are similar, though; the organized crime syndicate that represents the anarchy of the thinly settled region is eliminated to make way for well-regulated white settlement and economic development. Although mound-building indigenous cultures existed in present-day Mississippi since the Woodland Period (500 BCE to 1000 CE) and European exploration of the region began in the sixteenth century, the "Border" alluded to in the novel and in the series title refers to this retreating boundary between the social volatility associated with the "newly" settled frontier and the social stability characteristic of the older seaboard South. It represents the thematic "contest," explains David Moltke-Hansen, "between the expectations, norms, and mores of the settled, hierarchical, plantation South and the physical, psychological, and social rudeness of the frontier" ("Plantation" 12).

Mary Ann Wimsatt has observed that variations on the archetypical quest plot contribute to this thematic motif within Simms's Border Romances. The young aristocratic protagonist in each of the texts—in this case, the youthful lawyer Harry Vernon—leaves a more settled area of the South to travel south and west, but that journey is interrupted by the criminal activity of the outlaws. The latter are ultimately defeated by the protagonist, whose genteel, altruistic character symbolizes the forthcoming social order (*Major* 120). In *Border Beagles* (1855), the beginning of Vernon's journey into the "Yazoo neighborhood" of Mississippi is described in grandiose terms that echo this quest pattern of the Border Romances, if not the chivalric romances of previous centuries (87). The morning of his departure from Raymond, Mississippi, finds Vernon "booted and spurred, prepared to mount his good steed, on his journey of adventure" (92). His cavalier attitude toward the journey's incipient dangers likewise characterizes him as a knight-errant: "The duties of life and manhood, opening for the first time fairly upon his consciousness" led him to proceed enthusiastically, considering "he had little to lose in terms of positive possession, whether of wealth or affection; [yet] he had everything to gain in both respects" (96).

The specific objectives of this "adventure" are two-fold. First, Vernon is pursuing a fugitive named William Maitland and Maitland's two daughters at the behest of Vernon's mentor, Ben Carter. The young lawyer is to locate Maitland and secure the return of money that the older man had embezzled and for which Carter pledged security. Not at the risk of harming Maitland, though, for Carter does not want to ruin the reputation of Maitland's daughters, whose dead mother Carter also loved. This quest promises to lead Vernon into the territory of Saxon's Border Beagles, and the two characters' paths are guaranteed to cross when Vernon is also requested by the Governor of Mississippi to collect information about the criminal network and, if possible, to capture Saxon or any other bandits. The governor explains to the young lawyer that "many of our citizens, hitherto held in good esteem, are sworn confederates of these banditti," including magistrates and members of the militia, necessitating a stranger like Vernon to "work himself so adroitly as to sound those with whom he mingles, sift the worthy from the unworthy, and embody them in the proper moment for the capture or destruction of" the criminals (87, 88).

Vernon's blithe confidence is tested by a series of complicating actions that animate the plot and sensationalize the perils of the borderland setting. Like previous literary knights-errant, Vernon has a partner on his journey, albeit initially unwillingly. Tom Horsey, a naïve aspiring actor, is made to believe that Vernon is traveling to join a theatrical troupe in Vicksburg or Natchez. Horsey attaches himself to the young lawyer, liberally quoting Shakespeare as they travel through the woods and the swamps. Vernon manages to divest himself of the thespian after an evening at a remote cottage where Horsey becomes smitten with a young lady (and blackens the eyes of his romantic rival). In fact, Vernon leaves just in time to interrupt an armed robbery further down the road. Assisted by a new traveling companion, the woodsman Wat Rawlins, Vernon kills one of the robbers in defense of the victims, whom he discovers to be the fugitive Maitlands. But Vernon is wounded in their rescue, and he loses consciousness after not only discovering their identity but also becoming enamored with Virginia, the eldest daughter.

After briefly recuperating, Vernon continues to pursue Maitland to a nearby village. However, his newest companion is Saxon himself, traveling incognito. Suspecting the protagonist of being a spy, Saxon orders Vernon's arrest by Beagles posing as deputies for the alleged murder of Horsey, who has since wandered into the gang's secret swamp hideout. Vernon's gunshot wound is aggravated by the apprehension, and he becomes ill. He is nursed back to health by Virginia, whose father had taken up residency in the village, and he is attended to by yet another stout-hearted frontiersman, Dick Jamison. His true identity still unknown to Vernon, Saxon lurks around and becomes infatuated with Virginia as well.

When the outlaw realizes that Virginia returns Vernon's affections, he gives the signal for the protagonist to be transported to a magistrate in league with the Beagles. Fortunately, Horsey makes a timely arrival—following his escape from the swamp lair with his now-fiancée in tow—but that still does not free Vernon. Instead, Jamison and Horsey rescue him as the phony deputies lead him away from the magistrate. Now aware that he is a target of Saxon's gang, Vernon's daring plans for arresting the Beagles and the dramatic execution of his strategy quicken the pace of the novel's remaining chapters. Moreover, his resolve is fortified by a final plot twist: Virginia's abduction by Saxon, who spirits her away to the swamp hideout where she joins his former mistress, a woman whom Saxon had earlier seduced.

With the help of his faithful woodsmen, Vernon attacks the swamp hideout, rescues Virginia, and captures the outlaws alive, the only fatality being Saxon's old mistress, who melodramatically commits suicide after betraying her former lover. However, Vernon's attempt to bring the criminals to justice is foiled by the anger of the Mississippians whom the Beagles had victimized. The criminals are taken from jail and lynched by a mob, and with the death of Saxon née Foster "perished the spirit, the energy, and the capacity of the Border Beagles" (495). But the novel also ends on a pleasant note with the impending triple marriages of Wat Rawlins to Rachel Badger, Tom Horsey to Mary Yarbers, and Vernon to Virginia Maitland, whose father ultimately agrees to return the money that he had embezzled to Carter.

Six years after the publication of *Border Beagles*, Simms wrote editor Rufus Wilmot Griswold that "running through" the Border Romance series was "a strong penchant to moral and mental analysis" (*Letters* 2: 225). Simms's examination of the evolution of law and justice in an embryonic society seems the most prominent example of this moral analysis to appear in *Border Beagles*. It merits recalling that Simms began his professional life as a lawyer in Charleston, and John Cyril Barton illustrates elsewhere that Simms "stayed with law in theory if not in practice" after he gave it up to write (221). Familiar with both the established legal customs of Charleston and the frontier traditions of justice that pervaded the Old Southwest (the latter thanks to at least three trips he made to visit his father in Mississippi in the late 1820s), Simms was aware that there could be more incongruity than symmetry between these systems of jurisprudence. Simms's Vernon equivocates about this legal dissonance, particularly regarding the moral legitimacy of an individual's right to exercise justice. At the risk of mistaking the voice of a character for that of the author, Vernon seems to serve as an amanuensis for Simms's own beliefs—articulated elsewhere in his addresses and essays—about the importance of emotional discipline and respect for authority as preconditions for the growth of civilization.

On one hand, Vernon recognizes that there are circumstances in which justice could be exercised by private individuals when the civil legal system seems inadequate. His defense in Raymond of a farmer who assaulted a shopkeeper that insulted the former's daughter, and the jury's concurrence with Vernon's argument that awarding excessive damages would encourage the shopkeeper's ignoble behavior, testifies to the protagonist's qualified belief in mythical southern, if not frontier, codes of jurisprudence and honor. In the words of the defendant, if the public defamation of a young girl is not "provocation and injury enough to justify any father for licking the rapscallion that does it, then I don't know any sense in our having laws at all" (71). This apparent endorsement of summary justice is also underscored by the other virtuous characters in the novel. For example, after binding the phony deputies to a tree following Vernon's rescue, the woodsman Jamison returns to beat the outlaws with hickory sticks in order to "requite the rogues." Albeit discouraged by Vernon, Jamison rationalizes that "'Tain't every day that a rogue gets what he deserves" (446). The omniscient narrator spares us the scene of the violence but serenely comments that "[t]he hickories were not wasted; and, according to the usual ideas of border justice, in all parts of the world, the rascals met with their deserts" (447).

On the other hand, Jamison would have lynched the two Border Beagles had not Vernon intervened. The only reservation the woodsman has is whether to hang them in the woods or in the village, where they will "be a warning to all rogues, and gamblers, and abolitionists." Vernon dissuades the yeoman by offering not only practical reasons against it, but also "moral objections," for with regard "[t]o lynching, altogether, Vernon absolutely objected" (445). Barton offers a compelling case for Simms's opposition to capital punishment in Simms's other novels, but here Vernon's reluctance to resort to summary vengeance seems more characteristic of his symbolic function in the novel: to transition from unauthorized justice based on personal honor to its official legal, codified counterpart, thus creating the social stability and infrastructure that will foster a plantation- and town-based society.

Vernon and Saxon represent the opposing sides of this dialectic of justice. The criminal at one point scoffs to an accomplice that "I am the law!"; in contrast, the young lawyer forbears killing Saxon, reluctant "however deserving he might be of his doom" to "fling down from its erect place and posture an image so noble, made after the form of God, and filled with such godlike attributes and endowments" (448, 481). This triumph of morality over personal retribution exemplifies what Moltke-Hansen says was one "measure of civilization" for Simms: "the extent to which it provided liberty to those who were sufficiently advanced to use it properly" ("Plantation" 10–11). In other words, the emergence of law and order entailed a set of rights and responsibilities that constituted freedom in a mature society in contrast to the tenuous independence enabled by the absence of governance on the frontier. Though the outlaws did meet a grisly "unlawful" fate at the hands of a mob "[g]oaded to madness," the trajectory of Mississippi's future is nevertheless oriented away from self-interested amorality toward humane communal order (494).

To balance the gravity of his exploration of justice, Simms utilizes humor in *Border Beagles* more than he had theretofore attempted in his long fiction. John Caldwell Guilds also speculates that the author "attempted to substitute comedy" for graphic violence, for which he was criticized in reviews of *Richard Hurdis* (*Literary Life* 97). There are indeed scenes of gore and impropriety in *Border Beagles*—the "blood and brains [of the dead robber] covered [Maitland's] face and garments" after the thwarted robbery, and Saxon's mistress displays her bosom—but slapstick and comic incongruity are much more prevalent (181, 403). Simms foreshadows as much in his "Advertisement" to the 1840 edition. He tells the reader that "[m]y first book was held objectionable by many as too stern and gloomy in its character. The present may be in some respects censurable for the other extreme. . . . Let them balance each other."

Simms mined both older European and more recent regional traditions for the humor in *Border Beagles*. The novel begins with a description of court day in Raymond, a scene of "utmost commotion" featuring country lawyers "who cumber themselves with no weight of law, unless it can be contained in moderately-sized heads, or valise, or saddle-bag, of equally moderate dimensions" (11). Also in attendance are "swaggering" planters on the brink of bankruptcy and bullies eager for a fight, some of whom "had lost an eye, some an ear" (12). Legal satire has a long tradition in British prose fiction, including in Fielding, Smollett, and Scott, but Simms was also familiar with rowdy court day and militia day scenes in the pages of John Pendleton Kennedy's *Swallow Barn* (1832) and Augustus Baldwin Longstreet's *Georgia Scenes* (1835). Also coming from the tradition of Old Southwestern Humor were Simms's boisterous frontier characters Wat

Rawlins and Dick Jamison. The latter especially is from the "ring-tailed roarer" school of frontier comic characters, and was "clearly of [the] opinion that the fun was quite as great to drink, as to fight" (247). Jamison's dialect-filled speeches are filled with comic colloquial exaggerations, including one describing Polly Whitesides, "a lady" who is "six feet in her stockings, with cheeks red as gobbler's gills, and an arm . . . that would put your thigh out of countenance" (250). Horsey's pugnacious romantic rival Ned Mabry is also a familiar character from the ludicrous fight scenes of the regional humorists. Prior to an assault on Horsey, Mabry "bounded from the earth, ran round his enemy, slapping his thighs with his hands the while, in the most savage fashion, and at length, with a whooping shriek . . . he threw a sommerset [somersault], his feet aiming to strike the breast of the actor" (123).

But it is Horsey himself who is the source of most of the humor via the incongruity between his behavior and the novel's setting, leading to an endless series of situational ironies. On one hand, the aspiring actor's enthusiastic, florid, and often inaccurate quotations from Shakespeare are a stark contrast to the primitive frontier and uncouth society that surround him. Moreover, Simms accentuates this absurdity in scenes that juxtapose Horsey's theatrical pretensions with the outlaws' skullduggery. For example, Horsey not only sleepwalks in the Yarbers family's cabin, he also performs *Romeo and Juliet*. Simultaneously, Saxon enters the room through a trap door in order to steal Vernon's bags. Horsey arrives at the scene in Act Five in which Romeo challenges Paris, and Shakespeare's dialogue—"Wilt thou provoke me?—then have at thee, boy!" takes on an unintended meaning to the intruder, who throws the charging, sleepwalking actor into bed with the sleeping Vernon, who also tumbles him via a "very unscrupulous movement, backward upon the floor" (142, 143).

Moreover, like Don Quixote, Horsey is unable to distinguish reality from fiction. The most sustained and best-developed comic scene in *Border Beagles* occurs when Horsey wanders into a swamp and is taken by the outlaws to their hideout. But to keep him there—so as to make his alleged murder more plausible so that Vernon may be incarcerated—Saxon's lieutenant tells Horsey that they are a troupe of itinerant actors. Horsey is delighted, but the ruse is always on the verge of collapse thanks to the incongruity of the dirty ruffians and the primitiveness of the swamp hideout. One of the outlaws, Bull, almost blows their cover with a violent denunciation of tragedy as Horsey prepares to perform the title role of *Hamlet* for them:

> Tragedy be d—d. . . . that's all in my eye and Betty Martin. There's no fun in that, no more than in thunder and hoxy-doxy. Who wants to see a fellow get up and blow out his cheeks, and roll up his eyes, and growl and roar and choke, and shake all over as if he had an agy? . . . I was once down in Mobile, when I

> saw them making tragedies, and, darken my peepers, but the bloody b—hes made me mad enough to swallow 'em, they were so cussed rediculous. (335)

The farcical clash between Horsey's elevated fantasies and Bull's pedestrian tastes later devolves into a slapstick brawl.

In the "Advertisement" to the 1855 edition of *Border Beagles*, Simms claimed that Horsey's character was based on reality: "I can confidently affirm that all the leading characters are drawn from the life. Even my actor, absurd as such a character may seem, emanating from the wild woods of Mississippi, is no less real as a personage than any of the rest." Guilds offers that "Simms apparently modeled him on James H. Caldwell, an early manager of Edwin Forrest in the South and Southwest," an assertion supported by Simms's own claim in 1840 that "I knew [Caldwell] years ago in New Orleans" and that what he "said & shewn [*sic*] of him is the strict result of my own observation" (*Literary Life* 97; *Letters* 1: 188). However, there is a long history of characters misinterpreting reality for theater or misrepresenting theater in reality, beginning with Cervantes but also including Shakespeare's character Pistol in *Henry IV* and *Henry V*, according to Edward P. Vandiver, Jr. ("Shakespeare" 139). Yet Simms's Horsey marks one of the first appearances of this character type in American letters, anticipating Twain's and others' later comic use of thespians in fiction.

It took Simms at least two years to write *Border Beagles*, a process that was delayed by his habit of simultaneously writing multiple texts and by the repeated disappearance of the manuscript in the mail. The first indication that Simms had started *Border Beagles* was in November 1838, when he wrote to publisher Edward L. Carey that he would send him "some portions of a Tale of Mississippi" (*Letters* 5: 334). He had finished ten chapters by the next month but told Carey in February 1839 that he had "to throw aside" that manuscript to finish "other & pressing tasks," which may have been either the preparation of *The Damsel of Darien* (1839) for print or the start of *The Kinsmen*, published in 1841 (*Letters* 6: 15; Guilds, *Literary Life* 94, 95). The next month marked the first of two "miscarriage[s]" of chapters in the mail (the second in October), forcing Simms to re-write parts of the novel (*Letters* 6: 16). In June 1839 the first part of *Border Beagles* was at the printer in Philadelphia as Simms continued work on the second half of the novel (*Letters* 6: 18–19). Finally, *Border Beagles* appeared in two volumes by Carey and Hart, anonymously, in 1840.

Simms's choice not to attach his name to *Border Beagles*—it was attributed to "the author of 'Richard Hurdis'"—was a consequence of his awareness of, and sensitivity to, the partisan nature of literary criticism. On one hand, Simms's correspondence reveals his career-long frustration with "the bedevilment of a small tribe of underling critics," some of whose judgment were "hampered by convention," others by "injustice" (*Letters* 1: 316, 5: 152, 1: 156). On the other hand, even by 1840 he was already experienced enough to understand that the new novel would be evaluated as much on his reputation as on the text's individual merits. In order for *Border Beagles* to be reviewed as objectively as possible, he wrote his friend James Henry Hammond that the novel and the rest of the Border Romance series were "published by me anonymously with some design to try an experiment upon the critics." He added "[t]hey have effected their purpose, and have given myself & friends an ample opportunity of laughing at the wide-mouthed of that miserable pack," perhaps a reference to a previously hostile critic who was deceived by the anonymity into praising Simms's work (*Letters* 1: 299).

But it is debatable how many critics were actually fooled by Simms's "experiment." The 29 August 1840 review of *Border Beagles* in *The New-Yorker* attributed it to Simms, "though we believe this fact has never before been published" (Rev. of *Border* 381), and the October 1840 *Knickerbocker* speculated that it was the work of "the popular novelist and poet, SIMMS, of South Carolina" (Rev. of *Border* 364). But *The Knickerbocker* also wondered why "an author of Mr. SIMMS's reputation would be willing to publish anonymously, and thus lose the advantage, in a pecuniary point of view, if no other, of his name" (364). Modern critics share the periodical's doubts about the advantages of Simms's decision. Guilds theorizes that doing so "was depriving his steadily climbing reputation of some of its momentum" (*Literary Life* 96), and Wimsatt speculates that the absence of his name may have led to the novel's being reviewed less frequently than it would have been otherwise (*Major* 98). Ultimately, Simms did acknowledge the authorship of *Border Beagles* and *Richard Hurdis* at a public dinner in Tuscaloosa on 17 December 1842 (*Letters* 6: 59–60n).

As a consequence, when New York City publisher J.S. Redfield re-issued *Border Beagles* in 1855, the title page bore Simms's name on the "new and revised edition." The textual changes were minor, mostly revisions to dialogue. The major differences in the Redfield edition (and the eight subsequent reprints of the novel through 1891 by various publishers, all of whom used the Redfield plates) were that it was now a single volume, it included two illustrations drawn by Felix O.C. Darley, and it bore a new dedication to John A. Campbell, an Alabama judge and sometimes-contributor to Simms's *Southern Quarterly Review*. The 1840 Carey and Hart edition of *Border Beagles* had been dedicated "To M—L—, of Alabama," to whom Simms entreats, "Let this tribute remind you rather of the affection which always keeps you in thought . . . on the part of him who prays still for your kindliest memories." The identity of "M— L—" has never been established, but given the desire of Simms—by this time a twice-married man—to trick critics, the dedication may have been a red herring. A German edition of *Border Beagles* also appeared in 1858, titled *Die Grenzjagd*.

In contrast to the mystery of "M— L—," many of the characters and the events of *Border Beagles* would have seemed familiar to American readers, especially southerners, in 1840. In the "Advertisement" to the Redfield edition of the novel, Simms claimed that like *Richard Hurdis, Border Beagles* "is no less truthful. The history upon which it is founded, is beyond question." Simms meant that Saxon and the Border Beagles were loosely modeled after the John A. Murrell crime syndicate and its illegal activities in the Old Southwest. In the "Advertisement" to the 1855 edition of *Richard Hurdis,* Simms claimed to have known "[Virgil] Stuart [*sic*], the captor of Murrell, personally" as well as other "*dramatis personae*, during my early wanderings in that then wild country" (11). However, Wimsatt argues that it is unlikely that the novelist ever met Murrell's captor (*Major* 97–98). She concludes that it is more likely that Simms read about the criminal's career in published accounts that appeared throughout the mid-1830s. Likewise, scholars including Floyd H. Deen (in "Comparison") and Dianne C. Luce have compared the plot and characters of the Border Romances to 1835 and 1836 texts that focused on Murrell's capture and have concluded that Simms made significant departures from the historical record. Luce contextualizes the discrepancies, explaining that "Simms was less concerned with the historical personalities of the clan's leader . . . than with the nature and workings of the confederacy itself," and that the novelist "chose to present a more generalized warning of the danger to his society from within" rather than depicting historically accurate crimes (239, 241).

Had he been called to account for specific historical inconsistencies in *Border Beagles*, Simms would have argued that these distinctions were spurious in the context of the genre of the Romance. He wrote fellow editor John Reuben Thompson that "[m]y novels aim at something more than the story. I am really, though indirectly, revising history" (*Letters* 3: 421). This is because Simms disdained scholarly accounts of the past, claiming that they failed to convey what he thought was most meaningful about history—the genealogy of a region's identity and the character of its people. In fact, in his 1845 essay "History for the Purposes of Art," Simms claimed, "We care not so much for the intrinsic truth of history" than for what it revealed about its participants and what history could teach its readers (*Views* 1: 27). Consequently, Simms's version of history may be more reflective of what Raymond Williams says is a "structure of feeling," or "the lived experience of the quality of life at a particular time and place," in this case, of the Old Southwest in the 1830s (qtd. in J. Taylor 670).

For the social fluidity and the legal vacuum depicted in *Border Beagles* were indeed characteristic of the frontier after Removal and during subsequent white immigration. If Simms himself had not witnessed how law and order were slow to catch up with those sufferers of "Mississippi Fever" during his trips west to visit his father, the young novelist would certainly have read about the economic speculation, political corruption, and general volatility of the region during this transitional period. The appearance of Methodist lay ministers like William Badger and theatrical troupes like that pursued by Horsey had historical equivalents and were harbingers of stability and decorum, but as Moltke-Hansen explains, Simms believed "[o]nly gradually, fitfully was society establishing the order and hierarchy necessary for true civilization—a condition that was more of a promise than a realization of Southern history to date" ("Plantation" 14). Until then, there were the violent Border Beagles and their survivors, the latter who flourished in the "Flush Times" via "shaving, speculating, and banking. . . . [and] the invention of fancy stocks; the designs of which they will dispose of to the numberless associations of humbug, which cover this scheming nation as with an eighth plague" (Simms, *Border* 495).

This literary record of the sensibility of the Old Southwest may be *Border Beagles*'s critical saving grace. Otherwise, the novel has not fared well in comparison to others in Simms's *oeuvre*. Its anonymous publication in 1840 made it difficult for Simms to capitalize on the novel's reputation, and critical tastes had already evolved by the time of its re-issue under his name in 1855. Nine years earlier Nathaniel Hawthorne had denounced Simms's vision of historical fiction as producing novels "cast in the same worn mould that has been in use these thirty years, and which it is time to break up and fling away" (qtd. in Guilds, *Literary Life* 182). Even Simms's biographers were lukewarm, if not hostile, in their judgment of *Border Beagles* compared to his other works. Simms's first biographer, William Peterfield Trent, denounced it and the other Border Romances as "marred by a slipshod style, by a repetition of incidents, and by the introduction of an unnecessary amount of the horrible and the revolting" (88). Guilds also expresses doubts about the text, admitting *Border Beagles* is "not [Simms's] best-sustained or most stirring novel" (*Literary Life* 99).

This assessment of *Border Beagles* was anticipated by critics during Simms's own lifetime. On one hand, there were some laudatory reviews of *Border Beagles*, especially for its realism and stirring plot. For example, *The New-Yorker* review of 29 August 1840, commented that both *Border Beagles* and its predecessor "*are true portraitures of southern life*, and as such we commend them to all who are curious to know the social and moral condition of the Southern States" (Rev. of *Border* 381). Likewise, the *Casket* of October 1840 complimented Simms: "The story is well managed throughout, and though the language is often coarse, it is not more so than the reality would warrant" (Rev. of *Border* 192). The otherwise-hostile *Knickerbocker*, echoing the *Casket*'s critic, lauded *Border Beagles* for its "scenes . . . of unusual power and beauty, and incidents of great interest, that win a close attention" (Rev. of *Border* 364).

On the other hand, even some of the novel's admiring critics had reservations about its decency. *The New-Yorker*, for example, classified *Border Beagles* as belonging to "the Jack Sheppard school, so far as its teachings are concerned," a reference to the most famous of the "Newgate Novels," which critics feared glamorized violence and romanticized criminals (Rev. of *Border* 381). Likewise, *Burton's* criticized the novel for its "amplification of the details of villainy," which "is a degradation of the intellect, and its effect upon the mind of the reader is to render him familiar with every grade of vice" (Rev. of *Border* 157). Poe, no stranger himself to the macabre, also admonished Simms in the pages of *Godey's* for "a certain fondness for the purely disgusting or repulsive, where the intention was or should have been merely the horrible" (Rev. of *Wigwam* 41).

However, the most recent—and more theoretically inclined critics—have transcended the Victorians' obsession with propriety and their successors' prioritization of unity and form to esteem *Border Beagles* in the contexts of structuralism and cultural studies. For example, with respect to the novel's relationship to the genre of the Historical Romance, Caroline Collins claims that it and other Border Romances challenged the standards of the era. She highlights how Simms "broke free of the confines of romance by selecting conventions from various types of romance and by learning to use those conventions in new and different ways. . . . Simms's realistic frontier, then, derives at least as much from his ability to exploit romantic conventions as from his graphic depictions of violence" ("Simms's" 81). Masahiro Nakamura likewise approaches *Border Beagles* from the vantage point of genre studies, coming to similar conclusions about the forward-looking qualities of the Border Romances. He claims that "the mode of romance recedes into the background to be replaced by a realistic representation illustrating how unsuited ['southern ideals'] are to the violence and bloodshed of the frontier" (106).

Other contemporary critics have explored *Border Beagles* using the Russian theorist Mikhail Bakhtin's perspectives on language and power. Scholars such as Thomas L. McHaney, Nancy Grantham, and David W. Newton (in "Border") value *Border Beagles* and Simms's other narratives set in the Old Southwest for their broad catalog of class-inflected discourse. On one hand, this diversity of language realistically mirrors the variety of voices on the frontier, from the bourgeois Vernon to the rustic Jamison. More importantly, though, Bakhtin argues that different voices and the competing ideologies that they represent have the potential to challenge the power of elite culture and its self-sustaining system of values, a conflict the Russian critic says is represented in the pages of novels. McHaney pursues this approach to *Border Beagles*, saying the novel's polyphony enables Simms to illustrate "a vital disorder, an open society, a folk risibility that diminishes the artificial codes of the higher classes" (*Border* 103).

However, McHaney may be mistaking the presence of lexical variety for the subversive qualities of alternative voices, particularly the latter's revolutionary or revitalizing possibilities. Simon Dentith points out that the "mere presence of linguistic diversity does not make for a polyphonic novel." Quoting Bakhtin, Dentith emphasizes that "what matters is . . . [how] these styles and dialects are juxtaposed or counterposed in the work" (47). In other words, the degree to which the ideologies represented by these voices are in dialog with and challenge one another is more important than just the textual presence of classed or raced language. Moreover, the resolution of these interactions is always preordained in historical romances such as *Border Beagles*, no matter the uncertainty leading up to their conclusion. As Moltke-Hansen observes, "[t]he reader is never in doubt . . . about the ultimate outcome of the story" ("Ordered" 135). And given Simms's whiggish interpretation of history—that "history is the final arbiter of the success of . . . societies," according to Moltke-Hansen—the novel and its conclusion validate a meta-narrative favored by the dominant elite culture of the South; progress toward an orderly, paternalistic plantation society similar to that which Simms belonged ("Ordered" 126).

As a result, alternate perspectives on justice and authority are silenced by the plot—in the case of Saxon and his gang—or the voices representing other marginalized groups are symbolically assimilated into the dominant social order. For example, the novel's independent woodsmen—Wat Rawlins and Dick Jamison—almost immediately defer to and pledge their services to Vernon, whose profession, gentility, and values symbolize the forthcoming southern planters whose presence will make the woodsmen anachronisms. In other words, opportunities for the non-elite characters (and the class identity, interests, and values that their voices symbolize) to challenge the symbolic representative of a professional and agricultural society are precluded when Rawlins admits that "I love the lad" and Jamison experiences "[a] sudden regard for Vernon" that the narrator characterizes as "first love" (190, 252). This hierarchical, symbolic union between elite whites (or aspirational white elites) and non-elites is also symbolically reinforced at the conclusion of *Border Beagles* in the forthcoming marriages among the characters. These new families promise to not only provide a domestic structure for the soon-to-be gentrified borderlands, but also to populate them (Wimsatt, *Major* 120–21).

Regardless of the novel's ostensible faithfulness to history or its alleged fidelity to representations of class conflict, *Border Beagles* still merits study. As Moltke-Hansen explains, Simms played no little part "before the Civil War to make the South what it has *since* been: a commodity as well as a place, a creation as well as a birthright, and a global fascination as well as a domestic preoccupation" ("Plantation" 4, emphasis added). The conflict and especially the resolution of *Border Beagles* represents the desire of the plantation South to duplicate itself, at least on the page. Consequently, *Border Beagles* demands our analysis, if for no other reason than for how its outcome offered a compelling whiggish perspective on the settlement of the Old Southwest, on justice, and on the teleology of southern history. For, as Moltke-Hansen observes, the legacy of this simulacrum trumped and outlasted historical reality in the American, if not the southern, imagination. *Border Beagles* helped create an ideological, imagined South for Confederate soldiers to defend, Thomas Nelson Page to memorialize, and for William Faulkner to dismantle ("Plantation" 16–17). Moreover, as long as white-authored southern literature is characterized by its special relationship to place, by the tension between honor and authority, by violence and humor, and by the attendance of the past in the present, formative texts such as *Border Beagles* should have a place on the shelf.

Carl Werner, An Imaginative Story; With Other Tales Of Imagination

SAM LACKEY

By the time *Carl Werner, An Imaginative Story; With other Tales of Imagination* was published in New York City at the end of 1838, William Gilmore Simms had established himself as a major figure in the world of American letters. However, as the 1830s marched on, new troubles mounted. He broke with his New York publishers, the Harper brothers, his wife was debilitated while pregnant, and he began to feel the effects of changes in the publishing industry and book marketplace that would soon contribute to an extended hiatus from his novel writing. And in October of 1838, shortly after the release of *Richard Hurdis*, he and his wife Chevillette lost their first child, Virginia Singleton. *Carl Werner* was born out of this dark period, and its sales and reception did little to brighten the dreariness. Though it received a smattering of positive reviews, the work did not circulate widely and failed to make a significant impact on the literary scene. It was Simms's second short story collection and, like his first, 1837's *Tales and Sketches*, which comprised the second volume of *Martin Faber and Other Tales*, it bore a strong imprint of German influence (or "Teutonic extravagance" as Simms called it). There is also an intense focus on the interiority of the protagonists, as Simms takes great interest in probing their mental states and exploring "the origins of sin" and "social pathological complexes" (Thomas, "German Literature" 9). This focus also shows up in both volumes of *Martin Faber* and later works such as *Marie de Berniere* and *Southward Ho!*, and it seems often to accompany stories infused with the irrational and supernatural elements that Simms associated with German legends and literature.

Carl Werner consists of two volumes. In the first are the title story "Carl Werner. An Imaginative Story," "Ipsistos," "The Star-Brethren," and "Onea and Anyta," all novellas between sixty-five and ninety pages long. In the second volume is the novella "Conrade Weickhoff," along with the short stories "Jocassée," "Logoochie; or, the Branch of Sweet Water. A Legend of Georgia," and "The Cherokee Embassage." Aside from differences in length between the five novellas and the three short stories, a clear line divides this collection into two groups. The first three stories of Volume One and "Conrade Weickhoff" in Volume Two are set in European locales and heavily influenced by a loose collection of German literary motifs and mythology; "Onea and Anyta" and the second, third, and fourth tales of Volume Two feature Native American characters and indigenous communities. Though separated by setting and content, the tales all function as prime examples of the "moral imagination," a protean idea that guided much of Simms's fiction thematically and continues to affect the ways in which scholars classify and discuss his expansive canon.

John Caldwell Guilds has shown that Simms believed all forms of fiction share certain purposes, such as achieving truthfulness and presenting a moral. For Simms, "truthfulness is never without its moral" and it requires "the treatment of vice as well as virtue, of low and vulgar characters as well as noble and generous ones" (Guilds, *Writings* xvii). As a romancer, he believed in dialectic narratives and symbolic structures that created character doubling in which moral opposites battled one another (Wimsatt, *Major* 39). As Mary Ann Wimsatt explains, Simms favored "the central romance procedure" of weighing the dialectic in favor of the side representing right conduct," which seems to be another way of saying that he delivers a moral lesson or example to his audiences (*Major* 39).

He may have pursued this goal in all of his fiction, but his "moral imaginative" tales place special emphasis on the "strifes between the moral principles of good and evil." The strife is usually carried out in mysterious realms and the narratives are clearly influenced by legends and myths emanating from medieval Europe and indigenous North America. He conceived these stories to be more fantastical, sublime, and purely imaginative than his historical romances, evidenced by his letter to Rufus Griswold in which he described *Carl Werner* as "marked chiefly by the passion & imagination—by the free use in some cases of diablerie and all the machinery of superstition, & by a prevailing presence of vehement individuality of tone & temper" (*Letters* 2: 224). Guilds points out that short fiction provided Simms with the latitude in subject matter necessary to indulge his "love of the marvelous" and his long-standing admiration of German romantic literature. And as J. Wesley Thomas has deftly demonstrated, "Simms's understanding of the German romantic tradition was inexorably tied to bizarre and irrational elements" ("German Sources" 129). This association of imagination with superstition, supernatural occurrences, and "vehement passions" is somewhat limited in scope but undoubtedly important for the study of Simms. To him, the moral imagination was the use of creative faculties defined in the above terms and utilized to deliver moral instruction and examples of proper conduct.

The Charlestonian often divided his work into two large groups: the "domestic tales" or "tales of the South," and the "moral imaginative," encompassing "stories under the influence of German (and Spanish or other European) Romanticism, usually with exotic settings and heavy philosophical or psychological undertones" (Guilds, *Writings* xxi). Half of *Carl Werner* clearly falls under this category, but Simms viewed all of the stories in the two-volume collection as works of the moral imagination, and to be sure the four Native-American-themed tales contain many of the same components and lessons that animate the stories staged in Europe. The versatility of a tale like "Jocassée" was later indicated by its presence in 1845's *The Wigwam and the Cabin*, a collection that Simms classified under the headings of both domestic and imaginative. In all of his stories of the moral imagination, he seems to connect the wild flights of fancy involving ghosts and ancient legends with a well-defined moral allegory depicting the triumph of good over evil.

Edmund Burke is often credited with coining the idea of the moral imagination in *Reflections on the Revolution in France* when he described the crimes against civilization perpetrated by the revolutionaries: "All the decent drapery of life is to be rudely torn off. All the superadded ideas, furnished from the wardrobe of a moral imagination, which the heart owns, and the understanding ratifies, as necessary to cover the defects of our naked shivering nature, and to raise it to dignity in our estimation, are to be exploded as a ridiculous, absurd, and antiquated fashion" (qtd. in Kirk 36). In his own treatise on the moral imagination, Russell Kirk sees Burke as referring to "that power of ethical perception which strides beyond the barriers of private experience and momentary events" (38). This power is best expressed through art, and was the "gift and obsession" of figures such as Plato, Virgil, and Dante. Kirk goes on to declare that the moral imagination, maintained by men of letters acting as standard-bearers of tradition, helps to elevate us above the apes and manifests itself as "right order in the soul and right order in the commonwealth" (Kirk 39). Though he never made explicit reference to Burke's concept of the moral imagination, Simms deployed the idea in much the same fashion as his predecessor.

Simms's inclusion of moral lessons in his fiction corresponds with Burke's desire to maintain the "civilizing manners" supposedly targeted by the revolutionaries in France. For both men, these manners appear to consist of respect for women and nobility, taste, elegance, and the principles founded on Christianity. Such touchstones of civilizing morality certainly permeate the lessons found in *Carl Werner*. Simms concurs with the general notion that artists are the most well-equipped to maintain moral standards through his belief that wild and often mystical flights of fancy are best-suited for the conveyance of clear-cut moral instruction. Even if he was not intimately familiar with Burke's writings on the French Revolution, Simms was undoubtedly tuned into many of the same conservative wavelengths and equally invested in maintaining moral standards that hearken back to older traditions of European chivalry and valor. As a phrase, the moral imagination has been put to work in a number of ways and applied to a number of different fields, from political science to theology to literature. Sociologist John Paul Lederach recently found three recurring threads linking the diverse contexts of the term: the ability to "perceive things beyond and at a deeper level than what initially meets the eye," the necessity of the imaginative act, and the quality of transcendence (26–27). Writing in 2005, Lederach approached the term from the arena of conflict-resolution, a specialization completely different from that of Simms. Yet they share an interest in the powers of ethical perception and creative ingenuity while also subscribing to the belief that the moral imagination can transcend its surroundings and transport people to a higher plane of existence.

Simms endorsed the moral imagination's capacity to reach these lofty heights, and he regarded *Carl Werner* as one of the best examples of the concept's application and narrative expression. In the aforementioned letter to Griswold, he groups it alongside *Martin Faber*, *Castle Dismal*, and *Confession* as the moral imaginative tales constituting "the best specimens of my powers of creating and combining" (*Letters* 2: 224). Released on the heels of his successful early novels, the collection was dedicated to Prosper M. Wetmore, a minor New York writer and friend of Simms. An association such as this one reveals the South Carolinian's participation in an expansive literary network and speaks to his growing cosmopolitanism and burgeoning reputation. While Simms seemed to be operating under the assumption that *Carl Werner* would continue his ascendency in American letters, the wider reading public did not share his enthusiasm. As Guilds notes, Simms was not satisfied with the circulation or reception of the story collection. Years after it faded from memory, he continued to "feel that *Carl Werner* never received its due, either in criticism or in sales" (Guilds, *Literary Life* 91). Having recently split with the Harper Brothers, Simms worked with a new publisher in New York, George Adlard, whom he branded incompetent and guilty of overpricing the book. Simms also blamed the unfortunate timing of the release: the collection appeared in the midst of the so-called "money pressure"—a probable reference to the Panic of 1837—and at a point in which "the great revolution in cheap literature" meant that "books of Tales at $2" were simply "not to be thought of" (Guilds, *Literary Life* 91).

Wimsatt has demonstrated that the effects of the panic and the economic collapse that followed lasted well into the 1840s and damaged the careers of many antebellum writers, including Simms (*Major* 136). With cheap paperbacks readily available and newspapers often pirating popular British texts, there was little market left by the end of the 1830s for lengthy romances from the likes of Simms, Cooper, and Bird. After his income from long fiction began to drop precipitously, Simms turned to the rapid production of history, biography, geography, essays, and tales for magazines. According to Wimsatt, this development harmed his long-term reputation, as he was pushed out of his major field into "varied, occasionally trivial projects that gave the corpus of his writing a distinctly miscellaneous cast" (*Major* 144).

Despite the author's frustration and the financial trouble he saw on the horizon, *Carl Werner* was received rather favorably by critics upon its release (Guilds, *Literary Life* 90). The *New York Mirror* cited the "power and brilliancy" of the imagination on display, while the *New York Review* considered it "a production of no common order in the class of works in which it belongs" ("Literary Notices"

207; qtd. in Guilds, *Literary Life* 90). Similarly, the *New Yorker* declared that the volume would help "elevate the American Romance to new heights," and the *New York Gazette* claimed that the collected tales were "equal in many of their parts to the best things [Simms] has yet presented to the public" (qtd. in Guilds, *Literary Life* 90). *The Boston Traveler* struck a slightly different, but still positive, note in stating that the tales do not exhibit traces of Simms's previous works, and thereby demonstrate his unique "versatility of talent" (3). The review from the *Traveler* also picked up on the influence of the "German school," though it maintained that Simms's treatment of the subject was still "wholly original." Conversely, the German influence was viewed less favorably in the *Boston Quarterly* and the *Knickerbocker*. Most of these appraisals date from December 1838 or January 1839, and subsequent months saw few additional ones. Notwithstanding the positive reviews, the book was beset by poor sales and limited circulation and thus did not make a lasting impression. Simms made several attempts to reissue the collection and proposed various new editions featuring "Carl Werner," "Conrade Weickhoff," and "The Star Brethren," either singly or together, but the only members of the collection destined for republication in his lifetime were "Jocassée" in *The Wigwam and the Cabin* and "Carl Werner" in book form under the title *Matilda* in 1846. Despite its undistinguished history and persistent obscurity, the collection, perhaps more than any other entry in the Simms catalogue, truly exemplifies the author's commitment to the moral imagination and his employment of unique narrative methods to convey it.

As the title story and the finest example of the goals and techniques that run through the collection as a whole, "Carl Werner" demands to be examined first. The tale begins with a frame story: the narrator and his companion walking through the dark recesses of a German forest discussing superstition and belief in the supernatural. Because they are in Germany, a land renowned for its "wild fancies" and "marvelous imaginations," the narrator's friend deems it appropriate to tell the story of the eponymous Carl Werner and his friend Herman Ottfried. Herman is described as a "good natured, laughing, and mischievous creature . . . ready always for fun and frolic" but who lacks faith and has slight regard for a ghost or a sermon. Carl, on the other hand, is "superstitious to the last degree," with a memory "perfectly crowded with legends the most extravagant" and a "feverish and perpetual desire" to increase his knowledge of the bizarre, irrational, and supernatural (1: 10–11). This desire is stoked to a dangerous extent when, on the eve of Herman's departure from their native village, the two young men make a pact that should death come suddenly to either, the departed spirit must return to the still-living friend. As soon as the pact is sealed, a "hollow laugh resound[s] from the dismembered vault of the aged abbot" where they sit, signifying the blasphemy of their pledge (1: 29).

Throughout the story, the narrator takes pains to portray the long-ago German setting as a shadowy, spirit-filled realm. Before beginning the narrative in earnest, the narrator describes how the German mind has been affected by the land's ghosts, its ancient lore, and its landscape of "sinking valleys," "dense forests," "wild wastes," and "deserted ruins" (1: 9). Such a setting is prime terrain for a tale of diablerie (sorcery and the representation of devils), which is exactly what the tale becomes following the friends' pact. Herman does indeed return after suffering a sudden demise, but in the form of a demon whose features are "hell-stamped" (1: 56). The demon forces Carl to confront the terrifying fact that he prayed for Herman's death in order to learn the secrets of the afterlife, and the young dreamer, who earlier found himself literally covered with Herman's blood, must acknowledge his transgression and repair his damaged morality. But first he must fight an unstoppable compulsion to visit the ruined abbey and learn the demon's intelligence. Just before Carl falls victim to his dark impulses, an old man with strange clothes and a long white beard helps set him back on the right path. Carl confesses his sin to his wife Matilda, the sister of Herman, and together with the old man they bravely face the fiend. The moral object in this story is transparent; Thomas called it a "Faustian story dealing with the strife between the principles of hate and love for a man's soul" ("German Sources" 132). The demon obviously represents hate, and the old man symbolizes the forces of love that eventually lead Carl back to his wife and domestic felicity. The old man's mystical and almost holy benevolence also cures the title character of his susceptibility to melancholy musings and the longing for forbidden knowledge. Carl's weakness leads him to the brink, but love and duty ultimately restore him to the good graces of home and society.

Thomas confirms that the tale imitates the "German manner" in terms of mood and style, but states that it does not closely resemble any specific German story ("German Sources" 132). Those supposed characteristics of German Romanticism of which Simms was so fond—superstition, supernaturalism, irrationality, and vehement passions, along with a wild landscape and desolate ruins—function here in the service of Carl's supernatural adventures and the story's overriding emphasis on the importance of humility, temperance, and love. While many nineteenth-century critics responded positively to Simms's approximation of this German manner, others claimed that Simms's depictions of German scenes and personages were a bit short on substance. The review in the *Knickerbocker* says as much when it states that Simms lacks "the proper study of the language," an appreciation of the literature, and "the knowledge of the superstitions of the people," all important prerequisites for understanding the "character and peculiarities of the Germans" (qtd. in Guilds, *Literary Life* 90). The review acknowledges that the external style is present and even cites a well-done passage, but ultimately asserts that style is not enough.

The interest in personal guilt and social responsibility that characterizes some of Simms's more psychologically-inclined fiction like *Martin Faber* also figures prominently in "Carl Werner," and it may prove to be a more substantive influence than the diablerie and superstition that Simms assigns rather generally to all things Germanic. Indeed, the most compelling moments of the story involve depictions of Carl's interior state: the "irresistible spell" and "unholy curiosity" that temporarily take control of him and the "guilty fear" he experiences when confronted by the demonic Herman. His agonized feelings and mental afflictions are probed to dramatic effect, and the characterizations in the tale remain strong, albeit occasionally overwrought. The setting is conventional but appropriately eerie. And the weakness most likely to be identified by modern audiences—the convenient happy ending and the *deus ex machina* represented by the old man—can be explained by an understanding of Simms's moral purpose. In order to affirm the triumph of civilization and man, Carl must return to the proper track after a hair-raising adventure, and the heavy-handed symbolism is a symptom of the unapologetically allegorical nature of the text. Many modern readers may reject such obvious moralizing, but in this tale, unlike others in the collection, the outdated technique does not obscure the aesthetically-pleasing qualities of a story well-told.

Having the protagonist learn proper conduct and values is necessary for the type of moral instruction Simms was looking to provide. The flights of fancy, the supernatural, and the fascination with dark impulses may serve more as accoutrements than the primary focus, but they remain indispensable in many of Simms's moral imaginative tales. By establishing a peculiar mood and presenting the threat of terror and destruction, these elements of the German style increase narrative tension and create an unmistakable contrast between the forces of light and darkness. This dynamic is equally visible in "Ipsistos" and "The Star Brethren," the second and third stories in Volume One. In the case of the former, the German influence is direct and unmistakable. Thomas claims that the tale is "little more than a prose version of Goethe's poem 'Zueignung'" in which the eponymous protagonist rejects the worship of the false deity who rules over his ancient society (the setting is far less specific here than in "Werner") and instead pursues the ideal of truth represented by the beautiful goddess who appears to him in a vision ("German Sources" 133). The irrational and exotic is again utilized to strike fear and animate unsanctified superstition: examples include a burning mirror, serpents, gigantic figures of black marble in the magician Bermahdi's chambers, and of course an avaricious goddess with her "voluptuous involutions" and "eyes issuing streams of fire" (*Carl Werner* 1: 99–112). The overall effect, however, is hardly more than insipid. There is no forward momentum to the plot or life to the portrayals on display—just a recycled fable rendered vaguely, set in an undistinguished locale and peopled with flat characters.

Like "Carl Werner," "Ispsistos" supplies clear symbols and a conclusion that affirms the triumph of goodness and truth. "The Star Brethren" performs the same task but does so through a bleaker lesson. Originally published as the "The Spirit Bridegroom" in 1837's *Tales and Sketches*, this novella centers on the doomed love of Albert and Anastasia. After Albert is killed at the hands of an evil rival, a fallen angel inhabits his body and resumes his relationship with Anastasia. The two young lovers then seem destined for happiness. But Albert's perpetual sadness and midnight rambles spark a powerful curiosity in Anastasia; she yearns for the ability to share his sorrows and understand his condition. The angel in the form of Albert tells her not to seek his secret and warns: "Thou wilt lose what thou hast, in grasping at what thou has not, and the very hope which tells thee of a blessing to come, steals a blessing from thee while it does so" (1:183). Eventually, Anastasia's pursuit of knowledge destroys her union with the angel and forces her to seek a new companion in the form of a mortal who does not repine or desire change, the exact condition the spirit was seeking in her. A clever ending partially atones for the tale's underdeveloped characters and derivative subject matter, as Simms once again follows Goethe's lead and liberally borrows plot points and themes from *Faust* and Burger's "Lenore" (Thomas, "German Sources" 130–31). Anastasia falls victim to the same quest for unlawful knowledge that plagues Carl, and, much like he did in his longer fictions, Simms suggests that moral wrongdoing is often due to folly, not innate perversion (Thomas, "German Literature" 9). Both Carl and Anastasia are merely guilty of misplaced priorities and over-exuberant imaginations, but unlike her male counterpart, Anastasia's higher moral perception and attempts at atonement come too late.

The final story in *Carl Werner* that wholeheartedly adopts the so-called German manner is "Conrade Weickhoff," the opening novella of Volume Two. Unlike its aforementioned kindred stories, this *Tale of the Imagination* offers a relentless portrayal of evil and horror with no redemption, hope, or respite of any kind. There is still a moral at work, but it is not presented through the demonstration of right conduct; rather, it comes solely through the depiction of moral depravity and despair. The setting is cloaked in grotesquely Gothic gloom and the mood is slow-burning dread and discomfort. Nowhere else in this collection is the diablerie Simms associates with German fiction quite as evident, and he boldly presents scenes and ideas that remain disquieting even for modern readers. It should come as no surprise that this tale was also inspired by German antecedents; Thomas points to one scene especially redolent of Foque's *Undine* ("German Literature" 8). Nevertheless, the story comes across as a mostly original creation, and if the lead characters are relatively conventional and the German manner quite familiar, Simms at least supplies a memorable villain, an atmosphere of legitimate menace, and a plot that is far darker than it initially appears.

Simms returns once again to a Faustian bargain: impoverished nobleman Rodolphe Steinmeyer, on the brink of suicide after failing to win the hand of fair Bertha, makes a deal with his friend Conrade Weickhoff, who has strangely reappeared in their native district after a long absence and a rumored death at sea. In exchange for the fortune needed to marry his beloved, Rodolphe must pledge to commit suicide if his name is drawn in an annual ceremony held in honor of a perverse and dissolute count named Oberfeldt. It soon becomes clear that Conrade is actually a demon or some agent of the devil who strives to possess Rodolphe's soul through their awful suicide pact, and Rodolphe suffers great mental anguish as he attempts to start a life and family with his wife. The tale is marked by the familiar supernatural style of the other Germanic stories—dreary forests, disembodied laughs, and supernatural visitations—but the emphasis here is squarely on the grotesque and profoundly perverse. For example, in chapter twelve the narrator describes the terrible aftermath of the first ceremony in Oberfeldt's castle: "the body of the suicide lay in state in the centre of the apartment, which was illuminated with an intense glare, shooting out from strangely large torches, borne up by sable figures standing in its many niches and embrasures." The corpse's head "had been nearly severed from the shoulders," the eyes were open, and the lifeless hand still grasped the bloody knife (2: 28).

More horrifying still is the calmly malevolent Weickhoff, a portrait of subtle evil. As the narrative progresses, Rodolphe increasingly notices his friend's bright, cold glance, his ironical yet conciliating smile, and his "strange, taunting laugh" which "goes like a cold wind" into Rodolphe's bones. The beautiful Bertha, who much like Matilda of "Carl Werner" is a patient vessel of suffering, also observes Conrade's loss of human sensibilities and his "staring sort of contempt," which puts her, "for all the world, in mind of the Mephistopheles" (2: 38–43). Here, Simms creates a villain whose scornful attitude, poise, and cold formality throughout the story are just as frightening as his supernatural machinations at the end. The author also manages to include a denouement featuring tragedy and unmitigated misery on a scale rarely seen in nineteenth-century American popular fiction. While the moral lesson is clear, Simms amplifies the portrait of vice and evil required by the moral imagination and allows it to overwhelm the forces of good and love, thereby creating a genuinely frightening reading experience.

It is fair to grant that Simms's German-inflected tales were grounded in more than just an idle interest or curiosity. Wimsatt has shown that Simms was immersed in German literature from the 1820s onward: he learned the language during his brief time at the College of Charleston, studied the literature with a group of friends under the tutelage of a German professor, and printed essays and reviews of works by Goethe and other German writers in the *Southern Literary Gazette* and the *Southern Quarterly Review* (*Major* 229). The knowledge he acquired surely informed his German manner, but in the four stories above there persists a level of generality and haziness that sometimes renders many of the settings and characters hackneyed or indistinct. The American-themed stories in *Carl Werner*, however, evince more particularity of place and more nuanced characterizations, and because of their novel subject matter, they avoid the derivation that pervades the European-set texts. In the case of tales like "Jocassée" and "Logoochie," the exoticism Simms associated with the moral imagination is found in America, and the familiar moralizing and romanticized symbolic structures serve new modes of American regionalism.

In terms of enduring appeal, "Jocassée" is the most successful of the tales found in the collection. Guilds and Peter Murphy have noted that it demonstrates Simms's desire to depict a native setting in all of its natural beauty and wonder while also melding familiar romantic ideas to Native American materials. Murphy, in particular, has demonstrated how this tale of inter-tribal strife set among the Cherokee Indians in the South Carolina mountains can be read as both a prose romance typical of the American Romantic period and a myth rooted in native tradition ("Virtues" 40–41). He goes on to say that the plot and theme of the text "relate closely not only to the morphology and nature of Cherokee myth and legend, but also their religion and cosmology" ("Virtues" 45). The basic outlines of the myth—a pure-hearted young girl remaining eternally true to her noble lover—are common and appear in many permutations in the traditions of many different tribes. Simms may have been inspired by an Ojibwa legend that he picked up from reading Henry Rowe Schoolcraft's work, but he is known for occasionally confusing the tribal legends he learned from Schoolcraft, or in some cases simply making them up himself as approximations of the real thing (Mielke 63). Nevertheless, he still allows for the inclusion of genuine Cherokee spiritual beliefs and oral traditions, such as the feminine Sun-spirit, the purifying qualities of water, and the importance of naming and signifying physical objects (Murphy, "Virtues" 44–46). Perhaps most importantly, "Simms lets a Native American legend stand on its own merit, providing a story that all can appreciate" and breaking the mold of typical Indian Romances of the period in which native characters are almost always viewed in relation to white characters (Murphy, "Virtues" 47).

Indeed, there is a noticeable absence of white characters in this text, aside from the narrator who relates the story and his host who takes him on a tour of the Cherokees' old haunts. There is also very little mediation or influence from the white world. Jocaseé, the brave warrior Nagoochie, and the girl's impetuous brother Cherochee dominate the narrative and fully inhabit the diegesis. Therefore, they are allowed to develop as fully-formed personages, or at least as fully-formed as most of Simms's romance characters, and are not forced to pose as points of comparison to similar or superior whites. As Murphy puts it, the characters and their culture must "be dealt with entirely on their own terms" ("Virtues" 74). Thus Simms imagines the region as an entirely Indian space, inhabited by supernatural figures and governed by Indian religion and cosmology. And though virtue and faith, here personified by the lovely maiden, are again rewarded while the forces of hate that infect Cherochee are shown to be destructive, this time the moral lesson is not necessarily Simms's own. He borrows it from an amalgamation of native myths and legends and does his best to recreate it faithfully. His reverence for Cherokee traditions and interest in native terrain reveal his well-documented attempts to fashion a distinctly American mythology grounded in the land's own ancient past. But there is more going on here. He also historicizes the warring bands of Cherokees in "Jocassée" by grounding their story in a specific physical space consisting of real landmarks like Jocassée Lake, Keowee River, and Whitewater Falls. By mythologizing Cherokee history and representing a physical location that is distinctly native and unmediated by white influence, Simms achieves a level of innovation that is markedly absent from forgettable efforts such as "Ipsistos" and "The Star Brethren" and even from better tales like "Carl Werner" and "Conrade Weickhoff." He reimagines the old American frontier and grants his native characters a degree of narrative autonomy and humanity that is exceedingly rare in Indian-related nineteenth-century romantic literature.

Similarly, "Onea and Anyta" takes place in a distinctly native space, but the story begins after the domains of the proud Yemassee tribe have been overrun by white settlers. A valiant chief named Echotee and the few remaining survivors strike off into the "deeper western forests" where "the shadows of evening soon sank behind them like a wall, separating them forever from their native homes" (1: 220). The narrative then shifts to two young Creek warriors who discover a broad lake with a verdant island in the middle. On this island they find two beautiful maidens and instantly fall in love. The main narrative thrust is comprised of the young brave Onea's attempts to marry Anyta despite her native tribe's wish that she wed another, and it eventually becomes apparent that the maiden belongs to the lost Yemassees, who have taken up residence on the secluded island and with whom Onea must battle if he hopes to win her hand. The tale features some striking descriptive passages and an exciting wedding abduction, but Simms would have been better-served devoting more time to Echotee and his wandering flock as opposed to focusing almost exclusively, until the very end, on the rather ordinary love story. Echotee's identity as Anyta's scorned suitor is barely mentioned and Simms misses an opportunity to plumb the pathos of a potentially more interesting character than Onea, who functions much like a standard romance protagonist. Still, the natives display a range of emotions and personalities, from the courage of the young braves, to the strength of Anyta's convictions, to the treachery of her friend Henamarsa. As is the case in "Jocassée," Simms attempts to fashion native people who are recognizably human and more than simply stereotypes of the noble savage. Onea's bravery and Anyta's dutiful purity may be rewarded at the conclusion of this uneven tale, but the most compelling, though maddeningly underdeveloped, thread is the elegiac portrayal of the lost Yemassee.

In "Logoochie; or, the Branch of Sweet Water. A Legend of Georgia," Simms's native setting is a more heterogeneous site of the cultural confrontations that typify much of his frontier fiction. Like the previous text, this is a story of displacement. Following the encroachment of white settlers along the banks of St. Mary's

River in south Georgia, the Creek Indians depart for the safety of more remote swamps and rivers, leaving the trickster deity Logoochie behind. Unable to part with his beloved Branch of Sweet Water and the "old woods and waters to which he had been so long accustomed," Logoochie stays put and soon grows attached to the white settlers, particularly the family of fair Mary Jones, and decides to serve them "just as he had served the red men before him" (2: 95). This service entails preventing Mary's young lover Ned Johnson from setting sail with the nefarious Yankee steamboat captain Nicodemus Doolittle (Old Nick).

Although Mary and Ned assume narrative primacy as the tale proceeds, it is Loogochie who remains "the presiding genius of the place" and his mystical influence secures the youths' happiness. The deity represents truth and virtue in the text; if nothing else, he stands in stark contrast to many of the white settlers, who Simms often refers to as "squatters" and are said to wreak much desolation with the "sharp edge of the biting steel" (2: 70). Logoochie's desire to serve Mary may seem dubious, but it is based on the likeness he perceives between her family and his former Creeks. He is drawn to Mary due to their shared principles and conceptions of moral responsibility, and after she helps him out of a bind, he resolves to return the favor (2: 81). He must first deem Mary and Ned worthy of the land and his friendship before he rights the moral path of Ned, a kind soul who almost succumbs to the temptations of Yankee avarice and materialism plainly represented by the steamboat captain. Because Simms bestows such moral authority on a native character and seems to align reader sympathy with Logoochie rather than the whites, Peter Murphy sees the tale challenging the necessity and humanity of Andrew Jackson's 1830 Indian Removal Policy. Whether or not this is an actual preoccupation of the tale, there is no question that Simms delivers his moral lesson and deploys supernatural, legendary elements in an aesthetically-pleasing, well-wrought fashion. He also constructs a compelling account of an American region and pays homage to the native culture. The likably "uncouth god" may eventually leave the Sweet Water Branch to rejoin his countrymen, but he forgets to remove the spell he placed on the waters, ensuring that the river and its surroundings will continue to be associated with and sanctioned by the Indians who originally called them home.

If in "Logoochie" Simms hints at a certain degree of subversiveness through his sympathy with the Indian deity and his distrust of the obtrusive white woodsman, "The Cherokee Embassage," the final story in the collection, sounds the loudest cry over the iniquities of the white man's dealings with the natives. This tale is differentiated from its brethren by a relative lack of the supernatural elements that Simms usually favored in his works of the moral imagination. More than the rest of *Carl Werner*, this tale is grounded in a real historical event: in 1730, a delegation of seven Cherokee chiefs sailed to England for a meeting with King George. The narrative begins with Sir Alexander Cumming [*sic*] and his military retinue traveling through "a wilderness, seldom, if ever before, trodden by

European footsteps" en route to the Cherokee town of Keowee, where they meet with the seven chiefs and convince them to make the journey across the Atlantic (2: 178). Much of the action takes place at sea as the chiefs encounter several new experiences: seasickness, alcohol, and a sportive monkey named Jacko. Simms also details the "bustle and exhibition" that greet their arrival in London, but the real narrative focus is on the unfortunate agreement signed by the chiefs at the urging of their "brother George" (a probable reference to the real-life Whitehall Treaty of 1730).

The narrator tells us that the treaty is a "precious specimen" of an "unfair relationship between parties originally contracting on an equal footing of advantage" (2: 197). The "cunning" Englishmen are clearly shown to deceive the Cherokee nation, and at one point the whites are referred to as "selfish traders." Worse yet, the return voyage proves disastrous for the stately Cherokees. The frank description of the unjust treaty and the unmistakably mournful tone of the narrative's latter stages distinguish the story and lend it lasting power. The characters are mere sketches and many fascinating scenes in London are glossed over, but the two sequences at sea are noteworthy: the trip to England for comedic value and the voyage back home for its harrowing depiction of loss. Furthermore, the moral lesson of the story supplies a subtle critique of European colonialism that continues to resonate today.

Whether it was due to the Panic of 1837, the uneven quality of work, or Simms's habit of churning out texts faster than audiences and critics could consume them, *Carl Werner, an Imaginative Story; with Other Tales of Imagination* was not particularly successful upon its release. It is not a central component of Simms's canon, but it is a collection that deserves more consideration than it has hitherto received. Not only does it provide an excellent example of Simms's German manner, it also features a unique brand of romantic, often supernatural regional short fiction centered on Native American communities and characters. Though the former suffers from some triteness, the latter mode has recently begun to garner more critical attention and promises to remain a popular subject for scholarship in the years to come. Though not all the stories have aged exceedingly well, the collection still stands as a testament to Simms's conception of the moral imagination, an idea that for him was both a genre of romance and the articulation of the fiction writer's higher calling. Ultimately, the collection needs to be read for two reasons: the insight it offers into Simms's techniques, goals, and innovations, and the fact that much of it is quite enjoyable.

The Cassique of Kiawah: A Colonial Romance

KEVIN COLLINS

Published in 1859, just over a year in advance of the Civil War, *The Cassique of Kiawah: A Colonial Romance* is the last novel that Simms published in book form during his lifetime. Many critics argue that it is also among his best works of fiction. In addition, because it was likely composed and revised slowly over the course of the author's career, this work is unique in the ways that it reveals the philosophical evolutions Simms underwent over the decades in matters related to the individual's responsibilities to his collective, the values of legality as well as personal and national loyalty, the relationship between European Americans and the Native peoples they displaced to create the United States, and other concerns central to American identity. But *The Cassique of Kiawah* is most notable for the complexity of its often dark characters and plot. Harry Calvert, the novel's protagonist, is similar to many of Simms's earlier romantic heroes with regard to the depth of his thoughts, to the boldness of his actions, and to his stalwart sense of justice. Yet unlike most of Simms's earlier heroes, Calvert is beset with disturbing character flaws. Likewise, while there are also characters who are purely evil, Calvert is in conflict mostly with essentially good people who are corrupted by office or who cannot or will not see the dangers facing them. The cast of characters matches the description that Yeats would later make of the world in his poem "The Second Coming": "The best lack all conviction, while the worst / Are full of passionate intensity." For these reasons and others, *The Cassique of Kiawah* is—even as Simms specifies in his subtitle that it is a Romance—an experiment in the form of the Realistic novel that was already being produced in the Old World by 1859, the form that would dominate literary America in the decades following Simms's death, and that would do so much to define the literature of the twentieth and twenty-first centuries.

This introduction focuses on the work itself, the text, the history of its composition and publication, the placement of the work in Simms's *oeuvre*, and the critical response to it over the decades. In addition, it includes a new critical analysis suggesting that—if not for the unfortunate timing of the novel's release, after the tensions that would result in the Civil War had reached the point of no return—*The Cassique of Kiawah* and its author might today have a much more significant place in the American canon of literature because of the ways that the novel foreshadows American literary Realism.

It should also be noted for purposes of clarity that as an honorific title for two of the novel's characters, the cassique of Kiawah (alternatively spelled "cassock," "casique," and "cacique") was originally the anglicized title of a prince of the Kiawah Indians. The Fundamental Constitutions of Carolina of the late 1600s suggested the title for use by the hereditary representatives in the upper house of the bicameral Carolina Assembly. The Fundamental Constitutions were never ratified by the Carolina Assembly, though, and the title effectively ceased to exist by 1700. There are two cassiques of Kiawah in the novel: Edward Berkeley and the Kiawah prince who is killed in the climactic battle for Berkeley's estate.

Plot Summary

The novel follows its protagonist's and lesser characters' pursuits of the tangible and intangible goals that motivate all people: love, honor, reputation, identity, a home, and wealth. These pursuits are complicated, however, by the work's setting in early colonial America: though none of the characters would likely identify themselves as Americans, all understand to some degree that their national identities are different than those of their Old-World parents.

This uncertainty of identity comes through most clearly in the character of Harry Calvert. Calvert (a *nom de guerre*) is the second son to the British noble house of Berkeley. He knows, as a second son, that the family's wealth will go to his older brother, Edward Berkeley, so he sets out in the novel's narrative past to make his own fortune, in service to King Charles II as a privateer reminiscent of Sir Francis Drake, raiding Spanish treasure ships from his own ship, the *Happy Go Lucky*. He is successful enough in this pursuit to develop a reputation: he is admired by the British and feared by the Spanish. Earlier, Calvert had fallen deeply in love with Olive Masterson, and the couple had planned to spend their lives together.

Calvert's professional and romantic lives are shattered by a single act of treachery when Charles II, as a ploy in his negotiations with the Spanish king, condemns the privateer as a pirate and puts a price on his head. Calvert is injured, and his ship is hobbled, in a battle with a Spanish fleet, and he undergoes a long convalescence at a private estate on the isthmus of Panama, primarily under the care of the proprietor's daughter, Zulieme de Montano. Knowing that he cannot return to England and to Olive, Calvert marries Zulieme upon his recovery, more out of gratitude than passion, and gathers his new wife, her maidservant, and his long-idle crew onto the *Happy Go Lucky*. The novel opens as the ship enters an unpopulated inlet near Charles Towne, in the British colony of South Carolina.

Leaving his wife and crew, Calvert slips into the city where he meets briefly with some old acquaintances, primarily Quarry, the colonial governor, and Mrs. Perkins Anderson, the doyenne of the young city's social life. From Quarry, he learns that a newly arrived English noble and his wife are building an estate that they hope will benefit the local Indians. Calvert hears enough clues to determine that the new arrivals are his older brother, Edward Berkeley, and his true love, Olive, who had been convinced by her mother that Calvert was dead and that she should marry his wealthier brother. From Mrs. Anderson, Calvert learns much about the social and political intrigues of Charles Towne. Calvert is aware that both of these people, out of loyalty to their king, ought to seek to capture or kill the pirate, but each has a corrupt motivation for accommodating him: Quarry accepts rich bribes from Calvert, and Mrs. Anderson hopes for a romantic liaison with the famous pirate. Calvert is vaguely disturbed by the disloyalty of each, but he recognizes both that he himself benefits from it and that the circumstances of each is remarkably similar to his own: though nominally servants of the king, each has been altered by his or her colonial status so that fealty to the king is less natural given the ocean that separates them and that Charles Towne is developing into something other than a remote outpost of the realm.

Calvert also visits with Old Gowdey, a former shipmate who has settled into old age as a backwoods hermit. Gowdey confirms a suspicion that Calvert had already held: whatever benign appearances they may present, the local Indians will certainly slaughter Edward, his family, and his servants at the first opportunity. Calvert determines to lead his crew in defense of the estate of his brother and his true love, but his plan is complicated by events that reflect again on his own alienated position as a servant of his king.

Calvert returns to the *Happy Go Lucky* to discover that a mutiny plot is afoot. His third officer, Edward Molyneaux—under the influence of a seaman who had sailed on pirate ships in the past—plans to take over the ship and sail it under the Jolly Roger, that is, to live up to the cynical edict of Charles II. With little hope of wealth by other means, much of the crew is ready to join with Molyneaux.

This scheme further complicates the central conflict of *The Cassique of Kiawah*: if Harry Calvert is justified in revoking his sworn allegiance to his king, and if Governor Quarry, Mrs. Perkins Anderson, and others are justified in pursuing self-interest over national loyalties, what is so different about the ethical position of Molyneaux and the rebellious crew? This question and others like it, though never answered explicitly in *The Cassique of Kiawah*, are the essence of both the novel and the 150+ year experience of British colonial occupation of North America.

Having already settled Zulieme in town with Mrs. Perkins Anderson, Calvert acts to thwart the mutiny. With the help of officers and men he knows to be loyal, he divides the committed mutineers and attacks each separately, killing Molyneaux in hand-to-hand combat. He then accepts the renewed allegiance of the members of the crew who had wavered, and together they set out to protect Edward and his family.

At the estate, Olive is bound to a sickbed, seemingly suffering from the condition that has afflicted so many romantic heroines in other works: heartsickness.

She alternates between lament and swooning, she neglects her young son, and her condition only worsens when Calvert arrives. Her husband denies the possibility that the Indians he had committed to helping could be planning an attack, and Calvert works around him to arrange for a defense. Calvert's intricate plan succeeds in thwarting the attack, but shortly after Calvert's force wins the battle, Olive dies.

In the final chapter, Calvert—having arranged a formal pardon for most of his shipmates—sails with his wife and a skeleton crew toward the isthmus of Panama.

The Text

Though some serial publications from the postwar years would later be released as books, *The Cassique of Kiawah* was the last novel-length work published as a book during Simms's lifetime. It is also the last of the author's Colonial Romances, novel-length works of fiction treating the evolution of European civilization in North America from a society dependent on and loyal to its European parent cultures to a distinct culture prepared for the independence that the American Revolution would bring. The first edition of *The Cassique of Kiawah*, the 1859 Redfield edition, is marred by over 90 accidental errors likely attributable to the printer, not an unusually high number for mid-nineteenth-century American books of comparable lengths. The most notable error, almost certainly a printer's error, is the inaccurate layout of pages in some, but not all, printings of the first edition. Page 561 was followed by 564, 563, 562, and 565. In addition, the text is marred by errors that Simms likely made. When using Spanish words, he was inconsistent in his use of tildes and of the Spanish letter Ñ. He spelled the name of one secondary character fairly consistently as "Eckles" in the first half of the book and fairly consistently as "Eccles" in the second half. In Chapter 37, Simms's narrator seems to intend to refer to Edward Berkeley as "the cassique of Kiawah," the character's honorific title, and refers to him instead as "the cassique of Accabee" ("The Cassique of Accabee" is the title of a narrative poem Simms published years before this novel). There have been several reprints of the first edition since 1859, the earliest through purchase of the 1859 Redfield plates by other publishing houses, and the more recent ones through photocopy processes. A new edition was produced by the University of Arkansas Press in 2003, which corrects many of these original errors.

Not much is known with certainty about the history of the composition of *The Cassique of Kiawah*. There is, however, a tantalizing bit of evidence in one of Simms's letters, a suggestion that the author may have begun the work at a very early age, prior to his earliest known publication. One of Simms's letters refers to "10 or a dozen chapters of a novel called 'Oyster Point' founded on the early history of Charleston" that he began at age eighteen (*Letters* 1: 285–86). There is no clear evidence that the work begun as "Oyster Point" is the same work that was later published as *The Cassique of Kiawah*, but the circumstantial evidence is strong: no other published Simms work focuses so intensively on the early colonial history of Charleston. If *The Cassique of Kiawah* began as "Oyster Point," then it is, in a very real sense, a reflection of Simms's entire literary life: of both the youthful Simms who took a locally unpopular pro-Union stand during the Nullification Crisis and the older author who issued some of the most strident calls for succession in the 1850s.

Many of Simms's novel-length works feature protagonists who are avatars of the author himself. If *The Cassique of Kiawah* is indeed the product of thirty-five years of Simms's intermittent labors, then it is hard to avoid the conclusion that the stalking horse for the Simms point of view is actually two different protagonists: the optimistic-but-naïve Edward Berkeley, who remains on his estate to contribute to the building of what would become the United States, and the darker and more realistic Harry Calvert, who, disgusted by the cynicism and hypocrisy of the colonial administration, "secedes" with his wife at the end of the novel as they sail together toward Panama.

Critical Response

Contemporaneous notices were few, but they were almost unanimously positive. Because of the timing of the novel's publication, positive notices were perhaps predictable in journals based in the South. Positive notices in national journals, especially those headquartered exclusively in the North, were surprising for the same reason: for years prior to 1859, Simms's reputation as a political advocate for the interests of his region perhaps eclipsed his reputation as a fiction writer, so even the most objective of northern critics may have looked for reasons to disapprove of his works.

Critical discussions of *The Cassique of Kiawah* were rare over the century following the author's death, but brief discussions of the novel were included in more general treatments of Simms and/or southern literature in works such as Vernon Parrington's *The Romantic Revolution in America: 1800–1860* (1927), Jay B. Hubbell's *The South in American Literature 1607–1900* (1954), and Jon L. Wakelyn's *The Politics of a Literary Man: William Gilmore Simms* (1973).

Critical interest in the novel was revived just before and following John Caldwell Guilds's 1992 biography, *Simms: A Literary Life*, with introductions to reprint editions written by David Aiken and Sean Busick, and with the latter's discussion of the work in his *A Sober Desire for History* (2005). An essay by Anne M. Blythe devoted exclusively to *The Cassique of Kiawah* was included in a collection entitled *"Long Years of Neglect": The Work and Reputation of William Gilmore Simms* (1988). My own 2002 piece in *The Southern Literary Journal*, "Experiments in Realism" (excerpted below), treats the novel as an important work in the development of American literary Realism.

"Experiments in Realism"

Even very early in Simms's career, there were some hints in his Romances of a Realistic mind-set, most of which were to be found in the earthy and often comical dialect scenes featuring characters who were "close to the earth": backwoodsmen, slaves, and poor squatters. These scenes, however, were often incidental to the central actions of the Romances, which concerned the loves and battles of high-minded and highborn protagonists in conflict with unmitigated evils. Given the prominence of elements of Romance in Simms's early fiction, it is remarkable that a few critics recognized the elements of nascent Realism as a strength of Simms's work even as the bulk of the critics celebrated his conventional Romanticism. In *Simms: A Literary Life*, biographer John Caldwell Guilds exemplifies these two views in William Peterfield Trent, "who believed that Simms's best work followed the romantic traditions of Scott and Cooper" and Vernon L. Parrington, "who insisted that Simms was at his best . . . [when] depicting life as it really was, not as it should be." Guilds concludes that "Simms the writer defies classification," but the fact is that critics will continue in their attempts to classify him, and these attempts will likely always say more about the critics and their proclivities than they will about Simms and his (304).

A particular chronological aspect of the Realist-Romanticist dichotomy, though, is demonstrable: in terms of technique, Simms relied far more heavily on romantic convention early in his career than he did later on. Nearly all of his novel-length works from the 1830s and the early 1840s use then-common techniques that would be castigated a quarter-century after Simms's death by Howells, James, and the other prophets of literary Realism: the establishment of conflict by means of unrealistic contrasts between wholly noble heroes and wholly base villains, the use of extended and often intrusive and pedantic asides in which the narrator abandons his tale to make philosophic or historic points, and the glorification of romantic sensibility that can be exemplified by the gradual deterioration and death by heartbreak of a character. Through the late 1840s and the 1850s, Simms came, with mixed results, to rely upon these conventions less and less. By the time *Woodcraft* was published (1854), Porgy, the Simmsian hero, was spotted with notable (and comical) vices; still-present philosophical asides were mostly taken out of the mouths of narrators and placed, less intrusively, into dialogue; and the widow Eveleigh, the novel's heroine, was presented—quite intentionally, it seems—as too pragmatic and tough-minded to be prone to the swoons and heart-sicknesses that dogged many of her romantic female forbearers in Simms and elsewhere.

In *The Cassique of Kiawah*, Simms makes an even more thorough break from these tiring Romantic conventions. First, Harry Calvert is not just flawed; he has a dark side so prominent that it takes even readers familiar with Simms's Romances hundreds of pages to determine that he is indeed the hero. Second, while philosophical asides are still important to *The Cassique of Kiawah*, few are made either by the narrator or by characters; instead, the most important are suggested by Simms and actually take place only in the minds of his more active and astute readers. Third, while a character dies of a broken heart in a manner that may be parodistic of that romantic cliché, her suffering and death do not save her virtue, spare her loved ones a horrible fate, or even teach a valuable lesson to a morally redeemable character. In short, there is no sign of the "dark victory" or transcendent truth that so often seems to accompany a lingering and tragic death in Romantic fiction.

A significant factor in the near-total break with these conventions that Simms achieves in *The Cassique of Kiawah* is his use of doubling, or presenting two characters who fill the same role in some way. Doubling obviates some of Simms's habitual romantic techniques, and it takes the place of others; more importantly, though, the technique involves readers more actively in the telling of the story and thus allows some of the lessons or morals Simms hopes to impart to be implied rather than stated. Though doubling would not in itself become a constant in Realistic novels, all of the functions that it serves in *The Cassique of Kiawah* had somehow to be fulfilled after Simms's death by the authors who brought the Realistic movement into being. In this way, then, Simms experimented with the techniques that would characterize Realism before that movement became prominent, even before the social, historical, and scientific conditions that would make it inevitable had crystalized in the awareness of its founders.

The most prominent pair of doubles in *The Cassique of Kiawah*—Harry Calvert and Edward Berkeley—share not only experience and morality, but the same parents as well. The two scions of the House of Berkeley are alike in their calm, manly demeanors, in their common sense of justice, and in the depth of their love for Olive Masterton Berkeley. Despite these common heroic traits, though, each of the brothers in marred by a character flaw: Calvert's life experience has made him too cynical and pessimistic, while Berkeley's has made him too trusting and optimistic. These opposing tendencies come into conflict with regard to an issue central to the American experience—the treatment of the American Indian—in a way that forces readers to choose which of the two potentials heroes has the traits that will most benefit the emerging American nation. After allowing readers to consider the question for several hundred pages, Simms settles it in favor of a particular combination of the two.

Benefitting from primogeniture, Berkeley arrives in the New World as the Cassique of Kiawah, "one of the newly-constituted Carolina nobility," and begins building his colonial estate (*Cassique* 123). A man who had always known good luck, wealth, and ease, he envisions an estate that will benefit himself and his family, the colony as a whole, and especially the local Indians who had been dispossessed by the arrival of the English. Berkeley's blind optimism, a proverbial trait of some early Americans and an asset for characters elsewhere in literature, is shown to be a liability here as he ignores repeated warnings from Calvert, from the colony's governor, and from others, even as the Indians prepare to attack his estate and massacre his family.

Just as artfully depicted by Simms, Calvert's most serious character flaw is the opposite of his brother's: rather than too open and trusting, his life experience has made him too cynical and distrustful. Having to earn his own way in life, he served his king as a privateer raiding Spanish ships until, without warning, Charles II redefined his service as piracy in order to please the Spanish king and condemned Calvert in absentia. In addition to this betrayal, he has been pushed to cynicism by losing his true love to his brother, a circumstance that he initially reads as another betrayal, this one by two of his intimate companions. Since faith in his king, his brother, and his lover has stung him, he has no faith in humanity generally, much less in the Indians specifically. He is suspicious of them early on and prepares for their attack despite his brother's nonchalance.

Clearly, in juxtaposing Berkeley and Calvert, Simms is not asking readers to make the easy choice between a Romantic hero and a villain. Instead, he presents two good but realistically flawed men—men, in other words, like those the reader might meet in real life—and in effect asks, "Which will be more instrumental to the development of a great nation?" The choice is made more difficult by the fact that the brothers are doubles in terms of their overall honesty, virility, and good-heartedness. This overwhelming similarity makes their most notable difference even more significant.

Simms masterfully manipulates readers' opinions on the question throughout the novel. Early in the story, hoping that a common humanity can overcome racial and cultural differences and lead to peace between the Indians and the English, readers want to side with Berkeley. Eventually, as clue after clue make the malign intentions of the Indians ever more clear, Calvert appears to be the wiser of the two, and the readers' sympathies grudgingly shift. In the end, though, after Calvert's cynical but necessary forethought allows them both to survive the Indian attack, it is Berkeley who stays to build Simms's ideal America, his optimism very much tempered by the example of his brother. Despite the fact that Simms clearly admires Harry Calvert—notwithstanding the fact that Calvert's necessary self-reliance seems to reflect the author's own—the cynic does not remain to make American history. Though Calvert's pessimism, like his brother's optimism, is somewhat tempered by the close of the novel, Simms seems to say, in setting Calvert's course for Panama, that his deep distrust of his fellow man disqualifies him from a lasting place on the American scene, that a degree of faith and trust is essential to the American character, even though trust taken to the extreme of gullibility—such as Edward Berkeley's trust of malevolent Indians—can be a liability. Calvert does influence the American character, but he does so primarily by his ability to modify Edward Berkeley's blind optimism.

Simms juxtaposes other pairs of doubles in *The Cassique of Kiawah*—some vital to the work's central conflict and others seemingly irrelevant to it—and the result is always essentially the same: the technique frees Simms from the different conventions of Romantic fiction, often transferring pedantic historical and philosophical asides from the voice of his narrator to the minds of his more astute readers. Governor Quarry is paired with Charles II to imply that, even if all royal authority is corrupt, local authority is more reasonable than distant and centralized authority. A foppish cavalier (Keppel Craven) co-exists with a hypocritical puritan (Job Sylvester) in order to denounce both sides in the English Civil War and especially to denounce doctrinaire factionalism in general. Old Gowdey and Sylvia are juxtaposed as the grateful and ungrateful servant. The Kiawah chief and Edward Berkeley, each bearing the title "The Cassique of Kiawah," co-exist in the novel without any explicit mention of the fact that they share the same title. Merely by placing two cassiques into the novel—one central to the action and the other marginalized and essentially anonymous—Simms encourages his readers to consider the inevitable but unjust progression of American history.

The last pair of doubles to be discussed here and the pair whose treatment most strongly presages the Realist mindset are Zulieme de Montana Calvert and Olive Masterton Berkeley, who co-exist as lovers of Harry Calvert. Olive (whose "troubles" are that she is intensely loved by two desirable men) falls completely apart: she becomes ill, neglects her husband and child, loses her will to live, and finally dies. Zulieme, told by her husband that she is, in effect, of secondary importance to him, reacts very differently: she amuses herself in society but remains faithful to Calvert by rejecting the advances of some would-be swains; in the end, she announces to her husband that she is carrying his child, and she adds, "[Now] you will love me as you loved her" (599). Calvert, still stung by the death of Olive, kisses Zulieme and—by all outward signs—obeys her "command." They sail toward the isthmus and the rest of their life together.

The delicate sensibility that brings Olive Berkeley to die for love is typical of the Romantic heroine (or even—as with Goethe's Werther—the romantic hero). Such a death was once considered worthy of sympathy, but it becomes truly a waste in *The Cassique of Kiawah* as it devastates the lives of the widower, of their infant son, and of Calvert, who had endured years of separation to find Olive, but succeeds only when she is in the throes of her death. That death does not solve any problems—Calvert and Berkeley had already reconciled while she lived—or even uphold a worthy principle. Readers eighty-five years earlier admired and even sought to emulate Werther, but readers twenty-five years after *The Cassique of Kiawah* would come to question whether Goethe's tragic hero's—and Olive Berkeley's—reaction to disappointed love is more pointlessly self-destructive than admirable.

Olive is fair-haired and fair-skinned, and Zulieme is a swarthy brunette; Thomas L. McHaney has noted that Simms reverses the convention of the fair-haired heroine's triumph over her darker double (as in Cooper and elsewhere), but does Zulieme really triumph over Olive? While Olive lives, both Berkeley and

Calvert dote on her and ignore Zulieme. The latter's "triumph" amounts to two conditions: her survival and her acceptance, even her embrace, of a less-than-ideal consummation. These two conditions in Zulieme—made all the more prominent by the fact that they were precisely what Olive, her double, could not muster—are among those that grew greatly in importance as the Romantic movement gave way to the Realistic. Through Olive's death and Zulieme's life-affirming compromise, Simms can be said—both literally and figuratively—to have killed off the Romantic heroine in *The Cassique of Kiawah* and to have brought into prominence the Realistic heroine a quarter century in advance of Howells's Persis Lapham or James's Maggie Verver.

Clearly, there are criteria under which Simms can be said to have remained a Romanticist until his death. This tendency is evident in *The Cassique of Kiawah* in its historical themes and settings, in its scores of gratuitous classical allusions, and in the florid language employed in its most emotional moments. Just as clearly, though, Simms relied less and less upon Romantic conventions as his career progressed, and he came more and more to anticipate what would later become the conventions of Realism. To Howells, James, and others, Realism was perhaps an inevitable response to the social conditions and scientific developments of the later nineteenth century as well as to an historical perspective that allowed them to critique Romanticism decades removed from its heyday. Simms, though, had none of these advantages in 1859. To the extent that he looked forward in *The Cassique of Kiawah* to the conventions of literary Realism, then, Simms did so not as a sociologist or a literary historian, but as a creative artist.

Castle Dismal; or, The Bachelor's Christmas

JOHN M. MCCARDELL, JR., AND BRIAN K. FENNESSY

"I have been scribbling another story," wrote William Gilmore Simms in early January 1841, "called 'Castle Dismal, or a Bachelor's Christmas in Carolina.'" The Christmas season had just concluded at Woodlands, the plantation where Simms and his family resided from the first frost of November through late May. As the new year dawned Simms, at 34 already an accomplished editor, poet, novelist, and critic, described, in a long letter to his New York friend and regular correspondent, James Lawson, his most recent achievements and his latest plans. A novel *The Kinsmen; or, the Black Riders of the Congaree*, was to be published in February. A short story, "Murder Will Out," had been sent off to "Miss Leslie" for publication in *The Gift*. Another story, "The Muse of the Ballet," was under review for publication in *Godey's*. A series of essays, accurately described by Simms as "very scorching & searching," on the topic "Southern Literature," had begun to appear in the monthly magazine *Magnolia* in December and would continue for three more installments (*Letters* 1: 209–13).

Indeed, Simms was in the midst of an enormously productive period. In 1840, the year just past, he had published a series of poems in the *Southern Literary Messenger* and *Godey's* and an "Apostrophe to Ocean" in the *Democratic Review*. He had published, to enthusiastic reviews, his *History of South Carolina*. For six weeks in June and July, after settling his family in Charleston for the summer, he had visited New York for the first time in three years. There he saw Lawson, met with publishers, and renewed acquaintances with that city's lively artistic and literary community. He had en route stopped for brief visits in Washington, Baltimore, and Philadelphia. In November his agricultural oration at Barnwell Courthouse evoked a demand that it be published and also suggested that the orator might have a future in politics (*Letters* 1: 170–71).

The preceding twelve months, in other words, had shown all of Simms's protean talents on display. And his energy and creativity did not appear to be flagging. He continued to write and publish poetry, to compose essays and stories, to make notes for proposed biographies of "worthies of Carolina Revolutionary History," and even to try his hand at drama. He concluded his letter to Lawson by requesting back copies of *Knickerbocker* magazine and newly published anthologies of poetry, edited by George Pope Morris and William Cullen Bryant, the latter including two of Simms's works. Hoping, as always, for a prompt response in the form of "a budget of personal & literary news to enliven me," Simms sealed the letter and returned to his literary labors (*Letters* 1: 213).

The past year of activity, and that in which Simms now found himself engaged, offered revealing suggestions about his temperament, his work habits, his remarkable range of interests and, also, why, to so many critics over so many years, the most accurate assessment of his status as an American author has remained his own self-composed epitaph: "Here lies one, who after a reasonably long life, distinguished chiefly by unceasing labor, has left all his better works undone" ("Personal").

I

"Castle Dismal," published under the pseudonym G.B. Singleton, appeared in monthly installments in *Magnolia*, beginning in January 1842. No chapter appeared in May. The editors explained the hiatus as simply a decision "to defer the publication of the Sixth Chapter . . . in order to conclude that of 'Turgesius,'" a Viking chief who plundered Ireland in 832 A.D. ("Editorial Bureau" 320). Doubtless readers were on the edge of their seats to learn how this came out.

Though the story resumed in June, it was preceded by distressing news:

> An unexpected and grievous domestic calamity in the family of Mr. Simms—the loss of his youngest daughter—deprives us, to a certain extent, of his assistance in the present number, and will no doubt abridge considerably the amount of his labours for that ensuing. This event impairs several of the literary and other arrangements of our work, but we trust that the interruption . . . will be only temporary ("Editorial Bureau" 320).

Indeed, Simms was shattered by the sudden loss. "In the moment of my greatest seeming security, when everything was calm around me," he lamented to his friend James Henry Hammond, "the bolt fell at my fireside." Mary Derrille Simms, 2½ years old, succumbed to scarlet fever in late April 1842. "Of four [children] I have but one left," he continued, adding, significantly, "of the 3 children of my present wife not one. . . . I am almost wholly baffled and broken up" (*Letters* 1: 303–04).

The "present wife" of whom Simms spoke was his second. He had married, first, Anna Malcolm Giles, of Charleston, in 1826, and she had borne him a daughter, Anna Augusta Singleton. But Anna died, and, in 1836, Simms remarried, this time to Chevillette Roach, age 18. Chevillette was the daughter of Nash Roach, a planter with two plantations in Barnwell District. By this marriage Simms, age 30, had become a member of the planter class. For the rest of his life Woodlands, one of the two Roach plantations, would be his beloved home (*Letters* 1: lxvi-lxviii, lxxvii). Yet, in 1842, that home was devastated. All three children by Chevillette had died. Simms, clearly, was undone.

When the *Magnolia* noted the most recent of these deaths, it also mentioned "literary and other arrangements" referring to Simms's agreement, in March

1842, to take over as editor of that publication and move its offices from Savannah to Charleston (Guilds, *Literary Life* 134). The fifth installment of "Castle Dismal" appeared in the June 1842 issue. The sixth and final chapter never was published.

Editorial demands and family grief undoubtedly delayed completion of the story as well as its revision for publication as a book. Simms sailed from Charleston to New York on 31 July 1843. He returned to Charleston in mid-September and soon after forwarded to Lawson the finished manuscript of "William Potter, or a Christmas at Castle Dismal—a Ghost Story," which he asked Lawson to deliver to the Harpers for publication (*Letters* 1: 363). Thus, it is clear that by the end of September 1843 Simms had completed the hitherto incomplete tale and had also made revisions to the *Magnolia* version.

The Harpers declined to publish, and there was likewise little interest among other of Simms's and Lawson's contacts. Finally, in February 1844, increasingly concerned to get the story "off my hands without positively giving [it] away" (*Letters* 1: 404), Simms asked Lawson to deliver the story to Burgess and Stringer, a new publishing house that had also secured the rights to James Fenimore Cooper's works. Burgess and Stringer published the tale in the autumn of 1844 (Guilds, *Literary Life* 168).

II

Castle Dismal, the title of the published volume, is subtitled *A Bachelor's Christmas*, which suggests several contexts for the work. One, of course, is the author's intimate knowledge of the South and his desire, and ability, to bring that knowledge to light and life. Simms's dedication of *Castle Dismal* notes that the story is "illustrative of the traditions of the Southern States" (iii), and the narrator begins his tale with sentimental praise for "the song and the dance, the frolic and the festival" of Christmas in South Carolina (10). Images of the "fatted turkey, the selected ham, mince pies, and the unfailing egg-noggin" lure the reader into what might be a colourful, if superficial, paean to southern customs and the coming together of an entire household around a single table at the holidays (10).

Yet these festivities are not what "The Bachelor's Christmas" is all about. Nor is the tale properly placed in the tradition of "bachelor fiction," though aspects of that genre are also evident. A familiar theme in nineteenth century writing, a protagonist or narrator identified as a bachelor frequented periodicals prior to the publication of *Castle Dismal*. A brief listing of titles appearing in the *Southern Literary Messenger* alone would include "The Bachelor's Death-Bed," "Dorcas Lindsay: or, the Bachelor's Writing Desk," "A Stray Leaf from a Bachelor's Note-book," "The Bachelor Beset: or the Rival Candidates," and "Bachelor Philosophy." These stories, as well as longer works, exemplified the growing uncertainty over the place of the bachelor in a society dominated by ideologies of domesticity.[1]

Ned Clifton, the story's protagonist, describes himself as a "veteran bachelor" (10), and his "terror of the sex" (20) stems from a fear that marriage "destroys many a good heart and generous spirit," turning man into a "tame cur" (12). Clifton is modeled on Benedick, Shakespeare's misogynistic bachelor in *Much Ado About Nothing*, who eventually admits to his love for Beatrice once he is tricked into thinking that she loves him. In Simms's story, Clifton and Elizabeth Singleton do eventually confess their love for each other, freeing Clifton, in his words, from the "melancholy dependencies of bachelorism" (11).

Nor is *Castle Dismal* much of a Christmas story. The joys of this particular Christmas prove illusory. The charm and mirth of the season provide a recognizable backdrop against which Simms can in fact subvert domestic expectations through the unnatural—a bachelor living in the home of married friends, the appearance of ghosts, and an inner story of infidelity and murder that has been hidden by previous generations of inhabitants. The association of Christmas and ghost stories grew through both print and popular custom during the 1830s, although "Castle Dismal" predates Charles Dickens's use of the supernatural to restore the spirit of reunion and joy in such works as *A Christmas Carol*. For Simms, the Christmas ghost story instead casts a heavy gloom over modern, nineteenth-century notions of the home as a haven from a heartless outside world.[2]

Though each of these themes is clearly evident, the most significant context for understanding *Castle Dismal* is found elsewhere. Horace Walpole's *The Castle of Otranto*, first published on Christmas Eve 1764, introduced a new literary genre that came to be called Gothic. Walpole established terror as the dominant element, with its source not only in the presence of ghosts, prophecies, and plot twists, but also in the conflict over lineage and succession. The irrepressible threat that, through the supernatural intervention of God or fate, long-buried secrets of the past will come to light, drives the plot forward in *The Castle of Otranto* and most other Gothic texts. Often this instigating force is the result of some crime committed in the distant past, which must be avenged in order to achieve justice. The transgressor's fears about the disruption of patriarchy and domestic order allow the author to explore extremes of anxiety, cruelty, and passion before the crime is ultimately punished and contemporary conventions of morality are restored (Bleiler vii–xviii).

Walpole exerted considerable influence on the direction of Gothic literature. On the most basic level, the word "Castle" became part of the title for hundreds of novels over the next century, each time suggesting a labyrinthine architecture that complemented the imprisonment of the structure's inhabitants within a claustrophobic world of futility and despair. Themes of terror and horror, guilt and innocence, oppression and persecution were further elaborated in the works of Ann Radcliffe and Matthew "Monk" Lewis. Chiaroscuro became a recurring and almost predictable technique in such Gothic works. Nineteenth-century authors brought an increased amount of supernaturalism, the replacement of ancient castles with more familiar domestic settings, and a greater focus on psychological complexity (Bleiler xiii–xvii).

In the United States, some of these themes could be found in the early work of James Fenimore Cooper, Washington Irving, and Nathaniel Hawthorne, as well as in one of Simms's early novels, *Martin Faber*. The most accomplished American writer of supernatural tales was, of course, Edgar Allan Poe, who emerged in the forefront of Gothic literature in the 1830s with such tales as "Ligeia" and "The Fall of the House of Usher." Poe demonstrated a remarkable ability to unify the elements of character, setting, and mood in the short story to achieve a disturbing portrayal of the neurotic, Gothic mindset (Savoy 181). Thus, the beginnings of Gothic literature in America, according to the literary critic Allan Lloyd-Smith, exhibited a "preference for a more domestic unease and a psychological Gothic, with close relation to the uncanny and the ghost story" (94).

Yet despite evidence that Simms recognized the extent to which he was working within the wider body of Gothic literature, it remains difficult to say what specifically led Simms to choose *Castle Dismal* for a title and the name of the house where the ghostly plot unfolds. Simms may have been aware of a "Castle Dismal" in Robert Bisset's novel *Douglas; or, the Highlander* (1800), or he may have been simply continuing the Gothic themes begun by Walpole. Descriptions such as "this dismal old castle" (2: 6) and "these dismal galleries and halls" (4: 18) can be found in Radcliffe's *The Mysteries of Udolpho*. So perhaps it seemed natural to Simms to employ the already well-accumulated discourse of the Gothic in choosing a title. Moreover, Hawthorne gave his boyhood home the appellation of "Castle Dismal" when he returned to it with his wife in the 1840s, although he may have used the name earlier. It seems unlikely that Hawthorne would have taken this name from Simms, since the Salem writer never admired Simms's work. Nor is it likely that Simms would have been aware of Hawthorne's residence. It is more likely that both were inspired by the same Gothic sources but chose the appellation independently.

Traditional elements of the Gothic pervade *Castle Dismal*. The advertisement preceding the first chapter states Simms's intent to paint events in the lights and darks of chiaroscuro (v). As the narrator, Ned Clifton, approaches his friend's homestead on a "dark and cloudy day" (14), even the lantern at the end of the closed avenue of trees "tended rather to increase than diminish the tone of gloom and coldness" (18). The exterior of the house is likened to a prison or dungeon, and, although the current inhabitants provide a refreshing contrast of mirth, the ghosts of Mr. and Mrs. Potter demonstrate their own imprisonment "by decided and conflicting passions" (54), such that their re-enactment of some past scene must be intended in order that the narrator carries out his duty of bringing them to justice in the present. Clifton ominously declares, "I felt sure that what I had seen had been vouchsafed for some special object—that I was to become an agent in some drama of the future, having an immediate connection with some terrible drama of the past" (70–71).

This description of the house and the sensation felt by the narrator upon arriving there are remarkably similar to Poe's setting of the scene in "The Fall of the House of Usher." Though Simms developed his own plot, he retained themes often employed by Poe. The conflicting passions and moral agony of the transgressor or villain, William Potter, and his adulterous wife, would have been familiar to readers of Poe. Ned Clifton reveals even greater complexity in his various moments of interior torment, melancholia, and misogyny. He exclaims that if he had not thought to seek out his boyhood friend, Frank Ashley, for the holidays, "I might have committed suicide, drunkenness, or some other felony" (11). Yet Castle Dismal offers no surcease. The disruption or secret perversion of a place of supposed domestic bliss becomes evident to Clifton, and the relentless heightening of terror grows to encompass not only the suspected, and then confirmed, infidelity and murder that the ghosts re-enact nightly, but also a terror of marriage itself.[3]

In Gothic texts, as in the works of Shakespeare, the characters must either die or marry by the end of the story. For Clifton, the sight of Castle Dismal is not an augury of his own death, but something possibly worse, a dark presentiment "that I might fall into some snares of marriage on this visit." He dismisses this fear "as being quite too dreadful for contemplation" until it becomes apparent that Frank's wife has discovered his "terror of the sex" and determined to match him with one of her friends (19–20). Perhaps it is not surprising, then, that the theme of bringing justice to the ghosts of the haunted chamber is complemented by the story of Ned Clifton's reformation into a soon-to-be-married man.

III

Critics lavished high praise on *Castle Dismal*. Edgar Allan Poe called it "one of the most original fictions ever penned. . . . No man of imagination can read this story without admitting instantly the genius of its author" ("Critical Notices"190). A contemporary critic, Evert Augustus Duyckinck, a close friend of Simms, deemed it "one of the best ghost stories we have ever read. . . . We question whether there is anywhere a better manager in the construction of a tale" (*Castle* 1). William P. Trent, Simms's first biographer, though less inclined to Poe's praise for the story's "supernatural portions," found more appealing "the descriptions of the old homestead from which it took its name" (150). In his 1992 biography, John Caldwell Guilds pronounced the story "excellent" and continued, "in establishing atmosphere, tone, and mood, it is superb" (*Literary Life* 167). The work was also one of Simms's favorites. He believed it one of the "best specimens of my powers of creating & combining, to say nothing of a certain intensifying egotism, which marks all my writings written in the first person" (*Letters* 2: 224).

The warm critical responses to *Castle Dismal* were matched by strong sales. By mid-January 1845, Simms reported to Lawson, Charleston booksellers had "been compelled to order fresh supplies several times" (*Letters* 2: 13). By June 1845, more than 500 copies had been sold in Charleston (*Letters* 2: 82). The success of the work prompted Simms to propose to Lawson, in November 1845, a second edition. He added, suggestively, "I have an introduction to C.D. which will improve it I fancy. It is humorous!!" (*Letters* 2: 113). Soon thereafter a second printing did appear, but with no changes and no introduction. Again, in 1846, Simms suggested to Duyckinck a new, illustrated edition: "its diablerie, illustrated, . . . would make a hit" (*Letters* 2: 234). Yet again, in September 1849, Simms urged Putnam to bring out a new edition "from my stereotype plates, to be sent forth with broad margin & fine paper as [a] 50 cent [book], but he never answered me" (*Letters* 2: 557–58). A year later Simms wrote Lawson, "I wish you would get Stringer to put up for me the plates of 'Castle Dismal'" (*Letters* 3: 67). In April 1855, he tried once more, this time with Henry Carey Baird. "Don't you think," he wrote, "that an edition of . . . Castle Dismal . . . printed on thick paper . . . and put in neat colored paper at fifty cents, would be a good speculation? Bad as the book publishing season is, people must buy & read something" (*Letters* 3: 382).

At the same time he was pressing Baird, Simms was preparing *Castle Dismal* for inclusion in a series of "Novellettes" to be published by J.S. Redfield as part of a uniform edition of all of Simms's works that had begun to appear under the Redfield imprint in 1853. Unfortunately for Simms, Redfield temporarily suspended publication during the financial Panic of 1857. As a result, neither *Castle Dismal* nor any other title Simms hoped to include in this series of novellas ever appeared, and the Redfield Edition remained incomplete.

In 1863 Simms made one last effort, seeking the assistance of his old friend John Reuben Thompson, editor of the *Southern Literary Messenger*. "Having conceived the idea that a series of my minor tales or novels," including *Castle Dismal*, "would be good selling books, especially now, & for reading in camp and along the highways—(small volumes each of 150 to 200 pages,—& bringing from 50 to 75/100)," Simms had sent a proposal to West and Johnson publishers. But they did not respond. Simms asked Thompson to make sure they had received his letter, because "[i]f received, their silence is perhaps sufficient answer" (*Letters* 4: 420).

IV

For some hitherto inexplicable reason, *Castle Dismal* has never been republished since its second issue. How curious. Repeatedly cited as an excellent example of Simms's skills as a story-teller, almost always offered by name to support Simms's claims to a higher literary status than he has generally occupied—yet never republished, even though many of his stories, most of them inferior to *Castle Dismal*, have been reissued, sometimes multiple times.

A recent discovery, described elsewhere, offers tantalizing clues. At various times during the period 1845–1857 Simms worked on what he might have intended to use as the "humorous" introduction to a new edition of *Castle Dismal*. This manuscript fragment, bearing the title "Rawlins' Rookery," tells a story about the writing of *Castle Dismal* and also provides startlingly revealing glimpses into the life and mind of its author. An edition of "Rawlins' Rookery" is currently in preparation for publication, with extensive annotations, and it promises to shed additional light on *Castle Dismal* and its author.

That light will further illuminate the autobiographical elements clearly present in the story. Simms spent the Christmas season of 1835, as well as much time after the death of his first wife, at the Clear Pond plantation of his friend since boyhood, Charles Rivers Carroll. Carroll's father and Simms's father had both come to Charleston from northern Ireland, and together they became neighbors and members of St. Paul's Episcopal Church. Simms had studied law in Charles Carroll's office and, after the death of Anna and a fire that destroyed Simms's house in Summerville in late 1833, Carroll took Simms and his young daughter Augusta into his household. Thus, for extended periods of time, Simms's address was "Charles R. Carroll, Midway, Barnwell District" (*Letters* 1: xcvii, 68). In 1834 Simms dedicated his romance *Guy Rivers* to Carroll: "true friend, who from boyhood to manhood, has always maintained for me the same countenance—whose friendship no change of situation or circumstance has impaired or affected—whose advice has counselled—whose regards have cheered—whose encouragement, when I would have desponded, has stimulated and strengthened—who would not let me fear, and who taught me a familiar habit of hope—I dedicate this book with a single wish,—not to seem extravagantly selfish,—that it may appear as worthy in the sight of others as he is estimable in mine."

From Clear Pond, Simms began to court Chevillette Eliza Roach during the winter of 1835–36. After her brother was killed in a duel at South Carolina College, Chevillette was the only remaining child of Nash Roach. A widower, Nash Roach had acquired Oak Grove, where, styling himself as an English gentleman, he also found himself a neighbor of his first cousin—Charles Carroll. Though Simms may have met Roach and his beautiful daughter previously in Charleston, where both father and daughter sang in the choir of St. Paul's, it was through the aid and mutual friendship of Carroll, and on the grounds of Carroll's plantation, that Simms wooed and won Chevillette (*Letters* 1: lxxvii-lxxviii).

Thus, the courtship story in *Castle Dismal* is remarkably like the Christmas courtship of Simms and Chevillette. Detail after detail in the story reveals an intriguing and sometimes humorous connection, as the reader finds out that Ned Clifton and Elizabeth Singleton (not only the surname under which he published the original magazine version of the story but also the maiden name of the mother he never knew) are 30 and 18 years-old respectively (the same ages as Simms and Chevillette that winter); that Clifton discovers that Elizabeth is an only child; and that he wishes to know if the lady is of a good surname, for he would not marry a woman with an ugly one. Perhaps Simms's own reassurance with regard to Chevillette's maiden name—Roach—was the same reassurance offered to Clifton: "I trust she will suffer you to alter it to your liking" (21). Clifton's host and his spouse also bear close resemblance to Carroll and his wife, Sarah Fishburne.

Simms described Chevillette in a letter to Lawson in 1836: "She is young—just 18—a pale, pleasing girl—very gentle and amiable—with dark eyes & hair, sings sweetly & plays upon piano and guitar." An almost identical description appears in Simms's description of Elizabeth Singleton in *Castle Dismal*. In his letter to Lawson, he goes on to note that, "in marrying the lady to whom I am engaged, I should be at no expense while living in the South, the case would be very materially altered if I wished to carry her with me to the North during the Summer, as my desire and my pursuits alike would render it necessary to do" (*Letters* 1: 90–91).

After their marriage, in November 1836, Simms and Chevillette moved to Woodlands, the property across the Edisto River from Oak Grove, both owned by Nash Roach. He thus could be financially secure as a full-time writer living on a plantation belonging to his father-in-law. This security would tie him to Woodlands and make him dependent on his father-in-law, a widower with but one living child.

To what extent Simms may have actually discussed with Mr. Roach or Chevillette his wish to "carry her North during the Summer" will never be known, but what is known is that Chevillette made the journey only twice, once in 1837, when she was six months pregnant, and a second time in 1844. The first visit included travel by stage coach through the mountains of western Massachusetts as well as time in New York City. Chevillette's experience on this arduous itinerary is not known, but according to Simms, "Madame was somewhat fatigued . . . but she bore it better than I expected" (*Letters* 1: 102–03). The second involved a long visit with the Lawsons in New York, during which the Simmses seriously pondered a move north (*Letters* 1: 404). Yet the move never occurred, and Chevillette never ventured north again.

One may only surmise how often the topic of removal to the North may have arisen in the Simms household. Less surmise is required to determine why Simms and his family remained in South Carolina. In 1846 Simms confided to his friend James Henry Hammond, "My wife is an invalid—breeding every year—is an only child—her father advanced in life—unwilling that she should leave home even for a week's visit. . . . To leave my family, when such a relation subsists between us, is not easy" (*Letters* 2: 247).

That same year Simms wrote to Lawson, "I seriously deliberate upon the propriety of transferring myself, family or not, to Philadelphia or New York" (*Letters* 2: 197). Seven years later he confided to his fellow writer George Frederick Holmes, "My true policy is to live in one of our great Northern cities. Yet my wife is an only child; her father is in declining health & years; she cannot leave him, and I cannot separate from her & my children. . . . I am thus compelled to remain here, in my stable, when I ought to be speeding down the track" (*Letters* 3: 245).

Finally, there is the evidence provided by the manuscript fragment, "Rawlins' Rookery," a story about the writing of *Castle Dismal* and the unsuccessful effort to track down its author, who has disappeared. In the course of a long discussion of the life of the missing author, his closest friend at last reveals the uncomfortable truth that explains the flight:

> Woman . . . in her pure state, is the grand necessity of man. She alone can yield the proper sympathy—can surrender herself to a kindred soul. . . . If truly loving, she can appreciate any intellect, however subtle, however exalted, and minister to any sensibility, however exquisite & tender. In this craving he has been disappointed. He chose too soon—chose in the blindness of his need—chose from faith rather than knowledge—chose under his impulse, and not with his soul, and chose through the direction of his boyish passions, at a period of life when choice was scarce possible. . . .
>
> We see such mistakes made daily, and need not wonder. They are the easiest of all mistakes which man can make in life. . . . You simply deceive yourself. You find pleasure while doing so; and would find the same pleasure, to the end of the chapter, if she, having won, were as solicitous to keep as she has been to catch. But there's the rub. This is not always the case. Perhaps seldom. She, too, has her fantasies and raptures. Marriage undeceives both parties. You find each other out. The Fancy is no longer permitted to contend with the sullen experiences of reason, and Indifference, if not loathing, succeeds to love (72–76).

Confined in his own Castle Dismal, from which there was no escape, and trapped in an unfulfilling marriage, just as Ned Clifton had feared would happen to him, Simms could only dream, and occasionally write, of flight. Begun as a "humorous" introduction to a new edition of *Castle Dismal*, "Rawlins' Rookery" became an outlet for Simms. Misfiled in a folder labeled "Drama" in the Charles Carroll Simms Collection at the South Caroliniana Library at the University of South Carolina in Columbia, it has, for more than 150 years, been either overlooked or consciously ignored by scholars working in that rich source. Its discovery may help explain why *Castle Dismal* has never been republished. It surely affords new and valuable insights into both the story and its author.

V

Castle Dismal, then, may be read as a southern work; as a work of bachelor fiction; as a Christmas story; and as a Gothic tale. But perhaps more than any of these, and especially in light of "Rawlins' Rookery," *Castle Dismal* is an autobiographical statement and, more specifically, a commentary on Simms's own marriage, which embraces and subsumes all other interpretations. The South is not as it seems. Bachelorhood has its benefits, courtship its rituals. Christmas is not always joyous. Horror lurks just beneath the surface. Marriage is a dismal castle. It deceives and eventually imprisons.

And justice, however cruel and slow to work its will, finally prevails. At long last, and after too long a wait, *Castle Dismal* is again available to readers, to whom now is conveyed the pleasure, and the privilege, and also the challenge, of doing not simply the story, but also its author, justice.

NOTES

1. See, for example, Howard P. Chudacoff.
2. See Penne L. Restad (75–76) and Tara Stern Moore (82–83).
3. For more on the connection between *Castle Dismal* and other nineteenth-century Gothic works, see especially Lloyd-Smith (7, 32–34) and Molly Boyd.

Confession; or, The Blind Heart

TODD HAGSTETTE

The grimness that attended William Gilmore Simms's literary imagination was frequently on display during key moments in his historical romances and short stories. He often was accused of sensationalism for his attachment to murder, licentiousness, and mayhem of every variety in crafting his literary panoply of American history. It was also undoubtedly this strain in his fiction that helped produce his success with the reading public. Marketing considerations aside, there was a darkness that lurked in Simms's mind, one that the author tried to exorcise occasionally in print. Even his notoriously unsympathetic biographer William P. Trent was acute in perceiving the author's penchant for the macabre, noting that Simms's plantation "Woodlands was quiet and domestic enough, but whenever he shut himself up in his study he fell to talking with thieves and outlaws and brothers eager to kill one another" (121).

Despite this fascination in the author's mind, Simms only produced a handful of works wholly devoted to the Gothic, the criminal, and the psychological. Of these, *Confession; or, The Blind Heart* is one of the most fully realized. In his study of the literary aesthetics of crime, John Cyril Barton notes that "novels didn't become a dominant form through which crime and criminal behavior were critically explored in the United States until Simms began writing them" (222). Though earlier writers, most notably Charles Brockden Brown, dramatized villainous behaviors in America, Simms helped to pioneer the contextualization of these acts as legal transgression, in addition to Gothic sensationalism. *Confession* marks one of the earliest attempts in American fiction to trace the psychology of the criminal impulse through the unreliable first-person perspective of the murderer, who is unambiguously aware of the legal implications of his anticipated act.

Simms designed his novel to be experimental in its structure. In an introduction to the 1856 edition of the novel, he clarified his intentions for the work: his was a deeply psychological project, an attempt to "analyze the heart in some of its obliquities and perversities; to follow its toils, pursue its phases, and to trace, if possible, the secret of its self-deceptions, its self-baffling inconsistencies, its seemingly wilful [*sic*] warfare with reason and the sober experience." Ultimately, *Confession* was to be the declaration of "one single soul . . . put in bonds, put to the torture, and made to declare its dreary experience through its groans" (*Confession*

9–10). Simms hoped to demonstrate how the passions of man, specifically the monomaniacal exercise of a single passion, can unseat a person's otherwise healthy faculties. To make the experience tangible, he offered the reader direct access to the afflicted mind. This effort—to narrate a full novel through the limited first-person perspective of a character whose perceptions are increasingly unreliable as he is more and more corrupted by his own jealousy—was only partially successful. Some natural limitations with such a point-of-view trapped and stultified the narrative. Overall, Simms struggled with the task of retaining sympathy for a narrator whose judgments and mental processes, by necessity of the plot, were becoming increasingly erratic. Simms himself acknowledged the shortcomings of his style when, in his introduction, he apologized for the youthfulness of the novel's prose and for the sensationalism of its content. Nonetheless, both for its successes and for its ambitious failings, *Confession* deserves recognition for its innovation.

Simms attempted a partial justification of the gratuity of the novel's plot with claims that some of the instances from the story were based on his own observations in the West. Given his assertion that *Confession* originated in some of his earliest prose writing, Simms likely learned of the putative source material for his novel during visits he made to his father in Mississippi in the mid-1820s. What specific event inspired the novel, though, is unknown. More intriguing than the suggestion of a real-world analog to the plot is the possibility of an autobiographical component to the spirit of the story. Like his protagonist, Simms was functionally orphaned at an early age. His mother died in childbirth when the author was less than two years old, and his father in despondency left Charleston and his son to seek his fortunes in the West. Though Simms's upbringing in the care of his maternal grandmother was loving (unlike that of his fictional counterpart), "the sense of intolerable isolation from family ties was so intense with him that it haunted him almost to the point of obsession" (Salley, "William" lxii). The novel's focus on the redemptive potential of the frontier also emanates from this source.

Despite Simms's reluctance at age ten to live with his father in Mississippi, he took from the elder Simms's adventures the lesson that fresh starts, absolution, and opportunity lay in the West. Critics like Lewis M. Bush have gone so far as to identify individual referents for specific characters in the text (126–27). Many of these hard biographical associations are vaguely appropriate or somewhat inconclusive. Yet the potential for psychological touchstones is intriguing. In his 1856 introduction, Simms himself characterized the novel as "the natural progress of the author's mind to the solutions of his problems" (7). One has to wonder, then, at the turmoil and angst lurking within the author's mind. The Gothic impulse, the psychological structure, and the autobiographical hints of the text all make *Confession; or, The Blind Heart* deserving of greater critical regard than it has thus far received.

The Work

In its experimental content and structure, *Confession* marks Simms's efforts to craft a psychologically realistic depiction of burgeoning madness. The specific lens through which he situates his exploration of the mind is the impact of childhood trauma on adult development and behavior. As such, the novel is the extended confession of Edward Clifford who is orphaned at an age when he is "just young enough to wonder why" his loving parents are gone (*Confession* 12). In this emotionally precarious state, he is sent to be reared by his aunt and uncle in Charleston, where his upbringing is marred by his foster parents' preference for their natural children. His siblings wear the finest new clothes, while he is garbed in hand-me-downs; they attend the city's best prep academy, and he is sent to the local charity school. This preference crosses into neglect and emotional abuse of young Clifford following the untimely death of his adoptive brother. He grows up with his cousin and foster-sister Julia as his only repository of familial affection.

Rising above the scorn of his adopted home and particularly his uncle's attempts to relegate him to a blue-collar vocation, Clifford becomes a lawyer and an increasingly prominent citizen. This triumph is effected through his own hard work and the patronage of the father of his boyhood companion William Edgerton. Eventually, Clifford elopes with Julia, much to her parents' chagrin. With a burgeoning career, a doting wife, and an optimistic financial outlook, Clifford has apparently succeeded in spite of his rearing. His turbulent childhood, though, leaves him emotionally scarred and suspicious of human relationships. When his wife develops a friendship with Edgerton based on their mutual artistic impulses, Clifford's jealousy silently erupts within him. Under the influence of his unfounded suspicions, the husband goes to great pains to orchestrate scenarios in which his wife and friend can be ostensibly alone, though under his scrutiny. He witnesses little in Julia's behavior that is directly damning but plenty that he can irrationally misconstrue. As Clifford remarks at one critical juncture: "Seen through the eyes of suspicion, there is no truth no virtue; the smile is that of the snake; the tear, that of the crocodile; the assurance, that of the traitor" (248).

Clifford attempts to obviate his growing impulse to kill Edgerton, primarily out of a sense of devotion to his patron, by moving his family west to Alabama. In this endeavor, he follows his friend and confidant Frank Kingsley, a cavalier and candid bachelor. The move, though financially and socially regressive, placates Clifford and reinvigorates his relationship with Julia. This brief period of marital harmony is permanently disrupted, though, by an extended visit from Edgerton, traveling purportedly for his health. With a renewed effort to place the two assumed lovers into compromising situations, Clifford's monomania begins to consume him. Eventually, his corrupted perceptions convince him of infidelity, and Clifford poisons his wife and challenges Edgerton to a duel. Edgerton, however, commits suicide first. Thanks to posthumous letters from both Julia and Edgerton, Clifford realizes that though Edgerton did in fact pursue Julia, his advances were completely unwelcome. Edgerton had been tormented by his feelings, and Julia had been ever-hopeful of her husband's intercession. Anguished over the outcome of his mistaken assumptions, Clifford resolves on suicide. Yet, in the end, he is thwarted by Kingsley, who insists, "it is by living only that you can atone" (397). So, the end of the novel finds Clifford wandering farther west, into untamed Texas, in search of absolution.

Because most of the novel is psychological in its examinations, *Confession* is often considered a Gothic narrative, even with its distinct absence of the supernatural. Simms himself implied as much when he suggested to Rufus Wilmot Griswold that the novel belonged in a group with some of his more readily recognized Gothic works (*Letters* 2: 224). That said, placing *Confession* thematically within the author's canon is a difficult task. The novel exhibits characteristics of several of Simms's loose collections, but wholly belongs to none of them.

Some people have classed it among Simms's Border Romances, because of its plot's steady progression west; the most notable instance of this series assignment was in the 1856 Redfield edition of the novel, which grouped it under the series title "Border Novels and Romances of the South." In this group, *Confession* joined Simms's more clearly-defined novels of the southern frontier: *Beauchampe* (Redfield, 1856), *Border Beagles* (Redfield, 1859), *Charlemont* (Redfield, 1856), *Guy Rivers* (Redfield, 1860), and *Richard Hurdis* (Redfield, 1855). That these other works were crafted to dramatize the ethos of particular frontier states (*Beauchampe* and *Charlemont* for Kentucky, *Border Beagles* for Mississippi, *Guy Rivers* for Georgia, and *Richard Hurdis* for Alabama), whereas *Confession* was not, problematizes that text's inclusion.

Also in contradiction to this series assignment, Simms himself did not seem to have envisioned *Confession* as a Border Romance. In a 16 August 1841 letter to New York friend and informal literary agent James Lawson, Simms implied a distinction between the recently-completed *Confession* and the new novel he had underway (*Beauchampe*), for that latter work would "form one of the 'Hurdis' series" (*Letters* 1: 267). In other words, it was to be a tale of the border or frontier. Conversely, Simms did not object to the designation in 1846 when Taylor, Wilde and Company in Baltimore proposed publishing *Confession* as part of a collection of his "Border Romances" (*Letters* 2: 132n). Financial concerns might have trumped artistic ones in this instance.

Though in his biography of Simms, John Caldwell Guilds tacitly groups *Confession* with the Border Romances (*Literary Life* 168–69), elsewhere he explains why any such definition is fraught. After all, in categorizing his own fiction:

> Simms himself preferred to divide it into only two large groups: "domestic tales," or "tales of the South," by which he meant all those tales . . . dealing with regional themes and settings; and "tales of the imagination," by which

> he meant those stories under the influence of German Romanticism, usually with exotic settings and heavy philosophical or psychological undertones. (*Writings* xxi)

The fact that Simms, himself, included books such as *Martin Faber*, *Confession*, and *The Wigwam and the Cabin* (featuring his ghost story "Grayling") in both groups, however, "reveals that he did not always clearly distinguish between his 'domestic' and his 'moral imaginative' tales" (Guilds, *Writings* xxii–xxiii). This failure to distinguish, this melding of the two types, marks the very innovative spirit that characterizes Simms's experimental composition in *Confession*. Though the author once claimed that his novel was "marked chiefly by the characteristics of passion & imagination," he also gave it the subtitle *A Domestic Story* (*Letters* 2: 224). The Gothic, the frontier, and the psychological all merge in this distinctive tale.

The Text

Building out of his early experiences with writing in the psychological Gothic mode in such stories as *Martin Faber* (1833) and *Carl Werner* (1838) and anticipating his later work *Castle Dismal* (1844), Simms began to write the novel that would ultimately become *Confession; or, The Blind Heart* in late 1840 or early 1841. Though in his author's advertisement to the 1856 Redfield edition of the novel, he noted that the finished novel was constructed out of some of his earliest prose writings, to what material he was referring is uncertain. He first mentioned having begun the novel "in the winter" in a 24 February 1841 letter to James Lawson (*Letters* 1: 234). After composing approximately 150 pages, however, he ceased to make progress. This writer's block persisted at least into May 1841, where he cited vague "anxieties" as the reason for his inability to work. By August of that year, he finally managed to complete his text, and announced to Lawson on August 16 that the manuscript was now safely in the hands of the publishers (Guilds, *Literary Life* 104). The book was initially published in either October or November of 1841, by Lea and Blanchard of Philadelphia, as a two-volume work. Though not technically anonymous, the authorship of the first edition of *Confession* was left cryptic, which was not unusual at the time. Officially, the novel was attributed to "The Author of 'The Kinsmen,' 'The Yemassee,' 'Guy Rivers,' ETC." Later editions and printings were attributed to Simms by name, and the author freely discussed his writing of the book throughout his correspondence. The Redfield edition, which bore the name "W. Gilmore Simms, Esq." and was published as a one-volume work, was issued around 19 April 1856 (*Letters* 3: 385).

The first edition of *Confession*, issued by Lea & Blanchard, was un-illustrated. The Redfield edition, beginning in 1856, featured two illustrations by F.O.C. Darley and engraved by Whitney & Jocelyn. Darley's choice of subject matter for his illustrations is somewhat intriguing. The first image presents Julia sitting beside a river engrossed in painting. Meanwhile, a young man stands to her side and observes her work from over her shoulder. He wears an approving and engaged expression. Because of Julia's calm demeanor and the scene's similarity to the Alabama respite period of the plot, the young man is surely Clifford (rather than Edgerton). Darley's goal here was obviously to depict a moment of tranquil marital bliss as a set-up and foil to the Gothic action that concludes the story. Yet, Simms is diligent to present Clifford as too left-brained and pragmatic to engage much in Julia's artistic impulses. Edgerton comes into their lives specifically as a compatriot for Julia in the exercise of her creative side. By locating Clifford and Julia's contentment in a scene from which the former's fundamental estrangement can be inferred, Darley manifests a rather doomed portrait in the midst of potential success. The couple's position exacerbates this inference: Julia sits with her back to Clifford, and he scrutinizes her imaginative performance from the outside.

The second Darley illustration is equally interesting in its relationship to the action of the novel. Here we see a ruckus in a poker hall, with one man forcing another out an open window as onlookers stand by in evident astonishment. This is a clear depiction of Kingsley's outing of a cheater at the gambling hall. Darley's use of this character, in this rather tangential scene, as one of the hallmark images of the novel is a strange choice, at first glance. The oddity of its selection is mitigated by the psychological tenor of most of the work, this being one of the story's few action sequences. Nonetheless, Kingsley, while not exactly a minor character, is certainly peripheral to much of the novel's immediate drama. Yet this image of manly action contrasts fittingly with the picture of pastoral respite in the accompanying illustration. Together, these two images dramatize one of the central conflicts of the novel, the consequences of feminine versus masculine action. Kingsley, as the man of action—the man's man—is Simms's portrait of masculine resolve, particularly in its frontier expression. He disapproves of Edgerton, because he "wants manliness of character, and such a man always lacks sincerity" (*Confession* 319). Kingsley thus tries to spur Clifford. He criticizes him for allowing Edgerton into his marriage and for failing to play the man for his wife. When Julia is faced with Clifford's neglect and Edgerton's attention, "will she not become indifferent where she finds indifference—devoted where she finds devotion?" (*Confession* 320). The image of Kingsley's rough handling of the rounder at the poker table, then, is an analog for his recommended solution to Clifford's dilemma. Eject Edgerton. Face matters directly. The Gothic unraveling of Clifford's sanity and betrothal is the result of his voyeuristic inaction, when simply throwing the man out of the window would have sufficed.

Also of interest in the front matter of the novel is the dedication. Simms initially dedicated *Confession* to one of his earliest and closest friends, James W[right] Simmons. Fifteen years older than Simms, Simmons had joined the younger man to launch and edit the *Southern Literary Gazette* in 1828. Yet Simmons's presence at the front of this novel was not due to literary kinship, but because he ultimately "became comptroller general and treasurer of the republic of Texas, and was connected with the Galveston *Banner*" (*Letters* 1: cxxxvii). In his dedication, Simms is clear to point out that Simmons is "now of Texas." The novel was composed and published during the brief existence of the Republic of Texas, in the aftermath of the Texas Revolution and in the gradual lead-up to the Mexican War. Furthermore, *Confession* features a plot progression that moves ever westward and self-consciously into the promise of renewal on the frontier. Simms's conclusion is heavy-handed in its conflation of manifest destiny with individual actualization. Clifford, in the last passages of the novel, notes his and Kingsley's odyssey concludes in "the rich empire of Texas—its plains, rich but barren—unstocked, wild running to waste with its tangled weeds needing, imploring the vigorous hand of cultivation. Even such, at that moment, was my heart! Rich in fertile affections, yet gone to waste; waiting, craving, praying for the hand of the cultivator!" (398).

The dedication to Simmons would seemingly foreground the aspects of *Confession* that place it within the context of Simms's border series. And yet, interestingly, the dedication was removed for the publication of the Redfield edition of the novel, despite its designation in that edition as one of Simms's "Border Novels and Romances of the South." The reason for the removal is uncertain. Simmons would live for another two years beyond this later edition of the book, so his death had nothing to do with the change. Other works in the Redfield series—such as *Katharine Walton* (1856), *Mellichampe* (1854), and *Southward Ho!* (1854)—all bore new dedications with their publication, so house style or financial concerns over unnecessary pages were neither to blame. It could be that with the conclusion of the conflicts surrounding Texas years before, this dedication no longer held the gravity it enjoyed upon the novel's initial publication. Removing the Simmons dedication could also have been a subtle statement of Simms's reluctance to categorize his psychological experiment as another of his border tales. After all, it is the Gothic of *Confession* that marks its innovation.

The Context

Confession appeared at the front of what many critics consider to be the author's most productive period, the 1840s through the 1850s. The years following *Confession* saw the publication of the lion's share of Simms's Revolutionary War series, his most important short stories, the majority of his most well-regarded orations, all of his biographies, and his important two-volume essay collection *Views and Reviews*. This latter work would be cited as a fundamental text in the burgeoning Young American movement of the nineteenth century, "of which Simms was in effect the spokesman for the South" (Guilds, *Literary Life* 180–81).

Young America's hyper-nationalistic aims were on display in the majority of Simms's works from this period. *Confession* is no exception. In both his emphasis on the southern borderlands and his efforts to Americanize the European Gothic format, Simms sculpted *Confession* into a text *par excellence* of Young America ideology. Despite this position, the novel did not fare terribly well among critics.

Simms might have been justified in his introductory apology to the 1856 edition; the novel was not embraced by reviewers of the author's day, nor has it been since. A common tactic of the criticism is to brand the novel a poor imitation of the European psychological novel (helped in no small way by the epigraph from Goethe's *Faust* on the title page) or as a reinterpretation of William Shakespeare's *Othello*. Simms himself grouped the book "among the best of [his] performances" but was clearly aware of some of these potential complaints (*Letters* 2: 528). In addition to the epigraph, which acknowledges the thematic origins of the work while, at the same time, implicitly suggesting the novel's subsequent development, Simms has his protagonist exclaim, "I am no Othello—I have no visitations of the moon!" (321).

Of those nineteenth-century critics who treated the novel outside the confines of discussion of its predecessors, those who were most sharply divided were Trent, Simms's initial biographer, and Edgar Allan Poe, the author's peer and an especially discerning critic. Trent's 1892 biography is insistently regarded as biased and negative. This is nowhere more apparent than in its vitriolic assessment of *Confession*. Trent viewed the novel as a failed attempt "to rival Shakespeare in his greatest play [*Othello*]." He saw it as "made up of exaggerations and absurdities" and found in it "only a striking proof of the futility of attempting to write a novel in order to illustrate a pet theory, whether of psychology, or social science, or theology" (122–23). Poe, on the other hand, preferred Simms as a scribe of the ideological. In his 1841 review of *Confession*, he wrote of the author, "He should never have written 'The Partisan,' nor 'The Yemassee'. . . . His genius does not lie in the outward so much as in the inner world. 'Martin Faber' did him honor; and so do the present volumes. . . . We welcome him home to his own proper field of exertion—the field of Godwin and Brown—the field of his own rich intellect and glowing *heart*" (306; Poe's emphasis alludes to *Confession*'s alternate title, *The Blind Heart*). Interestingly, both writers mentioned Simms's evocation of Godwin yet assessed this inspiration quite differently.

The tenor of reviews subsequent to the novel's initial publication seems to have trended in a slightly more positive direction. An anonymous writer in 1845, in reviewing Simms's recently published *The Life of Francis Marion*, called *Confession* "extraordinary," and noted that the "genius and talents of Mr. Simms shine forth in their greatest splendor" in the novel's pages (qtd. in Butterworth and Kibler 59). Following its 1856 issue by Redfield, the novel was reviewed in *Godey's Lady's Book* as a "powerfully written tale" that "presents its author's genius in a novel light" (*Letters* 3: 385n). Simms wrote to Thomas A Burke in August of that year to thank him for a kind review that the editor had penned; Burke called *Confession* "one of the very best of all its author's productions," and doubted "if any reader of 'Confession' will care to put it a side [*sic*] until he has finished it" (*Letters* 3: 443n). These kinds of glowing reviews or, indeed, any reviews at all, were rather scarce, though. Some writers obviously found merit in the novel, but most readers and critics disparaged or ignored the book.

The twentieth century has done little to remedy this neglect and improve the novel's fortunes. Donald Davidson, the most accomplished of Simms's reviewers, was a bit undecided in his estimation of the work. On the one hand, he criticized *Confession* for seeming "too obviously worked up," that is to say too intently focused on being a literary production and not organic in its development. He censured the work for being "done with sheer literary muscle" without stemming, "like [Simms's] best work, from sources deeper than books and documents can supply." But, on the other hand, Davidson called *Confession* the author's "strongest psychological novel," a work exhibiting "clear merit" (li). Negative or mixed critical assessments of the past might be changing, though. Guilds declares that "*Confession* is a much better book than is generally acknowledged" (*Literary Life* 105), and Miriam Shillingsburg praises it as "one of the earliest convincing studies of domestic battery in American literature" ("Battered" 222). Simms is also increasingly being recognized as a forerunner of the southern Gothic genre, and *Confession* factors heavily in that regard.

A close reading of the novel reveals a number of themes and motifs that scholars have yet to treat in any great detail. Many of these elements contribute to Simms's experimental style in the book, especially his efforts to craft a more American version of the Gothic romance. For example, Edward Clifford, for all his psychological faults and behavioral foibles, is an expression of a quintessentially American character-type, the self-made man. His life is characterized by determination and success despite humble beginnings. Simms's treatment of this figure in *Confession* is complex and creative and marks his efforts at innovation. Not willing to allow his fictional rendering of the ideal American to be shallow and one-sided, though, Simms imbues his self-made man with duplicitous characteristics. Furthermore, though Simms ultimately celebrates this figure, he does so in a fashion that is subtle and ambiguous. His treatment of the self-made man gains depth also by his presentation of this character's antithesis in Edgerton. Indulged in childhood where Clifford was neglected, Edgerton lacks the discipline of his boyhood friend. Through the interaction of these contradictory figures, Simms offers a subtle portrait of the American character.

Clifford's ultimate rise in position from the feeblest and most tormented of beginnings draws on and reinforces the prototypical image of the American self-made man. Clifford is the epitome of this figure, not only because of his determination to succeed, but also because of his perseverance in the face of adversity. He survives the antagonism of his family, the lechery of his friend, and ultimately, the self-destructive nature of his own psyche. At the end of the novel, after the interplay of the Gothic disasters, Clifford, unlike most Gothic villains, lives through it. He is able to survive, persevere, and repent. His trouble begins, though, in the isolated nature of his upbringing, which renders it impossible for him to accept a natural love relationship with his wife or friends. Clifford, through his early education, has been taught that an untarnished companionship is a fantasy. Eventually, this influence brings about his apparently irrational jealousy of Julia and Edgerton's friendship. Referring to Clifford, Glenn M. Reed finds that Simms's "'self-made man' is so obsessed by the desire to have the unconditional love denied him by the death of his parents that he comes to scorn his social and material achievements and destroys the one thing he does prize, his wife" (xxi). So, though his origins have brought him to the full glory of the self-made man, they have also scarred him in such a way as to bring about his downfall.

Despite the tragic end to which Clifford brings himself and his companions, Simms ultimately validates the character of the self-made man through a comparison with his rival. Though subtly portrayed throughout the novel, Edgerton is a perfect example of the indulged character type. He comes from a prominent Charleston family and enjoys all of the benefits of position that Clifford has had to do without. Though the hysterical and suspicious tone of Clifford's first-person narration initially makes the reader suspect Edgerton's innocence, Simms actually reveals his deuteragonist in the end to be far from a hapless victim of Clifford's antagonism. In the confessional letter that Edgerton addresses to Clifford he admits to desiring Julia. He further claims that, though he attempted in earnest to suppress his dishonorable urges, he could not: "My education did not fit me for such a struggle. The indulgence of fond parents had gratified all my wishes, and taught me to expect their gratification" (368). Therefore, not only does Edgerton reveal that Clifford's suspicion of him has been justified, but his reasons for his behavior look back to his childhood development.

This interplay of characters, combined with the fact that Edgerton commits suicide, helps to redeem Clifford's villainy. He is not wholly condemnable. This duality in characters and ambiguity of guilt forges the complex structure of Simms's version of the self-made man. Clifford is celebrated in his achievement, justified in his suspicions, and yet still partially condemned as the murderer of Julia. Yet because of his perseverance, he is not wholly a monster. Bolstered by the positive facets of the self-made man, Clifford is able to live through the effects of the negative facets and hence is eligible for redemption.

One trait of Simms's novel that complicates the character types he establishes is the dual role Clifford is forced to play. As he begins to become his own nemesis, Clifford simultaneously portrays the protagonist and antagonist of the story's Gothic conflict. Edgerton's influence on the plot fades as Clifford increasingly wars with himself. The formative influences that give him the perseverance of the self-made man also wound him psychologically. The cruel treatment by his aunt and uncle prohibits him from understanding true companionship, and this inability leads directly to the jealousy that destroys his marriage and his friend. As *Confession* is an experiment in psychological unraveling, the majority of its later pages are devoted to documenting the decline in Clifford's tormented psyche.

Though the jealousy that Clifford feels for his wife's friendship with Edgerton is uncomfortable, it is his waggling beliefs about his wife's fidelity that make it tragic. Rather than confronting Julia, Clifford manipulates interactions between the two may-be lovers in order to spy on them. Even though encounter after encounter yields nothing incriminating in their behavior, Clifford, because of his wounded mind, remains unconvinced. In the face of no evidence, he begins to discern guilt in Julia's seemingly harmless behavior. Bush remarks, "Clifford, insane with jealousy, his tortured mind twisting even the most innocent actions of Julia, continued to throw them together again and again in order to test her, and to bring his own 'damning doubts to a final trial'" (125). These engineered situations harry all three participants until they are all, in some way, destroyed by them. Julia from the seeming neglect of her husband, Edgerton from his unconsummated desire for Julia, and Clifford from his self-destructive monomania, all converge in a Gothic implosion that leaves two dead and Clifford guilty, wounded, and alone. His own tormented psyche, in true Gothic fashion, not only brings his own downfall but destroys all of those around him as well.

Yet Clifford's story concludes with the possibility of expiation. Despite the hand-wringing efforts by readers to categorize Simms's novel as alternatively a border or a Gothic romance, the conclusion of *Confession* suggests that these styles are fundamentally interlocked in American fiction. Clifford's progression towards the American frontier is necessitated by his destructive behavior but also suggestive of the possibility of redemption. In Simms's presentation here, manifest destiny is important to the thematic conclusion of the novel. His endorsement of America's westward expansion is an early and lucid dissertation on this very American article of faith. Clifford's wanderlust, inspired though it is by Gothic dread, is a fictional realization of this policy. By leaving his hometown of Charleston for Montgomery, Alabama, he seeks escape from those elements that tax his frail psychology: the cuckolding impulses of Edgerton and the venomous ones of his aunt and uncle.

The West, for Clifford, offers escape from his tangible and immediate problems. At the end of the novel, though, the West takes on almost mystical qualities, and the healing it promises is more holistic. Texas is the place where Clifford seeks not only the isolation of a sparsely peopled land, but also redemption for his crime. Moving westward, ultimately, cannot provide balm for those problems within himself that Clifford imports; but, the remove from civilization suggests at least a blank slate onto which one might inscribe a new beginning, a new life, and a new soul. With the true American mentality of manifest destiny, Clifford faces the next frontier seeking just such an inauguration. The journey, both literal and psychological will be a struggle, though. As Clifford notes, from the commission of his crimes and throughout his search for redemption, "evermore an echo arose from the bottom of my soul; and my lips repeated it to my own ears only; and but one word was spoken; and that word was—'ATONEMENT!'" (*Confession* 398).

The Damsel of Darien

MICHAEL ODOM

William Gilmore Simms was the most prolific southern writer of the nineteenth century. Over the course of his illustrious career, he composed poetry, novels, short stories, essays, plays, biographies, letters, speeches, journalism, and history. By the middle of the 1830s, he had established himself among the most celebrated writers in American letters. Biographer William P. Trent claimed that the author's marriage to Chevillette Eliza Roach in 1836 and subsequent initiation into the planter class gave Simms "abundant leisure to lay his plans for new literary work." With new planter friends urging him not to "waste his time on such trivial subjects as legends and traditions of a country not two hundred years old," Simms turned his attention to Europe for "more dignified" themes (112). Literary biographer John Caldwell Guilds concurred a century later: "But the newly married writer, now a member of the very South Carolina gentry by which he had felt rejected since boyhood, was encouraged by his new peers—among others, his father-in-law, Nash Roach—not to forsake the great literary traditions of Europe, to which they still looked, with something akin to awe, for cultural verification" (*Literary Life* 81).

Already a voracious reader of European history, Simms set to writing about celebrated figures of ancient pride and character in these European settings; the result was the publication of *Pelayo*, a tale of medieval Spain, in the spring of 1838. That story, and a sequel, helped him explore the roots of the culture of the conquistadors who conquered much of the Americas. Spanish culture was profoundly important to the history of his region, a fact he later explored in *Vasconselos*, a novel based loosely on the expeditions of Ponce de Leon.

Simms first, however, treated another chapter in the history of the conquistadors, releasing another Spanish romance the year after *Pelayo*. *The Damsel of Darien* was published in two volumes in 1839 as an epic retelling of the life of Vasco Nunez de Balboa (c. 1475–1521), the first European known to see the Pacific Ocean. The celebrated conquistador was a fitting subject to bridge Simms's early forays into European historical fiction with his typical focus on the development of American identity. In his biography of the Spanish legend, Charles Anderson calls Balboa "the most attractive and tragic figure in the Hispanic conquest of the New World" (7).

Simms first mentioned his story of Balboa to his New York friend and informal literary agent James Lawson in a 2 September 1838 letter. He said that he "wrote during the first part of the summer some 150 pages of a new novel & there it sticks" (*Letters* 1: 135). Simms informed Lawson in January of 1839 that *Damsel* would be published with Lea & Blanchard of Philadelphia, who would pay $1,000 for a first edition of 3,000 copies; in the meantime, he was busy revising the "numerous errors of history & geography" committed while composing the first volume of the story (*Letters* 1: 139). In a 16 June 1839 letter, he indicated that he had finished *Damsel*, calling it "a romance based upon the events in the early history of the American settlements of Spain . . . and as the name somewhat implies, the scene is partly laid upon the isthmus of Darien and the material is drawn from the events attending the discovery by Vasco Nunez." He addressed this missive to James Kirke Paulding, whom he considered "one among the successful of our native authors,—as indeed, one of the fathers of our forest literature,—a leading Pioneer" (*Letters* 1: 144). Simms dedicated the novel to Paulding to show his appreciation for a "champion in the field of national literature" that he believed to be mistreated by critics (cxxviii). At the time of the letter, Paulding was serving in the cabinet of Martin Van Buren as the 11th Secretary of the Navy.

Despite the critical success and celebrated reception of a number of Simms's American romances, the few scholars who have considered these Spanish romances judge them of little consequence, and worse yet, a waste of the talented young writer's time. Guilds observes that while Simms endeavored to write "traditional European romance" to impress friends, his efforts ultimately "failed to arouse the degree of excitement among critics and readers that had greeted his best writing with American themes and settings" (*Literary Life* 95).[1] A text hastily dismissed and subsequently neglected for too many years, *The Damsel of Darien* needs to be reexamined particularly in light of contemporary movements in literary studies, as the author's incisive criticisms of European colonialism should provide currency among contemporary scholars.

Context

Stanley Williams has written about Simms's interest in Spain and its influences on his fiction. Dubbing Simms the "Hispanophile in the Carolinas," Williams illustrates how the author made Spain "a key to themes and backgrounds which were to be important in his fiction and poetry. Everything suggests his preference for Spanish, or at least a consciousness of its potential treasures for him as a novelist, either through a knowledge of Spain itself or of the history and legends of Spanish-America" (223). Spanish colonial history in America was of vital importance for the author. In considering the 1845 article, "The Epochs and Events of American History, as Suited to the Purposes of Art in Fiction," a revision of lectures delivered in 1842 at the Georgia Historical Society, Simms identified the three quarters of a century of imperial conquest and conflict after

Columbus's first landing in the new world as one of four epochs. Simms articulated his standards for historians by laying out preliminaries they must seek in recovering the spirit of these epochs:

> A profound inquiry into the moral and social characteristics of the several nations engaged in these discoveries—the English, French, Spanish and Portuguese—is an absolutely indispensable preliminary. Above all, he must *feel* their religious characteristics, in his own spirit, before he can boldly enter upon the delineation of the spirit of their time! This, alone, can lead to a just comprehension of their various motives—their strange phrenzies—their implicit faith—their sleepless jealousies—their fanatical enthusiasm—their curious inconsistency of performance—and the singular union, so frequently found in the same personage, of so much that is base and bloody, with so much that is magnanimous and great! (391–92, emphasis in original)

As Williams notes, Simms held historians to such standards when he reviewed books during his tenure as editor of *The Southern Quarterly Review* (1849–1854). Simms understood that to write about grand historical themes, one must ensure proper context. During the decade of the 1840s, he responded to the decline in the fiction market by writing and editing biographies of heroic men, such as Francis Marion (1844), the Chevalier Bayard (1847), John Smith (1847), and Nathanael Greene (1849), to celebrate as archetypes of virtue. Such great men, in Simms's estimation, often stood in contrast to their times—indeed all were regarded as exceptions who transcended not only their era, but history itself.

Washington Irving wrote two landmark histories that were largely responsible, before William Hickling Prescott, for informing nineteenth-century American understandings of Spanish colonialism in the western hemisphere: *The Life and Voyages of Christopher Columbus* (1828) and *Voyages and Discoveries of the Companions of Columbus* (1831). Simms, having read these volumes, relied heavily upon Irving's narrative history in writing *The Damsel of Darien*. Although the two authors became literary enemies in the cultural wars of the late 1830s and 1840s, Simms shared Irving's passion for history and the narrative recounting of it. Despite his great debt, however, Simms could not resist contradicting Irving in the first paragraph of the first page of *Damsel*. Simms took exception to a passage from *The Voyages and Discoveries of the Companions of Columbus*, in which Irving praised the "chivalrous, urbane, and charitable" dealings that the Spanish discoverers had with one another despite the "vindictive, blood-thirsty, and implacable" dealings they had with the Indians (qtd. in *Damsel* 13). Simms respectfully dissented from such a careless conclusion, noting of the Spanish that after "devouring the Indians for their treasure, they scrupled not to exhibit a like rapacity towards their own comrades, in its attainment, or upon its division; and that, in short, a more inhuman faithless, blood-thirsty and unmitigated gage of savages never yet dishonored the name of man or debased his nature" (*Damsel*

14). With this revision in mind, Simms established the context of sixteenth-century Spanish colonialism as a period of boundless greed and immorality. The Spanish conquerors, with few exceptions, exhibited what seems a total absence of virtue.

Text

In *The Damsel of Darien*, Simms advances an ironic depiction of the Spanish whose primary mission of proselytizing infidels had been discarded in favor of a mercenary strategy that devoured native cultures.[2] Rather than civilizing "infidels" of the unknown world with the light of Christian faith and culture, they proved the converse: "The vices of old Spain had been among the first of her possessions, which she gave, in exchange for its gold, to the New World; and the pander and the pimp, the profligate and the prostitute, were not wanting to the community, the mass of whose population was composed of the worn-out soldier and the wandering seaman" (*Damsel* 19). The Spanish devoured not only the Indians of the New World, but also one another. Simms depicts the Spanish as godless men, overrun by greed and envy. Treasure was for the taking, and these Spanish conquerors possessed no moral restraint. The Spanish during this period, the narrator insists, were "distinguished by a baseness and vindictiveness quite as shameless and unequivocal as marked their treatment of the Indians:—that nearly every departure from their usual faithlessness of conduct, was induced by fear, by favour, or the hope of ultimate reward" (13–14).

In the first chapter, Simms eschews any sense of gallantry on the part of the Spanish conquistadors: "Of the whole chivalry of this period and nation, but little that is favourable can be said" (15). By later placing the phrase "ocean chivalry" in quotes (130), Simms implies the absence of civilized culture as the Spanish ventured farther out in their maritime conquests; untethered from their home country, the more barbaric they became—in fact, more savage than the natives with whom they saddled such a label. Against such a backdrop, Vasco Nunez[3] shines forth as a virtuous knight who displays an ocean chivalry that is absent among his own colonial countrymen. Simms spends the entire first chapter establishing a setting in which his protagonist can be introduced in the second chapter as one who towers above the rest. In his first description of Vasco in the novel, Simms presses the contrast clearly: "It may be added here, though as yet we see none of these qualities, that he was already known as affable, frank, generous, bold, and adventurous, a skillful swordsman and an able commander. Qualities admired beyond all others at a time when the conquest of a new world invited the arms of ambition, and whetted the appetites of national and individual avarice" (25).

The story is set in Santa Domingo (or New Isabella, as Columbus named it) in what is now the capital of the Dominican Republic, a city on the Caribbean Sea at the mouth of the Ozama River. The city functioned as "the connecting link between two worlds; receiving and sending forth the pioneers of the old, and transmitting back, in requital, the wondrous and ill-gotten treasures of the new" (*Damsel* 22). The story opens at the beginning of November at the tail end of what had already been a tumultuous hurricane season, establishing an ominous feeling that another dangerous tempest could come at any moment in such an unpredictable climate. Micer Codro, an aged astrologer, overlooks the Ozama River, on which ride the fleets of ships, largely belonging to accomplished and rival cavaliers, Diego de Nicuesa and Alonzo de Ojeda. One other ship is moored in the Ozama, "one destined to achieve exploits and acquire glory" beyond even the "fondest hopes, and wildest imaginings, and most daring toils" of the rival fleets (*Damsel* 23). This ship belongs to Codro's ambitious young disciple, Vasco Nunez, who aims to achieve fortune and fame as a conquistador.

Codro provides an important father-figure for Vasco Nunez, fulfilling the role as a mentor who recognizes the leadership skills and unique virtue that make Vasco one who is destined for greatness; his continuous affirmation stimulates Vasco's ambition to achieve great acts and discoveries. As an astrologer, Codro possesses a supernatural discernment akin to a prophet who sees what the "stars" foretell about Vasco. Even though Vasco's star is bright and great, there is a haze behind it that foretells a tragic, untimely death that will follow fame and glory. As the narrative unfolds, it becomes clear that Vasco is one upon whom "fortune hath been less bounteous than heaven" (29). In fact, his dog Leoncico is one of the few valuable possessions belonging to the would-be discoverer, as the astrologer vividly illustrates: "You are known, Vasco, by good deeds and not by goods—by the stanch virtues of courage and courtesy, rather than by castellanos,"—or Spanish gold (29).

Because of Vasco's limited resources, Codro acquires a loan on Vasco's behalf from Felipe Davila, a rich scoundrel. It is to purchase a barque—a sailing vessel with several masts—for Vasco's quest. Davila also happens to be the uncle of Teresa Pedrarias, a beautiful young woman of nobility with whom Vasco is smitten. The young knight seeks to court her, although Codro doubts that Teresa reciprocates the same feelings and wonders whether she is worthy of Vasco's pursuit. Not only does Codro believe that Teresa is unworthy of Vasco's affections and that she will distract him from the ambitions of discovery, but he has also received a vision in the stars concerning a woman that troubles him greatly. Speaking to Vasco, he relays, "Yea, my son,—I have told thee out the truth—thou wilt triumph—thou wilt achieve conquest and fame: yet, in the same blessed volume which showed me thy success, did I also behold a danger which threatened thee and a fearful trial of all thy strength! . . . And the danger came to thee from the temptations of a woman, and the trial grew because of her" (34). Vasco, blinded by his affections for Teresa, ignores his mentor's advice. Eventually he finds out the hard way—by confessing his love for Teresa—that she does not consider him suitable because of his lack of prospects, family name, and wealth. As if this is not disaster enough, a hurricane then destroys Vasco's ship and crew just before they are to embark for the South Sea. Nature asserts itself regularly in the narrative, and Simms continually depicts it as a force powerful and indifferent to human aspirations, regardless of how noble or divine people believe them to be. Many characters—captains and cavaliers not exempted—suffer terrible consequences from the natural elements. The philosophy behind this presentation is that humans should expect calamity when they tempt the unknown cycles of the natural world. No human being can outsmart nature, which lays waste to anyone exploring unknown lands on the chaotic seas.

Fate also looms large over the events that take place, and much of the talk about destinies comes from Codro who regularly proclaims what he sees in the stars. While there is some lip service paid to religion, much of the discourse surrounding destinies, fate, and gods provides the narrative and its characters with a syncretic augmentation of Christianity with pagan spirituality. This syncretism is embodied in Codro, who is characterized as an astrologer rather than a priest. In spite of the elder's sage predictions, Vasco tempts fate and forces the hand of destiny. While he heeds Codro, he also is shrewd enough to perceive the limitations of prophecies, which are ambiguous and conveniently focused on ends instead of means; such ambiguity safeguards prophecy from being a falsehood by allowing details to be retroactively appropriated and reinterpreted to fit in the grand scheme of things. With this tension, Simms appears to assert that, while fate or providence certainly may play a role in a person's achievements, the great men of ambition in many ways choose their fate or destiny and make it happen, so to speak. While Codro urges Vasco on with his prophetic promises of achievement, Vasco himself creates his own destiny like many other great men of history.[4]

Yet, Codro's prophecy about the temptations of a woman eventually proves fatally accurate for the hero. Teresa returns to the narrative once Vasco has discovered the Pacific Ocean and set up a colony on Darien. The jealousies and greed of his fellow Spaniards continually assail Vasco when he is falsely accused of treason and imprisoned by Teresa's father, Don Pedrarias, who is appointed governor of the Darien colony by the king. Though he becomes Vasco's nemesis, Pedrarias is shrewd enough to understand the popularity of Vasco among the Spanish crew and inhabitants (as well as the Native Americans) at Darien; consequently, a bishop persuades Pedrarias that a marriage arrangement between his daughter, Teresa, and Vasco will secure the fulfillment of his greedy pursuits; by aligning himself with the beloved Vasco, Pedrarias can peacefully secure his position of power while enjoying the spoils of the explorer's conquests. The hero's ultimate downfall comes when Pedrarias is told that Vasco keeps a Native American damsel, Careta, and actually plans to marry her instead of his daughter (even though this is not Vasco's intention). When Vasco's life finally falls into Teresa's hands to have him spared from execution, her vanity lashes out punitively against the hero; her wounded pride leads her to view the beautiful damsel as her rival.[5]

This crucial plot point was certainly taken from Irving's account. In it, Balboa's fate was ultimately linked to his affections for a Native American damsel, whom the Spanish conqueror received as a peaceful tribute from a Darien chief:

> Careta returned joyfully to his territories, and his daughter remained with Vasco Nunez, willingly for his sake giving up her family and native home. They were never married, but she considered herself his wife, as she really was, according to the usages of her own country; and he treated her with fondness, allowing her gradually to acquire great influence over him. To his affection for this damsel, his ultimate ruin is in some measure to be ascribed. (Irving 144)

It is likely that Simms was inspired by this passage, as his historical romance centers its epic struggle upon a damsel from Darien upon whom Vasco places his affections; this forbidden love ultimately tips the balance of the corrupt Spanish scales of justice against Vasco, leading to his conviction for treason and his subsequent beheading. Simms not only names the damsel Careta (whereas it was the name of her father, the cassique, according to Irving), he also has Vasco marry her as one of the protagonist's final rites prior to last confession and his public execution.[6] Fittingly, Irving provided a summation of Balboa that encapsulates the moral of Simms's romance: "Thus perished, in his forty-second year, in the prime and vigor of his days, and the full career of his glory, one of the most illustrious and deserving of Spanish discoverers; a victim of the basest and most perfidious envy" (245).

Critical Reception

The early reviews of *The Damsel of Darien* were mixed and eventually proved to inhibit the work's reception over time. In a November 1839 review in *The Casket*, Edgar Allan Poe flatly declared the novel to be Simms's worst ever ("New Books" 283). The *New York Mirror* reviewed the work more favorably as "the most ambitious and successful incursion into the realms of romance the author yet made" (Rev. of *Damsel* 143). Guilds notes that most other contemporary reviews were "polite and respectful, rather than enthusiastic and laudatory" (*Literary Life* 95). Ironically, the most surprising source of critical mistreatment came from Lawson, Simms's friend and confidante (particularly during the composition of the book), who harshly reviewed the book in the November 1839 issue of the *Knickerbocker*. In the review, Lawson judged the work to be a failure for not only pleasure readers, but also for those who desire to improve their minds. Lawson accused Simms of careless composition, noting the repeated use of terms such as "speech," which he claimed occurred every twelve pages. Such carelessness led Lawson to conclude, "That The Damsel of Darien was written in a hurried manner, we think the proofs are numerous. In fact, Mr. Simms writes so much, and publishes so often, that it is next to impossible, with all his genius that he can always avoid incorrectness of phrase, and tautology in expression" (*Letters* 1: 152n, 154n).

Simms felt betrayed, and his lengthy 27 December 1839 letter was predictably defensive. After sarcastically lauding the "admirable" traits of Lawson's friendship—expressed by a negative review of the author's latest book that "damns its reputation & defeats its sale"—Simms proceeded to answer the charges. He accused Lawson of being "a very captious critic resolved upon nothing but fault finding." The ultimate fault, he continued, lay in confusing the work as a novel instead of a romance, thus unfairly saddling the work with standards inappropriate to the genre. Simms understood romance in the traditional literary sense as a genre originating in the medieval period that chronicles the legendary adventures of a chivalrous hero; while many were originally composed in verse, the genre later extended to prose narrative as well. As the novel emerged and proliferated throughout the seventeenth and eighteenth centuries, the new genre was frequently contrasted with romance, as its realism and complexity were meant to resemble actual life. Simms's rejoinder, rich with rhetorical interrogatives hurled at Lawson, proved an important defense for the writer's own work:

> Mere verbal correctness, good similes, and the simple exclusion of irrelevant matter do not constitute the only, or even the greater & more distinctive essentials of a novel or romance. Is nothing to be said of the invention which it displays, the fancy, the imagination—the creative faculty which makes the material to live, breathe, & burn. Is nothing to be said of that epic singleness of object which, in the Damsel, fixes the eye of the Hero & the reader, equally upon one great aim & purpose which is steadily pursued, amidst trials, & tortures, & persecution, to its triumphant close. Is nothing to be said of the felicity of moral, & natural painting in the description of scenes equally wild, wondrous & true—scenes of strife & repose—of passion & of tenderness—of hope, fear, shame, malignity, and every passion to which man & his nature are liable. All these appear in the Damsel. (*Letters* 1: 154–55)

Concluding that *Damsel* should be elevated to the higher standards of romantic composition, Simms ultimately labeled the work as a poem: "At least I have sought to make it such, and as such I require that it should be judged in all those essential respects which belong to the standards I have designated" (*Letters* 1: 155).

To better understand Simms's contention, it is important to turn to the author's advertisement in his 1835 romance, *The Yemassee*. Acknowledging the popularity and circulation of novels, Simms sought to disarm critics who might conflate genres in their reviews. Hence, the advertisement—better understood as a preface for today's reader—comprises a succinct explanation of the modern romance while pressing its distinction from the novel. Simms first advanced a crucial sentiment to critics that would be echoed in his own reply to Lawson in

1839: "I am unwilling that 'THE YEMASSEE' should be examined by any other than those standards which have governed me in its composition; and unless the critic is willing to adopt with me, those leading principles, in accordance with which the materials of my book have been selected, the less we have to say to one another the better" (*Yemassee* v).

Simms defined the modern romance as a substitute for the ancient epic—the standards against which such a composition should be measured. The novel, on the other hand, Simms considered an "altogether different sort of composition" that concerns itself with the "felicitous narration of common and daily occurring events" (*Yemassee* vi). He explained that the modern romance should be perceived as "a poem in every sense of the word." This perception must not insist upon poetry as necessitating rhyme; understanding this, the critic must equate the standards of modern romance with the ancient epic:

> It invests individuals with an absorbing interest—it hurries them through crowding events in a narrow space of time—it requires the same unities of plan, of purpose, and harmony of parts, and it seeks for its adventures among the wild and wonderful. It does not insist upon what is known, or even what is probable. It grasps at the possible; and, placing a human agent in hitherto untried situations, it exercises its ingenuity in extricating him from them, while describing his feelings and his fortunes in their progress. The task has been well or ill done, in proportion to the degree of ingenuity and knowledge which the romancer exhibits in carrying out the details, according to such proprieties as are called for by the circumstances of the story. (*Yemassee* vi–vii)

When the standards of the epic become operative for the critic of modern romance, extravagance can often be overlooked in the writer; Simms certainly hoped for such latitude and was largely granted that in writing his American romances. As for the Spanish-American colonial romance of *The Damsel of Darien*, Simms felt he never received the same margin, even from his closest friend. He lamented in a 6 December 1846 letter to Rufus Wilmot Griswold: "I do not think that the D of D ever had justice done it, though it received high encomiums from certain quarters. The theme was too stately for the taste of our day which at that time ran on the rough & tumble" (*Letters* 1: 228).

Postcolonial Reconsideration

The trajectory of literary scholarship today provides an opportune time to reassess *The Damsel of Darien*. A prominent contemporary approach to literature, postcolonial criticism, seeks to correct supposed historical biases of Western and European cultures that have established epistemological standards of truth and culture—a privilege that has accompanied such wealthy and powerful nations as they colonized weaker ones. Such colonization and subjugation of what postcolonial critics term "the subaltern" (i.e., the colonized and marginalized) for many years was framed as a civilizing institution, bringing the light of a superior culture to develop weaker nations. Ania Loomba asserts that the primary objective of postcolonialism is "to allow the voices of once colonized peoples and their descendants to be heard" (xi), and Leela Gandhi asserts that postcolonial critics seek to remain "sensitive to the long history of colonial consequences" still resonant today (3). While there are certainly many implications and varieties of postcolonial analysis that straddle various disciplinary fields, the upshot of its impact upon literary studies is the reexamination and interrogation of all past and recent literatures, and as Bart Moore-Gilbert notes, "bringing to the forefront of concern the interconnection of issues of race, nation, empire, migration, and ethnicity with cultural production" (6).

Published in 1839, *The Damsel of Darien* provides an early literary text that questions the assumptions of European empires, while also humanizing the subaltern culture laid to waste by such pursuits. Simms wrote his Native American characters as round and complex, imbuing them with a true sense of humanity. This compassionate portrayal of a conquered tribe reveals that Simms sympathized as much, if not more, with the colonized natives as he did with the colonizing Spanish. Simms's rendering of Vasco Nunez highlights the philosophical complexities and moral uncertainties of colonialism, as the protagonist's embattled words to his mentor explicitly illustrate: "By the blessed Virgin, Micer Codro, my heart bleeds for this abused people, even though we win such great profit from their wrongs; and sometimes I feel that I could join hands with the poor savages, and grapple in deadly strife in their behalf, with these worse savages whom I shame to call my countrymen" (55). Even the narrator exhibits such sentiments in a notable physical description of the Native American tribes, accompanied by stern value judgments against Spanish colonialism: "Overloaded with an unmeasured burden, which their cruel tyrants had accumulated upon their limbs, their frames, usually slight as they were erect and symmetrical, now freedoms, and the infantile joys to which their former condition had accustomed them! No wonder that they perished soon beneath the dominion of the Spaniards; the only wonder is, that they could do so much for their tyrants before death came to their relief." (64–65)

With this in mind, Vasco Nunez's troubles with his Spanish rivals, in several instances, center upon his humane views of the Native American people. Vasco's early rival, Jorge Garabito, is a sadistic Spanish cavalier who has a reputation for torturing and even killing the natives who are entrusted to him as slaves and human capital. Garabito also happens to be a rival suitor for Teresa; his outward displays of wealth attract her attentions and thus contrast him with the humbler Vasco who seems unconcerned with pomp. Garabito, upon a benign episode of public embarrassment involving a monkey knocking off his hat, takes up a trembling Native American boy named Zimi and beheads him in front of his mother and the entire Darien village. Vasco proceeds to publicly execute Garabito before Codro talks him out of an act of public justice, warning him of the consequences of killing such an esteemed cavalier over the life of a lesser native. Vasco instead publicly strikes Garabito across the cheek with the flat part of his sword to rebuke the cruel cavalier.

Garabito flees to plot with other jealous men such as the Bachelor Enciso (a cynical and opportunistic lawyer who works for Ojeda) to murder Vasco. Meanwhile, the slain boy's mother, Buru, ministers to Vasco after a hurricane dashes his ship and crew in Santa Domingo. With tears of mournful gratitude and gold from among the mountains of Darien, Buru pays her respects and makes an offering to reverse Vasco's fortunes. Biblical allusions to the "widow's mite" are present in Simms's depiction of Buru, who moves Vasco with her remarkable charity and compassion despite the loss of her son: "But such a proffer from the degraded Indian—from one of a people as yet unacknowledged as human, and but too commonly the victim of a licensed and legalized brutality filled his soul with mortification" (155). Such a tribute displays a remarkable spirit that not only transcends the expectations of Vasco but fills him with shame for the actions of his own people, as the narrator remarks upon the act as a "commentary upon the conduct of [Vasco's] countrymen was this noble and unexpected show of gratitude in the poor woman, whose best and dearest affections had been so wantonly and cruelly outraged. He felt that he could not receive her gold—he put it away from his sight" (155). Buru acts as an angel of God in the time of Vasco's despair, according to Codro, and she later saves Vasco from an eventual guerilla attack upon him and his men after they make further settlements in Darien.

Buru's husband and the slain boy's father is a mighty rebellious Darien cassique named Caonabo, who has managed to flee Spanish rule. He continually engages in guerilla warfare tactics to disrupt their occupation. Portrayals of Caonabo and his virtuous wife are the most moving episodes of the novel; moreover, Simms spent close to a quarter of the entire story treating them. He, thus, created a poignant story of Native American families and their struggles against Spanish tyranny. Simms shows them as husband, wife, father, mother, and most important, human beings who long to be sovereign and free. In the midst of Garabito's plot to assassinate Vasco, he is killed by Caonabo to avenge the murder of his son. Caonabo is a complex character suffering a tragedy of epic proportions in his struggle to fight for his tribe's freedom. In fact, Caonabo parallels Vasco in possessing the "hardy virtue" and "courage [that] never faltered," and thus displaying the noble and patriotic traits lacking in most of the European colonists (222–23). Simms lionizes the Native American chief for his will to live freely rather than captive to the Spanish. Through such characterization, Simms problematized Spanish colonialism by humanizing the subaltern who suffer grave injustices, eschewing savage caricatures that typically accompany a colonial viewpoint.[7]

Understanding Simms through a postcolonial lens, however, poses problems if we accept the author's own attribution of *The Damsel of Darien* as romance rather than novel. We can see throughout the text that Simms celebrates the virtue of Vasco Nunez, yet much of the commendation relies upon contrasting him not only with other Spanish explorers, but also within the context of the sixteenth-century zeitgeist of cupidity and subjugation. Simms attempts to establish a justified middle ground that commends European paternalism as a means of compassionate civilizing of Native Americans by teaching and modeling the Christian faith. This view is expressed most clearly through Codro's exhortation to Vasco in anticipation of his colonization of the Darien tribes:

> Vasco Nunez, my son, when thou hast trodden the green shores of that southern sea, beware what thou doest to the innocent people thereof. Of a truth thou has need to bring them to the tasks of labour, for without this, they can never learn the performance of those high and holy duties, taught by our religion; but task them not so that the limbs ache, and the heart desponds. Give them no tasks beyond their strength which shall impair their strength: but such only as shall increase it. Punish them when thou has need to do so, but never in thy passion; and never let thy punishments go to the taking of life, for life is of all things the most precious among the gifts of God to man. (66)

While Vasco Nunez is more humane to his Native American subjects, a more equitable leader among the Spanish colonizers, and even more concerned with teaching and exhibiting his Christian faith, the fact remains that he not only participates but leads in the subjugation and destruction of subaltern cultures, achieving fame and fortune in the process. Simms elaborated on such European colonial abuses in a December 1842 oration delivered at the Erosophic Society at the University of Alabama, which was published the following year, entitled *The Social Principle*. Simms critiqued the Spanish explorers' "inferior pursuits," which mingled religion with enterprise to create a zealous greed sanctioned by their sovereign rulers; Simms contrasted the "superior" British colonists, who sought another home in their destitution (10).

Though he acknowledged the humanity of his Native American characters and the cruelties of colonialism, Simms seems either incapable or unwilling to take the next logical step in the postcolonial view he initiated; he cannot see the natives as fully deserving of freedom and self-determination, rather than being the innocent victims of historical crimes against humanity. Of course, Simms was a man of his own time and place, the antebellum South. His largely sympathetic perspective on the condition of natives during the age of the conquistadors was certainly colored and corrupted by his own inborn opinions on the South's peculiar institution. It is noteworthy that later depictions of colonized natives in another Spanish colonial romance, *Vasconselos* (1853), were not as generous—perhaps illustrating a crystallization of the author's views regarding race and empire due to America's heightened tensions over slavery. Kevin Collins's recent introduction of the text treats two slave characters with African ancestry, Anita and Juana, observing how "their African beginnings, as Simms interprets them, are seen in their treachery and, in the case of Anita, in her mastery of the black arts. Juana, on the other hand, is very young and was likely born in Cuba. Simms may have used this contrast to reinforce the claims he repeatedly made elsewhere about the potential of the institution of slavery to ennoble godless and savage Africans" (this volume, p. 437).

As such, Simms viewed African slavery in the South as a "civilizing institution" that was overseen by paternalistic owners—himself included—while disregarding the moral contradictions in such a system. Simms was thankfully, though, able to remind his readers that great men like Vasco Nunez de Balboa also existed, confounding expectations and transcending their own dispensations. Ricardo J. Alfaro acknowledged the atrocities of Spanish colonialism in the "bloody days of the early sixteenth century," a time when "ignorance, fanaticism and ferocity were responsible for hideous crimes everywhere" (4). And while the Spanish have been rightly indicted for this dark period in their history, Alfaro was careful to point out the "redeeming light" of Vasco Nunez—an exceptional and pivotal conquistador worthy of our attention: "there stands Balboa as the friend and ally of the Indians, as the first Spaniard who associated in an immortal achievement the efforts of the white men and the bronze men, the first to lay the foundations for the fusion of the two races called upon to share in the future[,] the national life and the eternal destinies of Hispanic America" (4–5). Simms rightly believed that if great men who were models of virtue were written and read about, society would be better for it.

NOTES

1. Guilds considers the work an unmistakable waste of time and a departure from Simms's successful concentration upon fiction dealing with the southern frontier. A consideration that neither biographer seems to take into account for this shift in Simms's career is the financial crisis known as the Panic of 1837, which triggered a decline in book sales and readership and led many writers to diversify their output of literature.
2. Irving even took the opportunity to criticize religious hypocrisy in recounting Balboa's baptism of a Native American chief: "Before departing from the province of Comagre, he baptized that cacique by the name of Don Carlos, and performed the same ceremony upon his sons and several of his subjects;—thus singularly did avarice and religion go hand in hand in the conduct of Spanish discoverers" (148).
3. Henceforth, I will refer to him as Vasco Nunez or Vasco since I will be primarily discussing a character in a fictional story, not the historical figure; moreover, the narrator refers to him by his first name throughout the story, so my analysis will do the same.
4. Irving touches upon the boldness of Vasco Nunez in defying the stars of fate: "When he had launched his ships upon its waters, and his sails were in a manner flapping in the wind, to bear him in quest of the wealthy empire of Peru, he scoffed at the

prediction of the astrologer, and defied the influence of the stars. Behold him interrupted at the very moment of his departure, betrayed into the hands of his most invidious foe, the very enterprise that was to have crowned him with glory wrested into a crime, and himself hurried to a bloody and ignominious grave at the foot, as it were, of the mountain whence he had made his discovery! His fate, like that of his renowned predecessor, Columbus, proves that it is sometimes dangerous even to deserve too greatly" (245).

5. Irving goes on to detail the extremity of Pedrarias's vengeance upon Vasco Nunez: "not satisfied with the death of his victim; he confiscated his property and dishonored his remains, causing his head to be placed upon a pole, and exposed for several days in the public square" (245).
6. Simms omits this important factor that Irving recounts as having also contributed to the animosity that emerged against Balboa: "[Factions] broke forth into loud murmurs against Vasco Nunez, complaining that he had not made a fair division of the gold and slaves taken in the late expeditions, and threatening to arrest him and bring him to account. Above all, they clamored for an immediate distribution of ten thousand castellanos in gold, yet unshared" (160).
7. Simms used the same plot structures and elements earlier in *The Yemassee* (1835) where the colonists are British and, in Simms's eyes, justified. Simms thought of Americans as post-colonial and still too much under the cultural sway of Britain. Such Revolutionary romances expose the differences between the colonial mindset of the Tories and the self-reliance of the Patriots.

Dramas

Norman Maurice; Michael Bonham; and *Benedict Arnold*

ABIGAIL LUNDELIUS SMITH

On 8 April 1841, William Gilmore Simms confided in a letter to George Roberts, "My *penchant* is for another field very different from that in which I am more generally known to the public; and I will avail myself of the earliest leisure to send you a specimen of Dramatic Composition" (*Letters* 1: 244, emphasis in original). Confident in his ability, yet hesitant of its appreciation, Simms continued, "If the compensation for such labors were at all encouraging, I should perhaps, contribute one or two Dramas annually" (*Letters* 1: 244). Three years later, he was no less assured of the possibility of success when writing to James Lawson: "I am more and more inclined to the conviction that I am to prove my fate in the drama" (*Letters* 1: 428). Such was not to be. Despite his commitment to his dramatic endeavors, evidenced in part by their regular mention within his correspondence, Simms never garnered critical acclaim as a playwright. And by November of 1847, Simms seemed resigned to a far less illustrious fate for his plays. Writing to Lawson, Simms announced, rather dramatically, "I will make a volume of my Arnold, Michael Bonham, Locrine, Atalantis & adding this 'man of the people' [*Norman Maurice*], close my account with the Dramatic World in a single publication" (*Letters* 2: 369). As Edd Winfield Parks so succinctly notes, "The hoped-for glory never became a reality" (*William* 68).

The intervening years have done nothing to ameliorate the lackluster response to Simms's dramatic works. Writing about *Norman Maurice*, C. Hugh Holman says, "The effort to make a tragedy of the materials of contemporary life is admirable and daring; the effort to use the outmoded form of Shakespearean blank verse resulted in . . . absurdities" (*Roots* 80). Regarding *Michael Bonham*, he is even less kind: "to the present day reader it seems largely fustian bombast" (*Roots* 80). Simms's earliest biographer, William P. Trent, notes that "when read in the closet the play [*Michael Bonham*] seems to be the work of a precocious youth of eighteen rather than of a practical writer and constant student and spectator of the drama" (216). Critic William Hoole agrees: "by few, if any, standards, could *Michael Bonham* be considered a first-rate drama. . . . When read today it is slow and dull" (257). And, in the most recent of discussions, Erma Richter acknowledges, albeit more diplomatically, that *Michael Bonham* "was a failure aesthetically and financially" (108). Simms's last play fares no better. In her concluding remarks about *Benedict Arnold*, Miriam Shillingsburg suggests that the work has been "largely overlooked because of the inaccessibility of the play" ("Benedict Arnold" 287).

Given the lukewarm response of both contemporary and current critics, an obvious question arises: Why read these plays? First, it behooves the careful reader and scholar to consider the fullness of Simms's canon. This is not to suggest that the entirety of any writer's body of work is equally meritorious; that seems a hardly defensible assertion. Still, where possible, providing the opportunity for scholarly exploration is both appropriate and worthwhile. Second, although most critics concur that Simms's dramas are artistically insipid, they nonetheless agree that the plays remain historically and theoretically interesting. Note the remarkable shift in critical tone when the critics consider the plays as other-than-plays. Hoole argues that *Michael Bonham*'s "chief appeal is the interesting way in which the author altered historical facts" (257). Richter suggests that *Michael Bonham* reveals "the author's ability to merge fact and fiction to promote a political agenda" (109). Shillingsburg ultimately argues that, in its two-part structure, *Benedict Arnold: The Traitor. A Drama in an Essay* "is the most specific and detailed of Simms's works on the relationship between history and art, for he has opportunity in the Drama to develop his artistic rendition; yet in the Essay he plays literary critic discussing the handicaps to his art of adhering to the history" ("Benedict Arnold" 289). In another essay, Shillingsburg more generously suggests, "in several ways Simms's play represents an interplay of history and art that remains of lasting interest" ("Treason" 83). Perhaps the final reason to consider Simms's dramas comes from the playwright himself. Speaking of *Benedict Arnold*, Simms writes, "I probably see, quite as clearly as any other critic, the objections that may be urged against it" (*Benedict* 259). And yet, Simms offered it. That confidence, both in his dramas and in his audiences, deserves our attention. To that end, this edition offers readers the opportunity to explore the three long-form dramas completed by Simms. While other works within the Simms canon contain dramatic elements, particularly the poetry, these three are noteworthy for being fully-fledged, multi-act, book-length compositions ostensibly suitable and intended—at least in the case of *Norman Maurice* and *Michael Bonham*—for the stage.

Norman Maurice; or, The Man of the People. An American Drama

Published serially in the *Southern Literary Messenger* from April through August of 1851, *Norman Maurice* reappeared later that year in pamphlet form, published by John R. Thompson of Richmond. The following year, Walker and Richards of Charleston published it as *Norman Maurice; or, The Man of the People. An American Drama*. The 1852 publication included three additional one-act plays: "Caius

Marius; An Historical Legend," "Bertram; An Italian Sketch," and "The Death of Cleopatra."

Though enjoying numerous manifestations throughout the early 1850s, *Norman Maurice* made first mention four years earlier in a letter from Simms to James Lawson on 31 July 1847 (*Letters* 2: 341). By September of that year, Simms had finished the work: "I have been doing the tragedy. It is finished. Four acts have been sent to [prominent actor, Edwin] Forrest, . . . I have drawn the hero with F. himself in my eye—a portrait which I hope will not displease him" (*Letters* 2: 350). Apparently, the portrait did not please. In a letter written the following month, Simms admitted to Lawson that Forrest "speaks of it as not being as 'carefully elaborated' as it should be." And while Simms granted that the "style is not greatly elevated above that of ordinary conversation," he suggested that "this moderation of tone was deliberately determined on, in consequence of my wish to make the piece strictly a *domestic* drama." Simms continued, "The style was just sufficiently elevated to make it meet the exactions of rhythm. . . . [I]t will be quite easy to raise the style where it is necessary, & throw in those extraneous passages of poetry, which I rather suppressed" (*Letters* 2: 356–57, emphasis in original).

Not everyone found the play lacking in elevation. A review in the September 1851 edition of *The Literary World* praised Simms for his use of "blank verse" and suggested that he had "shown art and judgment." The review continued, "If [Simms] had given us nothing but prose, . . . the whole tone of the piece would have been let down . . . with the aid of skilfully [*sic*] delivered verse—[he has offered] a happy medium between slow-footed prose and the remoter elegancies of pure fancy" ("Mr. Simms's" 223). After reading *Norman Maurice* in 1852, fellow poet Thomas Holley Chivers offered this encouragement and advice to Simms: "I have received and read your Drama, and find it the best thing that *I* have ever seen of yours—in fact, I am now puzzled to know why you should ever have worn out your faculties in writing Novels. . . . You have shown in this Play that you are not unacquainted with the *true Dramatic Style*" (qtd. in *Letters* 3: 169, emphasis in original).

Norman Maurice tells the story of a young man's rise to political stardom. Written in the wake of the 1820 Missouri Compromise, *Norman Maurice* explores the political implications of statehood in America's border regions. By the play's end, the title character is the newly elected Senator from Missouri, a "champion of the people" who promises to defend the Constitution as a "ligament of fix'd, unchanging value, / Maintained by strict construction,—neither warp'd, / By the ambitious demagogue or statesman, / Who, with the baits of station in their eyes, / Still sacrifice the State!" (117). Certainly, *Norman Maurice* is a defense of the rule of original constitutional intent in the face of changing political sentiment. In proper Simms fashion, however, the curtain rises not upon the plot political, but romantic. Maurice has wooed the heart of young Clarice, and nothing can convince her guardian aunt of his worthiness. Mrs. Jervas has another suitor in mind, Robert Warren, Maurice's "kinsman and enemy" (5). Explaining Warren's hatred for Maurice, Simms writes, "Warren hates his cousin Maurice for several reasons. He has always proved his superior—has *proved* him a coward—has pardoned him a wrong, is his rival in love, and these rouse his *passion* for a vindictive triumph over him who has always triumphed hitherto" (*Letters* 2: 369, emphasis in original). Through an unexplained turn of events, Warren is in possession of documents that can devastate all of Maurice's aims. Though Maurice believes the papers destroyed, Warren reveals to Clarice that he maintains possession of the originals. The price of Warren's silence is Clarice's submission to his carnal desires. One fateful night, as Maurice wins nomination to the Senate, Clarice meets Warren in the woods where she stabs him and recovers the damning documents. Soon overcome by her act of violence, Clarice suffers a stroke. Maurice rushes to her side moments before her death, catching the ruinous papers as they "fall from her bosom" (125).

The intensity of Simms's drama is difficult to overstate. As one contemporary critic opines, "We unhesitatingly say that Mr. Simms' 'Norman Maurice' is one of the boldest literary ventures on record" (Hayne, "Dramatic" 242). Despite this lofty praise, the review concludes with a warning:

> There are so many ideas necessarily low and sordid, connected with the scenes through which Maurice, the lawyer and politician, *must* pass in his way to place and power, that no genius—not the genius of Shakspeare [*sic*] himself—could have *completely* harmonized them with the proprieties of High Art. Therefore, let the dramatist—bent upon writing tragedy—hereafter beware of contemporary *American* topics. (254, emphasis in original)

Ignoring this advice, Simms published *Michael Bonham* the following year.

Michael Bonham; or, The Fall of Bexar. A Tale of Texas

On 9 November 1843, in a letter to James Lawson, Simms made first mention of a new literary endeavor. Simms wrote "of a melodrama which I have been projecting as an experiment, for the Charleston Theatre—the scene in Texas—the subject the fall of the Alamo &c.—But of this, say nothing. 'I would not willingly be known'" (*Letters* 1: 387). Just over a week later, on November 15, Simms again wrote to Lawson, "I am preparing a melodrama . . . founded upon the conquest of the Alamo by the Texans & the subsequent battle of San Jacinto. . . . I am writing it just to see if I can accomplish the action of a drama. . . . Say nothing on the subject" (*Letters* 1: 388). Obviously enamored of his fledgling project, Simms wrote—again to Lawson and again after the passing of a week—to explain his foray into the dramatic: "I have half done a melodrama—my only object to test my powers of dramatic situation. I make no attempt at fine writing. There is much bustle in the piece so far & will be more" (*Letters* 1: 391). The following month, Simms mentioned his play once again to Lawson. "It is in five acts and has a melancholy conclusion, though the hero triumphs &c. This almost makes it a Tragedy. In parts, indeed, it rises into the dignity of one. . . . But do not mutter this even in your garden" (*Letters* 1: 393–94). Simms's curious secretiveness about this play continued with its anonymous publication.

Like *Norman Maurice*, *Michael Bonham* was first published serially in the *Southern Literary Messenger*, from February to June of 1852, and again as a separate volume by John R. Thompson later that same year. Unlike its dramatic predecessor, however, this latter play was published both times without the benefit of Simms's name, authorship credited simply as "By a Southron." In her fine essay on the play, Erma Richter offers a political, rather than personal, motive for this decision: "In spite of Simms's statements to Lawson that his interest in composing *Michael Bonham* was purely to test his ability to write a drama, significant evidence points to a broader, more political intent" (101). Richter notes, particularly, that this was quite reasonable "for one desiring annexation of Texas to strengthen the political position of the South" (101)—namely, its inclusion as a slave-holding state. No wonder, then, that Simms expected *Michael Bonham* to "make a rumpus, be sure, if ever it reaches light upon the stage" (*Letters* 2: 23–24). It was a drama intended to create some drama.

Michael Bonham is the story of a young hero keen on infiltrating and undermining the Mexican stronghold at San Antonio, all while wooing the heart of the Governor's daughter and securing a place in the annals of Texas history. The play opens with the Texans encamped outside Bexar awaiting their next encounter with the Mexican military force. Eager to assess the enemy's strength, the Texan commander, Milam, sends Bonham on a reconnaissance mission inside the city walls. Bonham is no less eager to penetrate Bexar's defenses—it affords him the felicitous opportunity of seeing his beloved Olivia once again. The romantic and political plots collide during a *Bal Masqué* hosted by Bexar's Governor, Don Esteban. Arriving in disguise, Bonham must contend not only with Olivia's spurned suitor, Don Pedro, but also with the woman whose love he has rejected, Olivia's cousin, Maria. Furious at his refusal of her advances, Maria unmasks Bonham, revealing his true identity as a spy. Summoned by Bonham's bugle call, the awaiting Texans overwhelm the city. With the political story concluded, the marriage of Bonham and Olivia offers a fitting dénouement. Simms complicates this comic end, however, with the stabbing of Don Pedro in the antepenultimate scene, the attempted murder and subsequent suicide of Maria in the final scene, and the swooning of Olivia into a dead faint at the curtain's fall. No wonder, then, that Arthur Hobson Quinn describes *Michael Bonham* as a "vigorous if lurid melodrama" (501).

Michael Bonham did eventually see the light of stage at the New Charleston Theatre in March of 1855. Although appearing without its intended political polemic—Texas having been admitted as a state nearly ten years before in December of 1845—the production, according to Simms, "was quite successful—greatly applauded, & played for 3 nights—which in our little city, is a great event—audiences rarely suffering for more than one" (*Letters* 3: 384). This reception might have surprised Simms. Three years earlier, when the *Southern Literary Messenger* serialized *Michael Bonham*, Simms seemed resigned to an unperformed play. In fact, he conceded in his introduction to the published edition, "The tale which follows, [*sic*] was originally prepared with a view toward performance. Subsequently, however, I have persuaded myself that it would read better as a story" (3). Part of the story's success must reside, as well, in its inclusion of a bit of local flavor. Although, as Hoole clarifies, there was "no 'Michael' Bonham," there was a South Carolinian Bonham "associated with the Texas Revolution . . . James Butler Bonham, of Edgefield, South Carolina, who died in the Alamo" (258). The discrepancies in historical detail pose no threat to Simms, though. While Simms acknowledged that he had "taken some liberties with the historical facts," he insisted that "the history will suffer little from my freedoms, while . . . the story gains by them" (3). Here, Simms provides an inkling of the theoretical framework defining his canon—an idea he would further explore in another drama, *Benedict Arnold*.

Benedict Arnold: The Traitor. A Drama in an Essay.

By May of 1863, with America deep into her civil hostilities, Simms was ready to present a drama not for the stage, but for the page. As the title indicates, the plot of *Benedict Arnold* details the events leading to the traitorous actions of the American Revolution's most infamous figure. Simms was not the first to attempt such a dramatic feat; as Shillingsburg summarizes, "Simms joined William Dunlap, James Fenimore Cooper, George Henry Calvert, and a score of amateurs who had attempted to use the Arnold-Andre conspiracy to surrender West Point to the British in 1780 in serious literature" ("Traitor" 273). Simms's treatment of this narrative is unique, however, in his exploration of the relationship between history and art. As with Simms's first two dramas, *Benedict Arnold* was published serially, this time by the *Magnolia Weekly* from May to August of 1863. Given the timing of its appearance and its Richmond, Virginia publisher, *Benedict Arnold* appears not only as Simms's retrospective on the American Revolution but his contemporary look at America's second great civil conflict.

It is quite clear that Simms intended Arnold to be the hero of the drama. In his introductory comments, Simms says, "The deeds of the hero are as brilliant as his treason is utter and unqualified. Arnold was no imbecile in action. He was only so in morals. His courage was unquestionable; and he exposed himself personally in battle, as was the case with the valiant man in ancient warfare" (165). Despite this approbation, it is worth noting that Arnold neither opens nor closes the play which bears his name. In the opening scene, Arnold's commitment to the Crown is the subject of conversation although he is not present to make his own defense; at the conclusion, Arnold has fled the stage, this time unwilling to mount any defense. In fact, like Simms's previous dramas, *Benedict Arnold* focuses largely on intrigues of the heart.

Throughout the course of the drama, three distinct love plots swirl around Mrs. Margaret Arnold. The first, of course, is her relationship with her husband, Benedict. Of their relationship, Simms offers this explanation, "Margaret Shippen was a fashionable damsel of the time—a *belle*. . . . She married, as such persons usually do, not a lover, but an establishment! . . . As for the *heart*, the less we say about that . . . the better!" (195). On the night of a *Bal Masqué* hosted by the Arnolds, in a plot move borrowed from *Michael Bonham*, both John Andre, Arnold's fellow conspirator, and Randolph Peyton, a young man in service to Washington, reveal their undiminished love for Margaret. Although she holds them both at arm's length, it is nevertheless clear that her affections once favored them. Love does not ultimately favor Margaret, however. By the play's end, she has been cruelly abandoned by her husband, watched helplessly as Andre is captured and sentenced to hang, and swooned hopelessly over the dead body of Peyton.

The response to Simms's final dramatic creation was limited and dismissive. A critic of the *Charleston Evening News* noted that the play suffered due to Simms's "too great *nearness* to the period in which he writes" (qtd in Hoole 256, emphasis in original). Simms himself acknowledges this dilemma in his prefatory comments to *Benedict Arnold*:

> All of the writers have been hampered, not by the barrenness of the subject, but the fear of violating the details of history. To be successful in this material, one must assert a certain degree of audacity—must be content with looking to the history for the main facts—the treason—the conspiracy—the detection and disgrace—but must boldly conceive for himself the events, incidents, and situations. . . . I was baffled by the details of history. I had no sufficient freedom. There was too much known to suffer invention its privileges. I was stopt by stern barriers of fact. (166)

At one moment, historical fact impedes dramatic action; in the very next, artistic license offends history's sensibilities.

That Simms, ever the historian and always the artist, found himself caught between an unusual irreconcilability of these two demands is evidenced long before the publication of *Benedict Arnold*. In a letter dated 4 March 1853, Simms wrote to Henry Carey Baird to inquire about Mrs. Benedict Arnold:

> Have you any thing in relation to the private life of Arnold while in Philadelphia? What was the christened name of his wife? Is there any thing in respect

> to her private history and character. . . . Were not all Mrs. Arnold's kindred loyalists & active as such. What were the names of uncles & aunts,—or is any thing known of them? Were they quakers [*sic*]; in other words, can I give her an uncle who is at once Quaker & Loyalist? (*Letters* 3: 226)

Over two years later, Simms was still in communication with Baird regarding the historicity of the Arnold saga. "[W]hat was Mrs. A's Christian name? And were her father & mother living then, either of them, and are there any descendants or connections now? . . . [I]s there any faith to be put in the alleged facts in a book about Arnold—a quasi historical fiction" (*Letters* 3: 407). Simms's line of questioning reveals his commitment to the facts. Over the course of two letters, in the space of a few lines, Simms asked eleven questions—most regarding Mrs. Arnold. And yet, Simms was not shy regarding his artistic intent. By the play's public appearance, Simms had christened Margaret Arnold with a Christian name and saddled her with a Loyalist Quaker uncle. Simms's justification for the artistic license of these decisions appears in the "essayical [*sic*] portions" (*Letters* 3: 7) of *Benedict Arnold* where he writes, "In this narrative, there is nothing improbable in the case, as reported by the dramatist. He does not really conflict with the Historian. He only knows *more* than the historian has been suffered to find in the written records" (430, emphasis in original). Herein lies the most unique theoretical aspect of Simms's play—a willingness to grant freedom to the artist while remaining faithful to the demands of the historian.

Simms and his Dramatic Women

The general response to Simms's treatment of women is one of tempered praise. In an essay exploring the relationship between gender and secession in Simms, Patricia Okker writes, "As much as Simms portrayed women as exerting a powerful influence on the forces of history, his ambivalence about independent women tempers his celebration of women's historical power" ("Gender" 26). Ultimately, Okker argues that Simms's "idealization of women as willingly subordinate to men undercuts his otherwise fervent celebration of independence" ("Gender" 30). Debra Johanyak agrees, suggesting that while "Simms somewhat softened his views toward feministic behavior late in his career, for the most part he held to his theory of domestic purity dominated by masculine authority as the structural framework for the society he believed in and upheld" (588). Shillingsburg attempts to give Simms a bit more credit: "Simms's opinion of women was not merely representative of the received opinion of his day that women were inferior and that too much education and accomplishment was a dangerous thing. He did sometimes reflect such received opinion, but he also had a deep respect for the talented and able women he knew" ("Battered" 219).

In her essay, "Toward a Feminist Reading of Simms," Caroline Collins paints a far different picture:

> Simms's strong women serve as enacters and enablers, providing important keys to the survival of individuals and cultures, and to the survival of the social order. At the very least, his later romances achieve a tension between 'man-centered' and 'women-centered' narratives. . . . [and indeed] are probably more 'woman-centered' than any other 'male-authored' works of literature in nineteenth century America. (6)

Collins sees Simms's women rejecting the notion of women as domestic dependents and embracing their role as active participants in not only their own destiny, but in the future of the world they inhabit. This freedom is not, however, without responsibility. Collins goes on to argue that Simms's female "characters' participation in their own undoing certainly evokes Shakespeare's notion of the tragic flaw, but also displays a desire for realism and a keen understanding of human psychology and behavior" ("Toward" 11). Not only is Simms willing to endow his women with freedom, he allows them a will of their own.

Looking at Simms's reimagining of Shakespearean characters, Charles S. Watson argues that Simms "expressed the Romantic view that Hamlet's will was defective. He stressed Hamlet's indecision and impulsive action as his principal traits, and . . . argued that Shakespeare's message in *Hamlet* is that action is the chief end of existence" ("Simms's Use" 21). If action is evidence of a robust will, the men of Simms's plays certainly seem to fit the bill. Simms's friend and protégé Paul Hamilton Hayne, in considering *Norman Maurice*, proposed that in "the hands of the author, an unpromising subject has been wrought into a work vivid in action" ("Dramatic" 254). Writing in 1869, James Davidson described both *Norman Maurice* and *Michael Bonham* as "vigorous productions" (525). As if to highlight Maurice's willingness to act, Simms places a particularly violent scene at the center of *Norman Maurice*. One evening, as Clarice and Maurice have just completed supper, Warren knocks on the door. During the lengthy exchange that follows, Maurice is violently active, as evidenced by the numerous stage directions: "*Laying his hand on Warren's shoulder*" (59); "*flinging him* [Warren] *away and rising*" (60); "*hurling the table over*" (61); "*Rushes upon him* [Warren] *and wrests the weapon from his hand*" (62); "*Takes Warren by the throat*" (62); "*Hurls him* [Warren] *out headlong*" (63). With every page, Maurice becomes more agitated and his reaction more pronounced.

In *Michael Bonham*, Simms clearly distinguishes between the man of words and the man of deeds. Don Esteban de Monteueros, the Governor of Bexar, first appears writing at a desk where his "sword lie[s] before him among papers" (10). Initially, it seems that Don Esteban might stand as the character who best unifies deed and word. In his opening speech, he says, "It is well done! It is written! The record is made. I may now take my rest. . . . The battle is over" (10). The letter in which Don Esteban lauds his efforts to Santa Ana, however, quickly reveals his passivity. He writes, "I have the honor to inform you of the complete defeat,—I may almost say, the total annihilation, of the Texian [*sic*] invading army. . . . This defeat, so utter and complete, is due entirely to the terror inspired by our arms! . . . Ours was a victory without a blow" (10). Within the Simms milieu, however, there is no victory without a blow.

Benedict Arnold also hears the call to action. In his opening soliloquy, he acknowledges, "The whole world sees my wrongs, yet I am silent! / The whole world know my claims, yet I ask nothing!"(186). Inaction will not always mark his course, however. By speech's end, he declares, "I cannot always be denied and baffled! / I feel it here!—a power and will to conquer, / Which will not be subdued;—yet, heart be still / While THOUGHT and subtlest WISDOM tutor will!" (186). And, of America's great traitor, Simms writes, "Arnold, as we see, has attained one of his objects, and that one of vital importance to all the rest. He has not suffered the grass to grow beneath the feet of his ambition" (219).

And yet, the men of Simms's dramas appear on the stage with words writ large and deeds largely unseen. At the close of the first act, Maurice promises to exact retribution on Warren: "But, let him dare / Once more to cross my path, and he shall feel / His serpent head grow flat beneath my heel" (32). Despite this explicitly Christological allusion, Maurice never crushes Warren's head—Clarice does. Michael Bonham's great action, rescuing Olivia and Maria from their captors, occurs prior to the play's beginning and Olivia tells the tale: "Señor, by that rancho—/ That scene of strife and dread, I still remember, / Never to lose it—when the wild Camanché, / Smote me to earth, and 'neath his savage fury, / Hopeless, I shriek'd for succor, and—I found it! / Nor succor only! You came, you conquer'd" (12). Even Benedict Arnold, America's great traitor, is remarkably passive. Prior to his dastardly deed, Simms claims that "Arnold, like Macbeth, is one to falter in decision—to show himself quite capable of conceiving the crime, but to be infirm of purpose" (330). This lack of resolve haunts Arnold throughout the play. Just before his capture, he cries out, "It is not yet too late! The damned deed, / That blackens me forever; wife and child; / Friends, country, honor'd name and ancient valor;—/ It is not beyond recall! I will recall it!" (186). And yet, he protests too much; by the soliloquy's end, Arnold has talked himself out of an honorable retreat and chosen cowardly flight.

With astounding clarity and conviction, it is the *women* of these plays who act. Consider, once again, *Norman Maurice*. Upon learning that Warren remains in possession of the infernal documents, Clarice agrees to a clandestine meeting in a "thick wood" where, as the text makes clear, Warren anticipates the long-awaited fulfillment of his passionate desire for her (108). Clarice has plans of her own. Answering Warren's call, she enters the wood and exits the stage. The stage direction indicates a struggle and "*a moment after a cry of agony, and then a sound as of a falling body. Rëenter Clarice with paper in her hand, and garments all bloody*" (111). Clarice exults, "He'll lie no more. / He wish'd for my embrace, and sure he had it! / Such close embrace, so sharp, so sudden, sweet, / It made him shriek and shrink with such a pleasure, / As men endure not twice" (112). In a rather shocking, and wholly unexpected reversal, Clarice's knife penetrates Warren. The victim has become the victor. Her act of violence is even more impressive when juxtaposed, in the very next scene, against Maurice's refusal to kill the man he has bested in a duel.

In *Michael Bonham* there are two women of action. The first is Ellen Harris. Disguised as a boy, Ellen has followed her husband to the Texas battlefield in order to reclaim his soul for heaven. Believing his wife unfaithful, Richard Harris murdered both the parson who witnessed their marriage and the brother who defended her honor. Upon learning of his error, he fled to Texas to die as honorable a death as possible. While all of Richard's actions occur prior to the opening of the play, Ellen spends the entirety of the play acting as "Billy" Harris. And, in their final scene, Ellen takes on her greatest role—that of intercessor. With his last breath, Richard beseeches Ellen, "Come closer—let me hear you; in my ears / Still tell me of forgiveness. Christ! Have mercy! / Look down upon me! Would that I had time / For pray'r; but no! I cannot" (30). Although calling on Christ for mercy, Richard looks to Ellen as the embodiment of that atonement. Ellen speaks absolution over Richard, saying, "Have mercy on him, Heaven! / Let not these murders hang about his soul, / Dragging it downwards" (30). Unwilling to let him die alone, she begs that God "take us both together" (30) and, in so doing, she pleads redemptive efficacy in her final act of sacrifice.

Also active, though not sacrificially, is Maria, Olivia's cousin who suffers an unrequited passion for Bonham. After hearing her pleas for his love, a love he has already given to Olivia, Bonham remarks, "Was ever so cruel a woman! Soul so proud, / And yet so passionate, was never seen! / . . . ready with her life, / To prove her heart's devotion; not less ready, / That heart's devotion set at nought or wronged, / Avenging it with life!" (23). A truer portent was never spoken. When it becomes clear that Bonham's affections lie with Olivia, Maria wastes no time in enacting her revenge. She attempts to secure Bonham's love by threatening to reveal his identity. When he refuses, she exposes him to the Mexican authorities. After the Texans take Bexar and Bonham secures Olivia's hand, Maria attempts to murder her cousin at their wedding. Failing in that, she stabs herself declaring, "[Olivia] cannot love as I have done. This hand, / That smote its kindred heart, had, in your cause, / Borne weapon 'gainst a thousand foes" (35). Both in life and in death, Maria's love for Bonham is marked by action.

Finally, Margaret Arnold appears as the most complete of Simms's dramatic women. In an essay looking at this play, Miriam Shillingsburg writes, "Simms made Mrs. Arnold the traditional virtue personified—a dutiful wife, a loving mother, a noble woman, and an innocent victim" ("Benedict" 278). Shillingsburg goes on to argue, "This entire characterization of Mrs. Arnold is . . . the product of the nineteenth-century veneration of womanhood" ("Benedict" 287).

Shillingsburg's reading of Margaret as the stereotypically passive victim, however, fails to watch Margaret in her final moments on stage.

In the penultimate scene of *Benedict Arnold*, and for the first time in the entire play, Arnold and Washington are in the same scene—it is not, however, the Arnold we would expect. In hot pursuit of the traitorous Benedict, Washington and several of his officers enter the Arnold home. Hearing a shot outside, Washington turns to the door but Margaret "rushes into the room, and places herself between Washington and the entrance" (258). Their initial verbal parlay quickly escalates:

> Washington.
> ... Let me go forward.
>
> Margaret.
> Only o'er my corse [*sic*]!
>
> Washington. (*Seeks to put her aside.*)
> Each moment lost.
>
> Margaret.
> (*Aside.*) Is a life-gain to Arnold! (*Struggling.*)
> Is this your manhood? To assault a woman? (258)

At no other time in this drama does Washington physically engage with another character. That Simms would have him do so with Mrs. Arnold is significant. She alone is his equal. Shillingsburg is correct when she argues that Washington "is the moral yardstick against which all characters must be measured, and, in all cases ... they are found wanting" ("Treason" 84). The men fall remarkably short—Benedict Arnold is a coward, Randolph Peyton is impetuous, and John Andre is a spy. Margaret, on the other hand, measures up to Washington. This moral fortitude allows Margaret to defend Arnold, intercede for Andre, and mourn over Peyton. Washington might be the iconic moral pillar, but with Margaret, Simms creates a character, a woman, who is far more real and far more good.

Further examination of the presence and power of the women within these dramas certainly seems worthwhile. Not only for their sake, but for the ways in which watching these women act on Simms's stage casts new light on Simms himself. As Caroline Collins suggests, "It seems unlikely, or at least contradictory, that someone who is not interested in women or who is interested in only keeping women down would create such a vast and intriguing array of strong, determined women" ("Toward" 7).

The Play's the Thing

This is, by no means, the fullness of what these three dramas offer. Numerous avenues of fruitful exploration remain—hospitality in *Norman Maurice* and

Benedict Arnold; the way in which food imagery shapes the conversation in *Michael Bonham*; *Norman Maurice*'s similarities to *Paradise Lost*; the parallels between Shakespeare's *Macbeth* and *Benedict Arnold*; the role of masking and unmasking in *Michael Bonham* and *Benedict Arnold*. Herein lies the value of the *Simms Initiatives*, the digital collection of the author's work, headquartered at the University of South Carolina, and their recent print edition of the author's selected works, issued by the University of South Carolina Press. They make Simms's long overlooked plays more readily available to a new audience, and allows them to argue, with greater vigor, for their place not only within the vast Simms canon, but also within the collection of American drama.

Egeria; or, Voices of Thought and Counsel, for the Woods and Wayside

DAVID S. SHIELDS

Egeria; or Voices of Thought and Counsel, published in 1853, was William Gilmore Simms's volume of apothegms—his positions on various philosophical and moral questions stated in cogent form. Composed of 295 pages of discrete paragraphs and epigrams, each headed by a thematic title, *Egeria* was Simms's attempt to communicate in the gnomic mode characteristic of the Transcendentalism authors, who stood as his intellectual rivals in the great contest for the hearts and minds of Americans waged in the 1850s. Because the ideas were presented as pure positions—that is as free floating conceptions untethered to a rhetorical program, a logical argument, or a scheme of suasion, the book appeared to contemporary readers as uncontentious. A reader's disagreements with the positions seemed differences of opinion, "of the sort only which music justifies and requires, in which a certain amount of discord is admitted as one of the most necessary ingredients of harmony" ("Notice" 2).

The book had a long gestation, predating by some years the first appearance of several aphorisms and observations as "Wayside Laconics," in the *Southern Patriot* over the twelve months from April 1846 to April 1847. Periodicals hungered for brief filler, and editor Simms began generating observations on manners and morals designed to arrest a general reading public. In 1847, he had composed sufficient material to warrant book publication, yet overtures to publishers, including longtime friend and literary collaborator Evert Augustus Duyckinck, failed to secure a taker. The original title, *Sybillane*, alluded to the mystic priestesses who rhapsodized prophecy in the late Etruscan and early Roman eras; yet the title misrepresented the contents, for there was nothing apocalyptic, occult, or mythogogic about Simms's thoughts. Indeed, in a letter to Henry Theodore Tuckerman in 1850, Simms characterized the volume as a "nice little gift of social morals," and he was sufficiently willing to present them as proverbial, rather than aphoristic, by withholding his name from the publication (*Letters* 3: 71). When E.H. Butler and Company of Philadelphia issued the volume in 1853, however, it appeared bearing Simms's name, and that name proved sufficiently potent to secure numbers of reviews, invariably positive.

Simms's willingness to appear without a veil of anonymity or pseudonymity may be accounted by his increasingly central placement in the republic of letters in the years between 1847 and 1853. His assumption of the editorship of the *Southern Quarterly Review* in 1849 placed him in one of the more conspicuous seats of literary power in the United States. His publication of the two series of *Views and Reviews in American Literature, History and Fiction* positioned Simms as a monitor of public affairs. By 1850 he possessed as forward a profile as any southern writer except Edgar Allan Poe. And his concerns with the fragility of civilization, the travails of leadership, and the conduct of life were laid bare in his Falstaffian novel, *The Sword and the Distaff* (1852), so the concerns of his aphorisms found a narrative counterpart in his curiously domestic novel about the knitting together of civil and familial life in the wake of the American Revolution's disruptions of life in the Carolinas.

The form of *Egeria* on first glance appears miscellaneous. Unlike a commonplace book of thoughts and sentiments, which one encounters in one's reading, Simms did not resort to an alphabetical organization of topics, although a topic index following the body of the entries permits one to pursue that sort of orderly investigation of matters. The title—"Voices"—suggests a kind of communal authorship of the contents, yet less than ten pieces paraphrased other authors' sentiments. More usually Simms crafted his own counsels employing his own approximation of the voice of wisdom. Indeed, his choice of Egeria, the mythical nymph who, according to Plutarch, instructed the Sabine King Numa Pomphilius, imparting to him principles, in a series of oracles, that he fashioned into the laws and mores of Italy, suggests Simms's desire to have the voice of authority behind his insights, yet no particular wise person.[1]

Egeria held a peculiar fascination for Western artists and intellectuals in the early nineteenth century. Unlike the muses, this feminine divine principle (she appeared in shadowy form to Numa) spoke more to the rational mind than the imagination. Like "Sophia" in the Book of Proverbs, her wisdom dealt with principles that governed the conduct of life and the ordering of society and the state. The truth of her oracles, according to Plutarch, were self-evident, positions so reasonable, so trenchant, or so commonsensical that one sought to internalize them immediately as a guide to personal performance. Byron, who visited the vale traditionally appointed as the scene of the conversations between King and nymph, composed a lyric that envisions the goddess as a projection of one's fondest attachments to one's most beautiful conceptions:

Egeria! sweet creation of some heart,
Which found no mortal resting place so fair
As thine ideal breast; whate'er thou art,
Or wert,—a young Aurora of the air,

The nympholepsy of some fond despair,
Or, it might be, some beauty of the earth.
Who found a more than common votary there.
Too much adoring:—whatso'er thy birth,
Thou wert a beautiful thought, and softly bodied forth. (*Childe* 4: 115)

In 1845 the sculptor Nathan F. Baker, a Cincinnatian who studied art in Rome, made his reputation with a marble incarnation of the nymph. Reports of the beauty of this "ideal union of gentleness, beauty, meekness, and loveliness" appeared on both sides of the Atlantic ("Astronomical" 3). This statue in turn inspired astronomer M. de Gasparis, in January of 1851, to name the newly discovered Asteroid (the thirteenth such body discovered) Egeria.[2]

Egeria was meaningful to Simms precisely because in her figure rationality and charm made counsel, or the imparting of thought, congenial: "Thought and Study are beguiled to the solitude, where Wisdom puts on the aspect of Love, for the better persuasion of the pupil" (*Egeria* 2). The problem of instruction is the natural resentment of the unenlightened to the imperative mood with which a mentor speaks. Maxims are commands. Rules are compulsions. Pride bristles at such demands, and an unreflecting resistance arises in the face of presumptive authority. Even in the Old Testament *Book of Proverbs*, the worldly commandments of the experienced father to the young man give way to the more affectionate and metaphoric instructions of the feminine spirit, Sophia. If worldly wisdom can be conveyed in a manner that permits even disconcerting truths to sound less discordant, less harsh, then they are more easily heard, internalized, embraced. Having labored as a public man of letters for over a quarter century, Simms knew "that the great part of mankind are not so easily taught" (*Egeria* 14). In the face of obdurate or contrarian people, an instructor has two choices in terms of exercising authority: the path of charm and poetic figuration (Egeria), or the aspect of an oracle, speaking with mysterious impersonality and a disregard of the audience, precluding its answer and responses. Simms felt uncomfortable putting on the mantle of a prophet or seer. He much preferred the path of charm.

How does charm manifest itself stylistically in *Egeria*? In a determined avoidance of the gnomic, or vatic isolated sentence. Brevity forces interpretation and application—its purity of position radiates the audacity of knowledge. So the Delphic Oracle spoke in single sentences, or cogent phrases: *Seek the protection of wooden walls!* Simms's insights are invariably elaborated with a provoking opening sentence, then a modifying, clarifying, or positioning series of elaborations. Indeed, when he finally permits himself a single-sentence thought—"Rational Liberty"—it has a complex internal architecture of clauses: "The only rational liberty is that which is born of subjection, reared in the fear of God and love of man, and made courageous in the defence of trust and the prosecution of a duty"

(49). The tensions of the God/Man, trust/duty reveal that Simms, even when striving for simplicity, presented a world defined by dialectic tension.

Indeed, the tensions in Simms's entries have sometimes the flavor of a conversation, in which the first sentence—a doxa—a conventional idea—or perhaps the position of another writer—undergoes exploration. Sometimes the conversation is explicit, as in "National Pride and Vanity": "National pride is, no doubt, as Schlegel calls it, 'a glorious fault,' but national vanity is very certainly a grievous folly. In the possession of the one, we may safely laugh at all the world, but the exhibition of the other only provokes the world to laugh at us" (51). The United States of the 1850s, fraught with its internal divisions and public ceremonies of sectional denunciation must have seemed to Simms a sorry spectacle in the eyes of the world. In 1853 the outbreak of talk among southern radicals of secession by whatever means possible must have troubled Simms, because his next entry, "Revolution" despaired at the prospect of violent communal action: "What are the revolutions which occur in a community, but the efforts of a people, who seek by madness to recover what they have lost by blindness" (51).

In entries such as "Revolution" one detects the reason for Simms to publish his book of counsel. The people lack insight. Their blindness, their stupidity, their passion have made them violent and self-destructive. Indeed, circulating throughout the entries is a vision of a hierarchical society in which an informed elite must deal with an unsettled and credulous populace subjected to volatile moods and opinions, and lacking fixed principles or certitudes of value by which to direct their actions. The distinctions existing within people, Simms believed to be an enduring condition; yet, capable by reason of moral ignorance to greater or lesser degrees of social and political disruption, given the state of communication in the body politic. Despite his willingness to put himself forward as a counsel furthering this communication, he entertained little faith in his contemporaries' capacity for moral progress:

> In morals, I suspect that the age is pretty much where it was a thousand years ago. In what is the morality of the British conquest over the Chinese, superior to that of the Norman sea-chivalry in the time of Charlemagne? How is the Christianity of the French conquest in Algeria, superior to the ordinary moral exhibitions of the British, French, Spanish, and Italian during the reigns of Louis the Twelfth, Henry the Eighth, Charles the Bold, Ferdinand the Catholic, and Pope Julius II? (*Egeria* 203)

For all the advances in technology and expansion of scientific knowledge, the West's capacity to cloak its most acquisitive and aggressive inclinations in the garb of ideals and its capacity to make philosophy an instrument of desire, instead of the love of Truth and Beauty, have doomed the greatest cultures of the West to recurring moral charades. There are moments in *Egeria* when there are intimations of the futility of counsel.

A malaise, stemming from the moral condition of the West, was not an unfamiliar mood in the mid-nineteenth century. For northerners the foremost sign of the age's turpitude was its tolerance of the enslavement of the African race. For Simms it was the delusion among westerners that their culture, economy, and politics served some higher good, when it simply mystified and excused greed and the will to power. The answer for certain male intellectuals on both sides of the Atlantic was eruption into history of the hero. Beginning with Thomas Carlyle's *On Heroes, Hero-Worship, and the Heroic in History* (1840), and finding an American culmination in Ralph Waldo Emerson's 1850 exploration of Plato, Shakespeare, Montaigne, Napoleon, and Swedenborg as *Representative Men*, intellectuals sought a remedy to the conventionality, timidity, and stupidity of the people through the influence of "great men," whose genius somehow communicated to the community in which they emerged. Simms, who had written biographies of Francis Marion (1844), Captain John Smith (1846), and Chevalier Bayard (1847), knew the attractions of the heroic and gave lip service to them at two points in the multitude of pages: "Great men are a common property. They form the solar system of the world of the mind, and shine more or less brightly upon all the nations" (*Egeria* 266). Yet there is much of the anti-heroic in Simms's counsel. For him the hallmark of genius was courage, yet those who dare suffer in the world and often experience neglect. Simms doubted the effectuality of the hero, particularly his ability to alter the frames of reference—the conditions, stations, positions, ranks, and offices that organized it. Hence his claim that "He is no slave, no matter what his condition, when that condition continues to improve in intellectual and moral respects." This subjectivist view also finds expression in his meditation on "Distinction": "Our distinctions do not lie in the places which we occupy, but in the grace and dignity with which we fill them" (20–21). That material circumstances or the coercion of law might delimit one's capacity at improvement or the exercise of grace is a possibility that Simms did not entertain.

As a subjectivist, Simms was decidedly not a jejune optimist believing humanity could find fulfillment in an imagined perfection. Indeed, he entertained a strong conviction that innate defects caused many, if not all, persons to conceive and perform evil, embrace stupidity, and perform error. Errors may recur in the conduct of life—to manifest repeatedly or haunt the imagination: the "errors of youth are the evil genii which wait upon our manhood, and the ghosts that make us tremble in old age" (*Egeria* 71). Yet for Simms error is not sin, an enduring debility that attaints human beings in a way depriving them absolutely from grace, insight, or happiness: "The man and the nation may equally fall into error; but this is one of the processes of truth, as skepticism first precedes faith. But the temporary lapse, or error, in man or nation, offers no good reason why they should not in the end come right" (*Egeria* 51). Yet the power of good counsel to stem error is limited by the form correction takes, for libraries are stuffed with books filled with wisdom and instruction. How can error persist? In answer,

Simms personifies "Error" and notes that "[h]ers is a strange vitality: we cannot brain her effectually with all our volumes. But here lies the mystery. The big books themselves help somewhat to explain it. This is the secret of the ineffectiveness; they are big, too big! Error is a subtle existence, small, compact and infinitesimally divisible" (183). Articulating an ethical system or explicating a sacred history of good and evil do little good in addressing the peculiarity of a defect. A more casuistic, precise, and disparate way of applying wisdom is needed—i.e. discrete oracles, cogent apothegms.

Evil in the traditional sense does not much operate in Simms's world. Lust, Sloth, Greed make no appearance in it at all. Pride, alone of the seven deadly failings of humankind, merits discussion. Evil prompts reflection: "The Audacity of Evil" insists that evil's difference from error lies in a conscious and willful embrace of error. The perversity of knowing something is faulty or wrong and affirming it, because it is, seems the only salient characteristic of evil. Indeed, *Egeria*'s thoughts are singularly distant from theology, even when considering topics such as prayer (a habitual performance).

Characterology supplants theology as the highest register of values. Instilling virtues, correcting errors, breaking bad habits of mind or performance take up most of the pages. The possibility of change being progress frames characterology; so it is not a surprise to see, in addition to musings on personal improvement, a strong conviction in communal and national progress. The baldness of Simms's commitment to a stadialist view of individual, communal, and national progress can be seen in his sonnet series "Progress in America." What is odd about Simms's progress piece, on national character and destiny, is his choice not to use the Germanic "spirit" as the figure metaphorizing the will toward improvement, but "blood." The blood's progress is further metaphorized in the headlong rush of a mountain torrent, purifying the waters as it gathers strength and impetuosity. Hindsight has made twenty-first-century readers of this turn in Simms's thought chary of the choice of metaphor. Purity of blood became the mantra of racism—and the "one drop rule" subjected many biologically diverse people into legal subservience in the nineteenth century, when no science could detect the racial constitution of blood.

The ambiguity of Simms's figure of blood is that it is a substance that is shared by humanity. Whereas genius is an innate gift of a remarkable few, blood operates in "the people." So its torrential flow to some better state is to some extent communal. The ambiguity is further mystified by the curious capacity of blood to respond to the promptings of wisdom. Books will make Blood better. And Blood will find expression in Books.

In the myth of Egeria, the book that results from Numa's communion with the nymph is a book of civil laws. Yet such legislation is not what Simms's book aspired to be. Virtually alone among the major writers and public intellectuals of his day, Simms had been an elected legislator. He had served in the assembly of

South Carolina. His experience did not imbue him with a high regard for legislators and legislation, produced by state and national governments. He saw the halls of government abound with "tinkerers" and "conservatives":

> The statesman who expects stability in the forms of government, while the people themselves are daily advancing to new conquests in mind, morals and machinery, might as well be an antediluvian. He certainly is no statesman for his day. Hence the absurdity, which we daily witness, of self-complacent politicians, who are continually insisting upon their superior pretension to govern the present, because of their superior familiarity with the past. (*Egeria* 251)

One must ultimately ask where progress is tending in Simms's imaginings of people, society, and nation, and what it is that conservatism is insisting be maintained? This book does not propose the telos of communal moral striving. From 1847 through 1853 Simms was evolving a concept of southern ethnogenesis—the formation of a new and separate nation. That notion would take a final, definite form after the failure of his northern lecture tour of 1856. But all of *Egeria* is suffused with a disquiet at the status quo. His wisdom is all about change. Not about the conditions of the enslaved, or of women; but of those persons in the republic who already possess sovereign powers and the freedom to exercise thought and will. The thoughtless procrustean southern grandee was fated for the scrap pile of history. The agrarian disbeliever in science and technology was doomed. The money grubber, the unpoetic tradesman, and the parochial jobber were the fools of the age, incapable of poetry and rapport with the place they claim to love.

Is the poet the enlightened man of Simms's world of wisdom-coming-to-be? Is he the true legislator of manners and mores, love and friendship—just as Percy Shelley had insisted? Certainly the amount of verse contained in *Egeria* suggests a kind of lyric attunement to one's place and one's fellows; it constitutes the mind of the oracle (or is it the Blood of the People?) better than the systems of the natural scientists or the engines of the technologist. It is perhaps germane to note here that Simms's other major publication of 1853 was *Poems: Descriptive, Dramatic, Legendary, and Contemplative*.

NOTES

1. See Plutarch, "The parallel lives, Numa Pompilius"; Livy AUC libri XXXVIII.
2. Given the associations of rationalism and political concern associated with the demigoddess, more than one woman author of the era embraced the persona. Mrs. Hemans perhaps had the greatest claim of any on the title.

The Golden Christmas: A Chronicle of St. John's, Berkeley

TODD HAGSTETTE

Although William Gilmore Simms is primarily remembered for his long-form romances—like *The Yemassee*, *The Partisan*, *Woodcraft*, and *The Cassique of Kiawah*—in many ways he was at his best when writing shorter works. Most of his tales exhibit a control and narrative effectiveness that can sometimes get lost in the sprawl of his novels; likewise, his novellas often display a sophistication that is on par with that of his romances but do not suffer from the verbosity that can plague the longer works. Counter-intuitively, Simms's style often feels freer and more unfettered when he operated within the confines of shorter forms. Such is certainly the case with one of the author's most enjoyable works, the comic novella *The Golden Christmas*. Rich in detail, extravagant in characterization, and feverish in plot, it is one of the author's most successful works when considered in terms of entertainment value or of overall quality. Set during the Christmas season in antebellum South Carolina, it joins two other Simms works, *Castle Dismal* (1841) and "Maize in Milk" (1853), in focusing much of its narrative attention on the customs of the season, especially as they are enacted at and around the southern plantation. For its comedy, *The Golden Christmas* lampoons cultural and ethnic conflicts of the families of the region, while the language of the story works luxuriously in puns and double-entendres. All is set against the story of a *Romeo and Juliet* style love plot. While some modern critics and scholars have argued for the novella's hidden seriousness and thus urged the importance of the literary and cultural themes at play in the book, *The Golden Christmas* can perhaps best be appreciated as a lighthearted and whimsical story of holiday romance.

So engaging are its storyline and characters that the tale drew the admiration of both of Simms's principal biographers, who rarely have agreed in their assessments of the author's work. William P. Trent, in his 1892 biography, suggested that *The Golden Christmas* demonstrates Simms's successful crafting of "descriptions of the social life of the Carolina aristocracy"; he found certain elements of the novella "very amusing," and declared the story overall to be "rather entertaining reading" (194–95). Remarking specifically on the plantation setting of the work, John Caldwell Guilds, in his 1992 literary biography of Simms, noted that with its "portrait of Christmas in the Old South" the novella "glories in presenting the sounds, tastes, smells, and other indoor and outdoor pleasures of the most festive season of the year" (*Literary Life* 203). Indeed, in the detailed depiction of the Christmas season in Charleston and the surrounding country, Simms provides a rather painstaking catalog of the customs and traditions of the plantation society of the Old South, one whose value is both literary and social-historical. In the same vein, by setting the bluster of the lowcountry Anglo-Saxon English community against the haughtiness of the French Huguenot, Simms's comedy is both amusing and insightful. In achieving these ends, *The Golden Christmas* exhibits the characteristics of several styles of fiction, including, among others, the comedy of manners, the plantation novel, the love romance, the Horatian satire, and the exposé.

The story opens with the narrator, Dick Cooper, being interrupted in his morning rituals by the frantic arrival of his friend and fellow bachelor, Ned Bulmer. Though at first Dick fears a duel is afoot, Ned assures him that, no, it is another matter entirely: "It is Venus not Mars, at this season of the year, to whom I address my prayers. It is an affair of the heart, not of pistols" (5). Ned, who comes from a proud English family that traces its lowcountry lineage far back into the southern past, is in love with Paula Bonneau, the petite and demure scion of the local French Huguenot tribe, which enjoys an antiquity to match the Bulmers. Based on deep-seated ancestral animosities, the current family alphas, Ned's father, Major Marmaduke Bulmer, and Paula's grandmother, Madame Agnes-Theresa Girardin, despise the other's family and would never concede to a match, in spite of Ned and Paula's desires. Ned thus calls in the assistance of his childhood friend and confidant, Dick, who is a lawyer fortuitously between cases at the moment—the "briefless barrister" of the novella's subtitle. More important, Dick holds a rare position in this community divided along family lines, as the Coopers are "an English cross upon a Huguenot stock" (*Golden* 17); the family cottons to none of the ethnic prejudice of either side, and thus Dick is a welcome visitor at both estates. Ned hopes to deploy his friend's bridging capacity to the fulfillment of his own uphill marital ambitions.

For his part, Dick is in seemingly reciprocal love with Beatrice Mazyck, daughter of one of the most prominent families in the region. Complicating matters is the fact that Major Bulmer has designs on securing Beatrice for his own son and has begun secret negotiations with the Mazyck matriarch. Once the Major informs Dick of his plans, the two enter into a wager of sorts to see who can win the young girl's hand, Dick for himself or Bulmer for his son. Of course, unbeknownst to the Major, the deck is heavily stacked against him, as Dick and Beatrice are already on the courting path and Ned and Paula are all-but-married in their minds. What follows is a comic series of subterfuges on the part of the younger generation as they foil the ruling generation's prejudiced pursuit of the romantic status quo. The action of the story is set against a dazzling panoply of southern holiday traditions and events; the reader is treated to shopping on

Charleston's King Street, an art show at famous Russell's Bookstore, a deer hunt, a wild boar hunt, a Christmas cotillion, and finally, the "Golden Christmas" itself, an all-night holiday party to commemorate the 100th Christmas celebrated at "The Barony," the ancestral plantation of the Bulmers.

The climactic moment on which the romantic storylines begin to turn occurs in the aftermath of the holiday dance at the Mazyck mansion. Seeing his plans for his son's betrothal unraveling during the course of the night, Major Bulmer gets rather intoxicated and flustered. Departing the party early with Ned, the Major belligerently insists on driving their buggy despite his inebriation. This is in part to spite Ned, who the Major correctly observes had been heavily instrumental in foiling the father's matchmaking plans. As Bulmer berates his son for his neglect of Beatrice and attendance on Paula, he loses sight of the road and crashes the buggy in the midnight, winter woods leaving both travelers senseless on the turf. Some time later, the two are rescued fortuitously by Madame Girardin and Paula on their way home from the same party. In gratitude for their timely assistance and upon the insistence of his son, the Major magnanimously invites the Huguenot clan to the Golden Christmas celebration. There, the frost between the two families melts, the romances resolve according to the wishes of the younger generation, and by the story's conclusion, the two bachelors who opened the tale are happily engaged, Ned to Paula and Dick to Beatrice.

Arguably one of Simms's finer efforts at short fiction, *The Golden Christmas* was published during the heyday of Simms's career as a writer. Yet discerning how the novella came to be written and what inspired its main action requires speculation. Simms did not refer to the composition of the story in any obvious detail in his extant letters. Judging from the circumstances and timing of the publication, though, it can be reasonably inferred that he was writing the novella at the same time as *The Sword and the Distaff*, the first version of *Woodcraft*, in 1851. Both works appeared initially in the same periodical within weeks of each other, and both were issued in book form by the same publisher. *The Golden Christmas* filled three weekly supplements to the *Southern Literary Gazette*, on 10 January, 24 January, and 10 February 1852. (*The Sword and the Distaff* began its serial run in February of that year). Walker, Richards and Company, the publishers of the *Gazette*, released the book edition of the novella immediately following its final periodical installment. The book seems to have appeared on, or at least by, 17 February 1852; the *Charleston Courier* on that day contained a note that the book had just been "received" at their offices (*Letters* 3: 212n).

Also on that day, Simms sent a letter to Francis Colburn Adams, former manager of the Charleston Theater, discussing the thespian's desire to have a drama version of the story prepared for the stage. This ambition was apparently communicated to Simms through J.D.B. DeBow, editor of the respected *DeBow's Review* (*Letters* 3: 161). Though Simms stated that he would "be greatly pleased, should a drama of the piece be made," he adamantly declared that he could spare no time to execute the rewrite himself. He offered some revision suggestions, including the need to beef up the role of Beatrice since Adams wanted beloved Charleston actress Julia Dean to play that role, and he concluded with the encouraging assessment that "the piece would prove quite susceptible of conversion into a Genteel Comedy, while the arrangements for a spectacle at the Golden Christmas would give a pleasant air of melodrama to the final act" (*Letters* 3: 161).

Sadly, that play version of the story never came to fruition. Simms's own unwillingness to have a role in its translation surely played a part. This was an odd turn-of-events given that Simms in the 1850s was eager to make a name for himself as a dramatist. In fact, he used the opportunity of corresponding with Adams to solicit the former theater manager's interest in his recently-published play *Norman Maurice*, even attempting to poach Dean for the lead female role. Also, shortly after this time, Simms's second major dramatic work, *Michael Bonham*, began its serial publication in the *Southern Literary Messenger*. As Simms had stridently, yet unsuccessfully, tried to sell *Norman Maurice* for a performance run following its initial publication in 1851, the chance to stage *The Golden Christmas* could have provided the solution to his theatrical ambitions. But, it was a chance he never took. *Michael Bonham* eventually was staged for three nights in 1855, and though that short run was apparently well-received by its Charleston audience, given its limited engagement, Simms's dreams of being a popular dramatist were never fully realized; and, *The Golden Christmas* lived only in print.

While the attentions of Adams and the local theater imply that regard for Simms's story was high, at least in his hometown, the sparseness of the reviews that attended publication suggests otherwise. Noticed in a handful of periodicals, North and South, overall the novella was not reviewed widely enough for an author of Simms's caliber and reputation. Those reviews that did appear were largely positive, if somewhat less vigorous in their praise than might have been hoped. Even the laudatory notices tended to treat the story and its execution as slight. The majority of reviews appeared in May 1852, with a write-up from no less a source than *Harper's* seemingly setting the tone. The reviewer complained that *The Golden Christmas* was stylistically "more careless than the usual writings of the author," yet despite its flaws in implementation, the novella's "ease and vivacity will make it a favorite with indulgent readers in search merely of amusement" ("Literary" 853). A similarly-themed editorial that same month in *Sartain's Union Magazine* remarked that the "story is rather common-place in incident, but pleasantly related, sufficiently amusing to redeem it from absolute dulness [*sic*], but not sufficiently brilliant to add any to Mr. Simms's literary reputation" ("Editorial" 439). In both cases, Simms's eminence as a writer actually detracted from the enjoyment these professional readers could take from the work.

Other reviews were more consistently positive, even if most came from publications with which Simms had standing relationships. The earliest, from March 1852, compared *The Golden Christmas* favorably to the rest of the author's output.

Calling it a "pleasant little tale," the reviewer for *The Literary World* ruminated that a "Southern Christmas is, it is well known, a season of great hilarity, and its genial scenes both of indoor and out, high and low life, are full of the vigor and animation we are always sure of having from Mr. Simms" ("Simms's" 206). Likewise, the widely-circulated *Godey's* recommended the book in a May 1852 review, based solely on the known quality of its creator, gushing that the "readers of the 'Lady's Book' will be pleased to recognize, in the author of 'The Golden Christmas,' an old and popular contributor, with whose merits as a writer they have had abundant opportunities of becoming familiar" ("Literary" 408). In August of that year, another publication that traditionally dealt favorably with Simms's work, *DeBow's Review*, gave the book a favorable if short notice, calling it a "lively and spirited tale, in the best style of the author" ("Southern" 211).

Far and away the most effusive review that *The Golden Christmas* received was in the "Notices of New Works" section of the *Southern Literary Messenger*, also in May 1852. After spending a "few hours very pleasantly in running over this little Christmas tale of Mr. Simms," the reviewer was able to state firmly that "[t]here is about it a freshness and healthiness of tone very agreeable, in these days of false sentiment, fabricated passion, and almost universal striving after the 'effective.'" Not only is the plot of the story engaging, but Simms's characters, which are "well and skillfully drawn," are relatable and true to life. Overall, the reviewer found *The Golden Christmas* to be a "very pleasant and readable tale" which had proven to be "far superior to the thousand and one strained and unnatural fictions which periodically inundate our booksellers' counters" (318).

Despite encouraging reviews like these and the inferred regard for the work that inspired the desire to see The *Golden Christmas* staged, robust sales, unfortunately, did not follow. Simms, who seems to have lived his entire professional life hungering for greater sales, increased notice, and enhanced respect, found no remedy with his plantation Christmas story. His awareness of the fact discomfited. In a November 1852 letter to his friend James Henry Hammond, Simms lamented some of his recent literary fortunes, noting especially that *The Golden Christmas*, which had been published in book form nine months earlier, "has not yet yielded me a cent" (*Letters* 3: 212). Sales of the book were such that when, only a few years later, Simms contracted with New York publisher Redfield to produce a multi-volume collection of his selected works, *The Golden Christmas* was not included, nor even apparently considered. Perhaps most telling of all, copies of the book were remaindered by William Gowans of New York City in 1858; this according to an advertisement placed by Gowans in the *American Publishers' Circular and Literary Gazette* on 20 February 1858, a sure sign of poor sales for the book (*Letters* 3: 213n).

In the twentieth and twenty-first centuries, a revival of sorts has been initiated on behalf of the novella. Beginning in the 1950s, select scholars have argued for the merits of the book, in terms both of entertainment quality and literary achievement. The first of these was Donald Davidson in his introduction to Simms's collected letters. Attempting to repair some of the damage done to Simms's reputation and legacy by Trent and other framers of the literary canon at the turn of the century, Davidson culled a selection of Simms materials to be advanced for canonical reconsideration. In that estimation, *The Golden Christmas* joined Simms's Revolutionary Romances, *The Wigwam and the Cabin*, *The Yemassee*, *Castle Dismal*, and a few other works to form what Davidson called "the massive body of Simms' real achievement." For Davidson, these works felt timeless and almost preexisting, as if they were "waiting to be told before they found in Simms the medium through which they burst into utterance" (*Letters* 1: li). In this way, works such as *The Golden Christmas* tapped into the cultural consciousness of the region and the country as a whole.

Building on Davidson's assessment, the novella received extended scholarly treatment for the first time in 1994, when James Everett Kibler, editor of the newly-launched journal *The Simms Review*, dedicated the third installment of that publication as a special topics issue focused on the book. That same year *The Golden Christmas* became the first book published in a proposed series, "The Southern Renaissance Collection," from Fletcher and Fletcher Publishing of North Charleston, South Carolina. Then again, in 2005, a new paperback printing of the book was issued by the University of South Carolina Press. Both publications, separated by over a decade were photo reprints of the original 1852 edition of the novella. Both featured introductions, and presumably were arranged for publication, by David Aiken. The latter text inspired the only known review of the book in the modern era, which appeared in the auspicious *Wall Street Journal*. In it, Stuart Ferguson offered an implied endorsement of the story, noting that it would "charm readers who have the slightest interest in Southern social traditions before the Civil War." Though "Simms today is not even on the back burner of the American literary stove," the republication of *The Golden Christmas* could be a step toward guaranteeing the author's proper regard in the American literary landscape; Simms's Christmas tale, Ferguson hoped, might "help to rehabilitate his reputation enough so that his virtues as a writer can be appreciated again" (13).

The small cadre of twenty-first century enthusiasts for the novella are correct that any reassessment of Simms as a literary artist and fit subject of academic study could profitably include *The Golden Christmas*. Though this holiday novella is perhaps less thematically consequential than some of the author's "bigger" works, it nonetheless offers several critical avenues that, when combined with its obvious merits in sheer aesthetics, make it a rewarding work for classroom investigation and critical discussion. Above all, *The Golden Christmas* is a story of contrasts. It relentlessly pits the younger generation against the older, the rising group of family heads against those currently holding sway. This contrast is played out primarily in the arena of the older generation's ethnic prejudice, where the Anglo-Saxon Bulmers and the Huguenot Girardins maintain a familial cold war that has lasted for decades. As Simms views things, the Carolina gentry of the nineteenth century was comprised of two basic classes:

> There was an English and a French class. The one was distinguished by frankness, the other by propriety;—the former was rough and impulsive, the latter scrupulous and delicate; the former was apt to storm, occasionally, the latter to sneer and indulge in sarcasm; the former was loud and eager; the latter was tinctured with propriety which sometimes became formality. In process of time, the two schools modified each other; at all times, they were equally hospitable and generous: fond of display, scorning meanness, and, accordingly, too frequently sacrificing the substantial securities of life, for the more attractive enjoyments of society. (*Golden* 29–30)

While the older members of the community hold to this division, the more progressive scions, Ned and Paula, augmented by their close associates, Dick and Beatrice (though she is mostly a background figure or symbolic character), strive to heal this ancient, clannish rift through their unrestricted romantic ambitions. Pursuing this goal, the younger generation ushers in a community more "tolerant, neighborly, and good-natured" than the one, deeply leveraged by "ancestral pride and prejudice," that they stood to inherit from their "bossy, stubborn, and arrogant" forebears (Kibler, "Pairing" 13). They also, by the novella's end, have not merely overcome ancestral prejudice but have successfully merged the houses. With the promise of offspring, the former separations will be cancelled by the mingling of blood, and Carolina society will take another step toward the noble and nonpartisan model of Dick Cooper.

Kibler views this ethnic conflict of the community as a dramatization of Simms's anxiety over the fate of the future plantation culture, with the happy resolution of the conclusion a suggestion that plantation life will continue. He sees the novella asking "whether or not plantation civilization and its traditions will survive," and, more specifically, "how such communities are kept whole and vital" ("Pairing" 13). Ultimately, Kibler sees Simms demonstrating that "plantation society survives only through close communal ties and loyalties" ("Pairing" 15). It is true that, aside from his comedic ambitions, Simms's chief fascination in *The Golden Christmas* was the theme of community reconciliation. The majority of the story takes place in various plantation settings, and the old-fashioned Golden Christmas celebration is the location of the final resolution of the long-standing animosities of the local families. Yet the Christmas atmosphere itself seems at least as instrumental as the plantation setting in producing, by the story's close, the reconciliation of the community. Operating within the open-minded season of the holidays, the members of the younger generation are progressive in their thinking; they are decidedly un-mired in the prejudicial habits of their ancestors, and it is their refuting of the traditions of their families that produces the community healing that the novella celebrates. In contrast to a nervous backward look at fading tradition, Simms seems to have been favoring a forward-focused hope for transformation. In doing so, he blended the romantic with the sociopolitical. Ned tells his father, "Hearts, sir, have a language in *our* day, which was denied them in yours. Perhaps this is one of the redeeming features of ultra democracy!" (86).

As an embodiment of the merged community, Dick is the character who can most easily be seen as an avatar for Simms's perspective. Aiken notes that in "Dick Cooper himself, Simms has created a narrator not unlike himself" ("Mock" 17). As such, Dick is comfortable in the manor house and skilled at traditional activities like the hunt; yet, he is a denizen of the city and seems to view the conventional ideologies of the reigning elite with, at best, suspicion and, at worst, disdain. When he encounters the decrepit and impoverished descendant of one of the formerly proudest houses of the region, he sneers that this was "a person well known about town,—one who had wasted his means like a fool, and had not the soul to recover them like a man, whose ancestors had exhausted the physical vigour of the family by a monstrous succession of intermarriages. . . . The natural consequence was physical and moral imbecility." Dick declares definitively that "the pity which his poverty and feebleness might have inspired, was all swallowed up in the scorn which I felt for such equal impotence and vanity" (23). Given that Dick is the ostensible hero of the story, his ridicule of the wasted traditions of the plantation aristocracy problematizes Simms's supposed adoration for the same.

In a later refinement of his plantation thesis, Kibler accommodated this disparagement with which the younger generation in *The Golden Christmas* seems to regard their sires. Considering the action of the novella in continuity with *Woodcraft*, Simms's other exploration of plantation community at the time, Kibler notes that *The Golden Christmas*, which is set over half a century later than the latter work, marks Simms's consideration of the new struggle of the community for continuance: "this time it is the prejudice and pig-headedness of family that might be the end of the plantation" (Introduction xxxi). Simms, of course, was not alone in casting aspersions on some of the empty traditions of the plantation. His friend John Pendleton Kennedy and others of that generation likewise interrogated plantation culture and enabled the exploration of ways that society could adapt and evolve in an ever-changing southern world. For Simms, this development relied in part on manhood, as represented by Major Bulmer and his eventual achievement of an updated level of social accommodation, even within the plantation community.

While the primary conflicts of the story involve young versus old and English versus French, myriad other contrasts are tested throughout the pages of Simms's text. One is aristocratic traditionalism versus modern progressivism. Simms also explores bachelorhood versus the married life, the rural versus urban environments, family ties versus the bonds of friendship, and, importantly, the masculine versus the feminine spheres. This last contrast, in fact, is a particular focus of Simms's social program in the novella. Mainly through the life philosophy of Major Bulmer and his interactions with his son and Dick, the reader is offered a kind of running commentary on the bounds of manhood. Bulmer himself, with the blustery audacity of his English blood, is offered up as a flawed but steadfast paragon of masculinity. Upon the commencement of their contest for Beatrice's affections, Dick is struck by the underlying gentlemanliness of Bulmer's carriage; he notes, "I was very deeply touched with his nobleness and generosity. Certainly, with all his prejudices, the Major is one of the most noble specimens of modern manhood" (53). This comportment is not the result merely of his skill in the hunt or generosity as a plantation host; rather, Dick and the reader are given glimpses of the man's integrity and fair-minded character, qualities essential for proper manly behavior in Simms's estimation. Neither is Bulmer's adoption of such qualities happenstance, as he steadfastly endorses the development of manliness of character as the premier commitment of southern men, like his son and Dick: "Manhood, Dick, is the first of virtues. It includes, it implies them all. Strength, health and courage,—these are the first necessities—without these I would'nt [*sic*] give a fig for any virtue. It could'nt [*sic*] be useful without it, and a stagnant virtue might as well be a vice for all the benefit it does society" (31).

It is on the ground of a failing of manhood that Ned first begins to push successfully his claim for Paula's hand. The patriarch's ancestral prejudice against the Huguenots begins to conflict with his sense of chivalric manhood as Ned more and more vehemently pursues the object of his affection. As the Major is forced to speak out in greater detail and more impassioned tone against his son's proposed mate, his language becomes increasingly offensive to the young lady who is its target. In a moment of exasperation, Ned finally calls out his father, crying, "I protest, sir, it is positively a reproach to your manhood that you should thus religiously maintain an antipathy, when its object is a sweet, young, artless, and unoffending woman!" (39). Though unrelenting for the moment, the Major must concede that attaching his perception of general vices inexorably and blindly to a single individual woman threatens to damage his gentlemanly *bona fides*. This concession of Paula's essential humanity and virtuous womanhood becomes an important first step in breaking down the enmity between the two families. If Simms does, in fact, worry over the plantation future in his narration of *The Golden Christmas*, his ultimate vision is perhaps one of a modified, rather than traditional plantation culture. He offers to the reader a fully self-actualized space where the manhood of the chivalric ideal overcomes the prejudicial customs of the past and makes of the plantation a more perfect social sphere that retains the positive ideals of the southern past while jettisoning those corrupted aspects of deep-seated ancestral animosity.

Of course, the white aristocratic owners are not the only members of the plantation community. One knotty scene in which Simms turns his literary imagination for the first time here to the slave quarters appears at the end in the tale of the narrative and cannot be left without comment. In an awkward insertion that follows the main story of Ned and Dick's courting travails and triumphs, Simms offers a rather slapstick tale of two slaves at The Barony who, following an altercation over one's theft of the other's prize pig, are subjected to a mock trial to settle the matter. The full interaction at the slave quarters is played for lowbrow laughs, and as such, this concluding moment of the novella glares with racial misappropriation. Some recent critics have made attempts to justify the sequence as thematically consistent, most forcibly Aiken's "The Mock Trial in *The Golden Christmas* and the Theme of Reconciliation" and perhaps most effectively Rebecca Sexton's contention that the "slaves' bickering and concern with social status clearly mirrors the actions of several of the white characters earlier in the novel. Through this parallel, Simms emphasizes the folly of . . . snobbery and prejudice and stresses that values (both good and bad ones) cut across racial lines" (6). These arguments notwithstanding, for many modern readers there is something that will feel problematic about the scene as well as the "Denouement" chapter in which it appears; it seems a clumsy, mercenary, and ultimately, unnecessary insertion of prejudicial caricaturing into a story that has otherwise steered refreshingly clear of racial politics.

The evocation of the "ham-loving darkie" stereotype mars the final moments of the story with an air of minstrelsy that, in twenty-first century estimations, can seem garish and tactless. Simms was writing his Christmas tale during the high point of popularity for the Minstrel Show tradition in America. Although some recent critics have pointed to a subversive element in those performances that subtly lampooned white plantation society and slavery, including valorizing runaways and other black characters, little evidence of this mindset is present in the concluding moments of Simms's novella. A fundamental humanity of any perceivable authenticity is not easily found in the characters of Zacharias and Jehu. So driven by meat-lust is the latter, for example, that he declares proudly as the last words of the novella that whatever punishment might come of it, he "can't help tief fat pig in sassage time" (168). This scene is doubly regrettable because it marks a departure for Simms from a tradition of crafting fully-fleshed black and Native American characters. Absent here is the essential integrity and skill of Tom from *Woodcraft*, the doomed tragedy of Sylvia from *The Cassique of Kiawah*, and even the complexity of Mingo from "Caloya; or, the Loves of the Driver" (from *The Wigwam and the Cabin*). This sequence also marks a diversion from the primary action of the story, one that is made more incongruous for its having been seemingly tacked on as the final moment of the narrative. This is in stark contrast to other works in which Simms's black characters are more integral to the overall arch of the story and thus have a role to play that is more representative of Simms's ideologically driven conception of the African-American presence in and effect on antebellum society.

One is tempted to wish that Simms had been less concerned with delivering the sensationalism he felt his audience expected, at least if his narrative voice can be trusted. Leading up to the pig-stealing sequence, as he offers a closing statement on the main action of his novella, Simms worries that "the reader is half inclined to blaze out at the presumption which dignifies, with the name of story, a narrative which has neither duel, nor robbery, nor murder—neither crime nor criminal" (165). Yet, truly, it is in part the absence of those more familiar tropes of exaggerated storytelling that brings much of the charm to Simms's Christmas tale. Despite his band-aid inclusion of a last minute criminal anecdote and the resulting racial marring of the decorum of the novella, *The Golden Christmas* is, overall, one of the author's finest accomplishments as a writer. A thoroughly engaging work that provides an important glimpse at plantation life in the antebellum South, this story of conflicts and reconciliations offers a mild and nuanced dissertation on progress, a catalog of traditions of old southern life, and a roadmap for how to successfully marry the two. All in all, a fitting and generous Christmas gift, indeed!

Guy Rivers: A Tale of Georgia

TODD HAGSTETTE

In the early 1830s, after spending the better part of a decade writing poetry almost exclusively, the young William Gilmore Simms turned his hand for the first time to fiction. This experiment in genre was accomplished through the simultaneous production of what would become two of the most well-known books in the author's collected works, not to mention two of his most significant contributions to American literature. The Gothic novella *Martin Faber*, published in 1833, became his first work of non-periodical fiction, but it was the publication less than a year later of *Guy Rivers: A Tale of Georgia* that marked Simms's emergence into what he would call, in the dedicatory epistle to the 1855 edition of the text, his "proper vocation" and the one on which he would build his reputation for the next 36 years (*Guy Rivers* 10). Published sometime between late June and early July 1834, *Guy Rivers* was the first of Simms's long-form romances, and the work that he considered the first of his "regular novels" (*Guy Rivers* 7); he reflected years later in a letter to Rufus Wilmot Griswold that "soon after the publication of Martin Faber, I gave my first *novel* to the public" (*Letters* 2: 224, emphasis added). After all, it was with the publication of this work that he "commenced a professional career in literature which has been wholly unbroken since" (*Guy Rivers* 7).

It is significant, then, that the first novel of this burgeoning fiction writer was also the first of Simms's many fictional frontier writings, collectively known as his Border Romance series. According to the author, these works were "meant to illustrate the border & domestic history of the South" (*Letters* 2: 224). Writing to James Lawson in December 1833, Simms described *Guy Rivers* as "a tale of Georgia—a tale of the miners—of a frontier and wild people." As such, the novel's "events are precisely such as may occur among a people & in a region of that character" (*Letters* 1: 55). More important than the content of the individual volume, though, is the function of the novel as a model for Simms's future work. Mary Ann Wimsatt notes that *Guy Rivers* established a template for the Border Romances, which she characterizes as a "clash between the ordered society of the plantation South and the unbridled license of the far frontier" (120). The narrative structure of the Border Romance typically involves a young protagonist (Ralph Colleton in *Guy Rivers*) from an established eastern society (South Carolina) who journeys into the wild frontier (North Georgia) and falls into the hands of criminals (Guy Rivers and Wat Munro); with the assistance of a rural farmer or backwoodsman (Mark Forrester) and, perhaps, a virtuous young lady enamored of the hero (Lucy Munro), the protagonist defeats the criminals and returns home to civilized culture, more mature and wise from his experiences.

Though Simms is not typically regarded as an autobiographical author, this standard plot template is nonetheless highly suggestive of a kind of imagined personal history of the author. Simms was raised in Charleston by his maternal grandmother, following his father's removal to the southwestern borderlands while Simms was still very young. He was an only child as a result of the infant deaths of two siblings, the second of whom died at birth, along with his mother. Bankrupted, Simms's father declared Charleston a "place of tombs" and moved west to seek opportunity and renewal on the frontier (*Letters* 1: lx). Several years later, when Simms was still a boy, his father sent for him, intending his son to join him in the West. But Simms refused; he chose the stability of aristocratic Charleston to the adventure and danger of the frontier. The borderlands of the South never left his imagination, though. A.S. Salley notes that when Simms was a boy he was fond of lingering around the campfires behind the Bull's Head Tavern in Charleston and delighted at the stories the cotton and tobacco wagon-traders told of their travels in the far regions of the country (*Letters* 1: lxiii). He also, in his youth and young manhood, took several trips to visit his father and see the frontier for himself. These were formative trips; he visited parts of Georgia, Alabama, and Mississippi, and perhaps traveled far west of the Mississippi River into what was at the time Indian Country. During these journeys, he saw Native Americans in their villages, he met pioneers and frontiersmen, and he witnessed embryonic civilization as it developed in the wild.

No wonder, then, that when it came time to craft his first romance, Simms drew on these experiences and spun a tale of adventure just beyond the edges of civilized society. It is likewise not surprising that his imagination would return to the borders of the country again and again throughout the course of his long career. From his father's exploits and the campfire tales he heard as a boy, Simms had been long primed to recognize the narrative potential of the frontier. On the other hand, he did not stake his life's fortunes in the wild but elected to stay in Charleston when given the opportunity to join his father. He was animated by the possibilities of the West but remained all his life a denizen of the urban East. When he visited his father on the frontier, the last trip of which led to his composition of *Guy Rivers*, he did so as a tourist. His depictions of life on the border had the stuff of reality about them because they were drawn from his first-hand encounters during his visits. At the end of the day, though, Simms returned home. So, in his vision of the frontier adventure, his protagonists are virtual analogs for the author: virile young men who leave their gentrified eastern homes to journey beyond the reach of civilization only to return home at the close of the story. The frontier might offer promise and possibility but, in the end, the law, the honor, and the culture of the plantation elite rule the day. In this way,

Simms reenacted his own life decision to privilege the city of Charleston over the wild edge of Mississippi with every Border Romance he wrote. The plot of *Guy Rivers*, the first full-length novel he ever envisioned, was the initial replaying of this psychological drama.

Besides the autobiographical elements of the book's origins, some key contemporary events also played a role in Simms's creation. In stories that Simms surely heard in both the official news organs of his day as well as via the informal gossip of the traveler's camps he frequented, he learned of the discovery of gold in the North Georgia mountains in the 1820s, which led to the country's first gold rush. As prospectors poured into the region to seek their fortunes, they began to push out the native tribes, primarily the Cherokees. Prior to Simms's writing of *Guy Rivers*, movements were afoot for the government to make this *de facto* dislocation official. As critic Rayburn S. Moore points out, Simms foregrounded both the gold rush and the Cherokee removal efforts in the opening passages of the novel, indicating their thematic importance to his work (55). The fictional village of Chestatee, Georgia, situated in the middle of the real-life gold country, presented the perfect setting for Simms's exploration of his border themes, as it dramatized life in the liminal space between the civilized societies to the east and the truly untamed territory of the Cherokee lands, or "the nation," as the characters in the novel consistently refer to it, to the west.

The novel opens with the romantic and financial fortunes of the protagonist, Ralph Colleton, in flux. Ralph is in love with his cousin, Edith, but is spurned in his courting by Edith's father, his uncle. Ralph has no fortune, his mother was not of the southern aristocracy, and his recently-deceased father had been frivolous, in the uncle's estimation, seeking his fortune through speculations in Tennessee, rather than setting up a respectable business enterprise in settled South Carolina. Ralph is suspected of favoring his father in this way. In exasperation, Ralph decides to make himself into the man his uncle fears him to be and heads west to seek opportunity. In the wilderness of North Georgia, though, he is waylaid by a mysterious stranger, who later is revealed to be the eponymous Guy Rivers. A leader of the Pony Club, whose notorious real-life counterpart "specialized in terrorizing luckless settlers and stealing their horses" during the westward expansion of the southern frontier, Rivers attempts to rob Ralph (Wimsatt, *Major* 123). In the tussle that ensues, Rivers has his cheek gashed open by the hoof of Ralph's fleeing horse, and Ralph takes a non-fatal bullet wound that causes him to faint and fall from the saddle just after effecting his escape. Luckily, he is discovered by the kindly backwoodsman Mark Forrester and nursed back to health in the latter's cabin near the frontier village of Chestatee.

Eventually, Ralph takes up temporary residence in the local inn, which unbeknownst to him is run by another leader of the Pony Club, Wat Munro. During his stay, Ralph witnesses and interacts with the various people who populate this part of the country and who are all engaged in some way with the gold rush in progress in the Georgia segment of the Appalachian Mountains. The cast of characters includes Lawyer Pippin, a shifty swindler with only the vaguest pretensions to his professional title, Jared Bunce, the Yankee peddler, and Lucy Munro, Wat's daughter who becomes infatuated with Ralph. Guy Rivers also seethes around the edges of the community, now with his face covered to hide the mark of his recent criminal dealings. The major dramatic action of the novel concerns the antagonism of Rivers for Ralph, the origins of which reach beyond the encounter in the woods to Rivers's former respectable life in South Carolina, during which he too loved Edith Colleton. This animosity becomes proactive following a particularly startling scene, in which the gold rushers of Chestatee brawl with another group attempting to poach their claim; ultimately the two sides join forces against the Georgia Guard who has come to both deal with the Pony Club and eject the squatters, who comprise both groups of gold hunters, from the land. In the resulting slaughter of the guardsmen, every major figure in the village, even the good Mark Forrester, takes part. Ralph, though, unwilling to participate in a quarrel that is not his, stands as a witness only to the crime but, due to his unfailing honor, avows to expose the deed if he is asked.

Rivers, with his true identity now revealed, attempts to ambush and murder Ralph, but carelessly slays the remorseful and fleeing Forrester instead. With Wat Munro's help, he pins the murder on Ralph, who ultimately turns himself in, believing optimistically that his innocence will save him. He is convicted of the crime, though. Lucy Munro, who knows the truth, intercedes on his behalf, first turning the heart of her wayward father and convincing him and Jared Bunce to help Ralph escape prison prior to his execution; then, she bravely escapes from the clutches of Guy Rivers, who has spirited her away to his forest hideout, in order to testify on Ralph's behalf. That, combined with Wat's dying confession, and Bunce's efforts to produce character witnesses on Ralph's behalf, all secure his ultimate release. Rivers is arrested and kills himself in prison. In the end, Ralph returns to Charleston with his newly-betrothed Edith and her father who, having heard of Ralph's troubles, arrived in Chestatee during the trial. Lucy and Jared travel with them, and all are set to begin a fresh start back in the civilized East, wiser and more experienced for their time on the border.

Simms worked on *Guy Rivers* for over a year, and the writing coincided with his drafting of *Martin Faber*. When exactly he made the decision to turn his literary attention to long-form fiction is unknown, but his childhood experiences with his father and his interactions with the wagoners passing through Charleston in his youth suggest that the impulse toward storytelling began early. The first mention of the composition of *Guy Rivers* is perhaps from a 13 November 1832 letter in which Simms observed to James Lawson that his "main work progresses—the first volume, in rough, is completed" (*Letters* 1:45). The editors of

Simms's collected letters indicate in a note that the author was referring to *Martin Faber* with this remark; however, because that work was a short, single-volume novella, not a two-volume romance, it is likely that Simms was, in fact, describing *Guy Rivers*. One year later, in November 1833, Simms indicated to Lawson that the "novel hastens pretty rapidly," and the following month it was "finished—bating corrections" (*Letters* 1: 53, 55). At that time, though, he had not yet sent it off to his publisher. Simms was silent about the remainder of the publication process in his extant letters, with the next mention of the novel coming after its appearance in the summer of 1834 from Harper & Brothers (*Letters* 1: 59).

Following the issuance of the first edition of the novel and owing to its popularity, *Guy Rivers* was published in several subsequent printings beginning later that same year. Though no known copies of it survive into the modern era, a foreign edition of the book was produced in England, reportedly as early as 1834. Simms mentioned in a 6 December 1846 letter to Griswold that *Guy Rivers* "rose to instant favor" when it first appeared and so was "republished in London in three vols." (*Letters* 2: 225). James Everett Kibler validated this claim in 1994 by tracking down London reviews of the novel from 1834, several of which used the known English title "*Guy Rivers, The Outlaw. A Tale of Georgia*" ("English Reviews" 558), which appeared on later British printings. Sometime between 1846 and 1854, a German-language translation of the book was published, though that text has not been located (*Letters* 4: 40n).

Nearly twenty years after its first appearance, *Guy Rivers* was one of the first texts Simms intended to include in what would be the Redfield edition of his selected works. He wrote to Lawson on 20 June 1853, "I propose this season to commence the publication of a uniform Edition of my writings." In the same letter, he initiated the process of transferring copyrights and obtaining printing plates from Harper & Brothers for *Guy Rivers* and five of his other previously-published works (*Letters* 3: 236–37). It was not until over a year later, however, that he was close to completing the revisions to the work that would update it for the Redfield series; this included editing it down to a single-volume work, revisions that, according to the author, "cost [him] a great deal of labour" (*Letters* 3: 340). He announced to Evert Augustus Duyckinck on 27 November 1854 that he "[s]hall finish the revision of Guy Rivers next week" and ultimately sent them to his friend and editor the following month (*Letters* 3: 333). By May 1855, Simms was correcting the proof sheets for the revised edition, and the work finally issued around 8 September 1855 as one of the first of the Redfield series (*Letters* 3: 385).

Early reviews of *Guy Rivers* were overwhelmingly positive and compared the novel favorably to the works of James Fenimore Cooper and Sir Walter Scott. Most noteworthy in this early batch of reviews was the overwhelming enthusiasm of northern, and specifically New York, publications. During the summer of 1834 alone, glowing reviews appeared in the *New York Evening Post*, the *New York*

American, the *New York Gazette*, the *New York Mercantile Advertiser*, and the *New-York Mirror*; in the same time period, the *Knickerbocker* praised the book, calling Simms "an acute observer of nature, and of human character" and declaring that "[n]o modern novel embodies description which can compare with this" (qtd. in Butterworth and Kibler 24–26). In contrast the reviews from southern publications, particularly Simms's hometown of Charleston, were fewer in number and more mixed in their praise. Simms noticed as much in a 19 July 1834 letter to Lawson, in which he marveled that the Charleston papers had not yet mentioned his book, either in praise or criticism (*Letters* 1: 59–60). Ironically, a notice in the *Charleston Courier* appeared that same day; it called Simms's narration the work of a "master's hand" and stated quite succinctly that the "plot is well arranged, and the interest of the story kept up throughout" (Rev. of *Guy Rivers* 2). On August 13, the *Charleston Mercury* followed suit, declaring that in spite of some flaws in the writing, *Guy Rivers* was "the best American novel, which has appeared of late years" (qtd. in Butterworth and Kibler 25).

Undoubtedly, the most extensive and gushing review of the novel was published in the *American Monthly Magazine* of 1 July 1834, almost certainly written by its editor, Henry William Herbert. He called *Guy Rivers* a " work full of a dark and terrible interest, [which] chains down our faculties as we read; yet in the most exciting scenes, we pause to admire the justice of the arguments, the correctness of observation which has given rise to such a tale" (297). Moreover, Simms's greatest success was his achievement of the very goal he set himself, to produce an accurate portrait of the southern borderlands: "we can imagine nothing more powerful, or more truth-like in its details, than the description of this frontier settlement, and its lawless inhabitants" (298). The oft-repeated coffin-nail comparison with which Herbert concluded his review established Simms within the pantheon of the nineteenth-century greats: "Cooper, great as he is in graphic detail, could not have written Guy Rivers had he died for it" (302). Though no review in the history of the criticism of *Guy Rivers* quite matched the enthusiasm of Herbert's, the novel continued to garner praise upon its republication in 1855, most notably from such landmark publications as *Godey's*, *Graham's*, and the *Southern Literary Messenger* (Butterworth and Kibler 101–02).

Of course, not all notices of the novel were entirely positive. Simms's first biographer, William P. Trent, took exception to the vulgar language and violence in the book, which he believed to be unbridled sensationalism meant to attract more readers and thus generate more revenue (88–89). Among early reviews of the novel, perhaps the most critical was one to be found in the December issue of *American Quarterly Review*. Claiming that *Guy Rivers* violated "every preconceived and well-settled role of propriety," the reviewer ultimately declared, "we have seldom met with a book in which so much labour and effort, with so little correctness, are exhibited." Several of the reviews of the 1830s, including the largely positive ones, sniped at the novel for its prolixity and its wooden dialogue. A typical claim along these lines, from a rather mixed review, appeared in the November issue of *New-England Magazine*, which complained that the "style is too verbose" and the characters are "terribly addicted to prosing" (qtd. in Butterworth and Kibler 26).

Whatever its perceived virtues or flaws, *Guy Rivers* certainly marked a new step forward for its author as well as a fresh direction for the larger landscape of American literature. Simms's novel emerged on the literary scene just as readers and critics across the country were beginning to petition for fiction that plied the American experience for inspiration, rather than relying on European models. Anchored securely in southern soil and peopled with a panoply of American characters, Simms's tale of Georgia answered this need. Plus, it combined a heady mix of Romantic sensationalism with unflinching Realism, making it not only an exciting tale but one with a true local feel. Trent, despite his hesitations about the novel's overall quality, noted of the reading climate of the time, "[u]ndiluted Americanism was what many readers were crying for, and they got it in 'Guy Rivers;' excitement, sentimentality, bombast were what others were crying for, and they got all three in 'Guy Rivers'" (86). By setting his work on the southern frontier, Simms gave vent to all the ambitions and anxieties that attended the great American migration west. As civilization steadily encroached upon the wild lands next door, the fiction writer had one of the best claims to the development of the mythology that would define that migration. American character was being forged on the frontier, and the frontier would be defined in the American novel. Guilds remarks that, with his composition of *Guy Rivers*, "for the first time Simms unloosened his verve and narrative power into the sustained creation of a distinctly American theme" (*Literary Life* 55).

The American contemplation of the western frontier, though, did not originate in Simms's writing. For decades, the national imagination sparkled with the optimistic possibilities that lay just over the horizon. Prior to Simms, writers such as James Kirke Paulding, Washington Irving, and perhaps most notably, James Fenimore Cooper had narrated accounts of the American frontier. For these writers and others, the borders of the country were romantic and largely bucolic spaces. Noble figures and the natural world operated in harmony as the nation pushed towards the "stabling place of the sun" (*Letters* 1: 49). In the South, the Appalachian Mountains marked the defining border of American westward expansion, and perhaps the ruggedness of that imposing barrier made Simms warier than his northern peers when he envisioned the frontier in his first novel. When Simms turned his gaze to the mountainous regions of Georgia, he saw a less romantic, grittier frontier than did the writers who came before him. The borderlands of the South were a place of great beauty and possibility, but also of great danger; they were populated as much by outlaws and ruffians as they were by pioneers and independent-minded Americans. It was the visitors from the planting societies to the east, like Ralph Colleton arriving from Charleston, who brought a romantic bent to the borders. The sentiment was an imported one for Simms, not something intrinsic to the national expansion, as the writers who came before him would have it. This is why his protagonists might become embroiled in the intrigues of the frontier, but would never get completely mired in them. The romantic finery of life was to be found in civilization, and they needed to see civilization in progress on the frontier, but then return to where it was already accomplished. In the rustic lands to the west, romantic and civilized perfection might be a possibility, but it was far from a certainty.

For this reason, Simms's frontier writing is sometimes thought of as pessimistic and needlessly grim. It does not fit comfortably with the American myth of manifest destiny and the idea of reinvention and rejuvenation on the frontier, the consistent possibility of heading further west to begin anew. Guilds discovers in Simms a belief in the "magic appeal of the frontier to honorable men with broken lives (but regenerated dreams)" (*Guy* 465). This is what draws the good-but-dislocated heroes such as Ralph out of civilization and into the action of frontier life; it is also in keeping with the promise of the West. But the frontier such men encounter is largely different from that of the American dream. John Cyril Barton finds that "Simms paints a picture of Georgia's borderlands that sets the stage for the landscape of crime, violence, and desperadoes" that would define his interpretation of frontier life for years to come (224). Because Chestatee is filled with members of the lower strata of society and their quasi-legal undertakings, *Guy Rivers* can be interpreted as being fundamentally hostile to the possibilities of westward expansion. Simms notes of the frontier: "In a country, the population of which, few and far between, is spread over a wide, wild, and little-cultivated territory, the chances of punishment for crime, rarely realized, scarcely occasioned a thought among offenders" (*Guy Rivers* 254).

Simms critic Masahiro Nakamura takes this quality of the narration a step further than Barton; he claims, "The frontier represents a lawlessness and social instability that is still a long way from 'law and order.' The romantic dream which Ralph (and the reader) reads there is utterly destroyed by its reality, and the civilization of South Carolina represented by him reveals itself as too impotent to transfigure it into a tamed and civilized world" (113). When the novel is considered as solely an expression of Romanticism, this view is consequential. Yet, Simms seems to be plumbing more than the Romantic ideal here; his frontier is nothing if not Realistic. Ralph is indeed confronted by a borderland unlike anything his romantic imagination prepared him for; given this, it is perhaps not realistic (or, Realistic) to expect his presence to transfigure the region entirely. Ralph is far from an impotent character: it is he, after all, who finally puts a stop to the villainous Guy Rivers and his parasitic Pony Club. Though the reader does not witness the long-term effect of that occurrence on the village of Chestatee, we can imagine that it is positive and instrumental in taking that wild place closer to becoming civilized.

Ralph's influence, in other words, is more subtle than the Romantic heroics expected. Simms judges, nonetheless, that "[h]e was a fine specimen of the southern gentleman—the true nobleman of that region, whose pride of character is never ostentatiously displayed and is only to be felt in the influence which it invariably exercises over all with whom it may have contact or connection" (*Guy Rivers* 370). Rayburn S. Moore takes the opposite tack to Nakamura, complaining of this very unflinching aspect of character. He protests that the frontier, despite the cataclysmic events that unfold there, renders no effect on Ralph's innocent character (57–58). This he reads as a flaw in the writing. Yet, as the romantic and honorable representation of civilization, Ralph's role is to be steadfast. He is unchanged by his experiences, because his character is stable. He might be informed and seasoned by his experiences in Georgia, but his fundamental being is unaltered. For Simms, the frontier is in transition, and resolute characters like Ralph help to usher in that change, rather than be transformed themselves.

Wimsatt exhibits a measured interpretation of Simms's view of the frontier in *Guy Rivers*; she explains, "the possibility of conflict between 'good' characters led by Ralph and the 'bad' ones headed by Rivers poses an ever-present threat to the harmony and stability of frontier life in Georgia" (*Major* 126). Rather than a failure of the frontier to alter character or of a character to alter the frontier, Simms's narrative dramatizes the fluidity of progress. His frontier is a place of binaries that need to be reconciled, and because of the realism of his writing, the solutions are typically compromises rather than victories. Above all, *Guy Rivers* is about the tension between civilization and savagery on the frontier, the confluence of society and the wild. The frontier is the testing ground for these things. Dianne C. Luce sees in the novel "Simms's early recognition that the raw life of the border communities was fertile ground for his imagination and that their frail connections with Southern institutions made them a perfect backdrop against which to play out conflicting impulses toward civilization and anarchy in Southern society" (242).

One of the opening scenes of the novel seems to amply demonstrate this strange conjunction of the civilized and the wild in the setting of *Guy Rivers*. Ralph's the first encounter with the outlaw Guy Rivers is rendered surreal by the extremely mannered and logical dialogue between the assailant and his would-be victim. Though negotiating for a violent criminal encounter, the language and bearing of both men is more suited to the civic spaces of gentlemanly society than to the backwoods crossroads where it occurs. Ralph even notes the oddity of the encounter to himself, finding it "excessively difficult, however, to account for the strange nature of the transaction so far as it had gone; and the language of the robber seemed so inconsistent with his pursuit, that, at intervals, he was almost led to doubt whether the whole was not the clever jest of some country sportsman" (29). Simms's pragmatic intention with the scene is to set up the revelation later in the story that his villain actually hails from the gentrified society of South Carolina and is a former lawyer and an educated man. Symbolically, though, it offers a telling glimpse at the nature of the borderlands and its people in Simms's imagination. As civilization pushes into the wild, the one is not immediately subsumed by the other; rather the two states mingle. Just as an aristocratic parley blends with a highway robbery, the budding of law and culture interlaces with the existing rough brutality of the untamed land.

The highly sensationalized and oft decried battle between the argonauts and the militia in the book's middle segment further demonstrates this aspect of the story. Those who people the village of Chestatee are revealed as squatters on government land and functional interlopers in Cherokee territory. They are a small step away from tribal aggression when another band of gold rushers enters "their" territory, and they cross into murderous savagery upon the arrival of the Georgia Guard. Even the noble Forrester participates, orchestrating the rockfall that obliterates the majority of the state army in one swoop. Yet only the villainous Rivers emerges from the scrape psychologically unscathed. Forrester, in anguish over his behavior, intends to disappear into "the nation," and silently throughout the back half of the book remorseful villagers likewise disappear. Their behavior is that of the frontier, but their beliefs are those of civilization. A comic analog is to be found in the farcical trial of Jared Bunce, the Yankee peddler. The kangaroo court in which he is tried for the crime of swindling the villagers may be more a harlequin of justice than a bedrock institution of society. Lawyer Pippen is a joke, and the destruction of Bunce's property is a travesty; but, the impulse towards law is germinating in Chestatee. Slow, halting inroads of civilization are suggested in these violent and comic moments of the novel.

This is ultimately what Simms's *Guy Rivers* seems to say about the borders of the nation: they are fuzzy. Westward expansion is not a tidy process. The frontier is not a clean line of infrastructure and culture. The push of civilization into the wilderness involves a negotiation between progress and regression, one in which the former eventually succeeds, but not without blood and toil. Simms's view of the frontier was not focused on futility, but realism. The nation could succeed in its westward destiny, but there would be consequences—this is the real world, not the fantasy of American inevitability. The romantic dreams of the American frontier could be realized, but they were not automatic or free. Southern society offered a plausible solution to the need. The harmonious marriage of man and nature in the agrarian community of the region and the crucial integrity of honorable character that defined the southern gentleman could lead to the acquisition of the wild lands of the West. Ralph and his ilk need to journey to the borders *and* return to the plantation. They, and the readers of *Guy Rivers*, need to remember the civilization from which they sprang and, when they travel out of the bosom of their homes, never forget "that you are in the wild abiding-place of men scarcely less wild—with natures as stubborn as the rocks, and with manners as uncouth and rugged as the woodland growth which surrounds us" (*Guy Rivers* 403). It takes the pioneer *and* the settler to conquer the frontier; it takes a Romantic impulse *and* a Realistic acceptance to domesticate the wilderness; it takes the South to civilize the West.

Helen Halsey; or, the Swamp State of Conelachita. A Tale of the Borders

JILLIAN WEBER

Early in his career, William Gilmore Simms wrote several works that would become part of his Border Romance series, including his 1845 novella *Helen Halsey; or, The Swamp State of Conelachita: A Tale of the Borders*. Well-known Simms scholar, Mary Ann Wimsatt, conceives a subset of the border series as a collection of several major works—*Helen Halsey*, *Guy Rivers*, *Richard Hurdis*, and *Border Beagles*—which are often, though not exclusively, set in the Gulf South. This is a region with which Simms himself was familiar and so provides the setting for much of *Helen Halsey*. When Simms was two years old his father moved west to the southern frontier of Mississippi while Simms remained in Charleston with his grandmother. The author made several trips to visit his father years later, and his appreciation for this region is obvious in many of his works. Much detail in the Border Romances, such as descriptions of the land, the inhabitants of the backwoods areas, and the traditions of the areas, are taken from Simms's personal experiences on horse rides with his father and uncle through the southern borders even beyond Mississippi. He made three major visits to the area, spanning from the mid-1820s to 1842. He noted the great changes in commerce and business between his visits, and the large timeframe over which he traveled to the area allowed Simms to "judge the progress of settlement in the area and also to voice his comments on the developing relationship between civilization and the frontier" (Wimsatt, *Major* 87).[1]

Helen Halsey, the shortest of Simms's border tales, encompasses many of the qualities associated with the border series, most notably the male protagonist's journey from his native plantation society to the frontier, during which time he comes into contact with criminal activity. At the end of the novel, matured by the crimes he has seen, he returns to society, ready to live responsibly in genteel antebellum culture. (Wimsatt, *Major* 120). *Helen Halsey* depicts this journey through a portrayal of the clash between frontier and plantation society. This clash manifests itself in differences between the physical landscapes, the sociocultural attitudes of the residents, and the laws and morality of each geographic region. In the novella, Simms uses these differences to draw attention to the disappearing space of the frontier and the contrasting views on moral and ethical issues between people from backwoods areas and plantation residents. This frontier space offered the perfect setting for Simms to voice his views on progress and morality, as the 1840s provided a space for much discussion of expansion, ethical progress, and legal action in these areas.

The Work

From 1842 to 1850, Simms wrote no novels and, instead, chose to publish novellas, short stories, biographies, poems, and essays.[2] John Caldwell Guilds posits that this change in genre was due, in part, to the Panic of 1837, which weakened the book market throughout the 1840s and put large, two-volume novels out of fashion. Instead, authors and publishers took advantage of faster printing techniques, inexpensive paper, and the absence of international copyrights, to produce shorter, cheaper books (Guilds, *Helen* xv–xvi). Despite shifting away from his primary genre—the novel—Simms produced some of his best works during this period and dealt with a variety of themes, with American self-identity remaining the dominant focus of many of his works. Published in 1845, *Helen Halsey* was one of these.

Simms's novella deals with violence, crime, and law enforcement in frontier areas on the verge of being conquered and settled in the mid-eighteenth century. The story begins as the eighteen-year old protagonist, Henry Meadows, sets out from his parents' home in Tennessee, on a journey to travel and discover some sense of self-identity. As he makes his way south, Henry stops at the inn of Jeph Yannakers and meets a young woman, with whom he is immediately enamored; however, she is skittish and afraid of the man with whom she is traveling. Though she and Henry share some brief intimate moments, her male companion pulls her away shortly after Henry promises her he will find and rescue her, no matter the peril. The next morning Henry sets off, despite Yannaker's warnings, to find this woman, having ascertained that the man who whisked her off was her uncle, the criminal Bud Halsey.

Henry travels toward the outlaw swamp of Conelachita where Bud Halsey leads a colony of criminals. To gain trust from the outlaws he encounters there, Henry claims to have murdered a man because of an argument over a horse. He is greeted by Bush Halsey, Bud's brother. An intelligent, well-traveled man, Bush is being held in the swamp against his will by his brother. Joining him in his captivity is Bush's daughter, Helen, who it turns out is the woman Henry encountered at the inn. She lives on a small island in the swamp with her father. Henry hopes to join this society in order to be close to Helen. What he does not realize, however, is that due to the group's secrecy, members of the society are essentially themselves prisoners of Bud.

Henry's presence is made more complicated still by Bud's suspicion of him; he believes Henry is a spy for law enforcement officials with plans to reveal all of the swamp community's secrets and illicit activities. Henry is forced to stay (though in his mind, he is a guest), so Bud can keep an eye on him. Over the following weeks, Bud observes a romance developing between Henry and Helen and plans to use their relationship to his advantage. At this point, Bud has uncovered Henry's real identity, including the fact that he lied about killing a man. This means that Bud will never allow Henry to leave. To prevent Henry's escape and cement him into the swamp community, Bud forces Henry to marry his niece, Helen. Though the two young lovers feel great affection for one another and want to marry at some point, Henry resents being forced into marriage and subsequently feels trapped in the swamp and the relationship. His initial happiness over finding and spending time with Helen changes to bitterness, and he renews his efforts to find a way to escape the swamp.

Henry befriends the outlaw parson, Mowbray, who sympathizes with Henry's frustrations. He tells Henry about his own choice several years earlier to abandon his wife, children, and congregation to live a life of crime and corruption. Their conversations only serve to exacerbate Henry's unease. Eventually, Helen and Bush discover Henry's plan to escape the community and express their own wish to join him. Though he feels burdened by the presence of two more bodies, he agrees to take them with him and is excited by their energy. Bush helps devise the plan that will allow all three to escape together by canoe, but the plan goes awry. Bud's men surprise the trio, shooting at them on the river. Helen is shot and dies. Bush cannot fathom leaving his daughter's body, so he remains in the swamp for the rest of his life. Henry, however, is able to narrowly escape and hide out for a time in an abandoned swamp hut. Bud's search party tracks him there, and Mowbray, who is ahead of the rest of the group, decides to help Henry ambush Bud. Though the plan works, Bud is able to kill Mowbray right before Henry's bullet ends his life. Ultimately, Henry returns to his parents' home and has become a more mature, but grave, man. He shares none of his recent experiences with his loved ones at home, choosing instead to live with the weight of those two months in the swamp on his own.

The Text

Simms first mentioned *Helen Halsey* in a June 1843 letter to James Lawson, who was serving as his New York agent. At that time, Simms called the work "Ellen Halsey, or My Wife Against My Will." Simms's early vision for the project was to include it in a collection called "Tales of the South," which he intended to be a compilation of seven tales. Many of these stories came to fruition, but in various forms separate from Simms's original intention. For instance, *Castle Dismal* was published just two months prior to the publication of *Helen Halsey* as a short novel, while many of the other proposed stories were included in the well-known collection *The Wigwam and the Cabin* (*Letters* 1: 354–55). Simms planned for *Helen Halsey* and *Castle Dismal* to be about 100 pages each and for the five other tales to number fifty to sixty pages a piece. Just a few months later, in September, Simms wrote to Lawson again about the work, but at that juncture the name had been changed to "Helen Halsey-a Border Tale, a Tale of Mississippi" (*Letters* 1: 369). By October 1843 the novella assumed the name it has today.

When Simms initially imagined this project, he wrote to Lawson that he was hoping to fetch similar compensation as Theodore S. Fay's payment for *Hoboken: A Romance of New York*. He was aware of how much various publishers were paying other authors for their works and sought equal or greater payment for himself. Simms seemed to have little doubt that many people would want to publish *Helen Halsey*, and instead focused on how much he would demand of each publisher. He wrote to Lawson that, "The Harpers will in all probability be willing to publish [*Helen Halsey*]. . . . If they positively decline publishing [the collection of stories], obtain them from them, and offer them to Winchester on the terms which Benjamin offered me, viz $125 for each tale that will make a number of the New World" (*Letters* 1: 375–76). In other letters Simms alluded to the Harpers and their willingness to publish the work, threatening likewise to take *Helen Halsey* elsewhere if they did not want it. Simms felt that some competition between publishers might goad the Harpers into publishing the work.

By November 1843, the tone of Simms's letters changed, gaining a greater sense of urgency. He wrote to Lawson again and implored him to get Mr. Benjamin, another publisher, to issue the novella. This time he only requested $100 for the book. At this time, Simms was working to have *Castle Dismal* and *Helen Halsey* published, each as its own novella, no longer as parts of a larger collection. This attempted manipulation of publishers backfired, and neither the Harpers nor Benjamin released *Helen Halsey*. Instead, Simms was able to secure Burgess & Stringer as the eventual publisher, and the work appeared in January 1845.

The Context

Helen Halsey was published on the heels of *Castle Dismal* and by the same publisher; yet it was received and reviewed more poorly than its predecessor, despite Simms's opinion that it was a stronger work. He noted to Lawson, "I am sorry that Burgess & Stinger put forth [*Castle Dismal*] first, for I think 'Helen Halsey' much the best" (*Letters* 1: 436). In an effort to attract early attention to the book prior to its publication, Simms's close friend, Evert Augustus Duyckinck, published a plot synopsis in the 29 November 1844 issue of the *New York Morning News*. A brief notice of the book's publication appearing in the *Charleston Southern Patriot* on 2 January 1845 called *Helen Halsey* a "most attractive and thrilling romance by our talented townsman"; but this kind of positive review was the exception (Guilds, *Helen* xvii). The novella received little attention from major northern or southern literary journals, though Simms wrote to Duyckinck that it was selling well and that, in Charleston, "the favorable opinions of many of our best men console me" (*Letters* 2: 20). Contributing to this lack of reception was the fact that the story "experienced but a single small paperback printing (selling for twenty-five cents)," though Simms pushed for its republication in hardback (Guilds, *Helen* 127). While few accounts exist of how the work was received by Simms's contemporaries, his own assessment can be found in a letter to Lawson on 30 June 1844. In it Simms stated, "Indeed, as a rapid and truthful domestic story I think it one of my most successful performances. Besides, its style is, I am disposed to believe, particularly good" (*Letters* 1: 420).

More recent critical reception of the work has also been rare, perhaps because the novella has long been unavailable. Guilds has been the most outspoken advocate for the work, expressing particular interest in and appreciation for the story, its influence on other authors, and the character of Mowbray. Simms biographer William P. Trent, notoriously critical of the author, was predictably harsh in his consideration of the Border Romances generally, declaring:

> It cannot be denied that these 'border romances,' the scenes of which are laid in nearly all the Southwestern States, are sometimes as rough in their construction as the people described were in their manners and customs. All are marred by a slipshod style, by a repetition of incidents, and by the introduction of an unnecessary amount of the horrible and the revolting . . . he might have avoided, at least, introducing brutal murders not necessary to the action of the story. . . . When all is said, one is forced to wish that Simms had written fewer or none of these stories (88–89).

Trent's assessment of Simms's border series, though not out of step with late nineteenth-century opinion in general, has not been shared by modern critics, many of whom see much to admire in these border works. Scholars like Guilds, Wimsatt, and J. Wesley Thomas find in them characters that represent the confluence of the untamed frontier and imposing modernity, questions of exploitation of the land, and scenes rich with convincing descriptions from Simms's own travels to visit his father.

Though *Helen Halsey* is a tale worth exploring and offers an important rendering of criminality and morality in the 1840s, it is not the first book of its time to introduce central themes surrounding crime on the frontier. Simms appears to have been influenced by an earlier tale published in a Charleston journal. "The Outlaw's Daughter," written by Edward Carroll in 1833, appeared in *Cosmopolitan: An Occasional*, a journal which Simms coedited. The framework for "The Outlaw's Daughter" is one of a sensitive girl, Ellen, and her loving relationship with her outlaw father, which ultimately leads to her death. Simms changed some aspects of the story, setting his tale in the nineteenth century, rather than during the Revolutionary War, changing Ellen's name to Helen, and moving the setting from South Carolina to the swamps of Louisiana (Guilds, *Helen* 128). The swamp setting that Simms uses is essential to his story, as well as to the larger themes of frontier justice that his story contains, because it shows a space where different cultures and social beliefs were converging and producing unexpected results.

While "The Outlaw's Daughter" influenced Simms, *Helen Halsey* influenced the 1862 German tale *Germelshausen*, by Friedrich Gerstacker. J. Wesley Thomas, who has written about German literature in conjunction with many of Simms's works, traces this influence to Gerstacker's time spent traveling through the American frontier and translating many of Simms's texts, particularly those published in 1845. *Germelshausen* tells the story of a young man who falls in love with a woman and becomes a part of an outlaw swamp society to be with her. When he leaves the swamp he leaves this woman behind and, reminiscent of *Helen Halsey*, returns to the swamp area years later to find much of it gone (Thomas, "German Sources" 143).

In addition to his influence on Gerstacker, Simms may have inspired Nathaniel Hawthorne's character Arthur Dimmesdale in *The Scarlett Letter*, which was released five years after *Helen Halsey*. Guilds observes that both characters are religious leaders who sin and abandon their families in some way, only to repent and confess at the end of the novel (Guilds, *Helen* xix). While this assertion of influence is difficult to substantiate, there are several factors that leave open the possibility that Hawthorne drew inspiration from Simms. First, many of the characters in *The Scarlett Letter* are based upon historical figures—Puritan community members and ancestors of Hawthorne. However, scholar Charles Ryskamp notes that Dimmesdale is one of just four characters in the novel for which no historical evidence or lineage can be found, leaving open the possibility that Hawthorne was influenced by Simms's fictional character, Mowbray (198). Additionally, both Sean R. Busick and Matthew C. Brennan have published articles in which they trace the relationship between the two authors (Simms and Hawthorne were acquainted and read and reviewed each other's work from time to time) and the parallels between social and political themes in their various works. Both authors had a "distrust of America's blind faith in industrial progress," criticized the pursuit of wealth at the expense of beauty, and grappled with the confluence of refinement and civilization in harsh environments (Brennan, "Hawthorne" 15). These shared political and social views make it plausible that Hawthorne would have found inspiration in a Simms character that embodied many of the themes about which he wrote and pondered so frequently.

More specific to *Helen Halsey*, Simms explores the ways in which the characters struggle with their own morality and how law can be counterproductive, exploiting a person's code of ethics. He provides the reader with a depiction of Mowbray's internal moral struggle and then contextualizes the violent relationship between Henry and Bud through the lens of morality and the gallows. Simms's portrayal of certain characters, like Helen and Bush Halsey, are fairly one-dimensional. They often exhibit qualities that are either innately good or bad and are the less interesting for it. Conversely, characters like Henry Meadows or Reverend Mowbray fall into a moral grey area and provide depictions of the nuances of moral consciousness as Simms saw it. Mowbray is a corrupt priest who was forced into priesthood by his family as a means of financial stability. He married, had children, and preached every week, but never felt sincere in his spiritual guidance. Instead, Mowbray's strongest and most convincing sermons came after he thought about or committed some immoral act. Struggling between the feelings of entrapment and moral responsibility towards his family and congregation, Mowbray left and entered the outlaw community. In this new context, he gambles, drinks, and commits crimes, yet still offers spiritual relief to his fellow outlaws. In Simms's deft hands, Mowbray is a man who is tragically torn between morality and immorality, with the nuances of this struggle depicted in startling and poignant detail. Simms based many of his descriptions of criminal networks on the bandit, John Murrell, who operated along the Mississippi River in the early nineteenth century. Interestingly, Murrell often assumed the persona of a traveling preacher in order to commit his crimes, a detail that suggests Simms could have been compelled by Murrell's story and this guise of morality. *Helen Halsey*, and Mowbray in particular, offer accounts of the internal struggle for morality and the outward perception of this virtue.

The rich descriptions of the swamp community and its extensive crime network speak to some of the issues that were at the forefront of American minds in the mid-nineteenth century and provide an interesting space to consider nineteenth-century law enforcement in conjunction with the characters of *Helen Halsey*. The editor of an influential law review, John Cyril Barton traces the history of crime and capital punishment during the nineteenth century, showing how the proliferation of crime fiction boomed at the same time as the push to abolish the death penalty in the decades before the Civil War. John L. O'Sullivan became the spokesperson for the anti-gallows movements in the 1840s, writing *Report in Favor of the Abolition of the Punishment of Death by Law*, and presenting it before the New York legislature in 1841 (Barton 226). This book instantly became popular, particularly its claims that the death penalty failed as a deterrent. Simms was undoubtedly aware of this well-publicized capital punishment debate and included scenes dealing with it in nearly all of his Border Romances. Barton points out a particular iteration of this thought in Simms's first border novel, *Guy Rivers*:

> If for O'Sullivan the spectacle of law's violence produces more violence than it deters, for [Guy] Rivers it stems from the desire to commit murder. In this respect Rivers, the great criminal in the tradition of Jonathan Wild or John A. Murrell (the infamous land pirate after whom Rivers was likely, in part, modeled), sounds very much like a reformer, an abolitionist such as O'Sullivan, in his denunciation of executions as a blood sport rather than an effective means of deterrence (226).

Simms worked through these ethical questions in his novels, and "[i]nsofar as they draw from the dramaturgy of the death penalty, Simms's Border Romances were shaped by and helped shape a popular aesthetic that represented or responded to crime and capital punishment—one of the dominant cultural aesthetics of the day" (Barton 222).

These questions of whether capital punishment and law fail to deter violence or instill a desire to commit more violence are present in *Helen Halsey*, particularly in the characters of Henry Meadows and Bud Halsey. When Bud discovers that Henry's father is a judge, rather than being fearful of the law, Bud is compelled to commit further violence and harm Henry. He threatens the boy with hanging, saying:

> I tell you that I now know you to be the son of one of my deadliest enemies, one of those men who have made me what I am, and to whom I owe nothing but undying hate. Your father, in his official capacity, as Judge of the Supreme Court of Alabama, robbed me, by an unrighteous decision, of lands and fortune. . . . You see the men are in waiting, the cord is ready, and you are already under the tree from which you may be suspended. It has borne as stout a man before (94).

While it is ironic that Bud, an outlaw, sees himself as "upholding" justice, the death penalty sentence he assigns to Henry works to make him the judge, jury, and executioner. He takes the law into his own hands but puts on a veil of legitimacy while disregarding the due process aspects of the legal system that validate its decisions. In the outlaw system of Conelachita, Bud and his followers have their own system of justice, though it seems to only encourage more violence. To combat violence and detection by law authorities Bud orders more violence and harbors a deep desire to harm others, his own followers included. Bud and his followers have effectively created a community that needs violence to operate and stave off law enforcement. However, this violence becomes deeply ingrained in the minds of the community's residents and perpetuates itself. For community members to affect violence upon others they must first have it affected on them, instilled in their minds as something that is acceptable and necessary for survival.

Henry also displays an internal struggle with morality and violence. Bud Halsey tells Henry that he must marry Helen or be hanged to death. Henry's pride initially prevents him from marrying Helen, and so Simms paints a vivid picture of the near hanging, again demonstrating his interest in the anti-gallows movement. In fact, Henry goes through with the hanging and is only saved by Bush and Helen at the last moment. The question of whether or not exposure to violence instilled in Henry a propensity to inflict violence and cruelty upon others is one that Simms raises. After this incident, Henry slowly begins to be affected by the outlaw community, deceiving his wife and father-in-law, finding enjoyment listening to Mowbray's stories of crime and corruption, and eventually killing Bud to secure his escape from the colony. While some of these actions were part of Henry's plan to gain Bud's trust and trick him into thinking Henry was part of the outlaw colony, a constant tension exists between Henry's sense of morality and the crimes he is forced to commit. He rightly recognizes that his new family initially accepted him with open arms because he appeared to be of high moral character. Now, there exists a tension between them, in part, because Helen and Bush see that Henry's character has pluralities, and he is not *just* virtuous, but struggles with his own moral consciousness. Henry notices this and states, "But the circumstances which gave [Bud] satisfaction now, afforded none to his brother, Bush Halsey, or my wife. Their attachment to me, as I have intimated rather than said, arose in part from the tenacious firmness with which I had held to my virtues" (142). Henry's moral center shifts, and he becomes more inclined towards cruelty, which pleases Bud. In order for the swamp of Conelachita to function properly, Bud needs citizens with misguided or easily influenced moral compasses. Conversely, Helen and Bush were initially drawn to Henry precisely because of his virtuous qualities, which seemed to be in stark opposition with the other members of the outlaw colony.

By the end of the novella, Henry's actions suggest that the corrupt forces which he so strongly tried to resist have influenced him. When Henry lies in wait for Bud he thinks, "Could I have been sure of my man, nothing would have been more easy than to have shot him where he stood" (204). Does this aggressive sentiment suggest that Henry has transformed into an innately violent person at this point? This scene raises questions about Henry's taste for violence because he so actively tries to resist it throughout the novella, and he begins his entrance into the outlaw community with a lie about perpetrating violence upon another man. Whether or not he has been fully influenced by his violent surroundings remains ambiguous up to the very end. While he shoots Bud with no hesitation, Henry spares Warner, Bud's injured henchman, and even helps him onto a horse. This, again, emphasizes the notion that Henry is not merely good or bad, but struggling with his own ethical system. Does his mercy towards Warner vindicate him, much like Mowbray's last cry to God is meant to vindicate and resolve him of his immoral deeds? Henry did make the conscious choice to enter the outlaw colony, despite warnings from others about the dangers and criminal elements present. This would seem to make him indictable. However, Henry has entered into a complex and dangerous web of crime which creates the conditions that allow the criminal community to function but which are then utilized by characters, like Henry, to escape it. The violence used by the members of the outlaw community to carry out crime breeds resentment and becomes the mechanism that also destroys the community, as this same violence is what some of these members then utilize to resist and escape the society. Because of this, it becomes difficult to separate a character's own choices from those influenced by criminal forces acting upon him, making the question of Henry's vindication a difficult one to answer. Simms constantly asks what makes one a "moral" person and how one either atones for his or her transgressions or adopts a moral code that justifies a life of crime. Perhaps, though, the answer is not straightforward, and Simms does not, in fact, provide a clear response.

Ultimately, *Helen Halsey* challenges its readers to assess law and morality in nuanced ways, as Simms depicts the struggles between internal values and outward perception that characters go through. He illustrates ambiguous areas of morality and characters' struggles with this ambiguity. The law becomes integral in this struggle, as interpretation of the law and the consequences of punishment vary from character to character, but in each case, the question of ethics is present. Simms shows the ways that the law can be misrepresented, manipulated, and misinterpreted. What is ethical, what is not, and how much are characters influenced by the ethical codes of the law, as well as other characters? For Simms, law can be counterproductive and influential in unexpected ways.

At a time when the frontier was shrinking, Simms was drawing attention to the encroachment of modernity and the confluence of civilization and the wilds of the border. *Helen Halsey* is a work that brings these issues to the forefront and does so consciously, as Simms points constantly to these themes through his characters, their dialogue, and the settings that surround them. The convergence of various moral sentiments on the frontier muddies the water and prohibits readers from attaining a clear sense of right and wrong. Instead it forces them to recognize and evaluate the nuances of law and morality. The novella shares many qualities with other works in Simms's Border series, allowing it to serve as a strong representative of the collection. *Helen Halsey* is an enthralling story which Simms himself held in high regard, due in part to its formal literary strengths, but it is easy to imagine that he also felt the work should have garnered more attention because of the ways that it draws awareness to the ever changing frontier.

NOTES

1. Simms delivered a lecture at the University of Alabama in 1842, entitled *The Social Principle: The True Source of National Permanence*, in which he remarked upon the changed nature of the frontier in Alabama from his last visit there twenty years earlier. He used this gentrification of the area by the English colonists to explain the success of English colonial pursuits and failure of French and Spanish settlement attempts. While the English wished to "nest" in these areas, the French and Spanish wished merely to exploit the land for resources. This lecture was delivered just three years before the publication of *Helen Halsey*, showing that the changing frontier was at the forefront of Simms's mind while writing his border tale.
2. Though his novel *Count Julian* was published during this period, in 1845, the text had been composed years earlier. See Guilds's *Simms: A Literary Life* for a discussion of the book's composition and publication history.

Historical and Political Poems

Monody, on the Death of Gen. Charles Cotesworth Pinckney; *The Vision of Cortes, Cain, and Other Poems*; *The Tri-Color*; *Donna Florida. A Tale*; and *Charleston and Her Satirists*

JASON W. JOHNSON

Anyone interested in assembling a collection of the historical and political writings of William Gilmore Simms would no doubt look to the author's prose works: his fiction and nonfiction. Simms deals extensively with the political arena, and literature's role in that arena, in works as varied as his essay collections, reviews, cultural expositions, history books, biographies, and of course, his romances, especially those of the border and the American Revolution. Given the overwhelming bulk of the South Carolina writer's historical and political prose, one may be forgiven for overlooking the not insignificant body of poetry concerned with these two subjects. The historical and political poems have remained largely untouched. Only James Everett Kibler and Matthew C. Brennan have written extensively on this breed of poems, but their treatments of such poems are not concerned primarily with history or politics and how those subjects are borne out in the texts. To date, John D. Miller's essay "The Business of Romanticism: Simms's Political Poetry" remains the only sustained discussion of the poet's political verse. No detailed discussion of Simms's historical poems as historical texts yet exists. While this essay cannot possibly remedy this lacuna, it does provide a few brief observations on five collections of verse devoted to historical and political subjects—collections, with the exception of *Monody*, that have been out of print for over a century.

Monody, on the Death of Gen. Charles Cotesworth Pinckney (1825)

Simms's first volume of verse, *Monody, on the Death of Gen. Charles Cotesworth Pinckney*, was published by Gray & Ellis in 1825.[1] Simms's name did not appear on the volume; instead the poet is referred to simply as "A South-Carolinian." Exactly why Simms chose to remain anonymous is unclear, as he never discussed the poem in any of his extant correspondence.[2] As to why Simms published the poem, profit in the form of cultural capital may have been foremost on the South Carolinian's mind. John Caldwell Guilds states, "Simms, it is not to be doubted, was sincere in his appreciation of Pinckney, but neither can it be doubted that the hard-working editor saw portrayal of national heroes as a profitable theme for future literary efforts" (*Literary Life* 23). If Simms had financial success in mind, then he would no doubt have been disappointed by the sales of the book, since "there is little reason to think that [*Monody*] was ever read by more than a few people among the nineteen-year-old poet's immediate circle in Charleston" (J. Meriwether, "Significance" 13). Despite lackluster sales and a small readership, the volume was received well by local reviewers, which must have encouraged the young poet still trying to find his voice and a place among the Charleston and American literati.

Monody's value persists today not necessarily because of the quality of the voice (it is, after all, juvenilia), but because it is an accurate barometer of Simms's early concerns, both aesthetic and political. Aesthetically, Simms was heavily entrenched in the neoclassical tradition, as Matthew C. Brennan has pointed out:

> Thus, steeped in the classics and in Dryden and Pope, surrounded by classical architecture on every street in Charleston, and no doubt wanting to impress his neoclassical elders such as Petigru and Legaré, the nineteen-year-old poet naturally turned to the closed heroic couplet for his first published book, no matter what misgivings he would soon feel about neoclassicism. (*Holy Craft* 15)

Simms uses all of the conventions one might expect to find in a stereotypical neoclassical poem: full or perfect rhyme (*course/force*, *mark/dark* [6]); inverted syntax ("Kings their crowns bequeath" [10]); consistently end-stopped lines ("Thou patriot sire! that shrunk not when thy land, / Was fiercely menaced by the invading band" [7]); punctuated elision between articles and nouns ("th' enraptured view") and prepositions and nouns ("T' enrich her bosom"). Simms also "adheres to the neoclassical conventions of the panegyric" (Brennan, *Holy Craft* 15), a laudatory mode that is best described as "gilding the lily."

Because he had not yet been caught up in the romantic movement, Simms's use of nature follows anthropocentric neoclassical convention. Consider the opening lines of *Monody*, for example: "When from the western sky, in purple robe, / The sun withdraws and leaves the azure globe, / Still o'er the vest of night we watch his rays, / As 'midst the wave his courser he delays" (5). The sun is not simply a star or celestial body; rather, Simms, with the word "courser," alludes to Apollo and his chariot, thus transforming nature into artifice. This particular maneuver was common in topiaries in both England and America, where hedges were carved and pruned in order to resemble sculptures. In line 3 the night is likewise transformed via the pathetic fallacy by the word "vest," through which the night takes on a certain artificial quality. This image metamorphoses night into human form, giving shape to the otherwise ethereal darkness. Finally, nature is used to reveal the strength of the hero, in this case Pinckney. Consider, for example, the second verse paragraph:

The hoary oak is scathed by many a year,
Its green hues faded, and its leaflets sear,
The tempest came, unmoved it met the blast,
Stretch'd its wide arms, and dared it as it past;
Mock'd the rude summons of the angry wind,
Nor sought in base submission, life to find,
Whilst all around bow'd to its restless course,
Nor dared to look,—that Oak withstood its force! (5–6)

In the beginning of the passage, the oak does not appear to represent anything, but is little more than one component of a larger scene. Not far into the passage, however, we realize that the tree is in the foreground of the scene and is therefore the speaker's focus. In order to draw further attention to the tree's significance, Simms capitalizes "Oak" by the end of the stanza. Clearly, the tree represents triumph in the midst of troubles; thus, the tree is a natural representation of the poem's hero. And while the poet does not mention Pinckney's name until late in the poem (with the exception of its appearance in the poem's subtitle), it is apparent enough that Pinckney is described and alluded to early in the text.

The political dimension of the poem appears simple enough: Simms praises a native son of South Carolina and a hero of the American Revolution. But this piece is not simply an encomium or a panegyric. Simms uses the poem to portray Pinckney as an example of right living, presumably one the poet's readers would be wise to emulate. Like so much doggerel verse of the time, *Monody* provides particular lines that function as morals, such as: "Live not for glory, but this one truth scan, / Who seeks for memory's note must live for man!" (12). For the first time in the poem, Simms makes clear his reason for composing the piece: Pinckney, who achieved fame with no concern for glory, serves not only as an historical figure or a great military man, but as a template for all human beings. The lines are a reminder that our *raison d'être* is not to serve ourselves or to fulfill our own desires but to "live for man" as Pinckney did.

Monody is also forward-looking. Not simply a patriotic poem, it foreshadows issues that would concern Simms for the rest of his career. Foremost the poem reveals a double concern with state and nation, both represented by Pinckney. Simms chooses his subject wisely, as Pinckney was not only a South Carolina hero, but also a part of the war effort that secured the new nation's independence. But again in this regard, Pinckney serves only as a representative of a larger issue, which is evidenced by the poem's dedication: "To the Patriot Dead of South-Carolina, this poem commemorative of the virtues of one of their illustrious fellows, is respectfully inscribed" (n. pag.). It is perhaps no accident that Simms, always so sensitive to the semantic potential of sound, chose the word "illustrious" because of its relationship to "illustrative"; if such is the case, then Simms is not simply celebrating Pinckney's "illustrious" career, but the career of all

South Carolina heroes. Thus, Pinckney becomes a composite of all the men who served and died in the American Revolution. And while he celebrates the nation's victory, Simms doubtless wrote the poem as a reminder to all of his home state's indispensable contribution to the war effort. Appropriately, Simms would return to this particular theme in his final volume, *Simms's Poems: Areytos, or Songs and Ballads of the South with Other Poems* (1860). In that collection, the poet includes a sequence celebrating the Palmetto regiment's contribution to the Mexican war. There is a difference between the motives behind such a state-centered view of national combat that upsets any symmetry one might otherwise find.[3] *Monody* is an encomium that praises both state and union. (It must be remembered that Simms was still a unionist at this point.) By 1860 (the publication date of *Areytos*), however, Simms's views of state and nation had changed. Simms used the Palmetto regiment poems, written decades before 1860, to voice pro-South Carolina and anti-union sentiments.

The Vision of Cortes, Cain, and Other Poems

Simms's fourth volume of poetry, *The Vision of Cortes, Cain, and Other Poems* (1829), is representative of the poet's early shift toward a romantic, but still European, aesthetic. *Visions of Cortes* was published under the imprint of James S. Burges, 44 Queen Street. As with *Monody*, Simms's fourth volume is not discussed in the letters. In reference to the conspicuous absence of any discussion of the collection in the correspondence, Kibler writes, "The poet makes no mention of the writing or publication of the volume in his collected letters, and of all Simms's titles, least is known about it" (*Poetry* 60). Without the prefaces to each of the volume's sections, we would have no idea about the genesis of the poems. Based on those prefaces, Guilds establishes that most of the poems were published in *The Vision of Cortes* for the first time (with obvious exceptions such as "The Lost Pleiad") (*Literary Life* 32). Simms would in later years, particularly during the last two decades of his life, assemble far more balanced volumes, including a more equal mix of old and previously unpublished poems.

The Vision of Cortes is unmistakably a product of English romantic influence, particularly that of Byron, a fact that Brennan explores in some depth. Brennan points in particular to the eponymous poem's epigraph, which is a quote from Byron, as well as to the second poem "Cain," whose name and content are drawn from Byron's poem of the same title (*Holy Craft* 94). In fact, it would be more accurate to say that Simms is not influenced by Byron, but is enamored of and thus imitates the English romantic poet. And while Simms is almost entirely immersed in Byron, his subject matter is American in nature, and would prove, like *Monody*, the beginning of later concerns, particularly his interest in the collision of European and Native American cultures. The dominant piece of the collection is the title poem, "The Vision of Cortes," and thus is worth discussing in some detail. It is a retelling of Hernan Cortes's incursion into the new world in general and Mexico in particular. Simms describes the battle between the Conquistadores and the Aztecs (Simms refers to them as Mexicans) in great detail. But it is not the battle that is of prime importance; of course the Spanish take the field. Rather, Simms focuses his attention on Cortes's conversation with the "chieftain" Guatimozin and the explorer's actions that result from that exchange. Cortes demands that Guatimozin "Go, bid thy followers quickly bring, / The splendors of thy favour'd land, / Without delay, with lavish hand" (24). The king refuses to acquiesce and is summarily burned to death. But just as important as the events Simms relates are the embellishments to the story, additions that reveal the poet's real concerns, which have little to do with reporting an objective history one might find in his historical prose.

Consider, for example, the way Simms describes Cortes and Guatimozin. Cortes is referred to in section 12 as "gallant" (19), giving one the impression that Simms favors the Spaniard, a reasonable expectation, particularly for a nineteenth-century audience who would have prized European values above those of the Native Americans. Simms undermines his previous description, however, in section 17 where he portrays Cortes in a different light: "And Cortes stands above [Guatimozin] now—/ A demon's fury in his eye" (24). The speaker vilifies and dehumanizes Cortes for his treatment of the chieftain, an unexpected turn to be sure. The depictions of Guatimozin are diametrically opposed to and more developed than the portrayals of Cortes. In fact, Simms places these disparate descriptions in such close proximity to one another that their differences appear even starker than they would otherwise: "And Cortes stands above him now—/ A demon's fury in his eye, / While calmness, on the monarch's brow, bespeaks a fearful apathy" (24). The European is in a demonic, frenzied state, while the king is the quintessence of placidity, a sign that he has accepted his fate with dignity. The words "fearful apathy" reveal Guatimozin's intimidating character, which he cultivates not with outward fury but with self-mastery, a trait Cortes lacks. Such a difference, Simms implies, is not localized to Cortes and the king, but is indicative of European (*viz.* white) and Native American attitudes.

But the differences do not end with their attitudes. Simms goes on to explore the views the two men hold for gold, a symbol in this context of material possessions. Cortes is willing to kill Guatimozin in order to take the Mexicans' gold. The king's reply to the Spaniard's demand fits nicely within the antimaterialist sentiment Simms would return to time and again:

> Greedy adventurer, dar'st thou say,
> Thy Gods have sent thee forth to prey
> With tiger lip, upon the brave,
> Whose land, by thee, is one wide grave,
> . . .

Seek'st thou the yellow ore, the spoil,
For which, thou'st borne uncounted toil,
Worthy, in better cause, to claim,
More than thou hast, or cravist, fame? (25)

In Simms's poetic imagination, Guatimozin refers to Cortes as a "Greedy adventurer," accusing him of seeking "the yellow ore" in hopes of gaining "fame." In order to vilify Cortes further, Guatimozin reminds him of the cost of his greed—the casualties of war. The chieftain does not share the Spaniard's materialism, referring to gold as "this furniture of hell." Rather than hoarding the gold á la European pirates, Guatimozin buries the gold in order to take it out of circulation. His concern is for the common good, not for his own gain. It is the monarch's expectation and hope that the gold will one day be used to "Glad poverty, destroy disease, / And lend the needy, life and ease" (26). Simms ensures that Cortes pays for his conversely greedy ambitions when he is haunted by a fearful vision of the Aztec dead, a lucid dream from which he never recovers.

In much the same way as *Monody*, "The Vision of Cortes" lays the groundwork for issues to which Simms would return often over the course of his career. His discussion of fame hearkens back to the moral of *Monody* and foreshadows his discussion of the same subject at the end of his career in sequences like the Palmetto regiment pieces. His critique of materialism was to prove a central subject of his work, in his later poetry and nonfiction alike. But it is the volume's concern for and praise of Native American culture that relates most obviously to Simms's future work in every genre the poet attempted. By the end of his career, Native American culture became synonymous with a native literature, one entirely divorced from "European models." And while Simms does not demonize Europe as he did Cortes, he does view European literature as a dangerous temptation.

The Tri-Color; or, The Three Days of Blood in Paris. With Some Other Pieces

Of Simms's early volumes, *The Tri-Color; or, the Three Days of Blood in Paris. With Some Other Pieces* (1831) has the most complicated and misleading publication history. The confusion lies in the book's imprint. According to the title page, *The Tri-Color* was published in London by Wigfall and Davis, Strand in 1830. That the year of publication is incorrect is not unusual. Often publishers would list the year prior to the actual publication date. The peculiarity here is the place of publication. According to Simms in a letter written to James Lawson in 1831, *The Tri-Color* was "published in our city," presumably Charleston, rather than London (*Letters* 1:38). Kibler agrees, suggesting that the book's real publisher was James S. Burges: "the type-font used to set the dedication to James S. Burges in Simms's *The Vision of Cortes* . . . appears to be the same as set the title page of *Tri-Color*" (*Poetry* 62). The second peculiarity of the title page is the absence of an author's name.

In the same letter to Lawson, Simms explained the work's anonymity: "I am not, nor do I wish to be known as its author, for a variety of reasons, none of which are of importance even to my friends" (*Letters* 1: 38). The question then becomes: Why would Simms conceal his name and that of the Charleston publisher? Kibler again provides the most reasonable explanation:

> The purpose of Simms's attempt to hide his authorship and of the pose of a London publisher may have been to place his work in front of American reviewers in order to escape any bias against him or American publications in general. . . . Another possibility is that since the volume praises the free press as it had been instrumental in bringing political reform in France, it would have been taken as a statement by Simms who had just become a Unionist newspaper editor in Charleston with numerous enemies. Giving the book a London imprint would have lifted it above local politics. (*Poetry* 62–63)

The second reason is perhaps the more plausible possibility. Simms may very well have been concerned that Charlestonians would think that he would use his unionist paper as a similar impetus for revolution. Whether or not Simms ever had such hopes is doubtful. If Kibler is right, Simms was attempting to protect himself from the barbs and slanders of his "numerous enemies."

There is a third explanation for the book's misleading title page. While Simms conceals his name, he does not conceal his nationality. In the "Advertisement" he writes:

> The work, now offered to the notice of the British Public, is by an American Citizen. It has grown entirely out of the recent events in the French metropolis, and may very well be considered the natural ebullitions of feeling in the citizen of a nation, the practice of which, in all revolutionary matters, it has been, to exult in each overthrow of oppression, as one more stride taken by human nature, towards the attainment of that still remote, but as events have shewn, far from ideal state of existence—the exercise of their own will in so much as relates to their individual control, and in society, their free self government, as a class of equal and rational beings. For the imperfections of the volume, he has no apology to offer beyond the patriotic feeling, to which it owes its origin. (n. pag.)

The "Advertisement" may function as a not-so-subtle reminder of the British defeat in the American Revolution. The author claims that the July Revolution kindled his patriotism. Not unexpectedly, Simms draws a parallel between the French desire for liberty and American revolutionary tendencies. Simms explains that it is the American citizen's "practice" to "exult in each overthrow of oppression." Also of interest is the way Simms uses the word "apology" near the end of the passage. "Apology" has at least two meanings, the first of which refers to a defense and the second to a request for forgiveness. However we choose to define the word in the "Advertisement," "apology" signals a rebellious, unapologetic attitude on the part of the poet. No defense is necessary, and the poet sees no need to be forgiven for his book, which according to Simms, is an outgrowth of "patriotic feeling." There is an unadorned audacity in Simms's desire to offend his audience, the British Public, the subjects of a tyrannical government he and his countrymen have not likely forgiven.

The advertisement is certainly more than an insult, though, and it is far more than a celebration or an expression of admiration of the French public's revolutionary zeal. The advertisement may also function as a guide or key in which Simms implicitly reveals to the reader the book's true purpose. By all appearances *The Tri-Color* is a poetic account of the July Revolution; certainly the dry, factual introduction supports such appearances. Yet Simms is not simply concerned with relating the events of the revolution; rather, he uses language reminiscent of American independence to suggest that the poem is not only about France but about America as well. In these poems, Simms establishes a link between the two nations, creating an alliance founded on liberty. There are echoes of bellicose language one might expect to find in writings and propaganda of the French revolutionary period: "Then rose the hymn of vengeance high, / And in his glowing song portray'd, / Were seen the sons of Liberty, / In panoply array'd" (35). The phrase "sons of Liberty" is a direct reference to the group of men responsible for the Boston Tea Party. The French rebels (referred to as "citizens") are Americanized, now part and parcel of the same revolutionary spirit begun in New England sixty years before what Simms later in the poem calls "freedom's cause" (43).

Simms tackles a number of other issues in the volume as well, a brief list of which may give some indication of the constellation of subjects and themes that inform the book and the author's poetic imagination. One such concern is the role of the poet in revolution, exemplified in the boy poet who relates the story of the July Revolution to the people, so that they may not forget. Another idea that informs the book is that of the wilderness versus the urban setting. Simms develops this particular idea in "The Tomb of Napoleon." He disapproves of the removal of Napoleon from St. Helena to a tomb in Paris. He discusses the "natural sublime" as the appropriate home for the emperor's remains (51). He discusses nature again, but this time as a revolutionary force in "Ode on the Late Popular Successes." It is nature, the poet contends, "who taught her children to rebel, / Against the Tyrants who would make them slaves" (58). Also of interest to Simms is France's relationship with other non-European countries in general and the city of Algiers in particular. Unfortunately, the poem is little more than a racist attack on an often abused other. There are, of course, other issues at stake here, but the central focus of the book is the cause of liberty, one that Simms presents within an American context.

Donna Florida: A Tale

Though published in 1843 by Burges and James, the date of composition of *Donna Florida: A Tale* is much earlier. Kibler points to a composition date of "no later than mid-1832, when Simms read 'portions' of it to Willis Clark in Philadelphia" (*Poetry* 69). Brennan concurs, proposing a possible reason Simms might have kept the text from the public for so long: "Simms's decision to publish *Donna Florida* as late as 1843 underlines how his early allegiance to Byron remained a poetic resource he could recur to from time to time" (*Holy Craft* 31–32). There is another possibility, however, one that Simms suggests in the preface to *Donna Florida*:

> The poem . . . was chiefly the work of the writer's youth. This fact, however, scarcely suggests any sufficient reason why it should be given to the public in his mature years. But his object is explanation rather than apology. The poem was begun, but not finished,—indeed, it still remains unfinished,—at a time when the too famous production of Lord Byron, DON JUAN, then of recent publication, was a subject of constant remark and criticism, particularly in connection with the premature and lamented fate of the unhappy writer. (1)

It is possible that Simms was concerned about the reception of the poem, but not necessarily for the reasons given here. He may have put the poem aside for so long because of its obvious influence. He may have felt the poem too derivative for publication. Perhaps he was trying to avoid the unfortunate, though accurate, label of "imitator." By the time he published *Donna Florida*, he had found his own voice and could no longer be accused of living in the infamous romantic poet's shadow.

If ever Simms wrote a more Byronic poem than *Donna Florida*, it has yet to be found. A number of indicators, aesthetic and otherwise, mark the poem as falling squarely in Byron's lineage. For one thing, Simms employs *ottavarima*, the same eight-line stanza used in Byron's *Don Juan*.[4] Second, like Byron, Simms uses exotic rhymes. Consider, for example:

> Our damsel waits—her charms demand attention,—
> I left off at her eyes, and hardly *gave 'em*
> Due share of that fierce glow which young lads mention,
> As the first thing in beauty to *enslave 'em*.
> Strange that so lovely, they should bring dissention,
> Still making it most terrible to *brave 'em*.
> (Canto 1, stanza 35, emphasis added)

These three rhymes are hardly the stuff of Wordsworth or Coleridge, who would have shirked at including anything of the sort in their own poetry, at least the poetry they would be willing to present to the public. But Byron regularly used colloquial, "unpoetic" rhymes like this in *Don Juan*. There are a number of other such examples of similar Byronic rhymes in *Donna Florida* such as *duty/foot he* (1: 24),[5] *idea/free a/see a* (1: 57), and *quiet/cry at* (1: 33). Aside from the formal similarities, the content also mirrors closely Lord Byron's mock epic. Most obvious is the title and location of the poem. One need not be gifted with an interpretive mind in order to see that *Donna Florida* is an allusion to *Don Juan*. The most interesting difference here is Simms's feminization of the title, which creates a diametrical opposite to Byron's often effeminate male hero. Simms also paraphrases or intentionally misquotes Byron, the most obvious example of which is the opening of Canto 4: "I want a Muse, as Byron did a hero" (4: 1). The latter half of the line is drawn from the opening line of the first canto in *Don Juan*: "I want a hero, an uncommon want" (1: 1). There are a number of other similarities not discussed here. Brennan gives a much fuller account of all such overlaps, including but not limited to Simms's Byronic digressions as well as his alterations/versions of classical references (*Holy Craft* 30–31).[6]

Beyond the Byronic influence, Simms's portrayal of an explorer whose voyage was doomed to fail is of particular interest in this work. This version of Ponce de Leon is quite different from that of Cortes in *The Vision of Cortes*. The latter explorer is vilified to the point of becoming a one-dimensional character. He ceases to be a flesh-and-blood individual and becomes a symbol of European excess, greed, and brutality. Don Ponce, as Simms often calls him, is a more fleshed out and sympathetic character. To start with, Simms casts Ponce de Leon as a comic figure, focusing on attributes otherwise ignored in more heroic accounts. For example, Simms discusses, however obliquely, Ponce's bodily functions: "His beard had something of a grizzly hue, / And sallow was his shrivell'd up complexion; / His shoulders caught a stoop at fifty-two, / And his good form had lost its old erection" (1: 38). Though the narrator ostensibly is describing the signs of Ponce's old age, including his stooping posture, he also is describing in the subtext of the passage more personal elements of physiology, ones that cannot be stated outright, given the mores of nineteenth-century readers. Both "shrivell'd" and "erection" indicate that Don Ponce is impotent, a fact that underscores the explorer's sexual inadequacy, particularly with regard to a woman as young as Leonora. This passage also draws into question Ponce de Leon's heroism. A nineteenth-century audience, had they picked up on the joke, would not have thought of Ponce as a hero in light of this revelation. The comedy of the passage results from the reality of the situation—that is, the divide between how Ponce sees himself, a dignified man of good breeding versus how Leonora, the narrator, and the audience see him.

Of course, Ponce is not all comedy. In fact, Simms manages to create a character for whom the audience feels pity. Few examples reveal the poet's gift of pathos more than the moment Ponce meets the Portuguese gypsy and the moments following that interview. Upon hearing the Portuguese's news about the Fountain of Youth, Ponce is filled with excitement: "The knight's faith soon was yielded—he got well;—a / Happy fancy banished all his care; / And off he darted suddenly and soon, / 'Revisiting the glimpses of *his* moon' (2: 21, emphasis in original). When he relays the good news to Leonora she laughs, knowing that the fountain must be apocryphal (2: 23). Her doubt sets in hard relief Ponce's gullibility. Yet his is not a chronic gullibility, but one brought on by desperation. Portions of their conversation may be humorous, but it is difficult to laugh at an individual so enamored as Ponce obviously is. In fact, the narrator does not blame Ponce for his situation, but Leonora: "If o'er his fate that maiden had not cast / Her wicked spells and held with wanton sway, / That made him all unfit,—and daily worse,— / For his own business, and perhaps for hers" (2: 15).

Charleston, and Her Satirists; a Scribblement

Published with James E. Burges in two installments (November and December 1848), Simms's *Charleston, and Her Satirists* seems an unusual turn—or return—in the poet's career; but given the subject matter of the piece, Simms's formal choice could not have been more appropriate. Now committed to romanticism more than ever, Simms knew that the content of his poem demanded influences other than Wordsworth, Coleridge, or Shelley. Apparently even Byron was inappropriate for such a piece. The South Carolina poet cast the poem as a satire, a literary vein he had not explored with any consistency since *Donna Florida* written more than decade earlier. What poetic form, then, could better communicate the wit and humor of satire better than the neoclassical heroic couplets of Alexander Pope's *Dunciad* and John Dryden's *MacFlecknoe*?

In a letter to Nathaniel Beverley Tucker, Simms explained the impetus and targets of his "local satire":

> [*Charleston, and Her Satirists*] was written at a couple of sittings—standings rather—and at the request of some Gentlemen of Charleston;—the people of that godly city being greatly outraged at a spiteful pamphlet which purported to be from the pen of a Yankee woman, who revenged herself on the community by a lampoon, in resentment at the loss (it is said) of a love—a lad whom she chased from college. (*Letters* 2: 504)

In the preface to the book, Simms questions the sex of the author, arguing that "In all probability, the quill of this goose came from a bird of masculine gender" (n.pag.). Simms defends this assertion, saying, "there were certain passages of the satire which could scarcely be ascribed to a female pen. It contained allusions to subjects of a nature quite too delicate to suppose that they could be discussed in the mind of a woman, and one who claims to be an unwedded one" (ibid.). Not surprisingly Simms took advantage of the occasion and composed a poem not entirely about the "spiteful pamphlet." As he explained to Tucker, "The portions of my scribblement that may interest you will be such as compare characteristics of North & South. The occasion was a good one for the utterance of some severities which were more legitimately bestowed by a native pen, and more appropriate to the deserts of our people" (*Letters* 2: 504).

The structure of *Charleston, and Her Satirists* is a complex one, beginning not with a critique of the author of the pamphlet, but with more general concerns: "Doubtless we need the lash—our virtues few, / Our foibles many, and our vices too" (5). The "Gentlemen of Charleston" may not have expected their inclusion in the satire; nonetheless, Simms reminds his audience that no one is innocent and that "Oh! Doubtless faults and vices both exist, / And well deserve the mighty satirist" (14). Here Simms qualifies his comments, explaining that the satirist does not lampoon for pleasure's sake or out of anger, at least not if he is to be effective: "No bitter selfishness must guide the pen / When satire speaks to touch the souls of men" (ibid.). Simms accuses the northern author, implicit as the accusation might be, of writing satire out of "bitter selfishness." And though much of his language borders on the trenchant, Simms makes certain concessions in the preface, stating, "With many truths, the aim [of the satire] was too feeble, the shaft too dull, to prove otherwise than innocuous" (n.pag.). Simms's ability to "confirm the justice of some of the satirist's points of censure" reveals an even temperament necessary for effective satire.

Before launching into a critique of the pamphlet, Simms examines the faults of a number of subjects. He examines, for example, England's condescension, xenophobia, and ethnocentrism via a personification of that nation, John Bull, stating, "There's Bull—our John—the prince of Pharisees, / Thanks God he is not like the men he sees" and "Fault-finding is his business,—'tis for this, / He travels only,—it perfects his bliss" (15, 16). John Bull is cast as a type Simms refers to as the "surface-traveler" (15). Another name for this type would be the outsider, one who does not understand a foreign culture, but does not hesitate to judge the customs and people of that region. Simms turns to the outsider motif again when he finally turns to the supposed subject of the satire, the female (or male) satirist more than a fourth of the way through the poem:

> The stranger, good at surface-seeing, knows
> But little that which 'neath the surface grows;
> Must live beneath our laws and feel their force,
> Ere he can judge their action and their course:
> At best, he gathers from some single voice,
> The opinion that he makes his own by choice,
> And mostly blunders, since, of all the crowd,
> The grumbler's first to clamor, long and loud;
> . . .

Her [the satirist's] little circle, narrow'd in its scope,
Without a purpose as without a hope;—
Bounded by walls of prejudice that keep
The stagnant thought in ever-bonded sleep;
. . .
She heard the groans about her, of the few,
And, glad to censure, joined the grumble too.

All that moved satire, or beguiled the sneer,
Was so much music to the Northern ear. (20)

Like the "stranger," another name for the "surface-traveler" leads into a discussion of the northern satirist who fits this description well. Her particular bias is informed by her own cultural mores as well as her ignorance of southern culture. Like the stranger, her view is "narrow'd in its scope." Because of her "little circle, she cannot see Charleston for what it is. She assumes that "groans about her, of the few" are representative of the truth. Unfortunately, her satire, informed by ignorance and prejudice, was "so much music to the Northern ear."

Thus far, Simms has moved from general to specific. He discusses the "surface traveler" and gives England as a specific example of the type. He then discusses the "stranger" in order to discuss the unnamed satirist specifically. Surely aware of the monotony that results from continuing in the same pattern, Simms also telescopes out, moving from specific to general. Consider his discussion of northern women poets:

Verse, such as yours, ne'er moved Pieria's hill;
Ne'er took by storm one mortal soul or sense,
Nor yielded patient hearing recompense. (25)

Few by write doggrel [*sic*]—all New-England scrawls.
Gould squeaks and squeals, Sigourney screams and squalls;
Scribblers inveterate—ardent, you would say. (25–26)

No genius moves them to the great design,
But the dull labor hobbles through each line. (26)

Doubtless, our Spinsters, when the rhyme is read,
Persuade themselves they ardently have bred;
They talk of passions which they do not know,
And, as they talk, believe indeed they glow. (28)

Simms begins by ridiculing the pamphlet writer's verse and then broadens his scope to discuss northern women poets in general. He then mentions in passing Gould and Sigourney, telescopes out again and finally specifies a particular type of woman, the spinster. By using these telescoping strategies (general-specific and specific-general), Simms uses general types (the stranger) to classify the female satirist and uses the female satirist as an occasion to discuss certain types (northern women poets).

One other component of the poem's elaborate structure is Simms's desire to instruct his audience, and presumably the female satirist, in the ways of successful satire. In order to do so, he satirizes some of the very "Gentlemen" who requested that he write the poem in the first place—i.e., the planter class. Of this class Simms writes, "Our southern planter, from the constant strife, / Secure, that clings to trade and city life, / Suffers his leisure to usurp his strength" (41). Not only is Simms addressing the planter's physical strength, but his atrophying mental faculties as well. He points out that "Letters and arts should flourish in his care, / Since time and wealth he equally may spare" (ibid.). Unfortunately, "His mental habit and his will constrains" (ibid.). The "store that college life bestows" is lost on the planter. His mind has been thoroughly weakened and regimented by his laborless existence and societal expectations or "the rule prescriptive chains" (ibid.). The poet warns the planter of the consequences of his "mental sleep" (43):

> Unless in season, resolute at last,
> He rises true to present as to past,
> Plucks from the ocean its escaping breath,
> And learns that idleness is surely death;
> That work alone is manhood, and that toil,
> Is needful to the son as to the soil. (42)

Simms explains the course the planter has set for himself is a fatal one, physically, intellectually, and spiritually. He also criticizes the planter's desire for material wealth, reminding him that "wealth is rather in the soul than soil" (44).

At first glance this particular passage appears out of place. Simms's aim is not yet clear. Only at the close of the planter section do we learn the poet's reason for incorporating this passage: "These are our faults and follies, told in part, / Deserving well the satire and the smart; / Our Lady Censor somewhat wastes her shot" (45). One would expect these two couplets to be placed in different verse paragraphs. That Simms places them in the same paragraph in adjacent positions gives the game away. Simms uses the planter passage as a way of revealing the failures of the "Lady Censor." The subject of his satire is the planter, a class Simms knew quite well. He does not approach his subject as the northern satirist does, as a stranger, but rather as an insider, thus fulfilling one of his requirements for good satire. Second, Simms does not insult the planter as the female satirist insults Charleston, and by extension, the South. Simms's aim is curative, as is evidenced by the advice he gives the planter class. His is a deep concern for the wellbeing of the planter and his culture. By expressing his concerns thus,

Simms fulfills another requirement for successful satire. Simms's opponent does not meet the southern poet's standards, a point he illustrates through his own constructive criticism of his class.

While *Charleston, and Her Satirists* contains none of the originality of Simms's style or voice; and while the poem is wholly derivative of neoclassical formulae, the subjects of the piece are handled with great mastery. He mixes well the mockery of Dryden's *MacFlecknoe* (his attack on northern women poets) with the dead seriousness of Pope's *Essay on Man* (his discussion of the southern planter), thus composing a composite poem wholly representative of the extremes of the literary neoclassical spectrum. And because he does not limit himself to an attack on the "Yankee woman," Simms provides readers with a Hydra-headed satire with multifarious concerns.

Conclusion

This collection—perhaps better referred to as a selection of collections—is representative, not comprehensive or exhaustive. A number of poems have been left out of consideration for at least two reasons. First, some of Simms's historical and political poetry is already in print in the series published by the *Simms Initiatives* and the University of South Carolina Press. The Palmetto regiment poems were recently published in *Simms's Poems: Areytos, or Songs and Ballads of the South with Other Poems*. A number of Simms's shorter political poems are well represented in recently published volumes. "Sonnet—The Age of Gold," for example is a part of the collection *Poems: Descriptive, Dramatic, Legendary and Contemplative* (1853). Second, the aim of this essay on Simms's *Historical and Political Poems* is not to evaluate all of Simms's poems in these veins; instead, it is to survey the landscape, for the first time, of those Simms poetry volumes the primary foci of which are either historical or political or both. Also worth noting is the number of poems published in these collections that were not discussed in this essay. These poems were omitted not because they are not worth discussing, but because they fall outside of the purview of this introduction. No doubt, many of the shorter pieces are too subtle in their political and historical commentary to be included profitably in the current discussion. Other scholars, I hope, will make those and other connections, using this paper and the works it discusses as a springboard for future research on Simms's historical and political *oeuvre*.

NOTES

1. The exact month and day of the book's publication are indeterminate. James Everett Kibler places the volume's release sometime before September 14 (*Poetry* 53). Matthew C. Brennan agrees with Kibler's assertion, explaining that the volume must have "appeared between August 16, 1825—the date Pinckney died—and September 14 when the *Charleston Courier* printed a favorable review" (*Holy Craft* 15).

2. John Caldwell Guilds has argued that Simms may have omitted any discussion of *Monody* in the letters as an indication of his low estimation of the poem.
3. For a more extensive discussion of *Aerytos*, see my essay on that volume in this collection.
4. *Ottava rima* is an eight-line stanza written in iambic pentameter and consisting of three rhymes. The rhyme scheme of the stanza is *ababab*cc_5.
5. Rather than using the long hand form, "Canto 1, stanza 24," I have abbreviated it to 1: 24, where the first number (1) is the canto number and the second number (24) designates the stanza number. I will use this citation method for the remainder of the discussion of *Donna Florida*.
6. James O. Hoge also provides a fine analysis of Simms's Byronic borrowings in his article "Byron's Influence on the Poetry of William Gilmore Simms."

History and Geography

The History of South Carolina from Its First European Discovery to Its Erection into a Republic and *The Geography of South Carolina: Being a Companion to the History of that State*

SEAN R. BUSICK

William Gilmore Simms's *The History of South Carolina* was first published by Charleston's S. Babcock and Company in 1840, bearing the rather cumbersome title *The History of South Carolina, from Its First European Discovery to Its Erection into a Republic: With a Supplementary Chronicle of Events to the Present Time*. Two years later Simms revised the book. Then in 1843 he published his *The Geography of South Carolina*, also with S. Babcock and Company. It was intended to be a supplement to the *History*. On the eve of the Civil War, Simms again revised and updated the *History*. This expanded and revised 1860 edition was published by New York's Redfield. Between the first edition of 1840 and the 1860 revision, the book grew from 319 pages to 437 pages.[1]

Unlike Simms's other books the *History* and *The Geography of South Carolina* were written primarily as textbooks for young students. He feared that the majority of South Carolinians, young and old alike, were largely ignorant of their state's history: "To say that the great majority of our young people know little or nothing of the history of the state, is to do them no injustice. We may equally charge this deficiency upon the old" (*History* 5).[2] Simms hoped to fill this need with a history that could serve as a textbook, while also appealing to interested older readers—a textbook that would be a pleasure rather than a chore to read. "I am now writing a History of South Carolina in a single volume, intended for the use of schools and for the general reader, who in these piping times, eschews heedfully all ponderous quartos," he wrote to his friend James Lawson on 20 July 1839 (*Letters* 1: 151). As John Caldwell Guilds has observed, "Since South Carolina historical data substantially provide the basis for the Revolutionary Romances and other fiction, Simms's assuming the role of historian *per se* was not an abrupt departure" from the sort of work he had been writing throughout his career (*Literary Life* 93–94).

In his preface to the *History*, Simms explained that the idea for the book came to him when he began to teach his thirteen year old daughter Augusta her state's history. It was then that he discovered that no existing book was suitable to his purposes. One problem with many of the existing state histories, was that they were "so cumbrous, and so loaded as they are with prolix disquisition, and unnecessary if not irrelevant detail," that they were inappropriate for "the unprepared understanding and the ardent temper of the young." The available state histories were simply too long and too dull for Simms's purposes. An unread, or unreadable, book did no one any good. The older histories tended to be encumbered with dry and dated political discourses on topics that were no longer of interest to the state's readers. "To the great portion of the reading community they are entirely useless," he wrote. (*History* 2)

The excessive length of the existing state histories, with many running to two volumes, also rendered them too expensive to reach a wide audience. Simms believed authors and publishers had a responsibility to make quality books available to the masses by producing inexpensive literature: "Books for schools and for the popular reader—the two objects for which the present history is designed—must be cheap as well as compact." With this goal and his intended audience in mind, Simms left out footnote references and all "unnecessary details," and tried to avoid excessive "prolixity" (*History* 3). He also scaled the project back as far as he thought he could, limiting himself to a relatively small one-volume history and a separate geography of the state. "In separating the political and social from the geographical history of the state" he wrote in the preface to *Geography*, "the object was to simplify the subject, and so to preserve unbroken the stream of narrative in the former work, as to make its perusal by the youthful reader, a pleasure rather than a task" (iii). What he believed was needed, was "to place the facts in a simple form, in a just order; to give them an expressive and energetic character; to couple events closely, so that no irrelevant or unnecessary matter should interpose itself between the legitimate relation of cause and effect; and to be careful that the regular stream of the narrative should flow on without interruption to the end of its course" (*History* 6). Simms was confident that a history and geography written according to this plan could accomplish much good in educating the public.

The Geography of South Carolina draws heavily from the work of Robert Mills, America's first professional architect and the designer of the Washington Monument. Mills also compiled an atlas of South Carolina which is still the most comprehensive source for geographical information on the state in the early nineteenth century. Simms's geography text might more accurately be thought of as a natural history of South Carolina; he wrote and organized it according to the conventions of natural history. This peculiarly American literary genre developed out of the need to systematically describe a vast new continent. It included the writings of John and William Bartram, Thomas Jefferson, John Filson, and many others with whose works Simms was familiar. Natural history would later engage the talents of writers ranging from Henry David Thoreau to Wendell Berry. Like countless earlier descriptions of America, Simms's *Geography of South Carolina* begins by surveying the state's physical extent, then moves on to enumerate its physical features, its flora, and its fauna, before describing its human inhabitants and their higher political and cultural attainments.[3]

Instead of a bibliography, Simms acknowledged his debt to several authors in *The History of South Carolina*'s preface. Those authors included Bartholomew Rivers Carroll, Jr., Alexander Hewatt, John Drayton, David Ramsay, William Moultrie, William Johnson, George Bancroft, William J. Rivers, Banastre Tarleton, "and several others" (*History* 5). He quoted freely from these authors, and though the quotes are not cited in footnotes, the text generally makes clear the source of quotations.

It is also worth noting that Simms used his sources critically, as any good historian must. When they were wrong or inconsistent, he did not hesitate to point this out to the reader. In one instance, for example, he noted that, according to some sources, "South Carolina was estimated to contain ninety-three thousand whites [at the time of the Revolution], when she could not possibly have contained sixty thousand" (*History* 199). In another instance, he pointed out what he believed was an error on the part of some historians who had said that General Nathanael Greene had been caught off guard by the Lord Rawdon at Hobkirk's Hill in April 1781 (*History* 299). And he was not afraid to admit his uncertainty when his research failed conclusively to settle an issue in dispute. "All the clues to argument upon doubtful or disputed points have been indicated," he told his readers (*History* 6). Because of that and his extensive research, Simms believed his own *The History of South Carolina* was "in many respects original, especially in the suggestion of clues; and it embodies much material which has escaped other historians" (*History* 6). Upon completing his *History* Simms could confidently write to his friend James Lawson on 25 October 1840 that "there is no Romance about it"—unlike some of his other books (*Letters* 1: 194).

His original research involved poring over all the relevant manuscripts in his extensive private collection and others that he could get access to, traveling to all portions of the state to see historic sites firsthand, and corresponding with authorities on local history. One such research trip was planned for the summer of 1847 to familiarize himself with the scenery, history, and manners of the upcountry for a revision to the *History*. Simms wrote in May 1847 to John C. Calhoun that he hoped to take a summer "jaunt" in South Carolina's mountains. "My purpose will be to pick up as much historical material as possible in relation to the events of the revolution in the interior, so that I may make my History of the State more complete, and more satisfactory to the upper country" (*Letters* 2: 318–19). In planning the trip he sought the assistance of Greenville's Benjamin F. Perry who was knowledgeable about upcountry Revolutionary history. "I am thinking of a new Edition of my History of South Carolina, in which I propose to incorporate all the matter that can be procured in regard to the up country history," he explained to Perry; "In this work I shall look to you for assistance" (*Letters* 2: 317). Simms's itinerary included the Cowpens and King's Mountain battlefields, and he hoped Perry would share his knowledge of local Revolutionary history and lore (*Letters* 2: 330, 333). As a result of this diligent research and careful revising, Simms felt confident that impartial readers of his last revised edition of the *History* would agree that he had "suffered nothing, by way of clue, suggestion, argument, or fact, to escape me" (*Letters* 4: 187).

The two main lessons of the book are that South Carolinians ought always to depend on native leadership and that they ought also to present a united front against external foes. These points are driven home in Simms's telling of the story of the American Revolution in the state. Though not strictly limited in scope to the War for Independence, *The History of South Carolina* deals extensively with the Revolution, and it is one of his most important treatments of the war. In the 1860 edition, 237 of the 437 pages are devoted to the story of the Revolution and the events from 1765 leading up to it. The American Revolution is the focus and central theme of the narrative. In fact, the full title Simms chose for the book indicates that the history of South Carolina culminates in the Revolution and the state's "erection" into a republic; subsequent events were mere epilogue.

As was the case with his other works on the Revolution, Simms sought to describe the war in South Carolina accurately, in a lively manner, to reach as large an audience as possible. In his narrative the Revolution is portrayed as the product of a long progress of social and ideological forces that nurtured and developed the colonies until they were ready for independence. Simms depicted the Revolution in South Carolina as a fratricidal civil war that was exacerbated by ethnic divisions within the colony, and much of the credit for the eventual victory, he emphasized, was due to irregular forces of partisans and militia. If *The History of South Carolina* can truly be said to have a thesis, it is that unity is essential in times of crisis and that South Carolina had been fortunate to have capable native leaders to see it through every emergency.

According to Simms, the Revolution began in South Carolina in October 1765 when the decision was made to resist the Stamp Act (*History* 158).[4] Previous to this tax, South Carolina had little reason for discontent with the mother country: "She had, on the contrary, many good reasons for loving her with undeviating loyalty." She enjoyed the protection of British arms and fleets and profited by her mercantile connection with the mother country. South Carolinians suffered lightly, if at all, under "the array of evils, wrongs, and abuses" that afflicted the northern colonies that had more substantial manufacturing and shipping interests (*History* 152, 153). Instead of finding herself in competition with English economic interests, South Carolina benefited from her connection with England: "She provided the raw material which the other manufactured, and she received the manufactured goods in exchange for her productions. The intercourse was simple enough between them, and the occasions for conflict were few and unimportant" (*History* 202). Neither had she felt the oppressiveness of British arms. On the contrary, British "men, money, and munitions" protected South Carolina from hostile Native Americans and Spaniards (*History* 181). Her causes of quarrel were not economic as much as sympathy with the plight of Massachusetts and chafing at British arrogance and the denial of a few abstract principles. "The duties on tea and stamped paper were not felt, regarding the amount; but as the assertion of an authority adverse to the rights of the people and the province," Simms explained (*History* 180).

South Carolina and Great Britain were bound not only by self-interest but also by an affection grown from sharing a language, a similar culture, and many of the same traditions. South Carolina's constitution and government were based on British models, and many of her citizens worshipped at Anglican churches and enjoyed reading English literature: "The people were especially fond of British tastes, manners, and opinions; their children had a British education, and they spoke of the mother-country invariably under the endearing appellation of 'home.'" They also inherited "the natural spirit of liberty and right which fills the bosom of an English stock" (*History* 152, 153).

In Simms's view, South Carolinians considered themselves Englishmen, possessed of the rights of Englishmen. These rights had always been jealously guarded, and they never shrank from asserting them. South Carolinians overthrew the colony's Lord Proprietors in 1719 for abusing the colonists' rights. Indeed, Simms believed that "the whole progress of the province of South Carolina had been calculated to nourish a spirit of independence among the people." Trial and strife had both strengthened them and made them aware of their strength. Most white colonists were freehold farmers who recognized no superiors, and "agriculture had taught them simplicity, hardihood, and a frank, bold, free speech and thought" (*History* 154). South Carolinians had no aristocracy and knew no restraints on their exercise of religion. Even slavery tended to make them more jealous of their own liberties while heightening their own sense of dignity. As the colony grew in population and wealth the colonists grew in local pride and boldness and were less content to be governed by a distant foreign court.

The period that witnessed Carolina's astounding growth and prosperity was an interval of salutary neglect during the reigns of George I and II that had fostered self-government and conditioned her citizens to expect little royal or parliamentary interference in their affairs. "The ascent of George the Third to the throne brought with it a change of policy in Britain, and with regard to the province, which awakened the anxieties of the intelligent and aroused the fears of the vigilant and jealous," Simms observed (*History* 148). Unfortunately for the cause of imperial rule, the cessation of salutary neglect coincided with the successful termination of the Seven Years' War, which removed the most dangerous threats to the colony's peace and safety. Then, free from foreign pressure, South Carolinians could begin to calculate the cost of union with England. Once this inquiry had begun, they "soon arrived at those convictions of political truth, law, and equity, which learned to question the tenure of foreign authority, and the legitimacy of these relations with the mother-country, which placed the provincials wholly at her mercy." From here, "The summits of republican freedom were not far from sight" (*History* 136).

After repeal of the Stamp Act, London tried again and again to increase the revenue from the North American colonies through the now familiar litany of taxes. These only served to confirm Americans' suspicions of imperial designs against their liberty and to widen the rift between the colonies and the court. Gradually, South Carolinians reached the conclusion that their interests and liberties would be safer in an independent American republic. Though they suffered relatively little compared to the people of Boston, they actively sympathized with their fellow colonists and saw in Boston's plight a real danger to their own liberty. In no colony, Simms wrote, was sympathy for Boston more passionately felt and expressed than in South Carolina. As Carolinians recognized, the unrestrained power that was allowed to subjugate one colony could subjugate them all. Safety could be found only in unity and concerted resistance to tyranny (*History* 160–61).

What was true for the colonies as a whole was also true for South Carolina. But her ethnic and cultural diversity spoiled hopes of internal unity against the external enemy. The colony's population contained large numbers of English, Scottish, Irish, Germans, and French Huguenots who brought their national prejudices to America and who were further divided by economic and geographic interests. Inhabitants of the backcountry for instance, had little in common with those who lived in the lowcountry. In the backcountry "a large portion of the people were foreigners, born British subjects, had been only eight or ten years in the country, had no intercourse, no sympathies, with the people of the seaboard, and were particularly jealous and resentful of the superiority which they asserted in arts, refinements, wealth, and education" (*History* 151). Having only lived in America for a short period many of them had not developed local attachments stronger than their ties to the mother country. And they certainly felt little loyalty to the haughty lowcountry Carolinians whom Simms's narrative places in the lead of the revolutionary movement.

In the backcountry also were large Scottish and German communities which provided many Loyalists. National differences among immigrants were compounded by the fact that they tended to settle mainly in close-knit communities, maintaining their language and customs and having little intercourse with outsiders. Simms wrote, "Here, in one place, were Scotch, loyal, intense in their loyalty, and stubborn in their prejudices." In another were Irish, "more eager, enthusiastic, impulsive, somewhat reckless, and never remarkable for their loyalty to the English dominion." In other places were German, Swiss, and French Huguenot settlements. The Germans were often loyal to the Hanoverian monarch on Britain's throne; many of them having been convinced by Loyalists that rebellion meant the forfeiture of their royal grants of land. The French, like the Irish, were relatively quick to amalgamate and held little sympathy for England (*History* 142–43, 183).

The antipathy of the colonists in the interior for the coastal leaders in rebellion furnished another reason for loyalty and disharmony. In fact, backcountry farmers often viewed the lowcountry planters in much the same way that American Whigs viewed the governing aristocrats in London. If America was the periphery to London's metropolitan center, then the South Carolina backcountry could with equal justice be regarded as the periphery to the metropolitan center in Charlestown. Seeking supporters of the crown in the backcountry, Loyalist leaders successfully appealed to the "natural jealousies" and "prejudices" of poorer settlers "against rank and wealth, the haughty assumptions of the citizens and planters of the seaboard, and their free expenditure of the public money." Whig complaints against virtual representation or taxation without representation did not resonate among interior settlers. They had the same complaint against the lowcountry: "The upper settlements had been little considered by the popular leaders, in the whole progress of the revolutionary proceedings; had been, until a recent period, unrepresented in their congresses and public meetings; and, but few efforts had been made to conciliate the more talented and influential of their leading men." Neglect of their interests, and fear that cavalier rebel leaders intended to dragoon them and their sons into service, earned the Whigs many bitter enemies who had not already embraced loyalty out of affection for the crown (*History* 179–80, 182).

Yet opinion in the lowcountry was also fiercely divided. In the early stages of the Revolution, a large portion of the mercantile community attempted to remain aloof out of concern that an active engagement in politics might be bad for business—"trade being always reluctant to peril capital upon the caprices of politics." Nevertheless, when eventually forced to choose sides, "they showed themselves in their true colors, as bigoted loyalists, hostile to all popular proceedings, a danger in the very heart of the commonwealth" (*History* 151).

Despite his description of certain loyal merchants as "bigoted," Simms's treatment of the Loyalists is relatively more charitable than that offered by many of his contemporaries. In his assessment, the Loyalists were wrong and stood in the way of progress. Generally, they failed to see the full picture, and sometimes this was because they were blinded by their own selfish interests, as in the case of the aforementioned merchants. Other times, however, loyalty sprang from pure convictions. As has already been shown, many colonists were reluctant to sever ties with Britain by virtue of having not long lived in South Carolina or because they were more afraid of a potentially tyrannical power in Charlestown than in London. Others simply did not feel oppressed and therefore found the arguments for independence unconvincing. After all, "South Carolina had, indeed, been a favorite plantation of the crown, and the reluctance of thousands to sever the friendly bands which had linked them together, was not less honorable to their principles, than natural to their affections" (*History* 181).

Simms's analysis of the divisions within South Carolina closely follows that of David Ramsay, one of the first historians of the Revolution, and has been confirmed by later historians as well. Ramsay wrote that "Country religion, local policy, as well as private views, operated in disposing the inhabitants to take different sides" (*American* 625).[5] The Irish generally favored independence. The Scotch were disposed to loyalty, as were backcountry settlers.

There were strong arguments in favor of loyalty and, as far as Simms was concerned, adherence to one's convictions did not make one a villain. He did not doubt that "many of the loyalists were persons of little principle . . . but, that the people who were subsequently degraded, under the general and opprobrious term of 'tories,' were, in many instances, moved only by an honest and loyal, if not a wise and just sense of duty." They may have been less far-sighted than their adversaries, but if their loyalty was based on honest motives the Loyalists were no less respectable (*History* 181).

Not only were the Loyalists, as described by Simms, not necessarily men with black hearts, they also did not necessarily have feeble minds. In fact, "the loyalists possessed numerous citizens of talents and real worth, who might have been conciliated, at least, to acquiesce in the movement which they might yet refuse to lead" (*History* 180). That they were not conciliated was due to the imprudence and indiscretion of patriot leaders. Unfortunately for South Carolina, individuals of both parties were guilty of indiscretions which made the conflict between them all the more harsh. Consequently, "the gulf through which they had to wade, to sympathy and union in the end, was one that dyed their garments in blood, the stains of which, to this day, are scarcely obliterated" (*History* 182).

Because South Carolina's heterogeneous population was so sharply divided within her borders, the Revolution more closely resembled a civil war than a war against a foreign foe. She "became one vast and bloody battlefield, in which nearly all of her sons contended," Simms wrote. "Unhappily," the citizens of South Carolina "too often contended with one another; and it is with a sentiment of profoundest melancholy that we record the fact, that the direst issues that ever took place within her borders . . . were those in which her own sons were pitted against each other." This war was especially savage, with both sides guilty of atrocities, and, moreover, it was utterly unlike anything experienced in the northern colonies (*History* 297–98, 216).

This sort of warfare, in a sparsely settled country, was particularly suited to the operation of small bands of guerrillas. In one of those fortuitous catastrophes that sometimes occur in war, South Carolina's defense was left to her militia after the capture of Charlestown and the defeat of the Continental Army under General Gates at Camden in 1780. Ill-equipped, badly outnumbered, and with the British and their Loyalist allies in possession of the most important posts, the militia fought a partisan war against their enemy.

Simms attributed much of the militia's success to their habit of serving under leaders of their own choosing, who like the citizen-soldiers they commanded were natives of South Carolina, knowing intimately her land and people. Local partisan leaders such as Marion, Sumter, and Pickens met with greater success than generals Lincoln and Gates, who held national commissions, partly because they had "a better knowledge of the temper, character, and interests of those whom they would lead, and a proper knowledge of the soil, the situation and circumstances of the country which they undertook to defend." Therefore, they were better able to adapt their tactics to their circumstances than were either national or British commanders. Lacking local knowledge, "commanders, otherwise brave and skilful [*sic*], have led thousands of gallant men to defeat, whom a better judgement [*sic*] and a native genius might have led to victory" (*History* 224).

For Simms, South Carolina's greatest partisan leader was Francis Marion. He boldly yet cautiously led his little band of men through the swamps and forests, tirelessly harassing his foe, only giving battle when it was advantageous. By these means he succeeded in disrupting British communications and supplies, forced the dispersal of British forces over the countryside, cheered independence-minded Carolinians, and extorted from the enemy "a bloody toll at every passage through swamp, thicket, or river." Marion was so successful, Simms argued, because, through his familiarity with his native state and her citizens, he employed tactics which were "peculiarly adapted to the peculiarities in Carolina, and consequently to the genius of her people" (*History* 267). Given adequate supplies and a suitable leader, like Marion, South Carolina's militia showed itself a match for the best drilled European regulars (*History* 256–57, 325).

With both the worsening sectional conflict and the young readers for whom he wrote *The History of South Carolina* undoubtedly in mind, Simms closed the 1860 edition by noting that South Carolina had never lacked men like Marion, equal to the challenge of leading her through any trial. "We have every reason to hope and believe," he confidently wrote, "that she will never be deficient in the men who are to wield her power, assert and maintain her arguments, and defend her rights" (*History* 436–37). Simms believed South Carolina's citizens had always been one of her greatest resources, and he thought this would continue to be true.

Yet, with more than a hint of foreboding he listed in the 1860 edition those leaders his state had recently lost:

> It is with a mournful pride that we refer to the great names, in recent periods, which she has possessed and lost. [John C.] Calhoun, [George] McDuffie, [Langdon] Cheves, [Robert Y.] Hayne, [James] Hamilton [Jr.], [Thomas] Cooper, [William] Drayton, [Hugh Swinton] Legaré, [Thomas S.] Grimké, [Stephen] Elliot[t]—these are names of men equal to all the exigencies of a

> people, and capable of conferring fame upon any annals. They are gone! and South Carolina stands upon the threshold of a new era, and, we trust in God, a yet superior progress! Let us hope that each season shall produce its proper men. (*History* 437)

It is interesting to note here that Simms had once looked forward to Calhoun's passing, thinking that the void he left would be filled by younger men of equal, if not greater, abilities. Indeed, many of the men he listed at one time or another, most notably during the nullification crisis, were counted among Simms's political opponents. Nevertheless, he believed the talent and character possessed by these men, who inherited a tradition of patriotism and public service passed down through the Pinckneys, Rutledges, and Gadsdens, as well as Moultrie, Marion, Sumter, Laurens, and Pickens, proved the worth of studying history and "that the example of the past has not been chronicled in vain" (*History* [1840] 318). Perhaps one day, Simms seemed to suggest, some of his young readers' names could be added to the list. With an eye on the worsening sectional controversies, he hoped to inspire his readers' patriotism in anticipation of a renewed independence movement.

The History of South Carolina sold well and received favorable reviews in the press. A justly proud Simms wrote to James Lawson on 27 July 1840, "My History of South Carolina is published & promises to be very popular. I will send you a copy. The newspapers speak in flattering language, & individuals of worth, here & there do me honor in referring to it. The prospect is strong that it will answer the purpose for which it was designed, and become a school book throughout the state; in which event I shall probably have no reason to regard my labor as unproductive" (*Letters* 1: 179–80). According to a reviewer in the *Southern Quarterly Review*, "Dr. Simms' History of South-Carolina, is pronounced, by competent judges, the best history of the State, in a narrow compass, that has hitherto been published." This reviewer believed that Simms would "do the State more service" by his *History* and *Geography of South Carolina* "than by all the novels—and they are not a few—that he has written." He recommended Simms's *History* and *Geography* not only to South Carolinians, but also as an example to authors who might undertake to write school histories of their own states: "We commend them to critics, historians and teachers, for a candid judgment, and—on our own responsibility—we commend them to authors in other States, who are interested in the cause of education, as unexceptionable models for similar works, to be prepared by themselves; and to parents in South-Carolina, generally, we commend them as worthy of patronage," he wrote ("History" 249). *DeBow's Review* praised the revised history as a "work of industrious research and sterling merit" (Heriott 658). The public and critical reception appeared poised to fulfill Simms's hopes for the volume.

Much to Simms's disappointment, *The History of South Carolina* was not adopted by the legislature for use in schools. This is not to say, however, that he was dissatisfied with his work, only with the legislature's failure to adopt it. As he told William Porcher Miles, he believed it was as "necessary to the public man, as to the pupil" (*Letters* 4: 186–87). Certainly he would be satisfied to know that in 1917, long after his death, his granddaughter Mrs. Mary C. Simms Oliphant heavily revised the book and, in this form, won its adoption for use in the state's public schools. *The New Simms History of South Carolina* went through multiple printings and editions, and remained in use by schools into the latter twentieth century. Thus, indirectly, Simms's work helped several generations of South Carolina schoolchildren learn their state's history.[6]

NOTES

1. See Busick, *Sober*.
2. Unless otherwise noted, all citations are to the 1860 edition of *The History of South Carolina*.
3. For the history and organization of American natural history writing, see Regis.
4. It is worthy of note that Simms's description of South Carolina's road to independence in the *History of South Carolina* does not differ substantially from the summary of the Revolution written over 100 years later by George C. Rogers, Jr. (*Chronology* 30).
5. See also Weir.
6. Differing definitions of precisely what a "public" school is make satisfactory numbers difficult to come by, but according to one estimate there were 746 "public" schools serving 9,061 students in South Carolina in 1826, and 757 schools serving 20,716 students in 1860. (Wallace 460, 464).

The Kentucky Tragedy Romances

Charlemont; or, The Pride of the Village and *Beauchampe; or, The Kentucky Tragedy*

TODD HAGSTETTE

Towards the end of his retelling of a notorious real-life murder trial in early nineteenth-century Kentucky, William Gilmore Simms offered a kind of deconstruction of literary homicide: "A murder in a novel, though of very common occurrence, is usually a matter of a thousand very thrilling minutiæ. In the hands of a score of our modern romancers, it is surprising what capital they make of it!" (*Beauchampe* [1856] 335). Of course, few made more capital out of the details of death and mayhem than Simms himself. Nowhere is this more apparent than in his expansive story of the Beauchamp-Sharp trial, popularly known as the Kentucky Tragedy.

Simms's original work on this sensational topic was published in 1842 as a two-volume novel titled *Beauchampe; or, the Kentucky Tragedy. A Tale of Passion*. Later, in 1856, Simms edited and expanded the work into two separately-titled novels. The first he called *Charlemont; or, the Pride of the Village. A Tale of Kentucky* and the second retained the title *Beauchampe*. In the aftermath of these revised editions, the relationship between the 1842 title and the 1856 books was misunderstood by some critics. *Charlemont* was not a sequel to *Beauchampe* (1842), as many assumed, but a slightly expanded revision of the first volume of the earlier work, with the 1856 version of *Beauchampe* an expanded revision of the second volume of the 1842 novel. This confusion, which originated in some of the 1856 reviews of the revised novels, was perpetuated egregiously by Simms's first biographer, William P. Trent in 1892 (118, 211), and lasted at least through the 1960s, when critics like Leslie Fiedler and Leonard Roberts repeated the mistake (Fiedler 219; Roberts 15).

To have this kind of misunderstanding in the publication history is perhaps fitting, though, for a set of novels so invested in misperception as a narrative device. Dramatic irony abounds as most of the major characters move around geographically, spend time in separate but blindly interconnected social spheres, and operate for at least part of the narrative under pseudonyms. As a result, the characters' endemic and inaccurate assumptions about each other and their world build steadily to the tragic conclusion of the story. Simms also imbued his story with a measure of moral complexity that is admirable considering his desire to structure his tale around definitive judgments of right and wrong. Though his antagonist is practically unredeemable, Simms nonetheless assures us that "no first villainy is ever entirely deliberate" and goes to pains to show the slow progress of that character's slide into evil (*Charlemont* 86). While the story's heroine is victimized and ruined, she orchestrates the tragic revenge under which so many will fall and is largely guilty of her own undoing. As Simms notes, by simply holding a "mirror before the eyes of her vanity" the villain conquered his young quarry. Most intriguing, the hero of the story, though ruled by honor and motivated by justice, is corrupted by his very virtues. Indeed, Simms aptly summarizes the conflicted atmosphere of his novels when he remarks that his is a "moral story . . . though our hero is not exactly so" (*Charlemont* 87).

The ambiguity that Simms interjected into the Kentucky Tragedy story is based not only on his own authorial viewpoint but also on an attempt to render his novels with the verisimilitude befitting their real-world origins. Late in the text of *Charlemont*, Simms offers a fourth-wall breaking excuse for the upcoming disappearance from the narrative of one of the heretofore primary characters. He tells his readers that "this story being drawn from veritable life, will lack some of that compactness and close fitness of parts which make our novels too much resemble the course of a common law case" (290). Regardless of how one judges the veracity of this claim—whether plot irregularities in the novels are indeed due to Simms's fidelity to the actual events of the story or whether the author merely cloaked narrative foibles in the guise of historical authenticity—any evaluation of *Charlemont* and *Beauchampe* must begin with an understanding of the historical murder trial on which the books are based.

The Kentucky Tragedy in History and Fiction

Early on the morning of 7 November 1825, in the town of Frankfort, Kentucky, a young lawyer named Jereboam O. Beauchamp crept to the home of the state attorney general, Solomon P. Sharp, and stabbed him to death in the vestibule of his house. The murder was orchestrated to avenge the honor of Anna Cook,[1] Beauchamp's wife, who, as a single woman living in a frontier Kentucky town, had been seduced, impregnated, and abandoned by Sharp.[2] By some accounts, Sharp attempted to deny his paternity with claims that the child was a mulatto. A savaged and shamed Cook agreed to marry her new young suitor, Beauchamp, with the condition that he avenge her lost honor. When Beauchamp failed to draw Sharp into a duel, the preferred method for an honor killing, he took the more nefarious route of assassination. The murder of Sharp was a national sensation immediately following its discovery and Beauchamp's capture days later. In prison, Cook and Beauchamp attempted a joint suicide, with first laudanum and then a knife, but botched both efforts. The former died of her stab wounds and the latter was marched, bleeding, to his execution on 7 July 1826. The events of the seduction, murder, trial, and punishment have since entered the realm of legend and come to be referred to as the "Kentucky Tragedy."

The resonance this story has had in the American imagination is due primarily to the sensationalism it displays. In one narrative, many competing binaries intersect to dramatize cultural concerns of the southern region and the nation as a whole. Here was a true story of the tragic yoking of sexual desire and death. It demonstrated the fatal consequences of both adhering too closely to and discounting the tenets of honor. It brought into sharp relief the cultural distinctions between city and town, between the settled interior and the still-wild frontier of nineteenth-century America. The story touched on such explosive issues as seduction, suicide, dueling, murder, racism, and the potential lethality of scorned womanhood. It was, in short, a real-life pot-boiler.

As such, the Kentucky Tragedy has inspired a spate of literary treatments from its own time to the present. Many of these treatments have been aided by the historical Beauchamp's own *Confession*, which narrated the events of his crime and capture with epic splendor. In his rendition, Beauchamp was a tragic hero, who had acted on principle, if technically against the law. His vengeance was enacted on behalf of all people everywhere who deserve justice. Casting himself as a martyr to the cause of virtue and honor, Beauchamp confessed,

> I die for pursuing, what the dictates of my clearest and most deliberate judgment had determined it was, at least justifiable in me to do, if not my duty to do: and for which, no guilty pang of conscience, has ever yet reproved me, or, the certain prospect of death, made me feel the least regret. And if my death, teaches a respect for the laws of my country, my example will be not less serviceable, in teaching a respect for those laws of honor, to revenge the violation and outrage of which, I so freely die. (3)

This characterization of the seducer as villain and the killer as hero colored the impression of the story in many of the narratives that emerged to retell this larger-than-life tale. In addition to Simms, writers such as Thomas Holley Chivers (*Conrad and Eudora; or, the Death of Alonzo*, 1834), Charles Fenno Hoffman (*Greyslaer: a Romance of the Mohawk*, 1840), Edgar Allan Poe (*Politian*, 1835), John Savage (*Sybil: a Tragedy in Five Acts*, 1865), and Robert Penn Warren (*World Enough and Time*, 1950) have all penned works based on these events.

Though these accounts of the same story vary in setting, details of characterization, and tone, they all, to some degree, merge into a central interpretation that exonerates the Beauchamp character and vilifies the Sharp figure. A narrative problem consequent to this interpretation arises in the characterization of Anna Cook. Seduction implies aggressive masculinity taking advantage of female passivity; yet, the vengeance of the Kentucky Tragedy is orchestrated by a highly proactive Cook. Additionally, if Cook appears too bloodthirsty, Beauchamp's heroism becomes eclipsed by a tacit romantic victimhood; he seems too much like Cook's pawn. Writers are thus tasked with realistically and sympathetically rendering a character of fatally ambiguous motives. In a 1989 essay for the *Southern Literary Journal*, William Goldhurst detailed the assorted methods that the nineteenth-century writers of the story employed to negotiate the pitfalls of Cook's character (*Sybil* is excluded from his analysis). These efforts are executed with varying levels of success. It is a fine line to walk in treating a lynchpin character.

Simms's own adaptation of the story succeeds where other interpretations fall short largely due to his portrayal of the female lead. Goldhurst calls Simms's version of the character the "most interesting, fleshed-out depiction of Ann Cook" (123). In fact, Simms biographer John Caldwell Guilds finds the author's characterization of his female lead to be the strong point of both novels. That Simms's Cooke[3] will not passively accept her degraded lot in life is a "bold statement of women's rights" for the time of the novels' composition. Simms was, thus, "surprisingly progressive in his view toward women" (Guilds, *Literary Life* 221). His protest on behalf of women was not merely in reaction to the extreme circumstances of seduction, though. He also "extended sympathy to the intellectually ambitious woman who chafed over social restrictions" (Watson, *Nationlism* 40). His female lead is troubled by the lack of educational opportunities in her frontier village home. Simms repeatedly portrayed the subtle animosity of the townsfolk to Cooke's passion for books, and it is this estrangement from her neighbors that makes the young woman susceptible to her seducer's citified charms. According to Fiedler, Simms's 1842 novel was "the first protest in our literature against woman's refusal in life to act out the humble, long-suffering part" that American culture assigned her (221). Simms, then, overcame the problem of Cook's characterization simply by making his heroine a complex and round character. He transformed what were formerly her paradoxes into conflicts and competing situational analyses. His Cooke reads like a real woman confronting complicated emotions in extreme circumstances.

Simms's take on the Kentucky Tragedy is also noteworthy for its contextualization of the story through the lens of the author's Border Romance series. As such, the conflict between Cook and Sharp is metonymic of the greater conflict between the residents of the nineteenth-century American borderlands and the citizens of the cities to the east. Like the rest of the author's border tales, these novels are also characterized by what J.V. Ridgely calls the "dark emotions and sentimentalism" of Simms's artistic vision in this venue (*William* 87). Truly, there are moments of real darkness in the plots and conflicted emotion in many of the novels' characters. Few instances in antebellum American literature are as grim and nihilistic as the ending portions of *Charlemont* in which the heroine looks at her newborn baby and, seeing in its visage the face of her seducer, feels a kind of surrogate hatred surge up in her breast. But Simms was also interested here in the cost of redemption, especially as a product of the nation's honor culture; Cooke's need for revenge, weighed against her growing love for her new husband, forms the major emotional conflict of the second novel.

Charlemont opens in the eponymous village, where Warham Sharpe catches a glimpse of village beauty Margaret Cooper as he passes through on business. Finding her "tall, erect, majestic—beautiful after no ordinary standard of beauty" and especially being struck by her haughty demeanor, Sharpe concludes that here is "just such a spirit as I should like to tame" (28–29). He resolves on his return trip to tarry in the village long enough to work his seduction. Margaret for her part is loved by her noble yet provincial neighbor, William Hinkley, but she is too proud of her intellect, artistry, and appearance to return his affections. A short time later, Sharpe returns to the village under the pseudonym Alfred Stevens. He masquerades as an apprentice journeyman preacher in order to ingratiate himself into the town and takes up board at the home of the Hinkley family. As Sharpe/Stevens begins the slow process of wearing down Margaret's sexual defenses through appeals to her vanity, Hinkley becomes increasingly suspicious of the interloper and eventually challenges him to a duel. This alienates the young man from his father, as it violates the southern guest-host custom. Subsequently exiled by his father, Hinkley leaves with his adopted, surrogate father, his former schoolmaster, Mr. Calvert. Sharpe's seduction complete, he returns to Frankfort leaving Margaret abandoned and ready to give birth. Disgraced and dispirited, Margaret swears vengeance on her seducer and, following the untimely death of her infant offspring, wanders from her village home in search of anonymity. So, by the novel's end, all of the major characters depart Charlemont and, as we later learn, the village is left in ruins.

Beauchampe picks up the action of the story five years after the conclusion of *Charlemont*. A new character, Orville Beauchampe, takes center-stage, and all the major characters from the first book have new names[4] and locales: Margaret Cooper in her bid for obscurity has changed her name to Anna Cooke and moved to an unnamed village outside Frankfort, which turns out to be close to the Beauchampe family home; Hinkley, who has adopted the name of his mentor and is now known as William Calvert, is a prominent lawyer and traveling political stump speaker; and the man known only as Alfred Stevens to the people of Charlemont, has returned to his real name of Warham Sharpe, residing in Frankfort, and operating as the chief political rival to Calvert.[5] Because of this widespread pseudonymity, none of the characters is at first aware of how intertwined their circles have become.

Beauchampe is a protégée of Sharpe's who, during a return trip to his family home, comes across Anna Cooke practicing with a pistol in the woods nearby and begins to court her. Anna rebuffs the infatuated advances of her young suitor at first but ultimately submits to marriage on the condition that Beauchampe find and kill "Alfred Stevens" (who unbeknownst to both is actually Sharpe). A brief period of marital happiness follows in which Anna's love for her new husband replaces the immediate sting of her desire for revenge. Their bliss comes to an end, however, upon Sharpe's arrival. Though Anna attempts to quietly eject her former seducer from her home in order to prevent Beauchampe from fulfilling his oath to kill the man, Sharpe's efforts to re-engage her sexually forces Anna to reveal the villain's identity to her husband. Unwilling to violate the guest-host custom, Beauchampe allows Sharpe to flee. The murder occurs offstage shortly thereafter when Beauchampe is unable to cajole his antagonist into a duel, in order to slay him honorably. Calvert re-enters the scene to defend Beauchampe at his trial, but he is unable to exonerate his defendant. Anna visits Beauchampe in prison and, following a botched joint suicide attempt, dies as her wounded husband is driven, fainting, to the gallows. Revealing his authorial inclination to view Beauchamp as a martyr, which makes him likeminded with other authors of the Kentucky Tragedy story, Simms has his hero revive momentarily on his way to his execution. Seeing the women of Frankfort looking on from the windows of the surrounding houses, the doomed man shouts out his triumphant last words: "Daughters of Kentucky! you, at least, will bless the name of Beauchampe!—"

Textual History

As early as a 16 August 1841 letter to James Lawson and following closely on the heels of his Gothic domestic novel *Confession*, Simms had a draft of the novel that would become *Beauchampe* underway. Even at that time, he had the work planned as an anonymous publication to be "one of the 'Hurdis' series," that is, a Border Romance (*Letters* 1: 267). It was Simms's custom at the time to publish all of his border series works without definitive authorial attribution. This was supposedly to bemuse the critics, with whom Simms often had a dicey relationship. In a 29 January 1842 letter, Simms informed James Henry Hammond that he published all of his border works anonymously "with some design to try an experiment upon the critics." He went on to assure his friend that these designs had "effected their purpose" and had afforded Simms and his "friends an ample opportunity of laughing at the wide-mouthed of that miserable pack [of critics]" (*Letters* 1: 299). During the summer of that year, in a letter to Benjamin F. Perry, Simms was even more sardonic about his relationship with his reviewers. The purpose of his anonymous authorship of *Beauchampe*, he claimed, was partly for "the bedevilment of the small tribe of underling critics, who are sagacious enough to detect a man's style in his sneeze, and his talent in a whisper." He reflected to Perry, "You perhaps are not aware that in my birthplace even to this day, nothing is more common, than to contrast the works of the author of Beauchampe, Rd. Hurdis &c, with my own greatly to my disparagement. My friends who have been in the secret have been chuckling for three years at the sagacious twittings" (*Letters* 1: 316). According to Guilds, though, in the case of *Beauchampe* at least, "the ruse misled few" (*Literary Life* 164).

How much of the novel had been written by August 1841 is uncertain, but as of September 10 of that year, Simms was already feeling pressure to complete it. He deferred a planned trip to New York at that time, telling Lawson, "I am to finish 'Beauchampe' before I can depart and this may take me until the 1st. or 10th. October. I am very much behind hand" (*Letters* 1: 277). His haste perhaps affected the quality of the product. In the same letter, he declared, "I write 15 to 20 pages per diem—write like steam, recklessly, perhaps thoughtlessly—can give you no idea of the work. Scarcely have any myself" (278). A little over a month later, Simms's anxieties obviously continued, as he lamented about *Beauchampe*, I have been "writing myself half blind & not done yet. It will be the most voluminous of my books" (*Letters* 1: 282). Ultimately published as a two-volume novel in the spring of 1842, its great size led to Simms's decision to split it into two separate works in the 1856 Redfield edition. This was necessitated further by the fact that Simms edited and expanded the story for the new format. Simms had made the decision to revise his 1842 novel by 21 February 1855, when he announced his intention to do so to Lawson (*Letters* 3: 366); less than one week later, he had apparently already completed the revisions to *Charlemont* and sent them off to Redfield (*Letters* 3: 368). By this time, he also had confirmed his intention to split the original novel into two separate publications. *Charlemont* was published around 1 March 1856, and *Beauchampe* was issued about the 22nd of the same month (*Letters* 3: 366n).

Both the 1842 two-volume *Beauchampe* and the double-titled expansion of the story are dedicated to the "Hon. James Hall of Cincinnati." In the 1856 edition, however, the dedication is only printed in *Charlemont* (where both books are mentioned in the dedicatory note). In the two cases, Simms inscribed his story to Hall "as one of the ablest of our literary pioneers; a genuine representative of the great West; whose writings equally illustrate her history and genius." Simms clearly revealed Hall's regional affiliation as the chief reason for his dedication. Throughout the mid-nineteenth century Hall penned several collections of short stories, a travel narrative, and a novel; he also edited various newspapers and a literary magazine, all detailing life in the American West. *The Dictionary of Midwestern Literature* notes that Hall "played a pivotal role in the construction" of the West, and specifically the Ohio River Valley (of which much of Kentucky is a part) "for Eastern audiences"; Hall's portraits, in both fiction and travel writing, represent the frontier as a "place of breathtaking beauty, unbelievable fertility, and relentless violence" (Noe 234). One of Simms's primary ambitions in *Charlemont-Beauchampe* was to represent faithfully the character of frontier peoples and life. For him, the story of the Kentucky Tragedy contained the epic potentials for both the beauty and violence of this region of the country that Hall so faithfully chronicled in his own work.

With that goal in mind, Simms began both 1856 novels with an "Advertisement" in which he declared, quite insistently, that his rendering of this well-known story was historically accurate. He noted that readers of his books might "find or fancy some occasional differences of fact and inference, date, place, and period" between his account and previous narratives of the Kentucky Tragedy; but, in the case of such discrepancies, his account could be safely regarded as "the only genuine article" (*Beauchampe* 7). His telling of the tale, after all, "has been very carefully prepared from and according to the evidence," and though penning a work of fiction, the author "seldom appealed to invention" in its creation (*Charlemont* 7). Notwithstanding these assertions, Simms certainly took some liberties with the Kentucky Tragedy story. While *Beauchampe* may employ most of the known details of the actual event, much else of the work comes from the author's imagination, and *Charlemont* is almost entirely fictional.

More central than the specifics of the historical story to this proclaimed authenticity is Simms's portrait of the American frontier people generally. Simms claimed that all his border novels, including *Charlemont* and *Beauchampe*, were "distinguished by great activity of plot, vehement & passionate personality, and pictures & sketches of border character & border scenery, in which [he] claim[ed] to be equally true & natural. There are running through all these works, a strong penchant to moral and mental analysis" (*Letters* 2: 225). His perspective on the Beauchamp-Sharp story was informed, in part, by the disparity between the frontier village and the settled city, especially in the development of their citizens. The isolation and lack of wealth that defined most frontier settlements of the early nineteenth century caused the denizens to treat strangers with less suspicion than was the case in larger towns. Because they lack the "resources of superior wealth, population, and civilization, the frontier people are naturally required to throw the doors open as widely as possible, in order to obtain that intercourse with their fellows which is, perhaps, the first great craving of humanity." Therefore, they are less discriminate than they should be in their admissions, so that a "specious outside, agreeable manners, cleverness and good humor, will soon make their way into confidence, without requiring other guarantees for the moral of the stranger" (*Charlemont* 8). Within the context of Simms's Kentucky Tragedy novels, the female residents of these remote places were especially susceptible to the potential harms of this blithely practiced guest-host custom.

The illustrations that decorate both 1856 texts attest to the emphasis on feminine sexual entrapment in Simms's view of the story. The four illustrations, two per novel, are all the work of Redfield artist F.O.C. Darley and all engraved by Whitney & Jocelyn. All of the images feature Cooke's courters, and all but one feature the woman herself. For Simms, the story hinged on amorous desire, in its honorable and dishonorable practice, and the ways its resultant problems were exacerbated on the borders. His female lead's imperilment, rescue, and fatal salvation are all orchestrated through the romantic or sexual drives of the men who desire her. Calvert fittingly pines romantically for Cooke, without the object of his affection appearing in the scene; Sharpe, as both voyeur and aggressor, seems to violate Cooke in two of the images; and interestingly, Beauchampe is depicted as a dashing, romantic hero in the only illustration that shows Cooke in a proactive romantic role, her kissing of Beauchampe's hand in his prison cellar following the murder. Darley's etching echoes Simms's own validation of Beauchampe's action, contextualized as an expression of love revenge.

Criticism and Interpretations

Upon its initial publication in 1842, *Beauchampe* received mostly positive reviews. Many of these came from the author's friends and literary compatriots or were published in periodicals generally favorable to his past works. Regardless, some of these early notices featured passages that glowed in admiration. The most flattering of these was the May 1842 review that appeared in *Godey's Lady's Book* and was likely written by its editor, Sarah J. Hale. She noted that the "fearful history" of the Kentucky Tragedy had now been skillfully composed "into a form which will give it a permanent place in the national literature." The review lauded, "The subject could not possibly have fallen into abler hands. All its capabilities have been seized with a firm grasp, combined into a beautiful and imposing picture, and placed before the beholder, with the skill of a first rate artist, and the feelings of a stern moralist" (288). In that same month, the *Greenville Mountaineer* printed a review penned by Simms's friend Benjamin F. Perry. Perry called *Beauchampe* a novel of "surprising and wonderful ability," which contains "a power, a depth of thought, a delineation of character and a thrilling interest, which are rarely equaled and never surpassed" (qtd. in Butterworth and Kibler 54). Edgar Allan Poe, reviewing the novel for *Graham's* that same month, called Simms "one among the best of our native novelists—pure, bold, vigorous, original." Being familiar with the story of the Kentucky Tragedy from his own poetic efforts in *Politian* seven years earlier, Poe noted that "no more romantic tragedy did ever the brain of poet conceive," and in Simms's novel "the theme is skillfully handled" (Rev. of *Beauchampe* 300). Three and a half years later, in a review in the *Broadway Journal* for Simms's 1845 collection *The Wigwam and the Cabin*, Poe listed *Beauchampe* as one of the author's "best fictions" (qtd. in *Letters* 2: 106n).

Despite these statements of high regard, most of the early reviews of the book featured an odd mix of praise for the novelist's genius with reproof of the novel's flaws. A sense of uncertainty undergirds most of the otherwise positive reviews. Poe claimed that he was "not sure that the author" had "done right in the selection of his theme" as "[t]oo little has been left for invention" (Rev. of *Beauchampe* 300). Perry complained that the prose was too drawn-out, with too much dialogue at times; he also felt that Simms's depiction of the murder scene was "obnoxious" (qtd. in Butterworth and Kibler 54). An anonymous review in the ordinarily sympathetic *Charleston Mercury* parroted reports that supposedly came from unnamed reviews in New York and Boston that found two major faults with the novel. One echoed Perry in opining that the book lacks "condensation, that the author sometimes gleans tediously after his own mowing"; the southern reviewer agreed, noting that this was "a fault that we found with its predecessor the 'Border Beagles.'" "The second blemish," the northern reviewers levied was that the plot was altogether "too horrible, too little relieved, tragic beyond the reach of sympathy" (Rev. of "Beauchampe" 2). Of course, the southern writer for the *Mercury* assured the paper's readers, "All the critics agree that in spite of its faults, the story is one of deep interest" (Rev. of "Beauchampe" 2). Any claims about uniformity of critical opinion, though, must by necessity make much out of little, as the 1842 novel actually received very few notices of any kind, a fact that in itself is revealing.

The problems that critics identified with the 1842 text were possibly the result of the novel's hasty composition. When Simms revised and expanded his book into two separately-published novels in 1856, he enjoyed the leisure to craft his story more deliberately and carefully. As a result, the reviews of the time were more uniform in their praise and seemed to imply that the "two-novel sequence represents a significant improvement over the 1842 two-volume novel" (Guilds, *Literary Life* 221). The 9 April 1856 edition of the *New York Evening Post* contained reviews of both *Charlemont* and *Beauchampe*, noting that the former "is worked up with the author's usual skill, and the materials used in its composition imparts a realness to many scenes which is not a common characteristic of works of fiction." Of the 1856 *Beauchampe*, it notes that the "dénouement is powerfully described, and might seem to transcend the limits of probability but that the main incidents are authenticated beyond doubt" (qtd. in Butterworth and Kibler 104). Two publications that had reviewed the 1842 novel updated their assessments with new insights into the 1856 double-novel work: *Graham's* followed its Poe review of the earlier edition with an anonymous notice of the 1856 books that declared them an "exciting story written in Mr. Simms' best style of narration and characterization" (Rev. of *Charlemont* 467); the "Literary Notices" of the June edition of *Godey's Lady's Book* called them "two of the most effective novels of an American author whose distinguished merits are now universally acknowledged" (563).

The longest and most-admiring of the later reviews was from Simms's friend and protégé Paul Hamilton Hayne, writing for the June 1857 *Russell's Magazine*. Among his detailed discussion of the strengths of the novels, Hayne singled out for praise Simms's handling of the "delicate ground" of some of the more potentially salacious and gratuitous moments of the narrative. He boasted of his friend, "Not one writer in a hundred could have managed the succeeding scenes, without either violating the proprieties, or veiling his descriptions with some sort of vapory conventional feebleness, mysterious and unsatisfactory. But the true artist rises with the difficulties of his subject" (254).

In the twentieth century, the novels fared more poorly, though recent critics have begun to find merit in them again. The reviews from the first half of the century were perhaps unduly influenced by Trent, who panned the novels.

Though the biographer misunderstood the relationship between the two books, he was unequivocal is his derision of both, calling *Beauchampe* "repulsive and uncalled-for" (123) and *Charlemont* "a romance which should never have been begun" (211). In an article for *American Literature* in 1960, scholar W.B. Gates offered a compendium of reviews from the first half of the twentieth century. Leading lights of literary criticism from this period, such as Carl Van Doren, Vernon Louis Parrington, and Arthur H. Quinn, were all cited. Gates noted that all shared Trent's basic animosity for Simms's Kentucky Tragedy novels (159). The reputation of the novels was dealt another serious blow by J.V. Ridgely, writing two years after the appearance of the Gates essay in the Twayne United States Author Series. Capping a scathing assessment of the works, Ridgely declared that Simms's treatment of the Sharp-Beauchamp story "fails simply as a story" (*William* 87).

Others of the mid-century period were more measured in their evaluation. Alexander Cowie, for one, though finding the works "lacking in restraint and crude in artistry," nonetheless believed they contained a "good deal of power" and exhibited "the most sustained emotional tension" of any of the author's novels" (236). This trend of finding value in the novels continued to rise throughout the second half of the twentieth century, culminating in several serious studies of the works in the 1980s and '90s, including Guilds's own endorsement in his 1992 biography of Simms. Guilds praised the "swift-moving narrative" of the story and found a particular strength of the books to be Simms's "multidimensional portrayal of the self-centered village beauty, Margaret Cooper," who is one of the chief protagonists of both novels (*Literary Life* 221, 164). More recently, historian Dickson D. Bruce, in his 2006 book-length study of the events of the novel, named Simms's *Beauchampe* (1842) the nation's "most significant antebellum treatment" of the Kentucky Tragedy story (66).

The historical account of the Sharp slaying hinges on notions of American honor, which explains the reason that an otherwise unexceptional murder case would so invigorate the artistic imagination of a writer like Simms. When Sharp dishonored Anna Cook in her Kentucky village, he put himself on a collision course with frontier justice, which was ultimately personified in Beauchamp. For his part, Beauchamp's downfall resulted from his decision to pursue retribution even outside the bounds of honorable acceptability. Cook herself manipulated the fates of both her transgressor and her avenger through her understanding of the southern honor code. This context informs the larger cultural memory of the story and undergirds Simms's retelling. According to Charles S. Watson, the Kentucky of Simms's fiction is an "embryonic society on the frontier, which finds its model in the chivalric ideal" (*Nationalism* 38–40). While this dynamic is exacerbated in the small village of Charlemont, it is also prevalent in the comparatively large city of Frankfort. The heroic ethos of the borders thus geographically and culturally unites the action of Simms's two novels.

The chivalric ideal also draws together Simms's two defenders of his heroine; its opposite impugns his antagonist. Beauchampe was a man of "high, manly bearing, and honorable purpose" (*Beauchampe* 79), and Calvert similarly is a man of "high bearing, ... courteous defiance, ... [and] superior consciousness of strength and character" (*Charlemont* 261). Conversely, Sharpe is a "man of loose principles," whose dishonorable behavior begins in his seduction of Cooke and ends when he refuses Beauchampe's attempt to duel him for retribution (*Beauchampe* 161). The latter act elicits the aghast objection from Beauchampe's second, "Colonel Sharpe—this will never do! You are a Kentuckian! You are regarded as a Kentucky gentleman!" (*Beauchampe* 308). The assumption has proven to be false.

Yet, interestingly, it is Sharpe who draws out the chivalric ideal in his opponents, even as he himself disregards it. In defending Cooke's honor, the highest calling of the noble southern gentleman, both Beauchampe and Calvert achieve a kind of honorable apotheosis. As he faces Calvert in a pending duel over Cooke shortly after the affair has come to light, Sharpe marvels at the "singular and imposing change which a day, almost an hour, had wrought in the looks and bearing of the young rustic." In fact, even a "choice military school, for years, could scarcely have brought about a more decided expression of that subdued heroism, which makes mere manliness a matter of chivalry" as Calvert's defense of Cooke had done (*Charlemont* 261). Later, Beauchampe too is transformed by his love for Cooke and the posture as defender of injured womanhood that he will eventually adopt: "From the rough, sturdy, confident rustic ... at a single bound he became a gentleman" (*Beauchampe* 117). For Simms, the honor of the gentleman is incubated on the frontier in the simplicity and direct goodness of the so-called "rustic," but it takes an act of attempted violence, one committed for noble purposes, to bring him to his full form. The tragedy and majesty of Beauchampe is that his honorable purpose must turn to a kind of fanaticism as it bumps against the fundamentally unprincipled Sharpe. The avenger ironically is forced to sacrifice his honorable practice in order to fulfill his honorable ideal. Calvert, as Simms's only entirely fictional major character, stands as the knight errant who, though achieving less glory than his historical kindred spirit, nonetheless comports himself as an unflagging gentleman.[6]

Even though Calvert keeps his honor unblemished, Beauchampe is Simms's hero. His sacrifice, despite its taint of dishonor, makes Beauchampe a martyr to a higher cause than merely his wife's spoiled virtue. Cooke lauds her imprisoned husband in the story's final chapters, crying "you have not been my champion merely, you are the champion of my sex. The blow which your arm has struck, was a blow in behalf of every unprotected female, of every poor orphan—fatherless, brotherless, and undefended—who otherwise would be the prey of the ruffian and the betrayer" (*Beauchampe* 346). Ultimately, for Simms, this is the meaning of the Kentucky Tragedy story. Beauchampe made of himself a champion for the disenfranchised women of the nation, especially those in the lightly populated and largely un-policed border regions. The hero saw in his disgraced wife not just the misfortunes of one person, but the failure of a culture to adequately protect and uplift sacred womanhood in its most vulnerable context. The aggressions that the frontier could not forestall were antithetical to the very progress the frontier represented. Beauchampe fought not just for victimized femininity or southern honor, but for the undefended American. His tragedy is that the burgeoning nation, at its edges, killed him for it. Thus, Simms drew out the momentous consequences of what would otherwise be a simple tale of murder and seduction. In *Charlemont* and *Beauchampe*, the Kentucky Tragedy became an epic of America itself.

NOTES

1. No consistent version of the names exists in the historical record; she is most often referred to in the way we do here, but is also called Anne Cook, Ann Cook, and Anna Cooke (this latter is Simms's character's name).
2. Sharp denied the paternity.
3. Simms adds an "e" to the last names of all of his historical characters: Cook becomes Cooke, Sharp becomes Sharpe, and Beauchamp becomes Beauchampe.
4. In the interest of simplicity and as a default position, I will refer to all characters by the name they adopt in *Beauchampe* unless the specific context of the discussion calls for the other.
5. Though he does not harp on the details explicitly, Simms is obviously referencing the Old Court—New Court Controversy of 1820s Kentucky as the political backdrop of his novel. Sharp was a leader of the New Court group, and his murder by Beauchamp was rumored by some to have been politically motivated. The characters casually refer to Desha in their political dialogue, which is highly suggestive of Joseph Desha, the New Court governor of Kentucky from 1824–1828. In the context of the novel, the fictional character of William Calvert (Hinkley in *Charlemont*) is apparently an Old Court advocate. See Bruce.
6. For this reason, some critics, like Charmaine Allmon Mosby, find Calvert to be the key figure in the story. Others, such as Marietta Patrick, though acknowledging Calvert's significance, do not accept him as the ideal cavalier hero and an alternate to Beauchampe.

Library of American Books

Views and Reviews, First & Second Series and *The Wigwam and the Cabin*

DAVID MOLTKE-HANSEN

It was a testament: William Gilmore Simms had two works in Wiley and Putnam's Library of American Books. That was more than most of the contributors to what, in the judgment of some literary scholars, is "the most important series of original works of American literature ever published" (Greenspan, "Evert" 678). Started in February 1845, the Library continued to issue titles for nearly three years. Simms's friend Evert Augustus Duyckinck had proposed and would edit the series. It was he who negotiated Simms's contribution to the Library of both a collection of short fiction, *The Wigwam and the Cabin*, and a collection of criticism, *Views and Reviews in American Literature, History and Fiction*. As Simms had been trying to market a short story collection without success for several years, he quickly had it ready. He also was able to edit his criticism promptly, using off prints as a basis. Each title appeared in the Library's typical, two-volume format, issued in paper for fifty cents per volume.

Like Simms, many of the authors included were affiliated in a loose network of writers and politicians. By mid-1845 the group had come to be styled "Young America," after Young Italy and similar European movements. Edgar Allan Poe, Nathaniel Hawthorne, and Herman Melville since have become among the best known members, having been elevated to canonical status before the Second World War. Yet, aside from the indefatigable and persistent Duyckinck and his frequent collaborator, William A. Jones, none did more to promote Young America's cultural agenda than did Simms. At the time, he was better known than, not only fellow southerner Poe, but also Hawthorne and Melville. Those two facts together made him a particular target as well as a partisan in the cultural wars centered in New York, but raging from Charleston to Boston in the decade following the Panic of 1837.

Those wars pitted the Democratic nationalists of Young America against the culturally conservative, cosmopolitan, religiously orthodox, and Whiggish group known by one of its principal journals, *The Knickerbocker* (subtitled *New York Monthly Magazine*). This cultural arbiter first appeared in 1833. Shortly thereafter Lewis Gaylord Clark became editor and remained so for more than a quarter of a century. Early in Clark's tenure, Simms, although an ardent Jacksonian, was a contributor, and his works received favorable reviews. Yet by 1838, Clark started issuing disparaging critiques of Simms's new books, and "the alienation" of the two "became final in 1839" (P. Miller 105). Two years later, Clark attacked a series of articles, in the *Magnolia*, in which Simms argued "vigorously for a national literature on native subjects." In part, he was responding to Simms's contention there that Knickerbocker Washington Irving was not "truly an American writer" because of the English caste of his work (Holman, Introduction xxiv). Within months, Simms took over editorship of the *Magnolia* to carry forward the war and to earn money in the face of the lingering consequences for the book market of the recent financial panic, one of the worst in the nation's history.

His new position pitted Simms even more directly against Clark but also put him in the company and on the side of several of Clark's enemies. Clark's ire had been building since the 1837 founding of John O'Sullivan and Samuel D. Langtree's *United States Magazine and Democratic Review*. It was bad enough that Langtree, O'Sullivan's brother-in-law and a fellow Irish immigrant, had founded *The Knickerbocker*. Worse, their new monthly was Democratic in its politics and nationalist in its cultural agenda. In its first issue, the *Review* called for "a new literature which would be filled with the 'animating spirit' of our democracy" (Stafford 60). Clark also turned on Cornelius Mathews and Evert Duyckinck, the editors, from 1840 to 1842, of the literary journal *Arcturus*, whose cultural agenda reflected the same nationalist and Democratic orientation. Battle lines drawn, between 1844 and 1846 Duyckinck served as cultural editor of the *Democratic Review*.

Views and Reviews

In contributing volumes to the Library of American Books, Simms was intent on demonstrating and analyzing what Alexander B. Meek of Alabama had called *Americanism in Literature*—this in *An Oration before the Phi Kappa and Demosthenean Societies of the University of Georgia, at Athens, August 8, 1844*. Simms's review of the oration appeared in January 1845 in the *Southern and Western Magazine* that he had just started and was editing in Charleston. With the addition of two long notes and other revisions, it became the lead piece in the first series of *Views and Reviews* (1–19). Perry Miller contended that Duyckinck particularly wanted to give this essay a wider audience, as it so well articulated the Young America cultural agenda. Miller added: "This was doing what Poe called carrying the war into Africa" (155).

Duyckinck may have been eager, but the publishers were slow. Both series, or volumes, of *Views and Reviews* have the publication date 1845, and "the first . . . was ready and the second under way by October" of that year (Holman, Introduction xxviii). On 19 November 1845, the *Broadway Journal* announced a November publication, and, then, on 4 December, a December one. Yet, to

Simms's frustration, the volume was still not out by February 1846 (*Letters* 2: 142). Indeed, it did not appear until the first of May. Two months later, the second series still had not gone to press.

Duyckinck told Simms that the publishers had decided not to go forward. While lamenting that Wiley and Putnam showed "so little disposition ... to bring [the volume] properly to the view of the public," Simms insisted that his contract be honored, and the compromise quickly reached was to make a smaller collection (*Letters* 2: 170). Even after this decision, it was July 1847 before the second series was issued. Not included in the end were a number of essays that Simms had indicated, in the "Advertisement" to the first volume, would be part of the work. While he did have pieces in the two volumes drawn from the *Southern Quarterly Review*, the *Southern and Western Magazine*, the *Magnolia*, and the *American Quarterly Review*, he did not include the pieces he had planned from the *Knickerbocker*, the *American Monthly Magazine*, the *Orion*, and "other publications of like character."

Even in delayed and truncated form, the two volumes of critical essays drew the fire of the cultural warriors. Simms's lead piece was only part of the provocation. After it there followed the substance of orations that he first gave before the Georgia Historical Society in Savannah in 1842 and, in revised form, later also included in six installments in the 1845 *Southern and Western Magazine*. In its last iteration, in *Views and Reviews*, the merged piece, nearly a hundred pages long in print, considered "History for the Purposes of Art." The leading question it asked was: what were "The Epochs and Events of American History ... Suited to the Purposes of Art in Fiction?" (*Views* 1: 20–101).

Simms used the rest of the essays in the two series to further explore the question. Two pieces in the first volume considered archetypal historical figures—Daniel Boone and Hernando Cortes. One treated the other successful American writer of historical fiction—James Fenimore Cooper. One considered "Literature and Art among the American Aborigines." The second series widened the focus. There were other essays on historical subjects suitable to writers on America—for instance, "The American Sagas of the Northmen" and "The Case of Major Andre," the British officer hanged as a spy during the Revolution, after he was caught assisting the American traitor Benedict Arnold. There also was a piece on another principal shaper of America's historical consciousness—Parson Weems, whose biography of Francis Marion Simms had just supplanted with his own, enormously popular treatment of the "Swamp Fox" of Revolutionary War fame (S. Smith, "Imagining").

Together with those pieces, however, were essays that broadened the idea of Americanism in literature to other aspects of Americans' cultural heritage—humor and domestic life. What, for instance, Simms wondered, were the peculiar, arresting, and distinguishing features of American humor, in contrast with British, assuming one could accuse the British of humor? To this end, he examined writings of fellow Young American Cornelius Mathews, editor of *Yankee Doodle*, and others. He also used a review of an English woman's acerbic account of travels in America, Frances (Fanny) Trollope's *Domestic Manners of the Americans*, to answer a caustic critique of American manners and learning. American books, Simms retorted, were appearing at an accelerating rate and were improving as the country developed. For all America's deep history, he continued, much of the country still was undergoing birth pangs. Yet, at the same time, America did not produce England's poverty and emiseration. Consequently, it was a much healthier society with a much brighter future in letters as well as life.

The Knickerbocker was savage in its review, taking the opportunity to denigrate both Mathews and Simms. Harvard College's Eliot Professor of Greek Literature, Cornelius Felton, attacked not just Simms, but the whole Library of American Books, in a review essay in the October 1846 issue of *North American Review*, the Boston ally of *The Knickerbocker*. According to Felton, *Views and Reviews* "breathe[d] an extravagant nationality, equally at war with good taste and generous progress in liberal culture" (376). In Britain, *Blackwood's* concurred, judging that "in every page" Simms "has quite liberated himself from all those fetters and prejudices which, in Europe, go under the name of truth and common sense" ("American Library" 576).

Even fellow Young American Nathaniel Hawthorne worried that "the themes suggested by [Simms], viewed as he views them, would produce nothing but historical novels, cast in the same worn mould that has been in use these thirty years"—that is, since Scott began publishing his historical fiction in 1814 and James Fenimore Cooper followed suite in the '20s. In Hawthorne's judgment, issued in the 2 May 1846 *Salem Advertiser*, it was "time to break up *and* fling away" those old molds. Hawthorne was making the recurrent case for literature's advance through change. Many in *The Knickerbocker* circle instead were arguing for the perduring qualities of fine literature, touting the polish, elegance, and wit they found in such English contemporaries as William Hazlitt, Thomas DeQuincey, and Charles Lamb (P. Miller 29). Simms, too, thought that art was what endured—*ars longa*—and he much admired DeQuincey, especially, but he preferred passionate narrative to lapidary observation (Simms, "Tuckerman's"). He also advocated for and pursued literary change—for instance, being a much earlier proponent of English and German Romanticism than such celebrated later champions as Ralph Waldo Emerson (Kibler, *Poetry* 5–36; Brennan, *Holy Craft*). Scholars argue, too, that, in his fiction of the 1850s, he was one of America's first social realists (Wimsatt, "Realism"; Bakker, "Frontier").

Yet, in *Views and Review* Simms was making a different point about literature. Yes, he was promoting the subjects and approaches that had been his, and James Fenimore Cooper's, bread and butter. The intent, however, was less to argue for continued employment of an outdated form of fiction than to assert the broad social and cultural functions of literature. His case was that of National Romanticism: "The moral objects of the poet and the historian," he insisted, "concern not the individual so much as the race," or ethnic group, whose members are the basis of a nation (*Views* 1: 30). Consequently, "the true and most valuable inspiration of the poet will be found either in the illustration of the national history, or in the development of the national characteristics" (*Views* 1: 40).

The rationale for this approach, Simms insisted, transcends politics and literary fashion, because, at its best, literature does. It does so by not only expressing the ideals and aspirations of a culture, but by making the time-bound transcendent. Thus, "to write *from* a people, is to *write* a people—to make them live—to endow them with a life and a name—to preserve them with a history forever" (*Views* 1: 6). Hawthorne was not writing historical romances such as those by Cooper and Simms, but he too exemplified the commitment to making his native place's historical and cultural, as well as geographic, location and nature central in his fiction.

The Wigwam and the Cabin

Simms did not write the stories he included in *The Wigwam and the Cabin* primarily to illustrate this commitment. Yet, published in earlier forms in multiple venues for varied readerships over nearly two decades, the tales did. Simms made the point in his dedicatory letter to his father-in-law in the 1856 Redfield issue: "One word for the material of these legends. It is local, sectional—and to be *national* in literature, one must needs be *sectional*. No one mind can fully or fairly illustrate the characteristics of any great country; and he who shall depict *one section* faithfully, has made his proper and sufficient contribution to the great work of *national* illustration" (4).

"Generally considered his best collection of short fiction" among the six published in his lifetime, *The Wigwam and the Cabin* was not what Simms first proposed to Duyckinck (Wimsatt, *Major* 145; Wimsatt, Introduction 4). Simms conceived of a collection of "Tales of the South" in 1843, when he asked his New York friend and literary agent James Lawson to offer it to Harper and Brothers (*Letters* 1: 353–54). Simms continued to revise his concept of what to include and, when Harper proved uninterested, took out two tales that became separate volumes, both published by Stringer: *Castle Dismal; or, The Bachelor's Christmas. A Domestic Legend* (1844) and *Helen Halsey; or, The Swamp State of Conelachita. A Tale of the Borders* (1845). Yet Stringer, too, proved not sufficiently interested in the short story collection. So it was that Simms turned to Duyckinck in March 1845 to see if there might be interest at Wiley and Putnam's (*Letters* 2: 43–44).

Keen to include his friend and ally in his new series, Duyckinck quickly got approval to offer contracts both for a short story collection and for a collection of criticism (*Letters* 2: 108). "During Simms's visit to New York in August 1845, author and editor . . . were able to work out the final details of publication," perhaps with the help of Lawson (Guilds, *Wigwam* xviii). By then, Simms had concluded that he really had two collections of stories in view, one set on the frontier and in the backwoods and the other set in the plantation South. The former, he decided in 1844, might be called *The Wigwam and the Cabin*; the latter he still called "Tales of the South" when first proffering it to Duyckinck. In the end, however, it was the first that the two men agreed on. One can only speculate, but it may well be that the frontier and backwoods focus better fit the ideological orientation and purposes of the Wiley and Putnam series: the frontier and backwoods were a common American experience and legacy, while the plantation was largely a regional phenomenon.

The Wigwam and the Cabin was one of three important collections of American short stories issued in rapid sequence by Wiley and Putnam in their Library. Poe's *Tales*, selected by Duyckinck, appeared in 1845, and Hawthorne's *Mosses from an Old Manse* a year later. All of these writers wrote short fiction through most of their careers, but, even though Simms, and to a lesser degree Hawthorne, derived much of their contemporary reputations instead from long-form fiction, there were multiple reasons for them to join Poe in writing tales that could be published in periodicals.

As Simms told a friend in 1841, "you will perceive that Irving now writes almost wholly for magazines and Cooper & myself are almost the only ones whose novels are printed" (*Letters* 1: 271). "After publishing four novels between 1840 and 1842, Simms reluctantly bowed to the effects of the recession [and] quit writing long fiction until the early 1850s" (Wimsatt, Introduction 9). Yet he continued producing books through the decade of the '40s at an astonishing rate—in all "twenty-nine . . . , among them eight volumes of poetry" in addition to the four volumes of stories and criticism in Wiley and Putnam's Library, four biographies, a history, a geography, and several orations (Wimsatt, Introduction 9). The one novel that appeared at mid-decade, *Count Julian; or, The Last Days of the Goth. A Historical Romance* (1845), did so as the result of an accident: Simms "had written the first five of its six books during 1836 and 1837," but these were lost, perhaps when the ship carrying them went down, and it was only upon their recovery, after their being washed up on shore, that he finished the work and saw it through the press (Wimsatt, *Major* 145; Guilds, *Literary Life* 393n).

The short story was growing in appeal to writers and readers for other reasons. The market was not just constricting, but changing. Periodicals were increasing in number, distribution, and importance. Between 1790 and 1840, there was over a thirteen-fold *per capita* growth in newspapers circulated by the U.S. Postal Service. In 1840 thirty-nine million copies went through the mails (John 4). Magazines added to that total at an accelerating rate and published even more stories per issue. Increasingly, therefore, novelists, like Charles Dickens, were turning to serial publication, as, more and more, would Simms. One reason is that the writer thus reached a larger audience. Novels often were published in initial runs of just 2,000 copies. Many newspapers had larger circulation, and even the literary monthlies had runs of 4,000 copies. The weeklies often reached many more—by the eve of the Civil War, 200,000 in the case of *Harper's Illustrated Weekly*, the most widely circulated.[1] Periodicals had other advantages as well. In their case, payment to authors ideally was up front and not dependent on sales volume, as were royalties on book sales.

The effect of periodical publication varied according to genre. Committed to so many words or columns or pages per issue, novelists wrote expansively—indeed, were often prolix. Short story writers rather had to compress their material. As Simms explained, when negotiating with a magazine editor after the Civil War: "Stories, complete in each issue, are . . . the most difficult of all compositions to write" (*Letters* 5: 77). They do not allow development of character and, therefore, require a plethora of incidents to carry forward the narrative. At the same time, the public prefers them to serialized novels, because one does not need to wait for later issues to learn what the outcome will be.

The tight constraints of periodical publication on short fiction did not pertain to book publication. For that Simms needed to plump up his short stories. This was to fill the standard two-volume format. Consequently, stories that had been relatively compressed in earlier, periodical iterations, sometimes sprawled in their final form in *The Wigwam and the Cabin* (Wimsatt, Introduction 10). To cite one example, in its original 1828 version, the "Indian Sketch" that became "Oakatibbe" was a short, seven-page periodical piece. "Later revised as 'The Choctaw Criminal,' in *The Book of My Lady* (Philadelphia: Key and Biddle, 1833)," it roughly doubled in length for inclusion in this gift book (Guilds, "Commentary" 387). Revised further as "Oakatibbe, or the Choctaw Sampson; an Indian Sketch" for publication in the November and December 1841 issues of the new *Family Companion*, it grew again. By the time it appeared in *The Wigwam and the Cabin*, it filled more than four times as many pages as in the original version.

Despite the expansive revision of numerous stories, the first volume of *The Wigwam and the Cabin* earned warm attention upon its publication in October 1845, four months before the release of the second series in February 1846. Apparently advance copies went quickly to the New York media. Famously, Edgar Allan Poe, whose *Tales* had issued from Wiley and Putnam just months earlier, lavished praise—not usually his habit. This was in the 4 October 1845 *Broadway Journal*, which he was editing at the time. Noting that "in a recent number of our journal we spoke of Mr. Simms as 'the best novelist which this country has, upon the whole, produced,'" he declared Simms's story collection "one of the most interesting of the Library [of American Books] yet published—and decidedly the most American of the American books." Poe continued: "in invention, in vigor, in movement, in the power of exciting interest, and in the artistical management of his themes, [Simms] has surpassed, we think, any of his countrymen" (Rev. of *Wigwam* 190).

Many others praised as well what the *New York Evening Mirror* of 29 September 1845 called "Simms'[s] Tales of the wild West, stories of daring adventure, stormy passions, dark deeds, and startling fortunes" (Rev. of *Wigwam*). In England, the December 1845 issue of the *New Monthly Magazine* judged that "the life of the planter, the squatter, the Indian, and the Negro, of the bold and hardy pioneer, and of the vigorous yeoman are given with a truthfulness that leaves the namby-pamby imitations, extolled as Cooper-like in this country, far, far in the background" (Rev. of *Wigwam*). Although the Valentine's day 1846 number of the *New York Mirror* thought Simms's tales better than his novels (Rev. of *Wigwam* 304), *The Harbinger*, exactly a month later, denigrated them as "what the Germans call bread-writing,—mere matters of trade, 'done to order on short notice'" (Rev. of *Wigwam* 218). In the same reviews that savaged *Views and Reviews*, the *Knickerbocker* and the *North American Review* heaped scorn as well on *The Wigwam and the Cabin* (Butterworth and Kibler 65–76).

Simms's short stories nevertheless contribute significantly to the author's modern reputation as a writer. John Caldwell Guilds, his literary biographer, contended that the stories in *The Wigwam and the Cabin* "represent . . . Simms at his very best," bearing "in part, in combination, or in entirety the earmarks of Simms's best writing: descriptive power; narrative skill; vernacular style; comic realism; controlled use of folklore and the supernatural" (*Literary Life* 170; *Wigwam* xxiii). Mary Ann Wimsatt has edited a collection of Simms's short fiction, taken from three of the story collections published during his lifetime—this under the title he once had thought to use: *Tales of the South*. Her belief is that these dozen stories are "Simms's best body of writing" (Introduction 4). Among them are five from *The Wigwam and the Cabin* and several, even more highly regarded pieces written after—for instance, "Ephraim Bartlett" (1852) and "How Sharp Snaffles Got His Capital and Wife" (1870). The weighting of the selections shows the centrality of *The Wigwam and the Cabin*, not just to Wimsatt, but to late twentieth-century and early twenty-first-century critics more generally. Of the works Simms saw through the press, *Wigwam* remains the best entry point to his short fiction.

While some critics give preference to Simms's realistic romances, *Woodcraft* and *The Cassique of Kiawah*, those who emphasize the short fiction insist that it is more accessible and engaging to contemporary readers. There are several reasons. Many in the computer age find the historical romance tradition and two-volume novels difficult to take. Then, too, Simms strikes many as better at rendering gripping and telling incidents than at exploring and developing character. Often, especially in his earlier novels, he used stereotypes common to the Romance genre to frame the natures and relationships of his principal (if not always his minor) characters. Those conventions, whether in the hands of Sir Walter Scott or Simms, his chief American disciple, no longer seem natural or appropriate to modern readers. The vividness of many of the protagonists in Simms's short stories (and also his gothic novels) make those characters much less alien, even in the face of their racism and sexism, so offensive to many in a post-modernist age. Finally, when working within the constraints of the short story or novella form, Simms often managed his narrative elements and movement with more economy and better control than is typical in his historical romances.

Which of the thirteen stories in *The Wigwam and the Cabin* have garnered the most attention? In Simms's own day, Poe and others pointed to the opening tale, "Grayling; or, 'Murder Will Out,'" as the "best ghost-story of modern times" as revised from its initial 1841 publication (Butterworth and Kibler 69–76). Like Simms's first novel, *Martin Faber; The Story of a Criminal*, published in 1833, it drew on the gothic tradition, in which Poe thought Simms excelled. Yet, Guilds concluded, "there are other, more skillfully handled tales of the supernatural in the collection"—especially several that "center upon the portrayal of Indian character or tradition," such as "The Arm-Chair of Tustenuggee," "a light-hearted tale with sinister undercurrents" (Guilds, *Wigwam* xxiii; Wimsatt, Introduction 12).

Not all of the Indian tales have supernatural elements. Also first published in 1841, "Caloya; or, the Loves of the Driver" was, in Guilds's view, "Simms's most controversial story," treating, as it does, "the attempted seduction of a young Catawba [Indian] wife by a lustful black driver on a South Carolina plantation" ("Commentary" 393–94). Simms's reply to early attacks on the story was to assert that the "'modes of life, passions, pursuits, capacities and interests of all,' including blacks and Indians, 'are as legitimately the objects of the analyst, as those of the best bred people at the fashionable end of London '" (qtd. in Guilds, "Commentary" 394–95). As Guilds noted, "of growing interest to today's reader . . . is the implicit comparison of black and red culture" that emerges both from the story's development and from the debate between Mingo, the driver, and Richard Knuckles, Caloya's husband ("Commentary" 395) That debate is about the kinds, limits, and meanings of freedom available to slaves, Indians, and other marginalized people. The intervention of the planter patriarch near the end of the story reasserts Simms's paternalistic assumptions and ideology as foundational to the South.

"The longest story in *The Wigwam and the Cabin*, 'Caloya; or, the Loves of the Driver' is not so well-structured, well-organized, or well-written," Guilds judged, "as, say, 'The Two Camps,' 'Jocassee,' or 'Lucas de Ayllon,' but it is a powerful tale, not only in its daring and audacious theme, but in the characterization of its chief characters" ("Commentary" 396). In his view, "perhaps the most artistically satisfying tale in the whole impressive collection . . . is 'The Two Camps,' in which Simms achieve[d] unity of tone and effect by employing a single vessel of consciousness whose credibility the reader never questions" (Guilds, *Wigwam* xxiii). "Contrasting with this humorous story, " Wimsatt said, is "'Oakatibbe,' a serious realistic narrative about the economic and social experiments" that led to the employment of Choctaw Indians to pick cotton alongside slaves (Introduction 12).

These, and other, stories illustrate Simms's remarkable commitment to exploring the South's non-English roots and peoples, as well as the life of the frontier. Charles Hudson contended that "Simms had experiences with Indians unmatched by any other man of letters of his time" (xxxviii); Guilds went further: Simms "wrote more about, thought more about, and almost certainly knew (and cared) more about the American Indian than any other man of letters of the nineteenth century" ("Literary View" xxix). This conclusion ignores writings by Native Americans. Moreover, because "Indian removal [from east of the Mississippi] was so important to the emerging expression of Southern political power and intellectual culture, as well as to the perpetuation of the Southern economic system," Laura Mielke argues, "Simms revise[d] the sentimental impulse of antebellum literature, embracing at the outset not the equalizing impulse of common emotion but the inequality created in the act of sympathy" (51, 53).

Conclusion

Despite the inclusion of *The Wigwam and the Cabin* and *Views and Reviews* in the Library of American Books, Simms's Young America days were ending by the summer of 1847. In the spring of that year, Simms complained to Duyckinck, no friend of slavery, that he could not bring his wife and children north with him on his annual summer visit, because "we have a colored nurse," and therefore, "your vexatious abolitionists forbid that we should cross the Potomac" (*Letters* 2: 291). Under this anti-slavery pressure, he told his friend James Henry Hammond, former governor of South Carolina, the people in Charleston were "restive" and "might be revolutionized" (*Letters* 2: 291). Then, in July—the same month that saw final publication of the second series of *Views and Reviews*—Simms wrote Hammond again to say "that dissolution of the Union is inevitable" (*Letters* 2: 332). From that time forward, Simms, the erstwhile American nationalist, would advocate as a southern nationalist.

This shift was of emphasis, not principle. Simms still wrote as a Romantic nationalist, still explored the diverse roots of the South emerging in his own day, and still sought to foster the self-consciousness and self-expression of his people, who were developing, he judged, as a distinct culture and society out of their historic divisions (Moltke-Hansen, "Horizons"). The program was ethnogenesis—the literary development of a people and a nation whose destiny was not yet, but in a beckoning future. Simms shared the agenda with Sir Walter Scott and, for a time Young America, but not with the twentieth-century critics who canonized Poe, Hawthorne, and Melville and relegated him as "a man of minor importance in terms of the intrinsic value today of his voluminous works," in Hugh Holman's words, but "of major importance in terms of the degree to which he embodied the attitudes and formalized the assumptions of a region" ("Status" 181). If that judgment is being overturned, it is because of the increasing inclination to read Simms together with, rather than apart from, his contemporaries writing in the North. When *The Wigwam and the Cabin* is considered alongside Poe's *Tales* and Hawthorne's *Mosses from an Old Manse*, one can see the different currents shaping emerging American fiction at the period when the American short story finally came of age in the Library of American Books. *Views and Reviews* provides critical perspective on those currents.

NOTE

1. See Scott E. Casper *et al.*, *The Industrial Book, 1840–1880*. Vol. 3 of *A History of the Book in America*. Chapel Hill: U of North Carolina P, 2007. 224–69, esp. 234; Frank Luther Mott, *A History of American Magazines, 1741–1850*. Cambridge: Harvard UP, 1938; and Mott, *A History of American Magazines, 1850–1865*. Cambridge: Harvard UP, 1966.

The Life of Captain John Smith. The Founder of Virginia

CAREY M. ROBERTS

Often portrayed as a sectionalist, a fire-eater, and an intractable defender of southern slavery, William Gilmore Simms held fame in his own day throughout the United States as a writer of historical fiction and prose. Much of his influence came through historical romance. He wrote volumes on colonial America, several more on the Revolutionary era, and tried his hand at virtually every English genre written in the nineteenth century: poetry, drama, humor, short stories, realism, and even detective capers. While popular as a writer of fiction, Simms also gained credibility as an historian, particularly as the writer of essays and biographies. Indeed, Simms's fictional writings may be slowly creeping back into the lexicon of American literature thanks to the efforts of scholarly attention. Yet considerably more attention should be given to Simms the historian in light of the pioneering efforts of historians Sean R. Busick, David Moltke-Hansen, and Jeffery J. Rogers. For modern readers with an interest in American origins and the antebellum understanding of the nation's colonial period, Simms's biography *The Life of Captain John Smith. The Founder of Virginia* is a fitting point of entry.

Simms's importance as an historian rests in how he directed American attention to its own history—away from the ancient world and even further away from relatively recent English history. Indeed, Simms caused Americans to take their own history seriously, understand it in imaginative ways, and ponder the importance of history in both building a nation and tolerating its cultural—and historical—divides. Building upon the works of a number of local historians, biographers, and collections of private papers, Simms taught Americans first, that it was appropriate and selfless to remember their own history and second, that studying the past enriches human happiness beyond merely providing moral examples. For Simms, history could be equally instructive and entertaining, a thought that occurred to few of his contemporaries.

Among early American historians, few equaled Simms in his acumen, attention to detail, dedication to historical documents and oral histories, historical essays, public lectures, and political treatises. Simms may not have produced a magnum opus like George Bancroft's *History of the United States* or a work so endearing as Francis Parkman's *Oregon Trail*. But he shaped the study of American history in countless, tiny ways, by providing works of rugged pioneers, dutiful soldiers, and inspiring heroes. He described his romantic settings with the literary flare of a novelist combined with the details of an historian. Always true to his sources, Simms exercised restraint from entertaining flourishes without smothering his readers in meaningless descriptions. To paraphrase Samuel Clemens's appraisal of James Fennimore Cooper, Simms well knew there was no need to tell his readers about every twig snapping under foot. While he was not alone in popularizing history, Simms played a critical role, if not the most important role, for antebellum Americans.

One key reason, perhaps the most important, for Simms to write his biography of Captain John Smith revolved around the scarcity of Smith's original autobiography. As a mercenary and explorer, John Smith offered no value to Simms's generation. But as the founder of the cradle of America and what was still one of the country's most populous and important states, John Smith held no equal. Furthermore, Smith was not merely the founder of Virginia: after he saved the settlement then abruptly left Jamestown, Smith sailed north to explore new territory. It was Smith who coined the name "New England" to describe the rugged shore of the northern coastline. In many ways, John Smith was the founder of all America, a man of singular importance who saved English colonization in the New World and paved the way for hundreds of thousands of colonists. This is how Simms would characterize the man in his biography.

At one time, learned colonial Americans read Smith's tale, but such was not the case for the Revolutionary generation and that of Simms. Uncovering what time nearly erased was no easy task in the mid-nineteenth century. As with his work on Francis Marion, Simms usually relied upon primary sources rather than popular myths. But in this case, rather than carrying around trunks of personal papers—as he did with other well-known Revolutionary era figures—Simms relied upon what primary sources remained, notably, Smith's rare autobiography.

Simms's biography closely followed Smith's own autobiographical account. At one level, Simms's account did little more than embellish the more charming episodes that Smith himself recounted some two centuries earlier. Simms can be faulted for too closely following Smith's account. No doubt Smith's stories about himself are of dubious authenticity—composed to engineer a legend of himself—rather than offer strictly factual reportage. Simms knew this but still traced Smith from his earliest youth through countless tales of adventure around Europe, Turkey, and North America. He emphasized Smith's own self-described heroic activities, whether fighting American Indians—the "forest monarchs of America"—or exploring the coastline of North America. Details are plentiful in Simms's account, and his attention to such details reflected the well-hewn eye of a master storyteller combined with the care of a trained researcher. He provided personal commentary from the Captain, then interspersed it with Simms's own analysis and reasoning. The commentary itself made *Captain John Smith* a brilliant work of both history and literature. Indeed, the book reads almost like a script for a modern video documentary with Smith's first-hand accounts serving as a formal interview and Simms's narration answering anticipated questions from the "viewer."

At a deeper level, Simms clearly understood Smith's story to be a compelling link between the emerging local history of early nineteenth-century America and a new, national history that Simms hoped to master. In doing so, Simms stumbled upon an incredible, intellectual connection. Scholars have noted the struggle between a pattern of local history writing in post-Revolutionary America and those who wrote national histories strictly from a local perspective. That is to say, early national histories, especially those created in New England, were nothing more than local histories writ large. In time, antebellum historians wrote lengthy, national histories, but pinpointing the leap between local history and genuine national history often eluded even the most serious students of the period. Simms may offer the missing link with his biographies: personal history was the key. Going from the local to the national without the baggage of local prejudice or the chauvinism of viewing one's local community as the epitome of the nation challenged many nineteenth-century historians. Simms, incidentally, is often lumped into such a group. But it was not Simms the historian who realized that biographies of great individuals could be appreciated both for their local characters and stories as well as for their meaning for larger, national audiences.

Simms confronted the problem of uncovering the unknown and remembering the nearly lost. Diligent research might reveal unknown characters and events, but these had meaning primarily as measures of local history. Early Americans had limited scholarly and institutional abilities to transition those things to the country as a whole. But if they could remember in a different way something once known across a wide spectrum of the populace, then a true national history could be told. In effect, Simms the historian practiced the same art as Simms the literary figure. As he wrote in his introduction to the 1856 edition of his short story collection, *The Wigwam and the Cabin*, "to be national in literature, one must needs be sectional" (4). That is, popular figures most important for their local accomplishments—the "founders" of Virginia, for example—contributed to the larger development of the American nation. Honest biography served that purpose; local history did not. Neither did the rising hagiography of national figures such as Mason "Parson" Weems's stories of a young George Washington. Equally unimpressive to Simms were the myriad local histories of New England towns written as if they were microcosms of the nation as a whole.

Not surprising, Simms's publication of *Captain John Smith* connected well with his publication of *The Life of Francis Marion*. In both cases, Simms retraced the steps of pivotal, but under-appreciated, characters in American history. In the language of today's historians, Simms brought attention to not only what was forgotten, but also to what was publicly unknown. Both Smith and Marion were soldiers, together they played indispensable roles in founding America at key stages of its development, and both quickly became the subjects of popular legend. Smith, the "Founder of Jamestown," and Marion, "the Swamp Fox," enjoyed widespread name recognition. But key differences remained, which Simms seemingly wished to correct. Marion became more than a household name in South Carolina; cities and counties were named after him. Indeed, Simms's own father was privy to some of Marion's popularity, as the elder Simms moved to Mississippi and lived in "Marion County," where he eventually died and was buried. John Smith enjoyed little initial popularity, admittedly because he spent scant time in Virginia, leaving behind a soon-to-be starving colony to explore the northern banks of the Atlantic. In fact, without the publication of his popular autobiography, Smith may have been remembered, if at all, as just another adventuresome buccaneer. As Simms remarked when describing Smith's death, "He probably died in obscurity, for none of the facts attending his demise remain to us" (373). While much remained unknown about Smith, much more simply needed to be remembered, as Simms knew.

Such was Simms's task, and it remains the task of all serious historians. They must do more than retell old tales, or chronicle extraordinary events like journalists. This mandate required Simms to convey a compelling story without further fictionalizing Smith's already larger-than-life legend. Here Simms belayed his commitment to solid history by turning to Smith's autobiography, which served as his only principle source. To be sure, Simms deliberately followed a different strategy with Smith than that which he took with Marion. With Marion, the Chevalier Bayard, and even his edited biography of Nathanael Greene, Simms remained dedicated to revealing what nobody knew, thanks largely to the treasure trove of personal correspondence and firsthand accounts he collected about these men.

But why did he refrain from taking a similar tack with Smith? The simple answer may be the best, which is that personal documents of the Captain were beyond Simms's reach on the other side of the Atlantic. Still, he could have written a forward for a reprinted edition of the original autobiography, commemorated a great hero, and quickly cashed in on the popularity of his Marion biography. And, indeed, Simms may have regretted taking on the task of Smith's biography. During the early spring of 1845, he complained to his close friend, James Henry Hammond, about "the pressure of one or two tasks of Biography, which I was ass enough to take upon my shoulders" at a time when he should have relaxed his endeavors (*Letters* 2: 45). A few weeks later, he explained to his literary agent, John Lawson, that his work on Smith proceeded slowly, but assured him that the work would be finished. He confided that "there is nothing in the subject to excite and interest me" (*Letters* 2: 49). Simms often was jaded and anxiety-ridden at the end of a big project, so these objections should not be given too much weight. Yet we might imagine that the taxes of the writer's efforts were particularly sharp in the case of this biography because of the added irritation of a paucity of sources. Indeed, the bulk of the writing of *Captain John Smith*, which occurred in 1845, corresponded with a year of events too pressed even for Simms's normally busy schedule. He simultaneously polished off the second volume of his *Views and Reviews in American Literature, History and Fiction*, commenced work on the Huguenots in Florida, and wrote portions of his biography of Chevalier Bayard, all while tending to his wife, who was pregnant with their daughter, Mary Lawson Simms. Yet Simms faced more than plantation chores, household duties, and writing tasks. While finishing the final pages of the Captain Smith biography, Simms lost his fifteen-month-old daughter, Valerie. He continued to write in the face of this tragedy but likely did not finish *Captain John Smith* until early 1846.

Amidst a year of personal tragedy and professional success, Simms also embarked on a new career. In 1845, he stood for election to the Carolina legislature. His subsequent victory in the fall legislative session taxed both his energy and his time. He would have preferred a political appointment from President James K. Polk, perhaps to a distant diplomatic post where he could repose himself to write at leisure and casually fill the duties of office. Lacking the President's favor, he happily accepted a place in the state legislature.

In the meantime, Simms endured a frustrating period of dealing with his publishers. Having just come off one of his most popular books, *The Life of Francis Marion*, Simms gained much needed attention from would-be sellers. Publisher J. and H.G. Langley offered to buy the copyrights to both *Marion* and *Smith* for $1300, which Simms accepted in the late fall of 1846. Alerted to the publisher's troubling financial situation, Simms realized Langley may not fulfill their terms. He sought alternatives and hoped to secure publication for the Smith book before winter set in. When he learned the ailing firm sold the copyrights to another publisher, Simms was outraged. Negotiations among various publishers, Simms, and his literary agent, Lawson, dragged on for months. But he reluctantly agreed to transfer the copyrights to George F. Cooledge and Brother for a slightly lower amount than that promised by Langley, but still a comparatively tidy sum for 1846. It would be March 1847 before Simms's Captain John Smith book was finally published in Cooledge's "Illustrated Library" as *The Life of Captain John Smith. The Founder of Virginia*. The same series also included a republication of Simms's *The Life of Francis Marion* and William Cutter's *The Life of Israel Putnam* (*Letters* 2: 184n, 189, 238–39, 249–50, and 306–07).

Simms repeatedly assured James Lawson that the Captain Smith biography would perform well and gain popularity. As he wrote to Lawson shortly after its publication, "It has life, spirit, energy . . . the essentials" (*Letters* 2: 306–07). While Simms thought highly of the finished product, the book received scant public attention, at least in terms of widespread sales. But there were exceptions. One was the favorable review published in the *Southern Quarterly Review*; the reviewer commended the work "to every generous heart" and praised Simms for "bringing . . . into light all the impressive and noble lineaments of his hero." *The Literary World* published a review possibly written by Evert Duyckinck that heaped even greater praise on Simms. The review described the book as "readable," "instructive," and "a fund of good humor." Best of all, the reviewer hailed Simms as a masterful novelist gifted with the historians eye for detail, familiarity with Indian life, and love for his subject (qtd. in *Letters* 2: 272n).

The publication history of *Captain John Smith* sheds little light on Simms's research strategy except to explain that pecuniary interests alone are not sufficient explanations. Yet again, a comparison of *Captain John Smith* and *The Life of Francis Marion* may answer several lingering questions. Simms handled Marion's biography with due diligence to uncovering primary documents. Simms conducted serious academic research, located personal letters, and even interviewed first-hand observers. With John Smith, Simms gathered some additional material, but rarely strayed from the basic narrative laid down in Smith's autobiography. As with his biography of General Nathanael Greene, Simms largely reproduced and slightly edited previous accounts. So, it was Simms's analysis, not research or new stories, that made *Captain John Smith* a powerful historical tome. Given the backdrop of Simms's personal life, his considerable stress under the weight of professional responsibilities, and his budding—but short-lived—political career, it would have been all too easy to patch together random passages of the Smith autobiography to garner fast money. On the contrary, he took extra care, perhaps too much care in the eyes of his associates, in reproducing Captain Smith's story for a new generation that needed to learn more about this important moment in our nation's history and the man who was at its center

Most of Simms's commentary on *Captain John Smith* revolved around publishing concerns, so any explanation of private motives he had for writing the work remains tentative. However, it is quite possible that Simms treated the book as slightly autobiographical. Given that the writing of *Captain John Smith* closely corresponded to his run for office and his new political career, Simms likely found little inspiration from Smith's narrative for the practical concerns for office. At the least, Simms did not view himself as playing the same kind of political role as Smith. For example, Simms portrays Smith as a prototypical, classical hero appropriate for nineteenth-century Romance. As Busick notes, in over sixty instances, Simms labeled Smith a "hero," considered his efforts heroic, or did the same for other characters in the biography (*Sober* 43). Smith was an adventurer, a man of the seas, and an explorer of a new world, all of which contributed to his greatness and played to the romantic heroes favored by Simms's readers. Yet in his own political career, Simms saw few examples of such heroism, given that American society long progressed away from its founding. Exploration and creating a new "home" required more than the steady, routine deliberation of the local legislator, which in Simms's day could hardly be described as heroic. Dedicated, practical, diplomatic, even strategic might serve to describe the typical nineteenth-century

American legislator, much as it illustrated General Nathanael Greene in Simms's biography of the Revolutionary leader. To borrow again from Busick, "Greene's practical brilliance was precisely what was needed to achieve the most wonderful results in the worst of times" (*Sober* 43). But it was not "heroic."

However, in periods of great crisis, such as imperial invasion, those called to defend hearth and home gained Simms's greatest admiration and earned "heroic" dignity. Great legislators, like great generals, served an unparalleled purpose and provided countless examples of model, professional behavior. But they did not inspire human beings in the same way as great heroes. To Simms, Francis Marion gained such respect. It was not by choice of career that Marion raised his gauntlet against the British. It was out of defense of those things that made his life worth living and a willingness to sacrifice everything, including one's life, for the singular purpose of protecting those things that mattered most.

Simms likely saw his task with Smith as particularly urgent, precisely because of its contrast with the current state of the antebellum world. Captain Smith easily highlighted the difference between the founding period of the country's progress with the demands of a settled society. The largely calm, deliberative political scene of a settled society routinely needed to return to first principles. It occasionally needed to resuscitate heroic virtues in order to maintain the progress already achieved. In short, the political progress of a society was neither inevitable nor guaranteed in the long term. To remain civilized, a settled society required more than political habit, procedural regularity, and the slow, steady beat of public festivity. In addition to these things, Simms likely believed a civilized society needed a kind of adventuresome militancy where its members tenaciously cling to their liberty as if their very survival were at stake. They need plenty of Nathanael Greenes in their legislative bodies, but an occasional Smith and Marion proved equally essential. Simms thus followed the common Jeffersonian approach to republican politics. Just as Thomas Jefferson believed every generation must undergo a revolution—meaning to return or revolve—Simms shared the Jeffersonian desire too for each generation to remove the political accretions of time and reconnect to the original principles of their society's origin.

It is, thus, probably no coincidence that in the middle of the 1840s, Simms simultaneously wrote a biography of a "creator" and a "savior" of America, Smith and Marion. It should also be noted that Simms's legislative career closely mirrored his admiration of Marion—a defender of what he knew best, those things he loved, and a person slow to combative resistance. Defending the patrimony of South Carolinians mattered more than creating a new southern nation. Likewise in the late 1840s, Simms's decision to call for South Carolina to secede—the first prominent legislator in antebellum South Carolina to do so—perhaps had most to do with Simms's desire to defend tangible customs of common life instead of fostering abstract, southern nationalism. Perhaps, too, Simms's personal preference for his biography of Marion over Smith reveals a theme all too common among Simms's writings—that people are most often called by duty and custom to defend what historically belongs to oneself. We are seldom the progenitors of those things or the traditions that sustain them. We are rarely a John Smith. But only by remembering the John Smiths of this world—of what was created in a wilderness—do we find the urge to become a Francis Marion.

The Life of the Chevalier Bayard; "The Good Knight," "Sans peur et sans reproche"

JEFFERY J. ROGERS

William Gilmore Simms was, as the great scholar of southern literature Jay B. Hubbell described him, "the central figure in the literature of the Old South" (572). The impetus, as well as the driving force, for this creative output was always a passionate fascination with history. It was his desire to see American history represented in fiction that produced what are arguably his greatest literary achievements. Among nineteenth-century American litterateurs who longed for a distinct American literature, Simms uniquely envisioned a national literary epic of vast scope which would chronicle, through the medium of fiction, the founding, maturation, and eventual independence of American society and the American people. As his *oeuvre* reflects, he substantially carried this project to completion. It was not only in fiction, however, that Simms sought to portray the stories of American history.

Although he is best remembered as a novelist and poet, Simms was also an important early American historian and biographer. In fact, of all the writers working in the South prior to the Civil War, Simms was "the central figure in historical studies," a recognition that has emerged only very recently (Busick, *Sober* xi). The notion of a novelist writing history may strike contemporary readers as odd, perhaps even suspect. The intermingling of the two forms, it would seem, makes it possible for history to dull fiction and for fiction to corrupt history. In the nineteenth-century, though, there was nothing unusual or suspicious about a novelist writing history or an historian writing fiction. Simms lived and wrote prior to the professionalization of the historical discipline when it became expected that, to be considered valid, historical scholarship should follow established, 'scientific' methodology, and that to be considered a genuine historian one must obtain the proper, university-level training. The beginning point of this transformation in how history was conceptualized in the United States is often marked by the founding of the American Historical Association in 1884, more than a decade after Simms's death. Yet, history as a mode of inquiry into the human condition extends back into antiquity, and nineteenth-century historians thought of themselves as working within that broad tradition.

Simms also lived in the age before sharp lines separating genres of writing had developed. Today, those lines separate 'history' from 'literature,' which is commonly considered to mean imaginative or creative writing. Nineteenth-century authors, however, could move from fiction to history (or biography) and back without raising the least suspicion that they were out of their proper sphere. For nineteenth-century readers and writers 'literature' encompassed a wide array of writings which today would commonly not be grouped under that term. History and biography were broadly considered to be literary works. Consequently, they were understood to be read, as well as critiqued, in much the same way as works of fiction, drama, and poetry. The aesthetic qualities of a historical work, its language, its narrative construction, its author's ability to provoke the reader's imagination, were viewed as essential criteria in assessing the quality of a work of history.

There were, nonetheless, recognized differences between fiction and history. Historical accuracy was a valid criterion in assessing the quality of a historical work, but it was not necessary for a work of fiction to contain this quality, even though it might enhance the value of the work. What distinguished Simms's writings, in all the genres in which he chose to write, was his dedication to making them fundamentally accurate, even when he granted himself license with incidental details in his fiction. Moreover, and crucial to Simms's understanding of history, was that accurate facts and details be combined with literary talent on the part of the historian to truthfully and effectively convey the character and spirit of the past. This can be seen in his series of Revolutionary War romances which respected historian George C. Rogers, Jr. described as actually giving "a better picture of the times than do the history books" (*Charleston* 48). In these novels, Simms depicted in compelling detail the social and political upheaval and partisan warfare which characterized the southern theatre of the American Revolution. Simms gave more critical thought to the use of history for the purposes of fiction than any other American writer of the nineteenth century, and this dedication to accuracy and artistry was certainly no less important to Simms when it came to writing history proper.

In addition to numerous historical and biographical sketches, essays, and articles published in a variety of journals, Simms wrote and saw published eight works of history and biography in book form during the course of his life. While there is debate among historians as to how precisely to categorize Simms's philosophy of history, it is clear that Simms, like other nineteenth-century intellectuals, viewed history as the unfolding story of human progress. This description, however, does not fully express the nuance and complexity of Simms's historical thought. Progress, for Simms, was measured by the growth of civilization, the advancement and maturation of the arts, literature, religion, morality, and better government. This type of progress often was facilitated by technological progress and geographic expansion, but these were ultimately of secondary importance. He made a distinction in his thinking between material progress, as praiseworthy and as desirable as it was, and moral progress. Qualitative progress, the type Simms most highly prized, however was slow, halting, and tenuous. It was not possible without social and political order which, in turn, was generated only when the fundamental institutions of society were functioning properly relative to the individual and to each other. Chief among these were the family and the local community. When these institutions failed—or when they themselves served to impede progress—conflict, revolution, and a new stage of historical development were the result.

These institutions were of such importance for Simms because they exerted the most profound influence in shaping the moral and intellectual character of the individual, and it was the individual whom Simms placed at the heart of history. Simms acknowledged the presence and relevance of forces larger than the individual in shaping history. Geography, for example, was readily accepted by him as a determining factor in history. Also, like other nineteenth-century intellectuals, Simms believed that factors such as ethnicity and nationalism strongly shaped history. Indeed, much of his literary project, both in fiction and in history, can be viewed as an effort to come to terms with, to capture with words and adequately describe, how deep-seated and long-developing historical processes had resulted in the creation of a new American nation with a culture and society distinctly different from its sources. Nationalism itself was, in point of fact, a progressive force freeing peoples from stifling oppressions and allowing them to pursue self-government. Attachment to a particular place and to a particular group of people was seen by Simms as a natural and healthy feature of human nature. Nevertheless, it was the individual who both lived out the consequences of these forces and shaped the course of history through choices and actions.

It is unsurprising then that biography constituted a large and significant part of Simms's historical writings. He believed that history is philosophy teaching by examples, and, consequently, no form of history was more effective in doing this than biographies of important individuals whose lives were worthy of emulation. To be valuable, history must teach lessons, particularly moral lessons, to its readers. This meant that Simms, an American writing in the second and third quarters of the nineteenth-century, wished to hold up examples of republican virtue to inspire his fellow citizens. The lives Simms chose to relate were models of exceptional character against which individuals and society could be measured. Nonetheless, these were still figures with whom readers could readily identify as Americans. *The Life of Francis Marion* (1844), *The Life of Captain John Smith. The Founder of Virginia* (1846), and *The Life of Nathanael Greene: Major General in the Army of the Revolution* (1849) all focused on figures who had been pivotally important in American history. They were also, in Simms's estimation, men of great virtue. Through their resourcefulness, tactical abilities, and capacity for leadership, Revolutionary War generals Francis Marion and Nathanael Greene were in great measure responsible for undermining the British 'Southern Strategy' to subdue the Carolinas and Virginia and thereby winning the American Revolution. John Smith, of course, is famed for saving the Virginia colony at its moment of crisis and, thus, the project of British colonization. These were American heroes who made the future of the United States possible, and their lives were worthy of remembrance. Standing somewhat apart in the list of Simms's historical writings is *The Life of the Chevalier Bayard; "The Good Knight," "Sans peur et san reproche"* published by Harper & Brothers of New York in 1847. It is a 401 page biography of Pierre du Terrail, Seigneur de Bayard, one of the most famous knights in French history. He was considered by his contemporaries and remembered ever since as the very personification of the chivalric ideal. As Simms's only biography and only major historical work which addresses a non-American subject, its presence among Simms's body of work seems oddly out of place. Why did Simms choose to write this biography, and how did he go about doing so?

Subject and Inspiration

The Chevalier Bayard was born in 1476 at the Château Bayard, the small family castle, located near Pontcharra in the province of Dauphiné. His family was a noble one, but modest by aristocratic standards. It was, nonetheless, distinguished by a strong military tradition. Heads of the Bayard family had fought and died at Poitiers (1356), Agincourt (1415), and Montlhéry (1465). Peirre's own father was severely wounded at The Battle of Guinegate (1479), never to take up arms again. The France into which Bayard was born was still largely a medieval society, but following the end of the Hundred Years' War and the departure of English troops from French soil in 1453, the country was at the beginning of a transformation which would make it a modern nation-state. Renaissance culture had moved across the Alps and was now strongly influencing the French court and French intellectual life. Under Louis XI and Charles VIII, France was increasingly prosperous as well as politically and militarily powerful. In the first half of the sixteenth century French kings would lead armies into Italy and would fight their Habsburg and Tudor rivals for hegemony in Europe. These Habsburg-Valois Wars, or Italian Wars of 1494–1559, began when Charles VIII invaded Italy in a quest to expand French territory, to limit Habsburg power in Italy, and to affect a more advantageous relationship with the Pope in Rome. They largely failed to win for the French monarchy these goals, but these were, nonetheless, the arenas in which Bayard won lasting fame and in which he died.

A key to answering the question of why Simms, a southern American writer of the early nineteenth-century, was drawn to Bayard as the subject for a biography can be found in these historical circumstances and in the details of Bayard's life. As a young man training as a page to Charles I, the Duke of Savoy, Bayard quickly earned a reputation for his honesty, generosity, cheerfulness, and devotion to duty, but of equal importance he also demonstrated extraordinary horsemanship. Chivalry required a knight to be not only a man of virtue and courtly manners, but a skilled warrior with a love of battle. By Simms's account, and those of Bayard's earlier biographers, Bayard achieved perfection in both these aspects. These qualities earned him the affection of King Charles VIII and inclusion into his Italian invasion force. At the age of 19, in his first taste of battle at Fornovo (1495), Bayard began his rise to military glory by demonstrating exceptional valor and capturing Italian battle flags. "He began his career in such a manner," Simms remarks, "as to confirm all the hopes which had been formed of his fearlessness and skill" (*Chevalier Bayard* 54). His fame would only grow. As Simms's biography relates, the list of Bayard's great deeds at arms and displays of honorable conduct is long and impressive, lasting right up to his ironic death in 1524. While fighting in Italy, Bayard was fatally wounded by an arquebus, the matchlock, smooth-bore precursor to the musket.

Simms was working on his biography of the Chevalier Bayard as early as the summer of 1845. In August and September of that year he published two sketches on Bayard in *The Southern and Western Monthly Magazine and Review*, a Charleston literary journal he edited. These included many of the details and some of the language which would later appear in the full biography. In a letter of 19 October 1845 Simms wrote to his New York literary friend Evert Augustus Duyckinck that he would have the biography completed by January of 1846 and that he planned to publish it under a pseudonym, a common practice at that time in the nineteenth-century albeit one beginning to fade (*Letters* 2:106). What initially and particularly drew Simms to Bayard is unknown. From his omnivorous reading, he was highly knowledgeable of European history, and as the editor of a Charleston newspaper in the early 1830s he included extensive notices of contemporary developments in Europe. He often brought his interpretations of ancient and medieval history to bear in his editorials and other writings prior to his composition of *The Life of the Chevalier Bayard*. These included two novels, *Pelayo: A Story of the Goth* (1838) and *Count Julian; or, The Last Days of the Goth* (1845), both set in early medieval Spain. Simms clearly had a special affection for medieval history, and as he was an author seeking an audience it is worth noting, as Simms surely would have, the Romantic Era's attraction to all things medieval. It is also worth noting that Simms's interest in medieval history remained strong well after the publication of *The Life of the Chevalier Bayard*. His 12,000 volume library at his South Carolina plantation home Woodlands contained enough material in French medieval history in the 1860s that it is said David F. Jamison, one of his close friends, bought a neighboring plantation in order to use it while writing his *Bertrand du Guesclin. His Life and Times, a History of the Fourteenth Century*, a biography of the great French knight of the generation prior to Bayard's.

After completing and publishing *The Life of Francis Marion* in 1844, the most commercially successful of his non-fiction books, Simms charged ahead researching and preparing the ones which would follow, and contemplated, but did not write, still more of Revolutionary War heroes Thomas Sumter and John Paul Jones. Simms saw important commonalities between these characteristically American figures and Bayard, which may explain his interest in the French knight. All of the men Simms chose to write about were military figures. They were men of action. In the opening chapter of his biography of John Smith, published the year before that of Bayard, Simms describes such men: "They seem to conceive and to think more justly while in action than in repose. It is the necessity which provokes the thought." "Such are the men," continues Simms, "who commonly appear to shape and regulate the transition periods in society; to time and to direct its enterprises; to infuse its spirit with eagerness and enthusiasm, and to meet, with the happiest resources and the most unfailing intrepidity, the frequent exigencies which hang about the footsteps of adventure"(*John Smith* 2).

While this may sound suspiciously like Thomas Carlyle's 'Great Man' theory of history, Simms's insistence that moral character mattered in making the man 'great' leads him in a different direction in assessing which historical figures were worthy of his pen. Marion, Smith, and Greene were all great because of their virtuous characters which inexorably lead them into action at the service of morally superior causes. In the case of Bayard, his illustrious family history and his natural endowments, "required him to go and be a soldier." It was quite simply Bayard's "destiny" to be a great knight (*Chevalier Bayard* 8, 6). Like Simms's other heroic military figures, Bayard was brave and courageous, but also a cunning and ferocious warrior. Marion, Greene, Smith, and Bayard were at their best when struggling against heavy odds. Where other men would have unquestionably failed, they conspicuously succeeded.

Francis Marion was Simms's ideal of the partisan warrior engaged in unconventional warfare, leading a small but determined group of guerrilla fighters during the American Revolution against the formidable British army. Through grit, guile, and an intimate knowledge of his native land, Marion and his men frustrated the British effort to conquer the Carolinas. Simms thought of Bayard too as a partisan. He repeatedly uses the word 'partisan' throughout the biography when describing the knight. Bayard was, Simms argues, "perhaps, one of the greatest captains France has ever produced—eager and watchful, observant everywhere, always secure against surprise himself, and always prompt to seize upon the error of his enemy" (*Chevalier Bayard* 5). These words just as easily could have been used by Simms in describing Marion. All that would be required is the replacing of 'France' with 'America.' Simms was researching and writing or editing biographies of Marion, Smith, Bayard, and Greene all in the early 1840s. The similarities between Marion and Bayard were apparent to Simms as he wrote his biography of 'The Swamp Fox' whom he described as, "the Bayard of the southern youth in the war of the revolution, uniting all the qualities of the famous chevalier, *san peur et sans reproche*" (*Francis Marion* 327). Although all of Simms's biographical subjects shared important commonalities, these two figures were particularly linked in Simms's imagination.

One important difference between Marion and Bayard was the historical context in which the two men lived. Francis Marion was of French Huguenot ancestry, a fact doubtless of some significance for Simms. Although of Scots-Irish ancestry himself, Simms was a proud South Carolinian who knew well the strong French influence in his state's early history. But, it was more important that Marion was a native-born South Carolinian, an American. With the coming of the American Revolution, Marion took up arms to defend his home and to achieve the independence of his country. While his character exhibited the qualities of a great late medieval/early Renaissance knight, he was nevertheless a man of the late eighteenth century, a man whose character and accomplishments on the battlefield had contributed to the birth of a new era in human history. The cause of Marion was the right cause, at the right time, and represented genuine human progress. The nature of Marion's character was reflective of the nature of that cause.

Bayard's circumstances were different. He was of aristocratic birth, of course, but both he and Marion gained fame being the men they were meant to be, doing what they were meant to do. Bayard, however, was a man at odds with his age. Marion was fully the man of his. Bayard was the product and perfect embodiment of all that was good in medieval European chivalry, but he lived in an age when, as Simms describes it, "chivalry was at its lowest condition in Christian Europe." "Everything," he remarks, "of that grace and magnanimity which had constituted its essential spirit and made it a peculiar institution—had given way to less imposing and less worthy characteristics" (*Chevalier Bayard* 1). The Age of Chivalry was on its death-bed as the old assumptions and expectations of the medieval world were giving way to modern realities.

New ideas about man's relationship to man and his relationship to God were unseating the old certainties. The state took on new forms and responsibilities while the Church, which was much like a state unto itself, and the heads of those monarchies struggled for power, with the Church increasingly on the losing end. Kings still fought kings for land and title, but the use of mercenaries and commoners as soldiers signaled something new. "It was even at such a time," Simms says, that the decaying institution of chivalry, "was destined to furnish to the world the happiest illustration, in a single great example, of its ancient pride and character, and of those virtues which had made it fruitful of good to humanity, in spite of many curious anomalies" (*Chevalier Bayard* 2). The chivalrous knight, committed to duty and honor, pious and respectful of women, mounted on a splendid horse, and expert with lance and sword was to become an anachronism, but in Bayard it had its finest example. Warfare in the medieval period was such that one great knight could turn the tide of battle, but there is no missing the pathos in the arc of Bayard's life. It is certainly clear in Simms's account of it. The last great knight, the representative of all that was best in the society of medieval Europe and its warrior code was, after a lifetime defined by that code, killed by a gun, a weapon of the future, one which can be effectively used with relatively little training by noble and commoner alike. Powerful enough, it could pierce the best-made armor. It was a weapon Bayard had disliked, one which rendered "skill, strength and individual" of "little account" (*Chevalier Bayard* 399). Honored in death by enemy and ally alike, in Simms's telling, Bayard's death is the coda for an age. In concluding his account of the life of the Chevalier Bayard, Simms declares "We feel sure, making due allowances for what belongs to the times rather than to the individual, that nothing of our picture was overdrawn or exaggerated. His merits, as a man and a soldier, were equally great and remarkable" (*Chevalier Bayard* 396). Bayard's example then, "shall still survive to the satisfaction and delight of the valiant and the true men that shall come hereafter!" (*Chevalier Bayard* 401).

There should be no mistaking Simms's favorable portrait of Bayard as a romanticized interpretation of the Middle Ages. Simms was very much a man of his time and saw it as more enlightened than that of Bayard. He was pointedly critical of many features of medieval society. The Church, for example, is not portrayed in an especially favorable light. The age itself was one, "in which religion was quite too frequently employed as the cloak for crime and idleness" (*Chevalier Bayard* 26). Of course, such criticisms of the Middle Ages were by no means unique to Simms. He was not attempting here to make a theological point against Catholicism or Christianity in general. Simms's tone in discussing these matters makes it clear that they must be understood in the proper context of their time. Along with its faults, Simms clearly sees chivalry, so intimately associated with medieval Christianity, as a civilizing force in a semi-barbarous age. This nuanced interpretation flows from Simms's peculiar version of historical dialectics in which moral and cultural contraries and contradictions in one age merge to produce the new ethos of another. And in Bayard, *le bon chevalier*, or the good knight, the personification of all that was good in medieval Europe, Simms even found some foreshadowing of the future.

Following the Battle of Garigliano Bayard's fame was such that the ambitious Pope Julius II offered him the command of his armies and a substantial salary. Bayard respectfully declined saying he would prefer to be but a humble soldier in the service of the King of France, his natural sovereign, rather than a foreign prince. Bayard's refusal is clearly seen by Simms as an expression of patriotic sentiment, of an attachment to a particular place and to a particular people. As such, it mirrored Francis Marion's patriotism in fighting for his homeland against the British, an invading foreign army. In this example it can be seen how in Simms's view of chivalry's insistence on loyalty, and Bayard's virtue in keeping his oath to his king, it served the cause of strengthening local affection and nationalism. Bayard chose France over even the Pope. It is little wonder then that Bayard has long been one of France's great national heroes.

Working intensely to finish *The Life of the Chevalier Bayard* during the winter of 1846/1847, Simms wrote to James Lawson, his closest New York literary friend, on 19 April 1847, to say that he had completed the manuscript (*Letters* 2:302). He had received a "considerable advance" from Harper & Brothers for the book, and took the manuscript with him to New York City to meet with the publishers (*Letters* 2: 260). Summer trips to the North were a nearly annual practice for most of his life. He reported that the book was through the press on 15 July 1847. It was released later that year under Simms's name. On the title page Simms included a passage from the English writer Sir Thomas Malory's *Le Morte de Arthur*, a text probably more familiar to his potential readers than the subject of Simms's biography. In the selection, Sir Lancelot is lauded as the best of knights. Simms doubtless chose this passage to link Lancelot, a fictional character, with Bayard, a historical figure, who truly was, in his estimation, Lancelot made real. Simms dedicated the book, however, to John Izard Middleton, of the prominent Middleton family who was born at Middleton Place plantation near Charleston in 1785. An artist with an interest in classical antiquity, Middleton traveled widely in France and Italy in 1808 and 1809 making historically significant observations and well-regarded drawings of ancient ruins. The tone of the introduction suggests that Simms knew Middleton and was an admirer of his work.

Sources and Evaluation

In critically evaluating any biography or work of history, it is necessary to investigate the sources and methods used. Unfortunately, there is no known letter from Simms in which he discusses in detail how he researched the *The Life of the Chevalier Bayard*, but in an "Advertisement" which follows the book's dedication he did list sources. The first three of these, set apart in roman numerals, Simms described as forming, "the basis" of his biography. The first of these is *Les gestes ensemble la vie Chevalier Bayard avec sa genealogie; comparaisons avec anciens preulx chevaliers: gentils, Israelitiques, et Chretiens. Enseble oraisons, lamentations, epitaphs du dit Chevalier Bayard, contenant plusiers victoryes du roys de France, Charles VIII, Loys XII, et Francoys permier de nom* by Symphorien Champier.[1] Published in 1525, this text is among the earliest accounts of Bayard's life. Champier (1471–1538) was the founder of a school of doctors in Lyon, France and a writer of histories. He was also related to Bayard through his wife. Simms gave credit for his access to this "rare and quaint old volume" to Alexander A. Smets of Savannah, Georgia who was a noted book and manuscript collector instrumental in the founding of the Georgia Historical Society (*Chevalier Bayard* [v]).

As for the other sources Simms lists in the "Advertisement," it is not known where he acquired them, but with what is known about his life one can reasonably speculate on how he might have obtained them. With his extensive connections within the transatlantic literary and publishing worlds it is not surprising that Simms was able to acquire what would have surely been rare and unusual books to nineteenth-century American readers. In addition to these networks on which he could rely, the bookshops of the major port cities of Charleston, New York, and Philadelphia would have been familiar places to him. What is known is that Simms never journeyed to Europe and thus could not have conducted archival research in primary documents. Therefore, all of his sources are, of necessity, secondary documents. Simms had an extraordinary aptitude for learning languages; he could read French and Spanish, both of which were obviously useful in writing *The Life of the Chevalier Bayard*.

The second of the sources Simms lists is *La très-joyeuse and plaisante histoire, compose par le Loyal Serviteur, des faits, gestes et prouesses du Bon Chevalier, sans peur et sans reproche* . . . by "Coleridge's daughter," who was Sara Coleridge (1802–1852), a noted author and translator in her own right, in addition to being the daughter of the famous poet Samuel Taylor Coleridge.[2] The text is a translation and reworking of the account of the 'Loyal Servant' whom scholars have identified as Jacques de Mailles (1475–1540), an archer in the French army and the secretary to Bayard. Mailles's account of Bayard was originally published in 1527 and is the most widely quoted source in studies of the Chevalier's life. It has been translated and republished many times. Simms too quotes liberally from the Loyal Servant. The third of Simms's major sources is *Historie de Pierre Terrail, dit le Chevalier Bayard, sans peur et sans reproche* by Jean Cohen (1781–1848), published in Paris in 1822.

Of the remaining sources, Simms gave only partial details. The manner in which he introduces them suggests they were significant in forming his understanding of the larger context of the period but were of secondary importance with regard to the details of Bayard's life. The casual manner in which Simms lists these sources also suggests he expected his audience to be familiar with them. Whether this was the case or not, the modern reader may find these names and works more obscure. Nonetheless, a list of these can be reconstructed and something about the works and their authors can be said. Philip des Comines (1447-c. 1511) was a writer and diplomat in the French and Burgundian courts. The work Simms probably used was his *Mémoires*, an edition of which was published in Paris in 1820. Comines has been considered by some scholars to be the first truly modern writer and the first critical and philosophical historian since classical antiquity.

Enguerrand de Monstrelet was born around 1400 and died in 1453. He was a French chronicler whose *La chronique d'Enguerran de Monstrelet, avec pieces justificatives, 1400–1444* mostly relates the later events of the Hundred Years' War. Jean-Baptiste de La Curne de Sainte-Palaye (1697–1781) was a French historian, classicist, and philologist. His *Mémoires sur l'ancienne chevalerie, chevalerie considérée comme un établissement politique et militaire* was published in Paris in 1781.[3] Gaspard de Saulx-Travannes (1509–1575) was a French military leader during the Italian Wars and the French Wars of Religion. His *Memoirs*, originally published in 1653, is still regarded as an important source for this period in French history. William Roscoe (1753–1831) was a highly respected and popular English historian. His *The Life and Pontificate of Leo the Tenth* was first published in 1805 with many subsequent reprintings.

Manuel José Qunitana (1772–1857) was one of the most popular Spanish poets of the nineteenth century, and many of his poems dealt with the theme of Spanish nationalism. The book by Qunitana which Simms referenced, however, is his *Vida de Gonzalo Fernandez de Cordoba, Llamado El Gran Capitan*, a biography of the famed Spanish general. It was published in Paris in 1827. The Scotsman David Hume (1711–1776) was one of the most influential philosophers of the eighteenth century. Less well known, however, is Hume's work as an historian. The first volume of his monumental *The History of England* appeared in 1754 and was considered the standard history of England until the publication of that by Thomas Macaulay. Born in Geneva, Jean Charles Léonard de Sismondi was an historian whose 29-volume *Histoire Des Francais* was published in Paris from 1821–1844.

The other works Simms mentioned were Robert Macquereau's *Histoire Generale de L'Europe*, published in 1841, James Bacon's *The Life and Times of Francis I*, published in London 1829–1830 and a prompt book on Shakespeare's *Henry VIII* by James B. Roberts. In addition to the above, Simms made reference in scattered footnotes throughout the text to works not included in the "Advertisement." Among these are Eyre Evans Crowe's *The History of France* and an article by the famed historian Edward Gibbon titled, "Critical Researches concerning the Title of Charles VII to the Crown of Naples." More often, however, Simms used his footnotes to add information not included in the text or, much like modern historians, to argue with and evaluate previous historians.

The contemporary reception of Simms's *The Life of the Chevalier Bayard* was generally favorable, with a notable exception. Interestingly, however, later critical assessment of the book as a part of Simms's *oeuvre* has been sharply divided. The first review of *The Life of the Chevalier Bayard* was in the 29 January 1848 edition of the New York *Literary World*, which, in addition to reviewing the book, carried a long excerpt. The reviewer wrote, "This appears to have been a labor of love to Mr. Simms. . . . His narrative is obviously arranged with judicious care, both in regard to the authenticity of the facts, and the sequence of the events" (Rev. of *Chevalier Bayard*). Famed poet, newspaper editor, and Simms friend William Cullen Bryant reviewed *The Life of Chevalier Bayard* in the 2 February 1848 edition of the New York *Evening Post* and had praise for it and Simms's skill at writing biography (Guilds, *Literary Life* 187).

Still, *The Life of the Chevalier Bayard* did not escape contemporary attack. In the March 1848 edition of *Holden's Dollar Magazine*, another New York literary journal, there appeared a short but brutal review which argued that, "Simms was just the last person in the whole world who should have made an attempt upon the Life of Chevalier Bayard because he has performed his self-imposed task in a more wretched, unskillful and beggarly manner than we had supposed possible." While claiming that Simms had given Bayard "the air of a snob and a paltroon [*sic*]" the reviewer concluded by saying Simms's *The Life of the Chevalier Bayard* was "a remarkably bad book," indeed, it was "the worst of all books that has yet been produced by the American press" (Rev. of *Chevalier Bayard* 182).

While the review in *Holden's Dollar Magazine* doubtless irked Simms, its hyperbole may have reflected more a personal grudge on the part of the editors, and the cliquish nature of the New York literary scene, than a fair reading of the biography. In May 1848, just two months after the appearance of the harsh review, the journal published an installment in an anonymously authored series titled "The Autobiography of a Monomaniac" in which the author subtly questioned whether Simms's popularity as a writer had more to do with his renowned sociability and skill at ingratiating himself with critics than his talent as a writer. Though anonymous at the time, the author was John Tomlin, a native South Carolinian, who had corresponded with Simms previously and favorably reviewed other examples of Simms's work in the past. Tomlin had even written to Edgar Allan Poe six years earlier that he had at one time considered Simms a friend and that, "the most pleasant walks I have ever taken in the fields of Literature, were made in his company" (*Letters* 2: 106n).

Though one can only speculate, it is possible that the over-the-top review was the consequence of a personal falling-out between Tomlin and Simms or that Tomlin wrote as he did in "The Autobiography of a Monomaniac" because he knew what was required of him to say about Simms in order for the editors of *Holden's Dollar Magazine* to publish it. Regardless, while it was not as successful as his earlier biography of Francis Marion, Simms's *The Life of the Chevalier Bayard* was popular enough with the public for Harper & Brothers to release a second edition in 1860.

In the years since Simms's death, *The Life of the Chevalier Bayard* has been treated with both praise and ambivalence by literary historians and Simms biographers. The first of these was William Peterfield Trent who, in his *William Gilmore Simms*, published in 1892 as part of The American Men of Letters Series, did much in his overly harsh treatment of Simms's career to marginalize Simms as the talented but ultimately failed literary man of the Old South. Trent's book was a benchmark in the decline of Simms's once high reputation and his judgments are ones against which Simms scholars have been arguing for over a century. Surprisingly, then, despite his almost flippant critiques of some of the author's novels and poetry, Trent found much good in Simms's biographies, especially *The Life of the Chevalier Bayard*. Prefacing this verdict by stating that, admittedly, there was no evidence of great original research in its pages, Trent nonetheless thought that the biography, "reads smoothly, that it treats of interesting men and times in an easy and acceptable way" (139). Trent's assessment may be due to his and his generation's preference for realism in literature and their consequent rejection of the romanticism of Simms and his contemporaries. In as much as biography attempts to show the reality of individual life, Trent may have been disposed to be more sympathetic to Simms's efforts in this genre.

A more recent biography of Simms, however, gives a very different impression. John Caldwell Guilds's *Simms: A Literary Life*, appearing exactly a century after Trent's biography, offered a complete reassessment of Simms's career, which effectively reintroduced Simms to modern scholarship. Sympathetic without becoming hagiographic, *Simms: A Literary Life* was the product of a slowly growing interest in the antebellum South's premier literary figure and public intellectual. Since the book's publication in 1992, literary and historical studies of Simms have proliferated. It is somewhat ironic, then, that in overturning so much of Trent's acrid criticisms of Simms's efforts in fiction and poetry, Guilds also dissented from Trent's appreciative reading of his biographies. For Guilds, Simms's efforts in biography amounted to a waste of "valuable creative energy" which resulted in nothing more than "conventional biographies now scarcely worth inclusion in his canon" (Guilds, *Literary Life* 187). This sweeping statement includes *The Life of the Chevalier Bayard* as much as the other biographies of Francis Marion, John Smith, and Nathanael Greene.

The only scholarly work which exclusively examines Simms's work in history and biography is Sean R. Busick's *A Sober Desire for History: William Gilmore Simms as Historian*. Busick makes a compelling argument that, because so much of Simms's writings are historical in nature, to fully appreciate Simms as a writer one must first understand him as an historian. Therefore, adequately assessing Simms's biographies is a crucial part of any study of Simms and his place in American literature. Of those biographies, Busick believes "the lives of Marion and Greene are better than the others" as they are based in "deeper primary research." This is unsurprising since Simms possessed in his own collection, or had greater access to, primary material from the Revolution than from seventeenth-century Virginia and medieval France. As a result, the biographies of Smith and Bayard, Busick concludes, must be "considered popular, not scholarly, biographies" (Busick, *Sober* 38).

This is a fair assessment of *The Life of the Chevalier Bayard*, but it is not quite complete. That Simms did not have access to the same quantity and quality of material in writing his Bayard biography as he did for those of Marion and Greene is undoubtedly true, and as a consequence those biographies do offer their readers a richer portrait of their subjects than does his life of Bayard. One might criticize Simms's judgment in writing a biography of a figure so distant from him in time and geography and about whom it would be difficult to find reliable information from which to work, but this would misunderstand the author's purposes in this project.

There are three ways in which one can critique *The Life of the Chevalier Bayard* and find it worthwhile reading and an important part of Simms's body of work. The first criterion is how well Simms rendered his portrait given the sources he had available and how well he managed those sources. A close reading of the text reveals a careful, thoughtful historian at work, making critical judgments about what to include and about what is certain and what is dubious.

The second criterion to apply is, by the standards which would have been familiar to Simms and his generation of writers and readers, to what extent is the biography written in an entertaining and engaging style. This is a highly subjective method of criticism, of course, but *The Life of the Chevalier Bayard* evidences the same gusto and energy characteristic of Simms's best work. It is a highly readable book. In this, Trent's opinion of it is well-founded.

The third criterion, one which is frequently applied to works of history and biography, is whether or not Simms's biography made a genuine contribution to scholarship. Despite the absence of original, primary research in its writing, *The Life of the Chevalier Bayard* did indeed make such a contribution. A fact that no commentator on the book has made mention of is that Simms's work is the first full, English language biography of Pierre Terrail, le Chevalier Bayard, which makes use of multiple sources and attempts to present Bayard in the larger context of his age. As such, Simms's portrait is the result of a serious historian working from a sophisticated philosophy of history.

Modern historians of medieval France will find interest in how a popular American author of the nineteenth century depicted one of France's most legendary military heroes. They might otherwise see little of value in the work which is not available elsewhere or which has not been superseded by more recent scholarship, but this is beside the point. The life of Bayard, as Simms interpreted it, was one which bridged the medieval and the modern worlds. He believed that life could serve as a vehicle by which what was good in the one could be transmitted to the other, and he hoped *The Life of the Chevalier Bayard* would be a conduit for that transmission.

NOTES

1. All of the actions of the life of the noble Knight Bayard with his genealogy; comparisons with ancient noble knights: Gentiles, Israelites, and Christians. Together [with the] prayers, lamentations, stories told of the Knight Bayard, containing several victories of the kings of France, Charles VIII, Louis XIII, and Francois first of the name.
2. The very merry and pleasant history, written by the Loyal Servant, of actions and exploits of the Good Knight, without fear and beyond reproach.
3. Memoires of the old chivalry, chivalry considered as a political and military institution.

The Life of Francis Marion

STEVEN D. SMITH

The Life of Francis Marion was William Gilmore Simms's "most commercially successful work of nonfiction," selling out within the first week of its publication in 1844 (Busick, *Marion* ix). By 1847 it was in its tenth edition, and it remains in print today (Busick, *Marion* x). There is no doubt that our national recognition of the Revolutionary War hero Francis Marion, widely known as the 'Swamp Fox' has been shaped largely by Simms—along with two earlier biographers, Mason Lock Weems (1809), using an original manuscript authored by Peter Horry, and William Dobein James (1821). It is Simms's biography, however, that has best stood the tests of authenticity and time, and undoubtedly has had the greatest influence on Marion's place in American memory.

Francis Marion

Simms's subject, General Francis Marion (1732–1795), was the most successful partisan warrior of the American Revolution (Stovall; Weller; Griffith; Tierney 42–43). His guerilla skills have been favorably compared with those of Mao Tse-tung (Griffith 5–7). Marion was also incredibly lucky and although fortune favors the brave, his luck was often due to events beyond his immediate control. From turning his ankle during the British siege of Charleston in May 1780, which allowed Marion to leave town honorably before it surrendered, to escaping a British surprise attack at Tydiman's Plantation in 1782, Marion eluded death, capture, or ruin, time and again.

Twentieth-century historian and biographer Hugh F. Rankin described Marion's life as "something like a sandwich—a highly spiced center between two slabs of rather dry bread" (ix). Indeed, there is little known about Marion's pre- and post-Revolutionary War life as is clearly evident in Simms's biography. Marion's initial military career began during the Cherokee campaigns of the 1760s. With this experience he came up through the officer ranks during the first five years of the American Revolution rising from captain in the Second South Carolina Regiment to Lieutenant Colonel and then its commanding officer by 1778. He was at the head of the failed American attack on the Spring Hill redoubt during the siege of British-held Savannah in 1779. After the injury to his ankle during the British siege of Charleston, he was released from command and hid along the Santee River until Charleston fell in May 1780. He then made his way to North

Carolina and was dispatched to Witherspoon's Ferry on Lynches Creek to take charge of the Williamsburg Militia.

Marion launched his career as a partisan there, the day after Major General Horatio Gates was defeated at the Battle of Camden on 16 August 1780. Marion immediately began harassing British forces in the northeastern part of the state using volunteers and militia. From August until December of 1780, he led an active partisan resistance from the Santee River east to the North Carolina border using Snow's Island along the Great Pee Dee River as his base of operation. When the new American southern commander General Nathanael Greene arrived in the South with a reconstituted Continental army to challenge the British in December 1780, Marion cooperated with Greene until the latter was forced into North Carolina in late January 1781. Again, Marion, now a Brigadier General in the South Carolina militia, was alone to resist British rule in the eastern part of the state. It was then that the British were able to focus on Marion, destroying his base on Snow's Island, and coming very near to destroying Marion's entire force. However, Greene and his Continentals returned to South Carolina in April 1781, and, together with Marion and others, went on the offensive against the British. Through the summer and fall of 1781, Greene increasingly relied on Marion to support his strategic campaign, ultimately honoring Marion with the command of the American frontline at the battle of Eutaw Springs in September 1781. In the later stages of the Revolution, Marion kept the British bottled-up in Charleston and helped to ensure American success in South Carolina. Yet despite his military prowess, Marion was not one-dimensional. His fame as the Swamp Fox has greatly overshadowed his equal talent as an able administrator of the northeastern district of South Carolina during the latter part of the Revolution (Stovall 112–13). Marion biographers, including Simms, have largely ignored this aspect of Marion's leadership skills.

Instead, it is the partisan or guerilla Swamp Fox that we remember today. Marion's tactics are supposedly still taught by the Department of Defense and have been labeled the forerunners of modern insurgent warfare (D. Wilson; S. Aiken). Contemporary enemies certainly agreed that he was a formidable foe. In the fall of 1780, Lord Charles Cornwallis, commander of the British forces in South Carolina wrote: "Col. Marion has so wrought on the minds of the People, partly by the terror of his threats & cruelty of his punishments, and partly by the Promise of Plunder, that there was scarce an Inhabitant between the Santee and Pee Dee that was not in Arms against us" (qtd. in Rankin 115).

More recently, historian John Tierney provides a typical summary of Francis Marion and his place in the history of guerrilla warfare:

> Francis Marion, in his late forties at the time, became the symbol of American guerrilla resistance. A teetotaling Huguenot, Francis Marion commanded a ragtag band of irregulars, including young boys and ex-slaves. They made

> their own clothes and weapons and shot their pistols with bullets made of pewter. Numbering no more than several hundred at its peak strength, Marion's force became skilled in night and dawn raids against British outposts. He and his men would ride as many as sixty miles at a stretch along clay paths and marches of South Carolina in order to surprise a Tory or redcoat force. After the war, many of Marion's guerrilla paths became permanent roads.... In one particular escapade... [t]he guerrillas swooped down on the [British] column and freed the entire lot of Americans, an incident which made the 'Swamp Fox,' instantly famous. (42)

Tierney's summary captures all the typical elements attributed to Marion's partisan warfare: 1) a force consisting of a few, overmatched, non-professional civilians or "ragtag" militia; 2) ingenious use of tactics like ambush and raid to terrorize and outwit enemies made up of regular or professional soldiers; 3) success despite continual lack of sufficient supplies and ammunition; and, 4) extreme mobility. As evidence of Simms's influence on our memory of Marion today, one only need compare Tierney's paragraph to selections from the first two pages of Simms's *The Life of Francis Marion*:

> Marion is proverbially the great master of stratagem: the wily fox of the swamps—never to be caught, never to be followed,—yet always at hand, with unconjectured promptness, at the moment when he is least feared and is least to be expected.... Unprovided with the means of warfare, no less than of comfort—wanting equally in food and weapons.... With a force constantly fluctuating and feeble in consequence of the most ordinary necessities—half naked men, feeding on unsalted pottage,—forced to fight the enemy by day, and look after their little families by night, concealed in swamp or thicket. (1–2)

There were other partisan commanders in South Carolina that harassed the British and won important battles that kept the revolution alive. Brigadier General Thomas Sumter (the Gamecock), Brigadier General Andrew Pickens (the Wizard Owl), Lieutenant Colonel Isaac Shelby, Lieutenant Colonel Elijah Clarke, and Colonel William Bratton are a few of the partisan and militia leaders that harassed the British. However, it is the Swamp Fox Francis Marion who is most admired, due in large part to William Gilmore Simms.

Weems, James, and Simms

Thanks to Simms, and the biographers who came before him Marion's fame remains secure in the "pantheon of America's Revolutionary heroes" (Busick, *Marion* x). As post-revolutionary Americans spread west across the mid-continent, 29 towns and 17 counties were named for Marion, and later, a university and an academy, not to mention unnumbered children (Bass, *Swamp* 4). A "selected" bibliography of works on Marion published in 1999 listed 21 biographies of Francis Marion, and there have been three since then (A. Moore 14–15). At least 14 books of fiction feature Marion as the inspiration. There are countless articles, chapters, poems, dictionary entries, internet sources, or other literature on Francis Marion and numerous discussions of Marion by military historians. Certainly Weems and Horry's book contributed to the early American popularity of Francis Marion as had Weems's biography of George Washington. However, once Simms's full treatment of Marion was published, the nation turned to Simms's *The Life of Francis Marion* as their source for Marion's career. Simms carried an authenticity that Weems and Horry could have never achieved for later antebellum readers. Simms obviously adored and admired Francis Marion. Besides *The Life of Francis Marion*, Simms wrote two other Marion tributes: a series in *Russell's Magazine*, "Marion-The Carolina Partisan" (1858), and a poem in *The Southern Literary Journal and Monthly Magazine*, entitled simply "Marion" (1836, 192).[1] Likewise, Simms made Francis Marion a main historical character in his novel *Mellichampe* (1854) and mentioned him frequently in *Katharine Walton* (1854).

As noted, Simms's biography was the third, and most authentic, of three nineteenth-century biographies devoted to Francis Marion. Peter Horry and Mason Locke Weems's biography, *The Life of General Francis Marion*, was the first and least historical. The story of how Weems came to publish the first Marion biography is important to understanding Simms's public distain of Weems as a historian and Simms's concerted effort to distance his representation of Marion from the Horry-Weems Marion. Peter Horry served as a colonel under Marion during the Revolutionary War and around 1803 completed a manuscript of his service with the general. Horry asked the Georgetown Library Society to publish the work, but they turned it down as being too costly to publish (S. Smith, introduction xxiv). Seeking another publisher, Horry met Mason Locke Weems in Georgetown, South Carolina (Wates 353). At that time Weems was a Virginia bookseller, the popular author of the first biography of George Washington, and a publisher of religious and moral tracts. Through his publications he actively sought to spread "republican and Christian principles, two concepts he equated" (Acree 2). Flattered that Weems was interested in his manuscript, Horry gave it to him while admonishing him to edit but not to alter its sense. Horry's delight was shattered when he saw Weems's version of his text. Weems had rewritten the manuscript into another of his "republican biograph[ies]" modeling it after the Washington biography (Acree 138). Wading through Weems's biography today is torturous. It imagines Marion engaged in long, stilted, and certainly fanciful orations to his troops or colleagues. The biography's chronological flow is confusing, and eventually the book becomes a series of dramatic anecdotes.

Horry was crushed to find his work now a "military romance . . . carved & mutilated . . . with so many erroneous statements" (Force). Weems was equally nonplussed. He thought Horry's demand for accuracy was secondary to the importance of teaching virtue, religious toleration, and republicanism through Marion as he had done in his Washington biography (Acree 243, 246). Ironically for Horry, his Weems-tainted biography became as successful as the Washington biography and was carried west by pioneer Americans after the Revolution. With the publication of Horry-Weems's Marion biography, Marion was "nationalized" (Marr).[2]

In 1821, William Dobein James published the second biography, *A Sketch of the Life of Brigadier General Francis Marion*. James was a soldier in Marion's partisan force, and his father was another of Marion's officers. Although historian George F. Scheer wrote "that no more accurate or valuable book on Marion exists," James adds to the Marion mythology, albeit in a different manner than Weems (Review 248). For example, James was not an eyewitness for much of Marion's partisan warfare (August 1780 to April 1781), but instead relied on his father and other acquaintances to relate that period (James vi). While James adds interesting details to Marion's military exploits, ultimately his book is also unreliable in its chronology and is deficient in scope.

Simms was unhappy with these two previous treatments and sought in his *The Life of Francis Marion* to find the correct balance between Weems's fanciful romance and James's dry and incomplete history. Simms wasted no time in his effort, dismissing both James and Weems in his Preface with a rather biting critique, all the more so for being accurate:

> Of the two works devoted to our subject, that by the Rev. Mr. Weems is most generally known—a delightful book for the young. The author seems not to have contemplated any less credulous readers, and its general character is such as naturally to inspire us with frequent doubts of its statements. Mr. Weems had rather loose notions of the privileges of the biographer; though, in reality, he has transgressed much less in his Life of Marion than is generally supposed. But the untamed, and sometimes extravagant exuberance of his style might well subject his narrative to suspicion. Of the "Sketch" by the Hon. Judge James we are more secure, though, as a literary performance, it is quite devoid of merit as pretention. Besides, the narrative is not thorough. It dwells somewhat too minutely upon one class of facts, to the neglect or exclusion of every other. I have made both of these works tributary to my own whenever this was possible. (7–8)

Thus Simms's goal was to write a Marion biography deconstructing Weems's mythological treatment yet still retaining a literary heart. In *The Life of Francis Marion*, Simms sought to combine history and literature, facts and myth, writing a "people's history, written in their hearts, rather than in their books; which their books could not write—which would lose all its golden glow, if subjected to the cold details of the phlegmatic chronicles" (Simms, *Francis Marion* 12). For

Simms, art was superior to historicity. As Lisa Kay Miller explains "Like [James Fenimore] Cooper, Simms believes that the creator of the American epic must be truthful, but of course not bound to mere fact. Instead, he is bound to truth in essence—the truth of human nature" (49). Simms thought there was a place for romance while remaining "true to the letter of history as research could make it" (Busick, *Sober* 7). Simms's representation of Marion thus could be described as the work of a literary Goldilocks, not too hot (like the romantic Weems), and not too cold (like the factual James), but just right (true myth Simms).

Perhaps the reason Simms was so hard on Weems was he saw a lot of Weems in himself. Indeed, they had nearly identical goals in writing their biographies of Marion. Weems was nation building in 1809. Likewise, "[s]tarting in the 1820s, he [Simms] joined wholeheartedly the efforts in progress to shape the culture, the politics, and the thought of the fledgling nation. His overriding objective was the development of a great nation, which need defer to none" (Watson, *Nationalism* 1). Again, like Weems, Simms saw this need not only as a historian but also as a member of the literati: "Simms perceived that his chief duty as a man of letters lay in the articulation of a distinctively American history and literature, distinguished from that of Europe" (L. Miller 44). Simms saw the American Revolution as a "confrontation between the Old World, with its traditional values, its established mores, and its rigid conventions, to which the Tories and Loyalists are committed, and the New World, with its fresh values, its emerging mores, and its unstructured freedom, to which the Patriots are committed" (Brown 72). Through some eight Revolutionary War novels, a handful of works in varying genres on the same topic, and obviously his *The Life of Francis Marion*, Simms championed the virtues of "honor, duty, integrity, compassion, fairness, [and] patriotism" (Brown 146). In an essay on the "True Uses of History" Simms wrote that the job of the romancer was to develop "national characteristics" (qtd. in Watson, *Nationalism* 2). Simms carried these virtues into his historical writings. Simms, like Weems, connected Marion with George Washington, pointing to their common birth years, their youthful desire for the sea, their self-drive for self-improvement, their common agricultural background, and similar even temperaments (Busick, *Sober* 46).

Despite Simms's overt attempts to distance himself from Weems, in the end, like all Marion scholars, Simms had to rely on Weems for some important details about Marion's life. Simms turned to Weems to demonstrate the human side of Marion. He quoted from a letter that only appears in Weems's book in which Marion described the burning of an Indian village:

> But when we came, according to orders, to cut down the fields of corn, I could scarcely refrain from tears. For who could see the stalks that stood so stately, with broad green leaves and gaily-tasselled stocks, filled with sweet milky fluid, and flour, the staff of life—who, I say, without grief, could see these

> sacred plants sinking under our swords, with all their precious load, to wither and rot untasted, in their mourning fields! (51–52)

The letter concludes, with Indian children asking their mothers "'who did this?' . . . 'the white people, the Christians did it!' will be the reply" (52). Without the quotation marks one might think it came from the pen of Weems.[3] Yet Simms treats the letter as authentic, noting that, "It is pleasing to be able to show that Marion felt, in this matter, as became that rare humanity which was one of the most remarkable, and lovely traits in his character" (51). Simms was not adverse to histrionic scenes if it suited his literary heart.

Simms: Southern Historian

Simms's *The Life of Francis Marion* is the first serious, full treatment of Francis Marion's life by an historian in the modern sense of the word. Though today Simms's biography may not meet the standards of modern academic scholarship, historian Sean Busick asserts *The Life of Francis Marion*, "contains some of the best history that Simms wrote" (*Marion* x) and "met the highest standards of scholarship when it was written" (*Sober* 50). Although Simms published his biography of Marion 35 years after Weems, and 23 years after James, it took Simms to methodically and thoroughly chronicle Marion's long and varied career during the entire war. While Weems and James created an American icon worthy of a new nation, Simms inserted the heroic Marion into an authentic past while maintaining Marion's virtuous nature.

Simms was a literary giant, and like Weems, explicitly sought to shape a national history or memory. As time passed, however, Simms found his nation increasingly hostile to his South. He lived in an era of growing national rift, which would eventually result in bloody Civil War. As the nation drew inevitably toward open conflict, Simms became a defender of the South and a secessionist; viewing the North as the nineteenth-century equivalent of Great Britain (Watson, *Nationalism* 74). From Simms's perspective, his sectionalism was nationalism. David Moltke-Hansen asserts that Simms was not first a nationalist then a sectionalist, but both simultaneously, and indeed, Simms wrote that to be national one must be sectional. According to Simms, to depict a section (ie. the South) faithfully was to illustrate the entire nation ("Horizons" 16). As Jeffery J. Rogers asserts, from Simms's first political "awareness" he "was a southern sectionalist who became a southern nationalist" ("Art" 71).

How much Simms's growing sectional nationalism influenced his portrayal of Marion in 1844 is difficult to assess. On the one hand, Simms did not drift into long passages defending the South in *The Life of Francis Marion*. On the other, Simms certainly assumed his audience knew not only who Marion was, but also what he symbolized. In the final chapter of his biography, Simms concludes, "Thus, while Marion is everywhere regarded as the peculiar representative in the southern States, of the genius of partisan warfare, we are surprised, when we would trace, in the pages of the annalist, the sources of this fame, to find the details so meager and so unsatisfactory" (331). Here Simms takes it for granted that the reader knows Marion's wartime activities, but not the significance of Marion's relationship to the South.[4]

The opposite question, and perhaps more important, is how much did Simms's representation of Marion further shape national and sectional memory of Francis Marion? Simms elevated Marion's reputation by providing the South with an authentic southern hero at a time of northern rejection of southern culture. Indeed, Simms's Marion was the paragon of southern virtue and honor. An underdog and an undefeated champion defender of South Carolina, Marion would be invoked by southerners throughout the war (Meitzen 113). As Lauren Pogue notes, "Marion biographers repeatedly used the legendary Marion to prove the South's martial past" (35). For example, the radical Virginian Nathaniel Beverley Tucker urged South Carolina to provide leadership in the move toward Secession, writing in 1851, "Is she not the land of MARION? Let his spirit animate her" (qtd. in Watson, *Nationalism* 110). Later, during the Civil War, guerilla fighters like General John Morgan would be likened to Francis Marion, enhancing the reputation of both (Meitzen 116). Likewise, John Blake White's famous painting of Marion and the British officer in camp was printed on Confederate money.

As noted, Simms's biography is much more complete and thorough than either Weems or James, and that alone secures its importance to modern Marion scholars. The biography opens with a detailed history of the Marion family and, like Weems and James, Simms attaches great significance to Marion's Huguenot ancestry. Simms was quick to assure the reader that Marion came from good stock: "They were a people of principle, for they had suffered everything for conscience sake. They were a people of pure habits, for it was because of their religion that they suffered banishment" (14).

Simms demonstrated how Marion's participation in the 1760s campaigns against the Cherokees taught him the tactics of irregular warfare that would gain him his Swamp Fox reputation in the Revolution. Marion's first command consisted of leading a small detachment of volunteers through an Indian ambush. Again, Simms, like Weems, took the opportunity to link Marion to George Washington. In describing Marion's surviving the ambush, Simms notes that, "He [Marion] seems, like Washington, to have been the special care of Providence" (49).

None of the three biographers detail Marion's career development from 1776 prior to his partisan command, but of the three, Simms devoted the most pages. This period, when Marion rose in the ranks from captain to lieutenant colonel, and when he really learned his military trade, is still underappreciated. Instead, most of Simms's biography consists of the "spiced center" of Marion's career as described by Hugh Rankin (see above). This is the 'swamp fox' period from

August 1780 to around May 1781, and the militia commander from then until the end of the war. It was this period that we are most familiar with today and which Simms details in Chapters VIII through XX. Here, Simms is more assured of his topic and proceeds apace, spicing his text with stories told by James and Weems, but also citing from his list of sources as he felt necessary to authenticate his text. Into this narrative, Simms inserted legendary anecdotes in keeping with his desire to write a "people's history, written in their hearts, rather than in their books, which their books could not write—which would lose all its golden glow, if subjected to the cold details of phlegmatic chronicles" (*Francis Marion* 12).

Simms is the first biographer to link Marion with the folk hero Robin Hood and Snow's Island, Marion's main partisan camp and hide-out, with Robin Hood's Sherwood Forest:

> Marion's career as a partisan, in the thickets and swamps of Carolina, is abundantly distinguished by the picturesque; but it was while he held his camp at Snow's Island, that it received its highest colors of romance. In this snug and impenetrable fortress, he reminds us very much of the ancient feudal baron of France and Germany, who, perched on castled eminence, looked down with the complacency of an eagle from his eyrie, and marked all below him for his own.... The love of liberty, the defence of country, the protection of the feeble, the maintenance of humanity and all its dearest interests, against its tyrant—these were the noble incentives which strengthened him in his stronghold, made it terrible in the eyes of his enemy, and sacred in those of his countrymen.... Art had done little to increase the comforts or the securities of his fortress. It was one, complete to his hands, from those of nature—such a one as must have delighted the generous English outlaw of Sherwood forest—isolated by deep ravines and rivers, a dense forest of mighty trees, and interminable undergrowth. The vine and briar guarded his passes. The laurel and the shrub, the vine and sweet scented jessamine, roofed his dwelling, and clambered up between his closed eyelids and the stars. Obstructions, scarcely penetrable by any foe, crowded the pathways to his tent;—and no footstep, not practised in the secret, and 'to the manner born,' might pass unchallenged to his midnight rest. (166–67)

It is on Snow's Island that Marion facts and myth combine most seamlessly. At the time of the Revolution, swamps were considered dark places, exactly like Robin Hood's Sherwood Forest, inhabited by the vilest of persons. Swamps were places where only a "vile swamp fox" would go (Weems 134). Marion himself saw the dark secretive places of the swamps. He wrote General Horatio Gates early in his partisan career that he chased the Loyalists into the swamps "impassible to all but Tories" (State Records of North Carolina 617). For Simms the swamp was a symbolic landscape for partisans. In his novels and in *The Life of Francis Marion*, Simms depicted the swamp as both a desolate place of gloom and disease but also lovely and inviting (Niemi 25–26). The swamp was "[h]istorically a symbol of the American resistance in South Carolina, for it was the partisans' primary shelter," and "[a]s a generous source of food, the swamp protects the partisans also from hunger" (Niemi 26, 28). In contrast, Simms describes the British as uncomfortable in or around swamps (Niemi 67). Thus Simms transformed the dark Snow's Island swamp into a picturesque and safe haven for Marion's expert backwoodsmen.

Snow's Island then becomes the proper setting for one of the most famous Marion anecdotes, first told by Weems. This is the story of the British officer who visited Marion's camp under a flag of truce to negotiate a prisoner exchange. After the meeting, Marion invited the officer to dinner. Seeing that Marion was about to sit down to nothing but sweet potatoes, the officer learned that this was the best food they had. Furthermore, he discovered that Marion's men were serving without pay. The British officer was so taken aback by the sacrifices of Marion and his men that upon his return to Georgetown, the officer resigned his commission exclaiming: "Why, sir, I have seen an American general and his officers, without pay, and almost without clothes, living on roots and drinking water; and all for LIBERTY! What chance have we against such men!'" (Weems 156). For Weems, the anecdote occurs at a camp near Georgetown (Weems 147). Simms places the exchange firmly on Snow's Island, a more suitable landscape for the Swamp Fox (76). Simms's version of the anecdote flows over four pages in which he contrasts an image of "portly" British officers as opposed to Marion's "slight" frame (179).[5] The anecdote had received national attention when in 1836 artist John Blake White painted the scene, further enhancing Marion's national memory, cementing his Swamp Fox image, and providing the visual link. The painting became a nineteenth-century mnemonic of Marion and Snow's Island. The scene has been copied and modified numerous times by White and others including, as mentioned, being used as Confederate currency (Scheer, "Francis" 260; Davies 20). A version of the scene is also in Simms's biography.

Sources

In *The Life of Francis Marion*, Simms presents the reader with a list of seventeen sources he consulted in writing his biography (Busick, *Sober* 39). For its time, this bibliography was a comprehensive list of the first histories of the American Revolution and included David Ramsey's history of the war published just two years after its end. Similar sources include what would have been at the time the canon of early American history like John Lawson's *A New Voyage to Carolina* and William Gordon's *The History, Rise, Progress, and Establishment of the Independence of the United States of America*. In citing these sources, Simms was building his work upon their authenticity.

Besides James and Weems, Simms's sources also include the writings of other Marion acquaintances including John Drayton, Henry Lee, and William Moultrie.

Thus Simms speaks of Marion through the voices of eyewitnesses. Simms also would have had the opportunity to interview members of Marion's partisans still alive in the 1840s (Busick, *Sober* 39). Again, these sources lend authenticity to *The Life of Francis Marion*.

One critical source was a five volume collection of Marion's (and other Revolutionary War figures') correspondence most of which was later published by Robert W. Gibbes as the *Documentary History of the American Revolution* (1853). Many of the letters came from the collection of our most unfortunate Revolutionary War hero, Peter Horry, and had been passed to both Weems and James before apparently making their way into Gibbes's possession. Gibbes allowed Simms to use them also, and Simms had plans to publish them after completing *The Life of Francis Marion*. Gibbes, however, felt that Simms had slighted Peter Horry by not giving him proper acknowledgement and asked for the letters to be returned. Today they make up a substantial part of the Peter Force Collection at the Library of Congress (Wates 357–58).

Besides the five volumes of letters, Simms cites Peter Horry's 134 page autobiographical "memoir" (vi), 76 pages of which related Horry's experiences during the American Revolution (Talbert and Farish xii). These 76 pages are now missing. It is quite possible that they were in Simms's possession and destroyed during the burning of Columbia in 1865. In any case, Simms was the last historian to see these pages. Thus, for modern Marion scholars, some of the most intriguing passages in Simms's *The Life of Francis Marion* are his quotations from Peter Horry's autobiographical memoir that may at least have had their basis in the missing Peter Horry manuscript biography of Francis Marion that was transformed into the Weems romance. Simms's quotations from Horry's autobiographical memoir are "among the best available record of Horry's firsthand knowledge of the war" (P. Shillingsburg 14). There are 16 separate references to Horry's memoir, including eleven anecdotes, five of which are direct quotes, and the remaining anecdotes based on the memoir interspersed with direct quotations (P. Shillingsburg, Appendix A). Brief as they are, these quotations display a command of literary form and flow that only serves to increase our sense of loss of Horry's memoir. Describing an engagement of several American officers against a lone British captain he writes:

> My officers ... in succession, came up with Captain Merritt, who was in the rear of his party, urging them forward. They engaged him. He was a brave fellow. Baxter, with pistols, fired at his breast, and missing him, retired; Postell and Greene, with swords, engaged him; both were beaten off. Greene nearly lost his head. His buckskin breeches were cut through several inches ... I almost blush to say that this one British officer beat off three Americans. (Simms, *Francis Marion* 160)

Peter Shillingsburg's analysis of Simms's sources for *The Life of Francis Marion* concluded that while Simms's quotations from Horry are substantially Horry's, "there is no guarantee that the anecdotes have not been dressed up a bit for dramatic effect" (13). Yet, the style in this quotation is nothing like that in Simms's biography and suggests that Horry could indeed turn a phrase. This is action writing at its best and salts Simms's biography with a taste that leaves us even more lamenting what we missed as a result of the unfortunate meeting between Weems and Horry.

Summary

For Americans today, Simms's Marion is *our* Marion. Weems's Marion is suspect; James adds important details in Marion's life; however, Simms captures, balances, and completes Francis Marion as both human and hero. It is safe to say that should he still be alive today, Simms would be quite proud to be singled out as the shaper of our modern memory of Francis Marion. While the Reverend Weems can be credited with rescuing Marion from obscurity immediately after the war (Acree 230), Simms can be credited with keeping that memory alive well into the twenty-first century.

NOTES

1. James Everett Kibler identified Simms as the unsigned author of this poem (Kibler 131, 332). I previously (S. Smith "Imagining" 32) attributed another poem entitled 'Marion' to Simms published in *Russell's Magazine* (1858), but have discovered that that poem, also unsigned, was written by William J. Grayson (Bass, *Autobiography* CCLXV, 26).
2. Weems kept Horry's name as the author, and did not add his own name until the fourth edition (Acree 153). From this point on I cite the book as Weems, but the reader should be aware that Weems used Horry's manuscript as the basis of his romantic biography.
3. Marion scholars would love to find that letter in the archives, as no other surviving Marion letter reveals such pathos.
4. In doing so, Simms unwittingly compliments Weems who had much to do with Marion's reputation and fame prior to Simms.
5. After Weems, Alexander Garden included it in his 1822 *Anecdotes of the American Revolution*, though again, not specifically placing it on Snow's Island. The story also dominated the entry on Marion in an 1831 book of "Military Biography" of Revolutionary War officers (Stavely 207–13). The entry also cites the story in reference to an earlier publication, the *American Biographical Dictionary*, the point being that while the story is part and parcel of the Marion genre, it is Simms that fixes the scene on Snow's Island.

The Lily and the Totem; or, The Huguenots in Florida

NICHOLAS G. MERIWETHER

What is history? Of all the questions William Gilmore Simms explored in his voluminous writings, none was more omnipresent, nor more insistent. It was an uneasy undercurrent beneath his evolving views of American nationalism and southern identity, and a recurrent theme throughout his restless explorations of every literary genre he assayed, from poetry to prose, from fiction to criticism. Indeed, as Sean R. Busick has reminded us, "Most of what [Simms] wrote, whether novels, poetry, biography or reviews, he would have classified as history" (*Sober* xii). As a result, scholars have found in that work a remarkable expanse of thought and practice that reveals how Simms approached the past, and used history to frame his understanding of the turbulence and travails of the present.

Yet in that voluminous corpus, one book-length work uniquely demonstrates Simms's ideas about history, the 1850 volume *The Lily and the Totem*. Throughout his work, Simms illustrated how he approached the writing of history, but only in *The Lily and the Totem* did he provide such a telling indication of how he read history. This essay places that accomplishment in the larger contexts of Simms's writing, thought, and career, discussing the book, its reception, and its place in Simms's *oeuvre*. The reissue of *The Lily and the Totem* by the *Simms Initiatives* marks the return to print of one of Simms's most ambitious yet neglected works, one that he championed throughout the last twenty years of his life and which remains a vital lens for understanding its author's thought and literary achievement.

While Simms's greatest claim to fame as a writer and historical novelist is his eight-volume series of Revolutionary Romances, those formed only one chapter of his life work "to envision, design, initiate, and consummate an epic portrayal of the development of our nation," as John Caldwell Guilds put it (*Literary Life* 333). Yet, in many ways, Simms considered the first era of European exploration of North America to be the most intriguing. "This was a time when the fountains of the marvelous seemed every where to be opened upon mankind," he wrote in an 1845 essay collected in his two-volume critical anthology *Views and Reviews in American Literature, History and Fiction*. "Never was era, in any country, more rich than this, in the one designated—in the abundant variety, the matchless beauty, the masculine pathos, the grace, the strength and the originality of its productions. Nay, never was period half so rich" (1: 60). Along with *Vasconselos*, his 1853 novel documenting the Spanish forays into Florida and the Mississippi

Valley from 1538–1542, *The Lily and the Totem*, which dealt with the early French expeditions of 1562 and 1564, demonstrated that conviction. Simms had long been fascinated by the Spanish contribution to the settlement of the New World: he published his poem *The Vision of Cortes* in 1829, and began another poem, *Donna Florida*, in his youth. As an historical topic, however, he considered the French efforts to establish Huguenot colonies on the southeastern seaboard an even more compelling story.

Simms came by his interests in the Huguenots early. As a boy, he listened to stories from his grandmother about medieval France (Guilds, *Reader* 7), and his native Charleston had a distinctive Huguenot heritage that exercised a strong influence in the city's culture. Simms also encountered admiring stories of Huguenot history through his reading. From Shakespeare, he learned how powerful Huguenot characters and themes could be in *Macbeth* and *King Lear*, as well as the appeal of the broader contours of their history, seen in the court of Henry of Navarre in *Love's Labors Lost*. Simms also admired the writing of Sir Philip Sidney, whose avowed sympathies led to his being dubbed "the English Huguenot" (Wiles).[1] And Milton, whose poetry was a life-long source of inspiration for Simms, wrote one of his most famous sonnets on the Huguenots, "On the Late Massacre in Piedmont."[2]

While Simms wrote about the Huguenot contribution to South Carolina history in many works, only in *The Lily and the Totem* did he provide such an extended treatment of the earliest French attempts to settle the New World. The first attempt, a colonial expedition launched in 1562 under the command of Jean de Ribault, succeeded long enough to establish a fort located on the coast of present-day South Carolina near Beaufort. It was abandoned shortly before a second expedition arrived in 1564, commanded by René Laudonniere, which established another short-lived colony, long thought to have been in present-day Florida, not where archeologists now believe it to have been, on the Georgia coast between Brunswick and Savannah (Mintz). Both voyages left fascinating documentary records, a web of evidence that commanded Simms's interest as a historian, as a collector of books and manuscripts, and most especially as a novelist.

Simms opens *The Lily and the Totem* with a detailed note on his method, a more than four-page explanation of his vision of the book's goals and narrative scheme. The "Epistle Dedicatory" to his friend James Henry Hammond outlined Simms's literary ambitions for the book and more. It prefaced twenty-five chapters, five of which he dubbed "Historical Summary"; these he interspersed irregularly through the latter part of the book, beginning with chapter 10, although two more—chapters one and nine—serve as historical summaries as well. Together, those chapters documented the two Huguenot expeditions and their fates, the first nine chapters covering the first expedition (about a fourth of the book), the rest detailing the better documented second expedition. Simms included his first attempt to tell the tale as an appendix, an unfinished 194-line poem that makes a revealing postscript to the project; it sketched the origins of the first colony and made it clear that Simms's conception was indeed an epic, albeit ultimately one best suited for prose, not verse.

The irregular placement of the historical summaries suggests that Simms was working out the structural balance between history and fiction as he wrote. Ranging from two to twelve pages, these chapters break the narrative flow at odd points, as chapters 10, 11, 13, 18, and 21, although the text is peppered with comments and even entire paragraphs of straight-forward historical exegesis. As he promised in the introduction, the goal was to make it possible for a reader to separate "the *certain* from the *conjectural*; and yet, I trust, that I have succeeded in so linking the two together as to prevent the lines of conjunction from obtruding themselves upon his consciousness" (v). That masks the more subtle play of history that winds throughout the book, with authorial asides within the text pointing out the connections between sources and authorities, often linked to footnotes that continue the debate, elaborate a point, or identify a source. Although the chapters of "Historical Summary" were extensive, Simms provided the most compelling précis of the story in an essay included in *Views and Reviews* called "The Settlements of Coligny" (1: 78–88). It provided a detailed synopsis of what would eventually become *The Lily and the Totem*, giving a summary of the history of the colonies, its appeal as a story, and the approach to it that he would eventually take when he finally began writing the book a few years later.

The sources for that history were largely fragmentary, scattered, and occasionally contradictory, but Simms did an admirable job assembling a coherent narrative from them. One of the most important authorities Simms cited was Richard Hakluyt's 1587 translation of *A Notable Historie Containing Foure Voyages Made by Certaine French Captaines into Florida*. The first three of those voyages' accounts were written by René Laudonniere and the last by Dominique de Gourgues, both central characters in *The Lily and the Totem*. Simms also relied heavily on Pierre François Xavier Charlevoix's 1744 work *Histoire de la Nouvelle France*, which he quoted extensively throughout the book, often in French. *The Lily and the Totem* substantially follows Charlevoix's account of the two expeditions, though Simms points out where he disagreed with or departed from it (Charlevoix 1: 135–236).

Simms cites a number of supporting works throughout the text. He praises James (Jacques) Le Moyne's account of the second expedition for its illustrations, noting that "To this painter are we indebted for numerous pictures of the people and the region, their modes of life, costume and exercises, which are now invaluable" (*Lily* 115). This is one of a wide range of narratives, documents, and histories that Simms drew on in the course of writing the book, including William Shergold Browning's 1840 *History of the Huguenots* (*Lily* 2) and Blaize de Montluc's chronicles (*Lily* 416). As was typical for the era, he did not identify those sources fully: although he cited some works by title, more often he provided only a last name. Thus he cited Verazzani to confirm the nature of the Indians (*Lily* 7); Caseneuve and Verdier added to his discussion of Huguenot history (*Lily* 2); Lescarbot helped to make a point about de Gourgues' explorations (*Lily* 418).[3] Although not explicitly mentioned, Simms also drew on years of reading about European exploration, the Huguenots, Indians, and related topics, reflected in other works. John Lawson's 1709 *A New Voyage to Carolina*, which Simms cited in his 1844 *Life of Francis Marion* (13n; 18n), would have also provided useful details for *The Lily and the Totem*.

Simms's use of his sources was astute. He favored works that provided transcripts of original documents. Hakluyt, for example, was not only reputable but indispensable, a major source that Simms had used before and would refer to for the rest of his life; he asked for it, along with James Adair's *History of the American Indians*, in a letter to Evert Augustus Duyckinck in January 1846, which may well mark the start of the project (*Letters* 2: 135). Simms's admiration for Hakluyt may have been for a fellow historian whose aims were largely sympathetic to his own. Hakluyt's writing also represented the search for a usable past, as scholars have recently argued (Olesen), and, moreover, it challenged the boundaries of genre (Sacks), just as Simms did with *The Lily and the Totem*. Adair, however, was controversial even in Simms's day, for his argument that American Indians were descended from the ancient Hebrews, but Simms recognized the utility of the book as a valuable compendium of description and analysis of Native American life and customs (Braund xi–xii). It was one of a few works he asked for by name after the Civil War, following the destruction of his library (*Letters* 5: 102).

Simms read those sources carefully, monitoring their bibliographic history and noting the appearance of new translations or editions. In 1847, he advised Albert J. Pickett, hard at work on his history of Alabama, of the major sources and repositories that would assist him, including several translations of Charlevoix's *Histoire* (*Letters* 5: 393–401). Though he peppered his letters and reviews with commentary on sources and histories, in *The Lily and the Totem* that critique is extensive and woven into the narrative itself. Some of Simms's criticisms read as modern: he anticipated recent scholarship on Hakluyt, for example, by presenting the competing justifications used by the warring colonial powers in the New World (Schleck 771). Even some of his minor sources, such as Le Moyne, have continued to attract modern critical attention (Bennett; Lorant; White).

Yet Simms departed significantly from his sources by attributing motive and inferring character from even scant information; thus Alphonse D'Erlach, only briefly mentioned and sparingly described in Charlevoix, becomes a major character in *The Lily and the Totem*. Simms also differed from Charlevoix in his depiction of the lessons—or moral, as he put it—of the French failures. Charlevoix ultimately chided the French for their reprisal against the Spanish, writing that "I do not hesitate to say, that the expedition of the Chevalier de Gourgues . . . would have been infinitely exalted by so acting, that his moderation and French generosity formed a noble contrast to the inhumanity of the Spaniards, rather than by closing it with the same fury that he detested in them" (1: 235). Sectarianism aside (Charlevoix was Catholic), in Simms's history, there is no hint of reservation. There the retaliation was entirely appropriate (*Lily* 462; *Views* 1: 87).

This understanding fit in with Simms's conception of the work of a historian: he subscribed to the whiggish view that history should elevate, and in his view the moral in the documentary record of the Huguenot colonies was clear, lacunae and contradictions notwithstanding. The colonists' failure to recognize the implications of the Edenic qualities of the land they found, and their myopic lust for gold and silver, were the seeds of their misfortune, a fate finally enacted by Menendez's reprisal against their encroachment on lands claimed by Spain (N. Meriwether, "*Lily*"). The frontier justice of that retribution was one of several literary themes in the book, but like the work as a whole, it also illustrated a point Simms had argued in *Views and Reviews*, where he outlined his vision for a strong and independent national literature. In these essays, Simms brought together his ideas about literature, history, and the role of the artist in American society. In particular, they show how committed Simms was to a Jeffersonian federal notion of both the American polity and its literature, and how deeply intertwined his political thought and his literary philosophy were, especially in the 1840s. Discussing the themes in *The Lily and the Totem* necessarily entails connecting them with his broader critical theory, and in particular with the essays comprising the two volumes of *Views and Reviews*.

Untangling the themes and connections between Simms's critical theory and practice is difficult. Except in *View and Reviews*, his articulations of the tenets of that theory are scattered throughout his many periodical contributions, the prefaces of his books, and his correspondence. Still, as scholars have shown, Simms's thought, though dispersed, shows remarkable cohesion and clarity (Pearce, "Metaphysical"; Moltke-Hansen, "Ordered"). This is especially true of his literary theory: it adds up to a powerful and cogent vision of what American literature could be, even if Simms, as an author, never quite managed to realize its full potential—and even as, in his lifetime, he saw emerge a more radical, enduring, authentically American literary vision in the works of Nathaniel Hawthorne, Herman Melville, and Walt Whitman, all fellow members with him in the informal literary circle associated with the Young America movement.

A key tenet of Simms's critical philosophy was the primacy of national themes and motifs in literature. "The true and most valuable inspiration of the poet will be found either in the illustration of the national history, or in the development of the national characteristics," Simms averred. "His themes, if unallied to these, will be very likely to lack permanence and general interest" (*Views* 1: 40). It was a reciprocal relationship: national themes were a requisite for great art, and a great nation could only be defined by a unique national literature. That was a cornerstone of the agenda advanced by Young America. Simms proved to be one of the group's most ardent exponents, and Duyckinck urged him to collect *View and Reviews* to advance Young America's argument. Simms obliged:

> Europe must cease to taunt us because of our prolonged servility to the imperious genius of the Old World. We must set ourselves free from the tyranny of this genius, and the time has come when we must do so. We have our own national mission to perform—a mission commensurate to the extent of our country. (*Views* 1: 3)

If Americans were to forge a nation, they had to have a national literature. To Simms and his colleagues in Young America, it was a question that went to the core of the young country's identity: "Are we to aim and arrive at all the essentials of nationality—to rise into first rank and position as a people—to lift our heads, unabashed, among the great communities of Europe" (*Views* 1: 7), Simms asked? The implications were clear.

So were the hurdles. One of the criticisms leveled at American writers—Simms included—by the British press and their American sympathizers was that they were derivative, and mediocre at that. These charges galvanized Young America, though to varied responses (Moltke-Hansen, "Horizons"). It fell to Simms to make the most sustained reply, advanced over the course of several essays published in 1845. First, Simms claimed the inheritance of European arts and letters for American writers and artists, phrasing it in pointedly nationalistic terms: "it is just as legitimate, on the part of our poets, to model themselves upon the great masters of the stock to which they originally belonged, and to employ their fashions and develop their conditions, as it is with those whose immediate sires preferred the more quiet and less courageous duty of clinging still to the ancient firesides" (*Views* 1: 43). Barbs aside, Simms believed that the model of those writers would not only adapt to the foreign shores of the New World, it would bloom anew, in a hybrid sufficiently exotic to be hailed as a new species: "That we should think and write, according to the examples and lessons of our ancestors, is not a whit calculated to impair our originality," he maintained. "As Americans, merely, the case is different, and there are peculiarities which we may engraft upon our ancient models, which would not impair their symmetry, and would not be remiss as regards our independence" (*Views* 1: 44).

Simms had theoretical problems to surmount as well, chief among them the often fractious and fragmented identity of the new nation. He drew his answer from his political philosophy, making his case for regionalism as the basis of an American literature. Indeed, the sprawling diversity of the country meant that the only way a genuinely national literature could form would be from strong representatives drawn from many states and every region. Although he made it clear why this was advantageous in *Views and Reviews*, it was not until the 1856 reissue of *The Wigwam and the Cabin* that he made his most cogent statement on that topic. In the "Epistle Dedicatory" prefacing the volume, Simms bluntly stated that "to be *national* in literature, one must needs be *sectional*. No one mind can fully or fairly illustrate the characteristics of any great country; and he who shall depict *one section* faithfully, has made his proper and sufficient contribution to the great work of *national* illustration" (4, emphasis in original).

If a strong national literature was necessarily a function of strong regional literature, then America offered her writers abundant opportunity. The diversity of the country could itself be a spur to originality, Simms believed:

> The very inequalities of things in moral respects, in employments, in climate, soil and circumstance, which we find these severalties, is at once calculated to provoke the mind in each to exertion, and to endow it with originality.... The very divergencies of our paths are favourable to the boldness, the freedom and the flights of the national intellect. (*Views* 1: 18)

While America's diversity was a strong point, its youthfulness was a problem. That was the central stumbling block for his theory of art, and Simms recognized it. It was not just that the new nation's past was recent; as Simms pointed out, the stories were still compelling, the lessons still clear. Rather, it was what that newness signified. For writers, the accuracy and the extent of the record of American history constituted "one of the leading difficulties in the way of American romance":

> What portion of our history remains unwritten? What portion of it is so obscure that all may not equally see?—for, it need scarcely be said to the reader, that, if the ordinary citizen is at liberty to contravene your facts and dispute your premises, there is necessarily an end to your story. There must be a faith accorded to the poet equally with the historian, or his scheme fails of effect. The privileges of the romancer only begin where those of the historian cease. (*Views* 1: 42)

The precision of that documentation had profound consequences. "The poet who sings of Anglo-American achievements, must sing in fear and trembling," he concluded, "and such a feeling, we need scarcely say, is a sad weight to be carried by the Muse. Her genius is nothing without her impulse, and the caution which ties her wings, keeps her back from that heaven of invention, the exploration of which is the only assurance of her fame" (*Views* 1: 46). Addressing that challenge was the task he set for himself with *The Lily and the Totem*, but he also sought in his critical theory a way of answering that challenge on philosophical grounds. If the nation's history was too proximate, and too detailed, to be ignored, then American literature would have to encompass it, facts and all—and perhaps even turn those strictures into strengths.

Simms's own reading of history suggested a mechanism for this approach, explaining how the arts emerged as society evolved: "No doubt that, in the beginning of a democracy, in that first wild transition state, which follows the overthrow of favourite and long acknowledged authorities, art and literature . . . will shroud themselves" (*Views* 1: 17). Civilization is what enabled the arts: "when the first rude necessities of a new condition are pacified, and the machine begins to turn evenly and smoothly upon its axis,—such will be the working of democracy. This is not less our faith than our hope. The natural conclusions of reason lead us directly to this confidence, even if the history of the past did not afford us sufficient guaranties for the future" (*Views* 1: 17).

History moved in great cycles. Great civilizations rose and fell. The task of tracing that course, and the reasons underlying it, fell to the historian. To Simms,

> history itself is only valuable when it provokes this inquiry—when it excites a just curiosity—awakens noble affections,—elicits generous sentiments,—and stimulates into becoming activity the intelligence which it informs! Hence, it is the artist only who is the true historian. It is he who gives shape to the unhewn fact,—who yields relation to the scattered fragments,—who unites the parts in coherent dependency, and endows, with life and action, the otherwise motionless automata of history. (*Views* 1: 25)

The prevalence of those "motionless automata" in American history carried particular dangers for writers. In the hands of a "rigid historian," those facts were only "the withered branches and the prostrate truths, the blasted forms and the defaced aspects, the dry-bones of perished humanity" (*Views* 1: 22). Being obsessed with—or blinded by—facts did not make for good history, or good writing.

These contradictory constraints required reconciliation, and in his theory of realism Simms found a way. Defining the ideal "as nothing more than the *possible real*" ("Bulwer's" 52), Simms believed that there was no inherent contradiction between fealty to fact and promotion of an ideal. Indeed, his argument in *Views and Reviews* was that inherent in American history were lessons tailor-made for epic treatment, and that expression of those lessons was possible without departing from that history. It was tantalizingly close to an explicit statement that realism could be the foundation for a uniquely American conception of Romanticism, one of the most intriguing ideas in his poetics and in his critical theory.[4]

Simms did address the topic obliquely, however. In *Views and Reviews*, he discussed the work of historians and novelists as not only driven by the same motive—the elevation of an ideal—but also as differing only in the restrictions they faced when dealing with history:

> The liberties of conjecture which are accorded to the historian, become, in [the romancer's] case, liberties of creation. So far as the moral is concerned, the difference of privilege is no ways important. Their privileges differ only in degree. We permit the historian to look from his Pisgah into the land of equal

> doubt and promise; but the other is allowed to enter upon its exploration and to take formal possession of its fruits. (1: 31)

For *The Lily and the Totem*, he had to fulfill both roles, historian *and* romancer—and that was the real challenge the book posed for Simms.

That exploratory sense informs the experiment in genre that *The Lily and the Totem* represents. The book was Simms's attempt to show how fiction and history could work together to tell a story, to interrogate a legacy—and to do so in a way befitting the new nation: innovative, compelling, and unique. With that, Simms turned American history from a hindrance to an asset for its writers, one whose riches were ample enough to support a national literature:

> The studies yielded to the master of fiction by our moral progress, are not less numerous than those which the painter may gather, on every hand, from the matchless forest land through which he wanders. He has but to follow a like direction—to cut away the under-growth—to cast down the offensive and obtrusive object—to bring out into bolder relief such forms as merit to be made particular—to be raised into superiority, and elevated by appropriate tributaries—and the work is done as he could wish it. The creation is here—already in our possession!—it is the *clearing*—the *clearing* only—which has need to follow. (*Views* 1: 88, emphasis in original)

He gave an outline of what that clearing would reveal in a long essay that divided American history into four periods. Simms described the first as "the most valuable in all our history for the general purpose of art in fiction" (*Views* 1: 78), and praised the "Settlements of Coligny" specifically, noting that "It is not so well known, however, what a fine series of romances belongs to this history, needing only the ordinary developments of art, to render them as highly distinguished and delightful as those of any history, the foundations of which were laid in the most adventurous and primitive periods of society" (*Views* 1: 79).

That setting allowed Simms to present many of the broader themes he saw in American history, from the centrality of the border to the eclipse of the Indians to the roles of religion, materialism, domesticity, and art in the growth of nations. Central to all of these was the idea of the border, which continued to exercise a defining force in the America of his own time; in an 1840 novel he memorably referred to it as "a region still wild, and still the abode of so much that was barbarous" (*Border* 51). But borders were also where the elements of a nation's future greatness were revealed. This is why the border was a shaping metaphor for Simms (Guilds and Collins; K. Collins). He viewed it as a liminal space where nations were born and ethnogenesis played out, a petri dish filled with contradictory and conflicting forces, all contributing to the messy, violent process of civilization.

Two central themes in that broader process as it played out in America were the steady eclipse of the Native Americans and the powerful impact of religion. Scholars have found Simms's depiction of Indians compelling (Guilds and Hudson), and Simms correctly saw the centrality of their story to the unfolding of the American epic. One lesson of their marginalization and defeat was the failure of their worldview, not just the inferiority of their technology. Part of the success of British colonialism, and of the second wave of European conquests in the New World generally, was the driving role of religion. The need for religious freedom was clearly expressed in those early Huguenot attempts, though Simms was careful to describe the inchoate nature of their belief and practice. Still, religion exercised a significant role; as he wrote in *View and Reviews*, "the religion of a nation is the most subtle and widely diffused element in its whole character and history" (1: 38). Only a force as powerful as religion could impel those colonists to leave their homeland—or turn that homeland into a place of oppression, such that they had to flee. The task of the historian, or the romancer, was to explain those motives and link them clearly to the moral of the story. It was inherent in the subject, as individual as it was professional, binding authorial identity with national character; as Simms put it, "there is very little substantial difference, in reference to what is individual in the revelations of the artist, between the several topics of one's self, one's country, and one's religion!" (*Views* 1: 38). That played out in history—and in his own life.

Simms wrote *The Lily and the Totem* at a point in his career in which his literary and editorial labors had their most pronounced political edge. His politics have posed problems for scholars ever since William P. Trent's 1892 biography (Watson, *Nationalism*; Wakleyn), but any discussion of his work in the 1840s has to take into account his active political involvement during that time, from his term in the South Carolina House of Representatives to his efforts on behalf of his causes, friends, and political allies. Chief among those was his friend, South Carolina politician James H. Hammond, to whom Simms dedicated *The Lily and the Totem*. Indeed, that dedication was something of a political statement, though only a part of a more complicated agenda. Simms wanted to honor his friend but also to support him against Wade Hampton; in 1850, when the novel was published, Simms's time in the legislature was still very recent history, and he continued to feel drawn to the political arena, convinced he had a role to play, even if only as a voice to be reckoned with.

Hammond recognized the gesture. "I appreciate most sensibly the kindness of your dedication to me," he wrote Simms after the book was published. "There are men who will abuse you & your work on that account *solely*, for I am getting to be awfully hated—more so I think day by day. It does not trouble me, but it will if my friends come to share it with me" (qtd. in *Letters* 3: 61n). It made a somber but revealing backdrop for the book's reception and for its place in Simms's career, as he entered his greatest decade as a writer, yet also the one marked by his increasingly strident sectionalism, a continuing descent into defensiveness and vehemence that began in the late 1830s as he felt his state, his section, and his way of life besieged.[5]

If the timing of the dedication was rooted in the moment, the idea was not. His biography of Francis Marion had provided an initial platform for Simms to explore his views on the Huguenot contribution to South Carolina history. Its opening chapter was entitled "The Huguenots of South Carolina," and in the second, Simms attributed that hero's qualities as a leader to his Huguenot heritage—"in his own mind and conduct, the most striking of these characteristics, which mark the community in which he had his early training"—and praising them for "the harmony existing among them, their purity of conduct, propriety of sentiment, the modesty of their deportment, and firmness of their virtues" (*Francis Marion* 24).

The work on Marion came at a peak of Simms's critical thought, as Guilds has argued: "Simms in 1845 was close to being at the height of his narrative powers: sure of his craft, bold in his concept, confident of his theory" (*Literary Life* 176). The mid-1840s were not only the apex of his political ambitions, it was a time when Simms's work as editor and writer and public intellectual seemed to coalesce and reinforce more than compete and distract. Arguments Simms advanced in *Views and Reviews* echo throughout *The Lily and the Totem*, and indeed, the book in many ways represents a canvas for Simms's ideas about history, literature, and fiction. To extend Guilds's 1977 assessment, *The Lily and the Totem* should be considered Simms's clearest demonstration of his practice; it is a critical counterpart to *The Wigwam and the Cabin*, a work that David Moltke-Hansen has insightfully analyzed from that perspective in his critical introduction to the Library of American Books in the current collection. Yet despite its episodic nature, *The Lily and the Totem* was a full-length work, and as such it provided an even more compelling example of the critical theory that Simms committed to paper in the 1840s, knitting together his ideas about genre, history, fiction, nations, peoples, and the role of the artist in society (Moltke-Hansen, "Horizons"; N. Meriwether, "*Lily*").

The book certainly answered one of the more stinging criticisms leveled at *Views and Reviews*. The *Boston Morning Post* had joined the hue and cry against Simms's call for a distinctive national literature in their 29 November 1847 issue, observing, "It is a pity that some of these gentlemen should not produce a work which would serve to show what this singular 'American literature' really is. One look at such a model would be more convincing than the perusal of scores of essays" (qtd. in Guilds, *Literary Life* 182). *The Lily and the Totem* was just such a model, and in its narrative strategy, it may have sought to answer a critique Simms took far more seriously. In the *Salem Advertiser* of 2 May 1846, fellow Young American Nathaniel Hawthorne's review of *Views and Reviews* praised Simms's essays as "all creditable to the author" but went on to worry that "[t]he themes suggested by him, viewed as he views them, would produce nothing but historical novels, cast in the same worn mould that has been in use these thirty years, and which it is time to break up and fling away" (qtd. in Guilds, *Literary Life* 182).[6] Simms saw history in America as fulfilling the same fundamentally universal human need that it evinced in Europe, but in its contours—its proximity, its gritty factuality, even its epic qualities—it demanded and elicited unique responses from its authors. Thus Simms could write history, but do so in a way that was unique, and uniquely American. "There is a great deal to be done in behalf of our literature. There are immense harvests to be reaped," he wrote Duyckinck in August 1845, but he also admitted, "To be great & successful, we must fling *convention* to the dogs, & how many Americans do you know prepared for this" (*Letters* 2: 99).

That convention was as much a function of readers as writers. As John Miller has observed, Simms "may have decried the marketplace, but he was a shrewd participant in it" ("Business" 143), and when the market wanted novels, Simms did not scruple to respond. Thus he abandoned his original conception for the story, as "a religious narrative poem" (*Lily* 463), "because of the indifference of readers; who, in all periods have determined the usual directions of the writer" (*Lily* vi). Yet Simms thought enough of his incomplete poem to include it as the appendix to the book, and given his lifelong belief in the primacy of poetry among *belles lettres*, it merits mention. Divided into three sections, it opens with God speaking to the French admiral, Coligny, who sponsored the expeditions, "That stern old Christian warrior," who tells him to "gird thy loins / For toils and perils better overcome / By patience, than the sword" (463–64). Though God tells him to flee France—a place where "Tyranny / Hath wed with Superstition"—for "A new world / Full of all fruits and lovely to the eye" (465), Coligny demurs, saying that his place is in France, where he can best protect the colony. The first expedition sets forth, "a little band . . . / Still resolute for God; —having no home, / But that made holy by his privilege" (469), and the poem ends with them finding the New World, "the native land of soul, / Where conscience may take speech,—where truth take root, / And spread its living branches, till all earth / Grows lovely with their heritage" (469–70). Although brief, the fragment clearly established Simms's basic narrative aims: Coligny's heroism, the colonists' religious purity, the Edenic nature of the New World, and its destiny as a God-given refuge for the Huguenots. Its place at the end not only allowed the poem to emphasize the major themes of the book, but also made the broader point that historical truth inhered in the story itself, regardless of form; as a story, the Huguenot effort was indeed "history for the purposes of art."

Simms also used the poem to emphasize the uniqueness of his method. "With these [lines], my original design found its limit," he explained in the "Epistle Dedicatory" (*Lily* vi), but his decision to include the poem can also be read as a more complex gesture, one that emphasized the challenge and the resulting power of the book's merger of fiction and history. That, too, suggests that the prose novel form was the only one sufficiently elastic to accommodate the strictures of that method: it fit with the arguments Simms had developed in *Views and Reviews*, but it nonetheless represented a dramatic statement from a writer who considered himself foremost a poet, and one steeped in classical and British forms.

It is difficult to date the poem, however, and only scant evidence dates the book's genesis, though certainly Simms was thinking of the topic by 1842. He first codified his thoughts in a series of lectures to the Georgia Historical Society in March 1842, entitled "American History, Its Epochs and Incidents, Considered With Reference To Their Employment for the Purposes of Art in Fiction," but aside from a teaser, published in 1844, it would be another two years before he committed it to print. That teaser was revealing, however: "The Huguenot Settlements in Florida" appeared in two installments in *Ladies' Companion* in August and September 1844. It was the first outline of the project, an eight-page piece that, after extensive revision, became chapter fourteen of *The Lily and the Totem*.

"The Epochs and Events of American History, as Suited to the Purposes of Art in Fiction" appeared in five installments in Simms's *Southern & Western Monthly Magazine and Review* that spring and summer, concluding with the September issue. As a postscript, "The Huguenot Settlements in Florida" appeared in November, reprising the teaser. All that year, Simms pushed the idea for the book. In April, he pitched it to Duyckinck as a candidate for Wiley and Putnam's Library of American Books: "If Wiley's plan [for the series] succeeds, and he will pay decently, I will prepare for him an original Romance of Florida, in one volume, the scheme of which is in my head" (*Letters* 2: 55). There it stayed while Simms completed other obligations, though it never strayed far from his thoughts. By October, it had become a priority. "It is barely possible that I may send you the 'Life of Bayard' by the first of Jany.," he wrote Duyckinck. "This I will follow up by 'The Huguenots in Florida,' getting ready *ad interim* the material for the 2d. vol. of 'Views & Reviews'" (*Letters* 2: 106), he explained, hoping to begin work on the book "about Christmas" (*Letters* 2: 111).

His *Life of Captain John Smith* filled his hours outside of his legislative duties that fall, but by November, he was confident enough to tell Duyckinck that "I propose, as soon as I return from the Legislature to prepare for you the Huguenots in Florida, and (anonymously) the 'Life of Bayard'" (*Letters* 2: 118). January 1846 may have seen Simms at work on the project; certainly he was thinking about it, writing Duyckinck for help with sources (*Letters* 2: 135), but that spring also represented a difficult time personally. In February he confided to Lawson that he was despondent of "my fears, anxieties, angers & apprehensions. I have nothing else to write about. My head is weary with profitless toils, and my heart is sad with vague expectations . . . I am struggling against renewed fits of depression, which impair my energies & baffle my successes" (*Letters* 2: 140). He even asked friends to look into the possibility of a diplomatic appointment abroad.

Part of his bleak mood stemmed from what he felt was the lack of critical acclaim his recent efforts had received. "I am almost the only literary man in the country who succeeds without a party, and in spite of the hostility of party," he wrote Lawson. "But I must not grumble. Enough, my friend, that I despond, & am weary. I wish to escape & find respite for a while" (*Letters* 2: 140–41). His depression may have slowed his work, but his enthusiasm for the project remained undimmed. "I am now on my Life of Smith and doing little else," he wrote Lawson. "But I hope that by that time [summer] to get ready my Huguenots & possibly something more" (*Letters* 2: 140). But he was also continuing his research, pressing Duyckinck for "the copy of Hakluyt, upon which I somewhat depend" and pledging "as soon as I can, to send you the MS. of Huguenots in Florida" (*Letters* 2: 143). Still, he could not resist a slight jab at his old friend: "I do not know that there will be any use in doing any thing as yet upon the 'Huguenots,' for your series comes forth with such angelic pauses between that they will scarcely be needed before next Christmas" (*Letters* 2: 147).

That was well, since his biography of Smith occupied the spring, but he was still optimistic for the book's prospects in May, reporting to Duyckinck that he wanted to see "the Huguenots" published in New York, presumably by Wiley and Putnam (*Letters* 2: 164). More than just other work intruded. On October 23, he wrote to Lawson that his wife was in ill health: "Sorrow & frequent brooding are the causes of her prostration. We have had enough, as you know, to overthrow any spirit less stubborn than my own. But mine is not wholly unshaken. The truth is, my dear Lawson, I have become greatly a discontent. Carolina has been a region of tombs for me" (*Letters* 2: 195). With his plantation's finances precarious, the idea of moving north to further his writing career appealed—but that required having a backstock of writing to sell. "I will go to work industriously for the next six months and get as much matter under weigh [*sic*] as I can make available next summer at the North" (*Letters* 2: 196).

That was the pressure that surrounded the start of the Huguenot project—and that helps to explain its final delays. On October 24, Simms promised Duyckinck that "I am going to work hard on my Bayard & my Huguenots" (*Letters* 2: 199), a pledge he continued to repeat through the end of the year. By then, however, he thought it "likely that I shall do nothing more, up to the summer, than prepare the life of Bayard and the Huguenots" (*Letters* 2: 234). He made good progress on the former, at least, writing Duyckinck on 25 February 1847, that "I have nearly finished my Life of the Chevalier Bayard" and "I think to get ready to bring on with me my Huguenots in Florida" (*Letters* 2: 273). By the middle of March he had almost completed *Bayard*. "Whether I shall attempt to get any thing else ready before I go North, is questionable" he wrote George Frederick Holmes (*Letters* 2: 284). To Duyckinck he was more optimistic, writing his old friend a week later that "I wish to get my Bayard, & if possible my Huguenots, ready before leaving for N.Y.," which he reckoned to be no later than early May (*Letters* 2: 286).

Simms's central concern was still the forum for publication: "Are W[iley] & P[utnam]. disposed to take the 'Huguenots' now" (*Letters* 2: 286)? The book's appearance in that series would make a powerful statement, one that connected it even more centrally to the arguments laid out in *Views and Reviews*, and Simms knew it. When that prospect foundered, he still persevered, and by the end of July 1848, he could inform Lawson that "I am in hopes next month to complete my Huguenots" (*Letters* 2: 414). The biography of Smith intruded, however, taking longer than Simms had hoped. Still, as he wrote Lawson by the end of August, he was hard at work "on my Huguenots in Florida." "But," he added, "I am writing 30 or 40 pages (letter sheet) per day, and feel perfectly prostrate by night" (*Letters* 2: 438). He nevertheless hoped to complete the book by mid-September, as he explained to James H. Hammond (*Letters* 2: 439), but by the end of November, it was still incomplete, though within "a few weeks of being finished" (*Letters* 6: 93). In his pitch to publishers Carey and Hart Simms described it as "a work, semi historical, upon which I have been for some time engaged," recounting "the history of a most exciting and interesting endeavor . . . all enveloped in an atmosphere of fiction" (*Letters* 6: 93). Interestingly, he had not settled on his final title, calling it "The Lily and the Wampum," and more significantly, he envisioned it as two volumes "of probably 300 or 320 pages each," more than twenty-percent greater than its final tally. This truncation, along with his circumstances and especially the rapidity with which he was writing, helps to explain some of the choppiness of the book's structure, in particular the increasingly dense blend of historical analysis and fictional exegesis that characterizes the last eight chapters.

The book finally went to press in the spring of 1850. In April, Simms reported to Lawson that it was slated for an August release (*Letters* 3: 34, 49), and the "Epistle Dedicatory" bears the date of 1 May 1850 (vii). When it came out, under the imprint of the New York firm of Baker and Scribner, it bore the title *The Lily and the Totem, or, the Huguenots in Florida. A Series of Sketches, Picturesque and Historical, of the Colonies of Coligni, in North America. 1562–1570*. Baker and Scribner did a modest job on the book, adding no illustrations and binding the 478-page volume in dark green cloth over heavily embossed boards with gilt lettering on the spine. It was a handsome, if plain, volume.

Simms rarely betrayed any sense of uncertainty about his projects in his surviving letters, but *The Lily and the Totem* must have given him more pause than most. Barbs could be expected; the *Knickerbocker*'s attacks on him and Young America were still recent, after all. But the bigger question was whether even a sympathetic critic would apprehend the statement the book made about combining history and fiction into a new genre that embraced the potential of a national literature. Perhaps just as important, would readers welcome something so structurally different from what they were used to encountering when they picked up a book, whether fiction or history? Simms stayed in Charleston that fall, but one consolation of his protracted absence from his beloved plantation Woodlands was that he was also closer to the news—and to the mails.

He need not have worried. The *Literary World* gave the book a two-page review in its September issue, praising it for providing "history as the facts of a record would be presented by an able lawyer, and not by the drowsy, matter-of-fact witness. The interest is awakened by raising the tone of history, warming it with the hue of fancy, and making it dramatic by the exercise of art" (Rev. of *Lily* 189–90). The only criticism leveled was against the unfinished poem comprising the appendix, but even that served as a platform for praising the book, saying that "just enough of the verse is given to allow our congratulations that so much of true poetry as may be found in the book has been wedded to a gracefulness of rhetoric, free to travel in any harness it pleases, at the sacrifice of rather constrained blank verse" (Rev. of *Lily* 189). The anonymous reviewer was especially impressed with "The Legend of Guernache," one of the vignettes in the book, but began by noting, at length, that the real value of the book lay in its regionalism:

> So many American writers have dealt in the Romance of Puritan history, after freely kissing the "blarney stone of America" (as the late lamented James Reyburn termed the Rock at Plymouth) that it is a relief to have a writer take up the history of other American settlements, and give it an exciting prominence; for really, it would seem to the limited reader, that the Puritan adventurers were the earliest at the New World settlement, and that their doings and sayings were the only rememberable occurrences in the primitive annals of the country. (Rev. of *Lily* 189)

The public affirmation of the book's artistic success—and its political agenda—must have pleased Simms especially. Writing Duyckinck on 11 September 1850, he could not resist rubbing it in: "You will have seen before this reaches you, the 'Lily & the Totem'—which was to have been one of your W & P. Series of American Books. I trust that it has given you satisfaction" (*Letters* 3: 60–61).

The accolades continued. *Harper's* reviewed the work in October, giving it a half-column in its "Literary Notices" section, calling it "romantic legends connected with the establishment of Huguenots in Florida, embroidered upon a substantial fabric of historical truth, with great ingenuity and artistic effect" (718). It singled out the "Legend of Guernache" as the best story in the book, "a record of love and sorrow, scarcely surpassed in sweetness and beauty by any thing in the romance of Indian history," but the notice also found valid Simms's overall approach of privileging the history, so that "facts are not superseded by the romance" (718). Simms, too, considered the tale "one of peculiar grandeur—bright with a lurid sort of brightness,—a strange wild mixture of glare and gloom" (*Views* 1: 84).

That same month, the *Democratic Review* gave the book an admiring paragraph, longer than many works received but only half as long as the notice of the revised edition of the *The Deerslayer*, which praised Cooper's "profound genius" ("Notices of New Books" 377). *The Lily and the Totem* came off well, however, with the anonymous reviewer noting that Simms "has long been before the public as a successful author, and his works have eminently illustrated some of the brightest pages in American history; and the present work contributes further to its romance" (379). Not surprisingly, it also praised the book's regionalist agenda, calling it "a very successful counterpart to the story of Puritan Deeds in New England, which is in everybody's mouth." *Sartain's Magazine* followed suit in November. Its positive notice, brief but still one of the longer ones in that issue, observed that Simms's "social and literary position among the Huguenot families of South Carolina have given him peculiar qualifications" as the book's author. The notice went on to compliment the work's status as a historical romance, concluding that "There is no class of books which we should more promptly welcome than those which revive and perpetuate the events of our early colonial history" ("Editorial" 318).

In November, *DeBow's Review* weighed in with the best review the book received, albeit brief: "This is generally admitted to be one of the very best productions of a man who has, at an early age, attained very high laurels in our literary world, and whose industry has exceeded that of almost any of his contemporaries" ("Literary, Editorial" 574). The next month, *Holden's Dollar Magazine* followed with a three-sentence note that praised the book and prefaced a long quote from Simms's "Epistle Dedicatory" (Rev. of *Lily* 758–59).

The critical consensus, if modest, was altogether positive. *DeBow's* may have been the most generous estimation, but all were favorable. "And it is with pleasure we commend it as a production which abundantly increases the fame of its author," the *Literary World* observed. "It is by such efforts of his pen that Mr. Simms will best answer the demands of a reading public, and always keep fresh the admiration of his countrymen" (Rev. of *Lily* 189). *Harper's* claim vied with the *Literary World*'s high estimation, observing that "With his power of graphic description, and the mild poetical coloring which he has thrown around the whole narrative, Mr. Simms will delight the imaginative reader, while his faithful adherence to the spirit of the history renders him an instructive guide through the dusky and faded memorials of the past" ("Literary Notices" 718). The *Democratic Review* was more measured, concluding only that "under the able guidance of Mr. Simms, a story of unusual interest is produced" ("Notices of New Books" 379). The brevity of *Sartain's* remarks, though more extensive than in the case of most works it noted, underscored the praise of the book as "a very charming fiction" ("Editorial" 318); it was a sentiment echoed by *Holden's* note, recommending the book as "a narrative of rare interest" (Rev. of *Lily* 758).

Holden's compliment made a fine grace note to the book's contemporaneous reception, but by then, Simms had moved on to other projects. In a December letter to Lawson, he wrote that "Recently I put forth a work, the Lily & the Totem, which is considerably praised and which I suppose you have seen" (*Letters* 3: 79). Yet it was only one in a list of recent and current projects. Simms did not forget about the book, but four months after its publication, *The Lily and the Totem* had receded from his mind and from the public eye as well.

Despite three more printings in 1850, 1854, and 1871, the book's obscurity became one of its most stubborn characteristics. After that first flush of reviews, it garnered some modern critical attention: two chapters addressed it, one in an unpublished 1966 dissertation and the other in Guilds's 1988 critical anthology *Long Years of Neglect*. Along with a few scattered mentions, that comprises the scholarly literature on the book. The consensus is that it is a good, if flawed, effort whose hybrid approach is its most noteworthy aspect, though it took decades for that estimation to emerge.

After its final publication, *The Lily and the Totem* went unnoticed until Trent's 1892 biography. There, a brief mention recounted the work's subject and skated over its genre by quoting Simms's introductory comment, out of context, that most people would view it as a "Romance of History." Trent's only assessment was the back-handed compliment that "one is certain that the prolific author did more credit to himself and to his subject by writing in prose than he would have done had he stuck to his original intention of writing in verse" (196). The book then dropped from sight until 1966, when it received its most extended treatment since its publication in an unpublished dissertation by Mary Crow Anderson. After surveying the literature, she concluded that "Simms' *The Lily and the Totem* remains, after well over one hundred years, the most significant of the novels about the early French Protestant colonies" (56). In 1977, Guilds considered the book in his early discussion of Simms's use of history, finding it superior to both *The Yemassee* and, more interestingly, *The Cassique of Kiawah*. In his estimation, the book "successfully blends history and fiction and contains some of Simms's finest writing" ("Simms's Use" 509–10). In particular, he singled out the introduction for providing Simms's "clearest statement concerning his technique for enhancing history with art" (510). Simms scholar and editor of the Centennial Simms series James B. Meriwether in 1988 considered it an "impressive, if hard to define book ("Theme" 21); that same year, my chapter on the book called it a flawed but interesting work that nonetheless offered much to Simms scholars. Judged by Simms's own criteria, it had to be considered successful, despite being "too much history to be fiction, too much fiction to be history, and us[ing] history in a different and more demanding fashion than does historical fiction" ("*Lily*" 82). Four years later, Guilds gave his final assessment in his biography of Simms, noting that it "is not Simms's masterpiece, but its power and originality cannot be denied." In particular, he singled out several chapters that "move[d] with the powerful narrative sweep of his best novels," and concluded that despite its weaknesses, "the book overall has remarkable vitality and readability, with stunning examples of realism" (*Literary Life* 194).

Historians have also tended to consider the book from a literary standpoint. Calling it "One of his most unusual experiments at blending history and fiction" (*Sober* 67), Busick nonetheless treated it as part of Simms's other historical writings, using it to preface his discussion of the Revolutionary War romances. Those, Busick correctly noted, represented Simms's "most ambitious foray into the field of historical romance" (*Sober* 68), but they also represented a less ambitious approach to writing history than did *The Lily and the Totem*. Still, Busick's critique raised the larger point of how the book should be treated. Exactly what kind of book is *The Lily and the Totem*?

While the book was in press, Simms called it "Semi Historical" (*Letters* 3: 36), and he was content for readers to view it as a "Romance of History," as he wrote in the book's "Epistle Dedicatory;" this, despite the book's more challenging embrace of the strictures of history than that genre connoted (v). That introduction is an important entry into Simms's larger argument about American history and literature. Indeed, that introductory letter extends the ideas advanced in *View and Reviews*, establishing the book as an example of an entirely new genre of historical fiction, and setting up the work as his most daring expression of that theory—or his most ambitious experiment to test it (N. Meriwether, "*Lily*").

In part informed by the work going into his critical essays of this period, Simms was also experimenting with his praxis. In 1849, *Father Abbot* gathered satirical columns published in the *Charleston Mercury*, one of several satires he produced during his career; another *sui generis* effort, the epistolary novel *Flirtation at the Moultrie House*, issued the same month as *The Lily and the Totem*. The stakes for those efforts were very different, however, and neither *Flirtation* nor *Abbot* carried the weight of the other's expectations. With *The Lily and the Totem*, Simms was exploring the limits of form, trying to assess how those strictures could inhere even more deeply in the text, going beyond subject into the very structure and aims for the work—into genre itself. Ultimately, the significance of *The Lily and the Totem*'s complex and ambiguous classification is also its great critical contribution, for it shows how, in Simms's reading of history, the gritty factual clarity of American history could still allow a genuine literature to flower—a grand epic as powerful, distinct, and distinctive as those of England were from their French counterparts.

Simms never attempted another work that so directly addressed both history and romance, although his subsequent novels reveal a heightened sense of the interplay between the two genres. Three years later, when he turned to the other major historical effort in that first period of American history, the Spanish explorations, he followed an equally rigorous methodology, though without the formal historical argument. In the introduction to *Vasconselos*, he admitted that "It is the province of romance, even more decidedly than history, to recall the deeds and adventures of the past." Indeed,

> [i]t is to fiction that we must chiefly look for those living and breathing creations which history quite too unfrequently deigns to summon to her service. The warm atmosphere of present emotions, and present purposes, belongs to the *dramatis personae* of art; and she is never so well satisfied in showing us human performances, as when she betrays the passions and affections by which they were dictated and endured. It is in spells and possessions of this character, that she so commonly supersedes the sterner muse whose province she so frequently invades; and her offices are not the less legitimate, as regards the truthfulness of things in general, than are those of history, because she supplies those details which the latter, unwisely as we think, but too commonly, holds beneath her regard. (1)

It was perhaps more of a response to Hawthorne's earlier critique than it was an admission of the failure of his earlier methodology. Indeed, the adherence to fact remained: "In the work before us, however, it is our purpose to slight neither agency. We shall defer to each of them, in turn, as they may be made to serve a common purpose. They both appeal to our assistance, and equally spread their possessions beneath our eyes. We shall employ, without violating, the material resources of the Historian, while seeking to endow them with a vitality which fiction only can confer" (*Vasconselos* 1–2). The echoes of his introduction to *The Lily and the Totem* still resounded clearly, but now Simms had tempered his approach. Though he continued to stress the obligations to history, he had abandoned the apparatus that showed how those obligations were acquitted. Never again would he merge history and fiction so clearly, so carefully, and so transparently.

In *Views and Reviews*, Simms wrote that "A certain degree of obscurity, then, must hang over the realm of the romancer. The events of history and of time, which he employs, must be such as will admit of the full exercise of the great characteristic of genius—imagination" (1: 42). Scholars have correctly pointed out how this belief not only informed but hindered Simms's fiction. Those dark parts in history—the gaps in the record—were more than just canvases onto which to project his imagination. They were also warnings of the fragility of the past, of the frailty of human effort. Most of all, they were warnings against complacency, mute reminders of the consequences of the failure to remember, like the mysteries made palpable by the ancient ruins that formed such a prominent symbol in his postwar unfinished novel, "The Brothers of the Coast." That was the work of America's writers: the sacred charge to remember, to record, to preserve—and to persevere. *The Lily and the Totem* represented a uniquely pointed expression of that charge. The book addressed a fragmentary record, a vanished heritage, and a failed enterprise—making it a vital example of what history *was*, in Simms's eyes, and how it could inform the new nation's literature. Simms understood that how writers filled those gaps was a complex task as well as a fundamentally moral act; nowhere else did he demonstrate that belief so explicitly.

That explains both the appeal and the problems of the book. For whatever reasons, artistic or political, *The Lily and the Totem* prompted Simms to step back and show more of his reading of history than he would in any other romance. Here he showed how historical judgment informed plot and narrative, and especially how it defined character; here he also showed how he used and interrogated his sources, quoting, translating, arguing with them. Simms's goal was to make that entire process visible, from the first lines of inspiration—seen in his inclusion of the unfinished epic poem in the appendix—to the final work, showing how it flowered and departed from the textual foundation of his sources. He recognized that this goal would largely escape most readers—who would consider it just another "Romance of History," as he wrote in the introduction—but his own ambitions for the book remained a high-water mark for him, for his critical philosophy, and for his corpus. Though he never revisited the topic of the Huguenot colonies, Simms continued to write about Huguenots for the rest of his life. In *The Golden Christmas* (1852), the character Madame Girardin comically illustrates the friction between South Carolinians of English and Huguenot descent, a theme that colored and in some cases informed, the dramatic conflicts of his Revolutionary War novels, epitomized by the character of Peyre St. Julien in *The Forayers* (1855) and *Eutaw* (1856). But *The Lily and the Totem* represented his most sustained treatment of the Huguenots, and that may help to explain why Simms made such an effort to give it a fourth and final printing.

After the War, Simms made considerable efforts to interest publishers in issuing a new and expanded edition of his complete works, one that would include *The Lily and the Totem*, which Redfield had not included. Less than a year from his death he was still seeking that end, writing his children to ask if Gilmore had "put up the set of my works; was the work 'The Lily & the Totem' among them; and have they been forwarded to Col. Evans" (*Letters* 5: 229). While the dire economic straits he faced certainly explain the appeal of the project, *The Lily and the Totem* was the only work he mentioned by name. It is a curious specificity. It suggests that the book still held a particular appeal for its author—that its republication meant, in Simms's eyes, that the book still held up, twenty years after its first publication. If so, its lessons now confronted a radically altered South—and a radically changed Simms.

The lessons of the Civil War shattered Simms's understanding of history; as Moltke-Hansen has noted, "The experience of the war radically challenged what he had thought and said over the first forty years of his literary career. In the aftermath he could not return to his antebellum worldview or its rendering" ("History Failed" 5). Reconstruction changed Simms from a historian who subscribed to a whiggish sense of history as moral progress to a writer who had lived through an inferno that destroyed that belief; in literary historian David

S. Shields's words, the War made Simms "a chastened witness to the potency of the brute application of resources and the ruthlessness of industrial-commercial culture" (xiii). All that remained was his conviction that the connection to that past perdured, and continued to shape the present; that even in that first epoch in American history, it was possible to discern "the small but impressive beginnings of a wondrous drama in which we, ourselves, are still living actors," as he wrote in the introduction to *Vasconselos* (2).

Thus the lessons—the moral—of his history of the Huguenot colonies took on a very different cast after the Civil War. If the South had been right—if the cause of southern independence had been justified—then its defeat demonstrated that material progress could indeed prevail over moral superiority. Viewed in that way, the lessons of the past could change, and perhaps Simms's Huguenots had simply perished at the hands of a more powerful adversary; perhaps their weaknesses were not fatal, and could have been overcome. Even in a shattered South, perhaps *The Lily and the Totem* could still offer advice, if not hope.

The loss of his copyrights—and the Redfield plates—may have nixed the chance for Evans to publish a complete edition of Simms's works, but a few months after Simms's death, the Charleston printing firm in which Evans was a partner, Walker, Evans and Cogswell, reissued the book, the fourth and final impression made from the original plates. It made an interesting postscript to a long career: a sole volume, snatched from the devastating loss of his other copyrights; a pet project, snatched from the oblivion that silenced so many antebellum books. And its appearance marked the last of the projects that he sought to complete in his waning days, finally coming to fruition.

Regardless of his motive, for Simms to have made such extraordinary efforts to see the book back in print lends particular weight to this republication. However fluid its lessons, whatever else it may have represented, this final printing of the book clearly gestured to its author's past and to his abiding concerns as a writer. Yet it was more. This last edition recast *The Lily and the Totem* as a literary epitaph for its author, a testament to the writer who had devoted his career to writing the story of the founding of the American nation, in the genesis of American literature. Now it became the capstone of Simms's career, a crowning effort that fulfilled the prediction he had set forth in *Views and Reviews*, more than a quarter-century earlier: "The spell of genius, in thus making sacred the ruins of time, preserves itself from oblivion" (1: 41).

NOTES

1. For Simms's opinions on Sidney, see *Letters* 1: 12; 2: 223, 308, and 396; 3: 260, 269, 278, 287, and 412; 5: 105.
2. For Simms's admiration of and influence by Milton, see, for example, *Letters* 1: 222; 5: 174. Scholars have explored Simms's debts to Milton; see Kibler, *Selected* (1990) and Brennan, *Romantic*.

3. Florentine explorer John de Verazzani's [or Verazzano's] account of his earlier expedition was included by Hakluyt. French antiquarian Pierre de Caseneuve was the author of *Dictionnaire Etymologique de la Langue Françoise*, and others; his "Origines au Etymologies Francoises" (1650) is a likely source for Simms's reference. Antoine du Verdier—not to be confused with Nicholas Verdier, a Huguenot captain identified by last name in the book—wrote *La Prosopographie au Description de Personnes Insignes* (1573), which discusses the Huguenots. Marc Lescarbot's *Histoire de la Nouvelle-France* (multiple editions, 1609–1618) is the likely source for Simms's references to this author.
4. For more on Simms's Romanticism, see Brennan, Kibler, and Nakamura. Scholars have also explored the significance of Simms's use of realism from several perspectives, but its place in Simms's complex attitude toward and relationship with Romanticism remains fertile ground for inquiry. Especially significant is Simms's insistence that American literature could accept and incorporate the country's history as a viable foundation for art—that its intensive factuality could be converted from a disadvantage, according to the traditional standards of European Romantics, into a strength that would be the basis of a unique, American instantiation and adaptation of British Romanticism and British theories of the historical romance; see Brennan, *Romantic* and Nakamura, especially his chapter 1.
5. David Moltke-Hansen has pointed to 1838 correspondence as the first sign of this process. At the time of the publication of *The Lily and the Totem*, Simms was editing the *Southern Quarterly Review*, dramatically increasing its political content (Kibler and Moltke-Hansen 1).
6. According to Guilds, this is the only known criticism of Simms by Hawthorne (*Literary Life* 182), although Simms reviewed Hawthorne and commented on him favorably in both his periodical contributions and his letters: see, for example, *Magnolia* 2 n.s. (Feb. 1843): 140; *Southern and Western* 2 (Aug. 1845): 128–31; and *Letters* 2: 89. No evidence proves that Simms read Hawthorne's review, though it was certainly possible, even probable; the connections between their circles would have made a report of it likely to reach Simms.

Marie de Berniere: A Tale of the Crescent City

W. MATTHEW J. SIMMONS

While William Gilmore Simms considered his full-length romances among his most significant contributions to nineteenth-century American literary culture, these works varied greatly in achievement and aesthetic merit. Often, the writer's prose was compromised by prolixity and his narrative development hampered by his inclusion of "big ideas," often at the cost of overall aesthetic effectiveness. Yet, on the whole, Simms's shorter fiction was relatively devoid of the flaws that could sometimes haunt his long works. While novels like *Woodcraft* and *The Yemassee* may be Simms at his absolute best—and strong enough to place him among the upper echelon of American writers of his time—the novella and short story are perhaps the writer's most consistently strong genres. In those forms, Simms was a disciplined author, crafting works marked by highly entertaining and effective narratives, memorable characters and situations, and sophisticated concepts presented in ways that complement the aesthetic achievements of the work. The strengths of Simms as a short fictionist are on display quite clearly in the three novellas that form the collection *Marie de Berniere: A Tale of the Crescent City, etc. etc. etc.*: the titular romantic ghost story "Marie de Berniere," the Caribbean morality tale "The Maroon," and the plantation Christmas story "Maize in Milk."

While each of these tales has its own textual history, the collection itself was first published by Lippincott, Grambo, and Co. of Philadelphia in 1853. The collection was well-received by critics, with *Harper's* calling the three tales "highly-wrought portraitures of Southern character," and Paul Hamilton Hayne, writing in the Charleston *Weekly News*, calling the collection's stories "some of the best of the author's minor tales," and selecting "The Maroon" and "Maize in Milk" to be worthy of especial merit (Butterworth and Kibler 88, 91). The book was a commercial success as well, as evidenced by Lippincott, Grambo, and Co.'s 1855 reissue of the collection, this time under the name *The Maroon: A Legend of the Caribees, and Other Tales*. The work also was popular in Europe, with German publisher W.C. Durgulin of Leipzig issuing at least three printings of *Marie de Berniere. Eine Geschichte aus New-Orleans. Und andere Erzählungen* in 1854. This proved a natural outlet for the collection, given the heavy influence of German romantic fiction on the individual tales. While there is evidence that Simms sought to republish these three novellas in value-priced standalone editions during the 1860s—intending these, and other similarly-sized short fictions, to be works "for reading in camps and along the highways" (*Letters* 4: 420)—only "Marie de Berniere" found another life in this form. However, all three works are included in the 1974 *Stories and Tales*, a scholarly collection that forms Volume V of the University of South Carolina Press's never-finished *Centennial Edition* of Simms's writings.

"Marie de Berniere; A Tale of the Crescent City"

"Marie de Berniere" is arguably the best, and certainly the most sophisticated, of the three tales present in this collection, and its textual history is appropriately the most robust. Over the course of seven years, Simms developed this work from a small "sketch" into one of the most significant short fictions in his canon. The germ of "Marie de Berniere" was originally published as "The Unknown Masque. A Sketch of the Crescent City" in the April 1845 number of the *Southern and Western Monthly Magazine and Review*, a Charleston literary journal Simms edited. Published under the pseudonym "E—," this was the only appearance of this short work until its inclusion in *Stories and Tales*. Nevertheless, "The Unknown Masque" began to evolve into a larger and more robust work soon after its appearance in the *Southern and Western*.

Simms had begun to expand "The Unknown Masque" for republication by late 1848, as indicated in a November 20 letter to his friend and literary agent James Lawson. According to this letter, Simms had been contacted by the New York-based editor Israel Post, who offered Simms "$5 per page" for contributions to a "new magazine." In this letter, Simms stated that he told Post he would send an "article probably next week" (*Letters* 2: 456). This "article" was a slightly expanded version of "The Unknown Masque," at this point called "The Egyptian Masque; a Tale of the Crescent City." The first installment of "The Egyptian Masque" appeared in the second and final issue of Post's *American Metropolitan Magazine* in February 1849 (*Letters* 2: 456n). John Caldwell Guilds, the editor of *Stories and Tales*, notes that the texts of these two early versions "are basically similar in content," and that, in some places, "the phrasing is identical," though the fragmentary second version is about two hundred words longer than "The Unknown Masque" (Guilds, *Writings* 700). These slight differences between these two early iterations belie Simms's larger goal for the tale, something that likely began to take shape soon after the aborted publication of "The Egyptian Masque." Writing to Lawson in May 1849, the author told his agent that if "Post has failed and his magazine has stopt [*sic*], it is highly important that I recover the portions of M.S. which remain unpublished" (*Letters* 2: 513). Simms, it seems, was ready to take that brief sketch and rework it into something much more significant.

While it is unclear whether or not Simms recovered these unpublished portions of manuscript, we do know that he was serious about the story's redevelopment, as he began to transform an entertaining short story into a significant and sophisticated novella at some point during the next few years. "Marie de Berniere; A Tale of the Crescent City" appeared in its current form in early 1852, published serially between February 14 and March 27 in the weekly magazine *Arthur's Home Gazette*. After this serialized appearance, the novella would be published three more times: as the lead story in Lippincott, Grambo, and Co.'s 1853 and 1855 editions of the present collection, and finally as *The Ghost of My Husband. A Tale of the Crescent City*, the second number in Chapman and Company's "Sunny Side Series" of value-priced reissues in 1866.[1]

In "Marie de Berniere," Simms gives us a tale of love, intrigue, and mystery, all the while providing a robust treatment of the expansive and complex social life of New Orleans. The tale is told through the eyes of "William," an eighteen year-old "humble rustic" from a "little village" in west Tennessee. William journeys down the Mississippi to gain worldly experience from a first-hand encounter with the sophisticated high society of New Orleans, traveling in the company of Frederick Brandon, another Tennessean whose travels, education, and experiences have made him into a sophisticated gentleman (Simms, *Marie* 13). Through introductions facilitated by Brandon's sister, Madame de Chateauneuve, the wife of a wealthy Creole aristocrat, Brandon and William become enmeshed in the life of the upper crust of New Orleans Creole society.

At the center of this life are parties, and the novella is appropriately built around the *bal masque* of the wealthy widow Marie de Berniere. Married at sixteen to a possessive, jealous, and violent husband, Marie is relieved when he unexpectedly dies. She quickly becomes the most eligible bachelorette in New Orleans, and Brandon soon assumes the role of her primary suitor. Their engagement is put in jeopardy at Marie's *bal masque*, where a mysterious man, costumed identically to Brandon, frightens Marie by presenting himself as the ghost of her late husband. This "ghost" threatens to reveal Marie as a criminal—an assertion based on the fantasies of killing her abusive husband she spoke aloud to herself in the privacy of her own closet—unless she ends her engagement with Brandon. Convinced that someone is out to manipulate Marie for her money, Brandon spends the novella both convincing Marie that this was no ghost and uncovering the identities of the individuals involved in the conspiracy. In crafting such a plot, Simms neatly mixes a love story, a detective story, and a ghost story into an entertaining and aesthetically pleasing tale.

But Simms is not merely providing us with a pleasant and satisfying entertainment; "Marie de Berniere" also presents the author at his philosophical best, challenging his readers with robust questions about the mutability of identity, the roles of faith and duty, and the ways in which these concerns connect individuals to themselves and their communities. Further, "Marie de Berniere" provides a detailed picture of New Orleans itself, showing the various influences the city has felt throughout its history. The novella presents a significant discussion of the social life of the Creole, the intrusion of the Anglo, and the contributions to both the physical and social constitution of the city by the Spanish, French, and English. Taken together, the illustrative, intellectual, and entertaining elements of the novella combine to make "Marie de Berniere" one of Simms's truly excellent works.

"The Maroon: A Legend of the Caribees"

Writing in the critical apparatus of *Stories and Tales*, Guilds notes that "The Maroon" has its origins in a "short sketch entitled 'A Legend of the Pacific' published anonymously in the *New York Mirror*, X (Oct. 13, 1832), 117–118, and shortly thereafter under the same title in *The Book of My Lady* (1833), pp. 244–256" (*Writings* 707). "A Legend of the Pacific," however, cannot be rightly considered an early version of "The Maroon," but rather Simms simply working through early interests in the subject matter he would begin to develop in earnest over a decade later, specifically notions of cultural contact, isolation, and social obligation.

Once the author did return to the ideas first set forth in "A Legend of the Pacific," it was under dark and troubling circumstances. The late 1840s was a period of financial and personal struggles for Simms, and he composed "The Maroon" against this background. In a 23 October 1846 letter to his agent, James Lawson, he first mentioned "a Tale in three parts, for each of which you shall demand $20 cash, unless you prefer the $3 per page arrangement." Simms opened that letter by putting forth a litany of complaints about his financial situation, the health of his family members, and his bad political fortunes, summarizing his frustrations by stating that "Carolina has been a region of tombs for me" (*Letters* 2: 195–96). Simms's use of this phrase is intriguing, as it echoes a similarly dark sentiment expressed by his father, William Gilmore Simms, Sr., years before.

Writing in his "Personal Memorabilia," an unpublished, unfinished memoir that Guilds notes was "written about 1864," the author recalled a conversation he had with his father when the two men were "traveling together in the Southwest." After being informed that his son planned to return to Charleston, the elder Simms responded with horror: "NO! Do not think of it. Stay here. Study your profession here. And pursue it, with the energy and talent which you possess, and I will guarantee you a fortune . . . Do not think of Charleston. Whatsoever your talents, they will there be poured out like water on the sands. Charleston! *I know it only as a place of tombs*" (qtd. in Guilds, *Literary Life* 12, emphasis in original). The antipathy the elder Simms clearly felt towards Charleston was based in the tragedies he suffered there years earlier, including business failures and, especially, the deaths of his wife and two other sons. Leaving the two-year-old Simms with the boy's maternal grandmother, the elder Simms abandoned Charleston for the West, never to return.

This echo suggests that the author was, at least subconsciously, thinking of his father and his father's tragic circumstances while re-working "A Legend of the Pacific" into "The Maroon." Just as his father had buried the author's infant brothers many years before, Simms had just recently buried his thirteen-month-old daughter Valerie, who died on 21 September 1846; she was the fourth of the author's children to die. Simms's recurring financial troubles had surfaced again, and his letters throughout the fall of 1846 and the winter of 1847 are marked by pessimism and anxiety. Despite these struggles, the author soldiered on in Charleston, that "region of tombs." Throughout his life, Simms was haunted by his father's abandonment, and he surely was aware of the differences between his and his father's reactions to similarly tragic experiences of Charleston. These contexts seemingly manifest themselves in the anxiety, melodrama, and worry over the nature of duty that figure so prominently in "The Maroon."

Simms's financial straits underlie the author's negotiations with publishers for the story, as well as its eventual form. While he had seemingly contracted for the novella's serialization with Lawrence Labree, editor of the *New York Illustrated Magazine of Literature and Art*, at some point in late 1846, the writer's communications with Lawson around the turn of the year expressed a difficulty in collecting his pay. While Simms had originally thought "The Maroon" would be, per his October 23 letter to Lawson, "a Tale in three parts," by January the work had doubled in length, and thus also in cost to Labree. Of course, speculating that Simms expanded the work to help offset his financial struggles would be just that—speculation. However, as evidenced by a 2 March 1847 letter to Lawson, it is clear that the author considered the value of "The Maroon" quite seriously; in this letter, Simms for all intents and purposes instructed his agent to hold the sixth and final section of the tale hostage until the author was paid what he was owed. Two days later, he sent a bill for a balance of $45 to Labree (*Letters* 2: 274, 280). "The Maroon" appeared in the *New York Illustrated Magazine of Literature and Art* across six installments, from January to June 1847.

Simms had mixed success with having the work republished. A version with minor revisions was serially published in the *Southern Literary Gazette* between 4 May and 8 June 1850, under the title "The Maroon. A Legend of the Caribees"; this work was reissued in Lippincott, Grambo, and Co.'s two publications of the *Marie de Berniere* collection. However, throughout the early 1860s, the writer attempted to republish "The Maroon," and these efforts were met with little success. While initially turned down by West & Johnson of Richmond and Sigmund H. Goetzel of Mobile during the early days of the Civil War, Simms had seemingly found a Columbia publisher by the conflict's waning days, as evidenced by a final, hand-corrected appearance of the tale. The South Caroliniana Library at the University of South Carolina holds a typescript of "The Maroon" to which Simms made several minor revisions, along with an accompanying handwritten title page that reads: "The Maroon:/a Romance of the Carib/By W. Gilmore Simms, Esq./Author of 'The Yemassee'/'Eutaw' 'The Partisan' &c/Columbia S.C./Evans and Cogswell/publisher/1865." This edition was never published, a fact that Guilds speculates was connected to the destruction and chaos caused by Sherman's February occupation of the capital city (*Writings* 709–10). Thus, despite the author's efforts, after its 1855 appearance, "The Maroon" was not republished until 1974's *Stories and Tales*.

Set in the Caribbean Sea during the early sixteenth century, "The Maroon" tells of the misadventure of the *Diana de Burgos* and its crew: the captain, Don Velasquez de Tornel, his mistress Maria, Don Velasquez's nephew Juan de Silva, the musician Lopez de Levya, and other minor crew members. The purpose of the *Diana de Burgos*'s Caribbean voyage is unclear, and other facts are similarly ambiguous—neither why Velasquez travels with his mistress nor why the musician is a part of the crew are ever explained. As the work opens, Velasquez has learned of flirtations between Lopez de Levya and Maria, flirtations that provide the captain with the first indication that his mistress and the musician are lovers. Despite Maria's attempts to assuage the captain's anger, Lopez de Levya is expelled from the *Diana de Burgos* and marooned on an uninhabited island Velasquez mockingly calls "the Isle of Lovers." Desperate to reconnect with her beloved, Maria manipulates both Juan, who lusts for her, and the crew, in a mutiny that puts her in control of the *Diana de Burgos*, so that she can rescue Lopez de Levya.

Meanwhile, the eponymous maroon has discovered that while the "Isle of Lovers" is uninhabited, it is used by a native Caribbean people for what appears to be a coming-of-age ceremony for young women. As a part of one such ceremony, an initiate is put through elaborate rituals before being left alone on the island for an extended period of time. After observing the ritual, Lopez de Levya reveals himself to the young woman, and they begin a romantic and implicitly sexual relationship. Lopez de Levya also discovers a huge cache of pearls, and hopes to find a way back to Spain, where the pearls will afford him wealth and position. While the maroon contemplates how long his idyll can continue, Maria's schemes put her on a course to rescue him, and the inevitable reunion results in a beautifully haunting conclusion to the tale. While the action of "The Maroon" is thus quite contrived, it is entertaining, and its plot allows Simms to craft a story that straddles both realism and fairytale. In this, Simms shows a significant debt to German Romanticism, a trait common throughout *Marie de Berniere*.

The morality of "The Maroon," and thus the work's general purpose, is largely an exploration of duty and the proper use of power. Lopez de Levya realizes that his sexual conquest and romantic manipulation of the young Caribbean woman are based largely in her thinking of him as a god, whose visitation is ostensibly a part of her ritualized transition to maturity. Simms deftly juxtaposes this abuse with Velasquez's mocking pronouncement of Lopez de Levya as ruler of the Isle of Lovers, creating a complex scenario readers are required to work through: do we find Lopez de Levya a sad, tragic figure put into a hopeless situation or a self-serving, manipulative, and morally lax opportunist? When he finds himself in a position of power—actually becoming the "ruler" Velasquez mocked him as being—do his moral obligations change? Are our perceptions of him affected by his access to power? Similarly, the machinations of Maria onboard the *Diana de Burgos* propose questions about duty, its reciprocity, and the consequences of its violation. These are complicated issues, and Simms thus does not tell a *simple* morality tale—but "The Maroon" is a morality tale, nevertheless, and readers will find it both beautiful and unsettling.

"Maize in Milk"

Based on a 17 March 1846 letter to Simms's friend and influential New York publisher Evert Augustus Duyckinck, Guilds posits that work began on "Maize in Milk" in that same month (*Writings* 763). While the writer originally submitted the work to Wiley and Putnam, Simms eventually contracted with influential periodical publisher Louis Antoine Godey to issue the work. "Maize in Milk. A Christmas Story of the South" was initially serialized in *Godey's Lady's Book* from February to May 1847. After this, the tale appeared only alongside "Marie de Berniere" and "The Maroon" during Simms's lifetime: in *Marie de Berniere: A Tale of the Crescent City, etc. etc. etc.* in 1853, and in that work's identical, renamed reissue *The Maroon; A Legend of the Caribbees, and Other Tales* two years later. There are no substantial differences between these appearances of the tale and its initial, serialized appearance. "Maize in Milk" also appears as a part of *Stories and Tales* in 1974; in that volume, editor John Caldwell Guilds speculates that Simms may have had "uncompleted plans" for reissuing the work during the 1860s, just as he had plans to republish "The Maroon," and as he had successfully reissued "Marie de Berniere" as "The Ghost of My Husand" (763).

In a 25 February 1847 letter to Duyckninck, Simms noted that "Maize in Milk" is "simply descriptive" (*Letters* 2: 273). While the editors of the *Letters* give further validity to this assessment, suggesting that this "Christmas Story of the South" is an "account of Christmas at [Simms's plantation] Woodlands," the tale nevertheless presents readers with an intellectual argument. Over a decade before the dawn of the Civil War, Simms was already engaged in presenting the moral and social superiority of the southern plantation system *vis-a-vis* a more crass capitalistic economy. Nevertheless, in "Maize in Milk" the author does not hesitate to present the hubris and myopia of his protagonist, an idealistic plantation owner, or that character's failings as a businessman. For a modern reader encountering "Maize in Milk," the story suffers from two distinct issues: first, it is not nearly as complex or intellectually challenging as the two other tales in this collection, and thus suffers in juxtaposition to "Marie de Berniere" and "The Maroon." Secondly, the tale's racial politics—Simms draws heavily on the trope of happy, contented slaves who exist in a familial relationship with their master—are unsettling and off-putting to contemporary readers. Despite these issues, readers who engage "Maize in Milk" charitably will find a charming, entertaining, and highly illustrative narrative of the attitudes and social conventions of the antebellum South. That Simms is also critical of the poor financial acumen of the plantation owner—who is blinded by his ostensible social obligations—further presents readers with an intriguing portrait of the author's attitudes towards the plantation as an institution, thinking that is interesting in light of his constant frustrations over his own management of Woodlands.

The tale takes place on the titular plantation, located in the vicinity of "St. Matthews" in "Carolina."[2] As the story begins, the aptly-named Col. Openheart is making plans for that year's Christmas celebration with his wife, Mrs. Emily Openheart. Aware of their recent financial and agricultural difficulties, Mrs. Openheart attempts to convince her husband of the wisdom in their family celebrating Christmas with her uncle, instead of engaging in their traditional holiday largesse. Col. Openheart will hear nothing of such an idea; as owner of Maize-in-Milk, his understood duty is to provide comfort and extravagance to those in his charge—not only his wife and their many children, but also their slaves and the better sort of poor whites who live close to them—and also to offer Christmas hospitality to wealthy neighbors who reside on other nearby plantations. After winning his wife over to his position, or at least making it clear that her protests are useless, Col. Openheart reveals that he has purchased all of the slaves of a recently-deceased friend named Butler, on credit and at an exorbitant rate.

Openheart's rationale behind this purchase fits his name, as he was concerned that the executor of the Butler estate, a crassly capitalistic lawyer appropriately named Skinflint, was prepared to sell these slaves—many of whom are elderly—"down the river." Assuming debt for the slaves' sake is thus understood as his aristocratic duty, his proper performance of *noblesse oblige*, so as to protect and provide for these individuals as the stereotypical kindly and paternalistic master. The rest of the story's action concerns the events of that Christmas day, which Simms relates in colorful, entertaining detail, and Skinflint's attempts at foreclosing on Openheart's debt two Christmases later.

In the end, a too-neat resolution and hackneyed romantic subplot lessen the overall power of the tale. Thus, while "Maize in Milk" is certainly the weakest of the three novellas gathered in *Marie de Berniere*, aspects of Simms's skill are still present. The descriptions of antebellum plantation life are lyrical and robust, and the story provides a useful illustration of the social attitudes of the plantocracy. Despite the work's limited achievement, Simms's always-intelligent social criticism is present here as well, as he juxtaposes the idealistic spendthrift Openheart against the avaricious Skinflint, showing both men, and their economic and social ideals, to be flawed. As such, though it lacks the aesthetic and intellectual achievement of the other two novellas in the collection, this "simply descriptive" Christmas tale is nevertheless entertaining, and illustrates Simms's usefulness in understanding and interpreting the attitudes and thoughts of aristocratic whites of the nineteenth-century South.

The Collection

While the three works that make up *Marie de Berniere* exhibit uneven quality, highly varied settings and action, and extremely different points of focus, they all fit neatly beside one another in the same volume. That these three disparate novellas work as a coherent collection is largely due to two things: their dealing with common themes of duty, including the role of the individual in a community, and their shared debt to German Romanticism. Further, these three tales provide readers of Simms with clear examples of the principles the author employed in crafting his short fictions, aiding us in understanding why these shorter forms were so consistently strong over the course of the writer's long and prolific career.

In introducing *Stories and Tales*, Guilds notes that "a close reading of [Simms's] critical writings" provides a "fairly adequate idea of [his] concept of the short story," and thus helps us to understand what the author has accomplished in this form generally (*Writings* xv). Guilds's general observations are equally apt when specifically considering the three tales that make up *Marie de Berniere*. As Guilds notes, one "of the main distinctions Simms made between the short story and the novel" relates to plot; "in plot or subject matter, the short story has more latitude than the novel because it may deal more freely with the supernatural, the improbable, or the unusual." Guilds goes on to say that though "Simms theorized that the short story, unlike the novel, may ignore probability—and even possibility—if it chooses to enter the province of fantasy," the short-storyist who is not aiming for evocation of the "wild and wonderful" must, like the novelist, "strive for verisimilitude" (*Writings* xv). Further, Simms saw the short story as similar to the novel, and all other literary forms, in its basic purposes. For him, literature must hold to the presentation of some form of the truth, and "literature faithful to truth serves a moral purpose" (*Writings* xvii). While Guilds's observations are sound and useful means of generally approaching Simms's fiction, the three novellas that comprise *Marie de Berniere* reveal the writer working through the consequences of the tensions between "verisimilitude" on the one hand and the "supernatural" and "improbable" on the other, as well as the possibilities these tensions provide the artist for exploring significant moral questions.

None of the three novellas collected together here is completely verisimilitudinous, nor are any of them totally fantastical. In the title story, Simms blends together a ghost story and a realistic portrait of Creole culture in New Orleans, while "The Maroon" features a (mostly) believable conceit that approaches the fairy tale in its final execution. Even the "simply descriptive" tale that closes the volume features dream-like descriptions and elements of exceptional coincidences that call into question the story's fidelity to a purely accurate presentation of the experiences of antebellum plantation Christmas. It is precisely this mixing of truthful, accurate presentations of real human experience, society, and community with improbable situations that allow Simms to perform the real and significant work we see across all three novellas in *Marie de Berniere*. By exploring how his realistically drawn characters perform under the demands of extraordinary circumstances, he presents readers with significant, distilled investigations of community and duty, themes that recur throughout Simms's canon.

This tension between the real and the fantastic recalls the influence of German Romanticism on Simms. German literature scholar J. Wesley Thomas penned several seminal essays on Simms and German Romanticism in the 1950s; the dearth of criticism on this aspect of Simms's work in the years since points to an opportunity for the contemporary critic, and the novellas of *Marie de Berniere* provide an accessible entry-point for this kind of scholarship. In the first of his essays, "German Literature in the Old South," Thomas notes that "[a]lthough Simms's literary antecedents were primarily Shakespeare and the English Romanticists, there are numerous instances in his works where the effects of his German reading can be detected." Thomas notes the particular influence of "Schiller's *Verbrecher aus verlorener Ehre* [*The Criminal of Lost Honour*] upon the American's concepts of personal guilt and social responsibility," especially in the manifestation of a tendency on Simms's part "to investigate the origins of sin and to portray it as the result of personal or social pathological complexes. Thus evil becomes the product of folly rather than of innate perversion" (9). This observation is useful when considering how Simms presents wrong-doing in the three novellas. Fr. Roquetti in "Marie de Berniere," Skinflint in "Maize in Milk," and any number of the Spanish characters in "The Maroon" are individuals whose folly is the result of poor understanding and interpretation of social codes, norms, propriety, and duty on their part, misreadings caused in part by the influences of various social systems. Thus, none of the "villains" in these novels is *ipso facto* evil, debased, or innately perverse. While Simms does not excuse them as mere "victims" of circumstance, he does charitably present their moral failings as based in flawed interpretation. Alongside this presentation is a suggestion that the proper role of the gentleman—that figure who is consistently Simms's true hero—is to correct these poor readings.

While such a general recognition of German romantic ideas may provide an approach to all three of these works, Thomas notes the specific impact of several specific German works on the tales collected in *Marie de Berniere*. In his later essay, "The German Sources of William Gilmore Simms," he notes that

> the detective story approach which [Simms] employs, as well as several specific incidents, recalls Schiller's *Geisterseher* [*The Ghost-Seer*]. . . . The secret passage-ways, particularly the one in the chimney, bring to mind those in the inn where Schiller's prince saw the bogus ghosts. . . . The Egyptian costume of Simms's unearthly visitor recalls the dress of Schiller's Aremenian. Of greatest

significance, however, is the fact that both stories are built around the ingenious plot of a fanatical priest to gain power and wealth for the church. (136)

Thomas also notes that the critical scene of "Marie de Berniere," the ghostly interview between Marie and the Egyptian at the *bal masque*, "was probably derived from an uncanny occurrence in the eleventh chapter of Eichendorff's *Ahnung und Gegenwart* [*Premonition and Present Time*]" ("German Sources" 136). According to Thomas, further influence of German sources upon the works in this collection is seen in "The Maroon," for which Simms "drew from Fouque's *Undine*," in that both tales explore the consequences of a "young nobleman" who is marooned on an island and falls in love with "a completely unsophisticated, waternymph-like creature," only to have such an idyll interrupted by the reappearance of a "former sweetheart" of the maroon ("German Sources" 137). And while "Maize in Milk" has no antecedent in German literature, its juxtaposition of two "worlds"—in this case, the paternalistic plantation and the crassly bourgeois world of mercantilism—does find a parallel in a long-standing technique of German Romanticism, with which Simms had already demonstrated fluency. According to Thomas, this technique is displayed by Simms as early as 1837's *Martin Faber and Other Tales*, especially in the story "Sweet William, a Tale of Faerie" (129–30).[3] Thus, whether Simms is directly drawing upon German sources or merely utilizing German romantic techniques, the imprint of writers like Schiller and Fouque on *Marie de Berniere* is clear.

Marie de Berniere may not be Simms's most important or best work, but it is one of Simms's major achievements. All three tales are aesthetically pleasing and enjoyable; while the politics and racial attitudes of "Maize in Milk" might be discomforting to some modern readers, even it still feels charming and lively. The questions of duty that run through all three works in the collection show the author's real achievement as a moralist who resists the simplicity of pedantry, and thus asks readers to consider complex, often ambiguous moral situations in a manner befitting their complexity. Finally, the German influences give credence to Simms's position as a transatlantic, and not just southern, man of letters, further showing him to be one of the more significant players in nineteenth-century literary and intellectual life generally. Perhaps most importantly, we are given a set of stories that inspire and entertain us, as well as challenge us intellectually and ethically; in this, Simms has done the work of great literature. For these reasons, *Marie de Berniere* must be considered a volume to be read, re-read, and studied.

NOTES

1. While not specifically naming "Marie de Berniere"/*The Ghost of My Husband*, Simms discusses submitting a "series of novellettes" for the *Sunny Side Series* in an August 1866 letter to George W. Ellis. Though little is known of Ellis, the contents of the letter suggest that he was a member of the publishing firm Chapman and Co. Several things are of interest in this letter. First, while Simms only publishes *The Ghost of*

My Husband in this series, that he speaks of a "series of novellettes" suggest he saw Chapman and Co. as a possible home for novellas like "The Maroon" and "Maize in Milk," works he also seemingly wanted to republish.

Secondly, the opening paragraphs of the letter contain instructions to be passed along to "the engraver," concerning how that individual should use photographs Simms had sent. Presumably, Simms is talking about an engraver working on an author portrait, of the sort that appears on a book's cover or frontispiece. This would imply that Simms had already entered into some agreement with Chapman and Co. about submitting work to their *Sunny Side Series* by August 1866, and had perhaps already contracted for the publication of *The Ghost of My Husband*. H.L. Penfield's engraved portrait of Simms on the cover of that work features Simms with the heavy beard he wore late in life, suggesting its basis was one of the photographs the author sent to Ellis.

Finally, the editors of Vol. 6 of the *Letters* also indicate that Ellis was a Freemason. Knowing that Simms had joined this fraternity during the Civil War, and that the organization was dedicated to sectional reconciliation between brothers during and after the war, it seems very possible that Simms's membership helped to facilitate the publication of *The Ghost of My Husband* during an exceptionally difficult period for the writer. See (*Letters* 6: 244–46).

2. Simms's obvious reference here is to the community of St. Matthews, South Carolina, though nothing in the story indicates that Simms is referring to this actual location.
3. Thomas erroneously identifies this volume as *Tales and Sketches*, likely because a half-title page reading as such appears after the close of the novella "Martin Faber" in the first of the two volumes that make up *Martin Faber and Other Tales*. "Sweet William, a Tale of Faerie," the story Thomas mentions, is the first work to appear after this half-title page.

Martin Faber, the Story of a Criminal; and Other Tales

TODD HAGSTETTE

As William Gilmore Simms's first published book of fiction, the novella *Martin Faber* tells a story of murder and the origins of evil, all from the twisted perspective of a criminally insane mind. In this "gloomy & passionate tale," the title character, the product of an indulged and coddled childhood, grows into a selfish, predatory, megalomaniacal sociopath who seduces a young country girl, Emily Andrews (*Letters* 2: 223).[1] After the girl threatens to reveal his deeds to his affluent fiancée, Constance Claiborne, Faber kills Emily and hides her body in the woods. Feeling invulnerable and wanting to watch his friend agonize over conflicting loyalties, Faber confesses his deed to William Harding, his boyhood companion. He changes select details of the actual crime, though, so when Harding publicly accuses Faber, he lacks the proper corroborating evidence and, thus, is discredited in the eyes of the community. In an effort to redeem himself, Harding turns detective, sniffing out the clues that eventually bring Faber to justice. The entire novel is Faber's death row confession. Though the plot, as a narrative, is rather simple, as America's first work of southern Gothic fiction,[2] the novella offered many innovations to the literature of the nation.

It also marked a critical juncture in the young writer's career and future production. Up until the publication of *Martin Faber*, Simms had primarily distinguished himself as a poet and a newspaperman. Beginning in the early 1830s, though, he started to invest himself wholesale in the writing of fiction, concurrently commencing production of his Gothic novella and his first work of long-form fiction, the border romance *Guy Rivers*. The former was ultimately published first by a few months. Simms's twentieth-century biographer John Caldwell Guilds notes the significance of *Martin Faber* for the author, as its writing and Simms's hopes for it, seemed to seriously alter his life upon its publication. Finding his literary ventures to that point of mixed success, Simms considered relocating from South Carolina to the western frontier, where his father and uncle had moved while the author was still a boy. But with the impending publication of *Martin Faber*, Simms functionally had found a new genre and a new life's work; as Guilds notes, "Ultimately, it was the publication of *Martin Faber* that changed a poet into a novelist.... At age twenty-six Gilmore Simms had found the genre for which his talents were best suited. Thereafter . . . he was primarily a writer of fiction" (*Literary Life* 43–44).

One of the most important works in Simms's development as a writer, *Martin Faber* has a rather long and intriguing publication history. Originally published as a novella by J. & J. Harper of New York in 1833, it was revised and expanded for re-publication, alongside nine short stories and a poem, as *Martin Faber, the Story of a Criminal; and Other Tales*, issued by Harper & Brothers in 1837. The 1833 edition of the book found popular success, and as early as 1834, Simms apparently had the go-ahead from Harper to begin editing for a subsequent edition. Simms wrote his friend James Lawson in July 1834, "I am to prepare a revised edition of Martin Faber & other things, making two volumes" (*Letters* 1: 61). Despite the book's early success with the reading public, though, the critical reception was more subdued. An October 1833 review in the *Knickerbocker* is fairly typical: it praises the exciting features of the book but also finds the work to exhibit "obvious defects in style" (qtd. in Butterworth and Kibler 23). By and large, reviewers tended to find in *Martin Faber* the promise, rather than the realization, of literary genius; most agreed, though, that the book foretold a bright future for an auspicious new voice in American letters.

This critical bipolarity continued when the 1837 edition of the work was issued. *Martin Faber and Other Tales* was reviewed more favorably than the 1833 single-novella publication, although the later book's defects were still noted. The *Knickerbocker* again provides a typical view, claiming that, while the reader will see "some things which he could wish were otherwise, he will find them but the rich superfluities of early genius" (qtd. in Butterworth and Kibler 38). Perhaps most significant of all, the book found an appreciative audience in no less a reviewer than Edgar Allan Poe. Though a fledgling writer himself at the time, Poe was already proving to be a formidable critic and tastemaker in antebellum America. Normally a biting critic of recent fiction, Poe was generally kind in his reviews of all Simms's Gothic work, beginning with *Martin Faber*. In fact, in stark contrast to modern critical consensus, Poe found Simms's Gothic to be his truly superior work and his historical romances to be substandard.

Poe's endorsement would become critical years later, as Simms continued to contend with controversy surrounding his book, beginning with its initial publication in 1833. Some early reviewers of the work levied charges of plagiarism against the young Simms. *Martin Faber*, in its first edition, bore a resemblance, in topic, tone, and mood, to English writer F.M. Reynolds's *Miserrimus*, a novel published in London and New York slightly earlier in the same year. Adding to the confusion was the fact that the American edition of *Miserrimus* was issued by the same publisher as *Martin Faber*, J. & J. Harper. So, as Simms sums things up in an "Advertisement" to the 1837 edition of the book[3] in which he addressed the charges: "The one was a tale of crime—so was the other. The one was published by Harper and Brothers—so was the other. The one filled about two hundred pages—so did the other. And, more unlucky yet, the same style of printing and binding was chosen for both publications" (v). As he goes on to discuss, though, Simms's novel was not influenced at all by the English work. Rather, Simms had based his novel on a short story he published earlier, in the 1 November 1829 issue of the *Southern Literary Gazette*, titled "Confessions of a Murderer." That story was composed, published, and revised all prior to the appearance of the Reynolds work. Aside from mere timing for vindication, Simms's work was also defended against the plagiarism charges on meritorious grounds. In his 1846 review in *Godey's* of *The Wigwam and the Cabin*, Poe noted, "[T]here is not the slightest ground for the charge of imitation. The thesis and incidents of the two works are totally dissimilar;—the idea of resemblance arises only from the absolute identity of *effect* wrought by both," and in fact, *Martin Faber* was "a more forcible story than its supposed prototype" (41, emphasis in original).

In addition to answering these plagiarism charges in *Martin Faber and Other Tales*, Simms substantially revised the title story for its 1837 second edition publication. He gathered his now-famous Gothic work with other stories that exhibit concerns with American history, the fantastic, and the romantic, "Indian, Pirate and Ghostly tales among them" (*Letters* 5: 157). In an "Advertisement" to introduce the nine short stories that comprised the total second volume and the second half of the first volume of the 1837 collection, Simms is rather dismissive of the contents. Calling them the "production of very youthful years" that are filled with "Teutonic extravagance," Simms opines that, as these stories were "[w]ritten in the wild exuberance of boyhood, the want of method will perhaps offend the severe mental disciplinarian." This was particularly so because, in most of the tales, "the fancy has been permitted a capricious play" (153–54). Ultimately, he asks that the reader "forgive these pranks of fancy and of boyhood" (159). Though the author was perhaps a bit too critical of the shorter tales in the collection, the title story is indeed the masterpiece of the book. It not only launched Simms's career as a fiction writer, but it brought together many of the thematic and political concerns that would occupy the author throughout his next three-and-a-half decades as a writer.

As a literary nationalist throughout his life, Simms would fervently urge American artists to escape what J. Wesley Thomas refers to as "the insolent sway of British cultural hegemony" ("German Sources" 127). Simms rejected the fact that, though America had become politically independent, it still looked to England for cultural guidance. For this reason, he encouraged, by example and through advice, American artists to employ native culture as the basis for their art. An American artist's chosen subject matter was far more than simply a function of taste for Simms; rather, it was a crucial factor in the development of national identity. C. Hugh Holman explains: "Repeatedly throughout his career, Simms was to declare that a nation was 'denationalizing' itself if it modeled its art on foreign forms or neglected to treat its native subjects" (*Roots* 4). In this spirit, Simms pulled away from British models in his own art and instead looked to American culture for his subject matter.

The beginnings of this trajectory are apparent in *Martin Faber*. Glenn M. Reed notes that, though *Martin Faber* draws somewhat on an earlier, European format for its Gothic action, what makes it "worth reading for a present generation is Simms's additions to and modifications of the work of his predecessors as he tempered his work to his perceived American audience" (i–ii). Much of American literature at the time was directly influenced by Old World literature, yet Simms interjected his fiction with certain innovations that helped usher in a new, American style. In his Gothic fiction, he borrowed some effects from his European counterparts. But it was his insistence, in practice and theory alike, on the creation of a national literature that caused him to branch out, seeking new effects appropriate to his country.

Reshaping the Gothic formula for an American setting was something of a revolutionary move. Many critics of the genre contended that the Gothic romance was unsuited to the newness of the American landscape. Charles Brockden Brown had earlier experimented with an American Gothic mode, yet still the New World was thought to be technically lacking in opportunities for traditional Gothic devices. As one critic summarized things, "the more Romantic parts of the American landscape were shockingly devoid of castles in a suitable state of disrepair; we possessed few ancient portraits that leered or winked or dripped blood; our manuscripts were likely to be either spurious or imported or embarrassingly modern" (Cowie 22). If the American Gothic was dependent on the traditional British formula then this kind of criticism would hold up; gothicism would have no purchase on American soil. But reproducing the British form was not Simms's intention; his goal, as with all of his writing, was to make his Gothic work characteristically American. What Gothic traditionalists identified as problems, Simms saw as opportunities. Instead of the dilapidated castle, Simms saw the labyrinthine forests of the American wilderness; instead of ancient, supernatural portraits, Simms created the oddly representative paintings of a backwoods murder; instead of prophetic manuscripts, Simms employed confessional, untimely letters. Because of the very nature of his project, to recast an old form from virgin clay, the "rules" of the British style were inapplicable. Teresa Goddu, in her evaluation of the form, notes that "a definition of the American Gothic depends less on the particular set of conventions it establishes than on those it disrupts" (4).

One of the conventions that Simms disrupted in *Martin Faber* was the supernatural. This shift in the perspective of the horror marked one of his major contributions to the form. No longer was the terror of the story of supernatural origin, as in the European models, but a product of the psyche. In time, this would become a key differentiator between American and European gothic modes. As Goddu argues, American Gothic literature "takes a turn inward, away from society and toward the psyche and the hidden blackness of the American soul" (9). The ghosts and haunts of the Gothic sentiment shift from real projections of the world to the products of a diseased or guilty mind. In other words, where the traditional Gothic featured "real" ghosts, demons, and other otherworldly events for its scares, Simms and the American gothic mode that followed him tended to explain the presence of these figures as outgrowths of genuine confusion or mental unrest. For this reason, G.R. Thompson refers to this psychological shift as "explained Gothic," and he asserts "it is hard to overestimate the importance of this characteristic, for it comprises an essential difference between American Gothic and British Gothic" (75).

The most visible proof that Simms was a conscious contributor to this shift in the Gothic format is in the changes he made between the two editions of *Martin Faber*. In describing the 1837 version of the novel, Reed notes that, while most of the changes made from the 1833 edition were minor stylistic improvements,[4] "more significant was the muting of the supernatural element which Simms achieved by placing increased emphasis on the role of the imagination in generating the specter that haunts the two central characters" (vi). Simms changed the wording in subtle ways to allow the possibility that the ghost of Emily is no more than a mental projection. For example, he added the italicized portion of the following to the 1837 edition, describing the appearance of Emily's spirit at the site of her murder: "I beheld, *under the influence of my imagination*, the distinct outline of her figure" (110).[5] Although Faber is not the only person to witness the appearance of Emily, the ghost might be merely a product of the guilt-ridden minds of both characters who see it: Faber's guilt over committing the murder and William Harding's guilt, as he does not see the ghost until after Faber has confessed his deed, over knowing about the murder. The actual resolution to this quandary, whether the ghost is "real" or imaginary, is left unanswered. Regardless, it is Simms's creation of the possibility of a psychological solution that typifies this American shift in the gothic formula.

Interestingly, Simms did not jettison the supernatural entirely; rather, he crafted his narrative to allow for the possibility of psychological origins for all the otherworldly action. He, in fact, suggests that the difference between the two possibilities is largely meaningless; the effect of the ghost's appearance remains the same. As Faber protests to the reader upon the appearance of Emily's ghost on his wedding day, "You will tell me, as philosophers have long since told us, that this was all the work of my imagination—a diseased and excited fancy; and in this you are probably right. But what of that? Is it less a matter of supernatural contrivance, that one's own spirit should be made to conjure up the spectres which haunt and harrow it, than that the dead should actually be made to imbody themselves, as in life, for the same providence?" (71). In Simms's Gothic imagination, superior agency works upon the characters' lives to dramatic effect; whether those agents are supernatural or psychological, their impact is the same.

Though this psychological shift in emphasis was one of Simms's major contributions to the American version of the Gothic romance, his desire for a truly national literature also can be seen through the multiple smaller changes he made in the traditional Gothic format. These innovations in character, setting, theme, and philosophy give the Gothic mode a more American, national feel. Many of his innovations in the genre, at the same time, also betray a distinctly southern feel. As he famously illustrated in his dedicatory epistle to *The Wigwam and the Cabin* in 1856, it was Simms's contention that in pursuing regional interests, an American writer was contributing to the development of a national literature. So, as Cooper did in the North for his border novels, Simms tilled his own native soil for the subject matter of his Gothic fiction. Thus, he helped to craft simultaneously a uniquely southern and a uniquely American literature, all of which began with the composition of his first major work of fiction, *Martin Faber*.

Not just a work of southern Gothic, the novella is also an early work of crime fiction. Some of its novelty lies in its first person narration from the killer's diseased mind, but it is also unusual in that Simms offers an early examination of mitigating circumstances in the development of the criminal mind. Because the defining features of character are typically acquired in the circumstances of childhood, for Simms the issue of early education became an important factor in determining the future adult. Reacting to the character of Martin Faber, Floyd H. Deen claims that Simms "intended to show the ruinous results upon character of improper education, over-indulgence by parents, and poor environmental conditions in general during childhood and early youth" ("Genesis" 317). In this sense, Faber's fate was set from his very origins. In the beginning moments of the book, Martin speaks of his family's position in his small hometown: "my father, each successive day, grew more and more supreme in the estimation of the people. He was the only active principle among them. He did their thinking, and they were very willing to depute to him a labour so excessively unpopular—not to say undemocratic. He was their oracle—their counsellor: his word was law, and there were no rival pretensions set up in opposition to his supremacy. Would this had been less the case!" (16). The affluence for which Faber's father has had to work is simply bestowed upon the son. Martin receives the benefits of position without any effort on his part to achieve them. This indulgence becomes most obvious in the interaction between Martin and his aged school teacher. After a strict but deserved disciplining, Faber, through false testimony and a manipulation of his inherited sway over the community, has the teacher exiled from the village. It is this kind of omnipotent influence unrestrained by formative discipline that twists Faber into a nearly remorseless figure of pure evil.

J.V. Ridgely writes, "Martin sententiously informs the reader that, though he had come of a good family and had every advantage, an inner power with which he could not contend had brought him to his own destruction" (*William* 43). Consistently throughout the novel, Faber attributes this "inner power" to the workings of fate, but this determinism is discredited by his own selfish whims. This inner power is nothing more than the psychological aftermath of his overindulged childhood. His own megalomania causes his murderous behavior. Despite his teacher's innocence, Martin has him banished; despite never intending to marry poor Emily Andrews, Faber lies and seduces her; and when she threatens to reveal his deeds to his wealthy future wife Constance, Martin, with selfish cold-bloodedness, murders her. Despite his insistence to the contrary, no impending fate is requisite to explain Faber's destructive behavior.

In contrast to Faber, William Harding comes from modest beginnings. Though he does work himself into prominence in the community with Faber as his ally, it is not until after he breaks from his friend that his true nature emerges. Martin, in his sadistic selfishness, confesses an altered version of his crime to Harding, knowing that his friend's sense of honor will necessitate notifying the authorities. His accusation, however, is fruitless, as the details do not match the actual crime, leaving Faber looking innocent and wronged and Harding seeming petty and dishonest. After this fall from status in the community, Harding, in an effort to regain his prominence, employs keen observation and logical deduction to successfully re-accuse Faber and gain back the admiration of society. Cleaving always to nationalistic themes, Simms's paired portrayal of these conflicting characters in *Martin Faber* seems to suggest his celebration of an archetypal American figure. Because of his raw determination to stake a place for himself in society, Harding is the epitome of the self-made man for whom the new nation seems custom-made. As such, he foils the indulged, aristocratic (perhaps vaguely Old World elite) Faber. Furthermore, his perseverance in the face of adversity allows Harding to continue to climb to affluence even after his set-back, and in striving for this social position he eventually upsets and disgraces the undeserving antithesis of his pioneering, "up by his bootstraps" American character. The supplanting of Harding's self-made man for Faber's privileged villain comes full circle by the novella's end, when Harding seemingly steps in as Constance's future husband.

In addition to native characterization, the landscape becomes an important element of Simms's Gothic vision in *Martin Faber*. The change in location from a traditionally European, even quasi-medieval setting to a southern township, though necessary for recasting a nationalistic Gothic form and seemingly simple, was actually problematic. Traditional Gothic literature, in setting and theme, is obsessed with time and history, with the ancient. The crumbling facades of various human ruins remind the reader, author, and hero alike of their own mortality. But because of the newness of the American landscape, many of the traditional Gothic "stock-in-trade devices, such as the lonely manor house, the winding staircase, the heavily curtained bedchambers, underground passages, [and] creaking hinges" were largely unavailable to the writer of southern Gothic fiction (Thompson, "German Sources" 73).

For Simms, however, this dearth was not an impediment to the transfer of the Gothic story; it simply meant a change in symbol was needed. Though America had no dilapidated castles, it did have the ancient forests of the untamed wilderness. For a story set in the South, then, the ubiquitous natural world became the perfect Gothic arena. Leslie Fiedler writes, "In the American Gothic, the heathen, unredeemed wilderness and not the decaying monuments of a dying class, nature and not society becomes the symbol of evil" (160). The wildness, the emptiness, and the uncertainty of the woods build fear in the mind. Just as early settlers on the continent looked with uncertainty upon the sprawling forests teeming with dangers and the relative inadequacy of their meager shelters, the American Gothic character is overwhelmed by the ruinous possibilities of the natural world that surrounds him. Because it is unsubjugated by man and therefore not subject to his morality, the forest is the setting where anything Gothic can occur.

Martin Faber makes extensive use of its wilderness setting. Indeed, practically all of the Gothic events of the novel take place in the woods that surround Faber's community. Simms imbues his setting of the southern forest with descriptions of Gothic blackness. The most dominant of these images, as Reed points out in his introduction to the book, are Simms's frequent references to abysses (x). The wilderness setting of *Martin Faber* is full of crevices, pits, and wells. These chasms all evoke the fear of standing on the edge and then falling—falling into insanity, falling into death, and falling into damnation. They foreshadow Faber's decaying psyche and plummeting morality. Significantly, Faber's first words as the novel opens are, "This is a fearful precipice, but I dare look upon it" (13).

The images of nature, like Simms's characters, are not simple and one-sided, but complex and varied. The majority of the story's action occurs in the wilderness, that portion of the southern landscape that is untamed by man's will. In fact, Faber's murder of Emily Andrews, the event on which the rest of the action turns, is committed in the deepest part of the woods. Though the wilderness is sometimes described with ominous Gothic darkness, at other times it appears with pastoral beauty. Indeed, Faber's first forays into the forest are described with tranquil pulchritude. It is not until after he commits the murder that the world turns predatory and accusatory. After he commits the dreadful deed, Faber concocts a personified wilderness to voice the accusation that plagues his own heart:

> The trees were hung with eyes that depended from them like leaves. Eyes looked at me from the water that gushed by us; and, as in a night of many stars, the heavens seemed clustering with gazing thousands, all bent down terrifically upon me. I started to my feet in desperation; and by a stern impulse I could not withstand, I pronounced audibly the name of my crime. "Murder!" . . . "Murderer!" was the response of the trees, which had now tongues, as well as eyes. The agony grew intolerable, and a lethargic stupor came to my aid. (62–63)

The setting reflects the mental unrest of the protagonist. Rather than fearing the ancient as the traditional Gothic would have it, American terror was of the new and the open-ended. The possibility of consequence torments the American mind from the unsculpted landscape that surrounds it. Yet a resolution is possible, as well. After all, it is through his assimilation of the woods, through his understanding of them, that Harding is finally able to bring Faber to justice for his crime. The wilderness setting, then, is the place for unrealized potential to be revealed; it can be the arena for Gothic dread or a force that eventually allows the light to prevail.

On this same note, though Simms makes good use of the southern backwoods for his exterior setting, the true setting for these works is the mind. Though the *mise-en-scène* is the South, the action of the story spans the mental landscape. This is Simms's great transplantation of setting—not so much from Europe to America, as from the external world to the internal. After all, where does *Martin Faber* take place if not in the twisted passages of Faber's megalomania and dying morality? Simms's portrayal of the outside environment, as well as the inner psychological one, seems to reflect a cultural belief in the ambiguity of extrinsic reality. The old conflict over America's landscape, whether sinister wilderness or paradisical garden, is resolved. It is both. Just like human nature, worldly nature is neither all good nor all bad. It exhibits the same complexity as the human mind.

Contrasted to the wilderness in Simms's book is the community, which plays an important part in both character development and the instigation of Gothic dread. In the traditional Gothic formula, fear often relies on the aloneness of the victim and the villain for its effectiveness; it is the anxiety of isolation that gives the Gothic work some of its teeth. Because of the southern literary preoccupation with the notion that a person is a member of a larger social structure and that the identity of the individual is understood in relation to the group as a whole, the characters in *Martin Faber* are not fundamentally isolated, but functioning members of the community. Though Emily Andrews lives with her exiled father in a lonely cabin in the forest, all of the other main characters live and operate within a larger social scene. Faber himself is a prominent member of his community who, outside of his Gothic complex, has normal interactions with ordinary people.

Rather than alleviating the fear of the traditional mode's isolation, locating the villainous sociopath amidst the normalcy of the community intensifies the unrest. The Gothic anxiety does not take place far away, but right in the middle of ordinary life. The reader is reminded that the human heart is an enigmatic thing. Murders can occur in the most benign circumstances, and the most stable human facade can conceal the mind of a psychopath. Never does a person feel as isolated as when faced with the realization that people are incomprehensible. By bringing the Gothic heroes, villains, and events into the community, Simms adds a menacing immediacy to the fear.

Simms developed his southern Gothic vision by combining what he considered to be the two categories of his fiction. Guilds notes that "Simms himself preferred to divide [his work] into only two large groups: 'domestic tales,' or 'tales of the South,' by which he meant all those tales . . . dealing with regional themes and settings; and 'tales of the imagination,' by which he meant those stories under the influence of German Romanticism, usually with exotic settings and heavy philosophical or psychological undertones" (*Writings* xxi). By taking the psychological fascination of his imaginative works and locating it within the domestic sphere, Simms helped engineer the transplantation of the Gothic formula to the American landscape. In order to craft American relevance in this genre, he crafted southern relevance. Simms was not the first American writer to employ the Gothic technique or to develop national literary flavors. Through his steady insistence on regional, for the sake of national, literary development and his inspiration from the European Gothic mode, however, he was, for all practical purposes, the founder of the southern Gothic genre. Teresa Goddu not only insists that "the American Gothic is most recognizable as a regional form," but that the region that lends itself most readily to the Gothic format is the South (3). This modern notion that the South is an area of "Gothic gloom and doom" can be at least partially attributed to the pioneering work of William Gilmore Simms, in his most youthful effort at fiction, *Martin Faber* (Goddu 3).

NOTES

1. For an earlier, longer discussion of this book, see: my master's thesis, "Screams from the South: The Southern Psycho-gothic Novels of William Gilmore Simms" (College of Charleston, 1998).
2. As *Martin Faber* was based on an 1829 short story Simms published in the *Southern Literary Gazette*, it predates Edgar Allan Poe's earliest tale with Gothic elements, "MS Found in a Bottle," by almost four years. Poe's tale appeared in the *Baltimore Saturday Visitor* in 1833, the same year as the first book edition of *Martin Faber*.
3. Unless otherwise noted, all subsequent passages from *Martin Faber* are quoted from the 1837, second edition of the book.
4. For a complete list of textual variants between the two editions of the work, see Simms, William Gilmore. *Stories and Tales*. Ed. John C. Guilds. Vol. V of *The Writings of William Gilmore Simms: Centennial Edition*. Columbia: U of South Carolina P, 1974. 601–54. Available online at the *Simms Initiatives* (simms.library.sc.edu).
5. For more on this specific scene, see Reed vi, though the text is misquoted through the use of superfluous ellipses, and the page citation is incorrect.

Poems: Descriptive, Dramatic, Legendary and Contemplative

MATTHEW C. BRENNAN

William Gilmore Simms was a prolific poet, who wrote nearly 2,000 poems. Though in his own time and in ours he is best known as the author of such romances as *The Yemassee* and *Woodcraft*, he always considered poetry his first calling; he proclaimed in 1860, "Poetry, I hold to be my proper province" (*Letters* 6: 213). He even thought that in time his verse would outrank his novels (*Letters* 3: 190). Consequently, to ensure that his verse would be "on record for future judgment," in 1853 he collected many of his poems into a two-volume work, *Poems: Descriptive, Dramatic, Legendary and Contemplative* (*Letters* 3: 262). The work forms the most substantial and important collection of poetry in his canon. As the subtitle indicates, the volumes not only cover Simms's entire career from *Lyrical and Other Poems* (1827) through his verse drama *Norman Maurice* (1852), but also subsume a diverse range of styles, subjects, and themes; moreover, Simms revised many of the poems, hoping to strengthen them and make them last. In the 1860s he had hoped to assemble an expanded edition, but as with so many of his ambitions during the war years, this plan was scuttled. Consequently, Simms's reputation as a poet has hinged largely on the appraisal by both his contemporaries and later scholars of this selection of poems.

The Work

Poems: Descriptive, Dramatic, Legendary and Contemplative appeared as the second release of the Redfield edition of his selected works, following on the heels of the novel *Vasconselos*. Though dated 1853 like the novel, *Poems* may have been published as late as January 1854 (*Letters* 6: 143); however, in letters of November 24 and December 17 Simms presumes that editors already possess the book (*Letters* 3: 261, 268). Volume 1 comprises 348 pages and four parts: (1) *Norman Maurice, a Tragedy*; (2) *Atalantis, a Tale of the Sea*, which he had initially published in 1832 with Harper and later revised for a second edition with Carey and Hart of Philadelphia in 1848; (3) "Tales and Traditions of the South," which includes "The Cassique of Accabee: A Legend of Ashley River," "The Last Fields of the Biloxi," "The Hunter of Calawassee," and "Vasco Nunez"; and (4) *The City of the Silent*, which he had published in 1850. Volume 2, 360 pages long, uses these headings for its four parts: "Southern Passages and Pictures"; "Historical and Dramatic Sketches"; "Scripture Legends"; and "Francesca da Rimini," a reworking of Dante. Simms selected many of the poems from his 16 previous volumes of verse, but some verses had never before been collected and some never published under his name.

The more than seven hundred pages of verse vividly display Simms's range of subject matter and forms. The first work of the first volume is a blank-verse tragedy depicting contemporary politics; Simms wrote *Norman Maurice* with actor Edwin Forrest in mind but clearly based the satiric character of Colonel Ben Ferguson on Missouri Senator Thomas Hart Benton, who unlike Simms opposed the expansion of slavery west of Missouri. The other long works in volume 1 veer in radically different directions. *Atalantis* is dramatic, but its subject is fanciful, going far beyond "the merely human sentiment," as Simms states in his headnote (*Poems* 1: 121). Indeed, the cast of characters includes a human—a Spanish knight—but it is mostly populated by Sea-Demons, Nereids, and Fairies. *The City of the Silent*, on the other hand, is a solemn occasional poem composed in closed heroic couplets for the public ceremony dedicating Magnolia Cemetery in Charleston. Other poems treat death and mourning personally, such as "At a Child's Grave," one of Simms's lyrics to draw on his autobiography as a father whose lost children outnumbered those who survived. And his numerous poems about children—such as "Blessings on Children"—no doubt draw on his experience of fatherhood.

Many poems fit squarely in the Romantic tradition and evoke various aspects of nature. In fact, the opening pages of volume 2 present the reader with "Flight to Nature," "The Brooklet," "Sabbath in the Forest"—a sequence of six sonnets using nature as a source of escape and nurture—"First Day of Spring," and "Sonnet—By the Swanannoa," one of Simms's most often anthologized poems and one that illustrates his realism in employing the specific place names of his southern environment. Indeed, many poems in the second volume are distinctly southern, from poems on the Edisto and Congaree rivers in South Carolina to "The Edge of the Swamp" (probably about the terrain of his own plantation, Woodlands) to a poem on western emigration. Simms rendered southern climate in "The Streamlet," "The Shade–Trees," "The Traveller's Rest," "Night Storm," "Summer in the South," "The Approach of Summer," and a host of other poems. Sometimes, like Wordsworth, Simms probed the enduring effects of his childhood experiences in nature ("Nature's Favorite," "Forest Reverie by Starlight," and "Autumn Twilight"). And also like Wordsworth, in "Inutile Pursuit" and "Mental Solitude," he tackled the theme of being idle in nature and receptive to its spiritual powers versus getting and spending in the utilitarian marketplace.

If the various poems on nature show Simms writing out of his own ecological niche, he also chose subjects from literary tradition. For instance, "Sonnet—The Old Masters" delineates the greats from the past, Dante, John Milton, and

"Michael Angelo." "Heads of the Poets" similarly pays tribute to Simms's artistic forefathers, who besides Milton this time include Geoffrey Chaucer, William Shakespeare, Edmund Spenser, Robert Burns, Walter Scott, William Wordsworth, and Lord Byron. The Bible also informs Simms's literary tradition and furnishes the content for "Saul at Endor," "Saul's Last Battle," and "The Rebellion of Absalom," three of the final four works in *Poems*. The poetic faculty itself more abstractly gives Simms his theme in "Imagination" and "The Bard."

Just as diverse as Simms's subjects are his poetic forms. Lyrics abound in the collection, including ballads and songs but especially sonnets. Simms was a master of this form and his rhyme schemes betray greater experimentation than the sonnets of any other nineteenth-century poet. As one would expect from a romantic poet, Simms frequently wrote blank-verse meditations, usually set in nature, as in "Moral Change" and "Autumn Twilight"; these are the types of poems Simms labeled "Contemplative." But if he showed the influence of romantic lyricism in the style of many works, he never turned from the past, as the topic of "Heads of the Poets" suggests. Hence, for "The City of the Silent," he revived the closed heroic couplet, the metrical form of his first book in verse, *Monody, on the Death of Gen. Charles Cotesworth Pinckney* (1825), which showed he had mastered Samuel Johnson and Alexander Pope. Significantly, too, Simms employs narrative, not just in dramatic works like *Norman Maurice* and *Atalantis*, but also in the poems that recount legends, such as "The Cassique of Accabee" and "The Hunter of Calawassee."

The Text

Simms first envisioned a collected edition of his poetry shortly after his 45th birthday. He told his friend James Henry Hammond, "When I can get $500 to spare, I will publish a complete collection of my verse, that the record may be ample, and all my material gatherable at a glance" (*Letters* 3: 127–28). Moreover, by then much of his poetry was unavailable. Both his first five books of poems and his most recent five were all published in Charleston; or as Simms clarified in his aborted preface to *Poems*, most of them "were printed rather for private distribution—than for sale—printed, in fact, without being *published*." Consequently, he said, these volumes "are not now to be had" (qtd. in Kibler, "Unpublished" 293). Surprisingly, he considered his poetic "career as pretty well over" and wanted "to revise" his work "and make" himself "as worthy as possible in the eyes of future criticism" (*Letters* 3: 155).

To this end, Simms entered into an agreement with Charleston publisher John Russell, who had brought out *Areytos: or, Songs of the South* in 1846. Russell had a prospectus printed in the *New York Literary World* on 16 August 1851, soliciting subscriptions to the planned two-volume collection. However, so few subscribers answered the call that Simms sought alternative arrangements. J.S. Redfield, whose New York firm would publish most of Simms's works until the Civil War, stepped in and published the edition. Besides an edition bearing Redfield's imprint, Redfield produced an imprint for Russell to satisfy the original subscribers. According to James Everett Kibler, "The two imprints represent two states of the same impression, the Russell copies likely being run off first, for in Volume I, page 220, last line, the first words are lightly inked in the nine Russell copies examined; whereas all nine of the Redfield copies show the impression of type but are not inked" (*Poetry* 96). The only key difference between the two issues is their bindings: Redfield's is dark green cloth while Russell's is dark brown cloth. The titles of both are stamped in gold on the spine, and "the cover has a multi-ruled blind-stamped box within a larger frame" (Kibler, *Poetry* 90–91).

In his unpublished preface to *Poems* Simms emphasized that he made many revisions in putting together his "best" verse: "In preparing this collection I have endeavoured to repair the defects of heedlessness & haste in the previous volumes" and "have sought to repair" as well the "faults of taste & temperament" since now he has higher standards for "nicety of finish" (qtd. in Kibler, "Unpublished" 293). Indeed, Simms had begun revising his early work in 1839 and was publishing improved versions "by the batch, in Magazines," such as the *Southern Literary Messenger*, "under the appropriate head of 'Early Lays'" (*Letters* 5: 356). Paul Hamilton Hayne was simply wrong when he wrote that Simms found revision repugnant and making corrections "distasteful" ("Poets" 159). In fact, while Simms viewed lyric poems as "*improvisations*" he insisted that they required later refinement "by exquisite art" (*Letters* 4: 432).

Many works selected for *Poems* from the books of his early twenties are significantly improved. One prime example, "Summer Night-Wind," was first published in the *Southern Literary Gazette* in 1828 and then collected in *The Vision of Cortes* the next year; but it was rewritten several times more, including for *Southern Passages and Pictures* (1839). Another example is "Night-Watching." It appeared twice in 1829, first in the *Southern Literary Gazette* and then in a longer form in *The Vision of Cortes*. Finally, it was revised for *Poems*. But other poems, as Simms mentions in the preface, are "fugitives" never before collected but now "reclaimed" for *Poems* (qtd. in Kibler, "Unpublished" 293). The chief sample of this type is "The Streamlet," written first in 1829 for the *Southern Literary Gazette* but revamped in 1835 for *American Monthly* and then revised once more for *Poems*. This final version deepens some effects, such as the vivid imagery of the natural scenery, but its added length perhaps introduces some redundancy as well. Considering the revised version in *Poems*, which consists of 22 stanzas, we observe the remnants of the earliest version in stanzas 4, 9, 12–17, and 19–21. The only modern reprinting of *Poems* is the edition of 1972, which forms part of the Arno Press series edited by Harold Bloom, The Romantic Tradition in American Literature. It was reprinted from a copy of the Redfield imprint in the Princeton University Library. Moreover, among its 193 poems Kibler's *Selected Poems of William Gilmore Simms* (1990; 2010) includes many works from the 1853 collection.

Although *Poems* was never reprinted in Simms's lifetime, he had entertained ambitions of publishing an expanded edition. In October 1867 Simms told Evert Augustus Duyckinck that he hoped to publish his "complete poetical & dramatic writings in 3 volumes" (*Letters* 5: 90–91); two months later, he planned to add two plays "to make 2 vols. of Dramas" and, by inserting his recent poems, "to make 2 vols. of Poems" (*Letters* 5: 100). However, his negotiations with Redfield's successor, William J. Widdleton, proved fruitless. To settle with Widdleton over unpaid royalties accrued during the Civil War, Simms had instructed James Lawson to take as compensation the plates of the two-volume edition of *Poems* (*Letters* 5: 99). The editors of *The Letters* note that "We do not know whether Simms got from Widdleton the plates for his *Poems* (1853); however, no collected edition of his 'poetical & dramatic writings' was published after" December 1867 (*Letters* 5: 91n).

The Context

Just before Simms started arranging for his collected poems, his reputation as a poet was mixed. The highest praise came in 1851 from James Warley Miles in the *Southern Literary Messenger*. Miles cited Simms's "originality of expression," "richness of imagination," and "command of language," coupled with "musical rhythm"—qualities found "in greater or less degree" in "all of" Simms's verse. Miles concluded, however, that Simms was capable of accomplishing much more than he already had (289, 291). The year before Duyckinck issued a harsher evaluation of Simms's poetry up to *The Cassique of Accabee* (1849). He asserted, "No man can deny that Mr. Simms is a poet; and yet no man in the country has sent before the world so much verse of doubtful character" (80–81). Between Miles and Duyckinck fell William Cullen Bryant, who thought Simms showed improvement in his poetry but had yet to fulfill his potential ("Simms"). These estimates surely reinforced Simms's desire to collect what he considered his best work so that his achievement could be fully and fairly judged. Indeed, just weeks before *Poems* was published he told Duyckinck that in his own mind his poems "exhibit the highest phase of the Imaginative faculty which this country has yet exhibited" (*Letters* 3: 261–62).

Compared to *Poems* Simms's earliest books were very well reviewed, a fact somewhat remarkable since, with the exception of *Atalantis* (1832), they were all published—or printed—locally in Charleston. The first two books attracted attention from two major voices in early American letters: Bryant in the *U.S. Review and Literary Gazette* and Timothy Flint in the *Western Monthly*. Moreover, the *New York Literary Gazette and American Athenaeum* also covered the books. Simms's third book, *The Vision of Cortes*, drew two reviews from Bryant in the *New York Evening Post*, as well as from two other northern sources, *The Yankee* and *The New-York Mirror*. The latter also reviewed *Atalantis*, one of the long works Simms later selected for volume one of *Poems*, as did *The Knickerbocker* and *New-England*

Magazine. Even more impressive, Thomas Campbell, author of *The Pleasures of Hope* (1799), reviewed it in the *London Metropolitan Magazine* and, while "disappointed" that the poem "is so thoroughly English," Campbell described it as "well-written" and "polished throughout" (12b).

In contrast, although *Poems* was published in New York by Redfield, only three northern publications noticed it: *Norton's Literary Gazette*, *Harper's*, and *Graham's*, which singled out only the play *Norman Maurice*, though also generally lauding the less known poems for their "sweetness and melody" as well as their "power of description" ("Review of Redfield" 546). If, in the midst of growing sectional tensions and changing literary tastes, *Poems* seems ignored compared to Simms's earliest volumes of verse, it nevertheless enjoyed three strongly positive responses in southern journals from George Frederick Holmes, Miles, and Hayne. Writing at length in the *Richmond Semi-Weekly Enquirer*, Holmes alertly underscored Simms's originality as an American poet: "Mr. Simms is truly an American poet—much more so than his more belauded northern brethren. English subjects are not re-galvanized by his pen." Instead, Holmes insisted, Simms "selects his themes for himself, from the diversified scenes and incidents of American nature and life." Hayne actually reviewed *Poems* twice, in the *Charleston Weekly News* when it first appeared and later and more fully in *Russell's*. In the newspaper piece Hayne stated that in its "power of passionate utterance" Simms's poetry is rarely "excelled." In the longer essay from 1857, "The Poets, and Poetry of the South," Hayne's criticism was more measured, faulting Simms for his diffuse style but finding his poetry ultimately worthy of lasting beyond his lifetime.

Simms's verse has lasted well past his own time, but till the 1970s it hung by a thread above the dustbin of history. William Peterfield Trent, whose biography *William Gilmore Simms* appeared in 1892, shaped the reception of Simms's verse until the recent scholarly renaissance fostered by Kibler. Trent bluntly dismissed Simms as a poet: His verse was a "failure" and has been deservedly "forgotten"; "Only by courtesy," Trent stated, can one call Simms's verse "poetry." Consequently, Trent considered the edition of *Poems* "needless" (327, 44, 143, 206). More surprising, and perhaps more damaging, were similar dismissals by critics who otherwise worked hard to revive Simms's reputation in the postwar era. T.C. Duncan Eaves served as one of the editors of the monumental *Letters*, but even he believed that "few of Simms's poems have any right of survival" (898). Donald Davidson, who wrote the introduction to the *Letters*, was hardly more sympathetic; in a sweeping statement he complained, "most of Simms' poetry" seems "too obviously worked up" from literary sources rather than from "deeper" origins (*Letters* 1: li). As a result, it is unsurprising that in the Twayne study of Simms, J.V. Ridgely announced that, since Simms's verse has "no significance," there is no need for him "to disinter" it (*William* 42). Not all critics were so harsh. Edd Winfield Parks suggested that culling Simms's complete works would produce "only a small volume of excellent poems" but one that would place Simms among "the better American poets" (*Southern Poets* xciii), and Allen Tate made a brief case for the neglected poetry when he affirmed that "by any test it deserved as much reading as" Simms's fiction (qtd. in Parks, *Southern Poets* 343). Though much more favorable, these last two critical judgments are merely generalizations and apply to no specific works, not even *Poems*.

The fortunes of Simms's poetic reputation began to turn only after the centennial of his death. In 1979 Kibler tracked Simms's canon and published an exhaustive bibliography of his books and poems, many of them unearthed and identified for the first time. This invaluable resource made modern scholarship on Simms's poetry finally possible. In addition, Kibler's introductory essay to the bibliography forms the first in-depth criticism of this verse since Paul Hamilton Hayne's. In contrast to Trent, Kibler remarked that Simms's two-volume edition of collected poetry "contains some fine poems" (*Poetry* 3). A significant discovery uncovered by the bibliography is that Simms wrote many of his romantic poems "during the great period of romanticism" and thus preceded Nathaniel Hawthorne, Ralph Waldo Emerson, and Henry David Thoreau in incorporating elements of the British romantics' verse into American literature (Kibler, *Poetry* 5). Kibler spent the next decade, the 1980s, assembling Simms's *Selected Poems* (1990), which made a cross-section of Simms's poetic canon, including many samples from the collected edition, easily available to contemporary readers. The first scholar to use Kibler's edition was John Caldwell Guilds. His 1992 biography mentions numerous poems and discusses not only many works within *Poems* but also the circumstances surrounding its publication. Ultimately, Guilds found that "the excellence Simms attained as a poet is overshadowed by his achievement as a novelist," but he argued that Simms ranks "somewhere between Bryant and Whittier" among nineteenth-century poets (*Literary Life* 346). Similarly, in his introduction to *Selected Poems* Kibler maintained that Simms in many ways is comparable to Henry Wadsworth Longfellow, Emerson, and Bryant ([2010] xxii). Sacvan Bercovitch's *The Cambridge History of Nineteenth-Century American Poetry* (1999) refrained from such a lofty judgment, but its chronology of important books of verse includes *Poems* among the four worthy collections published in 1853 (502). Thus, the time seems ripe for Simms's poetry to receive its due.

Building on the sturdy foundations of Guilds's biography and Kibler's bibliography and editing, a few recent scholars have begun analyzing works in Simms's *Poems* with a seriousness typically brought to more canonical poets like Emerson or Walt Whitman. In 2003, in an article analyzing Simms's "The Streamlet," David W. Newton argued not only that Simms's 1853 collection "anticipates Emerson's attempt to situate Romanticism within a uniquely American context," but also that the best poems in the collection suggest Simms "is Emerson's intellectual equal, and, at times, a superior poet" ("Enchanted" 24). Another essay supplying an extended discussion of a particular work in *Poems* is Jason W. Johnson's "'Dazzling Outlawries of the Imagination.'" It argues that Simms's innovations in the experimental sonnet "The Lonely Islet" help demonstrate both his "Americanism" and his artistry. Further analysis of many poems from the 1853 collection appears in my own *The Poet's Holy Craft* (2010). I argue for Simms's status as a pioneer of early American Romanticism, partly by showing his lifelong debt to Wordsworth and Samuel Taylor Coleridge, including the practice of writing contemplative poems similar to the British romantics' conversation poems; I also demonstrate how Simms's distinctly American and southern ecology parallels Wordsworth's Lake District environmentalism. And, like Johnson, I provide evidence of Simms's poetic craftsmanship, which often entails artful revision.

A recent issue of *The Simms Review*, edited by Nicholas Meriwether and based on papers from a conference organized by James Kibler, focuses on "Simms the Poet" (Summer/Winter 2009). Many poems never discussed before serve as subject matter for various articles, which is important, but only one article, Corey Mingura's on "The Western Emigrants" and the sonnet "The Age of Gold," centers on examples from *Poems*. The reprinting of the 1853 volume will ensure that scholars keep their eyes on the most important edition compiled by Simms himself. In fact, since most scholars know Simms only through *Selected Poems*, many overlooked works should now receive scrutiny. In a recent review-article Johnson sketched some aspects of Simms's poetry awaiting critical attention: "Simms and the Victorians"; "Simms and the Europeans"; "Simms and the ballad tradition"; "Simms and race/gender/ class, particularly in the narrative poetry"; and "Simms and Christianity and/or mysticism" (124). Many poems in the 1853 collection could advance this scholarship. Other long-needed studies would pair Simms and his contemporaries, for if we are to place Simms in his proper context as a canonical poet, we need criticism that compares him with figures such as Bryant, Emerson, Thoreau, Longfellow, John Greenleaf Whittier, Oliver Wendell Holmes, and Edgar Allan Poe. We need to test Simms's conviction that the poetry in *Poems* embodies "the highest phase of the Imaginative faculty which this country has yet exhibited." Simms knew his poetry would have to wait for posterity to receive a just measure of its value. Slowly, but emphatically, his judgment and ours are coming together.

The Remains of Maynard Davis Richardson, with a Memoir of His Life

JEFFERY J. ROGERS

Although it has not been considered a significant part of his literary legacy, *The Remains of Maynard Davis Richardson, with a Memoir of His Life* was a deeply personal project undertaken by William Gilmore Simms to memorialize a close and remarkable friend. As such, the attention paid to it will return a unique insight into Simms's early life as well as an appreciation of his earliest effort at book editing. During the nineteenth century editing was not only considered a respectable and necessary aspect of literary culture, it could even be prestigious. Newspaper editors could, and often did, gain tremendous fame and wide influence through the daily, weekly, or other periodic presentation of news, opinion, and entertainment which filled the columns of their papers.

Simms as Editor: Newspapers, Journals, and Books

The newspaper was the most commonly read literary medium in nineteenth-century America, and in the decades prior to the Civil War, Americans published an astonishing number of papers which were eagerly read by a widely literate public. Often openly partisan, nineteenth-century American newspapers presented a broad variety of types of writing, not simply reports of current events. Contemplative essays, poetry, and political polemics filled their columns in addition to news reports and advertisements for all the goods and services available in a dynamic country in the throes of the industrial and market revolutions. Therefore, newspapers were institutions fundamental to, and an integral part of, the social, cultural, political, and religious life of the early American republic. As a consequence, the editors of these papers were well-known figures in their communities and occupied positions from which they could lead, provoke, inspire, or anger, depending upon the nature and content of what they wrote and chose to print in their papers.

The literary culture of the early nineteenth-century did not recognize the sharp professional boundaries or distinctions which emerged later, namely those separating editor, publisher, and author, where those designations are understood to be specialized and exclusive. Instead, nineteenth-century readers would have viewed someone who produced and promoted or critiqued literature in any of its forms as, broadly speaking, a "man of letters." Implicit in this conception is an acknowledgement that each of these functions was vital to the literary enterprise, and therefore a litterateur could engage in one or more without appearing outside his proper sphere. It is unsurprising, then, that many notable newspaper editors in early America also wrote novels, poetry, and non-fiction books simultaneous with their careers as newspaper men. The reverse also happened: novelists and poets tried their hand at editing newspapers. Nor, for that matter, is it surprising that notable editors published books or other writings in long form such as pamphlets and tracts. There was a natural, even expected, connection between all of these activities. They were all considered simply part of a life in literature broadly conceived.

William Gilmore Simms was just such a nineteenth-century "man-of-letters." Over the course of his life, from 1806 to 1870, there was not a literary form or contemporary genre in which he did not write. And, like other literary figures of his time, he also edited a wide variety of publications. These included literary journals, newspapers, and books. The edited books fall into two primary classes. The first includes those which present the writings of a single individual. The second is made up of compilations which contain a selection of writings from multiple authors. This second class of edited books consists of works that were strictly literary in nature. For example, *The Charleston Book*, published by Samuel Hart in 1845, featured the writings (essays, poetry, etc.) of many in Simms's circle of literary friends and associates. It was intended to be a showcase for the vibrant literary scene in mid-nineteenth-century Charleston.

Of the former class of books, the common element was an effort to present to the reading public the writings of men Simms admired and whose thoughts and deeds should be more widely known. The last of the these efforts, published in 1867 by the Bradford Club of New York, was *The Army Correspondence of Colonel John Laurens in the Years 1777–8, Now First Printed From Original Letters Addressed to his Father Henry Laurens, President of Congress, with a Memoir*. This was a publication of a significant part of Simms's large collection of manuscripts by or relating to important figures from the era of the American Revolution. In the memoir which precedes the letters, Simms described aspects of war hero John Laurens's character which made him admirable and a fit model to be emulated.

While his edition of John Laurens's letters was preformed out of Simms's lifelong commitment to historical scholarship, the other two publications of a single individual's works contained the writings of men who were Simms's contemporaries. Although it was published with no named editor in 1866 by John F. Trow & Co. of New York, the *Selections from the Letters and Speeches of the Hon. James H. Hammond of South Carolina* is now acknowledged to have been compiled by Simms. Hammond and Simms initially met as newspaper editors on opposing sides of the nullification controversy in South Carolina. Hammond edited the

Columbia *Southern Times* while Simms edited the Charleston *City Gazette and Commercial Daily Advertizer*. In time, however, they became close friends.

Subject

The recipients of Simms's attention in these two efforts at documentary editing are well known to historians. Colonel John Laurens was an aide-de-camp to George Washington and died in battle during the Revolutionary War. James Henry Hammond was a prominent political and intellectual figure of the Antebellum South. Yet the figure to which Simms devoted his earliest such effort, Maynard Davis Richardson, is far more obscure and, sharing that obscurity with its subject, *The Remains of Maynard Davis Richardson, with a Memoir of His Life* may be the least read and, as a consequence, least commented-upon piece of Simms's work to have appeared in book form. This is unfortunate, for there is much in it that should be of interest to Simms scholars and to early American historians.

Nearly six years younger than Simms, Maynard Davis Richardson was born in Charleston on 1 January 1812. He attended the College of Charleston before transferring to South Carolina College in Columbia in 1828. There he was a member of the Clariosophic Society, one of the school's two literary and debate societies. By this time, Richardson had already evidenced the remarkable intelligence and literary talents for which he would be remembered by his friends. These were the "graceful and vigorous shoots of promise which so unhappily were denied fulfillment," as Simms reflected in the memoir he wrote of Richardson (*Remains* ix). The young man possessed a passion for debate, elocution, and classical literature and was, by what record remains, respected, and even somewhat envied, by his classmates for his erudition and diffident attitude toward formal academic honors. He graduated in 1830, third in his class.

Evidence of the close relationship between Simms and Maynard Davis Richardson can be found in the 19 November 1831 issue of Simms's Charleston newspaper the *City Gazette*. In a long article addressed "TO THE PUBLIC" Simms dealt with the subject of a rumor which had begun to circulate in the state that the *City Gazette* had been "bought over to defend and assert the principles and interests of the northern manufacturers" (2). The insinuation of this rumor, of course, was that, in the then intense and ongoing nullification controversy, Simms, the young newspaper editor, was essentially on the payroll of pro-tariff, northern interests. The article contains a full copy of the 25 October 1831 letter sent to Simms by Richardson from Camden which informed him of this rumor and which named as its originator Solicitor John Mayrant, Jr. who, Richardson said, had remarked just the day before at a public dinner at the hotel in Camden that a Col. James G. Spann had been informed by the well-known anti-tariff advocate Henry Lee of Boston, Massachusetts that it was known that Simms's paper as well as the Charleston *Courier* were the property of northern manufactures and served their interests. Writing as a friend, Richardson concluded by telling Simms, "Your character as an independent conductor of the Press is at hazard," and encouraged him to refute the accusation. In the introduction to the letter Simms described Richardson as, "a highly esteemed friend, whose well known character, talents and connexions, will render perfectly unnecessary, any remark which we might otherwise seek to offer in testimony on that score" (Simms, "To the Public" 2).

The rumor, Simms said, was "a lie—a base, wanton and deliberate lie," and he set out to refute it ("To the Public" 2). He wrote letters to John Mayrant, Jr. and Henry Lee asking them to explain their respective parts in the origination and perpetuation of this rumor and included these letters as well as their replies in the 19 November 1831 article.[1] In these letters a complicated saga of blame-shifting and denial unfolds. In his 4 November 1831 reply to Simms Mayrant said, "It is not true that I made such a statement." Instead, Mayrant claimed that Col. Spann had spoken to Henry Lee at the Free Trade Convention held in Philadelphia in 1831 from September 30 to October 7 and had been informed by him only that northern manufacturers were pleased with the positions taken by the *Gazette* and *Courier* and that "their agents in the state were instructed to patronize those papers." For his part, Henry Lee told Simms, "I certainly never did make the assertion attributed to me," but also admitted that while he remembered being introduced to Col. Spann at the Convention he also could not, "bring home to my recollection any such conversation held with him" (Simms, "To the Public" 2).

Believing he had successfully scuttled the rumor, one which challenged his honor and independence, and in the process humiliated his antagonists, Simms copied into the article another full letter from Richardson, from 2 November 1831, in which Richardson explained his reasons for coming to Simms's aid in the affair:

> To those who know you [the rumor] carries its own refutation with it, and to those who do not, the entire and uniform tenor of your Editorial labors ought to be a satisfactory answer. In the present instance, however, more is called for. The slander was obtaining extensive circulation, and, from the responsible source from which it emanated, an almost, proportionable credence. It was rung in my ears in several upper districts, and no reasons I could urge from your character and attitude of unvarying resistance to the American System; could root the impression from the public mind. ("To the Public" 2)

In not only the specific words said about him but in the attention given to safeguarding Simms's public reputation, we have a sense of the affection Richardson must have had for his friend. Evidence for that of Simms for Richardson is the work under consideration.

After graduation from South Carolina College, Richardson began the study of law, but in 1832 he too, like Simms, became involved in the newspaper business. Richardson established and served as editor and proprietor of the *Southern*

Whig, a Unionist, anti-nullification newspaper in Sumterville, South Carolina, where his father, John S. Richardson, was a judge. Both father and son, like Simms in Charleston, were active members of the Union and State's Rights Party, the political organization in South Carolina opposed to nullification. Through the editorial voice of the paper, Richardson attacked nullification and advanced the cause of his party, but the twenty-year-old editor's devotion to the principles of free thought and debate drew him into controversy and then conflict with John Hemphill, the rival editor of the pro-nullification *Sumter Gazette*. On 8 March 1832 Richardson, "without hesitation" printed a communication from a pseudonymous author, "W.E.," which critiqued slavery and called upon South Carolinians to question the institution (Freehling 84). While Richardson, as the essay "Negro Slavery" will verify, was no abolitionist, he did welcome a free and open debate about slavery, believing that such would force his fellow South Carolinians to clarify their views on the subject and allow them to respond more effectively to criticisms of their society.

The tone of the communication, however, printed as it was amidst the heated political atmosphere of the nullification controversy, was seen as dangerous by Hemphill. The nullifier attacked Richardson for allowing it to be published. The young editor, educated and urbane but also obviously proud, did not allow such an assault to go unanswered. He accused Hemphill of "the sickly sensitiveness and ridiculous squeamishness, about touching the subject of slavery which have ever been the subject of our misunderstanding abroad and of which there is not a nervous female who is not thoroughly ashamed" (Freehling 85). An editorial war ensued in which the issue of slavery fell away leaving the clash of personalities and egos. It culminated in a brawl between the two men on the streets of Sumterville, in front of the Sumter Court House. Richardson came with a knife and Hemphill a pistol. When it was over, both men were bloody and their clothes torn, but neither was killed.

As a member of the Union and State's Rights Party, Richardson was chosen to be a delegate to the 1832 Baltimore Convention which nominated Andrew Jackson as candidate for president. This was the first national convention of the Democratic Party. From Baltimore, Richardson traveled to Washington, D.C., where he wrote descriptions of notable political figures for the *Southern Whig*. With his father, Richardson also attended the Unionist convention in Columbia which began on 9 September 1832. He became ill on the return journey to Sumterville and the party stopped at the house of John Marshall in Richland District. He died there on 12 October 1832 and was buried at Bloom Hill in modern Sumter County, South Carolina.

Particulars of the friendship between Simms and Richardson are scarce. It is not known when the two first met, but there is evidence that the families of the two were long acquainted. In 1816, when Simms was ten years old, his father, William Gilmore Simms, Sr., an established planter in Mississippi, attempted to gain custody of the boy from his maternal grandmother Jane Miller Singleton Gates. The case was heard in Charleston before Judge Elihu Hall Bay who, after hearing the arguments of the litigants, allowed Simms to choose for himself with whom he would live. He chose to remain in Charleston with his grandmother. John S. Richardson, the father of Maynard, was one of the attorneys Jane Gates had employed to represent her. The other was future U.S. senator Robert Y. Hayne.

Conception and Composition

Writing to his New York literary friend James Lawson on 25 October 1832 Simms noted, "the melancholy intelligence of death of a very near & dear friend, Maynard Davis Richardson" (*Letters* 1: 42). These words speak to the closeness of the relationship between the two young men. Simms informed Lawson in the same letter that he had dedicated his 1832 epic narrative poem *Atalantis. A Story of the Sea: In Three Parts* to Richardson. Richardson traveled with Simms on his first trip to the North in the summer of 1832 and the two last were in each other's company in Washington, D.C. that year. Richardson left from the capital city to return to South Carolina sometime before Simms returned.

It was not long after receiving the news of Richardson's death that Simms began considering writing a memoir of his friend and publishing his literary remains. He wrote again to Lawson on 19 January 1833 that he planned to visit Sumterville in the coming days for the purpose of "procuring material" to accomplish this project. *The Remains of Maynard Davis Richardson, with a Memoir of His Life* was published by O.A. Roorback and printed by J.S. Burges, both of Charleston, sometime later in 1833. The memoir portion was 34 pages long while the writings of Richardson comprised 248 pages. Simms was not named as the editor. Instead, the compilation was attributed to labors "By His Friend." This suggests a genuine desire to ensure any attention the work received would be focused solely on Richardson. Simms expressed this desire at the beginning of the Memoir: "Though the transcripts and impressions of a mind and a life, scarcely yet active in their human career, and certainly, in great part, yet undeveloped, they carry with them, upon their faces, claims to the respectful consideration of all classes of readers, which may not go unregarded" (*Remains* vii). This, then, was an act of preservation and a memorial to a friend.

The edited contents of *The Remains of Maynard Davis Richardson* vary widely in genre. Simms divided that content into the categories of "Political," "Moral," "Literary and Critical," "Poetical," and "Epigrams." Clearly, Simms gave careful consideration to the structure of *Remains*. Although he did not mention it in his memoir, much of the volume's content originally appeared in Richardson's newspaper, the *Southern Whig*. For example, the political essay, "Calhoun's Exposition," appeared in 1832, from January 26 to February 16. "Jeremy Bentham and the Utilitarians" appeared in the issue of 2 February 1832 while "Mental Philosophy" appeared in that of 8 March 1832. Simms made slight modifications to the beginnings of some of the newspaper columns to make them more readable as essays in a book format. He also made occasional annotations to the essays which he denoted as being done by the editor. The notes accompanying the essays, however, are original to the newspaper versions.

Evaluation

The literary, critical, and political writings of Richardson which Simms selected for inclusion in the volume reveal an extraordinarily intelligent and intellectually ambitious young man. "They are of the true metal," Simms said of them, "and bear the stamp of a genius as beautiful and full of scent and promise as the first flower of the springtime" (*Remains* vii). Richardson had obviously read widely in the classics of literature and philosophy, and he clearly thought deeply about what he read. His love of debate seems to have sharpened his analytical abilities and his engagement with the main currents of early nineteenth-century intellectual discourse are manifest throughout this collection pieced together by Simms. The literary criticism and poetic works reveal a keen talent that, had he lived longer, promised exceptional achievements. Simms must have known Richardson's intelligence through personal interaction, but the quality of these writings must also have impressed him greatly. Knowing both the man and his intellect, Simms doubtless felt sharply the pain of Richardson's death at the young age of twenty.

One can easily speculate on the basis of their friendship. Although Simms was six years older than Richardson, the two had a great deal in common. Both were native Charlestonians. Both were precocious and intelligent young men with powerful literary ambitions. Simms had edited the *City Gazette* from 1 January 1830 to 7 June 1832. Richardson was the editor of the *Southern Whig* at the time of his death. Both men were also passionately engaged in the politics of nullification-era South Carolina, sharing the same Unionist side in that contest. In Richardson, Simms may have seen a reflection of himself, and by editing a volume of his friend's written remains Simms afforded posterity a perspective on the intellectual life of the Antebellum South and early America. The memory of Richardson remained with Simms for many years. He included Richardson's essay "Pursuit of Happiness" and two poems, "Winter Scene" and "Pursuit of Beauty," in *The Charleston Book*. He also apparently made an effort to have Evert Augustus Duyckinck include Richardson in his *Cyclopedia of American Literature* in 1854.

There are no known contemporary reviews of *The Remains of Maynard Davis Richardson*, and Simms biographers have given it only the scantest of attention. In his 1892 biography William Peterfield Trent asserted that Simms "probably did" edit the book and described the selection of Richardson's writings which Simms included in *The Charleston Book* as evidence that, "Simms's friend was not the least gifted of the *ignes minores* that lighted Charleston during the first quarter of" the nineteenth century (73). John Caldwell Guilds, in his *Simms: A Literary*

Life, published in 1992, makes no mention of the work at all, nor does he list it in his bibliography of Simms's works appearing in book form. Still, there is value to be found in a careful perusal of *The Remains of Maynard Davis Richardson*. With it we have Simms's first effort at book editing and gain an insight into what he thought the purpose of such volumes should be. In addition, a small ray of illumination is cast upon the young William Gilmore Simms, nearly as much, for that matter, as upon Maynard Davis Richardson, and the intellectual life of the Antebellum South, and Charleston in particular. Simms knew Richardson at a crucial, formative period in his life, and this friendship doubtless was an important one. It is interesting to speculate on what long term influence Richardson may have had on Simms. And, since the two men held so much in common, *The Remains of Maynard Davis Richardson, with a Memoir of His Life* also leaves us with the sad question of what might have become of the life and great talents of Simms's extraordinary friend.

NOTE

1. These letters are not included in *The Letters of William Gilmore Simms*.

The Revolutionary Romances

The Partisan; *Mellichampe*; *The Scout*; *Katharine Walton*; *Woodcraft*; *The Forayers*; *Eutaw*; and *Joscelyn*

DAVID MOLTKE-HANSEN

From the outset the American Revolution compelled attention from writers and artists. Yet fictionists were slow to follow advocates like Thomas Paine, poets like Philip Freneau, and painters like Jonathan Trumbull. When novelists finally did, Simms proved the most prolific. His series of eight romances remained unrivalled in its extent long after his death. Only in the wake of World War I, when the Revolution's sesquicentennial approached, did other novelists begin to treat more or less as fully as had Simms the subject of the War for Independence. Notably, in most of eight historical novels with characters from his native Maine, Kenneth Roberts turned to the subject, or the years just before and after, again and again. Van Wyck Mason did the same in the six volumes of his "American Revolution" series.

Still later writers followed suit as the war's bicentennial approached. Often this was in multi-generational family chronicles that included the Revolution but ranged much earlier or later. Among the most popular are Inglis Fletcher's "Carolina Chronicles" (12 vols.), John Jakes's "Kent Family Chronicles" (8 vols.), and Elswyth Thane's "Williamsburg" series (7 vols.). Several recent series with a more military focus treat just the Revolution. They include Edward Cline's "Sparrowhawk" (6 vols.), James Nelson's "Revolution at Sea Saga" (5 vols.), and Adam Rutledge's "Patriots" (6 vols.).

Simms paved the way for all these series, though not many authors have known their debt. At one level, his accomplishment was to give narrative form and force to the complicated ebb and flow of the Revolution in his native South Carolina. By doing so over a third of a century, starting just after the conclusion of the war's semi-centennial, he also helped claim the Revolution for America's imaginative life. Before considering his individual titles, their publication and reception, and their later, critical standing, it is important to understand what motivated him. Then one can assess the series as a whole and ask its value to twenty-first-century readers. (Because one work in the series, *Woodcraft*, has garnered more substantial attention than any other, this collection also has a separate essay on it, by James Everett Kibler.)

The Revolution's Changing Significance, 1815–45

To a remarkable degree, the Revolution framed Simms's boyhood. The future author was nine years old when America's so-called second revolution, the War of 1812, finished. During the conflict, his immigrant father fought under General Andrew Jackson in the Red Stick or First Creek War. That conflict led the budding poet to effuse in verse. Inspired as well by his Charleston, South Carolina grandmother's tales of his mother's family in the Revolution, the young Simms was in the habit of scouting old war sites in the surrounding countryside (Simms, *Partisan* [1835] viiv–iii; Guilds, *Literary Life* 7, 11).

This enthusiasm was further stoked by the fact that the American Revolution was gaining literary purchase. First came the hagiographies, memoirs, and historical accounts of the founders, together with reams of verse and documentary compilations. Then the story tellers started. Washington Irving's *The Sketchbook of Geoffrey Crayon, Gent.* appeared in 1820 and contained "The Legend of Sleepy Hollow" and "Rip Van Winkle," tales set immediately before and after the war. James Fenimore Cooper's *The Spy* came out in 1821 and his *The Pilot: A Tale of the Sea* two years later. Both these novels had Revolutionary settings—in the one case upstate New York (Irving's setting as well) and in the other the English coast and seas. It was in this latter environment that American naval hero John Paul Jones preyed on British shipping with storied success. Inspired by *The Spy* and by work editing a two-volume history of the Revolution, Mainer John Neal penned *Seventy-Six; or, Love and Battle* in just under a month in 1822.

At the time the sixteen-year old Simms thought of himself as a poet, not a fictionist. Despite his subsequent work as a journalist during the early 1830s, he did not shift his primary literary production from poetry to prose until after his 1832 trip to New York to launch a national literary career (Kibler, *Poetry*; Brennan, *Holy Craft*). He published his first Gothic novella, *Martin Faber*, the next year. Then, over the course of two years, he wrote three romances. These commenced the three series that occupied him much of the rest of his life. He began the Border series in 1834 with *Guy Rivers: A Tale of Georgia*, set during the gold rush that started in 1828 in the northern corner of the state. The series ultimately treated the westerning edge of southern settlement, from Georgia to Texas, as well as the southern backwoods, from the mountains of North Carolina to the swamps of Florida, in Simms's own lifetime.

The other series quickly followed. Simms started the Colonial in 1835 with *The Yemassee. A Romance of Carolina*, about a 1715–17 conflict between Native Americans and British colonists and their African slaves. The wider series broadly treated the periods of European exploration and colonization in the Americas from the 16th through the early 18th centuries. The third series, the Revolutionary, focused on that war in South Carolina. Simms delivered *The Partisan: A Tale of the Revolution* to Harper & Brothers, his publishers, just six months after the publication of John Pendleton Kennedy's Revolutionary novel *Horse-Shoe Robinson: A Tale of the Tory Ascendency*, set as well in the backcountry of South Carolina (Kennedy viii).

Simms subsequently wrote poetry, short stories, and novellas, as well as biographies and essays, in each of the subject areas of his series. Yet the majority of his output in all three was in long-form fiction—what he called romances. In making the move from poetry to romance, he followed the example of Sir Walter Scott. Scott died just as Simms's sixth volume of verse and first New York-published book, the 1832 dramatic poem *Atalantis*, was coming off the press to national critical acclaim. It was nearly 40 years earlier that the Scottish author began collecting and publishing the ballads of his country. Then, in 1814, he started his prolific and successful career as a novelist or romancer.

Scott judged fiction more accessible to broad readerships than poetry, and it was important to him to influence as many as possible. This was especially so in light of his goal of fostering a shared sense of British nationality among the Scots and the English—people of fraught histories, diverse origins, and deep antipathies. To this end, he examined not only the interactions of these ethnicities, which he did in *his* Border romances, set on the English-Scottish border. He also treated the earlier conflicts of Highlanders and Lowlanders in Scotland and of Anglo-Saxons and Normans in England. He did this to help people understand how Scottish and English identities had arisen out of the clashes and mixing of earlier ethnicities (Simms, *Views* 1: 40–41; Moltke-Hansen, "Horizons" 6–13).

The reason for such fictional narratives, Scott contended, was that ballads and other traditional lays do not have the same sweep as, for instance, *The Iliad*. A people's rise, conflicts, and conquests, myths, heroes, and villains, he concluded, need to be set and narrated on a large scale. Ancient bards did this formerly in epics chanted across generations. In a later and literate age, however, the surest way to provide people with a sense of their stirring past and mythic memories was in print. In type, prose carried the individual reader more effectively than poetry. The latter was supremely an oral and aural art.

Consequently, Scott, with others, developed the romance to tell epic stories in prose (Lukacs). It was different from the novel in both its purpose and its subject. As Simms put it in his "Advertisement" to *The Yemassee*, "the domestic novel [of Fielding and Richardson] . . ., confined to the felicitous narrative of common and daily occurring events, is altogether a different sort of composition." Its standards are not "those of the epic," but the romance's are. That is why, Simms also insisted, "the modern romance is a poem in every sense of the word" (vi).

Though deploying Scott's formula, Simms was not a copycat (Holman, *Roots* 50–60). His subjects were American (Simms, *Yemassee* [1835] vii). As Scott wrote of the ethnogenesis of the Scots, the English, and the British, Simms treated Americans' emergence as a people out of their diverse origins and historical experiences. He and Scott shared a genre, because it was the necessary and appropriate form for the subject matter and purposes of each. In time, Simms would have an elaborate understanding of what that meant. Yet, despite his clarity about the genre, he did not start with a grand plan to fictionalize Americans' rise and spread westward. His initial intention for the Revolutionary series was just a trilogy "devoted to the illustration of the war of the Revolution in South Carolina" (Simms, *Partisan* [1854] v).

While feeling his way toward a larger vision, Simms alternated among his three series. In the subset of his American-focused review essays and lectures, gathered in *Views and Reviews in American Literature, History and Fiction* and issued in 1846–47, he laid out his rationale for the three. The case he made was one trumpeted by his friends in the informal association of nationalist, Democratic writers centered in New York—the Young America circle (Widmer). Although adumbrated already in his 1835 preface to *The Yemassee* and elaborated over the next months in both his first two Revolutionary romances, *The Partisan* and *Mellichampe*, the argument he advanced was in a sense his *ex post facto* justification of his practice. He claimed that he was writing what the Alabama poet and politician Alexander B. Meek came to call, in an 1844 oration, *Americanism in Literature* (Simms, *Views* 1: 1–19).

Anticipating Meek, Simms lectured in 1842 on "The Epochs and Events of American History, as Suited to the Purposes of Art in Fiction." He explained that he saw American history divided into four epochs—that of initial European exploration and conquest in the three-quarters of a century or so after Columbus made landfall in the new world; the subsequent two centuries of British colonial settlement and continuing conflict with Native Americans and rival European powers; the two decades that saw the British American move from remonstrance to Revolution and independence; and the subsequent western expansion, self-development, and manifest destiny of the new nation and people (Simms, *Views* 1: 20–101). In treating each of these epochs in romances, Simms published at least two dozen long-form fictions—a third of them in the Revolutionary series.

While all three series shared common purposes, Simms had particular reasons to treat the Revolution as and when he did. A supporter of his father's old commander, President Andrew Jackson, and the Union during the bitter campaign of the early 1830s to have South Carolina unilaterally nullify federal tariffs, he was keen to assert the Palmetto State's role in the making of the American nation. The political passions of the nullification episode reminded him, too, that "the excesses of patriotism, when attaining power, have been but too frequently productive of a tyranny more dangerous in its exercise, and more lasting in its effects, than the despotism which it was invoked to overthrow" (Simms, *Mellichampe* [1836] v; Wakelyn 19–50). His early Revolutionary romances also "suggested clews [*sic*] to the historian . . . and laid bare to other workers . . . the veins of tradition which everywhere enrich" South Carolina. True, his "friends denounced [his] waste of time," but the result was that the Palmetto State had "furnished more materials for the use of art and fiction . . . than half the states in the Union" (Simms, *Katharine* [1854] 3).

These early Revolutionary romances reflected as well a commitment to realism. This was despite their conventional, romantic, chief protagonists. Indeed, many criticized Simms for the vulgarity and violence of his secondary characters. He answered the charge with a rhetorical question that reflected his dedication to historical verisimilitude: "Does the story profess to belong to a country and to a period of history which are alike known—and does it misrepresent either?" The implied answer to the first part of the question was "yes" and, to the second part, "no." Clearly, as he insisted, he had no desire "to make a fairy tale . . . in which none but the colors of the rose and rainbow shall predominate" (*Mellichampe* [1836] ix).

Rather, Simms's "object usually [was] to adhere, as closely as possible, to the features and the attributes of real life." Further, it seemed to him obvious "that vulgarity and crime must always preponderate . . . in the great majority during a period of war." Because, "to paint morally, the historic novelist must paint truly," Simms concluded that the fact that "the low characters predominate" should not surprise his readers (*Mellichampe* [1836] x–xii). The need to reiterate the point against a persistent strain in the criticism of his work may have been behind his observation in the historical overview with which he began his third Revolutionary romance, *The Kinsmen; or, The Black Riders of Congaree*: "That atrocious and reckless warfare between the whigs and the tories, which had deluged the fair plains of Carolina with native blood, was now at its height" (17). The romance that started there was his last in the series for almost a decade.

Southern Honor and the American Revolution

When Simms returned to writing Revolutionary romances in 1849, he still had these earlier motives and judgments. Yet, in the interval, his rationales for writing had shifted. He had developed new intellectual and political priorities. He addressed these initially in review essays penned between 1845 and 1852. He published three of the essays as *South-Carolina in the Revolutionary War: Being a Reply to Certain Misrepresentations and Mistakes of Recent Writers, in Relation to the Course and Conduct of This State* (1853) (Moltke-Hansen, "History Mattered"; *Letters* 6: 328n). There he argued that novelists, editors, biographers, and historians were mischaracterizing the course and conduct of the Revolution and of the Revolutionaries in the South—especially South Carolina. Even such an eminent southern writer as John Pendleton Kennedy had made material errors in his *Horse-Shoe Robinson*. These were not justified by the demands of his story or the faulty memory of the real Horse-Shoe Robinson. The consequence of such mistakes was to make the patriots appear less, and the British more, effective than they were (Simms, *South-Carolina* 60–72).

Even more galling was the critique of the patriots for excesses against the loyalists. Simms early acknowledged both the fact and, in particular instances, the unfortunate consequences. Yet he vehemently resisted reading those instances as normative (*Mellichampe* [1836] iv–v; Moltke-Hansen, "History Mattered"). Many loyalists earned the vigor of the actions against them. Many patriots were sorely provoked. The civil warfare between para-military forces of both sides inevitably produced violent interactions. To take the viewpoint of "the Descendants of the loyalists," as did Ann Pamela Cunningham, granddaughter of an upcountry South Carolina tory colonel, was to use "about the worst authorities . . . on the subject of the Revolution" (*Letters* 6: 330); for those descendants were seeking to assuage their "mortification" and to meet the need "to make out a case" for their own families (Moltke-Hansen, "History Mattered").

Simms argued the point so strongly because it was part of a larger debate about the role of the South in the Revolution. Northern editors and writers contended increasingly that it took northern troops to drive the British army from Georgia and South Carolina to Yorktown and surrender. This was because the South's population was divided in the conflict and, indeed, often resisted the patriot forces. To the contrary, Simms insisted, local partisans in South Carolina repeatedly saved the American army. Moreover, they did this while also fighting "all the tories who infested [the state], though these were mostly *refugees from all the States south of New York*, who had taken refuge in [British] Florida, & who followed in the wake of the British when they penetrated Geo. & S. C." (*Letters* 6: 330).

Simms contended that the South's leadership largely supported the Revolution but that the many recent Scottish and German immigrants tended to loyalism. Unlike the Irish and Scots-Irish, who often hated the English and also unlike the descendants of Huguenot immigrants, they owed too much to the British Crown (Simms, "Ellet's"). Further, at least in South Carolina, they made up "nearly half of [the colony's] population" and "had not been in the country 10 years" (*Letters* 6: 330). At the time, by contrast, New England was overwhelmingly settled by descendants of people who had arrived before the English Civil War over a century and a quarter before. The populations of the two regions therefore were very different in their make ups.

New Englanders, according to Simms, mostly were local patriots, not active on behalf of the larger cause of American independence. Consequently, South Carolina "sent, in proportion, more troops into the war than any other colony" (*Letters* 6: 330). Moreover, had it not been for southern leaders such as George Washington, the light of liberty would have been snuffed out. "You assailed my country . . . unjustly," Simms wrote New England historian Lorenzo Sabine. He then lamented Sabine's "abuse of partial facts; and the evident purpose which it betrayed, rather to goad, sting, wound & disparage, than to be historically just & true" (*Letters* 6: 328–29).

These points mattered not only because of the importance of historical accuracy. They had political ramifications. Charles Sumner of Massachusetts used the introduction to the 1847 edition of Sabine's *The American Loyalists, or Biographical Sketches of Adherents to the British Crown in the War of the Revolution* in his attack in a speech, in the United States Senate, on South Carolina and one of its senators, Andrew Butler. He characterized the Palmetto State as stained by "its imbecility from Slavery, confessed through the Revolution," and then "made the state out to be unpatriotic and un-American, not only in 1856 but at least as far back as the Revolutionary War," three quarters of a century and more before (M. Shillingsburg, "Failed" 185). That attack, Simms maintained, was what provoked the notorious "cudgelling" [*sic*] of Sumner on the Senate floor by Congressman Preston Brooks, Butler's South Carolina relation. Sabine "also misled Mr. [Daniel] Webster, who fell into a good deal of spoken blundering, in [his address to the New England Society of] Charleston, touching the vast number of New Englanders who perished in our battles" (*Letters* 6: 331).

Simms intended his fall 1856 lecture tour of the North, just months after Brooks used his gutta percha cane on Sumner, to set the record straight and to maintain the honor of South Carolina's role in the Revolution. Not surprisingly, given those intentions, the tour was a disaster and had to be cut short. His references to "Sumner's attack on S.C. as that of a deliberate & wanton malignant" antagonized his audiences (M. Shillingsburg, "Failed" 191). The newspapers replied in kind, claiming that Simms was "seeking to do, in the historical field, what Brooks had done in the physical" (M. Shillingsburg, "Failed" 194). The next year Simms lectured on his northern reception for a southern audience. Northerners, he insisted, were morally incapable of listening to southern viewpoints, because the "politico-social relations of the two great sections" were "in absolute and direct antagonism" (M. Shillingsburg, "Failed" 188; Hagstette, "Private" 52–58).

These intellectual and political conclusions were not the only developments that shaped Simms's return to his Revolutionary romance series. He formed new aesthetic goals as well. Although an early advocate of realism in fiction, he did not begin as a literary realist. Instead he regarded everyday life as being in the scope of the novelist; he was rather an epic writer of romances. Then it occurred to him that he could fuse these approaches, creatively using the tensions and differences between them (Ackerman 165).

Simms's fourth Revolutionary romance, *Katharine Walton*, reflected the change. Its purpose was "the delineation of the social world of Charleston, during the Revolutionary period" (Simms, *Katharine* [1854] 3). Simms still considered the work a romance but used its social realism to attack aristocratic prejudice in the manner of William Makepeace Thackeray (Watson *Nationalism* 92–93). According to Mary Ann Wimsatt, "the Loyalists, who controlled government, churches, and clubs, continued the city's glittering amusements—a fact that made [the city] ripe for treatment in the novel of manners vein" (*Major* 179). Consequently, "for the first time in the Revolutionary War series, . . . Simms [made] social hostilities rather than military maneuvers the backbone of a book" (Wimsatt, *Major* 179–80).

Because *Katharine Walton* was the first novel serialized in *Godey's Lady's Book*, the most widely circulated American cultural journal of the day, it presumably had more readers than any other of Simms's Revolutionary romances. Yet many scholars consider Simms's next his best. *The Sword and the Distaff; or, "Fair, Fat and Forty," A Story of the South, at the Close of the Revolution* appeared in serial form, too, but in Charleston. Publication started in February 1852. The book came out that fall—also in Charleston—before the conclusion of the serialization and its Philadelphia publication from the same plates the next year. Subsequently it became known by the title of its revised, 1854, Redfield edition: *Woodcraft; or, Hawks about the Dovecote. A Story of the South at the Close of the Revolution*.

In its serial form, Simms's work overlapped with the last segments of the serialization of Harriet Beecher Stowe's famous abolitionist novel *Uncle Tom's Cabin*, which ran for 40 weeks between 5 June 1851 and 4 March 1852. Simms contended shortly afterwards that his romance was the best answer to Stowe's work (*Letters* 3: 222). He did not mean that he wrote to reply to Stowe, as many others in fact eventually did. After all, he initially published for a largely southern audience—the only time he did so in his Revolutionary series. Moreover, he could not have been writing in reply because of the near simultaneity of the publications of his and Stowe's works.

Rather, scholars understand Simms to have meant either of two things. One is that the social world and relations conveyed in his domestic romance gave a radically more accurate and positive picture of slavery and the plantation South than did Stowe's sentimental domestic novel. Both works were critical of failings of the institution, but to different ends (Watson "Simms's Answer"). Social order wins in the one, and moral order loses in the other. The second reading of Simms's assertion is that his melding of sentimental domestic fiction with the romance was radically more effective than Stowe's appropriation of the romance structure for her work. In making this case, Zeno Ackerman argues that Simms and Stowe both dealt with responses to the disruption of the plantation idyll—by war in one case, by progressive, capitalist alienation in the other case (165). Whatever Simms meant, it aggrieved him that Stowe's book sold hugely, while his did not, published as it initially was in a small circulation journal and then in a North becoming more and more abolitionist in sentiment.

As Kibler argues in his essay on *Woodcraft* in this collection, Simms did not believe that the success of South Carolina plantation society was guaranteed. Rather, it had to be achieved again and again. To survive it also had to be protected from hostile influences. Yet historically the social order did carry forward. Once carved out of the wilderness and later restored after the disruptions and devastation of the Revolution, plantations remained the epitome of patriarchal order, and, under the guiding hand of plantation mistresses, the big house served as their moral center. This ideal, Simms understood, was not always the reality, but it was, he maintained, the cultural, social, and ethical norm.

Modern critics argue that Simms's patriarchal plantation purveyed a fantasy. Like other slave owners, Simms deceived himself about the bonds between slaves and masters. Most slaves did not happily think of themselves as members of their masters' families, black and white. Neither did they believe they owned their masters as much as their masters owned them. Nor did slaves all love their owners or, as happened repeatedly in Simms's romances, reject the chance of freedom (Fox-Genovese and Genovese, *Fatal*; Foley "Nimmons"; King 140; Shelton 77). At the same time as scholars criticize, however, they praise the verisimilitude of the details of Simms's renderings—not just in *Woodcraft*, but in all the Revolutionary romances.

Simms scoured the written record available to him in manuscript as well as print, conducted oral history interviews, sought out informants about incidents and places he did not know, and weighed the relative merits of his evidence. He began as a boy, musing about the stories implicit in "the local tradition, which, unconsciously, [his] mind began to throw together, and to combine in form." As he explained in the revised and expanded introduction to the 1854 edition of *The Partisan*, "even where the written history has not been found, tradition and the local chronicles, preserved as family records, have furnished adequate authorities." He concluded: "a sober desire for history—the unwritten, the unconsidered, but veracious history—has been with me, in this labour, a sort of principle" (vii–ix).

Even when he originally wrote *The Partisan*, Simms understood, as he rephrased the point in the 1854 edition, that "History . . . is quite too apt to overlook the best essentials of society—such as constitute the moving impulses of men to action—in order to dilate on great events,—scenes in which men are merely massed, while a single favourite overtops all the rest, the Hero rising to the Myth, and absorbing within himself all the consideration which a more veracious and philosophical mode of writing would distribute over states and communities, and the humblest walks of life." Although in his romance "the persons of the Drama, many of them, are names of the nation, familiar to our daily reading," the focus of *The Partisan* was not on them, but on "the little nucleus of the Partisan squad . . . first formed in the recesses of the swamp" (xi).

That preoccupation let Simms show "how the personal wrong . . . goaded the indifferent into patriotism . . . [and] the submissive into rebellion" (*Partisan* [1835] ix, viii). In doing so, he was explaining why things happened as and when they did. His purpose, as he observed in his 1835 introduction, was to "give a story of events, rather than of persons" (x). Events moved men and moved history forward. The treatment of events gave one the opportunity to explore history's unfolding and the consequences (Holman, *Roots* 35). The why of history, nevertheless, was different than the what.

Literary Realism, Sectionalism, and the Postbellum Turn

Simms's sense of the "what" of history shifted between the early 1840s and the '50s. The fundamental question in *Woodcraft* is not about the motivations and actions of the Revolution, which is finished, but about the restoration of a moral order and economy in the face of the war's social dislocations. Those disruptions challenged the character of both individuals and the community. In the process of shifting to this focus, Simms turned the historical romance into a novel of social realism and manners or a domestic romance (Dale). Indeed, Jan Bakker argues that *Woodcraft* is "the First 'Realistic' Novel in America" ("Frontier" 64–78). That may slight *Katharine Walton* (Wimsatt, "Realism"). In any event, the post-*Woodcraft* Revolutionary novels, although set in war-time, carried forward this social critical emphasis. Conservative, low country aristocrats continued to be objects of attack, as were the unworthy low-born, twisted by greed and hate.

Individuals of these castes at opposite ends of the social spectrum were too often tories. "Unable to lead themselves," according to Simms, they "threw themselves, as so many dead weights, about the car of *mouvement* [*sic*]; and it is no reproach to those who did lead, that they were passed over, or flung off, by the wheels" ("Civil Warfare" 260–61). "The language he used to describe the tyranny of the tories in 1780 was the same as he used to describe the tyranny of the nullifiers . . . and [also] the tyranny of Northern interests in the 1850s" (Moltke-Hansen, "Ordered" 138). Tory forces and their partisan opposition figure centrally in the last two of his antebellum Revolutionary romances, published in 1855–56. There they play key roles in the run up to, and the ultimate outcome of, the Battle of Eutaw Springs. This engagement is the event around which *The Forayers; or The Raid of the Dog-Days* and *Eutaw: A Sequel to The Forayers, or the Raid of the Dog-Days. A Tale of the Revolution* revolve.

The critique of the failures of leadership and allegiance in these romances grew out of deep frustration. Starting in the mid-'40s, Simms first ramped up this criticism in other writings. Like the tory elite, too many of the antebellum South's leading citizens were temporizing about the region's political future. Increasing Simms's sense of urgency was his apprehension about capitalism's growing and coercive influence. It infected not just politics, but also cultural life and other spheres. Avarice and the new, socially destructive methods of wealth's generation were undermining political resolve and corrupting arts'—and thought's—producers, productions, and consumers as well as social relations. His Revolutionary romances of the '50s all show this process. In doing so, they reflect what Amy Kaplan argues literary realism is: a "strategy for imagining and managing the threats of social change" (ix).

The disease of capitalism, Simms believed, had been at work longer and had infected more people and more of life in the industrializing and urbanizing North and Britain of his day than in his region. Yet, as his Colonial and Revolutionary romances show, the South was not immune. Moreover, capitalism progressively compromised the social, cultural, and political health of the region as the nineteenth century advanced (Mingura; Pearce, "All Aboard"). At least slavery, he contended, isolated the South from some of the worst consequences of the disease (Ackerman 165).

This belief was in part why Simms proposed the extension of the South's slave regime over countries on the Caribbean littoral. That goal, in Simms's view, was southerners' manifest destiny.Besides, Mexicans and others needed to be disciplined and civilized by the institution (Simms, *Self-Development* 22–23). This aggrandizing vision was part of Simms's design to protect southern rights against an overweening North. The South would do so by augmenting its influence and political power (Simms, "Southern Convention"). Simms's ambitions became greater still: establishment of the sovereignty and nationhood of the southern people. Only in this way, he eventually concluded, could the extension and preservation of his people's way of life and independence be assured. In his eyes as well, these were fundamentally the same motivations and objectives as those which animated America's Revolutionary founders.

The study of the Revolution, then, revealed the way forward, not just the heroics and necessities of an earlier age. History was about the future—until, that is, the Civil War created a chasm between the slave regime and its aftermath. In the process, the war turned the burgeoning South of Simms's Border Romance series, westward expansion, and manifest destiny into the Old South of beguiling and fading memories, timeless tradition, and social order. It also proved that the reasoning undergirding Simms's antebellum historical thought was wrong. The South was not destined for independence; white southerners would not become their own nation, and slavery was not the future of a Caribbean basin dominated by them (Moltke-Hansen, "History Failed" 27–30).

Yet even after Confederate defeat Simms continued the fight against capitalism. Shortly before his death in 1870, he told the ladies of the Charleston Horticultural Society that they must be resolute in their efforts to stem capitalism's corrupting and debasing influence. They needed to do this to preserve the South's distinction, culture, and values. The remembered patriarchal order of the antebellum plantation, centered on the big house run by the plantation mistress, might be no more; nonetheless it offered a model to inform his auditors' sense of a healthy society. At the same time, the sacrifices of the Civil War in defense of the southern way of life required the continuing commitment to that life (Simms, *Sense*; Georgini; J. Miller, "Sense"). Sadly, in Simms's view, what that defense could not do was free the South from Yankeedom.

The last of his Revolutionary romances, *Joscelyn*, serially published in 1867, reflected the shift in historical perspective and reality with which Simms had to deal after defeat. The chief protagonist, Stephen Joscelyn, is unlike earlier leading men of the series: he is a cripple, physically and psychologically. He is driven to fight against his demons as well as for the patriot cause. War is an inner tumult as much as an outward conflict. The notorious tory Thomas Browne, based on an historical figure, in effect loses himself and the last battle of the story in his parallel struggle. Joscelyn, though, finally affirms his manhood, his honor, and his sanity. His concluding victory is as much personal as military or political.

War's fortunes are uncertain, but a man can be responsible for himself. In the end, the inference seems to be, character is achieved (or lost), not simply a birthright and an example, as it was for Simms's early romance heroes. One's conduct is all one can control in the face of chaotic military and political conflict and social upheaval. Indeed, character is the fundamental measure of success and the chief bulwark against disorder and dissolution. Simms went on to suggest to the ladies of the Horticultural Society that, by this measure, the conquering Yankees had failed. This was because of how they behaved not only in the winning, but also in the aftermath of victory (*Sense*; Georgini; J. Miller, "Sense"). Morally and aesthetically, therefore, victory should still go to the South.

Joscelyn's story revealed Simms shifting from a social to a psychological understanding of war and literary realism. The move shaped all three of his last published romances, including two in the Border series—*Voltmeier; or, The Mountain Men* and *The Cub of the Panther: A Hunter Legend of the "Old North State,"* both serially issued in 1869. The move reflected as well Simms's preoccupation with states of mind back to his early days as a writer of Gothic tales (Hagstette, "Screams"). Unlike his late romances, however, those tales did not—could not—use the intellectual and aesthetic tools of the psychological realism just beginning to emerge in literature at mid-century. Furthermore, even among his last long fictions only *Joscelyn* and the unpublished and incomplete pirate romance "The Brothers of the Coast" deal with the impact of war on the individual or use war as a metaphor, as well as an occasion, for the inner conflicts and moral dilemmas of their protagonists (N. Meriwether, "Unfinished"). Some scholars even consider *Joscelyn* a proto-existentialist work (Moltke-Hansen, "History Failed" 29–30).

The Eight Revolutionary Romances

Joscelyn is the last written but the first in its chronological setting, treating as it does the Revolution's beginnings in the backcountry along the Georgia-South Carolina border in 1775. Before going back to the beginning, Simms thought of *The Partisan* as his opening, as well as his first, work in the series. He explained the relations of his earlier Revolutionary romances in the "Historical Summary" with which he introduced *The Forayers*. "The 'Partisan'," he observed there,

> closed with the melancholy defeat of the first southern continental army under [General Horatio] Gates, at Camden. "Mellichampe" illustrated the interval between this event and the arrival of [General Nathanael] Greene, with the rude material for the organization of a second army; and was more particularly intended to do honor to the resolute and hardy patriotism of the scattered bands of patriots, who still maintained a predatory warfare against the foe among the swamps and thickets, rather keeping alive the spirit of the country, than operating decisively for its rescue. "The Scout," originally published under the name of "The Kinsmen," occupied a third period, when the wary policy of Greene began to make itself felt, in the gradual isolation and overthrow of the detached posts and fortresses which the enemy had established with the view to overawe the people in the leading precincts of the state; while "Katharine Walton," closing the career of certain parties, introduced to the reader by the "Partisan," and making complete the trilogy begun in that work, was designed to show the fluctuations of the contest, the spirit with which it was carried on, and to embody certain events of great individual interest, connected with the fortunes of persons not less distinguished by their individual worth of character, and their influence upon the general history, than by the romantic circumstances growing out of their career.
>
> This narrative brought down the record to a period, when, for the first time, the British were made to understand that the conflict was doubtful; that their conquests were insecure, and that, so far from extending their arms over the interior, it became a question with them whether they should be able to maintain their hold upon the strong places of which they had so long held possession. . . . To maintain themselves in Charleston and Savannah, the necessity was pressing that they should contract their powers and concentrate their forces. Reinforcements from Europe were hardly to be expected. The British empire was in a state of exhaustion, and the army of the invader was now half made up of the provincial loyalists (4–5).

At that point Simms resumed the historical narrative in *The Forayers* and its sequel, *Eutaw*. In doing so, he continued to "seek to illustrate the social condition of the country, under the influence of those strifes and trials which give vivacity to ordinary circumstances, and mark with deeper hues, and stronger colors, and sterner tones, the otherwise common progress of human hopes and fears, passions and necessities" (5). *Woodcraft* followed chronologically, although appearing right after *Katharine Walton* and, so, before *The Forayers*. Together, the seven antebellum Revolutionary romances treat the period "from the fall of the city of Charleston, in 1780," to the months after "the provisional articles of peace, between the King of Great Britain, and the revolted colonies of America, were signed at Paris, on the 13th November, 1782" (Simms, *Partisan* [1854] vii; Simms, *Woodcraft* 5). At his death, Simms had plans for at least one additional romance for the series, presumably to help fill in the four-plus year gap between the action of *Joscelyn* and that of *The Partisan* (*Letters* 4: 625–26).

It only became possible to read all eight of the works in the series in book form during the bicentennial of the Revolution. Until the University of South Carolina Press issued *Joscelyn* in the Centennial Simms edition in 1975, that work had been available just in serial form. The next year, for the bicentennial, the Southern Studies Program of the University issued all eight romances. For the first time, they also were available with annotations explaining historical and literary references.

To recap, drawing on the introduction to the bicentennial edition, the eight novels of Simms's Revolutionary series first appeared in the following order:

The Partisan: A Tale of the Revolution. 2 volumes. (1835) New York: Harper & Brothers. Revised edition, entitled *The Partisan: A Romance of the Revolution*, New York: Redfield, 1854. Simms began this first novel in his Revolutionary War series early in 1835. He had a dozen chapters finished by June, and the book was published in November. He revised it extensively for publication, in January 1854, in the Redfield selected edition of his works. It deals with the 1780 Battle of Camden and its aftermath, especially the guerilla warfare by partisan forces under Francis Marion and other militia commanders. Like most of the other titles in the series, it was many times reprinted, first by Redfield and later by other publishers, but without further revision or correction by the author.

Mellichampe: A Legend of the Santee. 2 volumes. (1836) New York: Harper & Brothers. Revised edition, New York: Redfield, 1854. Simms's second novel of the Revolution was begun soon after publication of *The Partisan* and was issued apparently in October the next year. Revised for publication in March 1854 in the Redfield edition, it was many times reprinted but, as in the case of other volume in the series, without further revision or correction by the author. The story follows the fictional band of Francis Marion's partisans in their conflicts with loyalist and British forces in the wake of the Battle of Camden.

The Kinsmen; or, the Black Riders of Congaree: A Tale. 2 volumes. (1841) Philadelphia: Lea and Blanchard. Revised edition, entitled *The Scout; or, The Black Riders of Congaree*, New York: Redfield, 1854. Simms began writing his third novel of the Revolution early in 1840, and it was published in February 1841. Revised extensively for inclusion in September 1854 in the Redfield edition of his works, with its new title, the novel was many times reprinted in that form. It opens shortly after the Battle of Hobkirk's Hill, or the second Battle of Camden, in May 1781. The action ends with the British departure from the Star Fort at Ninety-Six, South Carolina the following month. A good brother is a partisan leader and chief protagonist; a bad brother is secretly the tory head of the Black Riders and a rival in love. Allied with the partisan leader is Supple Jack Bannister, the "authentic voice of the liberty-loving frontiersman," a recurrent figure in all three of Simms's romance series and also the Scout of the retitled and revised version of the novel (Ridgely, *William* 84).

Katharine Walton; or, the Rebel of Dorchester: An Historical Romance of the Revolution in Carolina. (1850–51) A shorter version was the first novel to appear serially in *Godey's Lady's Book* (February-December 1850), under the title "Katharine Walton; or, the Rebel's Daughter: A Tale of the Revolution." The initial book publication was by A. Hart in Philadelphia in 1851. The revised edition, entitled *Katharine Walton; or, The Rebel of Dorchester*, was included in the Redfield edition in 1854 and many times reprinted in that form. Although the work had been planned much earlier, the actual writing of this fourth novel of the Revolution apparently was not begun until the fall of 1849. Set in Charleston, the novel examines the social world there under British occupation and, because of this setting, has more unity of action and scene than other novels in the series. Simms called it the "most *symmetrical & truthful* of all my Revolutionary novels" (*Letters* 6: 120, emphasis in original).

The Sword and the Distaff; or, "Fair, Fat and Forty," A Story of the South, at the Close of the Revolution. (1852) Charleston: Walker, Richards & Co. Retitled issue, entitled *Woodcraft; or, Hawks about the Dovecote: A Story of the South at the Close of the Revolution*, New York: Redfield, 1854. First published serially in semi-monthly supplements to the *Southern Literary Gazette* (February-November 1852) and reprinted often from the Redfield edition, this fifth of the Revolutionary novels is set during the chaotic close and aftermath of the war, beginning with the British evacuation of Charleston in December 1782 and moving to Glen-Eberley plantation on the Ashepoo River south of the city, where the plantation community is striving to reestablish relative civil order and comity. Because the plates of the serialized version were used for the first Charleston printing of the book, that was called the second edition. Lippincott, Grambo of Philadelphia reissued the work from the same plates and with the same title in 1853. The Redfield edition was stereotyped by C.C. Savage of New York with modest emendations.

The Forayers; or, The Raid of the Dog-Days. (1855) New York: Redfield. This novel covers the British retreat from Ninety-Six and the lead up to the Battle of Eutaw Springs. Simms started the composition in November 1854, while finalizing the revisions for the Redfield edition of *Guy Rivers*. In February 1855, he claimed to be half finished. The novel appeared nine months later. In the interval, Simms staged his play *Michael Bonham*, gave an oration "On the Choice of a Profession" at the College of Charleston, revised *Border Beagles*, *Confession*, and *Beauchampe* for the Redfield edition of his selected works, and read proof on *Guy Rivers*. Like the other romances in the Redfield edition, *The Forayers* was reprinted many times.

Eutaw: A Sequel to The Forayers, or the Dog-Days. A Tale of the Revolution. (1856) New York: Redfield. This sequel completes the story of the British withdrawal from their outpost at Ninety-Six, including the Battle of Eutaw Springs, the last major engagement of the Carolina theatre, and that battle's aftermath. First reprinted by Redfield in 1858, the novel saw many subsequent reprintings.

Joscelyn: A Tale of the Revolution. (1867) Columbia, S.C.: University of South Carolina Press, 1975. First published serially in *The Old Guard* (January-December 1867), a copperhead (northern Democratic) journal. The serial publication stopped with several installments still to come. Consequently, this last of the Revolutionary romances is not quite complete. Simms conceived the work as early as March 1858, when he was making plans to visit Augusta, Georgia to familiarize himself with the setting (*Letters* 4: 41, 72, 82). Afraid of how he would treat the tories in their history, the local media reacted negatively, and Simms determined not to return (*Letters* 4: 83–4). Nevertheless, he intended to resume work on the book in 1860, before family issues, health, financial problems, and the secession crisis intervened. By October 1866 he had written 120 pages. The serialization of the work over the next year meant he was writing to deadline just ahead of the printers.

Critical Reception and Subsequent Reappraisal

The initial receptions of these eight novels reflected more than changing standards and tastes or the increase in sectional animosities. In the mid-1830s, when Simms began producing long fiction, the historical romance was a widely approved genre. By 1850, after Simms returned to romance writing, it was still popular among readers but becoming passé among the *literati*. In the English-speaking world Dickens was supplanting Scott as the dominant writer, while the novel was supplanting the romance, and literary realism was transforming Romanticism. Simms responded to these changes, incorporating social and then psychological realism in his fiction and appreciatively reading Dickens (Moltke-Hansen, "Critical Revolution"). Nevertheless, his continued adherence to the romance form made him appear increasingly as a member of an older literary generation (Holman, *Roots* 75–86; Wimsatt, *Major* 8–9).

The diminishment of Simms's currency is shown by the fact that, after 1860, the only new works he published in book form were three collections that he edited: one of Confederate poetry, one of his friend James Henry Hammond's speeches and writings, and one an edition of the Revolutionary War letters of Col. John Laurens of South Carolina. He also produced a couple of pamphlets: an account of the *Sack and Destruction of the City of Columbia, S.C.*, in 1865, issued by his own press, and his final address, *The Sense of the Beautiful*, which was locally published as well. His last romances appeared just in periodicals despite his efforts to see them issued in book form. Neither did he have success with the ideas for other books that he floated to his publishers (Moltke-Hansen, "History Failed" 14–19).

In effect, the Civil War ended Simms's career as an American author. The fact that the selected Redfield edition of his writings, including the first seven of his Revolutionary romances, continued to be reprinted emphasized all the more that Simms was an antebellum figure. He was regarded as a representative of the Old South, not the New. His world and slavery were in the past in the eyes of most postbellum publishers and readers. Yet, while true so far as it goes, this narrative is too simple.

After all, it was Simms's 1850 romance *Katharine Walton* that had the widest readership of all the works in the Revolutionary series. Furthermore, Simms always got mixed reviews even from his admirers, such as Edgar Allan Poe. Too, his sometime enemies, such as those in the *Knickerbocker* circle, did not review him in exclusively negative terms (Moltke-Hansen, *Views*). Indeed, the *Knickerbocker* praised *The Partisan* shortly after its 1835 publication, saying, "of all of the efforts of the author, we esteem this, in many respects, the best" (Rev. of *Partisan* 577). Yet it was just over a year later that Poe, in the *Southern Literary Messenger*, excoriated its "blunders," "bad taste," and "shockingly bad" English (117–21).

The next romance, *Mellichampe*, had the *Knickerbocker* thinking that Simms would "soon be at the front rank of American writers" (Rev. of *Mellichampe* 735–37). Upon publication of the third in the series, *The Kinsmen*, five years later, Poe concluded in *Graham's* that, "since the publication of the Pathfinder [by James Fenimore Cooper], we have seen nothing equal to" this newest work by Simms (143). In the interval, however, Simms had a falling out with the editor of the *Knickerbocker*, and that journal was becoming increasingly—though not consistently—dismissive (Butterworth and Kibler 39–54). In turn, Simms was becoming more vociferous about nationalism in literature.

The dyspeptic conclusion of the *Knickerbocker* in 1842 was that Simms's nationalism was a "device to secure an extrinsic and undue consideration for flimsy novels" ("Editor's Table" 199–200). Yet Poe's judgment in the *Broadway Journal* three years later was that Simms was "the best novelist which this country has, upon the whole, produced" (Rev. of *Wigwam* 190–91). As if this were not confusing enough, Charleston poet, editor, and young Simms protégé Paul Hamilton Hayne maintained, in his 1854 Charleston *Weekly News* reviews of the new Redfield edition of the early Revolutionary romances, first that *The Partisan* was "the nearest perfection" (2), then, months later, that *Mellichampe* was "more carefully elaborated, more artistic, and of greater sustained interest than any other romance belonging to that excellent series" (2). Fifteen years after Simms's death, however, Hayne called *Eutaw* the best ("Ante-Bellum" 257–68).

Also approving of *Eutaw*, *Godey's* nevertheless was rueful at the time of the romance's publication nearly thirty years before. This was because Simms's "commemoration of events" of the Revolution did not evoke "pleasant recollection" among the British ("Literary Notices" 84). His choice of subject did him honor, then, but hurt his trans-Atlantic sales and standing. Writing in 1856 as well, Simms's friend James Henry Hammond, former governer and future U.S. senator, went so far as to urge Simms to "cease to write novels." In his view his literary friend could not "better these last"—*The Forayers* and *Eutaw* (*Letters* 3: 425n).

On balance, the later Revolutionary romances were esteemed more and read less than the first four. This was despite the perception of both contemporary critics and subsequent scholars that the 1850s saw Simms at the height of his power as a fictionist (Guilds, *Literary Life* 191–233). His youthful enthusiasm was tempered and to some extent disciplined by experience. Shaping his works as well, as David Newton observes, was the fact that by then "Simms had spent more than a decade [as an editor and contributor] on a succession of failed Southern literary journals." Consequently, he was deeply frustrated "over the lack of an intellectually engaged readership in the South" (Afterword 496–97). This led him, Newton argues, to focus in his later Revolutionary romances "on acts of reading—both literal and imaginative" (Afterword 497).

By reading, Simms did not mean only the consumption of and response to literature or print. Woodcraft was a form of reading, and society and the political realm required reading every bit as much as the forest and books. Yet the need for and value of reading ran deeper. "The novels interrogate a culture," Newton continues, "where education possesses a marginal value at best, where economic, political, and material priorities overshadow the importance of a morally and spiritually informed imagination" (Afterword 497–98). That imagination was necessary for the creation of a country and advance of a people. "The reader's ability to recognize the signs and traces, both natural and human, thus become essential in making appropriate moral and imaginative judgments and in understanding the social and human complexities that are presented" (Newton, Afterword 500). As the motto on the crest that Simms designed for himself read, "*video volans*"—I see soaring.

The revolution advocated in these later romances is much deeper, therefore, than the pursuit of independence by bold and desperate bands of partisans. It is the achievement of self-worth, cultural independence, and moral and spiritual progress. The fruits of the political and military revolution were the civilization that Simms was helping to create and the character and community that he was helping to inspire, shape, and preserve. The artist made fully meaningful the promise of America's founding. Nationalism was not just the formation and perpetuation of a polity, but the expression and the achievement of a rising people and culture. That is why Simms insisted on nationalism in literature. It also is why the suppression of his new nation through the Confederacy's defeat meant the necessary re-imagination of both self-worth and cultural independence—the work he sought to advance in the last of his Revolutionary romances, *Joscelyn*.

The generally high regard accorded the later Revolutionary romances at the time of their publication did not carry forward after the Civil War. To judge by the number of reprints of the Redfield edition, Simms's works continued to sell for almost half a century. Yet, enthralled by modernism, postbellum critics were increasingly derogatory of Simms's historical romances. An early case in point is Simms's first academic biographer, William Peterfield Trent. His 1892 assessment was that, in contrast to Edgar Allan Poe, whom he later championed, Simms was too enmeshed in his slave society and in the romance tradition to write successfully according to modernism's aesthetic criteria. Although in some respects admiring, Vernon Parrington later also judged Simms as "essentially a failed realist," at once constrained and compromised by his literary and social environment (2: 119–30).

It was not until after World War II that C. Hugh Holman suggested that Simms's literary substance might be "of minor importance in terms of [its] intrinsic value today" but "of major importance in terms of the degree to which [Simms] embodied the attitudes and formalized the assumptions of a region" (Holman, "Status" 181). Holman subsequently called attention to the ways that the first seven Revolutionary romances explored the civil war of the early 1780s. What fascinated him was how Simms portrayed the war as a class conflict. Of the 98 characters, 30 were upper class—seven of them tories. Of the 21 poor whites, 18 were tories. Of the 25 middle class representatives, seven also were. Of the dozen slaves, only one was (*Roots* 35–47).

What Holman did not do in his essay, but others have done, is consider the impact of Simms's own times on his historical portrayals. It mattered that Simms was writing after the Palmetto State first was riven by the nullification controversy and then as it moved toward Civil War (Higham; W. Taylor; Wakelyn; Watson, *Nationalism*). While acknowledging the point, other scholars have contended that such readings have missed critical literary dimensions. After all, these later writers have insisted, Simms self-consciously used literary forms to literary ends. Moreover, his standing among his contemporaries put him at the forefront of American literature up through the so-called American renaissance of the early 1850s (Guilds, *Literary Life* 191–233; Wimsatt, *Major* 156–210).

Yet the only work in the Revolutionary series to receive substantial literary analysis from these recent critics is *Woodcraft*. Generally it is read alone rather than in tandem with other romances. There are three principal exceptions. Some scholars compare or assume differences between northern and southern romances (Simpson; Nakamura; W. Taylor). Some look for themes uniting Simms's different romance series or consider tropes, such as that of the hero, common to Simms and other antebellum southern writers (Grammer; Kolodny; Kreyling, *Figures* 30–51; Nakamura). Finally, there are those who ask how the changing politics of Simms's day shaped his writing (Higham; Kreyling, *Inventing* 93–104; W. Taylor; Wakelyn; Watson, *Nationalism*).

Despite these inquiries, many aspects of Simms's Revolutionary series have not been substantially considered. No effort has gone into comparison of more recent Revolutionary series with it. No one has juxtaposed Simms's historical romances with those of nineteenth-century European romantic nationalists. Indeed, American critics who have treated Simms have shown little awareness, beyond Sir Walter Scott, of the trans-Atlantic national romantic tradition. Instead they have privileged a different romantic strain, embodied in the romantic genius at odds with or critical of society (Rubin, *Edge*). The one book-length study of Simms's historical thought focuses on the non-fiction (Busick, *Sober*). Shrewd and deeply learned readings of historicism and historical thought in antebellum southern culture do not dwell on the theoretical and practical concomitants of Simms's historicist preoccupations and pursuits (O'Brien, *Conjectures* 2: 591–682; Fox-Genovese and Genovese, *Mind* 125–248).

The scholarly neglect is even greater for Simms's Revolutionary fictions than for his Border and Colonial romances. This is despite the relatively high regard given several of the Revolutionary works. One reason is that Simms's treatment of Native Americans has claimed much of the attention given to him since the 1835 publication of *The Yemassee*, the only one of his works always to have remained in print (Guilds and Hudson; S. Frye; Moltke-Hansen, *Yemassee*). The frontier themes, characters, language, and humor of the Border romances in turn fit into the study of the realism of Mark Twain and those in the southern and frontier humor tradition who influenced, or were influenced by, him (Parks, *Three Streams*; Wimsatt, "Evolution" and "Southwest Humor"). Too, these topics have shaped treatments of and courses in American exceptionalism, manifest destiny, and their literary refractions (Guilds and Collins).

Yet these same issues and elements occur in the Revolutionary romances. That fact, however, has not claimed attention except, in passing, from Wimsatt and Guilds (Wimsatt, *Major* 57–84, 156–95; Guilds, *Literary Life*). Rather than accept the point, Masahiro Nakamura argues that, on the one hand, the Revolutionary romances are about the construction of an ordered society, based on the plantation. On the other hand, the Border romances are about the challenge of the frontier and disorder to that society. The counter-argument is that Simms insistently explored the relationship of order to those conditions and developments that both threatened to undermine and made necessary social and cultural progress (Moltke-Hansen, "Ordered Progress").

Future Study

These debates may serve as background to the future study of the Revolutionary series. Yet those investigations will engage issues that earlier treatments did not: the relationship of colonialism to post-colonialism; the impact of the Revolution on gender, race, and class relations; the antebellum constructions and perceptions of these relationships and their rationales. Behind these sorts of questions are others about the purposes and original standing of such literature as Simms wrote and about the purposes of reading such works more than a century and a half after their production.

Holman did not emphasize part of the fascination of Simms's portrait of Revolutionary South Carolina society: that picture reveals a world dramatically at odds with the received view of the plantation South. Contrary to the stereotype, that world is not old, even though the environs of Charleston may be. Many of the characters there are recent arrivals rather than exemplars of ancient American traditions. They also are multi-cultural. Class and other divisions fissure the society, as well as destabilize conventional understandings of it. Some elite men are afraid to lead or incapable of leadership. When failed by men, women sometimes take matters into their own hands. Greed is a prime motivator and especially destructive of poor whites. So is willful ignorance. The frontier is close at hand, as is violence. America's birth pangs are dreadful. And yet liberty is won, and social order in the end is advanced, if only provisionally.

How did these awarenesses frame the thinking, by Simms and others, of developments in their own day? How and why did these white southerners decide that America's fragility could become the South's strength? In the end, the Revolutionary romances are about much more than their subject matter or the series' place in either Simms's *oeuvre* or the (former) American canon. Read with Simms's 16-plus other long fictions, they reflect a more insistent and influential epic vision of the American South than that of any other author. None of the twentieth- and twenty-first-century Revolutionary War series, even those set in the South, has had a comparable impact, although many of these later titles have sold much more than any of Simms's ever did.

The epic vision and ambition that came to shape Simms's work had historical consequences. More than a century later, Faulkner implicitly critiqued it in his Yoknapatawpha series, turning his southern vision into an anti-epic. The writing of the historical Revolution as an epic conflict meant that Simms and many of his readers came to see war as an instrument of progress, at least up until the Civil War (Moltke-Hansen, "History Failed" 5–10). Given Simms's complex understanding of the Revolution's divisions, course, and consequences, this was not simply the result of jingoistic pride. Compelling all the same, his epic reading and orientation made the Civil War in effect a reprise and a continuation of the Revolution (Watson, "American Revolution").

This belief helped shape and color Simms's enthusiasm for secession and the conflict that followed. During that conflict he continued his research and writing on the Revolution, completing his drama on Benedict Arnold as a meditation on the requirements of citizenship and patriotism (Moltke-Hansen, "History Failed" 10–14). This commitment to literature as a patriotic act and evocation had earlier, and has had later, American advocates. It fueled Confederate literature, as recent scholarship has shown (Bernath; Hutchison 18–98). It also was especially strong in parts of the Europe of Simms's day and later, a point that has long engaged students of nationalism (Moltke-Hansen, "Identity Politics").

In a post-modern and multi-cultural era, it is difficult to recover the intensity of the nationalist impulse in cultural production. Focusing on the epoch of America's political emergence, Simms's Revolutionary romances provide an opportunity to assess the impulse in his time and place. More, they invite consideration of the roles of history and art in framing identity. Because Simms privileged nationalism, he made it a political weapon. In his hierarchy of values, nationalism trumped racial, ethnic, and class interests that challenged its success. Simms confronted these conflicts by showing elements of them—for instance, the clashes between tories and patriots—while denying others—for instance, the African American impulse to freedom.

Simms used nationalism as well to perpetuate patriarchal authority and gendered roles, while critiquing those men who failed their responsibility in these roles (Simms, "Ellet's"). Treating history providentially, furthermore, he eventually made American liberty a basis to argue for southern independence. In doing so, he pointed to the path he believed the region's leaders should take in that pursuit. The complex negotiation of these multiple priorities and goals through his Revolutionary romances make those works rich sites for the recovery and critique of a long lost but once regnant artistic and political ambition. Simms did more to frame and to promote that ambition than did any other southern man of letters.

Richard Hurdis: A Tale of Alabama

JOHN D. MILLER

Seventeen years after the first printed appearance of *Richard Hurdis; or, The Avenger of Blood. A Tale of Alabama*, an anonymous reviewer for the *Southern Literary Messenger* recollected the "sensation" that accompanied the 1838 publication of William Gilmore Simms's violent novel about organized crime and revenge in frontier Alabama. The "sort of interest inspired by the life-like delineations of this wonderful narrative of blood and crime," wrote the reviewer in 1855, "has never been equalled [*sic*] by any work that has appeared from the American press" (Rev. of *Richard* 639).

Though bordering on hyperbole, the reaction noted by the reviewer was essentially correct. The novel's frank depiction of the danger and social instability accompanying the settlement of the Old Southwest did cause a stir among antebellum readers. Equally perceptive was the reviewer's recognition that *Richard Hurdis* was a memorable text in Simms's career and in American letters. It marked a return to the setting and the topics that the southern author knew best, and it heralded the emergence of Simms's theses regarding social progress and personal character for which white southerners, if not many white Americans, would embrace him during the rest of his long career.

Richard Hurdis belongs to Simms's series of Border Romances. The author had first made creative use of the Old Southwest, its outlaws, and its settlers in *Guy Rivers: A Tale of Georgia* (1834) and later relied upon these motifs for the settings, characters, and plots of *Border Beagles: A Tale of Mississippi* (1840); *Beauchampe; or, The Kentucky Tragedy. A Tale of Passion* (1842); and *Helen Halsey; or, The Swamp State of Conelachita. A Tale of the Borders* (1845). Like these other long prose works, *Richard Hurdis* is a romance, a genre that Simms distinguished from the domestic novel. The latter were more realistic in nature, illustrating recognizable settings, familiar types of characters, and commonplace actions or behaviors. In contrast, the romance, said Simms in his "Advertisement" to *The Yemassee. A Romance of Carolina* (1835)

> is the substitute which the people of the present day offer for the ancient epic. Its standards are the same. . . . It invests individuals with an absorbing interest—it hurries them through crowding events in a narrow space of time—it requires the same unities of plan, of purpose, and harmony of parts,

> and it seeks for its adventures among the wild and wonderful. It does not insist upon what is known, or even what is probable. It grasps at the possible; and, placing a human agent in hitherto untried situations, it exercises its ingenuity in extricating him from them, while describing his feelings and his fortunes in their progress. (vi)

The relevance of Simms's comparison of the romance to the epic helps account for the breath-taking pace and sometimes-incredulous nature of the "wild and wonderful" plot of *Richard Hurdis*, not to mention the novel's archetypal "human agent[s]." Mary Ann Wimsatt has recognized the pattern of the heroic quest in the basic structure of all of the author's Border Romances. Generally speaking, there is a brash young male protagonist in each of the texts, sometimes a member of the planting elite in the southeastern states, who leaves an established home to move west or south. That journey is interrupted by outlaws and their activities. However, aided by the upwardly mobile farmers, loyal yeomen, and good-hearted but comically bumbling rustics who also inhabit the frontier, the hero routs the criminal element, thus making the frontier safer for settlement and civilization; a stability that the protagonist, now wiser and more mature, has come to symbolize (Wimsatt, *Major* 120).

Richard Hurdis (1855) closely follows this structure. At an unspecified time in the early 1830s, the 21-year-old eponymous protagonist leaves his father's prosperous farm in Marengo, Alabama, for the new lands that opened in Mississippi following one of the Choctaw cessations of land to the U.S. government. At first, Hurdis claims he is motivated by the desire to "feel my freedom" from his father's oversight (16). Later he grudgingly admits the impetus for his exodus from home: a broken heart. He mistakenly believes that his childhood sweetheart, Mary Easterby, has betrayed him by becoming engaged to his older brother, John Hurdis, who stands to inherit the family's farm and slaves.

"The stubborn pride of my spirit was predominant," says Richard Hurdis, so he never queries Mary about the engagement, unaware that his brother had started the rumor (25). Hurdis is accompanied on his westward journey by William Carrington, a wealthy and amiable friend, who was "of good sense, and very fair education, [but] was not a man of mind" (27). Hurdis's naïve companion is also interested in purchasing lands in Mississippi prior to marrying his own sweetheart.

The two young men make a detour to Tuscaloosa so that Carrington can redeem a debt, and as they do so, John Hurdis commissions a neighboring squatter, Ben Pickett, to murder his younger brother along the route west. Pickett sets out to follow Richard Hurdis who, along with Carrington, is delayed in Tuscaloosa by bad weather, made worse by the presence of unscrupulous gamblers who try to cheat the young travelers. Their journey is also delayed by Colonel Grafton, a member of the local gentry, who encourages the two to linger at his frontier estate, where "[h]ospitality was a presiding virtue" (136). Hurdis and Carrington ultimately arrive at the house of the debtor, Matt Webber, who, unbeknownst to the genteel travelers, is a thief. Along with several other bandits, including the aforementioned gamblers, Webber plots to capture and rob both Hurdis and Carrington. Yet when the time for their apprehension arrives, Carrington escapes, only to be shot dead on the road to Grafton's by Ben Pickett, who mistook him for the younger Hurdis.

Hurdis is rescued by Grafton, who urges him to return to Marengo for the unpleasant duty of notifying Carrington's fiancée of his death. Hurdis does so, and the young woman's violent reaction to the news confirms his resolution to leave Marengo again to avenge his friend. In the meantime, Pickett also returns home to report to John Hurdis that he ostensibly accomplished his mission. However, Pickett has been followed from the crime scene by a member of the "Mystic Brotherhood." This emissary uses his knowledge of Pickett's and John Hurdis's scheme to blackmail them into membership in this shadowy crime syndicate, which "consists of a parcel of bold fellows, who don't like the laws of the state exactly, and of other societies, and who have accordingly associated together, for the purpose of making their own and doing business under them." The messenger claims that their chief crime is stealing and re-selling stolen slaves, and that "[w]e have our brethren in all the states, from Virginia to Louisiana, and beyond into the territories" (220).

Unaware of his brother's and his neighbor's culpability in the death of Carrington, Richard Hurdis decides to locate Matt Webber by returning to the border in the disguise of a gambler. En route to Tuscaloosa on board a riverboat, he meets Clement Foster, the leader of the Mystic Brotherhood, who is disguised as a minister. After Hurdis ingratiates himself with Foster, the criminal reveals his true identity and swears him into the Brotherhood. Foster leads Hurdis to the gang's swamp hideout, where the latter meets Webber and the other criminals involved in his abduction and Carrington's murder.

But fate adds another complicating action that temporarily thwarts Hurdis from exacting his revenge. He must prevent the marriage of Colonel Grafton's daughter to one of the bandits who has been wooing her in the guise of a gentleman. This he does in the nick of time, and along with Grafton and the other respectable planters and woodsmen of the area (to whom he has revealed his true identity), Richard Hurdis returns to the hideout of the Mystic Brotherhood to slay the criminals, which now include John Hurdis and Ben Pickett, who had rendezvoused with the main body of the gang. The only survivor is Foster himself, who laconically taunts Hurdis and Grafton as he makes his escape. Richard Hurdis then returns to Marengo to marry his childhood sweetheart and ostensibly to operate their families' estates.

The figurative qualities of these characters and the settings, as well as the plot itself, convey the major themes of *Richard Hurdis*. "[G]reat activity of plot, vehement & passionate personality" aside, "[t]here are running through [*Richard Hurdis* and the other Border Romances], a strong penchant to moral and mental analysis," Simms later claimed (*Letters* 2: 225). In particular, the elimination of the Mystic Brotherhood and the contrast between the lawlessness of the undeveloped frontier with the domestic tranquility of Marengo and Grafton's estate communicate the text's cautious optimism about the irregular and precarious transformation of the frontier to civilization. Moreover, the chief characters' emotional growth illustrates the personality attributes necessary for leaders to manage this evolution.

As the westward shift of settings in the Border Romances (from Georgia to Louisiana) suggests, the series narrates the South's emergence from a primitive state of development—i.e., inhabited only by Native Americans who ostensibly lacked any central governance, social customs, or infrastructure—to a stable, slave-based agrarian society characterized by paternalistic civil order and European-inspired cosmopolitan culture. But as critic David Moltke-Hansen explains, Simms believed "[o]nly gradually, fitfully was society establishing the order and hierarchy necessary for true civilization—a condition that was more of a promise than a realization of Southern history to date" ("Plantation" 14). At the heart of this anxious optimism was Simms's ambivalence toward the frontier. While he valued it for the animating effect that its ruggedness allegedly had on the character of the American people, he simultaneously worried that the temptations of frontier autonomy threatened law and especially order. Moreover, he fretted that the frontier would lead to the decline of already-established communities, the integrity of settler behavior, and the future prospects of the South and the nation. In particular, the South Carolinian worried that the availability of new, affordable land and the absence of tradition and central authority there would lead to personal selfishness and a disregard for the values of domesticity. As Moltke-Hansen explains, in Simms's mind, "[a]ttachment to home and family became the basis for devotion to, and work for, one's local community as both a place and a society" ("Plantation" 11). On the frontier, the continual temptation to move might instead take priority over this attachment to place, and individual interests consequently might trump altruism, public service, and the emergence of a stable community in the Old Southwest.

Hurdis's decision to abandon his family's prosperous farm, childhood sweetheart, and a doting mother foreshadows this conflict in the novel. What he expects to be a permanent separation from his family and his neighborhood is initially a liberating experience for the youth. He confidently tells his father that he will not return to the family farm; in Mississippi, "[t]here is no lack of employment when the pay is moderate and the work plenty" (55). The mood of the farewell scene with his mother is slightly more bittersweet, yet Hurdis is perversely honored by her anguish. He describes it as "mixed pain and pleasure. It grieved me to see how much she suffered, yet it gratified my pride to find how greatly I was beloved"

(57). Like many of Hurdis's historical counterparts, the exhilarating promise of a new future characterized by wealth and independence outweighed the emotional attachments of the past. In Simms's later texts, especially the 1842 oration *The Social Principle*, his warnings would become more strident about the cavalier disregard for place and family symbolized by Hurdis's blithe farewell. But here in its initial iteration in the Border Romances, the threat to the moral character and the attachment to place that Simms believed had fueled the sustained settlement and prosperity of the United States is more muted.

One of the first instances of Hurdis's growing awareness of the imprudence of emigration and the ambiguous effect that frontier life had on settler temperament occurs shortly after he and Carrington depart for Tuscaloosa. The protagonist's brash assurance is mollified and his emotional self-absorption is tempered by the scene of a party of Carolinians emigrating westward through Alabama. Though the travelers are characterized as enjoying "a perfect gale of delighted merriment," Hurdis pauses his narrative to reflect soberly that

> the social moralist may well apprehend the deterioration of the graces of society in every desertion by a people of their ancient homes. Though men may lose nothing of their fecundity by wandering, and in emigration to the west from a sterile region like North Carolina, most commonly, gain in their worldly goods, their losses are yet incomputable. The delicacies of society are most usually thrust from the sight of the pioneers; the nicer harmonies of the moral world become impaired; the sweeter cords of affection are undone or rudely snapped asunder, and a rude indifference to the claims of one's fellow, must follow every breaking up of the old and stationary abodes. (65–66)

The incongruity between the carefree attitude of the immigrants themselves and Hurdis's apocalyptic interpretation of their journey westward is the first step toward the gradual epiphany that leads the protagonist to return home at the end of the novel and embrace the domestic tranquility and communal stability that Marengo symbolizes. This scene is a stark contrast from the mood of the protagonist's own recent departure, suggesting that Hurdis may already be experiencing some misgivings about his impetuosity and his motives. Moreover, the valuation of "the claims of one's fellow" over "worldly goods," and the potential for "losses" to outweigh any "gain," suggests that the stimulating effect the frontier has on individuals may be offset by the costs to the future communities, not to mention the centers of civilization that are ostensibly being abandoned (even in a "sterile" society such as North Carolina).

The flourishing of the Mystic Brotherhood on the Alabama and Mississippi border in *Richard Hurdis* underscores the nihilistic effect that Simms feared the frontier could have on human society. On one hand, the Brotherhood's members characterize the secret group as a noble organization comprised of men who have been disadvantaged by the prevailing economic and social conditions of the

South. Foster, its founder and leader, was an orphan and poor laborer in west Tennessee. He tells the disguised Hurdis that his vision for the syndicate was "a brotherhood of those who have learned to see, in the principles which ostensibly govern society, a nice system of cobwebs, set with a double object, as snares to catch and enslave the feeble and confiding, and defences [*sic*] for the protection of the more cunning reptiles that sit in the centre, and prey at ease upon the marrow and fat of the toiling insects they entangle" (314). Mixed metaphor aside, Foster's characterization of and proletarian resentment toward not only a predatory planter elite, but also the professional class and religious establishment who support the dominant economic and social power structure, foreshadows Marxist analyses of ideological state apparatuses by more than a century. Similarly, the members of the Brotherhood explain their criminal activities as means of resistance in order to achieve socio-economic parity where the status quo prevents it. The "emissary" who reveals the Brotherhood's existence to Pickett and John Hurdis explains that its members are "simply seekers of justice; and we only differ . . . in the means which we take to bring it about" (238).

But here, too, there is a contrast between the Brotherhood's self-proclaimed identity as socially righteous vigilantes "who redress the wrongs and injuries of fortune, who protect the poor from the oppressor, who subdue the insolent, and humble the presumptuous and vain" and the ignoble nature of the Brotherhood's activities: robbing strangers and stealing and re-selling slaves (238–39). Again, this incongruity symbolizes the paradox that the frontier represented to Simms and the seaboard establishment: overcoming its rudimentary conditions was conducive to forging a robust American national character, and the newly opened lands encouraged the spread of an egalitarian society, yet emigration to unsettled areas had the propensity to warp conventional standards of civility and duty. Elliott West points out that Simms's misgivings were part of a collective wariness that "[o]n the frontier . . . people act not so much out of social purposes but from pure individual and natural instinct" (30). Consequently, the existence and then violent destruction of an alternative social and political structure like the Brotherhood—whose behavior was based as much on self-interest and expediency as on principle—is designed to be a cautionary tale of the degrading moral effect of the frontier on recent immigrants.

The exception to the amorality of the border region between Alabama and Mississippi is Colonel Grafton. Hurdis describes the design and atmosphere of Grafton's plantation outside of Tuscaloosa as reflecting "something of complete life—calm, methodical, symmetrical life—life in repose. . . . All testified to the continual presence of a governing mind, whose whole feeling of enjoyment was derived from order" (137). The planter's admirable material prosperity and familial contentment epitomizes the progress that diligence, modesty, and self-discipline can lead to if conventionally focused on replicating the domesticity and social propriety that Grafton and others left behind for the frontier. That

Grafton survives the bloodbath at the novel's conclusion and becomes a mentor to Richard Hurdis and, briefly, to Carrington (who boasts before he dies that he, too, will "become a public man"), suggests that the transplantation of the social traits of the original colonies to the frontier region is a blueprint for a stable, civilized Old Southwest (161).

Simms also emphasizes the importance of personal character to the transformation of the frontier through *Richard Hurdis*'s first-person narration. The author explains in the "Advertisement" to the 1855 edition of the novel that the "hero tells, not only what he himself performed, but supplies the events, even as they occur, which he yet derives from the report of others." To account for Hurdis's awareness of those events or conversations that he would otherwise have no knowledge of, Simms adds that "[t]he reader can readily be made to comprehend that the hero writes after a lapse of time, in which he had supplied himself with the necessary details, filling up the gaps in his own experience" (11).

The use of a first-person narrator is rare amid Simms's many novels, and it becomes apparent in *Richard Hurdis* why Simms did not utilize it more often in his long fiction. As John Caldwell Guilds observes, Simms "allows an omniscient author to intrude" for several chapters at a time, reporting the interior monologues and emotions of characters who died before Hurdis had any opportunity to hear their "report" (*Literary Life* 84). Perhaps aware of these inconsistencies between the first-person narrator and his detailed knowledge of sub-plots and other characters' psychological conflicts, Simms rationalized them by arguing in the "Advertisement" that "something is gained by such a progress, in the more energetic, direct and dramatic character of the story; and the rapidity of the action is a necessary result" (11–12).

Pace and mood aside, one of the interesting consequences of Simms's choice of perspective—at least for emphasizing the novel's message regarding the character required of leadership in the Old Southwest—is the dual voices of Richard Hurdis. Present in the text are the perspectives of a young, rash Hurdis as well as a slightly older but much more mature Hurdis. As Simms's aforementioned apology in the "Advertisement" explains, Hurdis is ostensibly narrating the story "after a lapse of time." This gap between plot time and that of the narration is especially evident in Hurdis's oblique, gloomy insinuations about the irony of Carrington's ambitions just prior to the latter's death as well as at the end of chapters where Hurdis cultivates dramatic suspense by alluding to the future significance of just-narrated events. The passage of time is further underscored in the conclusion of the novel itself. Hurdis explains that he had been "married to Mary Easterby about three years" prior to a final description of Julia Grafton, who dies yet a year afterward, suggesting that at least four years transpires between the events and their re-telling (402).

In that time, Hurdis evolves from a character that many critics found unsympathetic to one who symbolizes self-discipline, prudence, and sagacity. For example, Simms's close friend James Henry Hammond described the novel's protagonist as "as silly as he was surly" (qtd. in *Letters* 2: 548). Yet the voice of the older Hurdis reflects a man wizened by his youthful follies and the experiences of his two journeys to the border. This is the persona who pauses to gravely comment on the future consequences of the Carolinians' westward emigration. Moreover, aside from functioning as Simms's amanuensis on issues related to the Social Principle, the more experienced Hurdis's hindsight emphasizes the personal qualities inherent to responsible social and political leadership in the Old Southwest. Reflecting on his decision to humor Carrington's desire to gamble with the strangers in Tuscaloosa, for instance, the chastened narrator still rebukes himself years later:

> Bitterly do I reproach myself that I did so. But how was I then—in my boyhood, as it were—to anticipate such consequences from so seemingly small a source. But, in morals, no departure from principles is small. All principles are significant—are essential—in the formation of truth; and the neglect or omission of the smallest among them is not one evil merely, or one error—but a thousand. . . . Take care of small principles, if you would preserve great truths sacred. (125–26)

Given the subsequent death of Carrington due to circumstances involving the gamblers, the exaggerated solemnity of Hurdis's moralizing is understandable. But the "great truths" that he obliquely alludes to are those to which he owes his own improbable survival, not to mention the material and emotional success of Colonel Grafton: honor, modesty, and devotion to public duty. Exercising self-discipline in the pursuit of these "truths" (regardless of temptations related to gambling, familial jealousies, or the appetite for cheap western lands) will produce the principled leaders needed to direct the South's orderly march from raw frontier to cosmopolitan civilization.

Simms spent a year, probably less, working on this study of leadership and the effects of the frontier. Wimsatt offers that Simms began writing *Richard Hurdis* in 1837 (*Major* 98). Simms's correspondence indicates that he completed the last two chapters in April of the next year (*Letters* 6: 9). Prior to this, Simms had published seven novels with Harper & Brothers in New York City, but Guilds speculates that he had an unknown disagreement with the Harpers that led to a new relationship with the Philadelphia firm of Carey & Hart beginning with *Richard Hurdis* (*Literary Life* 82). With respect to the novel's release date, Simms balanced his need for money with his knowledge of the book trade in the rural South. He wrote Edward L. Carey in May 1838 that he was "dreadfully in want of some of the sixpences which a sanguine scribbler might look forward to secure from its rapid and extensive sale." Yet apparently in response to a suggestion that the book go on sale in August, Simms replied that "it strikes me as scarcely late enough. Books with us sell better as the winter is coming on, and when our country merchants are just visiting the city" (*Letters* 1: 130, 131). But Simms deferred to Carey's judgment, and *Richard Hurdis* did appear in two volumes in August 1838. It featured a dedication to John A. Grimball, Mississippi's Secretary of State from 1821 to 1833 and an unsuccessful candidate for governor there in 1837.

Simms's correspondence indicates that Carey & Hart printed a second edition of *Richard Hurdis* in the winter of 1838 (*Letters* 6: 14). Twice in the 1840s Simms discussed re-publishing "a new and cheap edition" of the novel with Carey & Hart's successor Lea & Blanchard as well as other firms—an unknown New York publisher in 1844 and the Baltimore-based Taylor, Wilde and Company in 1845—but nothing came of either attempt (*Letters* 5: 384, 2: 132). Four other editions of *Richard Hurdis* did appear in Simms's lifetime, though. The novel was re-issued in October 1855 (and a second edition a year later) as part of New York City-based J.S. Redfield's publication of Simms's early novels. The Redfield editions included illustrations of the fight between the Hurdis brothers in front of Mary Easterby and of Richard Hurdis's capture at Matt Webber's cabin, both drawn by F.O.C. Darley. The same plates were used by the New York-based publisher W.J. Widdleton, who issued an edition of *Richard Hurdis* in 1864. A German translation of the novel appeared in 1857. *Richard Hurdis, A Novel from Alabama* was published by the publisher Christian Ernst Kollmann in Leipzig as volume 280 in its "American Library" series.

Aside from the addition of the illustrations, the omittance of "The Avenger of Blood" from the novel's subtitle, and chiefly minor textual revisions, the most meaningful changes to Redfield's edition of the novel are the appearance of Simms's name on the title page and his explanation for its absence in previous editions. Early reviewers of *Richard Hurdis* had linked Simms to the novel, but the author's friend and fellow writer Alexander B. Meek was the first to confront Simms about it at a public dinner in Tuscaloosa on 17 December 1842 (qtd. in *Letters* 6: 59–60). Simms acknowledged his authorship, and in the much-expanded "Advertisement" to the Redfield edition, explained his reasons for its initial anonymity. He had been cryptic in his 1838 preface, offering that "I would not have any of my friends suppose the author and narrator to be one." But he also claimed to be indifferent as to whether his identity was known by readers, merely suggesting that "[o]ur acquaintance may be continued and increased to the profit and pleasure of both without disturbing the secrets of either" (vii–viii).

In contrast, Simms admits in the 1855 "Advertisement" that his earlier anonymity was designed to protect him from the judgment and interference of the public. He explains that "[w]ere I now, for the first time, beginning my own career. . . . I should not only keep the public in ignorance of my peculiar labors, but I should, quite as religiously, keep the secret from my friends and associates" (7). In addition to the risk of them "never separat[ing] *you* from your writings," Simms claims that knowledge of your work will license friends to offer unsolicited criticism of it. Furthermore, "they can give . . . no counsel, of any value in an art which they themselves do not profess, but which they are still very prone to teach; exercise no influence which is not apt, in some way, to prove pernicious; and, whether they praise or blame, are generally the worst judges to whom you could submit your productions" (8). He also suggests that professional jealousies affect a book's reception: "The instincts of mediocrity are always on the watch and easily alarmed; and it perpetually toils to keep down any growth which is calculated to fling a shadow over itself" (9). He concludes by reiterating his counsel to young authors to "[l]et the book win the reputation before you claim the authorship" (9).

Simms promised to one day elaborate on "the true reasons" behind his recommendation for authorial anonymity, but he never produced the autobiography that he occasionally pondered. Instead, his correspondence reveals his career-long frustration with "the bedevilment of a small tribe of underling critics," some of whose judgment were "hampered by convention," others by "injustice" (*Letters* 1: 316, 5: 152, 1: 156). Though in 1838 Simms had not begun his long-running feud with the New York City-based periodical *Knickerbocker*, by 1855 his pride had been wounded by that magazine's savage criticism of his novels, at least some of which was written by his friend James Lawson (*Letters* 1: 153–58). This may account for his warning about the opinions of an author's friends; but even in 1838, Simms was experienced enough to understand that his new novel would be evaluated as much on the author's reputation as on the text's individual merits.

In contrast to the mystery behind the author of *Richard Hurdis*, much of its content was familiar to American readers, especially southerners, in 1838. In the prefatory material to the 1838 edition of the novel, Simms claims that "[t]he events are real, and within the memory of men, though names have been changed, and, in some respects, localities altered" (vii). Foster and the Mystic Brotherhood were loosely modeled after the John A. Murrell crime syndicate and its illegal activities in the Old Southwest. In the "Advertisement" to the 1855 edition of the novel, Simms claims to have known "[Virgil] Stuart [*sic*], the captor of Murrell, personally" as well as other "*dramatis personae*, during my early wanderings in that then wild country" (11). However, these claims should be taken with a grain of salt, made, as they were, by an author seeking to emphasize the authenticity of a narrative whose sensationalism was a matter for criticism. To wit, Simms had defended *Richard Hurdis* on the previous page as "a genuine chronicle of the border region. . . . founded on well-known facts" (10).

Wimsatt has shown that it is highly unlikely that the novelist met Murrell's captor during his trip to Alabama and Mississippi in 1831 (*Major* 97–98). She concludes that it is more likely that Simms read about the criminal's career in published accounts that appeared throughout the mid-1830s. Scholars including Floyd H. Deen and Dianne C. Luce have compared the plot and characters of *Richard Hurdis* to 1835 and 1836 texts that focused on Murrell's capture and have concluded that Simms made significant departures from the historical record. Luce contextualizes the discrepancies, explaining that "Simms was less concerned with the historical personalities of the clan's leader or his captor than with the nature and workings of the confederacy itself," and that the novelist "chose to present a more generalized warning of the danger to his society from within" rather than depicting historically accurate crimes (239, 241).

Had he himself been called to account for specific historical inconsistencies in *Richard Hurdis*, Simms would have argued that these distinctions would have been spurious in the context of the Romance. For example, he wrote fellow editor John Reuben Thompson that "[m]y novels aim at something more than the story. I am really, though indirectly, revising history" (*Letters* 3: 421). This is because Simms disdained scholarly accounts of the past, claiming that they failed to convey what he thought was most important about history—the national character of a people and the continued relevance of major historical events. In fact, Simms claimed, "We care not so much for the intrinsic truth of history" than for what it revealed about its participants and how history could inspire its readers. Consequently, the author endorsed the use of creative license when translating historical material into fiction in his 1845 essay "History for the Purposes of Art":

> Assuming that the means of [an author's] refutation are not to be had, that he offends against no facts which are known and decisive, no reasonable probabilities or obvious inferences,—it is enough if his narrative awakens our attention, compels our thought, warms our affections, inspirits our hope, elevates our aims, and builds up in our minds a fabric of character, compounded of just principles, generous tendencies and clear, correct standards of taste and duty. (*Views* 1: 38)

In fact, Simms acknowledges these liberties in the "Advertisement" to *Richard Hurdis* in 1855, explaining that "I have exercised the artist's privilege" in adding, adjusting, or omitting certain details for the sake of "bringing out the heroic, the bold and attractive, into becoming prominence, for dramatic effect; and, filling out the character, more or less elaborately" (11).

Reviews of *Richard Hurdis* at the time of its publication universally recognized the "dramatic" qualities of the text, but critics were split about the propriety of them. On one hand, an 1838 review in the *New-York Mirror* applauded the novel's vigor and its vivid detail: "the author tells his terrible tale of retribution with a force and correctness of style, a power of description, and an earnestness and directness of manner" (qtd. in *Letters* 6: 11). Yet many periodicals wondered if there was too much "directness" in the novel. The *Knickerbocker* conceded in 1838 that *Richard Hurdis* was "undeniably a work of much power" but added that "it presents the most hideous distortions of character, and is enough to make a man sick of his humanity" (Rev. of *Richard* 367). Seventeen years did little to acclimate the public's taste, for in 1855, *Graham's Magazine* also admired the "boldness and strength" of the Redfield edition, but added the "objection still remains that an imaginative reproduction of real events and persons should be so managed as to give pleasure, not pain or disgust" (Rev. of *Richard* 469).

Ironically, though, it is this same verisimilitude that attracted twentieth-century critics to *Richard Hurdis*. Guilds argues instead that Simms "was ahead of his time, anticipating realism and naturalism" with his Border Romance (*Literary Life* 83). Caroline Collins also claims that the novel challenged the standards of the genre and its era. She highlights how Simms "broke free of the confines of romance by selecting conventions from various types of romance and by learning to use those conventions in new and different ways.... Simms's realistic frontier, then, derives at least as much from his ability to exploit romantic conventions as from his graphic depictions of violence" ("Simms's Concept" 81). Masahiro Nakamura likewise approaches *Richard Hurdis* from the vantage point of genre studies, coming to similar conclusions as Guilds and Collins about the forward-looking qualities and anti-romantic tendencies of the entire Border Romance series. He claims that "the mode of romance recedes into the background to be replaced by a realistic representation illustrating how unsuited ['southern ideals'] are to the violence and bloodshed of the frontier" (106).

Underlying all three of these later critics' arguments is an unspoken protectiveness of Simms and of the historical romance, both of which quickly fell out of critical favor after the Civil War. In fact, even prior to the war, Nathaniel Hawthorne had characterized Simms's concept of the genre as passé, commenting in 1846 that "[t]he themes suggested by [Simms in *Views and Reviews*, which included "History for the Purposes of Art,"] viewed as he views them, would produce nothing but historical novels, cast in the same worn out mould that has been in use these thirty years" (qtd. in Guilds, *Literary Life* 182). However formulaic or not, the relevance of the historical romance to post-structuralist literary studies ought to be taken for granted following the translation of Georg Lukács' *The Historical Novel* in 1962, which highlights the cultural function of this genre. More recent and progressive criticism has thus distanced itself from apologetics for Simms and has instead focused on other aspects of *Richard Hurdis*. John Mayfield, for instance, has illustrated that the alleged static qualities of Simms's male protagonists in novels such as *Richard Hurdis* reflect not artistic deficiencies, but Simms's "subversive" ambivalence about the adequacy of "patrician manliness" to maintain social and economic power in a rapidly changing era and region.

Mayfield's argument about masculinity shows how *Richard Hurdis* can profitably lend itself to New Historical and other contemporary theoretical analyses. We can now assume the inclusion of Simms in the canon (thanks in part to the efforts of Guilds and Collins) and can afford to be less apologetic about his choice of genre. *Richard Hurdis* has much else to offer its readers, especially those inured by representations of modern violence and vice to the novel's graphic descriptions of the frontier South: a time and place of conflict and transition that progress has made distant.

Sack and Destruction of the City of Columbia, SC

NICHOLAS G. MERIWETHER

Of all of William Gilmore Simms's works, none is more rooted in controversy than his account of the burning of Columbia, South Carolina, during the waning days of the Civil War.[1] The destruction of the city on the night of 17 February 1865 was the "greatest outrage" that Union general William Tecumseh Sherman was charged with, as historian James M. McPherson has written (474). Afterwards, the war of words over the event took on a life of its own, lasting far longer than other scars from the War. More than a century later, one scholar writing about the city's destruction observed that "Few events of the Civil War have produced more charges and countercharges, and have left a deeper, more persistent legacy of hatred" (Robertson). An eye-witness to the event, Simms wrote a lengthy account that he published serially in a triweekly newspaper that he edited (and largely wrote) in Columbia, revising it after the War as a pamphlet, published in October 1865. A new edition, published by the University of South Carolina Press in 2015, made that final, definitive text available in a facsimile of the final form that Simms saw through production.

Though historians have profitably used Simms's account to explore the events of Sherman's occupation of the city and the implications its destruction poses for our understanding of the War itself, the text's significance today lies primarily in what it says about Simms, not only in terms of his work but more centrally for how it outlines the difficult transition from war to Reconstruction that he had to navigate (N. Meriwether, "'A Scene'" 26–27). For literary scholars interested in Simms, the pamphlet is noteworthy as well for the effort required to substantially revise and recast it. Though published after the War, and despite the extensive revisions Simms made, the account retained enough of the flavor of its pre-Appomattox genesis to remain something of a representative of Confederate war writing as well, a status that fueled its later reissues. For historians, the text represents more than simply the genesis of one of the most contentious issues in Civil War historiography—for Simms's pamphlet represents the first sustained attempt to document what happened and assign responsibility for it—but also for its inchoate expression of several of the elements that would fuse together to form the myth of the Lost Cause.[2] And for readers interested in the Civil War, the text remains a telling dispatch from the embers of the conflict that came to define Simms and his last days.

Its 2015 reissue brought back into print an authorized facsimile of a work whose subsequent editions and impressions have all presented textual problems and often editorial deficiencies as well. A thoroughly annotated version is still needed, but until then, this new edition makes accessible a work that illuminates a number of critical issues for scholars. The scarcity of the work's first monographic issue, and the complexity of its subsequent textual history, have compounded the problems in its reception. With this reissue, the final text, as Simms intended it to appear, at last has a chance to speak to modern readers—and speak for itself.

This essay traces the textual history of the work, from its first serial issue through its later editions, outlining its contributions to our understanding of Simms and the challenges he faced as the South's leading public intellectual in the waning days of the War and immediately after. It also sketches how the text fits into the complex historiography of its subject and its place in Simms's life and work. Although framed differently and incorporating recent criticism, this introduction necessarily builds on the analysis of the text established by my earlier work (N. Meriwether, "'A Scene'"; "Civil War"), which usefully supplement this.

First serialized in the *Columbia Phoenix*, Simms's original account ran for the first ten issues of the small newspaper, beginning 21 March 1865 and concluding on April 10. Later that summer, he revised the text extensively, removing substantial portions, correcting and amending numerous details, and reorganizing several sections before supervising its production that fall. The final version appeared in time for legislators convened in the ruined capital to read, and they may have accounted for most of the copies printed and distributed; certainly very few have changed hands since then. Only a dozen have been catalogued by libraries, and fewer still have appeared in rare book catalogs and auctions (N. Meriwether, "'A Scene'" 25–26).

The subject and basic themes did not change when Simms revised the serial version. Both texts clearly set forth their aims: to provide a thorough accounting of what was destroyed, a catalog and chronology of the events before and during the destruction, a survey of the behavior of participants, both citizens and soldiers, and an assessment of who was at fault and where the final responsibility rested. Simms presented the broader context of the story with a discussion of the War, focusing on the immediate circumstances preceding the burning of Columbia, especially Confederate strategy and its deficiencies, and Sherman's march through South Carolina. Although the serial account appeared only a few weeks after the departure of Union forces, Simms also explicitly incorporated the charges he was answering; in time, this allowed the text to be viewed more as a part of the historiography of the controversy than a history of the event.

That confused identity also complicates the text's genre. In Simms's view, it was clearly a history, though his definition of historical writing was far more elastic and expansive than the modern scholarly sense of the term. As Sean Busick has noted, "Most of what [Simms] wrote, whether novels, poetry, biography or reviews, he would have classified as history" (*Sober* xii). But Busick also notes that, admiration for Simms's methodology and meticulous research notwithstanding, *Sack and Destruction* "lacks the retrospective viewpoint necessary for writing history" (*Sober* xii). John Caldwell Guilds, however, characterized it as "contemporary history" in his *Simms Reader* in 2001 (13), presaging the trend toward what historians have begun to call "recent history" (Potter and Romano). The original serial version is easier to classify: its genesis as a newspaper account, replete with all of the inflammatory, deliberately propagandistic elements that Simms elided from the pamphlet edition, clearly mark it as journalism. Though the pamphlet edition challenges modern notions of genre, even absent the earmarks of its journalistic origins, the presentation and nature of its prose make it a fine, early example of what literary scholars today call literary nonfiction. Regardless, the difficulties in its classification are integral to the work's literary merits as well as its defects, and are essential aspects of both its evidentiary value and its bibliographic placement.

Simms's goals structure the narrative. His argument was that Columbia could and should have been defended; that its destruction was, in essence, a war crime wholly assignable to Sherman, as the commanding officer of Union forces; that the destruction represented a tragic loss to the entire nation's cultural heritage; and that the event was the embodiment, if not the predictable result, of the North's dishonorable approach to war. Some of the prominent themes he highlighted prefigured ones that would play central roles in his postwar thought, ones that mark the text as an important, very early contribution to the creation of the Lost Cause myth. Foremost among these was the courage of the white women of Columbia in the face of incivility and abuse; as scholars have explored, this view of white southern women is central to the postwar fiction of a united, monolithic Confederate nation (J. Miller, "Sense"). While the incidents Simms compiled and the dialogue he quoted, documenting heroism in the face of the horrors of the event, cannot be gainsaid, his presentation speaks to this greater, albeit still inchoate, purpose.

Even more important to the myth of the Lost Cause was its recasting of the Civil War as a contest somehow removed from the obdurate centrality of slavery. Later accounts of the burning of Columbia address the agency of African Americans; in Simms's text, they are passive victims, treated even worse than white Columbians by Federal forces, with most hiding in fear for the duration of the conflagration. This is only part of the story, and it ignores the far more unsettling and complex reality of black-white relations that Simms could not apprehend (Foley, "Nimmons"). While Simms acknowledged the charge that slaves and freed blacks had a hand in the city's destruction, he had to deprecate it; indeed, his depiction of the suffering that African Americans endured was central to his view, that the War as waged by Federal forces was indiscriminate in its wanton cruelty, robbing the Union of any moral high ground that abolitionism claimed.

Any residue of that moral claim he believed was finally obliterated by the racism he charged to Union troops, albeit distinguished in degree and nature by their origins in the East or West.

Simms did not confuse loyalty to his state and region with blind adulation, especially when it came to their political leadership. He opened the serial account with a scathing attack on Confederate war strategy and battlefield tactics, using language that he toned down or removed entirely from the pamphlet. Nonetheless, even there he made plain that the city could have been defended, and suggested that Sherman's progress could have even been arrested and even defeated with the proper countermeasures. Though Simms's military acumen has been praised by modern scholars (Belser 285; Rogers, "Demands"), no historian has suggested that Sherman's army was anything other than remarkable in its prowess—a fact that Sherman's opponents admitted as well. By the time that army reached Columbia, it was nothing short of a juggernaut. Simms's belief that it might have been slowed or even stymied by essentially guerilla and small-scale partisan warfare seems willfully naïve. Neither does it fully square with his broader narrative aim, which was to reveal the recklessness, barbarity, and hypocrisy of Sherman's army. A rabble in arms could not have marched from Savannah to Columbia, covering that terrain at that speed, in the dead of winter. But Simms could not see his foe as superior in any regard.

If Simms discussed the work in his correspondence, those letters did not survive. The only mention is oblique, in his letter to South Carolina Governor Andrew G. Magrath shortly after the conflagration, in which he noted, "as copious statements of [the dev]astation & robbery of the city have already been put [in pri]nt, and accessible to all, we need not pause for [the menti]on of details here" (*Letters* 4: 497). What we know of the composition comes from the text itself, what Simms wrote in the *Phoenix*, and what can be gleaned from his circumstances.[3] On the night of the fire, Simms walked the streets of the city, talking to soldiers and citizens, taking it all in; he made it a point to include some of his own experiences in the narrative, such as attempts to steal his watch, and emphasized at the end that he was an "eye-witness of much of this terrible drama, and of many of the scenes it includes" (*Sack* 57).[4] Though the fire occurred on the first night, the destruction continued the next day, and Simms kept looking, listening, and talking.

When Sherman's army finally departed on February 20, the rubble, anger, and anguish left in its wake presented Simms with the most powerful story of his life. All he needed was a way to tell it. The destruction of the city's printers and newspapers created an opportunity, and Simms and Julian A. Selby, the former publisher of the *Daily South Carolinian*, decided to start a paper, with Simms serving as editor. Shortly after the fire, Simms visited the burned-out offices of the *Daily Carolinian*. Almost nothing had survived, but Simms found a composing stick in the ashes; it made a nice symbol for the new venture, dubbed the *Columbia*

Phoenix. Selby scoured the surrounding countryside for equipment and paper while Simms interviewed witnesses and gathered accounts for the lead story. A month later, on 21 March 1865, the first installment appeared in the first issue of the paper.

Called "Capture, Sack and Destruction of the City of Columbia," the story had no by-line, but Simms's authorship was assumed by his local readers, who knew him to be the editor (though even that was not acknowledged in the paper until after his resignation that fall[5]). Columbian Emma LeConte, whose diary was a good barometer of the rumors swirling in the capital, wrote shortly after the conflagration that "We are also soon to have a tri-weekly paper edited by Gilmer Sims [*sic*] and called 'The Phoenix!'" (82). Simms's meticulously compiled list of the properties destroyed and the owners and occupants dispossessed ran for the first three issues, with a few corrections published during the remainder of the serialization. Entitled "The Fire" in the *Phoenix*, it became "A List of Property Destroyed" in the pamphlet edition. The serial version is 24,362 words; "The Fire" is almost 4,000 words, including corrections.

The close of the serial version did not conclude the life of the story. At least one chapter was reprinted by another newspaper, a common practice, and others may have been as well (*Daily South Carolinian*, 29 April 1865). But Simms had grander designs for preserving and disseminating his carefully researched narrative, and spent considerable time and effort revising it over the summer and into the fall, not only to make it a better read, but one more in keeping with the radically changed landscape of the postwar South.[6] The resulting pamphlet, entitled *Sack and Destruction of the City of Columbia, S.C. to which is added a list of the property destroyed. Originally published in the Columbia Daily Phoenix*, totals 22,785 words; "A List of Property Destroyed," at 3,996 words, remained substantially unchanged from the three installments entitled "The Fire" in the serial account.

The nature and extent of the revisions Simms made are noteworthy—and revealing. A detailed analysis of these emendations has been published (N. Meriwether, "Civil War"; Simms, *Capture*), but it is useful to explore why Simms would take the time and make the effort to produce the final pamphlet edition. Clearly, he wanted to correct errors and did so, but the most important changes are in tone, reflecting the changed circumstances in which the revised version appeared. The serial form appeared before Appomattox, and part of its stated aim was to renew flagging war spirits and stanch the desertion that was increasingly sapping the South's war effort: "Encountered by a determined enemy, stung by the sense of loss and suffering, intensified by the stings of such a record of violated homes, *as is here written*, they will surely quail before our sons," Simms wrote in the April 8 issue (3, emphasis added). But the inflammatory rhetoric and calumny that characterized the tone of the serial edition had no place after the War, and indeed, it would have been irresponsible to continue to fan sectional animosity when the South's reintegration was now the paramount task facing the region.

Simms also must have had a sense that the story merited preservation. Newspapers did not survive well, especially in the postwar South where everything might be recycled or reused, and a pamphlet would have a far better chance of survival than a complete run of the first ten issues of the *Phoenix* (he was correct: only two runs survive today). And he may have felt a personal stake as well. Throughout the War, he had complained to friends that he felt his muse silenced; as early as 1861 he wrote that "literature, poetry especially, is effectually overwhelmed by the drums, & the cavalry, and the shouting. War is here the only idea" (*Letters* 4: 369). The serial version ended that silence. Indeed, it represents the most sustained writing on the War that Simms produced, and it represents one of only two major literary works he undertook during those four years, with "Paddy McGann." But "Paddy" he left in serial form, unlike "Capture, Sack and Destruction." One clue as to why he made the effort to revise and preserve it appears in a letter to his friend William Porcher Miles in 1861, where he complained that "one feels a little sore that there should be no record of a patriotism & a devotion to his country, which has left him little time or thought for any thing else, ever since the moment of secession, & for years before" (*Letters* 4: 355). *Sack and Destruction* made just such a record. Indeed, aside from "Paddy," his wartime literary output consisted of a few poems, numerous editorials and columns, and his customary correspondence—all ephemera that might not survive the vicissitudes of time. The pamphlet edition addressed that lacuna, in a form that would survive.

No extant records document the pamphlet's production. A notice in the *Phoenix* on September 26 stated that the booklet would appear "about the middle of October" (2), and its publication was confirmed in the October 27 issue, which noted that it had been "just published" (4). The only mention of its printing is by A.S. Salley, editor of the 1937 edition, in his "Foreword" to an anthology of poetry by Selby's son: "Mr. Selby once told me that he printed five thousand copies, with the price of 25¢ printed on the wrapper and that he sold only one copy" (xiii). Selby's recollection, or Salley's recounting of it, is problematic for several reasons. Given the acute shortage of paper, a print run of 5,000 copies is almost impossible to imagine; the price, clearly marked, was $1.00; and the one employee of the press, as Salley recounts Selby telling him, would have been unlikely to be able to print, much less bind, 5,000 copies of a 76-page pamphlet. Sales aside, given Simms's long report to Gov. Magrath, it seems likely that the other copies would have been distributed to legislators in Columbia, who needed to have an account of the destruction in order to consider redress.

The scarcity of the pamphlet did not relegate it entirely to obscurity. The first inkling of the text's tenacity appeared in 1870, when former Confederate Vice President Alexander H. Stephens published his *A Constitutional View of the Late War Between the States*. He reproduced several selections, introducing them as "written by the gifted and accomplished William Gilmore Simms, LL.D. The facts herein set forth by Dr. Simms are believed by the author to be entirely true"

(Simms, "Extracts" 2: 766). It was the first time the text was publicly attributed to Simms, and its appearance there marked the text indelibly as a participant in the Lost Cause narrative, which Stephens did much to foster. That did not have to happen. In 1905, Selby reproduced almost all of the pamphlet in his memoirs, where it stood simply as an example of the kinds of writing and publishing that Selby fostered, and that he believed were important stories about his time in the city. His version elided chapter breaks and headings, changing numerous paragraph breaks, and omitting parts of four chapters as well as abridging the "List of Property Destroyed."

Selby's republication may have lacked any deeper motive to engage in the controversy, but even the most optimistic assessment of the text's ability to reach a wider audience ended with the 1937 edition. Edited and introduced by A.S. Salley, this volume added a twenty-page introduction and twenty-four footnotes, marred by defensiveness and often polemical asides. One footnote explained, for example, that "Men of the intelligence of General Howard did not believe the Southern states were engaged in rebellion. They knew that they themselves were engaged in a war of conquest, which was but a more vigorous method of robbing the Southern States of their political and property rights than had been practiced theretofore. Rebellion was a term that enabled many cowards to vent the pent up hatred that had rankled in their blood and that of their ancestors for nearly two centuries" (48, n.4). Even the editor's own family stories serve as indictments of Union troop behavior (87, n.18). Originally published by Oglethorpe University Press, this edition spawned a number of later reprints, in various formats, both with and without Salley's introduction, and in varying degrees of bibliographic accuracy (N. Meriwether, "'A Scene'" 36–37). As dubious as some of these later reprints are, however, none of them republished Simms's first, inflammatory serial version.

That happened in 2005. *A City Laid Waste* brought back into print for the first time since its serialization Simms's original newspaper account.[7] As the first complete reissue of that original account, and the first new edition of any form of the work since Salley's 1937 effort, it merits scrutiny. Editor David Aiken adopted Simms's critical stance in his introduction, elaborating on the significance of the losses sustained in the city's destruction and reasserting the culpability of the Union army for its burning, as well as providing a detailed defense of Simms's work, reputation, and authorship. As Salley's edition demonstrated, that defensiveness is difficult to control, and can color the tone of even annotations, not just prefatory matter. Readers may find this edition vulnerable to that charge as well. For example, another heated, partisan account, Union Major George Ward Nichols's *The Story of the Great March* (also first published in 1865), is not held up as a mirror of Simms's own partisanry; instead, Aiken's introduction speculates that Nichols "may have been ignorant of the laws of war," and wonders if "perhaps he did not know what constituted a war crime" (38). Though confident of Simms's literary stature, the introduction confounds his prewar literary eminence with contemporary influence, asserting that "Only a concerted effort could reduce [the text's] power or the impact of its eyewitness testimony to the horrors of the Northern invasion" (40). This, for Aiken, explains Simms's later marginalization: "What started as an attempt to discredit [Simms's] reporting on the destruction of Columbia grew eventually into an attempt to discredit his work as a whole" (42). Others have concluded that Simms's literary fortunes were (and continue to be) the product of a much more sophisticated interaction with the processes that created the American canon after Simms's death (Guilds, "Long"; Moltke-Hansen, "Overview," especially xviii–xix). Likewise, the reception of his account of the burning of Columbia is rooted in the complexity of the historiography of that issue, which is not explored. However, the edition does bring back into print the all but inaccessible original, and its editorial apparatus documents and reflects the persistence of the sectionalism that infused the birth of the original account, and that continues to have cultural echoes that have bedeviled its author's reception ever since.[8]

The context of Simms's works is always complex, given the range of his interests, learning, and contacts, but for the *Sack and Destruction* it is paramount. In terms of its author's corpus, it is the only sustained example of his journalism we have, and the only one he prepared in his lifetime. (Volumes assembling his criticism and other newspaper writings, published by the *Simms Initiatives* in conjunction with the University of South Carolina Press, have helped to remedy this void.) Moreover, as the only journalism he revised himself and saw through to publication in monographic form, the pamphlet casts considerable light on his approach to writing history. Its contemporaneity allowed him to do the kind of research and writing that he could only dream of doing with his other historical topics, where the evidence was much more fragmentary, dispersed, and removed from its origins—and where his own impressions and experience could only imagine, instead of guide. Still, those long hours spent poring over manuscripts, assembling documents, and recording oral lore provided him with all of the skills that writing *Sack and Destruction* required, just as the success of the works produced by those skills gave him the gravitas and respect necessary for victims to trust him with their stories. The twists of fate that put the South's foremost public intellectual in the city whose destruction represented one of the final, deciding events of the Civil War helps to explain why the text has endured. It is Simms's status as public intellectual, writer, and fellow victim—or as scholars might say today, participant-observer—that makes his a unique voice in the literature on the burning of Columbia.

For Simms, *Sack and Destruction* was more than just his only sustained writing directly on the War: It also represented the recovery of his muse, and of his commitment to *belles lettres* after four years of fitful, labored, and diminished output (N. Meriwether, "Civil War"). Most of all, it marked the genesis of what would become his last great literary surge, an outpouring that remains impressive today for the straits in which they were produced, and for the tantalizing changes in their author's worldview they sketch (Guilds, *Literary Life* 304; Moltke-Hansen, "History Failed").

Those changes were shaped by the War. As the conflict stretched on, fewer of Simms's letters survived, but those that do provide telling insights into his life and mindset at the time. After a first flush of exhilaration, Simms's feelings about the progress of the War grew steadily more pessimistic. As fall turned into winter 1864, Simms confessed to Edward Spann Hammond that "I feel doubly alone. I have seen committed to the grave, year after year, children, wife & friends. The fiery circle of Fate is drawing rapidly around me" (*Letters* 4: 470). What that meant was not entirely clear. "All's very dark" (*Letters* 4: 471), he concluded, somberly.

That letter, dated November 20, is significant for several reasons. Although primarily a reflection on his friendship with Hammond's recently deceased father, whom he called "my most confidential friend for near twenty five years" (*Letters* 4: 469), his letter is more revealing of the circumstances he faced: "I have been too much staggered by recent events fully to command the resources of my mind. I can only fold hands, & wonder, and perhaps pray. What awaits us in the future, is perhaps foreshown to us by our Past, of trial and loss and suffering. Or it may be that God designs that we should surrender in sacrifice our choicest possessions, that we may become worthy of the great boon of future independence. Yet while I write, and hope, and pray, the day grows more clouded" (*Letters* 4: 471). He may have felt his view clouded, but what he suspected lay in store for South Carolina from Sherman was prescient: "[I]f Sherman had the requisite audacity—it did not need Genius,—he would achieve the greatest of his successes, by turning his back on the enemy in his rear, & march boldly towards the Atlantic coast. I fear that such is his purpose. If so,—what have we to oppose him? I dare not look on the prospect before us. It may become necessary for you, for me, & all to prepare as we can for the overrunning of Carolina!" (*Letters* 4: 471).

To his friend and fellow poet Paul Hamilton Hayne he was more succinct, writing him the following day to "pay me a visit sometime during the winter,—i.e. if Sherman does not smoke us out of our domain." (*Letters* 4: 472). By December, he was convinced that Sherman was headed his way, and he made plans to abandon his plantation Woodlands. Writing his son on December 27, he detailed his plans: "I propose to see the girls safely in Columbia, deposit them, my money & M.S.S., then return to the plantation, & urge forward the rest of my preparations with all possible speed. The probability is that Sherman will leave us very little time for loitering" (*Letters* 4: 474). He sent his children to Columbia on December 30, staying behind to supervise the packing of provisions, manuscripts, and other essentials. He was still at Woodlands on January 13, packing and making arrangements; to his daughter Augusta Simms Roach, he wrote, "I am resigned to whatever happens" (*Letters* 4: 477). Exhausted from his labors, he wrote his son on January 16, observing that "My notion is that Sherman means to take Augusta first, then seize upon the RR. send a column down upon Branchville, & press directly across the country for Columbia" (*Letters* 4: 481).

Still, he was sure that even that city represented a better chance of safety than anywhere else. His last known letter before Sherman's arrival in Columbia is dated January 24, from Woodlands. Written to Harry Hammond, it focuses on the task of gathering his father's correspondence for publication, but inevitably discusses the War, and ends, gloomily: "I begin to congratulate those fortunates who have escaped this crisis, and whom we still, perhaps unwisely, deplore" (*Letters* 4: 484). His next surviving letter is dated March 6, posted from Columbia. Written to well-known Unionist and old friend Benjamin F. Perry, he gave a terse overview of the city's destruction and subsequent straits, ending with, "All is wreck, confusion & despair" (*Letters* 4: 486).

Yet Simms did not allow himself to succumb to despair. As he wrote in the inaugural issue of the *Phoenix* on 21 March 1865:

> We must not despond, but let our citizens, rising, with heart and faith, firmly fixed on that Divine Providence, which suffers no sparrow to fall unnoticed to the ground, proceed to their labors manfully, each in his vocation, and all working together, until our city is renovated, renewed, regenerated, and springs with all her temples and palaces, her shrines of art and industry, into a strength and splendor superior even to the past. We must not sit and wring our hands idly, but go at once to our duties. The toil alone, honestly pursued, will heal all the hurts of fortune. ("Capture" 1)

His work for the *Phoenix* he frankly acknowledged was a way of putting food on the table for his family, but his writing—especially *Sack and Destruction*—represented much more. Not only did it show his determination to rebuild himself, his profession, and his state, it demonstrated his commitment to modeling the behavior he was encouraging.

Not surprisingly, no contemporary reviews of the pamphlet have surfaced: its scarcity and the general disarray in the region meant that it would likely not have reached surviving southern newspapers or magazines, and few northern readers would have been interested in an account faulting Sherman, widely hailed as a hero in the North. Indeed, the first real mention of the text is Alexander Stephens's; that republication also marks the first indication that the work's textual and bibliographic history would be the barometer of its reception.

There are exceptions to this, however. William Peterfield Trent praised it in his 1892 biography of Simms, saying that "Simms never wrote anything more graphic than this account" (281), and finding it persuasive. Interestingly, though Trent's biography is credited with having substantially damaged Simms's reputation, one eminent historian singled out Trent's praise for Simms's account in a

1902 article on the burning of the Columbia, complimenting Trent and finding Simms's pamphlet one of the few creditable authorities on the event (Rhodes).

The controversy persisted, however, and Simms's account continued to play a role in it. John G. Barrett's 1956 book, *Sherman's March Through the Carolinas*, used Simms's pamphlet (77; 88), but the text did not receive sustained scholarly attention until Marion Brunson Lucas's 1976 study of the event. His book, *Sherman and the Burning of Columbia*, remains one of the two modern, extended treatments of the subject. Lucas relied heavily on Simms's account, especially in his reconstruction of the fire's damage, but found its analysis, and especially Simms's fault-finding, ultimately unpersuasive. Lucas's conclusion—that the city's destruction was "an accident of war" (165)—was challenged by the other extended assessment of the topic, Charles Royster's opening chapter of his 1991 book, *The Destructive War*. Royster added another 150 sources to Lucas's bibliography, and wove a dense mesh of accounts, both northern and southern, to show that the city's firing was a deliberate goal of the army, in keeping with a much broader trajectory of a war mentality whose sheer destructiveness overwhelmed both sections as the War progressed. Royster did not address Simms directly as a source, he simply used his pamphlet, and often, corroborating it with dozens of additional accounts.

Royster's book had broader aims than merely settling old controversies, and his narrative strategy for the chapter on the burning of Columbia allowed historians to focus on the larger point of his magisterial history and gloss over the significance of what his portrait of the destruction signified for the controversy. Likewise, most—though not all—of Sherman's biographers have depended on Lucas as their authority for the question of who burned Columbia, finding Sherman blameless.[9]

If Simms's text failed to persuade these historians, it did find critics willing to defend its literary merits. Trent's admiration for the work is noteworthy, especially given the general tenor of his biography, and as Simms's reputation began its renaissance after World War II, *Sack and Destruction* received renewed attention. Both Guilds and James Everett Kibler praised it, Guilds calling it "an important and impressive document" (*Literary Life* 298) and agreeing with Kibler's assessment that it ranks "among Simms's best works." And Kibler correctly noted that its "stark and powerful prose style is memorable" (*Dictionary* 291). Most recently, Todd Hagstette has praised the work for its completeness and most especially its structure, which reveals a "true novelist's touch" ("Private" 62). Still, even Simms's most ardent admirers might hesitate at Aiken's assessment, which hailed the serial account as "a little-known masterpiece in American life and literature" (*City* 31).

Regardless of its relative merits, in both composition and tone the text is vintage Simms, and both versions are significant examples of his wartime writing. As historians continue to explore the literary output of the South during and immediately after the Civil War, Simms's narrative may well find its greatest audience as a window into how white southerners, like the survivors in Columbia, could embrace a romanticized vision of the Civil War. In Simms's narrative, the scorched earth of Columbia becomes fertile ground for the seeds of the Lost Cause to flower.

How the text stands as history is more difficult to assess. The account is sufficiently detailed, and the broader event sufficiently contentious, to require a thoroughly annotated edition to untangle its place in the literature on the event. An assessment of the accuracy of his charges and documentation requires situating the text in the broader historiography of the topic as well, a task that would require a full-length monograph. Some points can be made, however. In many details, Simms's reading of events was both accurate and prescient, as only in later decades would northern accounts emerge that corroborated his contentions, such as the numbers of Union soldiers killed by their own troops as they quelled the riot (Howard 2: 122; Osborn 129). Recent historians have generally accepted his catalog of the buildings and properties destroyed as substantially accurate. His larger purpose—to conclusively assign the blame to Sherman—remains disputed. Simms provided a list of final arguments at the close of the narrative that he believed settled the question, and those sketch how his narrative fits into the historiography of its subject.

Simms summarized his charges with eight points. His first, "Enough that Sherman's army was under perfect discipline," is the most problematic, and to modern readers even puzzling, for what he described is a riot by drunken troops clearly beyond the control of their officers. His second contention, if perhaps too absolute, nonetheless has ample corroboration: "That the fire was permitted, whether set by drunken stragglers or negroes, to go on, and Sherman's soldiers prevented, by their active opposition, all efforts of the firemen, while thousands looked on in perfect serenity, seemingly totally indifferent to the event." His third, "That hundreds of soldiers, quite sober, were seen in hundreds of cases busily engaged in setting the fire, well provided with all the implements and agencies, such as the most expert of city felons could conceive or devise," also dovetails with numerous other accounts, northern and southern, though it fails to distinguish between soldiers in ranks and those who were off duty—a crucial point, if invisible to a civilian. His fourth contention, "That they treated with violence the citizens who strove to arrest the flames" is probably more true than not, but Simms himself records the efforts of many Union officers and soldiers to extinguish fires and protect citizens and property. That, too, tends to undercut his fifth charge, "That, when entreated and exhorted by citizens to arrest the felons and prevent the catastrophe, at the very outset, the officers, in many cases, treated the applicants very cavalierly, and gave no heed to his [*sic*] application." Certainly that was true in some instances; but in others it was not, as Simms noted.

No scholar familiar with the diaries and records left by northern soldiers and officers questions the sixth charge, "That, during the raging of the flames, the act was justified by a reference to the course of South Carolina in originating the secession movement." But those records also complicate and largely undercut his seventh charge, "That the general officers themselves held aloof until near the close of the scene and of the night; were not to be found; and that Gen. Sherman's guard was not within the city; and yet no person could be ignorant of what was in progress. That Gen. Sherman knew what was going on, yet kept aloof and made no effort to arrest it until day-light on Saturday, ought, of itself, to be conclusive." Indeed, it seems clear that as Sherman and his senior officers became aware of the destruction, and most especially the riot, they responded, and far sooner than Simms realized.

The eighth charge repeats, for emphasis, the first point: "That, with his army under such admirable discipline, [Sherman] could have arrested at any moment; and that he did arrest it, when it pleased him to do so, even at the raising of a finger, at the tap of a drum, at the blast of a single trumpet" (Simms, *Sack* 55–56). Simms described what was clearly a riot, one that required fresh troops who had to enforce orders with bayonets and even bullets; this was not an army wholly under Sherman's or any other officer's command.

The best assessment of *Sack and Destruction*'s accuracy is that it is partly right and partly wrong—and given the horrors that Simms witnessed, and the litany of abuse and cruelty his witnesses recounted, that is noteworthy. And while it is important to note the care with which Simms built his case and marshaled his evidence, it is equally important to acknowledge the text's deficiencies—nowhere did he adequately acknowledge the role of the unusually high winds in the conflagration, a point that many other accounts highlight, for example. And some arguments then current were resolved over time, such as the question of Confederate responsibility for firing the cotton. Sherman admitted after the War that he had pinned the blame for the city's firing on Wade Hampton, charging his troops with starting the fires by burning the cotton as they retreated; as he explained in his memoirs, "In my official report of this conflagration, I distinctly charged it to General Wade Hampton, and confess I did so pointedly, to shake the faith of his people in him, for he was in my opinion boastful, and professed to be the special champion of South Carolina" (2: 287). But Simms was also writing to address what he thought was a cover-up of Sherman's culpability: In a line he elided from the pamphlet, he wrote in the April 10 issue of the *Phoenix* that "The attempt to lie it away, is as atrocious in its recklessness, as the deed which the falsehood is meant to palliate" (2). Had Simms been able to fully apprehend the events that he described, he might well have emerged with a more nuanced view, one that largely squares with the preponderance of evidence available today. That consensus suggests that Sherman never ordered the burning, nor did his officers, and they certainly did not countenance the riot and breakdown in discipline that the city's firing represented. However, by the time they reached Columbia, many Union officers and soldiers clearly believed that Sherman wanted the city burned, felt that it deserved such a fate, and were confident that they had the right to set the fires. Neither did they have any regrets afterwards, since the city's centrality to the waning Confederate war effort was the reason it had been targeted. Four long years of a war whose devastation had far exceeded all expectations made the destruction of Columbia merely collateral damage.

The controversy had already begun, and in Simms's words we can read the first sustained expression of the emotions that would fester long after, continuing to fuel a rancor that smolders on, however inexplicably, today (Moltke-Hansen, "Identity"). The tone and tenor of those words should remind readers that Simms's account is ultimately a document more of emotions and perspective than of facts and analysis: it is an honest expression of its author's feelings and of his best understanding of those horrendous events from the limited perspective of their immediate aftermath—and in response to what he saw as a whitewash of official misconduct.

Simms's motives were not entirely partisan, however—at least when it came to his revisions. Though he could not have anticipated how long the controversy would last, his principal aim with the pamphlet edition was to allow for healing. Only with a full and accurate record of the events could reconciliation occur; as he wrote to his friend Evert Augustus Duyckinck, "We may cherish regrets without becoming querulous over them, and may remember wrong doing with indignation, without desiring revenge" (*Letters* 4: 531–32). *Sack and Destruction* represented his effort, as a public intellectual, to create the environment in which white Columbians could have their story heard, and in so doing, embrace their new circumstances, however arduous, however unwanted, however unfair. This had long been a principal in his work as historian: only by understanding their history could a people build—or rebuild—their state. Only then could a real union emerge.

However laudable that goal was, the pamphlet failed to achieve it. The controversy persisted and even deepened over the decades. Official inquiries came to naught; well into the twentieth century, South Carolina politicians sought redress, even entering arguments into the *Congressional Record* (Blease). Recent historiography has also foundered on the issue—and on both sides of the question. When Lucas's study appeared, one reviewer used that event to invoke and dismiss Simms: "Despite the heroic and often friendly behavior of Union troops assigned to guard private dwellings and to fight the fire, prominent Columbians like William Gilmore Simms ignored the real actions of Union troops and created the myth that Sherman's men had destroyed Columbia" (Palmer 802). In this historian's view, "the success of many Columbians in salvaging their property indicates that Lucas is incorrect in attributing Columbia's fall to lack of Confederate planning. Wealthy citizens planned carefully, but about how to save their possessions rather than how to save Columbia. In light of this internal, unthinkable betrayal, it is not difficult to understand why South Carolinians had to mythologize Sherman's brutality. To accept the truth would have required admitting their own villainy" (Palmer 802). It is hard not to hear echoes of Simms's partisan vehemence continuing to reverberate, more than a century later.

Whether the topic of the burning of the Columbia will attract any new scholarship remains to be seen. Royster's chapter is the most definitive and recent treatment, but it has not changed the scholarly consensus on Sherman's responsibility for the destruction. The question of who is responsible for Columbia's firing remains an issue not so much unresolved as simply entrenched. For *Sack and Destruction*, that still-fraught context means that the best view of the work is as a compelling work of literary nonfiction, not as a dispatch from the War, nor a history of one of its greatest tragic events. This is in keeping with the broad trajectory of Simms studies, which for many years has been effecting a simultaneous reappraisal of the merits of Simms's work, and especially of his wartime and postwar work. That effort dovetails with other trends in Civil War literary studies, which in recent years have focused increasingly on southern wartime and immediately postwar literary production, and finding far more than earlier generations had seen (Fahs; Bernath; Hutchison). *Sack and Destruction* may benefit from this reexamination, but in this form, its status within Simms's corpus remains its best claim on scholars today.

After the war, Simms peppered his letters with pleas to northern friends to supply him with something—anything—to read. "I am also greatly in need of books," he wrote Duyckinck in August 1865, lamenting, "[I] have had nothing to read for 4 years. My library gone—and no books for study" (*Letters* 4: 516). His friends responded, and one of the books that may have been sent to him was a wartime edition of Thucydides' *The Peloponnesian War*, preserved today as a part of the Simms-Oliphant-Furman Collection in the South Caroliniana Library. Its presence in Simms's small library at the time of his death suggests what *Sack and Destruction* might have achieved had it incorporated that author's perspective, one that explicitly sought to present a nuanced, philosophical reading of the complexities of a bitter, pivotal war. That proved too much for Simms, or for any southerner of his generation; it would be another thirty-two years before that happened, in an essay by Basil Gildersleeve, the father of the discipline of classics in the American academy, entitled "A Southerner in the Peloponnesian War."

The parallels between the two wars are suggestive. When Thucydides described his enemy, the Spartan king Archidamus, as "a prudent and intelligent man" (Blanco 31), one whose speech before hostilities commenced counseled caution and stressed the loss of reason that drives nations to war, he could be describing Sherman's grief at the onset of the War (Kennett 93). Like Archidamus, he had a profound understanding for what war portended, and it was compounded by a genuine affection for much of the South and for many southerners who had befriended him before the war, especially those he knew to be Unionists (Fellman 79; 84).

But war reduces complexity into duality, as Thucydides showed, and for Simms, there could be no empathy for his erstwhile enemy. *The Peloponnesian Wars* reflects a mind bent on achieving understanding, especially of one's former opponent (Zagorin 139–61). *Sack and Destruction* made no attempt to see the War as anything except conquest and domination by the North, no effort to probe beneath the intensity of the feelings of even the Union soldiers Simms portrayed as good and honorable. His is a perspective as hardened as the worst of the Federal troops in his narrative, those whom he frankly described as having lost all feeling for civilians they could only see as traitors, guilty of violating the sacred compact of an indivisible union. That kind of understanding was not possible for Simms—nor was it a goal for his narrative. Documenting the event—its extent, emotional impact, and who was to blame—was the only understanding he could seek, the only responsibility he could shoulder as a writer, witness, participant—and all too recent partisan. This is why Simms alluded to Job, not Thucydides, in his opening:

> It has pleased God, in that Providence which is so inscrutable to man, to visit our beautiful city with the most cruel fate which can ever befall States or cities. . . . Humiliation spreads her ashes over our homes and garments, and the universal wreck exhibits only one common aspect of despair. It is for us, as succinctly but as fully as possible, and in the simplest language, to endeavor to make the melancholy record of our wretchedness as complete as possible. (*Sack* 3)

In this parable, Job endures a myriad of torments and tragedies, accused by his neighbors as meriting his misfortune until he is ultimately vindicated and rewarded. Simms chose his allusion carefully: like Job, Columbians were covered in ashes, signifying their misfortune (Job 42.6); and like the rest of the South, Columbians now had to rebuild and remember, following Job's example and learning from the grace and dignity they brought to their suffering. In time, that noble endurance presaged God's revelation and mercy. Revelation was a key part of that: the blessing of Yahweh's appearance granted Job understanding, which preceded his restoration, prosperity, and success.

That Simms hoped for the same comes as no surprise, and it is a key to understanding the text. In Simms's hand, *Sack and Destruction* represented the depiction of a calamity as incomprehensible and inscrutable as Job's torments. Job never wavered in his faith, despite his travails and the mystery of their onset and affliction; and that is why he was ultimately rewarded—with understanding, with restitution of all that he had lost, and more. It is the only literary metaphor that could frame and make comprehensible the epic tragedy that Simms experienced.

It was also a powerfully appealing model, one that allowed Simms to embrace reunion without questioning his antebellum beliefs and posture. The burning of Columbia, like the loss of the war as a whole, was a cataclysm to suffer and endure, not a lesson, much less a mistake, to learn from. Though he was prescient in perceiving Columbia's destruction as the result of two competing visions of the nation, he could not recognize any validity in the other—the one that he could finally only see as the treacherous despoiler of a surrendered, defenseless city, filled with noncombatants. To Simms, any shred of legitimacy to the North's view of an indivisible union was forever obliterated by what he saw that night. In that light, the care and restraint that he managed to muster for the revisions is significant. Modern readers may wish for greater balance, but what Simms accomplished was revealing, and even praiseworthy, within those narrow limits. Moreover, that he was able to tone down his rhetoric, and significantly so, shows that he had sincerely embraced the need for reconciliation and marks the start of that process, however far from its realization the text finally shows him to be. That, too, is a vital aspect of *Sack and Destruction*: the same emotional intensity in his enemy that so baffled Simms—that he so misread—he unconsciously mirrored in his own unrelenting stance.

Literary flaws and historiographical context notwithstanding, Simms's *Sack and Destruction* stands as a significant work in his corpus, not least for its centrality to so many of the critical issues that its author raises. David S. Shields is the scholar who most recently has reminded us that "Because the shape of history mattered so centrally to Simms's art, attention must be paid to his practice as a historian, to those occasions when he chose biography or civil history as his genre, rather than historical romance" (xiii). Questions of genre aside, it is especially important to remember that to Simms, *Sack and Destruction* was very much one of those occasions when he chose civil history, however recent.

Simms wrote and revised the text as a definitive answer to pressing but swiftly changing circumstances and needs, making it a useful lens into the nature of the challenges that the end of the Civil War and the onset of Reconstruction brought for the South. Simms believed that he was writing history, that his text would provide an enduring cornerstone that would help later generations and others understand what had happened and in so doing, provide a basis for reunion. In his time, that goal was eclipsed by the magnitude of the destruction and anguish he documented; later, it was obliterated by the continuing controversy his text ironically fueled, letting anguish congeal into bitterness and hate, instead of softening into understanding and forgiveness. Today, the book's enduring value lies less in what it says of its subject and more for what it says of its author: as a skeleton key to the changing thought, work, and role of the South's foremost public intellectual as he faced the tragic aftermath and devastating consequences of a war whose advent he had so ardently courted.

NOTES

1. This essay benefitted from thoughtful readings by David Moltke-Hansen, Todd Hagstette, and Alex Moore.
2. The literature on the Lost Cause is extensive and continues to develop. The first major expression is Pollard, in 1866; for recent scholarship, see Foster; Osterweis; Gallagher and Nolan; and Blight. Recently, Speiser has argued that Simms's writing in particular represents an antebellum expression of the perspective and themes that would later inform the Lost Cause.
3. For a thorough exposition of this, see N. Meriwether, "Civil War."
4. Unless otherwise noted, all passages are quoted from the 1865 pamphlet version of the text published by the Power Press of the Daily Phoenix.
5. Simms stayed to see the final pamphlet version through the press, resigning on October 1. Shortly after, the paper issued a formal announcement: In a column titled "Friendly Notice—Correction," the new editor responds to an item in the Charlotte (NC) *Times* on his assumption of the editorship of the *Phoenix*, saying that "it is due to Mr. Simms, who has conducted it from the beginning, to state that he withdrew from his connection with the paper before Mr. Johnston entered upon his duties" ("Friendly Notice" 2).
6. For a detailed discussion of these edits, see N. Meriwether, "'A Scene.'" For a textual comparison of those edits, see N. Meriwether, ed., *Capture, Sack and Destruction . . . A Collection of Documents*.
7. In 2003, a transcription of the three extant manuscript sources for the serial account, along with the full text of both the serial account and the pamphlet edition, was catalogued and made available at the South Caroliniana Library at the University of South Carolina as *Capture, Sack and Destruction of Columbia, SC: A Collection of Documents*.
8. Those cultural echoes reverberate today; for a thoughtful discussion of one such incident that directly addresses Simms and Sherman, see David Moltke-Hansen, "Identity Politics and the Civil War."
9. See, for example, John F. Marszalek, *Sherman: A Soldier's Passion for Order* (New York: Free Press, 1993), 325; and Stanley P. Hirshson, *The White Tecumseh* (New York: John Wiley and Sons, 1997), 284. For dissenting views, see Michael Fellman's *Citizen Sherman: A Life of William Tecumpseh Sherman* (New York: Random House, 1995), 228–31 and especially 449; and Lee Kennett, *Sherman: A Soldier's Life* (New York: HarperCollins, 2001), 268–69.

Selections from the Letters and Speeches of the Hon. James H. Hammond

ALEXANDER MOORE

In December 1861, nine months after the American Civil War had begun William Gilmore Simms received a letter from his great friend James Henry Hammond. Formerly governor of South Carolina and United States Senator, Hammond had considered Simms's suggestion that he publish a volume of his literary "Remains"; that is, his speeches, public letters, and other original documents. Hammond envisioned the book to be "a very select & rather undersized Volume & I would cheerfully make any compensation to the Publisher that you might think right."[1] Simms planned the book to become a volume for inclusion in a larger publishing enterprise close to his heart, a "Library of the Confederate States." Soon thereafter the author revealed to John Reuben Thompson, poet and former editor of the *Southern Literary Messenger*, that he was "revising Hammond's Essays & Speeches for the Press" as a title in the new series: "The volumes to average 400 pp. each, & sold at 1.00 or 1.25 according to bulk. New works to be interspersed as prepared, and wholesome variety to be sought in History, Biography, Statesmanship, Poetry & Fiction" (*Letters* 6: 223). Simms then elaborated his plan to William Porcher Miles:

> I have been suggesting a scheme of a Library of the Confederate States, to include only Southern writers in all departments, publishing a <u>single vol.</u> monthly. It will comprise Lives, with selections, of & from [John C.] Calhoun, [George] McDuffie, [Robert Y.] Hayne, [Nathaniel] Bev[erly] Tucker, [Thomas] Jefferson, [George] Washington, [John] Randolph, &c. with the miscellaneous writings of Hammond, [William J.] Grayson, &c. and be interspersed with original writings as they offer. I merely propose & will not edit. (*Letters* 4: 397)

By then Simms had already contradicted his statement to Miles that he would not edit the series; for, he was at work "revising Hammond now for the Press" (ibid.). *Selections from the Letters and Speeches of the Hon. James H. Hammond, of South Carolina* was published by John F. Trow in New York City in early 1866 under circumstances far different from those Hammond and Simms had anticipated four years earlier. Hammond had been deceased for nearly two years and the Confederacy had been extinguished in April 1865.

From the start of his literary career Simms had exhorted native writers to create an American national literature different in content and character from that of Europe and Great Britain. As sectional conflict between North and South worsened and eventually divided the Union, he shifted that advocacy to creating a distinctive southern literature—different in character and content from the literature of the northern states. Simms intended the Library of the Confederate States to be the vehicle by which the Confederacy would take its place on the world's literary stage. The Civil War and defeat of the short-lived Confederate republic prevented Simms from fulfilling his ambitious plan.

Book Plans

Sometime between December 1861 and his death in November 1864 Hammond composed a draft table of contents and began assembling copies of his pamphlet publications and official papers to use as texts for the anthology. Simms was at work early in 1862 on at least three speeches; so, it is likely that Hammond composed his list in late 1861 or early 1862. Hammond's list contained twelve items to be published "in one volume—large type—good paper. . . . It will make with large print an Octavo vol. of 250 or 300 pages."[2] When published in 1866 *Selections* was an octavo volume of 368 pages and contained eleven of the twelve items on Hammond's list, arranged chronologically in the order that he had proposed. However, by early 1862 preparation of Hammond's texts may have reached an impasse as the two men disagreed on some editorial issues.

At the close of 1861 Simms began editing and "correcting" pamphlet versions of three speeches. When he sent his texts to Hammond he received a reply on 18 February 1862 that revealed resistance to his editorial tinkering:

> I have read only the first page of the "Kansas speech." The corrections seem to be improvements, but glancing further over the pages, they appear to be so elaborate that when adopted it may be as much your speech as mine. I don't know how that would look as our styles are very different. My aim has always been <u>clearness</u> first, then <u>vigor</u> & for these I sacrifice elegance when necessary & sometimes grammar. . . . I will see whenever I can bring my self to the ungrateful task of looking over those Speeches again, how it stands & how far the adoption of your Corrections will estrange the style of these from my other productions.[3]

In other words Simms and Hammond differed on some elements of preparing the *Selections* text. To compare the *Selections* version of Hammond's "Speech on the Admission of Kansas . . . March 4, 1858" with the pamphlet version published in Washington, DC by Lemuel Towers reveals the sort of emendations that had caught Hammond's eye. Simms introduced qualifying words and phrases, changed capitalizations, and italicized some words for emphasis. These emendations may have tempered the "vigor" of Hammond's expressions but their effect was to clarify subject and verb agreement, eliminate superfluous punctuation, and to link accurately pronouns with their antecedent nouns.

James Henry Hammond's health had been declining through 1864 and he died on November 13 at Redcliffe, his Edgefield District plantation (Faust, *Hammond* 376–79). Amid his own wartime and personal losses, Simms mourned Hammond's demise. Writing to Edward Spann Hammond, Simms stated that "[Y]our father was my most confidential friend for near twenty years. Never were thoughts more intimate than his & mine. We had few or no secrets from each other. . . . There was something kindred in our intellectual nature." Simms then turned his thoughts to his friend's literary remains and intellectual legacy:

> Preserve all his papers. I hope some day to render a proper tribute to his memory. We have no chance for this now. There is no organ. There are no means. Do not suffer his revised publications to be mislaid. Have them carefully preserved, compactly put up & sealed against mischance. With God's blessing, I hope to put on record my appreciation of his claims and to illustrate them by his works. (*Letters* 4: 469–70)

Among his various accomplishments Hammond was foremost a politician and would-be statesman, who served South Carolina as governor and legislator in the United States House of Representatives and Senate. His activities in Congress—attendance, committee memberships, and voting record—are part of the public records of the nation. They were published in the official journals of the Senate and House of Representatives.[4] Hammond was elected to the Twenty-fourth Congress. He took his House seat on 18 December 1835 and resigned in February 1836 due to failing health. His House speeches and remarks are found in volumes of the *Congressional Globe* and *Register of Debates in Congress*.[5] Hammond's Senate term was longer and more noteworthy. He was elected to the Thirty-fifth Congress and took his seat in December 1857. Reelected to the Thirty-sixth Congress, he resigned on 11 November 1860, in response to the presidential election of Abraham Lincoln.[6] The *Congressional Globe* contains his Senate speeches and remarks.

In that era important Congressional speeches were widely published in newspapers and as pamphlets to reach a broad readership. Newspaper readers had insatiable appetites for lengthy columns of political speeches set in small type sizes. *Globe* texts were disseminated throughout the nation when they were reprinted in national and regional newspapers. Publishers occasionally gave Congressional orators opportunities to correct and revise their texts, thereby lending pamphlet versions greater literary authority than *Globe* versions. Hammond's Congressional speeches, especially those included in *Selections*, had also been published in the *Charleston Mercury* and other South Carolina newspapers. Newspapers were the chief tools in disseminating political views, establishing political party loyalties, and creating public opinion. As a young man Hammond had briefly edited the *Southern Times*, a pro-nullification newspaper in Columbia, South Carolina. Scrapbooks in the Hammond Papers at the South Caroliniana Library and Library of Congress contain clippings from newspapers throughout the nation reporting Hammond's political activities in Washington and South Carolina and printing his speeches with regularity. His other publications expand his legacy beyond the sphere of southern politics. Among those were speeches on southern politics and culture delivered on special occasions, periodical essays, and even some juvenile works of literary pretension (Tucker 485–86).

Hammond's pamphlets, journal articles, and newspaper essays ranged from scientific farming and plantation management to politics but the cornucopia of his diaries, plantation records, commonplace books, and thousands of letters is his chief legacy. Simms had known from their earliest acquaintance that Hammond was a consummate letter writer and diligent keeper of his personal and business papers. Even as Union forces devastated South Carolina in 1864–65, Simms persisted in his goal to preserve Hammond's papers and to publish a volume of letters to complement the planned *Selections*. A volume of Hammond's letters would add another title to the Library of the Confederate States and immortalize his late friend's talents.

Two months after Hammond's death Simms elaborated to Harry Hammond, his friend's eldest son, his plans for the volume of letters. He returned to Catherine Fitzsimons Hammond a bundle of her late husband's letters and encouraged other Hammond correspondents to return their letters to the family (*Letters* 4: 482–83). During 1865 Hammond's widow began to seek a publisher for the speeches and public letters volume. She wrote to her brother-in-law Marcellus C.M. Hammond that she had entrusted to her son-in-law James Gregg some pamphlets her deceased spouse had "corrected and arranged for publication" to carry to Great Britain in hopes of finding a publisher. These were likely texts that Hammond and Simms had labored upon in 1862 augmented by others edited since then. Gregg made the attempt, "but he writes that upon inquiry it could be published on better terms at the North. Spann advises that we defer as this is not the time to do it. He is deeply interested in it and will probably give it more attention than [my sons] Paul or Harry as his tastes are more in that line. I can't trust myself with the past" (Bleser, *Hammonds* 145).

As late as 1868—two years after *Selections* had been published—Simms described to M.C.M. Hammond his desire to publish an essay on Hammond "when I shall be able to undertake the article on J.H.H. for the present that must be delayed." He wished to thanks Edward Spann Hammond for sending a copy of *Selections*. An inscription in that copy was dated July 1866 with a note that "his [Simms's] name & that date in it."[7] This inscription is useful in narrowing the publication date of the volume.

Simms's counsel was heeded regarding the value of Hammond's papers. The James Henry Hammond Papers, Hammond-Bryan-Cumming Collection, and papers of other family members survive as a rich archive of the history of South Carolina and the South. First preserved by Hammond, his friends and supporters, then by family members and descendants, those collections are now entrusted to public institutions to preserve and make them available for study. The Library of Congress, South Caroliniana Library, and Southern Historical Collection at the University of North Carolina contain the majority of Hammond and Hammond-related collections. The major collections have been microfilmed and are available in published microform editions.[8]

Several published documentary editions contain Hammond's correspondence and diaries. Carol K. Rothrock Bleser's *Secret and Sacred* edition of Hammond's private diaries and her *Hammonds of Redcliffe* edited letters have demonstrated the value of Hammond's papers. Drew Gilpin Faust comprehended their breadth and depth to write an authoritative biography, *James Henry Hammond and the Old South: A Design for Mastery* and *A Sacred Circle: The Dilemma of the Intellectual in the Old South, 1840–1860.*[9]

A Measure of the Man

James Henry Hammond had a mercurial personality. Intellectually gifted and omnivorous in his interests, he struggled unsuccessfully to curb his appetites for wealth, public display, fame, and sexual license. His "design for mastery" was foremost a hopeless struggle for self-mastery. Simms once told his friend that "Were you as rarely good as you are rarely endowed, you would be one of the most perfect men living" (*Letters* 1: cxii). To this lack of self-control Hammond added a near-obsession to record on paper every aspect of his life and personality. In his introduction to the 1978 edition of *Selections* Clyde Wilson sought to give a context to Hammond's excesses and to rescue him from becoming a stereotype:

> Like any other man of strong intelligence, physical vigor, ambition, and sensitivity, Hammond suffered bouts of melancholy, indolence, self-pity, discouragement, indecisiveness, and lust. That his bouts are better documented than those of most of us does not necessarily prove anything in particular about Hammond or about his society—except that they were human. (Hammond, *Selections* xii)

Hammond or his heirs concealed some of the most revealing and embarrassing episodes in the man's life by redacting his most personal diaries. However, the obvious sparseness of these redactions suggests that just as his ego and sense of his place in history drove Hammond to document even his most foolish acts, that same self-regard prevented him from censoring those incriminating documents. What might he bother to conceal when he indifferently doctored his "secret & sacred" account of his sexual dalliances with his teenage Hampton nieces and his liaisons with Sally and Louisa Johnson, a mother and daughter enslaved at Redcliffe?[10]

Those episodes damaged Hammond's political career and family life. In addition, they undermined—at least for modern readers—many of his publicly-expressed views on society and culture. Perhaps the most glaring discrepancies between his public expressions and his private behavior related to the subject of sexual relations between enslaved women and their white owners. Sally Johnson and her daughter Louisa Johnson were acknowledged concubines of Hammond and his sons. He had purchased the mother and her two-year-old daughter in 1838. They both bore enslaved Hammond-fathered offspring. Henderson Johnson, his enslaved son by Sally Johnson, was fourteen years of age in 1856 (Faust, *Hammond* 317–18). His liaison with Sally was underway when Hammond asserted in a public letter to Thomas Clarkson that "some intercourse of the sort does take place. Its character and extent, however, are grossly and atrociously exaggerated. No authority divine or human has yet been found sufficient to arrest all such irregularities among men. But it is a known fact, that they are perpetrated here, for the most part, in the cities. Very few mulattoes are reared on our plantations" (*Two Letters* 136–37). He continued his remarks: "it is well known that this intercourse is regarded in our society as highly disreputable. If carried on habitually it seriously affects a man's standing, so far as it is known; and he who takes a colored mistress—with rare and extraordinary exceptions—loses caste at once" (ibid.). As Wilson suggested, few people can truthfully claim that their private lives and public utterances seamlessly complement one another. Likewise, Hammond's hypocrisies may have been no greater than those of most men. Yet he documented his own so well that he has become an easy example of the vices that contemporaneous abolitionists and later generations of historians have ascribed to southern slaveholders.

The 1866 Edition

The contents of *Selections* conform to Hammond's undated draft outline. However, the final arrangements for its 1866 publication remain unknown. Whether Simms or Hammond's sons had signed the publishing agreement and prepared the printer's copy text is also unknown. Perhaps Catherine Hammond or her son-in-law James Gregg was an active agent in New York City on behalf of the project. Harry Hammond had some role in the publication; for, he added a biographical essay on his father and began it with the statement,

> at a period when the entire obliteration of everything at the South seemed imminent and inevitable, these papers were hurriedly sent to the publishers in the hope of preserving some trace of what had been. One hundred copies were printed without preface, note, comment or correction. To remedy in part, these defects, the following sketch has been prepared for insertion in these volumes. (Hammond, *Selections* [xxvii])

Hammond then summarized his father's life and highlighted some features of each document in the book. He characterized him as an industrious, successful planter who was attentive to the physical and spiritual needs of his slaves:

> Lightly tasked, well clothed, well fed, their lives and persons protected, their sufferings alleviated by the kindest care, their domestic affections cherished with conscientious delicacy, a church built for them, Christian preaching with religious instruction in a Sunday School furnished, it would have been difficult to find a happier or more progressive body of agricultural laborers with greater local attachments, more trusting in, and trusted by those they worked for, than the slaves on his plantations. (ibid.)

Edward Spann Hammond's apparent ignorance of decisions regarding the book and, indeed, its publication date strikes a note of confusion on his part. On 13 November 1866, the second anniversary of his father's death and five months or more after *Selections* was published, he wrote to his mother his ideas for a book of his father's writings:

> While the great mass catch only at floating paragraphs in daily papers, there are great minds in their closets eager for the original and profound. These are the men that must soon be brought conspicuously before our people. It is those who would welcome a publication of Father's works, and would set store upon them if they possess the merit which he and we have always thought they possessed, and which has been accorded to them universally when an opinion upon them has been expressed. I would therefore suggest that steps be taken to have a carefully corrected edition, of considerable size, with picture and a brief biographical sketch, published at an early day. I have but little doubt that so far from its costing any thing, that several of the first publishing houses of the country would readily undertake it and pay to the family a percentage on every copy sold, or a handsome sum for the edition, for the privilege of making the publication. . . . I would suggest that Uncle M[arcellus] and Mr. Simms be consulted before doing any thing. (Bleser, *Hammonds* 155)

Living in Lynchburg, Virginia, E. Spann had perhaps not been kept up to date on efforts to publish *Selections*. By 1868 he had located and sent to Simms a copy of the work inscribed to him and dated July 1866. In three years he had not seen his father's letters that Simms had returned to the family in 1865 because his brother Harry had not shared them. E. Spann's apparent isolation might explain his post-publication remarks on its inclusions and omissions:

> Among Father's writings I must confess I fail to find the merit I hoped for in the first article in the book. A sentence here and there might be saved but the bulk of it seems to me dross to his other writings. There are some fine

> short passages in Anti-Debt and the Institute Speech. The last paragraph of the College Address is perhaps the finest he ever wrote. The last 10 lines of the Kansas speech nearly equal it in its prophetic solemnity. The exhortation in the Calhoun and Barnwell addresses are very fine—classic and polished—while the character in the former is intense in its vigor and thoroughness. (Bleser, *Hammonds* 157)

Selections contains eleven speeches and public letters. The earliest is from 7 July 1834, and the last is dated 21 May 1860. All had been published in some form during Hammond's lifetime, usually soon after they were written or uttered. A few were issued in more than one edition. Collected in a single anthology, they provided a primer to the political tenets and cultural values of the antebellum South, beginning with nullification and state sovereignty in the wake of the Compromise of 1833 and concluding with a Senate speech in May 1860 that reflected upon the failed promises of the Compromise of 1850. Clyde Wilson's introduction and textual endnotes to his 1978 edition elaborated the contexts of the items in the volume. These notes are reproduced in this *Simms Initiatives* edition. However, the 1978 edition lacked bibliographical information on some of the more significant selections. This new introduction adds to the textual information in that earlier edition. Some other facsimile editions of *Selections* have been published in the twentieth century. It was copied in microfiche by Lost Cause Press in 1976 and reprinted in a cloth-bound facsimile in 1985 by Reprint Company of Spartanburg, South Carolina. The HathiTrust Digital Library Record 000407865 has made available online copies of the 1866 edition housed in the libraries of Harvard University, Library of Congress, University of Michigan, and New York Public Library. An inscription in the Harvard Library copy reads "Gift of Harry Hammond, Beech Island, So. Carolina Ap. 11. 81." One of the South Caroliniana Library's copies was owned by Simms and later by his granddaughter, the author and editor Mary Simms Oliphant.

Speeches and Essays

The first item in *Selections* was "Report at a Meeting of the State Rights and Free Trade Party of Barnwell . . . July 7th, 1834." This address had its proximate context as a response to the June 1834 South Carolina Court of Appeals decision in the case of McCrady v. Hunt, the "test oath controversy." The decision upheld a lower court ruling that the state's 1833 oath of allegiance was unconstitutional. The Compromise of 1833 had defused the confrontation between South Carolina and the federal government respecting the Force Act of 1832 and the state's Ordinance of Nullification. In the aftermath of the controversy the state had required officeholders to take an oath that affirmed state sovereignty. Hammond was twenty-seven years of age when he delivered this speech to the Barnwell District State Rights and Free Trade Party members. The Barnwell speech placed

Hammond among the nullifier party allied with John C. Calhoun. It demonstrated his mastery of the constitutional and political issues involved in the crisis and his ability to express them in a clear, convincing manner. In October 1834 he was elected to the United States House of Representatives, his first elected office and the start of his political career on the national stage. Drew Faust observed, "It is significant that Hammond chose this as the first important statement of his political career when he was considering a collection of his works. In accordance with his wishes, it appears as the first item in the posthumous compilation of his works" (*Hammond* 154n).

Hammond's 1 February 1836, "Speech on the Justice of Receiving Petitions for the Abolition of Slavery in the District of Columbia" was one of his last acts in the Twenty-fourth Congress. On 26 February 1836 he resigned his seat for health reasons. This speech aligned Hammond with Calhoun in opposition to Representative Henry Laurens Pinckney on the issue of how Congress should respond to growing numbers of petitions from organizations and individuals seeking to abolish slavery. In the House, Pinckney instituted a policy called the "gag rule" in which abolition petitions were immediately tabled without discussion. The conflict was ostensibly a narrow one about House rules of procedure. However, Hammond and Calhoun recognized that the gag rule was inadequate to deter agitation in Congress. For, if the House had the power to table a petition it could later take it up from the table for consideration. Their position was that Congress had no authority whatsoever to receive these petitions or to take any action whatsoever upon them.

Hammond expostulated on the beneficial character of southern slavery. He contrasted the stabilizing role of slavery in human society with the chaotic consequences of abolition in the British West Indies and of unbridled industrial capitalism in Great Britain, the chief source of anti-slavery agitation during the 1830s. In addition to its publication in the *Congressional Globe*, Hammond's speech was published in pamphlet form as *Remarks of Mr. Hammond, of South Carolina, on the Question of Receiving Petitions for the Abolition of Slavery in the District of Columbia*.

Hammond's governor's messages of November 1843 and 1844 to the South Carolina General Assembly ranged widely in the number and variety of his recommendations for changes in the organization and operation of state government. In 1843 he recommended reorganization of state government by consolidating state offices in Columbia to obviate the "dual executive" maintenance of duplicate treasurer, state attorney, and secretary of state offices in Charleston. He also proposed eliminating the state surveyor general's post and permitting local districts to maintain their own land records. In both messages Hammond—a former teacher and a teacher's son—sought to strengthen public education by establishing state-funded academies in each election district. The state system would provide uniform standards and funding: "Every dollar which can be spared from the absolute want of the State, should be first offered to this great cause" (Hammond, *Selections* 71). Wilson observed that Hammond's messages demonstrate that "the antebellum South Carolina ethos was not pervasively hostile to progress. . . . Nor do these messages, closely read, confirm the portrait of Hammond the haughty aristocrat. They exhibit as sincere an interest in the welfare of all citizens as could be found anywhere at the time" (Hammond, *Selections* xviii).

Ninety-eight of the 368 pages in *Selections* were devoted to defending African American slavery in principle and practice. As such, these were the most frequently reprinted and widely distributed of Hammond's public pronouncements. His 21 June 1844 public letter to Reverend Thomas Brown of Glasgow framed part of its argument on his governor's pardon of John L. Brown, who had aided his enslaved mistress to escape from her owner. Brown's conviction and death sentence for slave stealing had become an international *cause célèbre*, eliciting appeals for clemency from British abolition societies. The letter was published in pamphlet form as *Letter of His Excellency Governor Hammond to the Free Church of Glasgow, on the Subject of Slavery*.[11]

His letters to Thomas Clarkson, dated 28 January and 24 March 1845 constituted a review of the history and present state of slavery in the American South, a defense of that institution from attacks by British and northern abolition societies, plus a review of biblical and constitutional justifications for slavery in human society. The author sought to demonstrate that slavery-based societies promoted stability and offered benefits to all classes in these societies. He criticized industrial capitalism in Great Britain and in the North because that system promoted conflict between social and economic classes unlike the natural, close-knit relationships between slaves and owners in the South. Turmoil in capitalist societies engendered reform movements—temperance, women's rights, workers' movements—that were anathema in the South. He wrote, "We have been so irreverent as to laugh at Mormonism and Millerism, which have created such commotions farther North; and modern prophets have no honor in our country. Shakers, Rappists, Dunkers, Socialists, Fourierists and the like keep themselves afar off" (Hammond, *Selections* 134).

Three pamphlet editions of Hammond's letters to Clarkson have been identified: *Two Letters on Slavery in the United States: Addressed to Thomas Clarkson, Esq. by J.H. Hammond*; *Gov. Hammond's Letters on Southern Slavery: Addressed to Thomas Clarkson, the English Abolitionist*; and *Cartas del Gobernador Hammond* [*sobre la esclavitud del Sur, dirigidas a Thomas Clarkson*]. The letters were also included in the influential anthology *The Pro-Slavery Argument: As Maintained by the Most Distinguished Writers of the Southern States Containing the Several Essays, on the Subject, of Chancellor Harper, Governor Hammond, Dr. Sim*[*m*]*s, and Professor Dew*.

Hammond's "Oration Delivered before the Two Societies of the South Carolina College, 4th of Dec., 1849" extolled education as the means for developing moral beings and good citizens, not simply as a means for training individuals to enter professions. An excerpt was published as "Intellectual Power" in Evert Augustus and George Long Duyckinck's *Cyclopedia of American Literature: Embracing Personal and Critical Notices of Authors, and Selections from their Writings*.

John Caldwell Calhoun died in Washington, DC, on 31 March 1850 and was interred in Charleston's Saint Philip's Churchyard on 26 April 1850. Testimonials, orations, and plans to create monuments to the deceased statesman's memory continued for several years after his death. Commemorative services gave politicians and political parties opportunities to appropriate Calhoun's life and views to their own uses. At seventy pages, Hammond's oration is the lengthiest item in *Selections*. Hammond examined the man's political career, demonstrating that Calhoun's views on the South and the nation had evolved from his youthful support of the Union and the tariff system that proved so destructive to southern planters. The longtime editor of *The Papers of John C. Calhoun*, Clyde Wilson observed that Hammond's oration was the "best concise account of Calhoun's career and also the best statement in brief compass of the history of antebellum American politics from the Carolina viewpoint" (Hammond, *Selections* xxi). It was published as *An Oration on the Life, Character and Services of John Caldwell Calhoun: Delivered on the 21st Nov., 1850, in Charleston, S.C. at the Request of the City Council* and a variant text was included among twenty five other orations and testimonials in *The Carolina Tribute to Calhoun*, edited by J.P. Thomas.

The "Speech on the Admission of Kansas . . . March 4, 1858" ranged over issues of popular sovereignty and the powers of Congress to regulate the admission of territories to the Union. In it Hammond boasted that the South could survive as an independent nation if the Union were divided by secession. The speech is famous because it contained two statements for which Hammond is most remembered. His challenge to British and northern industrialists became a slogan for southern nationalists: "What would happen if no cotton was furnished for three years? I will not stop to depict what every one can imagine, but this is certain: England would topple headlong and carry the whole civilized world with her save the South. No, you dare not make war on cotton. No power on earth dares to make war upon it. Cotton *is* king" (316–17). Hammond's second "quotable quote" was his expression of a "mud-sill" theory of human society:

> In all social systems there must be a class to do the menial duties, to perform the drudgery of life. . . . Such a class you must have, or you would not have the other class which leads progress, civilization, and refinement. It constitutes the very mud-sill of society and of political government; and you might as well attempt to build a house in the air, as to build either the one or the other, except on this mud-sill. (318)

The South's mud-sill was African American slavery; that of the North was "your whole hireling class of manual laborers and 'operatives,' as you call them"

(Hammond, *Selections* 319). According to Hammond, slaves in the South had been raised from African barbarism to the higher status of mud-sills while in the North white women and men were degraded from their natural dignity to the mud-sill class by economic and social oppression. The North's mud-sill was "galled by their degradation" but, despite their misery, possessed the power of the ballot box. When they discovered their power, they would revolutionize the North as thoroughly as abolitionists sought to revolutionize the South (Hammond, *Selections* 320).

The *Congressional Globe* version of this speech enjoyed considerable distribution in American newspapers. It was published in pamphlet form as *Speech of Hon. James H. Hammond, of South Carolina, on the Admission of Kansas, under the Lecompton Constitution. Delivered in the Senate, of the United States, March 4, 1858.* Excerpts were published in *To the People of the South: Senator Hammond and the Tribune* by "George Michael Troup" and *Are Working Men Slaves?: The Question Discussed by Senators Hammond, [David C.] Broderick and [Henry] Wilson.*

Commenting on Hammond's 29 October 1858 speech at the Barnwell Court House, Wilson suggested that "The moderate tone of the speech lends itself to the suspicion that on the eve of secession the lifelong Southern nationalist had come to accept the Calhounian vision of a united South within the Union. Noteworthy is his desire to do justice to those Northerners who had withstood the anti-Southern currents of the time" (Hammond, *Selections* xxiii). Two pamphlet versions were published: *Speech of Hon. James H. Hammond, delivered at Barnwell C[ourt] H[ouse], October 29th, 1858* and *Speech of Hon. James Hammond, delivered at Barnwell Court House, October 29, 1858.*

Because Hammond resigned from the United States Senate on 11 November 1860 in the wake of Abraham Lincoln's presidential election, his "Speech on the Relations of the States, . . . May 21, 1860" was one of his last public utterances on the sectional crisis. The immediate subject was another examination of the politics of admitting territories to the United States. Hammond disparaged "squatter sovereignty" which had turned Kansas Territory into a proxy war between pro- and antislavery settlers. He recapitulated his remarks on sovereignty and the defense of slavery with the telling observation that "The Senate is weary of it, the country is weary of it, and I, myself, am so weary of it that I have not listened or read, when it was the topic, for months" (365).

Hammond's weariness in 1860 did not afflict Simms or most of the Confederate South. The eleven states of the Confederacy and much of its white population asserted (and most must have believed) that the dissolution of the Union was the third American Revolution, a revolution that had already occurred, and it was time to recognize the fact. The North had revolutionized itself economically, culturally, and ideologically in ways that the South had not. The South had clung to a self-serving vision of the American Republic that bore little resemblance to the nation in 1860. Was the Civil War a "modern" nineteenth-century political revolution spurred on by the evolution of nationalism? Or, was it a rebellion driven by conservatives aiming to preserve an "original intention" version of the American Republic? No matter what lens was used to view the Civil War, by 1862, "weariness" was the pervasive squint. Simms and Hammond wrote each often during the last years of Hammond's life, exchanging lengthy letters on life, politics, and the pervasive "war news" that few could call optimistic by 1862.

Hammond never shook off his weariness with secession and war. He wasted declining energy to complain about Confederate taxes and confiscations and the ineptitude of Confederate generals on the battlefield. For Simms the weariness arrived in waves of misfortune in 1862: his infant daughter Hattie died in January 1862 and his beloved Woodlands Plantation was nearly destroyed by fire on 29 March 1862. The cause of the fire was never reported and may well have been an accident. Simms described the effects of the fire in letters to William Porcher Miles and Hammond, dated April 10, from "Woodlands in Ruins." With the assistance of his slaves he was able to save nearly all of his library and manuscripts collections—his own writings and historical documents—and many of the house furnishings (*Letters* 4: 399–405).

"Woodlands in Ruins" concludes this essay because it demonstrated Hammond's last act of benevolence to his life-long friend. Along with other friends of Simms, Hammond created a subscription fund to rebuild Woodlands. That effort was a gesture of support for the man who had stood by him for more than thirty years, defending his honor amid Hammond's dishonorable acts, and trumpeting Hammond's genius to the state and nation for those same decades. Despite the damage, Simms and his slaves saved most of the library, original and historical manuscripts, some furniture and household furnishings. On 10 April 1862 Simms wrote to Hammond lamenting the "Demonology" and misfortune that "haunts his steps & dogs his career, as tenaciously as ever the Furies clung to the heels of Orestes" (*Letters* 4: 402). Hammond and others lost little time starting a subscription to assist the author.

J. Dickson Bruns, David F. Jamison, George Sass, George A. Trenholm, William Gregg, and Hammond prepared a circular "to raise a purse to be placed at [Simms's] disposal."[12] By June they had raised $3,600 and a neighbor, John S. Jennings, had donated sufficient lumber from his nearby sawmill to enable Simms to begin rebuilding his home on a reduced scale. Simms publicly acknowledged these men's generous acts in a letter of 27 June 1862 published in the *Charleston Mercury* and *Daily Courier* of 8 July 1862. In it he boasted of the strength of his friendships and managed to express some of his characteristic optimism in the face of calamity (*Letters* 4: 409–12).

That optimism perished slowly but inevitably in the coming three years. James Henry Hammond died in November 1864. Three months later the rebuilt

Woodlands was pillaged and destroyed by Union troops and stragglers on 18 February 1865. Columbia and Charleston had surrendered the previous day, and Columbia suffered a catastrophic fire on February 17–18. War weariness became desolation.

NOTES

1. James Henry Hammond to William Gilmore Simms, 12 December 1861, James Henry Hammond Papers, Library of Congress, reel 2380, item 24798.
2. James Henry Hammond, undated, Hammond Papers, Library of Congress, reel 238p, item 25271.
3. Hammond to Simms, 18 February 1862, Library of Congress, reel 2380, item 24808.
4. *House Journal*, 25th Congress, 1st Session (Serial Set No. 285); *House Journal*, 24th Congress, 2nd Session (Serial Set No. 300); *Senate Journal*, 36th Congress, 1st Session and Special Session (Serial Set No. 1022); *Senate Journal*, 36th Congress, 2nd Session and 37th Congress, Special Session (Serial Set No. 1077).
5. *Congressional Globe*, 24th Congress, 1st Session, *Volume III*, 27–33; *Congressional Globe*, 24th Congress, 1st Session, *Volume III, Appendix*, 565–7; and *Register of Debates in Congress, Volume XI, Part 2*, 2492–500.
6. The *Congressional Globe*, 35th Congress, 1st Session, *Appendix*, 69–71, and *Congressional Globe*, 36th Congress, 1st Session, 1633, contain his Senate speeches and remarks.
7. Simms to Marcellus C.M. Hammond, 28 March 1868, *Letters*, 5: 121, n.57; E. Spann Hammond to M.C.M. Hammond, 2 March 1868, Bleser, ed., *Hammonds of Redcliffe*, 156.
8. Kenneth M. Stampp, ed., *Records of Ante-bellum Southern Plantations from the Revolution through the Civil War. Series A, Selections from the South Caroliniana Library, University of South Carolina* (Frederick, MD: University Publications of America, 1985) contains 15 reels of Hammond family material. Reels 13–15 include Hammond plantation journals and scrapbooks from the Library of Congress. Ira Berlin and others, eds., *Records of Southern Plantations from Emancipation to the Great Migration. Series C, Selections from the South Caroliniana Library, University of South Carolina* (Bethesda, MD: UPA Collection from LexisNexis, 2004), Part One contains 22 reels of Hammond family material from six collections. The James Henry Hammond Papers, 1774–1875, Library of Congress Collection MSS24695, fill 20 reels of microfilm available for purchase.
9. Carol Bleser, editor, *The Hammonds of Redcliffe* (New York: Oxford UP, 1981; Columbia: U of South Carolina P, 1997) and *Secret and Sacred: The Diaries of James Henry Hammond, A Southern Slaveholder* (New York: Oxford UP, 1988; Columbia: U of South Carolina P, 1997); *The Papers of John C. Calhoun*, 28 volumes, edited by Robert L. Meriwether and others (Columbia: U of South Carolina P, 1959–2003); *The Letters of William Gilmore Simms*, 6 volumes, edited by Mary C. Simms Oliphant *et al* (Columbia: U of South Carolina P, 1952–2012); James F. Jameson, ed., "Letters on the Nullification Movement in South Carolina, 1830–1834," *American Historical Review* 6, no. 4 (July 1901): 736–52 all contain Hammond correspondence. Drew Gilpin Faust, *A Sacred Circle: The Dilemma of the Intellectual in the Old South, 1840–1860* (Baltimore, MD: Johns Hopkins UP, 1977); *James Henry Hammond and the Old South: A Design for Mastery* (Baton Rouge: Louisiana State UP, 1982).

10. Bleser, ed., *Secret and Sacred*, 169 (Hamptons), 17–9, 231, 234 (Johnsons); Bleser, ed., *Hammonds of Redcliffe*, 9–10, 29–33 (Hamptons), 10–11 (Johnsons); Faust, *James Henry Hammond*, 241–5, 288–91, 302, 313 (Hamptons), 85–8, 303, 315–20 (Johnsons).
11. Recent scholarship on the Brown case includes Betty DeRamus, *Freedom by Any Means: True Stories of Cunning and Courage on the Underground Railroad* (New York: Atria Books, 2009), "Romeo Must Live," 51–67; and Caleb W. McDaniel, "The Case of John L. Brown: Slavery, Sex, South Carolina, and the Whispering Gallery of Transatlantic Abolition," unpublished essay presented at "Civil War—Global Conflict," Carolina Lowcountry and Atlantic World Conference, College of Charleston, 4 March 2011 (http://scholarship.rice.edu/handle/1911/37261, accessed 4 July 2013).
12. J. Dickson Bruns to Hammond, 20 April 1862, Hammond Papers, Library of Congress, reel 2380, item 24822–3.

Simms's Poems: Areytos or Songs and Ballads of the South with Other Poems

JASON W. JOHNSON

William Gilmore Simms once referred to *Simms's Poems: Areytos or Songs and Ballads of the South with Other Poems* (1860) as "a volume containing a selection from my fugitive pieces, song & sonnet, the growings of thirty years" (*Letters* 4: 193). His description is appropriate. The 416 page volume—second in length only to the 700-plus page *Poems: Descriptive, Dramatic, Legendary and Contemplative* (1853)—is a selection of poems, many of which had been published in newspapers and literary journals but never in a collection. These "growings of thirty years" come from every period, and represent well the arc of Simms's career, from the fledgling pieces of a novice to the more nuanced and sophisticated experiments of a wiser and more world-weary poet.

Simms framed these "fugitive pieces" with a title he had used once before, *Areytos; or, Songs of the South*. Though these two volumes bear the same title, the 1860 collection should not be mistaken for merely a second edition of the 1846 collection. More than a few poems from the 1846 volume appear in the 1860 collection (e.g., "My Forest Harp" and "Maid of Congaree"), but many others do not. "The Texian Hunter" and "The Land of the Pine," for example, were published in the first *Areytos* and in the second volume of *Poems*; neither was selected for the 1860 *Areytos*. Presumably, Simms used the title again not to indicate definitely a second edition but because a number of poems in the 1860 volume were "songs of the South." While these aspects of the collection problematize a view of it as simply a second edition, one could argue that it is a continuation of a project begun almost fifteen years earlier, a sequel meant to be read, or at least compiled, with the first collection in mind.

In both volumes Simms explained his choice of such an unusual title. In the dedication of the 1860 volume, he discussed the origin of the word "areytos":

> I need not say to you that the word "Areyto," or "Arieto" is borrowed from the aboriginal language of the island of Cuba. There, at the first coming of Columbus, the gentle race in possession of the soil, inspired by the smiling and blue skies which overarched them, the delicate languors of the

> atmosphere they breathed, the delicate fruits and flowers by which they were encompassed—with blooms and beauties scarcely equaled and seldom subject to change—had their songs of tenderness, of love, of passion, and enthusiasm, to which they gave the name of Areytos. This word, so very musical, belonging thus exclusively to our hemisphere, seems to me deserving of preservation and preference in our literature. It is quite as worthy of use as that of *lay, ballad, canzone,* or *sircente,* and as sweet and significant as any in the poetical dialects of OC and OU. The Provençal troubadour had none more appropriate, for such a collection, in all his melodious vocabulary. (v, emphasis in original)

According to him, then, "areyto" is another word for "song" or "songs of tenderness, of love, of passion, and enthusiasm." The poems in his final collection certainly run this particular gamut of subjects.

But Simms could have used another title to convey the same meaning, as he did decades before in *Early Lays* (1827). His real reason for choosing the title was that the origin was not European but specific to the New World, "belonging thus exclusively to our hemisphere." He here continued the work he began with "Americanism in Literature" (1845), in which he complained that American "writers think after European models, draw their stimulus and provocation from European books, fashion themselves to European tastes, and look chiefly to the awards of European criticism" (*Views* 1: 1). By using a word coined in the New World in a non-European language, Simms informed the reader that the poems or "areytos" that followed would not be imitations of European models, but American in character. He defended the "areyto" by explaining that it was "quite as worthy of use" as any European name such as "*lay, ballad, canzone,* or *sircente.*" In short, Simms's productions, while they might acknowledge their own European origins, were essentially American.

Background

Poems: Descriptive, Dramatic, Legendary and Contemplative (1853) is Simms's most important collection, if not his best.[1] When critics discuss Simms's poems—which, sad to say, is not often—they usually confine their comments to those pieces the poet selected for the two-volume *Poems.* There are a few good reasons. First, the majority of Simms's best work was selected for *Poems.* Second, because the collection surveys over two decades of Simms's output, it is perhaps the most representative of any volume published before or after 1853, with the obvious exception of James Everett Kibler's annotated edition of Simms's selected poems. Such a retrospective selection is convenient for the scholar looking to understand the poet's evolving aesthetic as well as to gain some insight into Simms's taste in his own poetry. Third, *Poems* and Kibler's *Selected Poems of*

William Gilmore Simms are the only extensive editions of the poetry. Therefore, if a scholar does discuss a piece not in *Poems*, chances are that he or she is using Kibler's edition.[2]

In a letter to Evert Augustus Duyckinck, Simms expressed the desire to add to *Poems*: "I am anxious to put forth my complete poetical and dramatic writings in 3 volumes" (*Letters* 5: 90–91). Unfortunately, for Simms scholars, the poet was unable to achieve his aim. Because such a complete edition was never brought to fruition, his last selected poems, *Areytos*, becomes that much more important to Simmsians seeking to better understand the arc of Simms's career.

Exactly when Simms first thought to gather a new poetry selection is uncertain, but he initially discussed the possibility on 18 June 1858 in a letter to J.T. Fields of the Boston publishing firm Ticknor and Fields: "I am thinking of a new collection of 'Southern Passages', & 'Areytos', & should greatly like an edition in blue and gold. When the poetical epoch comes round again, and the public feels a return of its periodical *furore* in behalf of verse, advise me of your readiness to avail yourself of the spasm" (*Letters* 4: 67). Apparently, Ticknor and Fields did not predict such a "poetical epoch" any time soon, as they never published the proposed volume. Simms spent the next two years assembling and revising the manuscript before submitting it to Justus Redfield, who agreed to publish it. Sometime during the summer of 1860, Simms went to New York to foster the book through the press. He believed he would finish the publication process by the first week of September (*Letters* 4: 238), but as Kibler points out, he "had received at least some of the proofs by Sept. 28, 1860" (*Poetry* 103).

Until this point, Simms had faced problems most authors encounter when publishing a book. But in addition to these common problems, Simms was beginning to contend with more than a little reluctance from his publisher. He reported the first sign of trouble to James Lawson in November:

> He, Redfield, wrote me that now was not the time for publication. In other words he was not in a condition to publish. But there would be a sale of the small edition I proposed, say 250 copies:—as I stated R & J. [Russell and Jones] had alone agreed for 100, or 200, and I wished 50 myself, to give away, resolving that the Publisher should not exercise the right exclusively of giving copies, & meaning to give them to such only as were worthy, and willing to read poetry. (*Letters* 4: 261)

Not only did Redfield not do a run of the book under the firm's own name, but the publisher did not pay for the stereotyping, leaving the cost to the author. Redfield owed Simms "over 600 dollars" in royalties (*Letters* 4: 269), and it was with this balance that the author paid for the stereotyping. In the same letter to Lawson, Simms wrote with obvious frustration, "What a commentary upon the way I am treated by all these men that after the book is stereotyped, there is no publisher among them" (*Letters* 4: 269). The change in plans meant that there would be further delays. The volume was finally released in December 1860, but its market was limited to Charleston.

Simms's troubles did not end after the small run had been released. Sometime before March 17, the author learned that a number of copies of *Areytos* had been destroyed by fire. In disbelief, Simms wrote to Lawson asking, "Are you sure that my books *were* burned"? Simms then reflected on the perpetual presence of fire in his life, both personal and literary: "It seems to be my luck to be always in danger of fire. My plates destroyed by fire in Harper's vaults; my House destroyed by fire; my books in Widdleton's hands by fire; my books (Areytos) in Redfield's hands destroyed by fire. What the d—l does it mean? Here is a chapter of mischances, all in my case, which should hardly occur in the case of any three other persons" (*Letters* 4: 350, emphasis in original). Apparently Simms had his doubts that this particular fire had occurred: "I fancy this fire is sometimes a false fire and an invention. See if Redfield approves of this faith in fire: If he believes in Widdleton's fire" (*Letters* 4: 350). Kibler argues that Simms's incredulity as to the fate of the copies is understandable and that he "had a right to question if Redfield was withholding the copies under the guise of their being burned," considering how the publisher had mistreated him only months before (*Poetry* 104).

Exactly why Redfield dealt so badly with Simms is not immediately clear. After all, as John Caldwell Guilds points out, Simms was the New York firm's "mainstay Southern author" (*Literary Life* 278). Guilds and Kibler argue that the reasons for such mistreatment were financial and political. Guilds contends that, "as sectional animosity grew, particularly after the secession of South Carolina, the New York publisher exploited the situation" by "withholding royalties" from Simms (*Literary Life* 278). Kibler writes that "the whole affair is revelatory of the quiet manner in which Northern business interest took advantage of a difficult situation" (*Poetry* 104). That is, Redfield realized that he could use the growing tension between North and South to save money at Simms's expense. This line of reasoning works if we are only concerned with explaining Redfield's refusal to pay Simms the $600 in royalties owed him, but it does not explain why the publisher printed the book for another imprint yet did not market the text in New York. After all, he had often published more-or-less simultaneously, with Simms's Charleston publishers, apparently printing the copies for both houses.

Though Redfield's printing and marketing decisions were in part financially motivated, the firm was probably not "trying to take advantage of a difficult situation"; rather, it was trying to avoid placing itself in a difficult situation by distancing itself from *Areytos*. As the title indicates, many of the poems were "Songs and Ballads of the South." Perhaps Redfield thought that poems about the South would not sell well in the North in a time of such regional tension. In fact, he surmised that "now was not the *time* for publication," meaning perhaps that the book's subject matter would impede sales. Also, Redfield might have believed that the northern reading public would be unforgiving of a New York publisher who allied himself with the South and with a writer who had been such an outspoken anti-abolitionist. Not only might he lose money on *Areytos*, but he might also lose across the board. Had the volume been proposed a decade earlier, the New York firm probably would have published it under the Redfield name. But the combination of the collection's southern subject matter, the author's proslavery stance, and the political climate of the time made the venture far too risky, especially given Redfield's precarious financial circumstances, which led to his bankruptcy within months.

Because of the collection's limited market and lack of popularity, *Areytos* never went to a second printing, much less a second edition. Consequently, Simms's final collection did not see the light of day again until the spring of 2012 when the *Simms Initiatives* digitized it and made available both a new print version and a full-text searchable online version on the *Initiatives* website. For the first time in its 152 year history, therefore, *Areytos* became accessible to anyone in the world, not simply to the residents of and travelers to the Simms holdings at the South Caroliniana Library in Columbia, South Carolina.

Characteristics

In so many ways *Areytos* serves as an excellent model of a collection of selected poems, particularly if a selection is supposed to represent the concerns and obsessions of the poet. A reader unfamiliar with Simms's poetry could become aware of the poet's concerns and obsessions simply by reading *Areytos*. Thus, in terms of both form and content, Simms successfully assembled a volume that accurately portrayed the recurring preoccupations of a long career.

His interest in poetic form is evident from the title of the collection. By focusing on the sonic quality of the aboriginal word "areyto," which he called "so very musical" (*Areytos* v), Simms directed the reader to pay close attention to the sonic qualities of the entire volume, as well as to the author's use of form to create a non-European American literature.[3] Consider Simms's experiments with the sonnet. While he followed the "European models" to the letter from time to time, he regularly—in fact, usually—deviated from the legitimate format and created his own.[4] Most of the sonnets in *Areytos* followed the latter trend. His innovations often mixed two different sonnet forms, such as the rhyme schemes of the Italian and English traditions. He also quite regularly departed even further by inventing a rhyme scheme out of whole cloth. Of course, Simms did not isolate his experiment to one form. Several poems in *Areytos* that bear the title "ballad" do not approximate in any way the ballad stanza one would find in *Percy's Reliques of Ancient English Poetry* or Sir Walter Scott's *Minstrelsy of the Scottish Border*. A number of "ballads" are written in non-ballad meters (iambic pentameter, for example) and rely on elaborate rhyme schemes that we might associate with the troubadour tradition Simms mentioned in the dedication.

Just as often as he tinkered and revised existing traditions, Simms created his own forms, stanzas, and rhyme schemes that have no European predecessor, or any precedent for that matter. Take, for example, "Come, While the Evening Sets Sweet and Clear," a stanza of Simms's own invention which runs $abab_4cc_2d_4ee_2dff_4$. These experiments with poetic form are one of the more distinctive characteristics of the collection. Unfortunately, in a number of poems, such experiments are the only redeeming quality. The best poems in *Areytos*, and they are numerous, rather are perfect syntheses of form and content.

Not only did Simms provide a variety of poetic forms, but he wrote about a wide range of topics. As Kibler has noted, "The world of Simms is indeed expansive; the scope of his art can in no sense be labeled narrow. In fact, a good case could be made for his being the most richly diverse of all our American poets, old or new" (*Selected* [2010] xix). Though lacking the expansiveness of *Poems*, *Areytos* is "richly diverse" nonetheless. A number of subjects appear briefly in the collection. Religion, for example, is only discussed directly occasionally but is represented well in "The Bride of Christ," a poem not critical of Christianity but of the Church (i.e., the manmade institution of Christianity).

A few of the poems are little more than versified advice, as in the case of "Strike!—As Said the Anvil" (58). The speaker tells a young man, "Speed to the work!—we'll all have time for sleeping, / When we have shuffled off these mortal coils" (58).[5] The poem—which echoes the cliché, "Strike while the iron is hot"—reminds us that only "seventy years [are] allotted to the best," so we must not procrastinate but fulfill our purpose now (58). The transience of this life is also dealt with in "Now, When the Spring Is Over" (62); unlike the previous poem, though, the speaker does not offer advice, but simply states that all is fleeting and that nothing lasts and that the young will soon grow old and die.

A number of other minor subjects and themes crop up, but most of the poems fall into only a few categories. One of the more prominent subjects in the collection is love. Most of these poems, however, lack the depth of much of Simms's best work. Repeated readings of these pieces generally are not necessary, as most of them suffer from transparency and univocality. "Serenader Implores His Mistress to Come Forth" (229) and "Why Meet Me with Aspect So Chilling?" (17) are good examples of the kind of love poems Simms selected for *Areytos*. Not all of such poems are quite so superficial. Consider, for example, "Now Weave Your Spells, Young Maiden," in which Simms alluded to "Sir Patrick Spens":

Now weave your spells, young maiden—
Love's sweet and mystic charms;
For the old moon now comes laden
With the young moon in her arms. (181)

The last two lines echo closely two lines from the Scottish popular ballad:

I saw the new moon late yestreen
With the old moon in her arms;
And if we go to sea, master,
I fear we'll come to harm. (Child no. 58)

By appropriating lines from a tragic ballad, Simms indicated that the spell cast by the maiden will have tragic results. A reader must be familiar with "Sir Patrick Spens" in order to fully understand the poem. Such an allusion adds depth to the piece and necessitates several readings, characteristics not shared by most of the love poems in the selection.

While Simms's love poems tend to be shallow, the majority of the poems concerning nature have a depth and sophistication one might expect to find in the mature work of Wordsworth and Coleridge. As Kibler points out, Simms "writes of nature and of nature's manifold roles as teacher, source of inspiration, restorer of a tired spirit, spiritual guide, aid to reflection, nurturer, and symbol of immortality" (*Selected* [2010] xxiv). In *Areytos*, Simms discussed all of nature's "manifold roles." The "Chimney Cricket" (173–179) is an example of nature as teacher and spiritual guide. According to the speaker, it is the cricket's job to "[t]each your young ones truthful seeing, / And conduct them to the beauty / That lies sure in homely duty!" (177). In "The Mountain Winds" (65–70), Simms celebrated the beauty of Mount Tyron, and frames the mountain, and nature, as teacher, as nurturer, as spiritual guide, as symbol of immortality, and as restorer: "and the exquisite repose / Of nature, from the striving world releases, / Taught me forgetfulness of mortal throes, / Life's toils, and all the cares that wait on human woes" (65). In all of his nature poems, nature is a source of inspiration and an aid to reflection.

Simms thus expressed his own ideas of Romanticism, a philosophy he learned from the British Romantic poets. He did not conceal his influences, but instead "[made] his debts explicit," often echoing poems by poets such as Wordsworth and Coleridge (Brennan, *Holy Craft* 78). In "My Forest Harp," Simms used the title to allude to Coleridge's "The Eolian Harp." As Matthew C. Brennan has noted, "Simms's use of the wind image draws especially on the associations of renewal and of imaginative power" (*Holy Craft* 90). In poems such as "My Forest Harp," in which the "wind image" signifies such renewal, Simms implicitly acknowledged Coleridge, who more than any of his British contemporaries, used the motif to great effect. A reader well versed in Coleridge would certainly trace Simms's image back to the author of "The Eolian Harp." Not only did Simms borrow images from his British forbears, but on occasion he quoted their work directly, as he did in "Chimney Cricket," when he called the insect "Thou best philosopher" (176), a direct quote from Wordsworth's "Intimations" ode (l: 110).

Even though these themes play an important role in the collection, they are overshadowed by the "Poems and Ballads of the South," for which the book is named. The bulk of these poems were written several years before the publication of the 1860 *Areytos*. A number celebrate southern landscapes; an example is "Oh, the Sweet South!," which describes the landscape and its maternal relationship with the poet (9). But the majority of these poems are patriotic pieces, some to the point of xenophobia. First published in 1856, "Elegiac.—It Is the Cause," for example, is a warning to southerners in general and to South Carolinians in particular to be mindful of foreign power. The foreign power Simms described was not England or Mexico, but the northern United States and the federal government. His poems about the Mexican-American War appeared in the late 1840s. His poems that address England as the enemy are about the American Revolution or the War of 1812.

Overall, the poems about these earlier conflicts give specific details that indicate the subject of the text. "Elegiac," on the other hand, offers no such clues. Simms's contemporaries would not have needed any, as a political and moral divide between North and South was well under way. Simms characterized "the Cause" (a word he capitalized throughout) as a crusade, writing that the South ". . . needs some noble martyr, / To bear his breast, and perish for his kind!" (63). The word "kind" suggests a xenophobia that had become common in both regions. The poem is a call to arms, an admonition to a people who have grown too comfortable and, as a result, are unaware of "the Destinies that wait" (63).

There are other poems like this one, but most of them are not as effective because they rely too often on abstract language rather than on images, a characteristic that makes "Elegiac" such a provocative piece. The better southern patriotic pieces in *Areytos* are instead about the Mexican-American War. Most of the poems in this vein are placed near the end of the volume in a sequence about the exploits of the Palmetto Regiment, called by Simms "our gallant little regiment" (*Areytos* v). The poems in this sequence are an encomium on South Carolina's contribution to the nation's victory in the conflict with Mexico.

The series begins at the end of the war with "Ode.—Welcome, Thrice Welcome," which, according to Simms, "was written to welcome the return of the remnant of the Palmetto Regiment from Mexico" (*Areytos* 381). The ode both celebrates their return and laments the loss of so many men. Following the ode, Simms related chronologically the movements and losses of the regiment, beginning with their organization before departure in "Carolinians, Who Inherit" (384) and continuing with "The March to Alvarado," which details the loss of soldiers on the march to Mexico. Simms detailed the regiment's desire to join the fight in "We've a Right from Ancient Valor" (391). But not all of the poems are about the regiment as a single entity. In fact, a few are elegies for individuals who died and those at home who bore the loss. "The Widow of the Warrior" (394), for example, describes a woman's grief over the loss of her soldier husband. Simms did not simply discuss the war and the army in terms of battles and casualties *en masse* but reminded us of the personal aspect of war. Such a nuanced and sophisticated depiction is lacking in Simms's other patriotic poems, which often suffer from a didacticism that borders on propaganda.

The majority of the regiment poems were first published in *Lays of the Palmetto: A Tribute to the South Carolina Regiment, in the War with Mexico* (1848). As Simms explained in the dedication to *Areytos*, "Most of [the poems in *Lays of the Palmetto*] were written at the moment when the event which they seek to honor first reached our ears" (v). These poems were not reflections but what Simms called in the advertisement to *Lays* "almost improvisations, outpourings of a full heart" (3).

Even though the regiment poems are not secessionist or xenophobic, Simms must have been aware when he selected them for *Areytos* that the public might very well read them with rising regional tension in mind. In a letter—the letter in which he relayed Redfield's decision not to issue the book—Simms discussed the timing of the book's release: "This is the very time for that vol. in the South, a large portion of the material being patriotic" (*Letters* 4: 261). Whether or not Simms included the lays in *Areytos* because of the growing regional tension, he clearly saw the necessity of such patriotic verse, which he hoped would galvanize and encourage his southern readers in uncertain times.

Reception, Then and Now

Despite the book's subject matter, it did not fare well with the southern reading public. In an attempt to justify the volume's relative failure, Simms explained to Lawson that "people here breathe nothing but war, & read none but military books now" (*Letters* 4: 326). That *Areytos* only achieved marginal commercial success cannot be blamed on negative reviews, but rather on a public that usually might be interested in a volume like Simms's but that at the time had other tastes and concerns. Yet reviewers, both northern and southern, had not lost their interest in Simms's verse, as is evidenced by their positive reception of *Areytos*. Not surprisingly, northern critics and their southern counterparts saw the collection quite differently.

The critic for the *Charleston Mercury* (22 December 1860) praised the book without qualification but only took interest in the southern patriotic verse. In this particular instance, *Areytos* was used for a larger political purpose, as is evidenced by the placement of the review. On the same page appeared an article titled "E Pluribus Unum," in which the anonymous author wrote: "The most impressive feature in the action of South Carolina is the concentrated unanimity of her people. Having long, carefully and deliberately considered her position in the Federal Union, and arrived at her conclusion, her people have come up to the work of her independence from vassalage and ruin under Northern rule" (Rev. of *Areytos*). Such vitriolic, stirring language was compounded by a piece on

"The Demonstration Last Night" in which the author reported: "A very imposing procession marched last night through our principal streets with flags and several bands of music. The Washington Artillery, the Zonaves, the Palmetto Riflemen, the Cadet Riflemen, the Carolina Light Infantry, the Union Light Infantry, the German Fire Company, the Minute Men and the citizens generally, participated."

These two articles and the patriotic speeches that follow all suggest that Simms's poetry was being drafted in service to the Cause. While Simms would have been happier had his southern reviewers discussed in more detail the complexities and nuances of the book, he must have approved of their conscription of the patriotic verse. The review ignored entirely all other aspects of *Areytos* in order to rally its readers around the Palmetto flag.

The *Southern Literary Messenger* likewise discussed the southern verse, writing that "Mr. Simms's muse is a patriotic goddess" (Rev. of *Areytos* 157). Of the patriotic verse, the anonymous reviewer paid particular attention to "Make Gay the Spear with Flowers" and "The Ballad of Old Hickorie." Of the former poem he stated, "[it] breathes a spirit of strategic defence, with stirring appeals to be prompt in action, nor let an opportunity slip, which may be mourned for when it cannot be recalled" (Rev. of *Areytos* 157). Of the latter, he wrote: "'The Ballad of Old Hickorie' hurries you along with it irresistibly as you read, producing the effect of lively martial music, to which your feet must keep time, whether your will go along or not, and you presently find yourself marching whether you will or not" (ibid.). Unlike the *Mercury* reviewer though, the critic for the *Messenger* penned a more comprehensive appraisal, taking into account not only the patriotic verse, but poems in other veins as well. For example, he quoted "The Lost Pleiad" extensively and praised Simms's handling of the theme of "[t]he obliteration of a world from the Universe" (ibid.).

Not only did the reviewer praise individual poems but he spoke well of the book in general: "Throughout a great portion of the songs in this volume there is a vein of exquisite sadness, which is apt to be the tone of all poetry which is not intensely young; of poetry which has had its boyishness, its huge credulity, its positiveness as to the heroism in man and the angelism in woman rudely chipped, rubbed, scraped off, by observant criticism, and daily contact with a world anything but the creation of a boy-poet" (158). The critic's balanced treatment suggests that the *Messenger* did not see Simms's volume primarily in service to the Cause, but judged it as a work of literature, not propaganda.

Northern reviewers were not critical of the patriotic verse; in fact, they did not discuss those poems at all. In the book notices for March 1861, Louis Godey praised the volume, focusing on the poet's formal gifts: "The lyre of Mr. Sims [*sic*] is one whose tones must always command approval. Classical without coldness, the poetic utterances in this present volume are such as will add to their author's already high reputation" (275). The reviewer for *Harper's* likewise praised the poet and his poems. While acknowledging Simms's "eminent position in American literature depends on his merits as a novelist rather than on his poetical productions, the latter, which are here collected in a volume, evince the genuine feeling of the poet, and powers both of imagination and expression of no common order" (Rev. of *Areytos* 411). Even when critical of the poet and his craft, as he was of Simms's versification, which he described as "unequal," he praised his handling of form as being "vigorous and spirited" (ibid.). Notice here that the reviewer did not frame Simms as a southern, but as an American, poet. In this regard, the *Harper's* review is more than fair.

Two points are worth considering about the North's response to *Areytos*. First, if these two reviews are any indication of northern reception of the book, then Redfield's apparent concerns were clearly unfounded. Kibler is right when he points out the attacks leveled at Simms by the northern press (*Poetry* 101). But, while northern newspapers may have been critical of Simms's failed 1856 lecture tour in the North, as well as of his anti-abolitionist attacks on Harriet Martineau, they obviously approved of his poetry. Such approval suggests a complex response to a complex human being.

Unfortunately for Simms, the critical attention to *Areytos* was brief, if generally favorable. Of course, the volume has received some attention by scholars more recently, but by and large it has been consigned to oblivion. There are three notable exceptions. The first scholarly consideration of the volume is Kibler's brief discussion in *The Poetry of William Gilmore Simms: An Introduction and Bibliography*, a seminal account of the book's origins and publication background. Any understanding of *Areytos* must begin with Kibler's entry. Guilds wrote the second treatment of the volume in *Simms: A Literary Life*. Like Kibler, Guilds offers a history of the book's conception, publication and reception (277–78). Matthew C. Brennan, in *The Poet's Holy Craft: William Gilmore Simms and Romantic Verse Tradition*, offers an invaluable discussion of Simms's revision strategies in *Areytos*. Like Kibler (*Poetry* 102), Brennan concludes, after consideration of Simms's letters about *Areytos*, that the poet did not find revision as distasteful as has been supposed (*Holy Craft* 50).

While no one has done a thorough analysis of the volume as a whole, a few of the poems in *Areytos* have received substantial attention from Kibler and Brennan. In *The Selected Poems of William Gilmore Simms*, Kibler offers thorough notes on poems selected from the 1860 collection, such as "Chimney Cricket" (397–98n) and "The Slain Eagle (Saluda)" (340–41n). His notes on these poems and many others from *Areytos* often go beyond historical and personal context into insightful analysis. In *The Poet's Holy Craft*, Brennan discusses a number of the poems from Simms's last volume of poetry. For example, he considers Simms's "Lamia.—the Beautiful Sin" in comparison with Keats's "Lamia," pointing out that "Simms's speaker despite his 'pall'd and palsied soul' successfully flees and ends his narrative in a distinctly un-Keatsian but conventionally Victorian way: He blesses 'the good God for the granted grace'" (*Holy Craft* 39). Brennan performs a number of other deft interpretations, but his discussion of "Lamia" is his most valuable contribution.

Kibler, Guilds, and Brennan have laid the groundwork for a reading of *Areytos*, but there is still much to be done if we are to understand the collection's overall affect. Thus far, the individual poems that have been culled from the book have not been read within the context of the volume. The very nature of the work, as a selected poems, lends itself to such a strategy, but a reading of *Areytos* as a single text would yield interesting results. How does one poem play off an adjacent poem? How does this poem relate to another of the same subject? Is there a continuous narrative that runs from the beginning to the end of the volume, or do the poems run at cross purposes? That is, do poems contradict each other or do they serve to support one another and in so doing generate a unified set of themes? Who are the notable influences on Simms in this book? How does form play a role, not simply in individual pieces, but in the collection as a whole? Are the same formal strategies used throughout and, if so, why? Does a particular meter recur in the text and, if so, why? The list of questions could go on and on. An attempt to answer just a few of them would serve to complicate an already complicated *oeuvre* and an even more complicated poet. Now that *Areytos* is available in print again, there is no reason why these inquiries cannot commence.

NOTES

1. The publication history offered here would not be possible without Kibler's researches in *The Poetry of William Gilmore Simms: An Introduction and Bibliography*.
2. Other resources have been available to the Simms scholar. *The Simms Reader: Selections from the Writings of William Gilmore Simms* edited by John Caldwell Guilds and *An Early and Strong Sympathy: The Indian Writings of William Gilmore Simms* edited by Guilds and Charles Hudson offer a sampling of the poetry, but with a few notable exceptions (for example, "The Mountain Tramp" in *An Early and Strong Sympathy*), the selections can be found in Kibler's edition.
3. For a more detailed discussion on the ways in which Simms uses form to establish a distinctive, non-derivative American literature, see my article, "'Dazzling Outlawries of the Imagination': William Gilmore Simms and the 'Americanism' of the Sonnet."
4. The most comprehensive study of Simms's sonnets is Brennan's *The Poet's Holy Craft: William Gilmore Simms and Romantic Verse Tradition*. In Chapter Three, "The Romantic Sonnet," Brennan offers several examples of Simms's formal innovations of the sonnet. Brennan also provides two helpful appendices in which he lists a number of rhyme schemes Simms used in his experiments in the sonnet tradition (141–43).
5. As there are no line numbers in this particular edition of *Areytos*, the citations refer to page numbers. Quotes from the texts of other poets such are cited by line number unless otherwise indicated.

Social and Political Prose

Slavery in America and *Father Abbot*

EHREN FOLEY

In 1833 William Gilmore Simms found himself an erstwhile Unionist newspaper editor who had sunk his own personal funds into trying to save the moribund Charleston *City Gazette*. As a champion of free expression and opponent of nullification, he had placed himself in opposition to two powerful political forces within South Carolina, H. L. Pinckney's Charleston *Mercury* and John C. Calhoun. Throughout the heated political debates, Simms and Pinckney would exchange increasingly vicious editorials, with Pinckney, especially, moving beyond the political and engaging in personal attacks against Simms's character. Simms would emerge from the Nullification debates badly bruised, both personally and politically, and as his *City Gazette* fell into oblivion, he retreated from the overtly political world of newspaper editing and instead focused his attention towards his work as a novelist, poet, and social critic (Wakelyn 19–40).

It was in the service of these more literary pursuits that Simms began editing *The Cosmopolitan*, a short-lived journal published in Charleston, in the spring of 1833.[1] In the first number he engaged in a dialogue about the value of historical romances to the creation of a national literature. His argument was that authors should focus their attention on those regions and places with which they were most familiar. On that basis he lamented that James Fenimore Cooper, in his most recent productions, had allowed himself to stray far away from the sketches of the people and landscapes of upstate New York that had defined his earlier career (*Cosmopolitan* 22–24; Wakelyn 54). This emphasis on the importance of local and regional literature to the creation of a truly American literature would become a powerful focus for Simms as he entered the next stage of his career as an author and editor.

For the next fifteen years or so, Simms, along with a cohort of American authors and artists—Edgar Allan Poe, Nathaniel Hawthorne, Herman Melville, Evert Augustus Duyckinck, and Thomas Cole among them—would pursue this cultural agenda with vigor. They were all members of the loosely affiliated movement that became known as "Young America," and they tended to be Democratic in their politics and nationalist in their cultural outlook.[2] Simms would champion this quest for an American literature through a number of literary outlets, from his historical romances, to his poetry, to his short fiction, and even through his voluminous writings as a review essayist. Two of Simms's seemingly distinct works—the first, *Slavery in America*, an extended review essay critiquing Harriet Martineau's *Society in America* (1837), and the second, *Father Abbot*, a series of dialogues between the fictional Father Abbot and his disciples—are unified in their attempt to describe, explain, and defend the society and culture of Simms's region, the American South. They both, in their own way, were part of the broader cultural agenda that Simms had pursued since at least the early 1830s, though they also hint at how his thinking would evolve by the eve of the Compromise of 1850. By the time he penned *Father Abbot* in the fall of 1849 his nationalism had transitioned into a commitment to sectionalism. In a letter to Virginian Nathaniel Beverly Tucker in January 1850 Simms made the point plainly. "The idea grows upon us rapidly, and we are pleased to think upon the Southern people," he wrote, "I have long since regarded the separation as a now inevitable necessity" (*Letters* 3: 8).

Intellectually the transition was significant, but, for Simms, it was not especially abrupt. Instead, the move was subtle, at least in his writing, as evidenced by *Slavery in America* and *Father Abbot*. He had always believed that sectional literature was the gateway to national literature and wrote in the dedication to the Redfield edition of *The Wigwam and the Cabin* (1856), "No one mind can fully or fairly illustrate the characteristics of any great country; and he who shall depict *one section* faithfully, has made his proper and sufficient contribution to the great work of *national* illustration" (4, emphasis in original). But the politics of the late 1840s, especially the tensions arising from the war with Mexico and the battles over the slavery question in the territories acquired as a result, had led Simms to believe that the nation as presently constituted could not long endure. These same tensions had also caused "Young America" to crumble under the weight of the sectional crisis. This disintegration was particularly evident in that more idealistic strain of the movement that was focused on the production of cultural nationalism through literature and the arts during the 1830s and 1840s, and that Simms had done so much to foster.[3] By the late 1840s Simms had effectively transitioned from a writer who believed that by writing sectional literature he, along with others, could produce an American nation, to one who remained committed to writing sectional literature, but who now did so in the service of what he hoped would become a unified southern nation.

Slavery in America

Simms's commitment to writing sectional literature—first in service to the American nation and later in service to a southern one—had, almost of necessity, included a willingness to interject the proslavery argument into his themes. In *The Yemassee* (1835), for instance, the character Hector, a slave, refuses to accept freedom when it is offered to him, explaining that he was unfit for it and incapable of handling such independence. These themes, the civilizing force of slavery and the potential dangers of unbounded freedom, had become a centerpiece of the proslavery argument as articulated by southern intellectuals, Simms among them. The argument rejected the more radical contentions about human equality that were finding increasing voice along the fringes of the northern free labor society, most especially by those caught up in the various idealist revolutions then underway—be they revivalist, socialist, transcendentalist, or abolitionist. Increasingly, though, southern intellectuals offered a critique of these emerging ideologies and developed an alternate worldview, one that celebrated individualism and human difference, and, of course, defended the perpetuation of human bondage.

Simms's most notable and sustained defense of southern society and southern slavery, at least in a work of non-fiction, came in 1837 when he was offered the opportunity to review *Society in America* (1837), written by the English social theorist Harriet Martineau, for the Richmond-based *Southern Literary Messenger*. His essay quickly gained wide circulation and newspaper articles throughout the South quoted from Simms's review (Wakelyn 65). Its popularity convinced the publisher of the *Messenger*, Thomas W. White, to issue a significantly expanded version of the review in pamphlet form, which he did in 1839. Like the original review, the pamphlet, released under the title *Slavery in America; Being a Brief Review of Miss Martineau on that Subject*, received warm notice. Two New York papers, both with a strong literary persuasion, the New York *Mirror*—where southerner Edgar Allan Poe served as a literary critic—and the New York *Evening Post*—where noted poet and Simms friend William Cullen Bryant was editor-in-chief—each noticed Simms's *Slavery in America* and offered favorable reviews (Butterworth and Kibler 43). Later, it was also included in the 1852 collection, *The Pro-Slavery Argument*, issued first by Walker, Richards, and Co. of Charleston and then, in 1853, by Lippincott, Grambo, and Co. of Philadelphia. That five-hundred page tome included essays by leading lights in southern society and politics, including William Harper, James Henry Hammond, Thomas Roderick Dew, and, of course, Simms. The essay's success, and extended relevance to southern thought, served to divorce it somewhat from the occasion of its original production, which was the review of Martineau's book. Indeed, it may represent that exceptionally rare instance where a review essay proves more significant, or at least more enduring, than the work it treats.

Harriet Martineau had travelled to the United States in 1834, and for two years she toured the country recording her observations, which she published in two volumes. *Society in America* was wide-ranging and discussed a number of topics, from government to agriculture to manufacturing, but in his review Simms focused special attention upon Martineau's chapter entitled "Morals of Economy," and more specifically upon the section touching upon the "Morals of Slavery." While Martineau began her chapter by recounting two extraordinary examples of slaveholders who went to great personal sacrifice to protect their bondpeople—one in South Carolina who personally nursed his slaves during a cholera outbreak and another who sold his slaves rather than have them abused by his young wife—the thrust of her chapter was the hypocrisy and degradation inherent within the system, which, she argued, infected all participants, both white and black (Martineau 2: 312–52). Her position as an outsider within both American and southern society gave her a unique perspective and one that remains worthy of perusal. For Simms, though, Martineau's foreignness utterly disqualified her to comment upon the southern social order. To contend otherwise would have run counter to his long-standing belief that to truly know a nation or a people an individual needed to be of that place. That was, after all, the rationale that led him to write, when not treating literature, almost exclusively about southern and western themes, and to argue that other writers should also explore the intricacies of their own regions. Simms's attack on Martineau's understanding of southern society, however, did not end with her foreignness. In fact, his arguments ranged far beyond Martineau's text, and he used the review essay instead as a vehicle for exploring and articulating his own views about proper social order, civilization, and race. It is the expansive quality of the essay that makes it worthy of study today.

For Simms, slavery was merely one facet of a properly ordered society, one built upon organic hierarchy and the interconnectedness of labor and capital. It was this organic whole that Simms envisioned when he viewed southern slave society and that was threatened by the various –isms and –ologies then being spawned in Europe and the American North. The very basis of this organic society, however, was inequality, and Simms made clear his break with Jefferson's dictum that all men were created equal. Of course that was a fallacy, he argued, as even a cursory study of either nature or human society would reveal. Interrogating this notion of fundamental equality, he wrote:

> The stars are lovely in their inequalities, the hills, the trees, the rivers and the seas; and it is from their very inequalities that their harmonies arise. Were it otherwise, the eye would be pained by the monotony of the prospect everywhere. As it is, we love to look abroad upon nature, and it is with a pleasure no less sensible than that of the savage, that we learn 'how to name the bigger light and how the less.' They have their names only as they are unlike and unequal. It is because these shine *in their places*, however inferior to other orbs, that they are lovely. (*Slavery* 62, emphasis in original)

It was the organic hierarchy offered by slavery, Simms argued, that was the key to a properly ordered society and that provided the remedy for the social fissures that had prepared the way for the downfall of older nations and empires. By uniting the interests of labor and capital, slavery protected against the urban riots and social upheavals that invariably led to the imposition of dictatorships and the destruction of republican liberty. Even more than that, a hierarchical society recognized something fundamental within nature: that each individual within a society had different capacities and abilities. Or, to reverse another Jefferson quotation, some were, in fact, born booted and spurred and others born with saddles on their backs. Obviously this construction appealed to members of the master class, but, perhaps just as much, it also appealed to southern intellectuals like Simms. Not only did the logic justify holding some men in bondage, but it also suggested the superiority of a man of letters within a society that too often neglected his talents.[4] In the era of the "common man" and the expansion of political democracy within the nation, the proslavery argument served not only to defend black bondage, it also served as a full-throated defense of social hierarchy more generally at a time when that notion seemed under attack.

The point was an important one for Simms and others who contended that the founders "were democrats, not levellers." To properly understand the founders' republic, and to establish proper social harmony, it was necessary to recognize that:

> Democracy is not leveling—it is, properly defined, the harmony of the moral world. It insists upon inequalities, as its law declares, that all men should hold the place to which they are properly entitled. The definition of true liberty, is the undisturbed possession of that place in society to which our moral and intellectual merits entitle us. *He is a freeman, whatever his condition, who fills his proper place. He is a slave only, who is forced into a position in society below the claims of his intellect.* (*Slavery* 65, emphasis in original)

It was this logic that allowed Simms to conclude at the end of *Slavery in America* that it was improper to apply the appellation of slave to the servile in the South. "He is under no despotic power," Simms argued, "There are laws which protect him, *in his place*, as inflexible as those which his proprietor is required to obey, *in his place. Providence has placed him in our hands, for his good, and has paid us from his labor for our guardianship*" (82–83, emphasis in original). Every man in his place, each fulfilling his divine sanction, this was the true definition of liberty for Simms. It was the social order described by Hector in *The Yemassee* when he refused his freedom, and it was a social vision outlined in countless other of Simms's writings. Unbounded individualism was a path to chaos and disorder. It threatened to rend asunder the Great Chain of Being and destroy the God-inspired social order that southern intellectuals identified within their own society.

These divergent visions of the relation of the individual to society lay at the heart of the emerging conflict between pro- and antislavery thought. It was an area where intellectually, and even religiously, the North was beginning to divide from the South. The evangelical fervor that swept through places like upstate New York, carried by charismatic purveyors such as Charles Grandison Finney and that spawned countless religious movements, including Joseph Smith's Latter Day Saints, tended to carry with it a more optimistic vision of human nature, one that celebrated the possibility for individual and social perfectibility. It was the spiritual and intellectual fuel behind so many of the social reform and social utopian movements that Simms identified as threatening the very fabric of society. Like many other southerners, even under the influence of the Second Great Awakening, he tended to subscribe to a more orthodox Christianity. These southerners retained a belief in the innate sinfulness of man and averred that only through a social order that imposed proper discipline could man truly thrive and achieve his proper station in life. They worried about, and wrote withering critiques, as Simms did in *Slavery in America*, of a social order that accepted the exploitation of laborers without the guidance of a ruling class that would provide material aid and spiritual guidance. Slavery, Simms and other southern intellectuals argued, offered a different path. It protected labor under the guiding hand of the master. It was a patronizing view of slaves, one grounded firmly in a deeply held paternalistic worldview, and it also offered a skeptical view of human nature. But it was at the same time a worldview grounded in a particular understanding of Christian morality (Fox-Genovese and Genovese, "Divine" 211–33).[5]

Because of the centrality of Christianity in the development and articulation of the slaveholders' worldview, and of the proslavery argument, it is worth paying special attention to Simms's use of religion in both of the following texts. It is implicit throughout *Slavery in America* through Simms's continual insistence upon the civilizing effect of enslavement. Throughout the text he made the argument that many races had passed under a period of enslavement on their path towards civilization and lamented those instances where slavery was not employed and civilization lagged as a result, most notably through his discussion of Native Americans. In several instances he made the connection more explicitly, pointing towards the end of the pamphlet to the direct Biblical sanction of slavery, noting that if the historical examples he had offered "were not enough, for the purposes of authority, God himself, we are given to understand, actually in two remarkable instances, placed a favorite people in foreign slavery" (71).

He continued, just a few pages later, to make the connection to his narrative of progress and civilization, arguing that "our native North American savage . . . needed nothing but an Egyptian bondage of four hundred years to have been saved for the future, and lifted into a greatness to which Grecian and Roman celebrity would have been a faint and failing music" (73). The implication, of course, is that lacking that period of bondage Native American societies lagged far behind their Euro-American counterparts, but Simms at least held out that possibility for progress. It is a possibility that he extended also to African American slaves, writing, "The time will come, I doubt not, when the negro slave of Carolina will be raised to a condition which will enable him to go forth out of bondage. When that time comes, it may be, that we, like Pharaoh, will be loth to give him up," though he concluded, "that time is very far remote" (78). Here again, Simms turned to Biblical allusion to justify and defend racial slavery. But orthodox Christianity was not simply a crutch used by cynical slaveholders to defend their peculiar institution. It represented a deeply and sincerely held component of their broader worldview, a fact that is evidenced through Simms's deployment of religious elements in his collected series of dialogues between the titular Father Abbot and his group of followers. It was no coincidence that Simms chose a religious figure to serve as the main character in his series of essays that would extol the virtues of southern society.

Father Abbot

Father Abbot originally appeared as a series of newspaper columns, entitled "The Home Tourist," published in the Charleston *Mercury* between mid-September and early November 1849.[6] In very short order Simms, working with publisher Miller & Browne, collected and published the columns in a pocket-sized edition that sold for twenty-five cents a copy. Despite the hurried nature of its publication, the collection generally received warm reviews, both in the Charleston papers and by former Charlestonian J.D.B. DeBow, whose *Review* said that the imagery brought the reviewer back to "the banks of the Ashley and the Cooper" where they could "hear the waves beating up against the beach of old Sullivan's" (Butterworth and Kibler 77, 79; "Editor's Department" 312). A review in the *Literary World*, a publication edited by Simms's friend and fellow Young America booster E.A. Duyckinck, was more mixed. While the reviewer lamented that Simms seemed to dilute his literary prowess by issuing such a vast amount of material, some of which they judged unworthy of publication, they also noted that, though segments of *Father Abbot* bore evidence "of a hurried communication to the newspapers," others remained "as clear, strong, and highly-finished as anything we know of in the language" ("Simms's *Father Abbot*" 80–81).

Interestingly, none of these contemporary reviews made note of the political dimensions of the work, yet the primary reason for its hurried publication seems to have been Simms's belief that the collection might advance his electoral prospects in South Carolina. He admitted as much in an 1849 letter to his friend and former South Carolina governor James Henry Hammond, writing, "The articles to the *Mercury* had an object beyond what was apparent on the surface," and suggesting, "they contributed to the nomination to Congress" (*Letters* 2: 563). Simms, though, ultimately would decline that nomination and never would win a seat in the U.S. Legislature. Still, the late 1840s marked the most politically active period of Simms's career and *Father Abbot* was part of that political engagement.

Following his experience during the Nullification Crisis, Simms had turned to literature and cultural criticism as a way to shape, indirectly, the course of southern politics. By the late 1840s, however, he attempted once again to interject himself more directly into formal politics. In 1848 he served as a campaign organizer for Zachary Taylor, hoping both to hasten a political realignment that would generate a united southern party and also to elect a president who would be sympathetic to the expansion of slavery into the western territories. Following Taylor's victory, Simms thought he would be in line for an ambassadorial post and turned down an appointment as South Carolina's Lieutenant Governor so that he could accept a foreign posting, but the ambassadorship never materialized (Wakelyn 137–49). It would not be the last time that Taylor would disappoint Simms. Like other southern expansionists, Simms became disillusioned by Taylor's presidency, especially when his behind-the-scenes maneuvering to admit California as a free state became public (Levine 190–92). At that point, Simms turned his attention back towards his previous attempts to develop a unified southern party. He supported, and sought election to, the Nashville Convention that was held during the summer of 1850 for the purposes of generating southern unity. While his support for the convention was unwavering, here again his electoral ambitions resulted only in frustration (Simms, "Southern Convention"; *Letters* 2: 574–77; *Letters* 3: 8–13).

It was amidst this political fervor that Simms penned *Father Abbot*. Despite the political motivations behind its production, however, it is not entirely surprising that many of the contemporary reviewers failed to appreciate its political dimensions. While *Father Abbot* does contain policy statements, they are embedded within a much richer narrative and remain subordinate to the dominant themes of place and progress. It is for this reason that *Father Abbot* rises above simple campaign propaganda and has enduring value beyond its original position as campaign ephemera.

"The Home Tourist," which was the title of the column in the *Mercury* from which *Father Abbot* emerged, also served as the subtitle for the pamphlet, and this is significant. It gets right to the core of Simms's mission, which was to display for his readers the virtues of their region and home place. Simms's own loyalty to place had shaped so much of his literary and political career, and *Father Abbot* represented another attempt to write a regional literature that vividly described his local environs. The character of Father Abbot leads his followers, and Simms's readers, on a journey to Sullivan's Island, a place so near at hand that they had for too long taken it for granted. Father Abbot laments that southerners, even Charlestonians, have ignored the virtues of their home and instead "plodded annually to that vulgarest of all social places, Saratoga"; he hopes that soon they might "begin to discover that Sullivan's is a much more famous place" (58). In the heated political environment surrounding the debates over the fate of the territories acquired from Mexico, what was at stake was more than just the capture of revenue from tourists; it was a matter of civilization's survival. By promoting

Sullivan's Island as a destination that might hold southerners at home rather than having them travel to New York, Simms was again beating the drum for southern unity in the face of increasing sectional tension.

Another area where Simms melded immediate policy concerns with broader philosophical arguments is during his discussion of the hotel under construction on Sullivan's Island. That discussion dominates the narrative, and it likely references the Moultrie House, a hotel designed by the Charleston architect Edward C. Jones, which was completed in 1850.[7] The immediate utility of the building was obvious: it would house the tourists whom Simms envisioned coming to Sullivan's Island. But for Simms, the hotel represented something more than a utilitarian structure. It was, he said through Father Abbot:

> one more step to our emancipation. It is a gain upon our former condition. It will do something towards curing us of that self-disparaging weakness, that of *absenteeism*. It is the infirmity of a provincial people that they have no faith in home. But the Hotel proves something more. . . . Now, when you show me Carolina going into her own manufactures, sending her own ships upon the sea, and providing for her own people home places for refuge, you show me the first three steps taken towards an indefinite progress. (203–4, emphasis in original)

It was nationalism, which by this time Simms was voicing as a sectional idea, expressed through architecture. This project extended further, though, as when Father Abbot describes the *tableaux vivants* that might be staged at the hotel, drawing inspiration from a "series of studies, from Southern History and tradition," rather than "the stale repetitions of Dukes and Marquisses; Macbeths and Hamlets; Queens and Shepherdesses; Turks and Banditti" (197). Here the character of Father Abbot is essentially endorsing the program of cultural nationalism that Simms had pursued over the course of his literary career, and that he was continuing to develop in the present volume. His celebration of local themes and local artists also extended to his endorsement of the amateur Charleston painter Auguste Paul Trouche, who is mentioned several times in the text and who, one imagines, might have produced artwork that would hang on the hotel walls, at least if Father Abbot had his druthers.

This discussion of art and architecture was important for Simms; and it was no coincidence that included among the fellow-travelers who accompany Father Abbot to Sullivan's are Pictor, the painter, and Beauclerk, the poet, because Simms was throughout the text making the argument that literature and the arts are of central importance to the project of creating national identity. They were all necessary figures for illuminating to their fellow citizens what Simms called "The Home Secret"—only these artists could demonstrate to their people the virtues of their home place. They were the ones who would "discover what a people are, what they need, and what they may become," and without whom "the race, after a certain period of gestation must die out" (*Father Abbot* 17). Here Simms was emphasizing the connection between loyalty to place and societal survival. It was a theme that he had explored in numerous other writings and that he extended in *Father Abbot*. Simms was also, of course, making the case for his own significance within his society and within the life of the nation. For the nation, he proposed, could not survive, indeed, could never come into being, without the man of letters.

But *Father Abbot* was not simply a celebration of the Carolina shoreline. Simms also included social criticism within his text. He lamented, especially, the lack of industry that he saw within his home state. "Enthusiasm," he wrote, "has been crushed out of us by frivolity," making "life a mere drowse in the lap of vanity" (145). Sloth and vanity were precursors to social decay and Simms, through Father Abbot, instead advocated a mission of commercial development and a future where domestic manufacturing, commerce, and agriculture could all exist in harmony. Yet he was not just imagining the New South that would be endorsed, decades later, by boosters like Henry Grady. His social vision, as outlined in *Father Abbot*, was more subtle. He did not want Charleston to become another Lowell or Waltham; he instead hoped to braid elements of progress and modernity with the conservatism and order that he so valued in southern society. While he admitted that "[c]ommerce is, perhaps, the greatest of civilizers," he also warned that "no man must seek to revenge himself upon society for its seeming neglects, by abandoning his soul to Mammon. This is to sacrifice the substance for the shadow; the soul for the purse" (185). Here was the great dilemma for the southerner and slaveholder living in the era of the Market Revolution. How could he maintain the social order and organic hierarchy that he believed preserved society and at the same time stay competitive with modern, industrial, free labor societies?

The answer for Simms, as it was for other southern intellectuals who grappled with these problems, was measured progress that came on their own terms and that was devoid of the democratizing and, from their perspective, deleterious, effects of free labor. It was a progress that brought industry, but retained agriculture; that incorporated elements of modernity, but maintained organic hierarchy. So Father Abbot, towards the conclusion of the text, advocates experimentation and innovation in agriculture, but does so by looking back to antiquity and referencing Edward Gibbon's chapter on Roman economy in his *Decline and Fall of the Roman Empire* (218). The juxtaposition is significant. Innovation is vital to survival, but so are a proper appreciation of the past and a veneration of tradition.[8]

Conclusion

This tension between innovation and veneration marks the chief linkage between *Slavery in America* and *Father Abbot*. For southern intellectuals like Simms, it was slavery, and more specifically proper Christian slavery, that pointed the way through their dilemma. Slaveholding became the means of slowing down the processes of social change that accompanied modernity. It allowed southerners, they argued, a way to escape from the social decline and chaos that plagued free labor societies. They studied Ricardian theories of rent and diminishing returns on agriculture, as well as Malthusian predictions that population would outstrip society's ability to provide for it, and they saw in them predictions of the destruction of free labor societies. Working classes exposed to these privations would rise in revolt and topple society, leading either to anarchy or despotism. In either case it would mean the destruction of freedom and republican liberty. Men like Simms watched world events closely and in the European revolutions of 1848 they saw these predicted outcomes coming to fruition.[9] It was only a matter of time, they believed, before the American North would suffer the same fate. But Christian slavery offered a way out of this cycle of destruction. By protecting and providing for the working class, and thus avoiding the inevitable working class revolutions, slavery not only made measured progress possible, it also protected freedom for those individuals capable of handling it.[10] It made possible the melding of industry with agriculture and southern society's participation in a modern world economy, as Simms advocated at the conclusion of *Father Abbot*. It did so, however, without sacrificing their social values or social order.

Of course it was easier to articulate this worldview from a plantation office than from the slave-quarter, and it was also deeply self-serving, but ideologies, then especially those articulated by a ruling class, oftentimes are. One need not, however, deny the enormity of slavery to appreciate the intellectual work that was required to defend that social order. Both *Slavery in America* and *Father Abbot* represent, in different ways, bricks in that intellectual edifice and are important and sophisticated elaborations upon the worldview that was articulated by southern intellectuals in the generation preceding the American Civil War. That Simms mentioned slavery only once in *Father Abbot*—towards the beginning of the text when he suggested that slavery is a seemingly necessary condition for making a nomadic people stationary and inculcating in them "The Home Secret"—suggests also that the defense of southern society was not merely a cynical defense of a profitable labor system.

Southern intellectuals like Simms believed they were engaged in an epochal clash of civilizations and that at stake was nothing less than the survival of American society and republican liberty. If they failed they predicted a decline into social decay and anarchical chaos. If they prevailed they might escape from this fate and secure a future marked by social harmony and ordered progress that would endure for a millennium. Doing so would require a recognition of the peculiar advantages of the southern political economy and also the creation of political unity within the region, two missions that Simms sought to achieve through his writing and editing work, including the production of the two texts reproduced herein.

A close reading of these texts reveals the intricacies of this intellectual project, one to which Simms would devote ever more time over the course of the following decade. While he was continually frustrated by his efforts to gain entrance into formal politics, Simms would continue to use the power of the pen as a way to create national identity. It was a role that he had advanced first as a member of Young America, writing in service of the American nation, but it was one that he would continue, and which is evidenced in the writings below, as a moral philosopher of southern nationalism. He did not work alone in that project, but he remained the most significant southern man of letters in the years of growing sectional tension that would finally explode in April 1861, fittingly, just off the coast of Sullivan's Island, where Simms's alter-ego, Father Abbot, had extolled the virtues of southern climate and southern society—in service of creating a southern nation—just over a decade before.

NOTES

1. For the best discussion of Simms's engagement with the *Cosmopolitan* see Guilds, "Simms and the *Cosmopolitan*."
2. For more of the Young America Movement see Widmer, Lause, and Eyal.
3. See especially Widmer.
4. Drew Gilpin Faust most fully articulated this interpretation of the connection between the proslavery argument and the alienation of southern intellectuals in*A Sacred Circle*. See, too, her edited collection *The Ideology of Slavery*.
5. Historians Elizabeth Fox-Genovese and Eugene D. Genovese collected, synthesized, and most fully articulated their interpretations of the worldview of the southern master class, with special attention on the role played by their reading of both history and religion, in *The Mind of the Master Class*.
6. The dates of publication were September 18–22, 27, 29; October 1, 3, 6, 10, 13, 16, 23, 27; November 3, 5 (*Letters* 2: 565n).
7. Simms was familiar with the Moultrie House, attending a ball there on 29 August 1850, and it also appeared in a novella, *Flirtation at the Moultrie House* (1850), that John C. Guilds has attributed to Simms (*Letters* 3: 60n; Guilds, *Stories and Tales* 780).
8. For discussion of slaveholder's attempts to grapple with modernity and progress see Moltke-Hansen "Ordered," Genovese *Slaveholders' Dilemma*, and Smith *Mastered by the Clock*.
9. See, for instance, William Gilmore Simms, "Guizot's Democracy in France."
10. The argument about the slaveholders' dilemma derives from Genovese, *The Slaveholders' Dilemma*, which is a characteristically erudite, complex, and concise statement on this tension in antebellum southern thought.

South-Carolina in the Revolutionary War

SEAN R. BUSICK

We should not be surprised to learn that, in his day, William Gilmore Simms was widely recognized as one of America's foremost historians. The most important man of letters in the Old South, he was also the central figure in historical studies of the period. He worked with practically every historian writing in or on the Old South, either assisting with research or in his capacity as magazine editor and book reviewer (Hubbell 572). He was far and away the leading southern interpreter of the American Revolution. He was one of the nineteenth century's most accomplished, popular, and prolific writers of historical romances. He wrote more history of high quality than anyone else in the South. His biography of Francis Marion is one of the best historical biographies written in the Old South and still contains much to reward curious readers. His school history of South Carolina taught generations of children their state's history. He accumulated one of the finest private collections in the United States of historical manuscripts relating to the Revolution. He was a thoughtful and respected commentator on the nature of history and its relationship with fiction. Today, as people accustomed to the specialization (or, perhaps, compartmentalization) of labor, we expect the writers of fiction to stick to the writing of fiction and historians to stick to history. Consequently, Simms's work as a historian is not always appreciated as it should be.

The genesis of Simms's *South-Carolina in the Revolutionary War: Being a Reply to Certain Misrepresentations and Mistakes of Recent Writers, in Relation to the Course and Conduct of this State* lies in two lengthy reviews of Lorenzo Sabine's *The American Loyalists*—"South Carolina in the Revolution" and "The Siege of Charleston in the American Revolution"—which Simms published in the July and October 1848 issues of the *Southern Quarterly Review*. Later Simms combined the two reviews under the current title. This volume was published under the pseudonym "A Southron" by the Charleston firm Walker and James. Sabine's volume accused South Carolina of being a hotbed of Tory activity during the Revolution and claimed that the state owed its independence largely to the heroics of New England soldiers. Simms considered these charges to be not only untrue but also offensive, and he worked to correct Sabine's misrepresentations in these reviews. Thus began his battle with New Englanders over South Carolina's role in the Revolution, a battle which would last until the Civil War.

Simms was caught off guard by Sabine's charges against South Carolina's Revolutionary heritage. "In the midst of our serenest sky," Simms later explained, "the bolt has fallen among us!" ("The Social Moral"). New Englanders had always written American history as if it were simply New England history writ large, but never before could Simms recall one section actually attacking another's Revolutionary War heritage. Even during the most bitter sectional disputes, South Carolinians never suspected that their history and ancestors might fall under attack. The Revolution, after all, was sacrosanct as the great unifying event in the nation's past. Or so they thought.

It is understandable that Simms and his fellow South Carolinians might have been surprised by Sabine's book. The first generation of American historians to write about the Revolution had lived through and, as was often the case, actively participated in the events about which they wrote. Therefore, they were passionately committed to the Revolution and the young republic to which it gave birth. This commitment showed up in their histories as a strong sense of nationalism. Dedicated to national unity and cultural independence to go along with America's political independence, they produced for the United States a national history. Well versed in classical history, these early historians knew that republics were fragile creations and large republics were supposed to be untenable. Therefore, when diverse conditions within the United States spawned party battles that seemed to threaten their young republic, American historians responded by stressing their nation's unity (Shaffer, *American* 109).

One example of this devotion to national unity and the patriot cause is their treatment of the Loyalists. The historians of the Revolutionary generation were generally predisposed to promote the idea that the Revolution was a unified—and unifying—national movement by treating the Loyalists as a small, insignificant minority. With the notable exception of South Carolina's David Ramsay, who treated the Loyalists realistically and with sympathy, early historians tended to portray the Loyalists as short-sighted, mean-minded, corrupt men (Shaffer, *Politics* 120).

Despite its bias toward national unity, the history produced by the Revolutionary generation was colored by localism. The majority of their histories were local histories, partly because of the difficulties involved in research (it was easier to access local sources) and travel. But this was also partly due to the strength of local loyalties, which sometimes had deeper roots than did loyalty to the newly-created nation. Indeed even "the most cosmopolitan writers commonly used a particular locale as the backdrop for defining the nation's character and past" (Shaffer, *Politics* 15). Their enthusiasm to demonstrate America's political and cultural unity led them into committing the logical error of generalizing from the specific; they drew conclusions about the national experience from the particular experience of their own specific locale.

Since most early historians were from New England, the history of the Revolution took on a decided Yankee flavor. Even some Southerners such as David Ramsay and Chief Justice John Marshall of Virginia were not inclined to rebut the notion of New England's cultural and moral superiority (Shaffer, *Politics* 19). Indeed, although there was a vigorous tradition of southern historical writing dating back to John Smith and Robert Beverley of Virginia, no one produced a southern interpretation of national history until 1854–1858, when George Tucker's four-volume *History of the United States from the Colonization to the End of the Twenty-Sixth Congress, in 1841* was published (R. Davis 278). As historian Michael Kammen has correctly observed, "the hegemony of New Englanders over the writing of American history," perpetuated (and perhaps exacerbated) social tensions. New England's hegemony has been resented by Midwesterners and New Yorkers, "but nowhere has it been despised so much as in the South" (158). Nevertheless, the work early historians produced was national, not sectional, history since it stressed America's unity. While writers may have displayed local biases, no section was subjected to criticism for not conforming to the nation's ideals or the ideals of the writer's section.

Unlike their predecessors, the second generation of American historians did not live through and write in the shadow of the Revolution and the divisive battles over ratification of the Constitution. Therefore, even though travel was easier and they had better access to sources than earlier historians, they were not as concerned as the Revolutionary generation historians with promoting national unity. These romantic era historians produced the first sectional, as opposed to regional or local, American histories. Before the ratification of the Constitution there were no national politics to draw the states and regions into sectional disputes. The repudiation of literary nationalism was mirrored in "the changing emphasis of political writing of the period. During the 1810s and 1820s, statesmen-writers . . . continued to advance the vision of a unified America typical of the colonial and revolutionary periods" (Werner 84). By the 1830s, however, the increasing sectionalism of literature reflected the changing tone of political discourse. Similarly, their distance from the Revolution made it easier for romantic-era historians such as Lorenzo Sabine to sympathetically, if not romantically, write about the Loyalists.

Like his predecessors among the Revolutionary generation of historians, Simms was a strong nationalist. This is not to say, however, that his history was not colored by local prejudices. In the introduction to the 1856 edition of *The Wigwam and the Cabin*, he explained, "to be *national* in literature, one must needs be *sectional*. No one mind can fully or fairly illustrate the characteristics of any great country; and he who shall depict *one section* faithfully, has made his proper and sufficient contribution to the great work of *national* illustration" (4, emphasis in original). By faithfully depicting the history of his state Simms, in his estimation, was contributing his share to the creation of a truly national history, as others had done before him. Yet as national politics became more poisoned by sectionalism, so too did the writing of history. Some historians began to stress America's diversity instead of its unity, conflict instead of consensus. Healthy local pride began to degenerate into bitter sectionalism. New Englanders, in particular, started to view slavery as evidence of the South's deviance. For the first time, the South's role in the Revolution was under attack.

Lorenzo Sabine's *The American Loyalists* was just such a sectional history. An abolitionist politician from Maine, Sabine berated the South for not contributing its fair share to the struggle for American independence. He argued that South Carolina's patriots were hampered by the presence of slavery in their state. Sabine tallied the number of troops each state contributed to the Continental Army and found that nearly 68,000 of the over 230,000 men who served were from Massachusetts while the combined total for all the states south of Pennsylvania was less than 60,000 (Sabine 30). However, it should be noted that he counted enlistments rather than troops. If one man enlisted four times, as some did, he was counted four times. But according to Sabine's math, South Carolina was full of Loyalists and contributed little to the cause of American independence, while New England provided greater than her share of patriots.

Indeed, according to Sabine, Charleston's surrender to the British was attributable to a lack of commitment to American independence and was thus an early manifestation of that city's secessionist impulses. South Carolina, he claimed in *The American Loyalists*, "could not defend herself against her own Tories; and it is hardly an exaggeration to add, that more Whigs of New England were sent to her aid, and now lie buried in her soil, than she sent from it to every scene of strife from Lexington to Yorktown" (32). The southern colonies, and South Carolina especially, according to Sabine, owed their independence to the heroic sacrifices of New England soldiers.

Simms initially replied to Sabine's criticism of South Carolina's role in the Revolution in an article for the July 1848 issue of *The Southern Quarterly Review* that was also published in *South-Carolina in the Revolutionary War* in 1853. Then, during his northern lecture tour of 1856 and southern lectures of May and June 1857, he again defended South Carolina against Sabine's indictment. In the *Southern Quarterly Review*, he praised Sabine's historical essay at the beginning of *The American Loyalists* for being clearly and forcefully written. Though he doubted the utility of a book on the Loyalists, he was not "prepared to quarrel with that taste, or passion for novelty, which, of late, seems disposed to busy itself in rescuing the memories of the American Loyalists." Very few of the Loyalists were "distinguished by remarkable endowments," and he questioned the moral object of praising people whom he considered lacking in patriotism. But "many of them, doubtless, were very worthy people," and "some of them had respectable talents," so he could understand the need to study them. "Let the deserving have their dues," he wrote (Simms, "Revolution" 44, 38, 39).

His major objection was to Sabine's charge that South Carolina was so enfeebled with Loyalism that she owed her independence to New England soldiers. This error, Simms wrote, sprang from a common fault of Yankee historians and politicians. For a long time, New England regarded "her children as the saints, to whom the possession of the earth has been finally decreed." Therefore, they naturally assumed that all good deeds were performed by New Englanders: "They have all the talents, all the virtues, and perform all the achievements." Reading only their own historians, they have no reason to believe otherwise (Simms, "Revolution" 45).

Simms thought his review might serve as a corrective. If he could not change Yankee minds, he might at least persuade honest people in other sections and give South Carolinians ammunition for defending their ancestors. He still believed he might do good by meeting Sabine's charges head on in 1856. Just eight days before he first delivered "South Carolina in the Revolution" to a northern audience, Simms optimistically wrote to George Bancroft, William Cullen Bryant, and others that he trusted that through his lectures he would "be able to disabuse the public of the North of many mistaken impressions which do us wrong" (*Letters* 3: 454).

Yet he greatly underestimated northern resentment against slavery and South Carolina, the epicenter of treason. His proposed route—through Buffalo, Rochester, and Syracuse—took him through the heart of the "Burned-Over District." So named because it had been so hotly evangelized during the Second Great Awakening, the "Burned-Over District" was the epicenter for northern radical reform movements. A quarter century before Simms, Charles Grandison Finney arrived in Rochester to lead an important series of revivals. He preached Arminianism and perfectionism to New Yorkers and "said flatly that if Christians united and dedicated their lives to the task, they could convert the world and bring on the millennium in three months" (P. Johnson 3–4). They became convinced that Christians had it within their power to eradicate sin from the world by perfecting themselves and others, and that by doing so they could hasten Christ's return. High on the list of sins that needed to be eliminated were sloth, intemperance, and slavery. So, lazy southern slaveowners were at least doubly cursed and in need of reforming, by force if necessary, as they stood in the way of the millennium (Tuveson 195–96).

Simms's northern lecture tour "proved a failure." He later confided to James Chesnut, Jr. that after delivering his lecture defending South Carolina's role in the Revolution three times, "my Committee reported to me that such was the public hostility, such the rancour occasioned by my revelations, . . . that they—the Committee—could neither sell nor give away the Tickets" (*Letters* 3: 472). For the sake of his friends on the committee who would lose money if he continued the lectures to empty halls, he cancelled the rest of his engagements. Interestingly, though, when Sabine revised his book in 1864 he conceded that no New England troops actually saw service below the James River in Virginia. He reaffirmed, however, that Charleston's surrender was attributable to its citizens' loyalty to the Crown and that the surrender of Charleston constituted an early attempt at secession from the American Union (38–45).

Though Simms's northern lecture tour has received some scholarly attention as an episode of worsening sectional tensions on the road to disunion, *South-Carolina in the Revolutionary War*, his formal, published reply to Sabine, has not. Interested readers will be best served by consulting Miriam Shillingsburg's "Simms's Failed Lecture Tour of 1856: The Mind of the North," Clyde Wilson's "Tiger's Meat: William Gilmore Simms and the History of the Revolution," and Sean R. Busick's *A Sober Desire for History: William Gilmore Simms as Historian*.

Historiographically, Simms straddled the gap between Revolutionary and romantic historians. He wrote with the literary flair of the romantics and his sympathy for the Loyalists was closer to them than to the Revolutionary generation of historians. In his nationalism and his ideas of historical causation, however, Simms was much closer to his Revolutionary predecessors who were less likely to believe that history was driven by impersonal forces than were nineteenth century historians. Like his contemporaries, Simms believed that "the chief value of history consists in its proper employment for the purposes of art!" (Simms, *Views* 1: 34). Yet, he was much closer to the Revolutionary historians in his desire to create a national history and "to put Americanism in our letters" (Simms, *Views* 1: 7).

Southward Ho! A Spell of Sunshine

JILLIAN WEBER

In 1854 William Gilmore Simms's *Southward Ho! A Spell of Sunshine* was published, the author's only "new" publication of that year. At the time of its release, Simms was already a prolific southern writer, editor, and poet. Well known as a native and champion of the South, as well as a staunch supporter of slavery, Simms allowed feelings of southern nationalism to shine through in his novel. *Southward Ho!* has a broad subject matter and an extensive publishing history, largely because all but two of the stories present in the work were published in newspapers and journals before they were collected in Simms's novel. The collection and publication of this text elucidate both the political and dire financial state of Simms's life at that time, allowing modern readers a snapshot of the political consciousness of the nation in the period shortly before the Civil War. Though it contains much literary and political merit, *Southward Ho!* was released to only lukewarm reviews and is still not considered one of Simms's seminal works; it does, though, warrant a closer look and greater appreciation for the historical moment and mindset which it preserves.

Structure of the Text

Southward Ho! is a collection of sketches and short stories, most of which Simms had previously published in other periodicals. It is, nonetheless, frequently considered a novel in the vein of *The Canterbury Tales* because the stories are told through the frame narrative of a group of travelers on a steamboat from New York to Charleston. During their journey they recount tales to one another to pass the time, often stories from or related to their native countries or states. Simms saw himself modeling the work after a fourteenth century allegory by Giovanni Boccaccio, comprised of over 100 tales told through a frame story. He described *Southward Ho!* as a "Southern Decameron" (*Letters* 3: 314).

The frame structure is comprised of a native Charlestonian recounting his travels with his New York friend, Duyckman, a name highly reminiscent of Simms's real-life friend, Evert Augustus Duyckinck. In fact, the trip from New York to Charleston was one that Simms made himself several times, and some of the characters within this frame story were modeled on his friends and acquaintances (Wimsatt, "Frontier" 154). As John Caldwell Guilds notes in his biography of Simms, "*Southward Ho!* contains observations on the people, politics, and geography of the various states along the eastern seaboard, but also as far west as Texas and Missouri" (*Literary Life* 219). These travels undoubtedly brought Simms into contact with many types of people from different areas of the country, making the use of his peers as stock characters clearer. The story content ranges geographically, culturally, and temporally, from tales of South Carolina's political upheavals, to legends of troubadours and nobility, to accounts of Native Americans.

Few scholars have explored *Southward Ho!* at great length, but those who have done so offer productive insights about how one might contextualize Simms's text with regards to his other works and the social conventions in which he believed. Though J.V. Ridgely's work on Simms is no longer representative of the critical currents, he notes an important pattern in Simms's writing generally, which also appears in *Southward Ho!*: the South as a structured society with three very distinct orders. As Ridgely sees them, the orders consist of the aristocratic class; the middle group of farmers, merchants, and frontiersmen; and the lowest class of slaves, outlaws, and misfits (*William* 26). Though elsewhere in his canon Simms exhibited a fascination with outlaws and frontiersmen, in *Southward Ho!* his focus was largely on the aristocratic class. The narrator in *Southward Ho!* is a gentleman from Charleston, his peers are of high social and financial stature, and the tales that these passengers tell deal with the aristocratic class more often than not. In his portrayals of this class, Simms emphasized southern paternalism and the *noblesse oblige* that he felt was necessary from leaders. He believed that the members of the aristocracy were responsible for discharging their roles as leaders with nobility and grace rather than tyranny. Their power could be given up, or rather, taken away, if they abused this duty.

Southward Ho! is also one of the author's more humorous works. He employed humor to dispel ideas about controversial political issues, like secession and slavery; in this way, Simms presented a more tempered version of his rather strong views in the turbulent political atmosphere of 1854. In *Southward Ho!* humor informs both the frame narrative and the embedded short stories. It is in the frame, though, that the more politically charged aspects of the text come to light. The short tales that the travelers tell, though at times entertaining, are disparate and loosely connected. The frame, on the other hand, consists of dialogue between passengers that serves to challenge common northern stereotypes about the South while reinscribing Simms's own views of his home region. It marks Simms's conscious efforts to paint the South in a positive light and change northern sentiment towards the area. Framed as character dialogue and often written in a rather didactic style, Simms's pro-southern frame narrative was designed not as an attempt at a genuine conversation about regional difference but, instead, as the author's attempt to influence the nation's views of southern politics, culture, and geography, through passionate moralistic rhetoric.

The Work

The stories in *Southward Ho!* deal with quite a large set of subjects, ranging across domestic and international matters, past and contemporary time periods, and class conflicts. Despite this range, there are some threads that recur throughout the travelers' tales: sagas of revolution, of feudal and medieval ages, of Native Americans, of pirates, and of humorous occurrences. Many are loosely unified through a focus on criminal or aberrant behavior and the resultant dispensation of justice for those who operate outside of the law. While the frame narrative offers a wide gaze at southern settings and cultures, many of the individual stories give attention to locations outside of the United States, in Europe or South America. For Simms, these international contexts allowed him to articulate national concerns by depicting societies going through revolutionary changes or upheavals of class systems, not unlike the United States in 1854. By so doing, he could avoid personalizing his message and viewpoints, likely in hopes of offering greater access to his novel for readers who may have held different political views.

The first traveler's tale in the collection is "The Maid of Bogota," a story of revolutionary spirit and action, which details the cruel Spanish rule of Colombia in the 1850s. Selina Burroughs, the narrator of the tale, described as having "a proper sense of justice naturally sympathizing with the threatened innocents," focuses on La Pola, a girl who becomes an inspiring symbol of spirit and patriotism for her native country through song (*Southward Ho!* 25). La Pola acts as a spy for Bolivar, the revolutionary figure known as "The Liberator" who fought against Spanish dominance. Ultimately, La Pola is captured and sentenced to execution, but not before making a lasting impact in the fight against Spanish colonization. Simms based this story on the historical figure, Simon Bolivar, who was influential in the Venezuelan struggle against Spanish oppression.[1] In doing so, he framed his message to encourage action over mere verbal affirmations of patriotism. This is a theme that Simms returned to throughout his novel when discussing southern nationalism and his view of active participation in the brewing fight for secession and southern rights.

Several other stories in *Southward Ho!* are united by a common focus: conflicts ignite between marginalized figures and characters who hold authority or operate within the higher echelons of a hierarchy. "The Story of Blackbeard," one of the strongest tales in the novel, is about the infamous pirate and his quest for power and riches. The buccaneer attempts to eschew all laws and regulations that may apply to him while he plunders and murders on the sea. Ultimately, though, Blackbeard is unable to sustain a life outside the law and cannot elude justice forever, as a young lieutenant captures and kills him.

"Legend of Missouri; or, the Captive of the Pawnee" is one of two stories about Native Americans in the novel. It depicts battles between the Omahas and the Pawnees, warring Native American tribes. What Simms ultimately makes clear in this tale is that the conflicts between these two nations pale in comparison to the larger wars between Native Americans and American settlers on the horizon.[2]

"Love's Last Supper" is a tale representative of Simms's stories of the medieval ages. It gives an account of interactions between a troubadour, Guillaume de Cabestaign, and members of the nobility, Lady Marguerite and her husband, Raymond de Roussilon. Lady Marguerite and Guillaume de Cabestaign engage in a romantic affair, of which Raymond de Roussilon is suspicious. Raymond de Roussilon becomes jealous of Guillaume and takes justice into his own hands, beheading Guillaume and feeding his cooked heart to Marguerite. Simms, by depicting Roussilon's subsequent trial, jail sentence, and condemnation by the community, ends the story with the message that there are clear conventions and means of justice by which each particular class must abide in order to maintain a sense of order. This notion is something that Simms believed in the context of the southern hierarchical system, and it is a thread that appears throughout many of the stories in *Southward Ho!*

"The Bride of Hate; or, The Passage of a Night," which Guilds deems to be the only story that stands apart in *Southward Ho!*, is the tale of Ulrica, the benefactress of a young boy, Herman. Ulrica, unbeknownst to the boy, is actually his mother. However, she wishes harm upon him because he is set to inherit all of her land and money. During her attempt to harm her son and prevent his inheritance, Ulrica is haunted by the ghost of a daughter she had drowned years earlier in a lake on the property. This haunting leads to her death, Herman rightfully inherits the property, and when he has the lake drained, he discovers the skeleton of his sister. This particular narrative reveals the strong Germanic influences present in much of Simms's work. J. Wesley Thomas identifies the German story "Das Majorat," by E.T.A. Hoffman, as the inspiration for "The Bride of Hate" ("German Sources"), though Guilds views the similarities between the two stories as exploitation, rather than inspiration. Gothic elements infuse "The Bride of Hate," with the decaying castle, surrounded by barren land, symbolizing the decay of a noble family. Both the German story and its American counterpart have nearly identical settings, parallel plots with few variations, and analogous climactic scenes. Guilds posits that "The Bride of Hate," though stylistically the strongest tale in *Southward Ho!*, remains cold and lifeless because the "borrowed" nature of the content prevents true creativity (Guilds, *Writings* 681).

Simms's stories, including "Dalton the Stranger," "The Bride of Hate," and "The Story of Blackbeard," often deal with wrongs being revealed and then righted. Justice prevails, and Simms showed the ways in which the past can both haunt and help us. Other tales included in the novel range from topics about the South, class conflicts within certain geographic spheres, regional clashes that come to a head over a battle for oysters, and the natural beauty of the southern landscape. Whatever the content of the stories, they have in common the treatment of class and geographic, social, and political structures. Rarely did Simms show class lines and hierarchies being displaced or eliminated completely. Instead, these social structures served as sites of conflict. Furthermore, geographic differences account for differences in class and mindset, which allowed Simms to both illustrate the discord that occurs from these distinctions and draw parallels to the North and the South during the moment in time that he published *Southward Ho!*

Of particular note in the frame narration of the novel is Simms's illustration of the South as an unrecognized place of beauty during the 1850s. He predicted that northerners would soon take note and migrate south. By Simms's estimation, northerners had limited exposure to this beauty because they stuck to industrial train routes between major cities and did not explore environments outside those designated paths, but he predicted this would soon change. Simms wrote, "Hear me prophesy! Fifteen years will not pass before the mountain ranges of the Carolinas and Georgias will be the fashionable midsummer resort of all people of taste north of the Hudson. They will go in search of health, coolness, pure air, and the picturesque" (*Southward Ho!* 8). Undergirding this contrast of the bucolic settings of the South with the industrial corridor was a notion that progress and technology were not unequivocally good. For Simms, this marked an important difference between the general thinking of the North from that of the South. The North was lacking in foresight regarding technology's demarcating power over geography and the consequences it would have on the national vistas. Jeffery J. Rogers, picking up on the material and moral progress in Simms, writes:

> [Simms] made a distinction in his thinking between material progress, as praiseworthy and as desirable as it was, and moral progress. Qualitative progress, the type Simms most highly prized, however was slow, halting, and tenuous. It was not possible without social and political order which, in turn, was generated only when the fundamental institutions of society were functioning properly relative to the individual and to each other. Chief among these were the family and the local community. When these institutions failed—or when they themselves served to impede progress—conflict, revolution, and a new stage of historical development were the result (*Bayard* xxv).

Simms worked through many of the ideas to which Rogers gestures in "The Philosophy of the Omnibus."[3] *Southward Ho!*, then, is a seldom explored work that offers new ground for scholars to dissect Simms's philosophies regarding the ways technology and travel affect sectional preconceptions. It recommends a reconsideration of the South with this distinction between material and moral progress in mind. Throughout the frame story, Simms's characters pontificate on the oft-ignored natural beauty and wonders of the Shenandoah Valley, among other sites of the South. A North Carolinian stands up for his state when a fellow passenger claims that he saw little of note when traveling by train through the area. Here, the conflicts between North and South, as well as modernity and traditionalism, come to a head when the Carolinian responds, "You will form a very erroneous notion of this truly valuable state if you assume its general character from what you see along the railroad route. . . . Penetrate the interior even now, and you will be rewarded in a thousand places by the beauties of a careful cultivation, the sweets of a mild and graceful society" (*Southward Ho!* 314). In *Southward Ho!* Simms revered and placed more importance on the slow progress of the South, which revolved around tradition and hierarchies, than on the modernization of the North. In fact, for him, the focus by northerners on modernization actually inhibited them from appreciating many aspects of the South.

Composition and Publication History

Southward Ho! has a long composition and publication history, as it began as multiple independent short stories which Simms subsequently compiled into one larger work. Simms first mentioned the idea for *Southward Ho!* in a 25 February 1847 letter to Duyckinck, "his New York friend and informal literary agent," pitching it as a volume of sketches about the scenery and traditions of the South, titled "Slopes & Summits of the South" (Wimsatt, "Frontier" 155). In this letter Simms indicated his desire to publish the work anonymously, which he sometimes did to test the merit of a volume outside the influence of his famous name. Several of the stories from "Slopes & Summits of the South," later included in *Southward Ho!*, formed the basis for a series of nine chapters published sequentially in the *Charleston Evening News* on 12 June, 13 June, 18 June, 25 June, 2 July, 3 July, 16 July, 30 July, and 31 July 1849 (*Letters* 3: 314n). These chapters, entitled "Spells of Sunshine; or, a Summer in the South," would form the framework for *Southward Ho!*

Simms seems to have had largely financial goals in mind for writing the book, as he noted to James Henry Hammond in a 20 June 1853 letter, "I am collecting my scattered novellettes & tales. You have probably seen 'Marie de Berniere &c.' This will be followed up by other vols. of similar material; all of which will yield me a little money" (*Letters* 3: 240). Simms's hope for monetary gain from the publication of *Southward Ho!* was also evident in his timing for the novel, which he hinted at in a 17 July 1854 letter to Duyckinck: "In preparing my tales for the press, I am disposed to follow a suggestion of yours & make a Southern Decameron—a Christmas Decameron" (*Letters* 3: 314). His plan to make a holiday gift book out of the collection suggests that aesthetic decisions could potentially be compromised by the need for widespread consumption. Simms also suggested other titles for the collection, such as "Tales of Glow and Glamour, for a Christmas Fireside," presumably as a marketing strategy to increase sales in various geographic, political, and economic contexts. By excluding mention of southern geography from the title, Simms's novel may have been more marketable to a northern audience. Other than these concerns, Simms was, for the most part, silent in his correspondence on the composition of the book. In a 4 September 1854 letter to James Lawson, though, he noted that *Southward Ho!* was in press, with the author himself overseeing production. The volume came out later that fall, published by Redfield and stereotyped by C.C. Savage, both of New York.

As it is comprised largely of previously published material, *Southward Ho!* has an extensive textual history that spans two decades. Of the dozen or so stories within the frame narrative, six were previously published in *Graham's Magazine*, primarily in the 1840s; three appeared in Simms's 1833 collection *The Book of My Lady*; and several of the others were featured in such periodicals as *Godey's Lady's Book*, *Southern and Western*, *Magnolia*, and *Southern Literary Journal*. Only two of the stories, the pirate tales "The Ship of Fire" and "Blackbeard," appear to be new to the volume. Several of the individual stories in the collection have detailed publishing histories themselves, prior to their inclusion in *Southward Ho!*. For instance, "The Benefactress, or the Passage of a Night," was meant to be published initially in one of three proposed volumes of Simms's short stories by Harper & Brothers. These volumes were to be approximately 150 pages each, though *Helen Halsey; or, the Swamp State of Conelachita* is the only volume to fully come to fruition. "The Benefactress" was later renamed "The Bride of Hate; or, The Passage of a Night" (*Letters* 1: 375n). "Annihilation" was first published in the *Magnolia* and then later republished as "The Wager of Battle. A Tale of the Feudal Ages" in *Graham's* in February 1849 (*Letters* 2: 55n). "A Tale of the Etrurian" appeared in *Graham's* in June 1849 (*Letters* 2: 382n). Originally published in *Graham's* in 1848, "La Pola, The Maid of Bogota," was then released in *The Cosmopolitan*, followed by the *Southern Literary Journal*. It was later seen in *The Book of My Lady* and finally became part of *Southward Ho!* (*Letters* 2: 432n). As a complete text, *Southward Ho!* went through many subsequent printings, both during the author's life and for years afterward. Some of the major publishers who re-printed *Southward Ho!* after Redfield were Widdleton of New York, Russell of Charleston, and Donohue & Henneberry of Chicago.

Simms's reliance on recycled material in composing *Southward Ho!* was partially attributable to his editorship of the *Southern Quarterly Review* at the time. The *Southern Quarterly Review* was the last of three cultural journals that Simms edited during the 1840s and '50s, and his time with the publication was particularly rocky. Beginning in 1849, he worked tirelessly to shape the journal into a southern literary publication that actively promoted the literature of the South. He reached out to his New York friend James Lawson, asking him to help cultivate positive reviews of the journal in his area, knowing that southerners often looked to northerners for praise (Guilds, *Literary Life* 153). When Lawson informed Simms that the *Review* was nearly impossible to find in the North, Simms was discouraged. He did not achieve his goal of firmly establishing a distinctly southern literature in this venue and ultimately, after five years as editor, was unable to continue because of exhaustion and the magazine proprietors' inability to pay his salary and provide for the journal. Both the financial and physical tolls this editorship took on Simms appear to be large factors in the publication decisions surrounding *Southward Ho!* In many ways, Simms was too drained to produce a novel-length work of all new content, thus he gathered previously published stories together and hoped to gain maximum returns with minimal investment.

Simms as Southern Apologist

The primary strength of *Southward Ho!* is the insight it offers into Simms's political views during the early to mid 1850s. More than many of his other works, *Southward Ho!* displays Simms's southern nationalism and the vehemence with which he believed in the South as a place with an heroic past and an idealized future. He believed in the exceptionalism of the South and felt the region ought to be recognized as an entity distinct from the North. By the time of the Mexican War at the end of the 1840s, Simms had become fully pro-secession, views that are reflected in *Southward Ho!* and its references to South Carolina's "revolutionary spirit" (*Southward Ho!* 444). In the early 1850s he became a spokesman for the South and its hierarchical structure, particularly as it came under attack. Simms acknowledged the presence and relevance of forces larger than the individual in shaping history. Rogers notes that Simms readily accepted geography, for example, as a "determining factor in history. Also, like other nineteenth-century intellectuals, Simms believed that factors such as ethnicity and nationalism strongly shaped history" (*Bayard* xxv). In *Southward Ho!* the narrator often describes the sectional and regional differences between the passengers aboard the ship: North Carolinians, South Carolinians, Texans, Alabamians, and New Yorkers. Simms used these differences to establish conversations among his characters about various regions, which nearly always dealt with the history and grandeur of the South.

At times, the political frame of his pro-southern views becomes pointed. Simms introduced his own views on abolition in *Southward Ho!* through the conversations between his characters from different geographic regions. Simms felt that abolitionists dictated much of northern policy and without them, the South had the ability and opportunity to revitalize itself, continue institutional slavery, and become a global influence.[4] In one such example, an Alabamian character and a New Englander discuss their differing stances on slavery in the North and South. The Alabamian operates as Simms's amanuensis as he attempts to refute the North's attitude toward this institution. He asks of the abolitionists, "why do they shape the laws, dictate the policy, control the whole action of society?" (*Southward Ho!* 394). The framework for *Southward Ho!* provided an opportunity for Simms to use the dialogic structure of his characters and their geographical heritages to espouse these views. In another related example, Simms's narrator and fellow Charlestonian converses with a North Carolina farmer, urging him and his state to work together with South Carolina to promote secession.

Though the embedded stories are strong indicators of Simms's political consciousness during the mid-1850s, his characters, for the most part, fall flat and do little to represent the southern ideal in which Simms believed. Simms was largely unsuccessful in grounding his claims about the region in his narrative. For instance, in a novel that describes the natural beauty of the South many different times, Simms located his characters on a boat with very little scenery. His characters discuss the barren North Carolina coast in contrast to its interior topography and the Alabamian on deck notes "how little promise of this [southern beauty] there is along the Atlantic shore!" (*Southward Ho!* 382). Though he may have been trying to illuminate what he felt were the unknown natural wonders of the South, Simms contradicted this goal throughout the novel.

Simms also wrote of South Carolina leading the rest of the southern states against "federal usurpation" and claimed that the state "has a thousand foibles, faults—nay, follies—perhaps, but she has some virtues which power can not crush out of her, or money buy" (*Southward Ho!* 445); yet he offered few concrete examples. Instead, he relied on rhetoric laced with patriotic language, abstract ideals, and references to glorified ancient societies to inspire and influence his readers. While this language may have inspired southern audiences, it failed to show northern readers why the South was an entity that was misunderstood. The frame structure functions, rather, to estrange northern audiences and place blame on the North generally for the ways the South was perceived. The polarizing views present in the novel help to account for its varying reception in different areas of the country, particularly its greater popularity in the South than the North.

Critical Reception

When *Southward Ho!* was first released, the general tenor of its reception was lukewarm, though the response varied by geographic region. Simms himself was always curious about how the text was received in the North and South, as evidenced in his correspondences with friends. He frequently asked Duyckinck in letters, "Have you read '*Southward Ho!*' & how does it take?" (*Letters* 3: 340) and later remarked, "I have seen none of the notices of *Southward Ho!* except in our Southern papers, and am anxious to hear from you how folks speak of it in your quarter" (*Letters* 3: 351). Simms was correct in assuming that critical reception for the work would vary depending on geography. *Putnam's Magazine*, based out of New York, included the following review of *Southward Ho!*: "Magazine readers of moderate diligence will recognize most or all of the tales and poems, some of which are very well done ; but none of which, as here republished, need we examine. The thread of the story is merely a not very remarkable voyage from New York to Charleston" ("Literature" 213).

The southern papers in which Simms found reviews of his book were the Charleston *Mercury* on 27 November, the *Courier* on 28 November, and the *Evening News* on 30 November 1854. The review in the *Courier* was generally positive, particularly when juxtaposed with the review from *Putnam's*, noting the southern nationalism that dots the novel's pages. The reviewer called the book:

> A lively and agreeable survey of men and manners, as they are, executed in a style which shows both the author's shrewdness as an observer, and his abilities as a narrator.... The versatile and protean genius of the gifted author, here displays itself in its most sportful sallies, and yet ever and anon breaks forth in a hint, or lesson, or suggestion, of the deepest significance (*Letters* 3: 351n).

Southern reviewers seemed to view *Southward Ho!* more positively than elsewhere in the nation precisely because Simms verbalized the common concern at the time that the South as a geographic and political region was misunderstood by the North. As a member of the planter class, Simms understood the implications that this misunderstanding held, especially with the emergence of the Republican Party out of the North in 1854. This party championed modernization, which consequently placed the plantation system at risk. The drive to stop the expansion of slavery, the trumpeting of free-market labor over slave labor, and the desire to expand railroads and factories all threatened with extinction the aristocratic ideals of much of the South. In *Southward Ho!* Simms often alluded to northern industrialization and juxtaposed it to the longstanding bastion of "loyalty," "manners and customs," "sentiments and traditions," and "virtue" that was the South of Simms's imagination (*Southward Ho!* 444–45). It is in these instances that the author's view that the tradition and constancy of the South were superior to the chaos of change in the North becomes clear.

Several of the other reviews of *Southward Ho!* were written by Simms's friends, and so were generally favorable; Paul Hamilton Hayne, literary editor of the *Evening News* and fellow southern author, wrote that *Southward Ho!* was:

> a very entertaining collection of miscellanies, consisting of tales, sketches of character and poems, written in the author's happiest vein, and sufficiently various in style, purpose and expression, to keep attention and interest continually alive.... The activity of the author's mind is marvelous, and its versatility no less so. No doubt the present agreeable book will prove as popular as its vivid descriptive power and cheerful, genial humor entitle it to be (*Letters* 3: 351n).

John Esten Cooke, a fellow southern novelist and Simms protégé, wrote, "the best criticism of this entertaining volume would be the simple declaration that everything about it is *Southern*" (qtd. in Guilds, *Literary Life* 220).

Of course, not all of Simms's friends were quite as generous in their praise of the novel. James Henry Hammond wrote to Simms in 1853 expressing well wishes for his upcoming collection of stories but encouraging him to "use the knife freely" throughout the revision process (*Letters* 3: 242n). Simms failed to take his friend's advice, though, and did not make more than minor edits to *Southward Ho!*, which led to some of the later negative criticisms (Ridgely, *William* 40). William Peterfield Trent thought *Southward Ho!* was a gimmick, "a device to enable its author to publish long-forgotten stories" (209). While Trent is often considered to have been overly critical of Simms, the author's financial stress and exhaustion in 1854 might lend support to Trent's opinion. Reacting to the notion that *Southward Ho!* was written in imitation of Simms's oratorical style, Trent glibly declared, "I for one am willing to believe that the hearty, genial author was a much better raconteur over a glass of punch than I have found him to be in the pages of his pseudo-Decameron" (210).

The modern age has not been much kinder to *Southward Ho!*. As Guilds writes, the work "is a collection badly in need of editorial cutting and pruning. In *Southward Ho!* Simms attempted to hang disparate tales and sketches on the Chaucerian framework of storytellers on a common journey—in this case a sea voyage from New York to Charleston." Guilds continues: "Though in some ways visionary, *Southward Ho!* is nevertheless a mediocre book, a collection of stories and tales far inferior to those in [Simms's major short story collection] *The Wigwam and the Cabin*" (*Literary Life* 218). He attributes the narrow and unenthusiastic reception it received outside the South to these editing problems, in addition to the lack of new stories in the work (*Literary Life* 220). Wimsatt, conversely, believes that Simms's own comments about the work—that he put the work together fairly haphazardly—have encouraged twentieth century readers to rank the novel lower than many of Simms's other works ("Frontier" 154).

While critics today, like Guilds, view *Southward Ho!* as fundamentally mediocre, productive and valuable features of the text are also present, such as Simms's use of humor to illustrate his ideas about southern nationalism, secession, and the role of the South in the nation's future. Wimsatt describes Simms's use of several regional conventions of southern humor during the mid-nineteenth century. For instance, Simms put characters from very different geographic regions in dialogue with one another, speaking about topics that could be humorously and greatly misunderstood by the parties. His tendency to designate characters by their regional affiliations allowed him to exaggerate the characteristics of a region. In *Southward Ho!* he embellished characteristics of passengers from Alabama, North Carolina, and Texas, among others. Simms was raised in Charleston by his grandmother, but traveled to Mississippi and the Gulf South multiple times in the first half of the nineteenth century to visit his father. It is likely that during these travels he was exposed to local oral narratives and border humor, which were widely circulating in the 1840s. He also would have been exposed to cultural characteristics of people from a part of the country different than Charleston. Because of these travels, as well as Simms's contact with Augustus Baldwin Longstreet and other humorists, it is perhaps unsurprising that aspects of this comedy appear in *Southward Ho!*.

Most of the humor in the novel is genteel regional humor, likely because Simms was marketing *Southward Ho!* as a gift book that would appeal to a larger audience, but Wimsatt notes too the presence of the "green-spectacled Alabamian," a representative of border, or frontier, humor, which deals with flamboyant southern stereotypes and could often be quite bawdy in nature. The conventions of the "Arkansas Traveler" trope are present in this character, including a contrast between a sophisticated traveler and this wily native, depictions of poverty of the natives, a question-and-answer dialogue format known as thrust-and-parry, and clever tricks beside understated tales told by the native to the traveler in an effort to protect his home ("Frontier" 149). Throughout the novel, Simms's Alabamian character engages in silly and frivolous conversations with other passengers, like the North Carolinian, about different geographic regions. The Alabamian pokes fun at North Carolina, calling it "Lubberland" (a common dig during the nineteenth century) and otherwise "mercilessly gull[ing] the North Carolinian" about the state (Wimsatt, "Frontier" 158–59). Though Wimsatt focuses a great deal on these few instances of frontier humor in the novel, the occurrences are atypical and much of the humor is more mannerly. Simms's characters do not ever fully exhibit bawdy old southwestern humor or behavior. The thrust-and-parry conversational style allows characters to engage in humorous conversations about misconceptions of the South, but even these interactions remain decorous. Indeed, Simms's characters harp on the manners and morals of the South throughout their time on the steamboat.

Southward Ho! is perhaps most significant to modern readers for the entrance into a political and historical conversation that it allows them. It becomes a moment captured for readers that encapsulates detailed rationales for a southern mindset. Though it is not Simms's seminal work, the claims that it was assembled quickly with little cohesion are not fully justified. The frame narrative constantly works to address Simms's views that the South was oft ignored and bound to emerge in glory. Simms's characters remain constant throughout this frame and engage one another in discourses on the South as a geographic, political, and cultural entity. While interspersed with short stories, the frame remains consistent in its evocation of Simms's southern political agenda and provides a sense of unity to the novel. The individual stories, though at first glance disparate, all have at least one of three things in common: class conflicts and hierarchical structures, a sense of justice for wrongdoing prevailing, and elements of humor. Simms weaves these characteristics together with a pervading sense of southern paternalism and nationalism. Discussions that appear to deal with revolutions or troubadours on the surface, actually serve their greater function as metaphors for southern issues troubling Simms at the time.

NOTES

1. For further explication on Simms as a historian, see Sean R. Busick's *A Sober Desire for History: William Gilmore Simms as Historian*. Columbia: U of South Carolina P, 2005.
2. For further discussion of Simms's treatment of Native Americans in his works, see John Guilds and Charles Hudson's "Introduction." *An Early and Strong Sympathy: The*

Indian Writings of William Gilmore Simms. Columbia: U of South Carolina P, 2003. xiii-li.

3. Colin D. Pearce provides a more thorough discussion of "The Philosophy of the Omnibus" in "All Aboard! 'The Philosophy of the Omnibus' and the Problem of Progress in William Gilmore Simms." *The Simms Review* 18.1–2 (2010): 71–91.
4. Joseph Kelly traces the evolution of Simms's slave ideology in "The Evolution of Slave Ideology in Simms's *The Yemassee* and *Woodcraft*." *The Simms Review* 20.1–2 (2012): 53–68.

The Spanish Romances

Pelayo and *Count Julian*

W. MATTHEW J. SIMMONS

Traditionally two of the more critically maligned works of Simms's *oeuvre*, *Pelayo: A Story of the Goth*, and its ostensible sequel, *Count Julian; or, the Last Days of the Goth*, are nevertheless valuable resources to scholars of Simms and nineteenth-century literature generally. While their value may not be immediately apparent based on aesthetic merit, these works show Simms struggling to articulate some of his key philosophical concerns, and they provide two of the most fascinating textual histories of all of the author's many works. Also, *Pelayo*, at least, is a much better novel than critics have traditionally acknowledged. So, while these romances of Gothic Spain may be two of the author's minor novels, they nevertheless are among Simms's most intriguing attempts at writing historical, and even philosophical, fiction. Because of this, they deserve renewed critical attention, in spite of their limited aesthetic successes.

Simms's interest in medieval Spain may seem uncharacteristic for an author most well-known for his novels about the Revolutionary War and the early days of the American Republic. Yet, as Stanley T. Williams's excellent "Spanish Influences on the Fiction of William Gilmore Simms" points out, Spanish culture and language were "a key to themes and backgrounds which were to be important in [Simms's] fiction and poetry. Everything suggests his preference for Spanish [language and culture], or at least a consciousness of its potential treasures for him as a novelist, either through a knowledge of Spain itself or of the history and legends of Spanish-America." (223) Certainly, the hazy history of late Gothic Spain, with its tense mix of Germanic, Hispano-Roman, Jewish, and Moorish populations, provides rich fodder for romances of the type Simms produced. Yet, it is nevertheless curious that the author would leave his robust explorations of the American scene for such a radically different fictional setting, especially considering the great commercial and critical successes of his Revolutionary and Border Romances. To make sense of Simms's ambitions for these twin novels of "the last days of the Goth," we need to consider the origin of the novels and the possible social and personal pressures he would have been feeling in the late 1830s. Both novels point to what is perhaps the central theme in Simms's work, an issue *Pelayo* and, in its own vexed ways, *Count Julian*, would allow him to explore from a new perspective: the relationships between history, art, and the literary vocation.

Both *Pelayo* and *Count Julian* had their genesis in a short piece of juvenile verse-drama, a project Simms abandoned as a young man, only to find himself returning to in the late 1830s. Writing to his literary agent and friend James Lawson in October 1841, Simms recounted this part of his literary biography, noting that "I have in my possession now a Tragedy partly written when I was 17–18—founded on the apostacy [*sic*] of Count Julian. From the materials of this tragedy, my romance of Pelayo was evolved" (*Letters* 1: 285). As Williams's essay suggests, Simms did have a longstanding interest in Spanish culture and language, and thus his youthful foray is unsurprising. Yet, the question remains: why did he return to this project approximately a decade and a half after putting it aside?

Simms biographer John Caldwell Guilds posits an explanation for the author's choice by contextualizing it within the major social pressures Simms himself was likely feeling at this time: so recently married into the lowcountry gentry from "which he had felt rejected since boyhood," the author "was encouraged by his new peers . . . not to forsake the great literary traditions of Europe, to which they still looked, with something akin to awe, for cultural verification." (*Literary Life* 81) Always conscientious of the fraught position of a professional man of letters in the antebellum South, Simms needed to legitimize his vocation, especially amongst his new social milieu. By leaving his work on America and her history for the time being and taking up a project derived from European history, Simms, in Guilds's reading, hoped to show the Charleston elite that his work was of real and significant merit.

In *Conjectures of Order*, Michael O'Brien notes the singular importance of history, and historical literature and knowledge, to the southern elite in the early decades of the nineteenth century: during this time "historical literature grew in force as a species of knowledge deemed to explain the human experience and, in its ubiquity, came then to engross a greater share of Southern culture than before or since." (591) Southerners read a wide variety of historical texts, especially standard classical sources like Thucydides, Herodotus, and Livy. While most medieval historians were ignored, those of early modern Europe, like Edward Hyde, Earl of Clarendon, and Voltaire were regularly examined. Hume and Gibbon "were ubiquitous and even enjoyed" (O'Brien 594). These historians all evidenced a traditional view of the role of history, one that "told the stories that clarified the lineaments of this mixed human race;" they "told historical tales of transhistorical significance, whose value was to encourage the morally great and to warn against the immorally forceful" (O'Brien 597). Surely Simms was exposed to several of these historians, as his own approach to history reflects this traditional stance. Simms believed the role of an historical text was not merely to rehearse the significant actions and events of the age, but rather to reveal truths in expressing things of "transhistorical significance."

Thus, Simms's abandoning of eighteenth-century America for eighth-century Spain is perhaps unexpected, but not out of character for the writer who believed that the latter contained relevant truths about the former. Simms explored the ramifications of this fact in these two novels. The social pressures Guilds notes likely did weigh heavily on the author, yet these did not paralyze him. Rather, his understanding of the purposes of history as a humanistic pursuit and literary wellspring would suggest to the author that Medieval Spain could be just as valuable to the modern American writer as it would be to the Spanish or Islamic novelist of the nineteenth century. Further, orations like *The Social Principle* and *Self-Development* show Simms's view that the Spanish conquest of America was based in a culture heavily affected by centuries of warfare with the Moors, fighting that began at the time in which Count Julian and Pelayo lived. Thus, we can surmise that the author understood the two places and periods as, in some important ways, directly connected.

Backgrounds—*Pelayo: A Story of the Goth*

Pelayo was published by Harper & Brothers, in two volumes, in 1838. Though technically anonymous, it was attributed to the author of *Mellichampe*, *The Yemassee*, *Guy Rivers*, *The Partisan*, and *Martin Faber*. Because this is the only edition of the novel to emerge before the recent *Simms Initiatives* volume, the publication history of the book is not extensive. The story of *Pelayo* is nevertheless complex, providing an example of the struggles Simms often endured in realizing his artistic vision.

Simms's earliest forays into writing *Pelayo* were during his late teens in the mid-1820s, when he engaged in writing a verse-drama about the legend of Count Julian, influenced by poems on that and related subjects by Sir Walter Scott and others. At some point in the late 1830s, the adult Simms reconsidered this work. While there is no definitive evidence of when he returned to writing *Pelayo*, Simms's first mention of the novel in his extant correspondence was a March 1837 letter to James Lawson: "the Harpers . . . have the entire MS of Pelayo," he told his friend and informal literary agent. He also remarked that the book turned out to be a "much longer work than I had intended it to be, and has cost me more time & thought than I had anticipated" (*Letters* 1: 99). Simms's comment that he struggled mightily with *Pelayo*'s production provides evidence in favor of Guilds's argument that Simms was out of his element with this novel, perhaps indeed producing something out of social necessity, rather than out of artistic vision. Further evidence about the frustrations Simms faced are found in a letter to Lawson from September of the same year. He complained that he was "literally doing nothing, unless turning into prose, the verse passages of Pelayo be considered doing something. It is labor, but labor without profit" (*Letters* 1: 116). While it is unclear how much the publishers wanted changed from the time of their reception of "the entire MS" to this rewriting of the "verse passages" six months later, it is clear that the overall process was exceptionally taxing for Simms; while Harper & Brothers had the full manuscript in March 1837, *Pelayo* was not published until the spring of 1838, over a full year later.

Simms's reference to these "verse passages" of *Pelayo* alludes to the work's genesis as well as to possible reasons for the novel's uneven quality. In its published version, three poems, representing songs and ballads sung by characters at key moments, constitute all of the verse in the novel. Yet, the aforementioned letter shows that Simms reworked—with difficulty—more extensive verse passages into prose, suggesting a much larger initial presence of verse in the work. Simms seems not to have overhauled these extensive verse sections, but to have engaged in a sort of odd translation from poetry to prose. Mary Ann Wimsatt notes that the fidelity of *Pelayo* to its verse origins is seen most manifestly in the novel's dialogue, where "the speech of the characters is lofty and archaic, depending heavily on asides and soliloquies. That of Pelayo in particular is filled with metaphors, conceits, word-plays, and paradoxes, in attempted imitation of Renaissance drama, and is streaked with a grim humor redolent of the Jacobean stage." ("*Ivanhoe*" 259) The effect of this is often jarring, as characters often seem as if they fell from the pen of an Elizabethan playwright instead of a nineteenth-century novelist.

By choosing to use language in this way, Simms limited the novel's chances at real aesthetic success. He marred a sophisticated narrative and philosophically intriguing exploration of history, citizenship, virtue, and justice with prose that was too often prolix and leaden. If Guilds is correct, and Simms's proximate goal in writing *Pelayo* was to earn respect from the Charleston elite through invocation of European subjects and forms, then Simms certainly succeeded. However, this same success is also the chief source of the novel's failings; while *Pelayo* is a much more intelligent, challenging, and fulfilling novel than Guilds allows, Simms ultimately did not reach the levels such a sophisticated work would seemingly demand because of his myopic fidelity to the work's juvenile source and his resistance to deviating from the confines of the European traditions of the Romance and the stage.

Simms dedicated *Pelayo* to William Hayne Simmons, a Charleston-born physician descended from Henry Woodward, "the first English settler of South Carolina" (Simmons xi). While such a dedication seems to further validate Guild's reading, Simmons's precarious position in Charleston society complicates this straightforward picture. Although a descendant of Charleston's literal first family, Simmons was not a wealthy man. While a physician by trade, Simmons thought of himself as a man of letters. In 1821, at the age of 37, he "decided to pull up his roots" in Charleston and leave for Florida (Simmons xiii). Though Simms was then only 15, the two men maintained a professional and personal relationship over the years, something that was surely aided by Simms's close friend and literary collaborator James Wright Simmons, the younger brother of William Hayne. As late as the 1840s and '50s, William Hayne Simmons contributed poems to the *Southern Quarterly Review* while Simms was editor of that journal. Simms also included several works by Simmons in *The Charleston Book* and promoted Simmons's work to Evert Augustus Duycknick, another friend and an influential figure in the mid-century New York publishing world. Simmons wrote on the early history of Florida, and dedicating the book to him reinforced the connection between that history and the fall of Gothic Spain. Because Simmons, like Simms, also had greater ambitions than inheritance, Simms may as well have been including his Florida friend in the search for the cultural respectability that Guilds believes the novel represents.

Backgrounds—*Count Julian; or, The Last Days of the Goth*

Derived from the same juvenile source material as *Pelayo* and conceived of as its direct sequel, *Count Julian* soon took on a life of its own, and its publication history is perhaps the strangest in the entire Simms canon. Several striking delays resulted in *Count Julian* being published more than seven years after *Pelayo.* The extended breaks in composition were both frustrating and confusing to Simms, as the aesthetic failures of *Count Julian* bear witness.

Soon after the publication of *Pelayo*, Simms was already at work on its sequel, as evidenced by a January 1838 letter to Lawson. Work on *Count Julian*, though, proceeded "rather slowly" (*Letters* 1: 139). By March of 1839, Simms had made significant progress, but an unforeseen circumstance would severely delay the work, and perhaps ruin all chances of it being either a fitting sequel to *Pelayo* or a strong novel in its own right. In a letter of 30 March 1839, Simms asked Lawson to "call on the Harpers & see if they have received any M.S. from me, of the sequel to Pelayo" (*Letters* 1: 142). This manuscript contained the first five books of *Count Julian*, but was lost at some point before or during its delivery to the publishers. According to family legend, Simms was separated from the manuscript because he was instructed by a psychic to avoid the ship from New York to Charleston on which he had already booked passage (Guilds, *Literary Life* 393n). The author's luggage—including the *Count Julian* manuscript—was already on board. Though unable to retrieve his belongings, Simms followed the advice of the psychic and canceled his passage on that ship, which sank off of Cape Hatteras. Miraculously, the trunk containing the manuscript of *Count Julian* washed up on shore and eventually was found. Simms did not recover the manuscript until 1841, as evidenced by his noting in a letter from October of that year that the work "has now only recently been restored to me" (*Letters* 1: 281). Because the early 1840s was one of the most productive eras of Simms's career, he was busy with other projects when the manuscript finally made its way back to him. As a result, he did not restart composition on *Count Julian* for at least another year and a half. Thus, nearly four years had elapsed from the time Simms began work on *Count Julian* to when he resumed its composition in mid-1843.

These intervening years created a significant obstacle to the easy completion of *Count Julian*: quite simply, Simms seems to have forgotten his original plans for the novel. Despite this, he made arrangements, as he often did, to have the book published before it was completed. Park Benjamin was contracted to bring out the still-unfinished work by August 1843, thus giving Simms very little time to complete a work he now found unfamiliar. To make matters worse, Simms had to forward the incomplete manuscript to Benjamin as part of his arrangements with the publisher. Not in possession of the original manuscript for a second time, Simms wrote to Lawson that he hoped his agent would encourage Benjamin to make "immediate progress, with the novel, as it will be impossible for me to prepare the sequel until I get the printed sheets which precede. I have not read the thing for years" (*Letters* 1: 365). Perhaps predictably, Simms did not finish in time for August publication.

In October 1843, just as Simms seemed to be wrapping up the novel, new delays occurred. Benjamin seemingly had yet to print proofs. A vexed Simms wrote to Lawson to "see Benjamin on the subject of the novel. My understanding was that they were to put it to press instantly, or as soon as possible. Instead of this, here is 1 ½ months, and no proof yet. . . . Do see them about it, and unless they are willing to proceed at once, or if they show any reluctance, let the MS. be withdrawn" (*Letters* 1: 375–76). When he eventually did receive and review the proofs, Simms told Lawson "I very much fear that Count Julian will be a wretched failure. This is *entre nous*. It seems to me from reading some 40 pages of the proofs that it is monstrous flat. Heaven grant it may get better as it proceeds" (*Letters* 1: 416). By April 1844, Simms had still heard nothing about the novel's publication; ultimately, Benjamin never issued *Count Julian*.

While the business and legal details of the end of Simms and Benjamin's relationship are unclear, by early 1845 Simms had moved on to working with two other possible publishers for *Count Julian*: Burgess, Stringer and Co. and J. Winchester. The author continued to struggle with completion of the novel, and his relationship with these publishers was soon strained, just as it had been with Benjamin. He wrote to Lawson in February, "As soon as [Winchester] sends me the proof of what he has, I will finish the story. . . . This I cannot do, unless I rewrite and reinvent all that portion which he retains. You will also get from Stringer the printed volumes & retain them for me. I do not care to urge the work upon him, altho he was pledged for it" (*Letters* 2: 39). By June, both publishers were gone, and William Taylor had purchased the rights to *Count Julian*. Simms was soon able to finish the work, but there were still delays, as evidenced by his pointedly asking Lawson in November 1845, "Why has Taylor delayed the Count?" (*Letters* 2: 115) The nature of these delays is unclear. While the copyright was secured in

1845, it remains unclear whether the work was actually brought out to the public in late 1845 or early 1846; compounding this confusion is discrepancy in the date printed on the title page and cover. Though otherwise identical, the cover is dated 1846, while the title page reads 1845. Whatever the actual publication date, Taylor did publish *Count Julian*. While Simms's long ordeal was finally over, the novel's strange and troubled composition and publication history is reflected in its overall poor quality. Until the recent *Simms Initiatives* volume, the 1845/46 Taylor edition was the only publication of the novel.

One of the more curious features of *Count Julian* is Simms's dedicatory epistle to John Pendleton Kennedy, the Baltimore lawyer and congressman most famous as author of *Swallow Barn*. Simms invoked Kennedy as a sort of surrogate through whom he could offer an apologia for *Count Julian* to the public, in anticipation of the criticism it was sure to receive. In the dedication, Simms noted that Kennedy would "easily understand how much of the encouragement of the author depends upon the reader's sympathy, and how much the just decision upon his labors result from a correct knowledge of the circumstances under which he has toiled," (*Count Julian* v) circumstances Simms would soon relate. He described the work's beginnings as a drama and lamented the "absurdity" of "theatrical management in modern times" which lead to the work being "consigned to the closet" (vi). Simms then explained how this drama was later brought out of "the closet," and reworked to produce *Pelayo* and *Count Julian*.

Mentioning the latter work, Simms declared to Kennedy that while it was not "worthy of you, my dear sir, it is yet frankly laid before you as one of the best testimonies of my own abilities and of my respect for yours" (vii). Though Simms called it a testimony to his own abilities, he also seemed to know that there were things about *Count Julian* that could have been changed. The novel could have been made better, but "such an attempt would involve an entire remodeling of the structure—a change of plan and purpose—of elements and attributes—of scenes, places and characters—and, in the somewhat mournful language of Scott, in similar self-review, I resolved to 'let the tree lie where it had fallen.' That tree, my dear sir, is at your feet" (*Count Julian* viii). In many strange ways, this dedicatory epistle both admitted and tried to excuse the great flaws of *Count Julian*. It was Simms's hope that Kennedy "will find some fruits [within the novel] which, if not of the richest flavor, or the noblest size, will at least possess a not ungrateful relish for your lips" (viii). His friend could, thus, soften the harsh critical judgment he likely knew to be coming.

Critical Reception and Evaluation

In comparison to the great successes Simms had with other works in the 1830s and '40s, both novels were relatively unnoticed upon their release and have seen very little critical attention since. Wimsatt notes that of six journals that regularly reviewed Simms's works, only the *Knickerbocker* reviewed *Pelayo*; the causes of this dearth of criticism are unclear ("*Ivanhoe*" 251n). Nevertheless, the journals that did consider *Pelayo* provided generally positive reviews: though later often at odds with Simms, the *Knickerbocker* recommended the work, and described it as a novel that will satisfy readers that "kindle at passionate language, and stirring dramatic incident" (qtd. in Butterworth and Kibler 40). The same review also commented on the fact that Simms's narrative departed from pure, factual history—a prescient recognition, as the coming years would see Simms's intellectual energies deeply involved in trying to theorize the proper relationship between art and history. The *Ladies' Journal* also recommended *Pelayo*, noting that it "will not only be read, but will be remembered, for there are such scenes in it which cannot leave the mind" (qtd. in Butterworth and Kibler 41). In the case of *Count Julian*, the novel was critically damned from its first appearance, with the *Knickerbocker* caustically noting that "there is more life in the sleeping beauty of a wax museum" (qtd. in Butterworth and Kibler 67). Simms's Kennedy-invoking dedicatory gambit backfired, succeeding only in further compromising the work's reputation: reviewers saw Simms's apologetic stratagem as insulting to Kennedy, a novelist who was highly regarded at the time, and critics were vitriolic over this *faux pas*.

Both novels have been almost completely critically disregarded in the twentieth and twenty-first centuries. Guilds dismissively calls *Count Julian* "ill-advised" (*Literary Life* 195) and describes *Pelayo* as "a derivative piece below the standards of an author of Simms's caliber." He suggests that the positive reviews of the latter during Simms's life are "attributable to the taste of the time and the reputation of the author, not to the sagacity of the reviewers" (81). Mary Ann Wimsatt provides the fullest twentieth century treatment of each novel, devoting two essays to considering their place in Simms's canon, as well as their connections to works by other major writers.

In an essay exploring the parallels between the Spanish fictions of Simms and Washington Irving, Wimsatt finds *Count Julian* related to Irving's *Legends of the Conquest of Spain*, a work also about the "accession of Roderick to the Gothic throne of Spain, his various crimes which culminate in the rape of Count Julian's daughter, and Julian's subsequent betrayal of Spain to the Moors" ("Irving" 33). She notes that while "the influence of Irving on Simms is strong and evident," throughout the work, "Simms did not, apparently, make much specific use of Irving's story," in the first five books of *Count Julian*, and instead drew on the ninth-century account of the Moorish historian Rasis—the same account that Irving used as his source material. However, Book Six, the novel's final section, leans heavily on Irving's *Legends*, adapting phrases and descriptions from that work (*Count Julian* 33–34). Wimsatt agrees with earlier dismissive assessments of *Count Julian*, calling it "derivative, digressive, frequently melodramatic and tedious," and argues that it does "not challenge even the relative mediocrity of Irving's work" ("Irving" 34). But in an essay that examines the influence of

Scott's *Ivanhoe* on *Pelayo*, Wimsatt examines that work closely. *Pelayo*, she argues, is a novel that helps us understand Simms's place in the nineteenth-century Anglo-American intellectual and literary climate, and suggests that "Simms's indebtedness to Scott extends far beyond the fragmentary borrowings previous writers on the subject proclaim" ("*Ivanhoe*" 253). Wimsatt contends that these, and other, features help to redeem the work, despite its "prolixity, melodrama, and slightly salacious sexuality" ("*Ivanhoe*" 260), concluding that the work thus deserves wider critical attention.

Reconsidering *Pelayo* and *Count Julian*

Wimsatt's assessment of *Pelayo* leads in the right direction. While an imperfect novel that suffers from unnecessary digressions and jarring stylistic choices, *Pelayo* is nevertheless a generally exciting, readable book, with real adventure and intrigue. But what makes the work truly interesting are the ways Simms attempts to take it beyond an historical adventure story and make it into a novel of ideas. The work opens with a brief examination of the historical circumstances of medieval Spain, including a recounting of the degenerate kingship of King Witiza and his overthrow by Don Roderick. Simms shows that the downfall of Witiza, and other like governments, is due to misrule, excess, and an overall abandonment of virtue. The Goth, Simms tells us, "had sunk from all the attributes of that forward valour and manly simplicity of character" (*Pelayo* 17). Looking to illustrate transhistorical truths, the author prescribed revolution as the cure for such vicious government; though they are marked by violence, suffering, and "horrors" that are "lamentable," revolutions "are injurious to places rather than to people. The great bulk of mankind grow wiser upon them, and the discovery of a new abiding-place, like the discovery of a new truth, must always afford an added empire to thought, and a wider realm to the wing of liberty" (*Pelayo* 13).

Simms's concerns in this novel were not different from those he advanced in his romances of Revolutionary America—he asked how a government loses its virtue, and what the proper response of a people should be to a government marked by vice, excess, and loss of "manly simplicity of character." How do we understand the forward march of liberty, and what role do people from different stations of life play in this movement? How is government legitimized, and can a ruler who lacks in virtue still be a legitimate ruler? Perhaps most importantly, what is the role of singular great men in the progress of liberty? These last two questions are the most pressing explorations in *Pelayo*, as the novel sees the deposed King's sons, Pelayo and Egiza, conspiring to restore the rule of their family and overthrow the vicious and lustful "usurper." Yet, after his defeat of Witiza, Roderick is declared King by the Gothic nobles—not by himself. He thus is able to claim to be technically a legitimate ruler, who has the support of at least some of the people. This complication figures in the brothers' attempts to build a conspiracy against Roderick with the nobles who did not support his ascendancy.

They first attempt to persuade Julian, Count of Cueta and the most accomplished soldier in Spain, to support their cause. Yet the virtuous Julian refuses the princes' offer, as he sees Roderick's rule as legitimate, right, and proper because it has been proclaimed by a large number of his fellow nobles.

Despite his ostensible legitimacy, Roderick, because of his fundamentally lustful and tyrannical nature, is Simms's villain; Pelayo and Egiza's quest to overthrow him forms the novel's central action, as the brothers are Simms's representatives of liberty and nobility. In this way, Simms essentially wrote the history of Revolutionary America back onto that of medieval Spain. A key moment in the novel is when Pelayo is able to gain the political and military support of Spain's Jewish community, who answer to the leadership of the desert warrior Melchior. Under Roderick, the Jews continue to be a people in peripatetic exile; Melchior is certain that, under the rule of Pelayo, his people will finally have a place to belong, a country and a government that will provide them with the assurances of liberty, security, and justice. In talking to Melchior about the Jews' support of his bid for the crown, Pelayo makes promises to Melchior that a contemporary of Simms would have recognized as positively Jeffersonian. The young prince promises that, under his kingship, Jews would have "the same freedom with the rest, to hold their faith and their wealth—their several thoughts—to shape themselves in life—pursue their venture, whether in worship, or in toil, or in trade, each with his single mood, with no restraint, save of wholesome laws that all obey" (*Pelayo* 87). As Pelayo journeys throughout the Spanish countryside, he makes similar promises to other groups. Spain, then, is to be a multi-ethnic kingdom, ruled by a government based in notions of justice and liberty—ideals that would echo on the other side of the Atlantic a thousand years later.

As he reimagined eighth-century Spain as a prototype for the American Republic, Simms did a credible job of discussing virtue, liberty, and equality. This is especially apparent in his sympathetic and nuanced presentation of the Jewish characters and Pelayo's impassioned defenses of their patriotism to suspicious Christian Spaniards. The author's repudiation of the anti-Semitic stereotypes of avarice, licentiousness, and the hatred of the Christian are compelling and artfully done. Although one character, Amri, does indeed fit these stereotypes, his vices stand in stark contrast to the virtues of all the other Jewish characters. Furthermore, Simms linked Amri to the equally despicable Christian nobleman Edacer to show that moral degeneracy is the fault of the individual, not the race. Simms took a seemingly Aristotelian approach to virtue in the novel. While Amri, Edacer, and Roderick are clearly flawed because of their *lack* of virtue, the almost monomaniacal pursuit of justice and liberty on the parts of Pelayo and Melchior, at times, illustrates that an excess of virtue can itself become vice. Their pursuit becomes tedious, and the demands that Pelayo places on his brother Egiza, like those that Melchior places on his daughter Thyrza, do much to show a flaw of even heroic men—they can fail at simple human decency in favor of abstract ideals.

Simms's adherence to the conventions of the Romance leads to one of the most powerful *and* problematic aspects of the novel: needing a "dark lady" to parallel the virtuous and pure Thyrza, Simms develops a subplot around a Gothic prostitute named Urraca. This subplot presents her love for Amri, and her desire to leave her profession and commit herself fully to him. Amri, however, manipulates Urraca to satisfy both his lusts and further his political ambitions. Eventually finding her to be an impediment to his aspirations for power, Amri attempts to eliminate Urraca by convincing the enslaved Zitta to poison her mistress, a plot Urraca learns of and tries to turn back against Amri. Simms elegantly presents this series of events, using this subplot to provide readers with some of his most robust explorations of love, ambition, and, most interestingly, slavery itself. The relationship between mistress and slave is well-realized, moving, and morally nuanced; Simms here questioned the purposes and ethics of slavery, providing readers with a moving example of the complexity of his thought on the subject. As in other places in his *oeuvre*, Simms also shows himself unafraid to discuss sexual ethics forthrightly, a feature of his fiction that deserves greater critical attention. Finally, the closing scene of the subplot is incredibly beautiful, shockingly violent, and one of Simms's most emotionally realized scenes generally. Taken together, the story of Urraca, Amri, and Zitta is one of the real highlights of *Pelayo*.

Yet, this subplot is also vexing. It seems, at best, to be only tangentially related to the rest of the novel, and feels shoe-horned into the book. It does little to explicate or complement the main action of the story, and causes *Pelayo* to be seventy-plus pages too long. Finally, it seems a waste to use the incredibly compelling figure of Urraca in a context where her story is little more than a digression. Simms would have done much better to devote a short story or novella to telling this story; that he shoves it into Book IV of *Pelayo* is disappointing with regard to the narrative potential for Urraca's story, and frustrating as a jarring and emotionally demanding digression from the rest of the novel.

Taken as a whole, *Pelayo* offers a fascinating exploration of liberty, freedom, justice, notions of virtue, religious tolerance, and the inevitable flaws of great men participating in a great endeavor. It is, of course, full of aesthetic shortcomings, too: the tediousness of its dialogue, its overall prolixity, and the aforementioned subplot concerning Urraca, Amri, and Zitta. Yet, despite these flaws, *Pelayo* is a much stronger novel than has been previously argued. Reading its understanding of revolution and the pursuit of liberty and justice alongside Simms's more familiar romances would, I think, give us a deeper insight into the author's philosophy of history, government, and the artist's place in these pursuits.

Count Julian was billed as the sequel to *Pelayo*, and it in many ways wants to explore similar themes. Yet, the work is messy and often frustrating to the point of un-readability. The narrative jumps in unexpected and confusing ways. Pelayo himself is absent from *Count Julian* until its close, in what seems like a hackneyed attempt at continuity between the two works. Yet, perhaps the incredible composition and publication history of *Count Julian* suggests that we cannot, in any really reliable way, read this as a sequel to *Pelayo* except in terms of inspiration. Read as its own novel, *Count Julian* explores religious zealotry, romantic love, desire for power and money, and animal lust as obsessions that control an individual, leading to hubris and error. While there thus may be some similarities in theme and setting between the two books, Simms's work in *Count Julian*, especially with regard to religion, sets it significantly apart from *Pelayo*.

Count Julian's plot centers on Toledo, where Pelayo and Egiza's uncle, the Archbishop Oppas, is enacting his own schemes against Roderick from within the royal court. The morally degenerate Oppas is a holy man only in title, and shows no concern for either piety or the justice and liberty sought by his nephews. Rather, his goal is only the fulfillment of his lust for Roderick's queen, and he engages in complex machinations to achieve his goal. Chief among these are his manipulation of Romano, a mentally unstable religious zealot who harasses Roderick with Old Testament-style prophetic warnings. Oppas also seeks to manipulate Count Julian, who, at the novel's opening, is still loyal to Roderick. The twisted archbishop convinces Roderick to send Count Julian to fight the Moors, and persuades Julian to send his beautiful daughter, Cava, to Toledo for protection. Oppas knows that Cava's beauty will fire an insatiable lust in Roderick, and the twisted Archbishop predicts that the king's rapaciousness will lead to Cava's rape and Julian seeking vengeance against Roderick for the sovereign's vile action; in the ensuing chaos, Oppas hopes that he will be able to claim Roderick's queen as his own bride. Complicating matters is the presence of Prince Egiza, who met and fell hopelessly in love with Cava during the action of *Pelayo*. Having abandoned his brother in the mountains outside of Cordova, Egiza seeks to rescue his beloved Cava from the rapacious king. During his rescue attempt, Egiza makes an attempt on Roderick's life. This proves fruitful for Oppas's schemes, and the plot moves forward until Julian has, at the novel's climax, denounced his faith, declared loyalty to the Caliph, and joined forces with the Moors so as to effect his vengeance against Roderick for the rape and ruin of Cava.

The plot is convoluted, and *Count Julian* deserves its reputation for being an overwrought and tedious potboiler. Yet, in examining how positive impulses like religious devotion and romantic love can, in fact, lead to error and vice, *Count Julian* gives the reader pause, and asks us to reconsider what we know about Simms's overall project. Clearly Oppas and Roderick are evil. But several of the other characters, like the love-obsessed Egiza and the piety-obsessed Romano, are much more ambiguous in their morality and virtue. There are also unambiguously good and heroic characters. Chief among these are Egiza's jailer, Guisenard, and the muleteer Toro. These men are marked by a sober restraint that contrasts to the lustful excesses of Oppas and Roderick; by a sense of duty to others that nevertheless resists the destructively obsessive regard we see Julian and Egiza holding for Cava; and by a simple and humble Christian faith, in stark contrast to the irrational, bombastic, and dangerous zealousness of Romano. They are not the ridiculous, salacious caricatures that define the novel's other male characters, nor the helplessly pathetic shells we see in Cava and the Queen. Instead, Simms showed examples of real virtue in these men, and they seem to be the only fully human characters in the novel. Again, it is as if Simms was proposing true virtue in an Aristotelian sense, and only Guisenard and Toro, among all the characters in *Count Julian*, are able to find the golden mean.

Yet these two men are only minor characters, involved in plots merely complementary to the main action of the novel; that such liminal figures are *Count Julian*'s most heroic characters is deeply unsettling. What is even more disturbing is how quickly, and with what great and egregious violence, Simms killed these characters. Their deaths are the two most beautiful and completely realized scenes of the novel, on par with some of Simms's most powerful scenes generally, but Simms so jarringly ripped these characters from the narrative that readers cannot help but view them as literally hopeless. In this way, they seem to be a fitting metonym for the entirety of *Count Julian*.

Perhaps the difficulties in composing *Count Julian* made Simms unable to write a hopeful novel, and these scenes are the frustrations of the writer made manifest. Even if the hopelessness of the work can be attributed to the author's palpable frustrations, the Simms scholar must nevertheless contend with the darkness inherent in these scenes, especially with regard to religion. In *Count Julian*, prayers are not answered, except in death. Simms insinuated that the rape of Cava occurs underneath the gaze of an icon of the Blessed Virgin, and Toro's call to Mary to save him results only in death. Guisenard's simple, rational piety is destroyed by Romano's mad fundamentalism, and Oppas literally molests those who come to make their confession to him. A harrowing moment of mob violence results from attempts to convey the corpse of a "saint" to a church. All of these scenes of religious depravity lead to the novel's climax, Julian's apostasy, where he declares that all faiths are nothing more than "national superstitions." Faith, as Simms presented it, portends to be as much a sin as lust, greed, or wrath. The reader interested in understanding how Simms thought of religion must necessarily visit *Count Julian*. While Simms himself was broadly Christian, if not a churchman, the dark, proto-naturalistic world of *Count Julian* forces us to question just how orthodox his understanding of religion truly was, at least at this moment in his career. Exploring these questions makes *Count Julian* a worthy and rich source of study for the Simms scholar—even if it is, in many ways, a bad novel.

Both *Pelayo* and *Count Julian* have deep and profound aesthetic shortcomings, and the cynical reader could see their presentations of big ideas as attempts by the author to cover up their weaknesses as novels. Yet the truth of that is up to the scholar to decide. Both works, despite their flaws, deserve real attention, precisely because these two imperfect romances of medieval Spain try to explore some of the most profound questions that Simms took up in his *oeuvre*: the nature of virtue, the role of government, the purposes and ends of liberty, the place of faith in personal and public life, and the dangers that accompany all of these. Perhaps Simms could have explored these ideas sufficiently in a work of the Early American Republic, fictional territory on which he surely had much more aesthetic successes. But, convinced of transhistorical truths, he used his prerogative as an artist to explore other shores, and saw them as equally able to tell his society about itself and its moment, while at the same time telling about another people and their historical and cultural situation. If this is a flaw on the part of Simms, it is a flaw of ambition—the only flaw we would ever wish on our truly great artists.

A Supplement to the Plays of William Shakespeare

NAN MORRISON

Like many novelists, William Gilmore Simms was drawn to the dramatic genre on both the stage and the page. He wrote to F.C. Adams, "Dramatic writing was my first literary passion, and I believe it to be my forte" (*Letters* 3: 163). From 1825 to 1835 he wrote many dramatic fragments, one of which, "Pelayo," he completed at the age of eighteen (Watson, *Antebellum* 116). Another, "The Death of Cleopatra," took its inspiration from her tragic portrayal in *Antony and Cleopatra* by William Shakespeare, the dramatist who was his "first love," to use John Caldwell Guilds's description. Simms's letters, essays, and novels are sprinkled with phrases from Shakespeare's plays, but his study of his idol was not superficial. Hugh Holman and Ernest Vandiver have analyzed the ways in which Simms uses the dramatic techniques of Shakespeare to deepen the characterizations in his novels. Joseph Kenner believes that, in addition to imitating techniques, Simms appropriated from Shakespeare the defining concept of masculinity many of his male characters manifest. Holman and Vandiver argue also, and the epigraphs to the chapters of some of his novels support their analysis, that Simms's knowledge of Elizabethan and Jacobean drama was not limited to plays written by Shakespeare. Indeed, Grace Whaley has tabulated the many allusions in his novels to Ben Jonson, John Webster, and lesser-known playwrights such as Philip Massinger, George Chapman, and James Shirley.

Largely self-taught, Simms seems to have considered early English dramas as his textbooks. He advised poet Alfred Billings Street to "go through a course of the old blood and bone and sinew of the dramatists of the Shakspeare period" (*Letters* 2: 156). He admonished Thomas A. Burke "Acquaint yourself with the standard literature of the Shakspeare and Baconian period" (*Letters* 3: 447–48; of the six variant spellings of Shakespeare's name, Simms preferred "Shakspeare").

Perhaps believing that adaptation is the sincerest homage, Simms rewrote entire acts of Shakespeare's *Timon of Athens* and *The Tragedy of Locrine*, a play which was imputed to Shakespeare, changing the settings and context. His hope was that these adaptations would be performed by Edwin Forrest, the leading American actor at the time. Writing to James Lawson, his literary agent at whose house he met Forrest, Simms vowed that he would seal his "fate in the drama" and was "determined" to make Forrest his "colleague in glory" (*Letters* 1: 428). Early in his marriage to Chevillette Roach, in September 1837, Simms looked forward to taking her to New York "to see [Edwin Forrest's] Othello and Lear" (*Letters* 1: 117). When Simms saw Forrest perform on the stage in Charleston, he remarked on his "crudenesses," "defective tastes," and "disregard to details," but he realized that the "vigor," "courage," and "unique entireness" of America's first great tragedian gave him the attraction of a star. (Simms, "Thoughts") Unfortunately, Forrest rejected both of Simms's adaptations.

Simms went to the theater as often as he could in New York and Charleston, and he reviewed the New York performance of *As You Like It* by Ellen Tree and her husband, Charles Kean. He wrote the *Southern Patriot* on 26 September 1845, "I had the pleasure of seeing the two former in "As You Like it," [*sic*] and promise you that you will find no falling off in Ellen Tree. Her 'Rosalind' is quite as admirable and exquisite as ever. The 'Jaques' of Charles Kean is scarcely to my liking" (*Letters* 2: 130n). The next year he looked forward to seeing them in Charleston: "My wife will go to town (Charleston) with me sometime this month, as soon as we hear of the arrival of Mrs. Kean (Ellen Tree) whom she is anxious to see" (*Letters* 2: 130–31). At the age of twenty-one Simms had been confident of his opinions about the meaning, the acting, and the texts of Shakespeare. In an 1830 review of a performance in Charleston of *Julius Caesar* he saw "the enthusiasm of Liberty and the strong detestation of Tyranny" as did most Americans, but it is the southern ethos which is reflected in his praise of Thomas Abthorpe Cooper's acting: "All was manly and noble, passionate and grateful." But, strangely for a nineteenth-century southerner, he shows no understanding of the stoic Roman view of suicide and speaks of the guilt which should ensue from self-murder. His criticism of the script shows a poet's sensitivity to sound and rhythm. Simms decries the change the actor playing Cassius made in Shakespeare's text: "Mr. Southwell destroyed the music of the line—'Oh, I could weep. My spirit from my eyes! There is my *dagger*!'—by substituting the word 'sword' for that of 'dagger.' A Poet annexes no little import to a word—and the difference to our ear between these words is considerably in favor of the former" (Simms, Rev. of *Julius Caesar*).

Simms's interest in drama was not limited to stage performance. His letters to Lawson and Evert Augustus Duyckinck are littered with requests for early English texts. He was acutely interested in the variances in texts of the same work. To Richard Yeadon he explained the differences seen in *The Merry Wives of Windsor*: "In my English editions of Shakspeare, the language of Pistol is precisely as I wrote it. In my American editions it is as you copied it. The character of Pistol's usual phraseology and the purport of what he means to say, incline me to prefer the English as the true reading" (*Letters* 2: 62). He was one of the first subscribers to the publications of the Shakespeare Society and ordered texts from the Percy Society and the Camden Society, all of which were founded in 1840 and dedicated to the publication of early English texts (*Letters* 2: 67, 108, 124, 184, 190; *Letters* 3: 165). His library contained several editions of the works of Shakespeare, including the 1790 edition published by Stockdale, as well as editions by Hudson and Mason (*Letters* 3: 102, 379, 498). He frequently perused Samuel Ayscough's *An Index to the Remarkable Passages and Words Made Use of by Shakespeare* and Mary Cowden Clarke's *The Complete Concordance to Shakespeare* (*Letters* 2: 102, 107). He asked Duyckinck to secure installments of "the heroines of Shakspeare," a reference to Anna Brownell Jameson's *Characteristics of Women* first published in 1832 in England (*Letters* 2: 199).

The two editions of Shakespeare's works that influenced *A Supplement* are Charles Knight's *The Pictorial Edition of the Works of Shakespeare* published in eight volumes in London between 1839 and 1843, which Simms asked Duyckinck to procure for him (*Letters* 2: 180), and the 1780 edition by Edmund Malone, *Supplement to the Edition of Shakespeare's Plays Published in 1778 by Samuel Johnson and George Steevens*. The latter may be the edition he told James Henry Hammond he could purchase: "There is a copy of Shakspeare in N.Y. (or was) for $20 or $25, which was unique, being one of the best folio editions & containing all of the *imputed* plays . . . which Shakspeare was at one time supposed to have written & which he may have written when a boy" (*Letters* 2: 313, emphasis in original). Malone's supplement contained all of the plays Simms would edit except *The Two Noble Kinsmen* which was included in Knight's *Pictorial*.

Simms parodied his own love for texts in his depiction of Tom Horsey, a Shakespearean actor, from the author's 1840 novel *Border Beagles*. Like Simms, Tom flavors his conversations with snippets from Elizabethan and Jacobean plays. Like his creator, Tom also collects editions of Shakespeare and has an exaggerated interest in textual variances: "It was curious to see with what industry the youth had accumulated authorities on Shakspeare. He had Gifford, Malone, Steevens, Seymour, Rowe, Farmer, and some thirty or forty more at his finger-ends" and was able to entertain his companion "with a dozen different readings of all the disputed passages in Macbeth, Hamlet, Richard, and the rest" (1: 81).

Even though he extensively annotated his copy of Shakespeare's canonical works, Simms may have realized that editing a new edition of all thirty-six of the Bard's plays printed in the First Folio was a herculean task for someone who had to earn a living from his writing. The seven texts that comprised Shakespeare's apocryphal works would be more manageable. Further, there was no American edition of the disputed plays, and Simms could provide a service to the readers in his country and fill a niche in the literary market. Even seven plays proved to be more time-consuming than he anticipated. But, he achieved his goal in April 1848 when his volume became the first American edition of the Shakespeare Apocrypha. William Peterfield Trent may be correct in his judgment that Simms lacked the training and "life-long environment" (136) to produce a scholarly edition which would stand the test of time; nonetheless his introductions to the plays provide insight into the way Simms thought about his own art and the shape of a literary career.

The Work

A Supplement contains a general introduction, emended texts of and notes on the seven plays listed in the title, and an introduction to each play. The plays were selected because all of them except *The Two Noble Kinsmen* had been printed in Shakespeare's lifetime with his name or initials on the title page. *The Two Noble Kinsmen* had been printed after his death with the names of Shakespeare and John Fletcher on the title page. The authorship of these plays had been widely debated, but Simms states that a decision "upon their authenticity is not one of the goals of the author and publishers" who "prefer to leave the question, as they find it to future criticism and the sagacity of the reader" (*Supplement* 3). The dramas may be "changelings," "scarce half made up" and "sent into the world before their time," like *Richard III*, "but they need to be united in the same household." Simms immediately contradicts himself by arguing for their authenticity and, unfortunately, bases his argument on a false assumption. He says that Heminge and Condell, fellow actors who collected Shakespeare's plays after his death, included the plays in the First Folio of 1623 for which Ben Jonson, a rival playwright, wrote a dedicatory poem. This is the best proof of Shakespeare's authorship because "they and he [Heminge, Condell, Jonson] ought to have known whether these plays could properly, or should be, imputed to his pen. They include them without doubt or misgiving." Further, he says, six of the plays "are in the order of the old folio of Heminge and Condell" (*Supplement* 11–12). The First Folio, edited by Heminge and Condell, did not contain these plays. They were included in the second printing of the Third Folio in 1664 long after Heminge, Condell, and Jonson had died.

Simms is not as confident as his assertion suggests, but his thesis is that these plays may have been written in Shakespeare's youth, between the age of 18 and 25, because he had to have written something before he wrote *Titus Andronicus* at the age of twenty-five. They are, therefore, worthy of attention because they provide the aspiring writer an insight into how "his predecessor worked—from what small beginnings, against what obstructions, and with what inferior tools. It is important, indeed, that he should see where, and how frequently, the great master has faltered, or has fallen, in his experiments." Reading the plays gives a young writer an understanding of the growth of the mind and art of the dramatist, how "feebly, step by step, he has continued to struggle, upward and onward, until from awkwardnesses, he arrives at grace" (*Supplement* 4).

Both of these points may be projections of Simms's life. He wrote prolifically from an early age, and he thought that most of his early work was inferior. In a letter to John Pendleton Kennedy he described his early work with the same imagery of childbirth he used to describe the imputed plays: "I need not say to you with what doubt and disappointment we are apt to look back, after the lapse of a few years, on what has been the favorite achievement of our youth. . . . But an author's writings are always useful—even when abortive as works of art—to those who would study his career & properly analyze his endowments" (*Letters* 2: 160). When he sent Beverley Tucker copies of some of his books, Simms apologized for them because they were written "at an extremely early age, & under the pressure of necessities which left me too careless of any but present & momentary circumstances" (*Letters* 2: 528).

Even if his works were "disfigured by errors of taste and judgment," he hoped they showed "proofs of original force, native character, and some imagination" (*Letters* 2: 528). The tension between genius and artistry was one with which Simms was familiar because, according to even his best friends, he lacked the patience and temperament to polish the works which his fertile imagination provided him. James Henry Hammond frequently chastised Simms for squandering his natural gifts. It comes as a surprise, therefore, when Simms refutes the romantic view of Shakespeare as an untutored child of nature. Instead, he says, Shakespeare had well-off parents who provided him with a good education. His early works were influenced by the books he read, and his art was an acquired talent as well as a natural gift. This view accords with Simms's thesis that as Shakespeare matured so did his craft.

Simms also projects his life onto Shakespeare's in his discussion of *The Yorkshire Tragedy*. This play, based on an actual incident which occurred in 1604, did not obviously fit his thesis that the imputed plays were written during Shakespeare's youth. Reflecting his own hectic labors, Simms writes that "it is yet possible that he wrote it, in nightgown and slippers, scene by scene to meet the wants of the actors. The demands of a theatre, the hurried competition of rival houses, might easily prompt him to this drudgery, as an aside from his usual labors, at the very moment that he was most busy on his glorious achievements" (114). Besides, he adds, it is impossible to date Shakespeare's plays. While this statement is correct about some of the plays, it undermines Simms's thesis that the imputed plays show the artistic mistakes of a beginning writer while the canonical plays are the polished and sophisticated art of a mature writer.

Although his argument is contradictory, his description of how Shakespeare could write an inferior play at the same period in which he was writing *Macbeth* and *King Lear* reflects the way Simms often wrote about his own life and career. Describing the mismanagement of the cotton plantation on which he depended and his father-in-law's lethargy, he diplomatically wrote to Beverley Tucker, "These hints will enable you readily to understand why it is that I wrote so much, so recklessly, and still have an eye to the *quid*" (*Letters* 3: 11). Later, he wrote Tucker, "I am hurried and interrupted. . . . I am engaged in a drudgery which leaves me almost incapable of any thing else,—I am weary, vexed, and, as you phrase it 'out of heart'" (*Letters* 3: 95). When Hammond begged him not to squander his talent, he wrote, "I see nothing at present before me, but the necessity of toiling on, as I do now, assured that my drudgeries will, at least, provide me with the means of staving off necessities" (*Letters* 3: 194). If the inferior imputed plays were, indeed, written during Shakespeare's younger years or even later under pressure, then Simms's inferior works written during his youth and later under pressure might be prologues to greater works of art.

Despite his avowal that the purpose of the work is not to come to conclusions about authorship, Simms does. *The Two Noble Kinsmen* is "not the work of an apprentice" because "it is too confident a performance for the inexperienced writer, and too wanting in the higher freedoms of music and imagination, for Shakspeare in the day of his mature manhood." He agrees with Knight that the truth found in *The Puritan* is "not such truth as we find in Shakespeare," and, further, "the very meanest of [Shakespeare's] acknowledged and unquestioned writings is so infinitely beyond this performance as to make any attempt at comparison impertinent" (*Supplement* 118). Of *Thomas Lord Cromwell* he concludes, "There is nothing in the performance to entitle it, as a production of Shakspeare to the smallest consideration," but he agrees with Schlegel that some of its faults derive from its being a biographical drama (67–68). The author of *Sir John Oldcastle* "appropriated certain of Shakspeare's materials" but did not imitate him (88). Oddly, unlike most Shakespeareans, Simms rejects the evidence in the diary of Philip Henslowe, the Elizabethan theatrical impresario, that he paid Anthony Munday, Michael Drayton, and two other writers for *Oldcastle*. That could be a different play, Simms says, because rival theaters often presented "pieces on the same subject" (68). He will entertain the possibility that Shakespeare wrote *The London Prodigal* despite Knight's indictment—"the low moral tone of the writer's own mind produced the low morality of the plot and its catastrophe"—because it may have been "the work of his 'prentice hand" (qtd. in Simms, *Supplement* 45).

The play that seems to fit his thesis about juvenilia perfectly is *Locrine*, the work he spent some time in adapting for Edwin Forrest. Without equivocation he claims it as an early work by a "young beginner, fresh from his classical studies, who had scarcely yet begun to think for himself, and whose chief employment hitherto had been that maturing of all young poets—the acquisition of the act of utterance" (53).

Analyses of the individual plays vary considerably. The discussions of *The Two Noble Kinsmen* and *Locrine* are lengthy and perceptive. He engages with the opinions of German and English editors. The number and validity of his textual emendations vary in the same manner. One of his flaws as an editor is his lack of specificity. Instead of citing a particular source and previous editor for a reading of a passage he emends or accepts, Simms vaguely refers to "early editions."

The Text

In July of 1847 Simms wrote Lawson, "I shall go to work tomorrow on the Shakspeare" (*Letters* 2: 328). To Benjamin Franklin Perry, on 15 July [1847] he wrote, "I am now busy in editing the half dozen plays which have been imputed to Shakspeare" (*Letters* 2: 334). Only ten days later he complained to Duyckinck, "I have spent many tedious hours,—day & night in revising imputed plays of Shakspeare, a wearisome task which I am almost sorry to have undertaken" (*Letters* 2: 336–37). On September 5, he wrote Lawson, "I have sent to Cooledge's all the Dramas but one (*Locrine*) the analysis and correction of which I will have to delay" (*Letters* 2: 346). When he wrote Lawson on October 26, he still had not finished the introduction "to the play of Locrine, and to the whole body of the work," but it had cost him "immense labor" and he should be "moderately recompensed with $500," or, at least, with $400 (*Letters* 2: 359). In early February of the next year he wrote Duyckinck that he had "just finished reading the pro[of]" of the book (*Letters* 2: 397). On 8 April 1848, *Literary World* announced that *A Supplement* was "just published" (*A Supplement* 193).

Simms's dedication of "this humble labour, a First American edition of the imputed plays of Shakspeare" honors the textual scholar and editor, the Reverend Alexander Dyce, "The acute and laborious worker in the old, but still ample and green, fields of British Dramatic Literature" (*Supplement* [1]). Dyce had edited numerous Elizabethan and Jacobean plays including *Timon of Athens*, the play Simms adapted and offered to Forrest. Simms draws attention here to the tradition in which he now places his work after having told Lawson at least twice that he would dedicate it to Edwin Forrest who had rejected his stage adaptations (*Letters* 2: 359). He has chosen the textual scholar over the stage actor.

The excellent illustrations that accompany the plays in this volume were engraved by Alexander Anderson who is listed on the cover with Shakespeare. Anderson was an experienced illustrator of dramatic texts. The catalog of the works by Shakespeare which were collected by Thomas Pennant Barton, now housed in the Boston Public Library, includes an entry for the third publication of the Boston edition of the works of Shakespeare (1810–12) with the following information: "Each play is illustrated by a wood-cut engraved by Alexander Anderson, the first person in America who followed wood-engraving as profession." According to Jane Sherzer this was the first illustrated edition of Shakespeare in America (644). His and Simms's *Supplement* was not only the first illustrated edition but the first edition of Shakespeare's Apocrypha in America.

The second edition of Simms's *A Supplement* was published by Alden and Beardsley, located in Auburn and Rochester, New York, in 1855. The portrait of Shakespeare is different from the 1848 edition, and there is no illustration for *The Two Noble Kinsmen*. Another printing of the second edition was also produced in 1855 by James B. Smith in Philadelphia entitled *A Supplement to the plays, comprising the seven dramas which have been ascribed to his pen, but which are not included with his writings in modern editions, namely: The two kinsmen; The London prodigal; Thomas Lord Cromwell; Sir John Oldcastle; The puritan, or the widow of Watling Street; The Yorkshire tragedy; The tragedy of Locrine, Ed., with notes, by William Gilmore Simms*. Although the library catalog entries for this edition give the date as "[1848]," it is probably 1855. Despite his complaints about his editorial labors,

Simms wrote Lawson that he planned "a new and revised edition of Shakspeare entire, for which my studies for years have been silently preparing me" (*Letters* 2: 409). Cooledge and Brother publishing company did bring out an edition of Shakespeare in 1851, but Simms did not edit it. Instead they published the Johnson-Steevens text with "*a glossary and an account of each play, and a memoir of the author, by the Rev. William Harness. . . . and forty beautiful illustrations engraved on wood, in the seventh-seventh year of his age, by Alexander Anderson . . . from new and original designs by T.H. Matteson.*"

The Context

Simms published his volume at the height of Shakespeare idolatry in America, a veneration which began before the colonies fought a war to become a nation. James McManaway traces the beginning of American Shakespearean theater to 1750 with a production of *Richard III*, the popular adaptation of Shakespeare's play by Colley Cibber, in New York. The same play was performed in Williamsburg in 1751; in Annapolis in 1752; in Philadelphia in 1753, and "Charleston had a performance of *Lear* in 1764" (McManaway 514). Sarah Nalley has recorded the performances of twelve plays by Shakespeare which were presented in the 1773–74 Charleston season alone. (75). Even this early, texts of the plays were available in Charleston. Hennig Cohen found fifteen advertisements for the works of Shakespeare in the *South Carolina Gazette* from 1738 to 1775 (327). Allusions to Shakespeare were woven into the fabric of early American history. In the Stamp Act controversy John Adams famously compared the Mother Country's treatment of the colonies to the maternal practices of Lady Macbeth. Abigail Adams kept a copy of Shakespeare on her bedside table and referred to herself in some of her letters as "Portia." The majority of entries in Thomas Jefferson's commonplace books were from Shakespeare's plays.

After the founding of the United States the dissemination of Shakespeare grew as the nation expanded ever forward. As settlers made their way across the country so did Shakespeare performances: from *The Merchant of Venice* in Milledgeville, Georgia (1834) to *Hamlet* and *Othello* in Montgomery, Alabama (1835). Ascribing the popularity of Shakespeare to the embryonic state of American literature, Alexis de Tocqueville marveled, "There is hardly a pioneer's hut that does not contain a few odd volumes of Shakespeare. I remember that I read the feudal drama of *Henry V* for the first time in a log cabin" (58). Esther Dunn poetically described the westward democratic movement of the poet along with the people: "He echoed along the banks of the Ohio and Mississippi as the flatboats bore settlers and entertainers westward to the new frontier. He was familiar in mining camps" (4). It is not surprising, then, to read Woodrow Holbein's account of 600 performances of twenty-three plays presented in Charleston between 1800 and 1860 (88).

It is also not surprising that the number of American editions of Shakespeare's plays began to increase. Along with this increase came a new emphasis on textual scholarship and criticism. Sherzer writes, "It is interesting to observe the difference between the two Philadelphia editions. In 1795 we are informed that the American public cares nothing for annotation; in 1805–9 the text is almost lost under the mass of comment. Nor had any previous edition in America shown so much editorial work, both in text and annotation" (649). Thus, according to Andrew Murphy, in the nineteenth century "the Shakespeare text became—from a publishing point of view—a genuinely popular commodity, to be mass-produced, mass-marketed, and mass-distributed" (5). It was this market Simms confidently entered with a collection of plays the cover of which bore the name of William Shakespeare in bold letters.

Early reviews of *A Supplement* were brief but appreciative. Anonymous reviews in *Literary World* (Rev. of *Supplement* 203) and *Southern Literary Messenger* (Rev. of *Supplement* 333) praise Simms for providing the notes and comments. The anonymous reviewer in *Graham's* (Rev. of *Supplement* 119) contested Simms's thesis that the plays were written in Shakespeare's youth. Simms's loyal friend, William Cullen Bryant, published a short but favorable review in the *New York Evening Post* on 19 April 1848.

Later critics were less kind. C.F. Tucker Brooke, editor of the definitive *The Shakespeare Apocrypha* (1908) references Simms's emendations but dismisses most of them. In discussing a deletion from *Lord Cromwell*, Brooke says that his restoration of the line "is sufficient condemnation of Malone and his blind followers: Messrs. Simms, Tyrell, Hazlitt, and Moltke" (426). Even in a negative assessment, the company Simms was keeping was not negligible for a South Carolinian with little formal schooling.

Trent, following his usual practice, came down hard on Simms's shortcomings but excused them because of his milieu: "the editor's own work was slight both in quantity and in quality. The only play annotated with any fullness was 'The Two Noble Kinsmen,' and the notes and introduction to this were mainly derived from Charles Knight. Indeed, a cursory examination of the volume would lead to the conclusion that it was but a piece of hack work, and therefore scarcely worthy of mention" (135). But, Trent continued, this objective assessment should be tempered by a consideration of the author's intention and region: "Such a conclusion would be highly unjust to Simms. He really undertook the task as a labor of love, and his own editorial and critical deficiencies were due to his lack of education and to his Southern environment" (135). Guilds wanted to destroy the myth Trent constructed of Charleston neglect, but he devotes only one sentence to *A Supplement*. Alfred Van Rensselaer Westfall echoes the charges made by Trent but concludes "Simms' edition was the first critical reprinting of these seven plays in over sixty years. It deserves some consideration" (138).

Edd Winfield Parks condemns Simms's textual expurgations while praising his critical introductions: "The expurgations are carefully noted in all the plays, but they make the text worthless for the critical student or the general reader"; nonetheless, the "critical introductions should not be dismissed" because "they present an examination of the plays from the point of view of an experienced creative writer" (*William* 80–81). This view is echoed by C. Hugh Holman who concludes that in the "general introduction and the introductions to the individual plays he demonstrated a thorough and loving acquaintance with the drama of Shakespeare's age, even though he lacked the scholarly equipment needed for the task" ("British Dramatists" 359). J.V. Ridgely echoes Trent's judgment. Of the works between 1842 and 1851, including *A Supplement*, he says, "In the marketing of material Simms was a giant in these years. Yet all his pages are little more than hack work born of immediate pressure" (*William* 88).

Parks's view sums up what I see as the value of the volume. Simms had not the training or time to be a scholarly editor; yet he had the writer's ear to detect patterns of speech and rhythm. Not to be disputed is the critical claim that he provided a service to American readers in producing texts that had never before been collected and printed in this country. For the modern reader his textual emendations and notes present an interesting glimpse into the ways in which a nineteenth-century southern writer read and thought about Shakespeare. He loved words and imaginative flights of fancy, but he was not a systematic thinker.

Vasconselos: A Romance of the New World

KEVIN COLLINS

Vasconselos: A Romance of the New World (1853) was published during a period when William Gilmore Simms seemed most interested in putting into practice a combination of synergistic theories he had preached to authors, historians, and their readers eight years earlier in a collection of essays entitled *Views and Reviews in American Literature, History and Fiction* (1845), revisions of articles and orations from the three years just prior. These theories included the notion that a uniquely American literature was essential to the development of the nation, that authors could most effectively tell the stories of their own regions of the country, and that mere objective and demonstrable history—"the dry-bones of perished humanity" (Simms, *Views* 1: 33)—is rendered more palatable and more memorable for the everyday reader when embellished with human passion, with the stuff of Romance.

Before 1853, Simms had been putting these theories into practice for twenty years in Revolutionary and Border Romances, but most of the theories were by then altered or enlarged by the tensions that would lead to the Civil War. There had already been talk in southern drawing rooms that "the nation" might not forever be the United States. Whereas Simms had for years made secessionist statements, they had balanced before 1853 with reformist statements that could be interpreted as efforts to preserve the Union (e.g., references to the need to preserve States' Rights in the entire Union by enforcing more strongly the provisions of the 10th Amendment to the Constitution). The Kansas-Nebraska Act, discussed intently in 1853 and passed the following year, led many southerners, however, to seek out potential new slave territories, and the island of Cuba—the setting for the bulk of the novel—was near the top of many lists of candidate areas. At the same time, Simms's notion of "his" region became more and more expansive. He had used southern settings earlier in his career, but using them seemed an even more intensive and conscious focus in the early 1850s: in 1852, he produced *As Good as a Comedy* (set in Tennessee) and *Michael Bonham* (Texas); the following year, he published, in addition to *Vasconselos, Marie de Berniere* (short works with southern settings from South Carolina to New Orleans), and, significantly, a non-fiction work entitled *South-Carolina in the Revolutionary War*, the long subtitle of which makes clear that it was written in response to the northern marginalization of the role Simms's region had played in the Revolution.

Whether or not he consciously intended to, Simms presented in *Vasconselos* a broad geographical expanse—parts of Florida, Georgia, the Carolinas, Tennessee, Alabama, and Mississippi—as an adopted homeland worth fighting for, and he presented even treason as justifiable, given treachery that assaults the nobler aspects of humanity. But even as the notion of his home region and its significance was expanding, Simms remained consistent in *Vasconselos* concerning the need to transcend "the dry-bones of perished humanity," and the historical account in the novel was of secondary importance to the fictional tale of human love and misery—the best and the worst of human passions—that dominates the work.

Though "colonial" literary treatments invite disapprobation in a post-colonial era, Simms wrote three:[1] *The Yemassee* (1835), *Vasconselos* (1853), and *The Cassique of Kiawah* (1859). While not as technically or aesthetically elegant as Simms's other Colonial Romances, *Vasconselos* is significant as an indicator of its author's philosophical evolution, for its inclusion of American Indian ideals within the earliest American patchwork, and for its anticipation of key principles of modern psychiatry two years before the birth of Sigmund Freud. *Vasconselos* is a Colonial Romance (Simms describes it as "ante-colonial") that treats, in various levels of depth, a host of subject matters. The most notable is the Spanish effort to colonize the New World. Within this exploration, Simms treats the adjustment of Spanish culture from Medieval to Early Modern standards, the effects of imperialistic ethics upon that culture, ruling class corruption, the alienation of racial and national minorities, and the historic De Soto expedition to mainland North America. In addition, the opening of the novel focuses on young love corrupted by sibling rivalry and incest. The end of the novel treats the emergence of a new American national identity influenced by Native American culture and, especially, by the abilities of individuals to adjust themselves to an untamed frontier environment.

Vasconselos's plot is exciting: Spanish knights in Havana, Cuba (along with two Portuguese brothers, mercenaries) prepare for departure with the De Soto Expedition to mainland North America in 1538. Preparations include a bullfighting event and a jousting tournament. Protagonist Phillip de Vasconselos, one of the Portuguese knights, is denied credit for his accomplishments because of his national origin and considers resigning from the expedition. His brother, Andres, resents Phillip and attempts to please his Spanish comrades and lords. Meanwhile, Phillip courts Olivia de Alvaro, a mysterious and beautiful teenage orphan of noble blood in the care of her uncle, Don Balthazar. Preparing to seek Olivia's hand in marriage, Phillip discovers a dark secret: that she had been regularly drugged and (it is strongly suggested) sexually molested by her uncle for years. Unwilling to expose the crime because of the shame it would bring to Olivia, Philip joins the expedition, where he will serve under both De Soto and Don Balthazar.

The expedition (including Olivia, dressed in blackface, posing as a servant boy) encounters Florida Indians who welcome and help the visitors but who are betrayed and held as slaves. Don Balthazar, aware that Phillip knows his dark secret, has him arrested and tried on trumped-up charges. De Soto orders that the Portuguese warrior be stripped of his knighthood and left to die, but he is rescued by the Indians. Phillip, together with Olivia, whom he fails to recognize, helps the Indians to evade the Spanish, and eventually to fight them. Olivia has her revenge on her wicked uncle, who dies on the expedition. But one of the pair's hosts, a noble Indian woman named Coçalla, a relative of the historical figure Tuscaloosa, falls in love with Phillip. Unaware that Olivia is beside him, he returns her affections. With the Spanish nearly defeated, Olivia dies. Defeated and near starvation, the remnants of the Spanish force decide to head for the gulf and hope for passage back to Cuba. Together with his new Indian wife, Phillip establishes a (fictional) permanent white presence on the mainland of North America, well ahead of St. Augustine, Jamestown, and Plymouth.

According to biographer John Caldwell Guilds, Simms had completed a few chapters of *Vasconselos* as early as 1848,[2] and he inquired of *Godey's Lady Book* about the possibility of serial publication. Sarah J. Hale of *Godey's* praised some passages but objected to the passion and violence of the novel. Simms next tried Philadelphia publisher Abraham Hart in 1851, specifying that the project was not yet complete. Hart, who had just published *Katharine Walton*, also rejected the novel. The author submitted the first 15 (of an eventual total of 50) chapters to Redfield in January of 1853. Redfield, which had published earlier Simms works, asked for the remainder. Simms finished and submitted the manuscript, and it was published in December of 1853. Redfield reissued the novel in 1856, and a reissue—from the same plates—was produced by Widdleton in 1868 and by A.C. Armstrong and Son, New York, in 1882. Bedford, Clarke, & Co. of Chicago reprinted it again, also from the original plates, in the same year, as did Burrow Brothers of Cleveland in 1888. Donohue, Henneberry of Chicago reissued it in 1890. There were three microform editions, all using images of the original typesetting: in 1970, both the Redfield and Bedford Clarke editions were released in microform; and Adamant Media Corporation produced another microform version in 2001. The University of Arkansas Press released in 2013 the first new edition of the novel since its original publication—with critical analysis, emendations, explanatory notes, and textual notes.

Guilds indicates that Simms planned originally to publish the novel anonymously, but he accepted the suggestion of J.S. Redfield, its first publisher, to attribute the work to "Frank Cooper." The 1853 Cooper edition, was dedicated to Dr. John W. Francis of New York. When the novel was reissued in 1856, Simms was listed as the author, and the dedication was revised to include a discussion of the caprice that led him first to publish the work pseudonymously. In addition, Simms discussed in the dedication Dr. Francis's taste, generosity, and interest in history. The original Redfield edition did not contain any illustrations. The 1868 Widdleton reissue featured two in its front matter that, though unattributed, were almost certainly by F.O.C. Darley. One depicts two armed knights grappling over a spear, with a startled horse in the background. This appears to illustrate one of the emotional high points of the portion of the novel set in Havana: the contest between Phillip and Andre de Vasconselos during the knightly tournament sponsored by De Soto. The other illustration depicts three characters and a horse. On the left side of the illustration, a short and slender character—likely Olivia, disguised as Juan, the page—holds a crossbow and the bridle of the horse. In the center is a large and seemingly noble Indian character, possibly the historical figure Tuscaloosa (spelled "Tuscaluza" in the novel), holding a spear. To the right, a knight, Vasconselos, gestures to the other two characters in conversation. This illustration seems to depict an emotional high point near the end of the novel, the decision of Vasconselos to join forces with the Indians after Don Balthazar has attempted to murder him.

Vasconselos was begun by 1848 at the latest and completed in 1853, and this period includes the midpoint of Simms's more than forty-five year career as a published writer. It is a part of his explicit plan to tell the romanticized history of his nation for the entertainment and enlightenment of his people through novel-length prose epics: the Border Romances, the Revolutionary Romances, and the Colonial Romances. Ethnohistorian Charles Hudson notes that Simms relied for some historical details upon Theodore Irving's 1851 book, *The Conquest of Florida by Hernando de Soto* (xli). In addition, Simms refers repeatedly to "The Chronicler" of the De Soto expedition in the second half of the novel, and there is indeed an extant, though fragmentary, chronicle of the journey. It was produced by four individuals who took part: Luys Hernandez de Biedma (an agent of the Spanish king), Rodrigo Ranjel (DeSoto's secretary), a Portuguese officer who called himself "A Gentleman of Elvas," and a fourth author, Garcilaso de la Vega, who called himself "The Inca." Whereas Simms may have had some familiarity with this chronicle—he owned a translation of Elvas—his narrator refers to it dismissively: "The accounts of the white men are grievously confused and contradictory, for the simple reason that they labored to obscure, to modify, and even to pervert the details whose results were so disastrous to their progress, and, as they fancied, in their national pride and vanity, so discreditable to their arms" (487).

Instead, Simms's narrator refers to—and cites long direct quotations from—an imaginary Chickasah Chronicle of the events: "our version is drawn chiefly from the narratives of the Mauvilians themselves, as contained in the celebrated MSS. of the Great Iawa, or High Priest of Chickasah, Oolena Ithiopoholla, who wore the sacred symbols, somewhere about the year 1619, only about 70 years after this event. The narrative is written on the bark of trees, in the Choctaw character" (487). This passage is followed by a five-page translation from the "Chickasah Chronicle," one that is very similar in terms of style, tone, and syntax to "translations" of the Yemassee language found in an earlier Colonial Romance, *The Yemassee*. In addition, this Indian chronicler refers to Castile, to "the Blackamoor," and to De Soto's interior monologue in ways that make it seem less than authentic. (If it is authentic, Simms is even more significant to American history than he is given credit for!) Consistent with his theoretical preference for the imagination over objective historical accounts, over the "dry-bones of perished humanity," Simms seems to have invented the Chickasah Chronicle.

The reception of *Vasconselos* was neither wholly positive nor wholly negative at first. A contemporary notice in *Godey's Lady Book* (which had declined to publish *Vasconselos* serially) gave the novel a mixed review: "This is a powerfully written romance. . . . The style is energetic, and the incidents and the plot, though the latter is not altogether agreeable to our taste, are full of the spirit of the age and of the characters represented" (qtd. in Guilds, *Literary Life* 214–15). A review in *Graham's* praised the novel for the "tropical exuberance" of its style, "evincing that the author completely realized the period and the time which he attempts to represent. . . . It has the ingredients of a fine romance" (qtd. in Guilds, *Literary Life* 215). In a private review, a close friend of Simms—James Henry Hammond, who was often frank about what he perceived as Simms's literary flaws—wrote, "I think it is among the best if not the *very best one* of all your novels" (*Letters* 3: 256n). The rapidity with which the novel was reprinted—once within three years of its original publication and three more times in the 1880s—indicates that the reception with the reading public was at least moderately positive.

In the 141 years since Simms's death, *Vasconselos* has inspired less critical analysis than many of Simms's other novel-length works. In 1941, Raven I. McDavid published in *Modern Language Notes* a note entitled "Ivanhoe and Simms's *Vasconselos*," an argument—common in Simms studies—that the author was greatly influenced by Sir Walter Scott, perhaps inordinately so. McDavid points out the strong similarities between the chivalric games in the two works, including some that might be coincidental and others that are certainly examples of homage. In 1978, Charles S. Watson published in *The Alabama Review* a piece entitled "De Soto's Expedition: Contrasting Treatments in Pickett's *History of Alabama* and Simms's *Vasconselos*." The article does much to illuminate Simms's views concerning the importance of romanticizing history. Watson compares the objective portrayal of De Soto in Albert James Pickett's *History of Alabama* with Simms's stress in *Vasconselos* on the explorer's character flaws and the moral lessons to be learned from his experience. Watson also points out that it is an Indian character, Tuscaloosa—rather than De Soto—who represents Simms's ideal of Old World chivalry in the novel. In 2003, Peter Murphy produced for *Studies in the Novel* an article entitled "Simms's *Vasconselos*: A Multicultural Reading." Murphy points out that the ending of the novel—Vasconselos's marriage to the Indian princess Coçalla—suggests a vision of a racially hybrid America, a notion that seems distasteful to Simms considering some of his other writings but is undeniable in

Vasconselos. Murphy also stresses the notion that the Indian values and cultures are far nobler in the novel than those of the Spanish invaders.

Though it is the central focus of neither, *Vasconselos* is treated in some depth in two recent books: Mashahiro Nakamura's *Visions of Order in William Gilmore Simms* (2009) and Sean Busick's *A Sober Desire for History* (2005). In his chapter six, "Home versus Wilderness and Simms's Southern View of the Native American," Nakamura focuses on the differences between Simms's accounts of events and those of the Spanish and Portuguese chroniclers, and he points out that while Philip de Vasconselos is a purely fictional character, the chroniclers refer to an Andre de Vasconselos (Phillip's fictional brother is called Andres), implying a stronger connection between the historical and fictional accounts. Nakamura as well points out the differences between Simms's descriptions of settings in Havana and on the mainland frontier, arguing that the former consistently suggest a mixture of tranquility and corruption while the latter imply both struggle and purity. Nakamura also notes that Patricia "Galloway comments about Nuno de Tobar in Andrew Lytle's, *At the Moon's Inn* (1941), in which he is 'an authentic character who disgraced himself by seducing Soto's wife's companion, whom he was forced to marry'" (197). Busick's book, focusing on Simms as an historian, mentions that the author, at the start of *Vasconselos*, makes a case for the truthfulness and accuracy of historical romance that is nearly the opposite of James Fenimore Cooper's view.

Vasconselos is notably flawed as a work of literature. Many of its flaws, though not all of them, are attributable to Simms's writing habits, habits that negatively affected many of his other works. He developed the earlier chapters of the book—at least most of those set in Havana—at relative leisure, over the course of four years; he then rushed through the last chapters, under the pressure of a deadline, between January and October of 1853. As a result, the pacing of the whole novel is uneven. In addition, some of the most interesting minor characters in the book are developed with a level of detail that suggests that they will be essential to the ending, yet they are then killed off with a disturbing arbitrariness or, worse yet, merely abandoned without explanation. Of all of the novel's flaws, though, the most prominent one—the one that poses the greatest challenge to the willing suspension of disbelief in the general reader—may not at all have been the result of the author's writing habits, and it may even have been intentional on Simms's part. If so, *Vasconselos* is a very significant novel for the ways it reveals its author's insights into the human psyche. This most prominent flaw is the fact that the delicate and beautiful Olivia de Alvaro—the object of the ardent attentions of protagonist Phillip de Vasconselos for the first two-thirds of the novel—signs on in the final third in drag and in blackface as Phillip's page. The two travel together almost constantly in the New World, even sleeping side by side, yet the demonstrably intelligent, discerning, and love-struck Phillip never realizes either that his page is in fact his lover or even that she is a woman.

Of all of these flaws, the pacing problems might be the easiest both to explain and to justify. With the leisure he enjoyed for composing the opening of the novel, the lingering descriptions of the natural beauty of Cuba may have seemed appropriate, and comparable descriptions of the natural environment of mainland North America may have been quite impossible under the pressure of an approaching deadline.[3] Whether or not this difference was intentional—and despite the imbalance it imposes on the whole novel—this difference has a side benefit: it permits Simms to contrast not just the geographies but the cultures of the two sites, always to the benefit of what would become his own culture. The overgrown vegetation outside of Havana, which Simms describes as covering over, hiding, the island's man-made structures also hides the Old World moral corruption of the Spanish nobles who rule the island:

> Balthazar of *Vasconselos*, by contrast, rules over Olivia's "happy empire," which is situated on a "gentle eminence" of "the suburbs of the infant city" with "balm" breathing ever through its atmosphere. Her summerhouse is portrayed as a paradise and as the Christian church to which a temple image is given. Hallowed and softened by "the most blessed of all the angels who take part in the destinies of the earth," it turns out to be the place where Balthazar, who celebrates the Nativity, commits incest with her. The words "ripe," "lusciously," and "proximity" . . . show that dissipation contradictory to sacredness exists in this summerhouse. (Nakamura 146)

Such dissipation exists, hidden by tropical flora and fauna, throughout the scenes set in Cuba, exemplified perhaps most vividly in Balthazar's molestation of his niece—enabled by the exalted and inherited social status that makes him immune to charges of such depravity—but also apparent in the deference that social inferiors show to their betters before taking perverse joy in lording their own status over those lower than themselves on the social ladder.

Whether by choice or because of the pressures of his deadline—and with the exception of the extensive natural descriptions in chapter 42, Simms devotes far fewer words to the descriptions of the mainland settings despite the fact that, except for the absence of man-made structures, the settings would have been comparable—at least at the start of the journey, in Florida—to those in Cuba. As his Indian comrades will do near the end of the novel, Phillip avoids being lulled into a false sense of security by the presumably lush environment of mainland North America; when he notices it, he considers it first as a hiding place for potential dangers. The leaders of the exhibition, the Old World nobility, also seem somewhat aware that the rules are different on the mainland. No less perfidious, Don Balthazar must nevertheless be more transparent on the mainland when he arranges for what he believes will be Phillip's execution: he scarcely denies his wrongdoing even as he concocts a transparent story to justify the death sentence. De Soto chides the villain for his ham-handed assault on the

Portuguese knight even as he grudgingly approves of it in recognition of Don Balthazar's authority. To this point in the novel, De Soto is a morally redeemable character: accomplished, brave, and good-humored; once he permits Balthazar to railroad Phillip, though, he commits himself in the novel to the road to ignominy and eventual ruin.

Even given the opportunity they provide Simms to contrast the social and moral standards of the Old and New Worlds, the stylistic differences between the beginning and the ending of *Vasconselos* are disturbingly notable; equally notable is the series of secondary characters whom Simms seems to depict in three dimensions before abandoning them suddenly.

The first of these is Donna (i.e., Doña) Isabella, the wife of De Soto. From the very start of the novel, Isabella is presented as a paragon of even-handedness, even temper, and good humor. Though Isabella chides her husband for his follies and excesses, De Soto recognizes in her the qualities of an able administrator, and he announces that his wife will govern the island in his absence. Especially to readers concerned about the miseries that Olivia is enduring—that, presumably, other women in Cuba may be enduring—the rise of Isabella presents the hope of positive change that would also serve Simms's efforts to contrast Old World values with New. Nevertheless, when the expedition's ships depart from Havana harbor, Isabella departs from the novel. Though she is an admirable character, Donna Isabella eventually serves as little more than a distraction—one that harms the overall unity of the novel—and the work may have been a better one if Simms had written her out altogether.

Four other odd character-development choices concern Afro-Cuban characters: Anita, Sylvia, Juana, and Mateo. Anita is an old woman, a slave to Don Balthazar, who abets the pervert in his drugging and sexual abuse of his niece. Fairly early in the novel, Olivia briefly recovers enough of her wits to pretend to take her medication, and this inspires her to seek revenge on the old slave, to literally "give her a dose of her own medicine." Inadvertently, though, Olivia makes the potion too strong, and she kills Anita, who is replaced by a combination of Sylvia, another old slave who has earned the trust of Balthazar, and Juana, a younger slave. The change offers Olivia some hope; while Sylvia seems as dedicated to serving her evil master as Anita had been, Juana—through a combination of her greatest vice, laziness, and her greatest virtue, a sympathy for Olivia—improves somewhat the plight of the girl assigned to be her victim. One result is a greater awareness in the victim of her desperation. Meanwhile, Juana is visited by her brother Mateo, an audacious outlaw and escaped slave who will defy the price on his head by, among other things, showing himself before the entire city of Havana in order to reap the public glory of fighting a bull. Juana begs her brother to take her with him to his wilderness hideaway, but the outlaw is aware of his sister's limitations, and he advises her to remain on Olivia's estate, where he repeatedly visits her and forms relationships with Olivia, with Phillip de Vasconselos, and with Don Balthazar de Alvaro. He seems to make a deal with Balthazar to betray Phillip, but he has plans of his own: to join the expedition to Florida. Toward this end, he double-crosses Balthazar, introduces Olivia (in blackface) to Phillip as his nephew, Juan, who is anxious to work as the knight's page, but is bested in his effort to murder the villain and is himself murdered with the connivance of Sylvia.

Though each of these characters serves either the plot or Simms's philosophical outlook in some way, each is developed to the point of piquing the curiosity of readers only to be summarily dismissed from the novel. The contrast between Anita/Sylvia and Juana is particularly interesting because of the novel's setting-in-time, 1538, only 46 years after the first voyage of Columbus to the New World. Since both older slaves are in at least their sixties, both must necessarily have been born in Africa; their African beginnings, as Simms interprets them, are seen in their treachery and, in the case of Anita, in her mastery of the black arts. Juana, on the other hand, is very young and was likely born in Cuba. Simms may have used this contrast to reinforce the claims he repeatedly made elsewhere about the potential of the institution of slavery to ennoble godless and savage Africans. Juana's primary function in the novel, though, is to introduce Mateo, perhaps *the* paragon of the fair and adaptive New World mindset in the novel, possibly even more so than Phillip de Vasconselos. Mateo is proud of his independence, adaptive, and audacious. Having been abused in his youth by an overseer, he had killed the man and fled to the countryside with a price on his head. There, a legend grew around him as a daring but noble outlaw who regularly defied the slaveholding society to capture him but who always eluded it. The reader comes to know and like Mateo sufficiently to consider the implications of his plans to kill the evil Balthazar, his pursuer, and to join the De Soto expedition: he would be—like Phillip, Coçalla, Tuscaloosa, and Nuno de Tobar—one of the most "American" characters who sets foot on what would become American soil. It is perhaps true that, given Simms's role as a spokesman for the slaveholding South in 1853, he could not in conscious celebrate such a renegade as fully as many of his readers do, even with the odd pronouncement that Mateo makes following the single emotional high point of the section of the novel set in Havana. Just after Mateo has shown Phillip conclusive proof of Balthazar's sexual abuse of the girl he loves, the shaken yet grateful Phillip responds with disappointment over the fact that he has no reward to offer the outlaw. Mateo's reply is telling: "I ask no reward, Señor. I am only too happy to serve you. I wish I could serve you forever. I feel that I could work for *you*, and for any true man like you. But I can't work for a bad one, and a beast! I would be happy to go with you to Florida. But there, Don Balthazar would know me through any disguises. And yet, I might get over that. Let me go now, Señor" (317). Here, Simms presents even Mateo, the bold and noble mestizo who has not just challenged the institution of slavery, but essentially defeated it, as tolerating slavery given a kind master.

This contradiction in the character of Mateo muddles the otherwise clear depiction of the man's essentially American desire for freedom and self-determination. More damaging yet to the novel, though, is Simms's decision to eliminate Mateo just as the scene of action was moving to the land that would become the United States, just after Simms had developed his character into one that any reader would find interesting and one that exemplified the very American virtues that Simms was describing and prescribing to his readers. It is hard to avoid at least the possibility that Simms's decision was motivated in some measure by polemics, that as the national debate over the morality of slavery was intensifying, Simms "punished" Mateo for questioning, even with reservations, the righteousness of the institution of slavery. If this is the case, this decision comes closer perhaps than any other evinced in his corpus to justifying the conclusion of his first biographer, William Peterfield Trent, that Simms might have been a great writer had he not been smothered by the peculiar ethics and polemics of the antebellum South.

There are other egregious flaws in the novel attributable to the author's need to finish the manuscript quickly, including the unexplained decision to abandon his narrative completely in an important passage (362–64) and to express a key dialogue with character headings, as though he were writing a drama.[4] Even the worst of the flaws attributable to Simms's haste in *Vasconselos*, though, produce the mixed feelings of contempt for his carelessness and admiration for the focus necessary to complete a grand literary task in a very limited amount of time. But the single greatest flaw in the novel seems unrelated to the haste with which Simms finished *Vasconselos* even though it, too, occurs in the final third of the novel: Vasconselos, defined throughout the work more than anything by his discernment and the depth of his love for Olivia de Alvaro, fails to recognize Olivia on the Florida campaign despite the fact that she is almost constantly by his side and disguised flimsily, only with an herbal potion that darkens her skin.

Before he is murdered in Cuba, Mateo introduces "Juan" to Vasconselos as the son of his sister Juana, a free woman of the mountains. The knight remarks here and later that the boy seems familiar, but stunningly, he fails to see his sworn love through her thin disguise. Juan then accompanies Vasconselos on the voyage, staying with him almost constantly, sleeping beside him, yet the knight never recognizes him as Olivia until he pulls from the chest of Juan/Olivia the arrow that would kill the page. Only when he sees Olivia's bosom, and the unaltered color of her chest, does Vasconselos recognize how great his loss is.

Though this inconsistency in the protagonist's character is a flaw of the novel regardless of its explanation, it is mitigated to a degree if Simms were enacting in the novel the psychological condition known as Dissociative Identity Disorder (DID; formerly known—but only long after Simms's death—as Multiple Personality Disorder). Lauren L. Kong and her co-writers cite the common psychological view that the separate personalities associated with DID "define identities as separable person-like states with idiosyncratic memories, personal history, and personality traits" (687), and they point out that DID is a coping mechanism for traumatic experiences in childhood.

It may seem at first as though the character exhibiting symptoms of DID is Olivia: she takes on a new name and a new gender—both common in cases of DID—and she seems to develop her separate personality as a direct result of her lover's discovery of her childhood trauma, the years of sexual abuse by her uncle. In addition, the male gender of her new personality seems a very specific coping mechanism to the childhood trauma she endured: as a male she would be both less vulnerable to the predations of her uncle and more powerful to resist them. Nevertheless, there is also a strong argument to be made that Phillip de Vasconselos exhibits signs of DID in the novel. He takes on a new name—his Indian comrades call him Istalana—and he undertakes a mission that contradicts that of his youth: rather than serving the cause of Iberian colonization of the New World, he works to resist colonization, to permit America to undertake its natural development. Though the trauma he adapts to in emerging as Istalana is not specifically a childhood trauma—he discovers Balthazar's abuse of his lover when he is a young adult—it is a trauma that undermines his childhood values: the very values he had been raised to serve show themselves to be complicit in the most vile of abuses as Balthazar keeps his dark secret by repeatedly implying to Olivia that she would not be believed if she sought to raise a charge against a person as exalted in the colonial system as he is.

Though interesting in itself, the possibility that Simms enacted DID in *Vasconselos* is most significant in the ways it would account for the otherwise inexplicable failure of the astute and passionate Phillip de Vasconselos to recognize his doomed lover as she works at his side for months. Kong et. al. explore two theories regarding the transfer of memories between identities in DID subjects. According to the first, "one would expect compartmentalized memory processes to result in [interidentity amnesia] between identities" (686). This theory accounts for the experience of Vasconselos in the novel. Olivia, on the other hand, always seems very aware, even in her Juan persona, of the identity and presence of her former lover. The authors cite an earlier study in categorizing experiences like Olivia's as examples of "sociocognitive DID," i.e., "identities are constructed by patients who adopt the DID narrative as an explanation that fits their lives, resulting in self-construal of multiple identities" (ibid.), a theory of DID under which memories would pass intact from identity to identity. It is at least possible that Simms, without formal knowledge of the field of academic psychology, created characters who exemplify both of the prime hypotheses now used to explain interidentity memory transfer in DID: in the case of Olivia, she *created* Juan as an identity when her own identity as a woman shamed and victimized by the assumptions of the Spanish colonial system were no longer viable for her, so she kept her earlier memories; in the case of Vasconselos, his identity as Istalana was forced upon him by the trauma of the mutual rejections of and by himself and the colonial system he had been raised to serve, so all of his memories as Phillip did not follow him into his life as Istalana. In both cases—even though Olivia would not survive to contribute to the developing American culture—the adaptations made by the characters cause them to emerge as people more suited, as Simms saw it, to the meritocracy that American culture would eventually engender, less suited to the stratified social system of the Old World.

DID is an effective metaphor for the historical shifts in the identities of some individuals, begun in the sixteenth century, from Europeans to Americans, a shift that some chose and that merely happened to others, a shift that Simms explores in the other Colonial Romances. This shift culminates in the late climax of the novel, during which Phillip—in recognizing and mourning Olivia—reconciles his two identities, is "cured" of DID, and begins his new life among the Indians on the North American continent.

The fact that the publication of *Vasconselos* preceded the modern formal scholarly study of psychology is not particularly relevant to an analysis based in part on the minutiae of academic psychology: though it has been called by other names, the psyche has always been an important part of human character, and writers of imaginative literature much farther removed than Simms from the heydays of Freud, Jung, Adler, James, and their descendants have illustrated the principles of modern psychology for centuries in their works, some more accurately than others. As I have pointed out elsewhere, Simms himself, in *Guy Rivers*, explored behaviors and their consequences that look forward with remarkable accuracy to the causes and effects of self-esteem deficit as they are viewed by the consensus of twenty-first century psychologists.

Perhaps more significant than its demonstration of Simms's psychological prescience, the somewhat accurate illustration in *Vasconselos* of what is now called Dissociative Identity Disorder offers some explanation for the otherwise puzzling inability of the central character to identify his true love. Even with this explanation, though, *Vasconselos* is a flawed novel that nevertheless illustrates the author's life-long mission of producing a literature that is distinctly American and that can inspire American readers with the sort of national pride that might inspire them to achievements that match their potentials.

NOTES

1. Scholars disagree about which titles are or are not part of Simms's Colonial Romances; David Moltke-Hansen, for example, includes "The Damsel of Darien" in this collection, but John Caldwell Guilds does not.
2. Though he cites no evidence in support of the claim, C. Hugh Holman claims in his introduction to *Views and Reviews* that Simms had written much of *Vasconselos* in the 1830s.

3. One of the very few exceptions to the rule that Simms gives short shrift to natural descriptions in his mainland settings occurs in chapter 42 where, lashed to a tree and seemingly in his death throes, Phillip observes as Simms describes the surreal scenes of animals seeking to devour the protagonist. First a carrion-eating bird then a family of panthers approach Phillip as he drifts in and out of consciousness, and Simms goes into great descriptive detail here. This chapter ends with the arrival of the Indians, who scare away the animals and embrace Phillip as one of them. This chapter is important to the claim I later make concerning the psychological ramifications of Phillip's transition from a Portuguese knight in the service of Spain to an American. Especially since this chapter immediately follows one during which Simms explores Olivia's dual identities as a Spanish girl and a mestizo boy, these paired chapters amount to the most convincing evidence that Simms seeming anticipation of Dissociative Identity Disorder is no accident.
4. My own response to this passage, on my first reading, was to interpret it as "Note to self: develop this section later into a narrative that includes this dialogue." If that were Simms's intention, he never got around to the job.

War Poetry of the South

COLEMAN HUTCHISON

Of the many William Gilmore Simms texts that have suffered "long years of neglect," none may be as perplexing as his 1866 anthology of Confederate verse, *War Poetry of the South*. In addition to being one of the largest and most diverse contemporary anthologies of the poetry of the Civil War South, it is also, by a significant margin, the most important. Simms drew poetry from all of the Confederate States, as well as several Border States; he also included a good deal of his own verse. Not surprisingly, then, the 205 poems in the collection vary greatly in tone, topic, and literary quality. The result is a generous and more or less representative sampling of Confederate literary culture.

Yet historians and literary critics alike—both within and without Simms studies—have consistently underestimated this nearly 500-page volume. No major studies of Simms spend significant time discussing *War Poetry of the South*.[1] Moreover, Simms critics have tended to belittle his labors in the field of Confederate poetry. For instance, Edd Winfield Parks lumps the anthology in with other "hack work" that Simms undertook in the immediate postwar period (*William* 9); similarly, Mary Ann Wimsatt describes the editing of *War Poetry of the South* as a "literary chor[e]" (*Major* 218). As one might expect, other scholars of Civil War literature and culture have not done much better with the collection. Like so much of Confederate literature, the anthology is only occasionally cited and rarely discussed.

Nonetheless, the collection was of great interest to its editor, who took up the ambitious project while his personal and professional life lay in ruins following the dissolution of the Confederate States of America. Simms gave nearly a year of his late life to *War Poetry of the South*, which bears the marks of his editorial care as well as his vast connections to the southern literati. As such, the collection should also be of great interest to twenty-first century readers, since it grants extraordinary access to a largely evanescent phenomenon: the birth and death of a national literary culture.

Compilation and Production

It is no surprise that William Gilmore Simms deemed an anthology of southern war poetry worthy of both publication and his time. After all, Simms was a lifelong advocate for a distinct and distinctive southern literature. He also thought of himself first and foremost as a poet. The opportunity to collect and help preserve the poetry produced in the Confederacy must have seemed undeniable to the aging literary lion.[2] And by late 1865 Simms had taken up the project in earnest. On December 15, the *Daily South Carolinian* (for which Simms was serving as an Associate Editor, alongside Henry Timrod) announced and praised Simms's proposed anthology. In addition to his far-flung network of correspondents, Simms solicited work from the public. He wanted any and all Confederate poems, be they high-brow, low-brow, or somewhere in between.[3]

At the outset of the American Civil War, Simms was dubious about the prospect of a literary culture springing fully formed from the heads of Confederate nationalists. As late as October 1862, he begged patience from readers and writers alike in a letter to the editors of the *Southern Illustrated News*: "All our thoughts resolve themselves into the war. We are now *living* the first grand epic of our newly-born Confederacy. We are *making* the materials for the drama, and for future songs and fiction; and, engaged in the actual event, we are in no mood for delineating its details, or framing it to proper laws of art, in any province" (*Letters* 4: 413, emphasis in original). To Simms's mind, the exigencies of life during wartime—to say nothing of severe shortages of paper, ink, type, skilled labor, and printing presses—meant that a robust Confederate literature might have to wait until after southern independence had been achieved.[4]

And yet, the Confederate States of America was lousy with lyric. Poetry was a ubiquitous and at times tiresome part of cultural life in the Civil War South. As one beleaguered editor of the *Southern Literary Messenger* lamented in July 1863, "We are receiving too much trash in rhyme. What is called 'poetry,' by its authors, is not wanted. Fires are not accessible at this time of year, and it is too much trouble to tear up poetry. If it is thrown out of the window, the vexatious wind always blows it back" ("Editor's" 447). *Pace* Simms, Confederates may have been "*living* the first grand epic" of their new nation, but they were also producing an epic amount of poetry in the process. It was Simms's task to cull from the resulting mass a representative sample (Hutchison 99–142).

Simms compiled the anthology during a tumultuous and busy period for the southern man of letters *par excellence*. In a 24 March 1866 letter he complained, "I have the daily task of writing 3 or 4 columns in the Newspaper, answering a large Correspondence, editing the War Poems, and writing at snatches, when I can, a chapter of my new Romance" (*Letters* 4: 546–47). Money was also an ever-present concern for Simms, who was all but destitute following the burning of his plantation Woodlands and the defeat of the Confederacy. An exercised Simms wrote to Evert Augustus Duyckinck on 5 March 1866 to check on the financial arrangements for *War Poetry of the South* and a proposed collection of Mother Goose stories:

> I need present cash for present necessities, and any arrangement which will give me that, will be welcome. *I have no shelter of my own, in which I can lay my head*, & my children, at present, are living at the plantation in negro houses. A few hundred dollars now would enable me to *restore one wing* of my dwelling there, and give me a tolerable habitation. If I can procure this aid from these two volumes, I should feel comparatively at ease. I should then have an abode where I could live cheaply, write cheaply, & dying, be buried with little cost, among my kindred (*Letters* 4: 542–43, emphasis in original).

Such "present necessities" forced Simms to settle for a pittance from the New York publisher Charles Benjamin Richardson, to whom he granted the copyright for *War Poetry of the South* rather than "wait upon the lingering returns of sales for one or more seasons" (*Letters* 4: 536). In the end, Simms received only a few hundred dollars for his extensive work on the anthology (*Letters* 4: 581).[5]

This is not to say that *War Poetry of the South* was "hack work" or that Simms's interest in the anthology was merely commercial. From the beginning of the project, Simms was committed to making the anthology a "good book" (*Letters* 4: 555, 558). This may help to explain the remarkable time and energy he lavished on the project. As John Caldwell Guilds notes, "Simms was not content with publishing simply the best random selections sent to him; he recruited poems from the well-known writers, from various regions of the South, attempting to recognize the region's cultural and geographical diversity" (*Literary Life* 305). Playing on his well-known name, Simms was able to solicit manuscripts and revisions from southern poets both major and minor.[6]

To be clear, publishing the "best random selections sent to him" would have saved Simms a great deal of effort. He was flooded with poems and queries from like-minded collectors. On 20 February 1866, a snippy Simms wrote to Duyckinck: "The book will be quite creditable. There will be a very large mass from which to select. . . . I find the demand for these things very considerable, North & South; and have received letters from collectors & librarians begging duplicates & annoying me by a fruitless correspondence" (*Letters* 4: 540). One such "fruitless correspondence" with a John A. McAllister (seemingly of Philadelphia, Pennsylvania) reveals a great deal about Simms's editorial labors:

> The war poems of the South are still daily coming in to me, a large proportion of them in M.S. I have not yet attempted classing them, nor do I know what duplicates may be found, nor have I yet decided what selections I shall make from them for publication. It is at present impossible for me to say what I have and what I might wish to have, especially as it is impossible for me to know what things may be scattered over the country to be brought to my knowledge only by accident, or the occasional contributions of persons like yourself making collections. (*Letters* 4: 538)

The tone of this letter suggests just how overwhelmed Simms was by the prospect of sifting through the "rapidly accumulating" pile of poems (*Letters* 4: 542). Simms also confessed that, no matter how large this "very large mass" grew, the resulting archive would always be partial and incomplete. Such is the nature of collecting a popular culture. Finally, the fact that Simms was corresponding with someone from Philadelphia bears out his claim that "the demand for these things" was indeed "considerable, North and South."

Undaunted by the challenge, Simms worked on *War Poetry of the South* throughout the spring of 1866. By April, he could brag to his old friend Duyckinck, "The Poetry of the South, during the war, will possess (I think) a much higher character, than any thing that has yet been published" (*Letters* 4: 549). Simms traveled to New York in early June, where he was able to personally oversee the volume's composition and proof sheets (*Letters* 4: 590). His work on the anthology was completed by late September, and *War Poetry of the South* appeared in print some time between 10 and 23 November 1866 (*Letters* 4: 606, 622).

Text and Context

The resulting volume was remarkable for both its size and production values. Printed by George C. Rand & Avery, the 12 mo., 488-page *War Poetry of the South* was a respectable-looking book, with good paper, generally clean type work, plain green boards, and a large gilt stamp of Simms's signature—all for a reasonable $2.50. The publisher, Richardson and Company, hoped that the volume would "prove a family book, to be pored over, with various recollections, and fondly and frequently referred to, as embodying a record precious to the growing generations." As such, the firm also offered a fine edition, with "Morocco Cloth" and gilt edges, for $3.50 (*War Poetry* 483).

Richardson, who was known for his military titles, seems to have invested heavily in texts sympathetic to the Confederacy and an emergent Lost Cause ideology. During the war he brought out northern editions of John Esten Cooke's hagiographic *The Life of Stonewall Jackson* (1863) and Sally Rochester Ford's bestselling Confederate novel *Raids and Romance of Morgan and His Men* (1864). After the war, Richardson offered a single-volume edition of Edward A. Pollard's *Southern History of the War* (1866) (which was later republished as *The Lost Cause* [1867]) alongside titles like William Parker Snow's *Lee and His Generals* (1867). Indeed, both Pollard's and Snow's books were advertised in the final pages of the second printing of *War Poetry of the South*, suggesting the contours of the literary field into which Simms's anthology entered.

Even the casual reader—one ignorant of either Richardson's list or Simms's politics—could not mistake *War Poetry of the South*'s sympathies. The anthology's title page includes a melancholy engraving of a broken column, laurel wreath, harp, and discarded sword against the backdrop of a ruined garden. This is followed on the next recto page by a relatively hopeful dedication "To the Women of the South":

> They have lost a cause, but they have made a triumph! They have shown themselves worthy of any manhood; and will leave a record which shall survive all the caprices of time. They have proved themselves worthy of the best womanhood, and, in their posterity, will leave no race which shall be unworthy of the cause which is lost, or of the mothers, sisters and wives, who have taught such noble lessons of virtuous effect, and womanly endurance. (iii)

With its twin evocations of a lost cause and rhetoric of posterity, the dedication seems steadfastly focused on the future (Aiken, "Simms's" 16–17). The juxtaposition of the mournful title page with this sanguine dedication captures well the animating tension of the volume—a tension to which Simms gives further voice in his remarkable prose preface.

Dated "Brooklyn, September 8, 1866," Simms's four-page introductory remarks are both deeply rhetorical and deeply conflicted. Simms argues that the "emotional literature" he collects is "essential to the reputation of the Southern people, as illustrating their feelings, sentiments, ideas, and opinions—the motives which influenced their actions, and the objects which they had in contemplation, and which seemed to them to justify the struggle in which they were engaged" (v). Perhaps quietly echoing John Adams ("The Revolution was in the minds and hearts of the people"), Simms plays the disinterested intellectual historian here, urging readers to be sympathetic as they peruse his anthology. Stifling his strongly southern nationalist sentiments, Simms does not offer an apologia for the Confederacy; instead, he hedges a bit. Note the passive construction and use of the past tense here: these motives and objects "*seemed* to *them* to justify" the southern war effort (emphasis added).

The deftness of Simms's rhetoric betrays the delicate political position in which a postwar anthologist of Confederate poetry worked. How could she or he present aggressively nationalistic verse—poems that risk being "too 'fierce' and 'bitter' to suit the taste and temper of the present" (Mason 7)—to a newly re-United States? Abram Joseph Ryan, the author of the hugely popular Lost Cause anthem "The Conquered Banner," worried that his incendiary anthology of Confederate verse, *War Lyrics and Songs of the South* (1866), would be censored in the North. As a result, he had the collection printed in London (Ryan iii). Thomas Cooper De Leon, a Confederate veteran and older brother of Confederate diplomat Edwin De Leon, instead begged his readers' indulgence and made a familiar appeal to the historical record: "If poems, born of revolution, bore no marks of the bitter need that crushed them from the hearts of their authors, they would have no value whatever, intrinsic or historical" (vii).

But it is Simms who makes the most original argument for how to square wartime invective with postwar imperatives to reconciliation. One need only subsume Confederate literary nationalism under a broader American literary nationalism:

> Several considerations have prompted the editor of this volume in the compilation of its pages. It constitutes a contribution to the national literature which is assumed to be not unworthy of it, and which is otherwise valuable as illustrating the degree of mental and art development which has been made, in a large section of the country, under circumstances greatly calculated to stimulate talent and provoke expression, through the higher utterances of passion and imagination. Though sectional in its character, and indicative of a temper and a feeling which were in conflict with nationality, yet, now that the States of the Union have been resolved into one nation, this collection is essentially as much the property of the whole as are the captured cannon which were employed against it during the progress of the late war. It belongs to the national literature, and will hereafter be regarded as constituting a proper part of it, just as legitimately to be recognized by the nation as are the rival ballads of the cavaliers and roundheads, by the English, in the great civil conflict of their country. (*War Poetry* v)

It is as though the American Civil War never happened. Despite having strongly advocated for secession and steadfastly supported the Confederacy, Simms reverts to his antebellum agitations for a national literature. For instance, Simms had argued in a preface to the 1856 version of *The Wigwam and the Cabin* that "to be *national* in literature, one must needs be *sectional*. No one mind can fully or fairly illustrate the characteristics of any great country; and he who shall depict *one section* faithfully, has made his proper and sufficient contribution to the great work of *national* illustration" (4, emphasis in original).[7] After a hugely bloody and costly war for independence, the South was once again in the subordinate position, making contributions to a national literature that was not entirely its own. Looking to England for a model or precedent, Simms argues that nationalist poetry is, finally, a fungible good. The canon of Confederate poetry is just like the cannon of the Confederate army: a strategic asset that will benefit the newly re-United States (Hutchison 139–42).

Having established a way to read Confederate poetry in a postwar world, Simms then touts the representative nature of his anthology. He boasts that the poems are drawn from "all the States of the late Southern Confederacy, and will be found truthfully to exhibit the sentiment and opinion prevailing more or less generally throughout the whole" (*War Poetry* vi). In the same breath he also confesses the partial nature of his archive, noting that he had been unable to "do justice to, and find a place for, many of the pieces which fully deserve to be put on record" (vi). Blaming a shoddy interstate mail system for the exclusion of larger collections from Louisiana, North Carolina, and Texas, Simms goes on to promise a second edition "of like style, character, and dimensions" (vi).[8]

Simms also cannily acknowledges that *War Poetry of the South* was entering a crowded literary field. Anthologies of Confederate poetry began to appear as early as 1862 and continued to be published well into the twentieth century. Indeed, the cessation of Civil War hostilities resulted in a minor publishing boom, as anthologists in the South, North, and England used their collections to commemorate and make sense of the atrocities they had just endured.[9] Simms names in particular collections edited by Frank Moore and De Leon, before making a generous concession:

> There may be others still forth-coming; for, in so large a field, with a population so greatly scattered as that of the South, it is a physical impossibility adequately to do justice to the whole by any one editor; and each of the sections must make its own contributions, in its own time, and according to its several opportunities. There will be room enough for all; and each, I doubt not, will possess its special claims to recognition and reward. (*War Poetry* vii)

Even William Gilmore Simms, the most well-connected and esteemed southern man of letters, could not adequately capture in a single anthology the "genius and culture of the Southern people" (*War Poetry* vi). But a series of local anthologies of Confederate poetry might do the trick. Perhaps this is how Louisiana, North Carolina, or Texas could get their poetic due.

Simms closes the preface by briskly defending his editorial rationale and reiterating his belief that these poems are both "highly creditable to the Southern mind" and of great historical interest. The tone of these final three paragraphs is protean, but Simms's rhetoric is skillful throughout. Perhaps the most telling moment is in Simms's discussion of authorship. Speaking in the third person, Simms confesses that "He has been able to ascertain the authorship, in many cases, of these writings; but must regret still that so many others, under a too fastidious delicacy, deny that their names should be made known" (vii). The inclusion of anonymous and pseudonymous poems is an aspect of Simms's editing that has come under particular fire, with critics reading his "regret" as a dereliction of editorial duty. Yet such criticisms misapprehend the function of anonymity and pseudonymity in *War Poetry of the South*.

First, Simms may well have been confessing his own "too fastidious delicacy" here. After all, Simms published poems anonymously and pseudonymously throughout his long career (Kibler *Pseudonymous*, esp. 1–8 and *Selected* [1990], esp. xii–xiv). More to the point, Simms published poems anonymously and pseudonymously in *War Poetry of the South*—a great number of poems, in fact. His name appears next to seven titles in the table of contents. However, Kibler argues persuasively that the anthology includes another twenty-seven "proved" Simms poems and at least five "probable" Simms poems (*Poetry* 478). Thus, anonymity and pseudonymity worked to Simms's benefit in his anthology, allowing him to quietly publish a significant amount of his own poetry. Second, anonymity and pseudonymity were signal features of Confederate poetry, which often flouted the rules of polite literature. Indeed, many Confederate poets showed little interest in literary professionalism. They published their poems anonymously or pseudonymously, and the majority were "amateurs in every sense of the word" (Moss 15). Suffice it to say, Simms's decision to include anonymous and pseudonymous poems was in keeping with an important aspect of poetic culture in the Civil War South (Hutchison 99–102).

Simms also betrays his generic biases in the preface. He admits to having excluded a "large proportion of pieces . . . of elegiac character"—and with good reason (vii). The extraordinary losses occasioned by the American Civil War meant that elegy was a dominant poetic mode during this period. Given that one in five white southern men of military age did not survive the Civil War, Confederate elegies were particularly common (Faust, *Republic* xi). Thus, Simms includes elegies for only "the most distinguished of the persons falling in battle, or such as are marked by the higher characteristics of poetry—freshness, thought, and imagination" (*War Poetry* vii). In turn, he expresses some contempt for those "songs, camp catches, or marching ballads" collected by Moore in his *Rebel Rhymes and Rhapsodies*: "The songs which are most popular are rarely such as may claim poetical rank. They depend upon lively music and certain spirit-stirring catchwords, and are rarely worked up with much regard to art or even propriety" (vii–viii). As a result, Simms only includes a handful of popular song lyrics.[10]

Yet for all this high-literary snobbishness, Simms goes out of his way to say that the pieces he excluded from the *War Poetry of the South* are nonetheless "worthy of preservation"—even those endless elegies and spirit-stirring songs (vii). He closes his discussion of editorial rationale with a concession to literary taste: "Still, many of these should have found a place in this volume, had adequate space been allowed the editor" (viii). Such is the theory of *War Poetry of the South*; in practice, Simms is surprisingly egalitarian in his selection of poems. The collection opens with perhaps the finest poem produced in the Confederacy, Henry Timrod's Pindaric ode "Ethnogenesis." But the volume also features far less accomplished or ambitious poems, such as Albert Pike's revised lyrics to "Dixie": "Southrons, hear your Country call you! / Up! lest worse than death befall you! / To arms! to arms! to arms! in Dixie" (92). And while *War Poetry of the South* includes many competent sonnets, there are also a number of inept broadside tributes to Stonewall Jackson.

The uneven quality of the poetry seems to have been by design. Again, Simms claims to be preserving these poems for posterity, for the future "philosophical historian." Even bad poetry—perhaps especially bad poetry—will show "with what spirit the popular mind regarded the course of events, whether favorable or adverse; and, in this aspect, it is even of more importance to the writer of history than any mere chronicle of facts" (v). Simms even comes to the defense of those poets who cannot "claim poetical rank"; he argues that "we can also forgive the muse who, in her fervor, is sometimes forgetful of her art" (vi). Apparently the philosophical historian does not require good poetry, merely poetry that "glows or weeps with emotions that gush freely and freshly from the heart" (vi).

We might compare this editorial rationale to that of De Leon, who thought that the work of the postbellum anthologist was to protect his or her readers from the "rhymster of low degree," to select out only those rare blooms of poetic beauty: "The garland is to be gathered from a field extensive and teeming with a rank luxuriance of growth, that it must often puzzle the analyst to separate from the really valuable" (v). Calling the popular poetry of the Confederacy "ephemera that have lived out the day for which they were born," De Leon highlights "the quality, and not the quantity, of Southern poetry" (vi). As a result, he includes "few even of the most popular" poems in his *South Songs*, privileging instead "polite" poems by established poets (vi).

Simms's *War Poetry of the South* is by no means a popular poetry anthology. Many of the best known names in southern literature appear in its table of contents: James Barron Hope, James R. Randall, John R. Thompson, Margret Junkin Preston, Alexander B. Meek, Paul Hamilton Hayne, John Esten Cooke, and James D. McCabe, Jr., to say nothing of Timrod and Simms, among many others. Moreover, the anthology over-represents traditional verse forms. However, unlike De Leon's *South Songs*, Simms's anthology does include some of the Confederacy's poetic "ephemera," if not its "trash in rhyme." Once again, this is in keeping with the dynamics of a nascent Confederate literary culture. The poetry of the Civil War South was overwhelmingly occasional in nature. Whether popular or polite, low-brow or high-brow, Confederate poems were very much socially contingent productions, non-autonomous works of art largely inseparable from the circumstances in which they were created—especially those of privation, civil war, and emergent nationalism. In turn, a great deal of this poetry was written quickly and rushed to print; needless to say, it bears the marks of such hasty composition (Hutchison 7–8, 99–103). Simms's expansive anthology does well, then, to represent some of the diversity of Confederate literary culture.

One hastens to add, some but not all of the diversity of Confederate literary culture. As the above list suggests, male poets far outnumber female poets in *War Poetry of the South*. Moreover, as Johanna Shields has recently argued, Simms's selections may have been much more provincial and ideological than previous scholars have supposed.[11] Finally, the collection's more or less chronological arrangement—it opens with Timrod's ode to the convening of the Provisional Confederate Congress on 4 February 1861 and closes with a series of poems describing the final furling of the Confederate flag after Appomattox—limits its sense of multiplicity. While chronology may grant the diffuse collection a sense of narrative arc, it also makes the individual poems feel more connected or coherent than they truly are. But such limitations are part and parcel of any literary anthology. As Simms would learn in late 1866 and early 1867, anthologists rarely make everyone happy.

Reception and Appraisal

The reception of *War Poetry of the South* was generally warm in both the South and the North—though reviewers on both sides of the Mason-Dixon had complaints about Simms's editorial decisions, in particular his decision to let anonymous and pseudonymous attributions stand. Not surprisingly, the southern response to the volume was at times rapturous. The Georgia-based *Southern Cultivator* saw the publication of *War Poetry of the South* as critically important, since it might occasion a reassessment of southern literature writ large: "by it the literary tastes and talents of the Southern people will be largely measured." Echoing Richardson's puff, the *Cultivator* concluded that it was "a book for every Southern home—a book in which we cannot fail to take a personal and patriotic pride." ("Books" 273). *The Land We Love* was a bit more equivocal in its two reviews of the anthology. Both praise the "Nestor of Southern Litterateurs" (Rev. of *War Poetry* [May] 71) for his "commendable industry" and "zeal and ardor" in the face of the destruction of his homeland (Rev. of *War Poetry* [Feb.] 309). Yet both also complain that Simms excluded several well-known lyrics; misattributed several poems; and did not vigorously pursue questions of authorship. Indeed, the reviewer for the May 1867 issue seems to prefer the much smaller, more heavily curated De Leon anthology, since "each poem it contains is a gem" (Rev. of *War Poetry* 72). Nonetheless, *The Land We Love* concurs with *The Southern Cultivator*: this is "a book which no Southern family can do without" (Rev. of *War Poetry* [May] 74).

In the North, the reception was predictably quieter. *The New York Times* offered a somewhat begrudging review of this anthology of "belligerent literature." The *Times* reviewer was not at all surprised that the Civil War South had produced such "surplus patriotism" given the southerner's "[a]rdent, impulsive, and, indeed poetical" nature (Rev. of *War Poetry* 2). *The Round Table* went further, suggesting that the volume compared favorably with northern anthologies edited by Frank Moore and Richard Grant White and showed "the southern poets to have been as much in earnest in celebrating their view of the war as ours were in celebrating ours, and considerably more vehement, not to say vituperative at times" ("Literariana" 244). New York's *Old Guard: A Monthly Journal Devoted to the Principles of 1776 and 1787* concurred in a particularly red-blooded, southern nationalistic review: "Whatever might have been said before the War, it can no longer be affirmed that the South has not a literature of its own—a literature which has been born of a struggle that imparted to it the freshest and most endearing elements of immortality" (Rev. of *War Poetry* 202).

The only truly negative southern review came from New Orleans's *Crescent Monthly*, which offered some of the harshest criticism—North or South—of

Simms's editorial acumen and taste. The anonymous reviewer claimed that Simms's anthology betrayed "too much Palmetto partiality" and "too great a sympathy for mediocrity in verse" ("Book" 77).[12] Up north, the *New Englander and Yale Review* thought Simms had made "as good a selection as could be made" but rejected outright the claim that such sectional poems would contribute to a national literature: "But we cannot agree with him. They seem to us to be the second-rate effusions of the day, and hereafter they will perish from the knowledge of all but the most curious investigator of the history of these wonderful times" ("Notices" 383).

Following this initial flood of reviews, few writers of the late nineteenth and early twentieth century remarked on Simms's monumental anthology.[13] As Simms went from being a man "more respected than read" to a man neither respected nor read, his anthology of Civil War poetry was mentioned less and less often. Over the past 150 years, there have been a number of cheap facsimiles but no scholarly edition of *War Poetry of the South*. And, with the notable exceptions of Aiken, Busick, and Shields, few contemporary historians or literary critics have taken up Simms's anthology in earnest. What, then, is one to do with *War Poetry of the South*? Richardson never commissioned additional volumes from Simms, and there is no conclusive evidence that *War Poetry of the South* went beyond a second printing. Given these "long years of neglect," one might be tempted to leave this collection in the dustbin of literary history.

Doing so would be a mistake. *War Poetry of the South* remains the most diverse contemporary anthology of the poetry of the Civil War South. Guilds rightly deems it the "best anthology of its kind" (*Literary Life* 306). Among other things, it was "creditably" edited by one of the leading lights of nineteenth-century American literature. Moreover, each of its pages embodies the "feelings, sentiments, ideas, and opinions" of Confederates who thought they were in the process of creating a nation and a national literature that would endure. No matter how wrongheaded or offensive those "feelings, sentiments, ideas, and opinions" may seem to twenty-first century readers, they are certainly worthy of critical consideration. In sum, *War Poetry of the South* has a great deal to teach people within and without Simms studies.

In recent years, scholars have begun to rethink the image of Simms as a mere "literary casualty of the Civil War" (Davidson and van Tuyll; cf. Moltke-Hansen). As James L.W. West III has recently argued, some of Simms's best work was produced after the war (6). It is time that *War Poetry of the South* be considered alongside that best postwar work. A more robust engagement with the volume will, in turn, help to draw attention back to Simms's poetry and literary criticism—two sites of ongoing critical neglect (Busick, "Simms's" 52). Finally, the volume can also help to answer longstanding questions about Simms's postwar philosophy and outlook.[14]

More broadly, it is well past time that *War Poetry of the South* be recognized as a treasure trove of Civil War-era literature and culture. Because poetry anthologies almost always serve a retrospective function—a backward glance over roads traveled, as Walt Whitman might have it—they have the ability to collect, preserve, and make available exuberant and diverse poetic cultures. Anthologies are, as the Australian poet and critic Jennifer Strauss suggests, "essential to the transmission of poetry from the relative ephemerality of periodicals and slim volumes into a more mainstream communication with readers" (87). To read the pages of an anthology like Simms's is to encounter in a single setting poems that likely appeared in a number of other venues and media.[15] Thus, *War Poetry of the South* grants scholars and students intimate access to a short-lived and understudied literary culture. It captures as well as any other single volume the great expectations and stultifying disappointments of Confederate literature.

NOTES

1. For instance, *War Poetry of the South* warrants just two paragraphs in John Caldwell Guilds's standard literary biography, garners no mention in J.V. Ridgley's influential introduction, and appears only in the bibliography of Trent's foundational study. For a persuasive call to action, see Busick, "Simms's."
2. As Aiken notes, Simms also had an abiding interest in the poetry of war ("Simms's" 12).
3. See Guilds, *Literary Life* 305–06. Wakelyn echoes Simms's claim that he had begun collecting the material for his anthology during the war (258). It is not known whether this wartime collection found its way into *War Poetry of the South* or was lost with the plundering and destruction of Simms's library in February 1865. See Simms, *War Poetry of the South* vii.
4. On the material hardships faced by Confederate litterateurs, see London; M. Massey; and Fahs, esp. 1–15.
5. On the postwar marketplace for Simms's writings, see J. West. See also Simms's 12 July 1866 letter to his son (*Letters* 4: 580–82).
6. A 20 March 1867 letter to John R. Thompson suggests Simms's sense of responsibility to his fellow poets: "I regret that the "Burial of Latané" was imperfectly given in the War Poems. *Mais, mon ami,* what would you have? You were out of the Country, and I had to rely on a newspaper copy. Please send me a revised copy in MS. if you have none in print, and you shall be put *rectus in curia,* through the next edition" (*Letters* 5: 31–32).
7. I am not the first scholar to point out that this marks a return to Simms's pre-war arguments about the South's contributions to a national literature. See especially N. Meriwether, "Civil War" 117; and Busick, "Simms's" 51. Moltke-Hansen, *Unfinished* is particularly good on Simms's preface. See especially 18. Both McCardell and Current-Garcia comment on Simms's ability to "reconcile the conflicting demands of section and nation" (McCardell, *Idea* 147; Current-Garcia 325). The subject of Simms's movement from "nationalism to secessionism," as Charles S. Watson describes it,

has engendered an enormous body of criticism. See especially Watson, *Nartionalism* passim; Parks, *William* 89–109; and Wakelyn 158–87.

8. This seems to have been more than just poetic sabre rattling. Simms wrote to Duyckinck in August 1866 claiming that the volume "will be quite 450, and yet more than half of the collection will be omitted." (*Letters* 4: 596).
9. Like *War Poetry of the South*, the majority of these anthologies argue for the historical importance of the "emotional literature" of the Confederacy. To read Confederate poetry—in the South, the North, or even England—is to better understand what brought about a conflict with wide-ranging and catastrophic effects. See Shepperson, 3–5; F. Moore, v; *Lays of the South*, 1. See also Hutchison, 139–42.
10. This is a missed opportunity for Simms, especially in light of recent scholarship that underscores popular song's crucial cultural role in both the United and Confederate States of America. See McWhirter, passim; Hutchison, 143–72; and F. Barrett, 17–40.
11. J. Shields's characteristically incisive essay takes Simms to task for under-representing "reluctant but loyal Confederates" like Alexander B. Meek and William Russell Smith (both Alabamians) "who represented southwestern townspeople of a different character from that of the formidable lowcountry elite to which Simms belonged" (112). In turn, Shields wants us to see the collection as "less a reflection of popular opinion than one important part of a larger effort by staunch Confederates to shape public memory in their image" (126). While that may have been Simms's unstated intention, I do not know that the poems bear out this claim. Because of their composite nature, it is often difficult to characterize an anthology in purely ideological terms. As Franny Nudleman notes, anthologies from the postwar period pulled together "a diverse body of poetry that cannot be read through the lens of homogenizing nationalist abstractions" (90).
12. The previous April, the *Crescent Monthly* had called into question the ethics of Simms's decision to publish his collection while William G. Shepperson was planning to bring out a second edition of his 1862 *War Songs of the South*. See 1 (April 1866): 168. Southern periodicals like *Scott's Monthly Magazine* were similarly dubious about the ethics of publishing such a southern book "at the North" (3 [Jan. 1867]: 82).
13. In an influential 1891 essay for *Lippincott's Monthly*, "Literature in the South Since the War," Thomas Nelson Page championed *War Poetry of the South* as an important collection in the history of southern literature: "A considerable number of the poems possess not only force, but merit of a high order, whilst a fair proportion of them are by their manifest sincerity and feeling raised above the plane of mediocrity. Some, indeed, are poems which, notwithstanding the local significance which narrowed their scope, and despite the perils of unceasing quotation and of hackneyed application, will make their place permanent in the literature of America." (48 [Dec. 1891]: 741–42).
14. Among other things, there is no critical consensus about the cultural work that Simms's anthology takes on. For instance, Aiken claims that *War Poetry of the South* was "more a second call to battle than it was a capitulation" ("Simms's" 11). In contrast, Brennan argues that Simms aimed in the volume to "fulfill the public function of elegy, a collective witnessing that lends healing and understanding" ("Trauma" 134–35). Such claims could and should be put into closer conversation.
15. On nineteenth-century poetry anthologies, see Hutchison and Renker.

Woodcraft; or, Hawks about the Dovecote

JAMES EVERETT KIBLER

Woodcraft is the fifth novel composed in Simms's saga of the American Revolution. Set during the chaotic close and aftermath of the war, it is the last (eighth) Revolutionary Romance in terms of chronological action. As the work opens, the British are evacuating Charleston in December 1782. Then the novel shifts to a ruined rice plantation, Glen-Eberley, on the Ashepoo River south of Charleston, where the plantation community is striving to establish relative civil order and comity. To resist being stolen by the British, some of the plantation's slaves have hidden in the swamp, and as their master, Porgy, returns, they come forward to seek normalcy and put in a crop to feed the near starving. In achieving order, some of the "woodcraft" maneuverings of both war and survival in wild nature must be utilized. Hence the title. As Porgy will state, life, even in peace, is eternal civil war. Proper woodcraft is necessary at every turn and juncture if people are to survive as whole human beings.

The general critical consensus for the last hundred years has been that *Woodcraft* is among Simms's best novels. Many, in fact, deem it his masterpiece. Donald Davidson, perhaps still the most perceptive critic to have written on Simms, for example, wrote in 1952: "It is not too much to say that *Woodcraft* is Simms' highest achievement. Certainly it stands . . . without a rival in its day and time, and hardly excelled or even paralleled later in its peculiar vein" (*Letters* 1: xlv). It is a many-faceted, exceedingly rich and complex work. Critics have rightly discussed it from a multitude of vantage points, but the full measure of the novel has yet to be taken.

Like its themes, the composition history of the novel is among the most complex of Simms's works. It first appeared serially in the Charleston *Southern Literary Gazette* a year after the serialization there of *The Golden Christmas*, to which it bears some thematic affinities and related imagery (Kibler, "Pairing," 13–16). Its title in the *Southern Literary Gazette* was *The Sword and the Distaff; or, "Fair, Fat and Forty," A Story of the South, At the Close of the Revolution*. The novel ran from February to November 1852. In a letter to James Henry Hammond on 18 August 1852, Simms reported the novel finished (*Letters* 3: 193). Before the last section of the serialized version appeared, the complete novel appeared as a separately published work in Charleston from Walker and Richards (publisher of the *SLG*) in September 1852. It was still entitled *The Sword and the Distaff*, and bore on its title page "Second Edition," which is actually the first book edition, created from the typesettings for the *SLG*. It was reissued by Lippincott, Grambo of Philadelphia from the same plates and with the same title in 1853.

This early title effectively represents the complicated mesh of contrasts and opposites that fill the novel. The sword here is emblematic of war and the male world. The distaff (a part of a spinning wheel, or in heraldry, the distaff or female side of the family) stands for the peaceful domestic sphere, the home and hearth, and the female world. In other words, the novel is Simms's *War and Peace*, seventeen years before Tolstoy. The subtitle "Fair, Fat and Forty" refers most specifically to the Widow Eveleigh, Porgy's love interest and plantation neighbor, who stands in contrast to him. As a British officer says of her, she is more of a man than some men, while Porgy is inactive, passive, and of less than heroic nature. Like Falstaff, who is partly a model, he is a likeable comic, mock heroic figure. His unusual name likely derives from a scrappy fish common off the Carolina coast. Its shape, like Porgy's, is round and fat-bodied. The fish was usually only eaten by the poor, owing to its boniness. Just as the worlds of male and female get blurred by Porgy and Eveleigh, the world of domestic peace gets mated with the maneuverings of war.

Simms asked his friend Hammond to comment upon the work, and in a letter of 8 July 1853, he called it "fully equal to any of your novels." He went on to advise Simms to "strike out" the subtitle "Fair, Fat and Forty," because it was "decidedly vulgar." He also noted several inconsistencies and a "fault in your geography" (*Letters* 3: 243). Simms revised the novel, subsequent to its Lippincott, Grambo appearance in 1853, along the lines Hammond suggested. The new, revised edition appeared from Redfield in late September 1854 as *Woodcraft; or, Hawks About the Dovecote. A Story of the South at the Close of the Revolution*.

William P. Trent, Joseph V. Ridgely, and later critics could see no apparent reason for the change and felt the new title had no bearing on the text. Yet it is equally effective, perhaps even more so than the first. It broadens the focus. Woodcraft is the figurative image of maneuvering through life, full as it is of pitfalls and dead ends. In this way, with his new title, Simms highlights the *Bildungsroman* novel of character development (especially for the main character Porgy) and in general broadens the psychological implications outside the smaller (albeit still epic) panorama of war and peace, of the "soldier's pay" of coming back to normalcy in a ruined, war-ravaged land. In twentieth-century fashion, the outer world of the landscape mirrors the scarred inner world of the characters, especially the returning veteran Porgy, who in the early stages of the book, is fatalistic, self-indulgent, and self-pitying, and says that he might best slit his own throat. Simms's belief in the flawed nature of man and his insistence on human frailties and limitations has always been a hallmark of southern literature.

Likewise, Porgy's overseer, Sergeant Millhouse, is only a partial man, most literally, as reflected by his loss of an arm. As in Flannery O'Connor, physical deformity is an outward sign of an inner lack, a spiritual deficiency. Although he may seem more "practical" than Porgy in his thorough-going materialistic attitude toward the world, he is close to being a grotesque. It is no wonder that slave Tom can assess his shortcomings. He concludes that Millhouse lacks the proper balance for dancing, which Millhouse forswears as frivolous.

In addition to the new title, Simms made a few substantive changes and cleared up inconsistencies. For example, Corporal and Sergeant Millhouse become consistently Sergeant Millhouse, as suggested by Hammond. Unfortunately, the Redfield Edition also bears Redfield house-styling and what appears to be some substantive editorial tampering. The Redfield Edition has two unsigned illustrations by F.O.C. Darley, engraved by Whitney, Jocelyn, and Annin in South Carolina. The title page verso indicates that the text was stereotyped by C.C. Savage of New York.

Both editions of the novel are dedicated to Joseph Johnson, MD. Johnson (1776–1862) was a Charleston friend and author of *Traditions and Reminiscences Chiefly of the American Revolution in the South* (1851). To Evert Augustus Duyckinck in 1854, Simms declared Johnson to be "one of the best living reminiscents" of the war (*Letters* 3: 343). In the dedication, Simms suggested that the novel is a *roman à clef*, peopled with fictional portrayals whose real-life antecedents Johnson would surely have no trouble recognizing: "The humorists of 'Glen-Eberley' [Porgy and his comrades at his plantation] were well-known personages of preceding generations, here thinly disguised under false names and fanciful localities, which, I am inclined to think will prove no disguise to you. I shall keep my secret, however, as a matter of course" (*Woodcraft* 3). Simms went on to state that Johnson was under no similar obligation to remain silent about the true identities of the characters, and in fact, was encouraged to name them.

George Hayhoe writes that Johnson's *Traditions* describes "a widow lady of great respectability,—'fair, fat, and forty,' —who entertained the soldiers, and one young officer who flattered himself that he might acquire her wealth by marrying her" (524). Hayhoe feels that this "description is quite probably the germ of the novel," considering the fact that Johnson's "fair, fat, and forty" became the subtitle of *The Sword and the Distaff*. The phrase in Johnson, incidentally, likely derives from Sir Walter Scott's *St. Ronan's Well* (1823) and/or *Redgauntlet* (1824). Hayhoe might also have used the fact that *Traditions* had just appeared the year before Simms wrote his novel to explain it as the impetus for Simms's composition.

As for the Eveleigh surname, the Eveleighs were well-known in early Lowcountry and Charleston Revolutionary War history. Legend has it that it was from the window of the George Eveleigh house on Church Street in Charleston that Francis Marion leapt to avoid capture by the British. A Nicholas Eveleigh of Charleston had an illustrious revolutionary history.

Of Porgy, Hayhoe writes, while he bears resemblance to Falstaff, "it is likely that much of the inspiration for Simms's portrait . . . is derived from a sketch of Dr.

Alexander Skinner of Lee's legion in Alexander Garden's *Anecdotes of the Revolutionary War in America* (1822). Garden describes Skinner as 'an honest fellow, just as ready to fight as eat' (136) and points out his 'strong resemblance to Falstaff' as well as Sancho Panza" (Hayhoe 527). Hayhoe continues: Garden also notes that Skinner was unsuccessfully trying to court the widow Mrs. Charles Elliott of "Sandy Hill" plantation, but even though she refused him, the fact that he had "a kind invitation to feel himself at home" in her house, "the most hospitable mansion in the State, made Skinner the proudest and happiest of men" (Garden 138; Hayhoe 527). These details fit Porgy perfectly.

Simms's character Colonel Moncrieff is based upon James Moncrieff (1744–1793), a Scot who served as a military engineer for England during the siege of Charleston in 1780. He supervised slaves stolen from outlying plantations for resale, and in March 1782, Colonel Balfour suggested he lead a brigade of blacks against the Patriots. Moncrieff is known to have shipped eight hundred slaves to the West Indies, where he sold them as his own property. According to Hayhoe, "such exportation of slaves was illegal but was such a common offense that Cornwallis had issued orders forbidding it without his express permission on 2 August 1780" (524). M'Kewn is likely based on James McKloun, a Scot and loyalist, whom the Patriots did not banish after the war.

Porgy's body servant and cook, Tom, as well as slaves Jenny, John, Jupe, Maum Sappho, Charlotte, Betty, Sally, and Bob, "may be based on or named after Simms family slaves" (*Letters* 1: clii, 2: 590–91). The novel is peppered with allusions to historical figures such as Harden (Colonel William Harden) and Withers (William Withers), Captain Henry Barry, General Francis Marion, General Henry Lee, Horatio Gates, Nathanael Greene, General Charles Cotesworth Pinckney, General Alexander Leslie, Colonel Nisbet Balfour, Major John André, and others. Porgy's consistent praise of the Patriot militiamen of South Carolina reflects Simms's attitudes toward the South's role in the Revolutionary War.

There is no known counterpart for Samuel Bostwick, Dory Bostwick, or Lance Frampton, though their family names are common in the time and place. There is a Frampton plantation ("The Hermitage") near Pocotaligo, whose master, John Edward Frampton (1810–1896), was a state senator from 1842–1846, while Simms was in the legislature. He was one of the largest planters in Prince William's Parish of Beaufort District and had ties to Simms's Barnwell District. He married there in 1842. Long active in the Nullification Movement, Frampton attended the Southern Rights Convention of 1852, and signed the Ordinance of Secession. Lance Frampton, an admirable, sober, common-sensical farmer-soldier, may have been either an ancestor, or a tribute to the senator from one who obviously shared his political beliefs. In courting, Frampton is Porgy's superior. The Widow Griffin, Millhouse, Absalom Crooks, Dr. Oakenburg, and Geordie (George) Dennison may be purely fictional creations, though as Hayhoe suggests, "it is possible that, although Simms used published anecdotes and traditions such as Johnson's [and Garden's] as the basis for some of his characters, he modeled others on figures he had heard Johnson and others talk about" (521).

Woodcraft appeared during a period incredibly fruitful and rich for both Simms and American literature. The decade of the 1850s has been named the American Literary Renaissance by historian and literary critic F.O. Matthiessen (1902–1950) in his landmark volume *American Renaissance: Art and Expression in the Age of Emerson and Whitman* (1941). Although Matthiessen makes no mention of Simms, *Woodcraft* would be legitimate there squarely in the middle of the brief period that produced *The Scarlet Letter*, *Moby Dick*, *Walden*, and *Leaves of Grass*. Interestingly and significantly, if placed there, Simms's work would be the only humorous novel of the decade, and well before *Huckleberry Finn*. A persuasive case has been made by recent critics, most particularly Jan Bakker, that it is as well the first realistic novel in America.

The novel incorporates a complex system of character contrasts, pairings, and comparisons in what later would be called a Faulknerian manner. As in Faulkner, plot and action are driven in this way; and character provides order, structure, and themes. Themes grow out of character rather than the other way around. The centrality of character is likely what lifts the work from the rhetorical to the dialectic and accounts for its literary stature. In general, abstractionist theme-driven, rhetorically conceived fiction is not as effective, and *Woodcraft* escapes these limitations by a Shakespearian, Dickensian focus on the nuanced complexities of human personalities in conflict with themselves and each other.

This is not to say that ideas and views and philosophies are not present, but they grow out of character that is alive (not flat cardboard), believable, engaging, and memorable. Captain Porgy had first appeared in *The Partisan* (1835) as a rather simple supporting figure and, frankly, at times something of a bore. He makes a cameo appearance in *Mellichampe* (1836), is resurrected fully and effectively in *Katharine Walton* (1850), and later appears briefly in *The Forayers* (1855) and *Eutaw* (1856). But here he takes central stage as chief protagonist. He is the most beloved character in Simms's work but nevertheless elicits debate as to just how sympathetically we should see him. Mary Ann Wimsatt has made a good case for Porgy as very sympathetically human despite his exasperating self-indulgence and self-pity early in the novel (*Major* 168–72). William Taylor has him the perfect embodiment of the Cavalier plantation South, with all its strengths and defects (288).

Wimsatt treats the novel's "dominant mode" as a "comedy of plantation manners" (*Major* 167). One question *Woodcraft* poses is whether plantation civilization and its traditions will survive. Involved in this focus is a definition of community and how such communities are kept whole and vital. For the community to persist, there must be hospitality, neighborliness, tolerance, good naturedness, and nurturing through food, fellowship, and friendship—as opposed to self-centeredness and extreme individualism outside society (Kibler, "Pairing" 13).

Beyond these considerations, *Woodcraft* bursts with life in all its infinite possibilities. Its world is full of miracles and mystery. The spiritual suffuses the empirically real. As Porgy says, the "devil is at our elbow" (410), ready to delude, defraud, degrade, and destroy. He continues, and "with foes among those who surround us, and the vices and vanities at our own hearts to second their labors, unless Heaven help us in season, and with all its angels, hope and humanity stand but a poor choice for happiness" (410). In this struggle to survive and maintain community, life is war, civil war, very much like the military conflict that has just ended. It is chaotic, confusing, contradictory, paradoxical, violent, and absurd enough in its particulars. It requires the maneuverings of woodcraft to get through it, often in a dark wood, and along winding, circuitous, and dangerous paths. The novel's sometimes tedious first hundred pages, set in the woods, are necessary to frame the figurative comparison. There are all sorts of snares and false paths throughout the novel, false "ologies" and "isms" that lead to dead-ends and sometimes to death. Two such are atheism (as expressed by the squatter Samuel Bostwick) and utilitarianism (as demonstrated by Millhouse), but there are numerous others as well. Many times the novel's paths (in and out of the woods) go in circles, leading nowhere.

What Simms provides here, beyond "ology" and "ism" or specific concerns (like, for instance, answering *Uncle Tom's Cabin*), is a way of seeing the world, a *Weltanschauung*, that encompasses and transcends topical issues. This way of seeing opens doors to possibilities rather than closing them with easy explanations that oversimplify and thus distort truths. Simms felt, and had his omniscient narrator suggest, that transcendentalism, abolitionism, utilitarianism, hedonism, realism, naturalism, empiricism, determinism, Marxism, spiritualism, positivism, and other passing ideological approaches all, in the final analysis, are flawed by shortsightedness and single-mindedness. Any angle of truth, held too tightly, becomes a falsehood. "My writings are not to be estimated by things of a clique or of a day," he wrote (*Letters* 4: 461). He was aware of literary trends, but was equally the possessor of a strong historical consciousness and was cognizant of the broader context and the constants of literature, which a grounding in the Classics gave him. In the final analysis, in this instance, if not always in his fiction, the shifting fashions, while they made an imprint on his work, seem only superficially secondary when placed against these constants.

The novel's doors indeed open to mysteries, unexplainable riddles, and miracles that are at the heart of life. This world has miracles at every turn of the path. The characters learn practical woodcraft in going down the novel's paths, but real wisdom comes from the particular way of seeing man as finite, flawed, and imperfectible, but yet still capable of transcendence of his animal nature. It is a book that centers on transcendence and transfiguration, both sought and rejected, both accomplished and not achieved.

Man's animal nature, determined by animal desires in an animal world that ends in death, is a part of this novel's realistic universe; but equally realistic is man's capacity for salvation through faith. The character Dory Bostwick is essential in this respect. A faith in miracles is essential to the anti-empiricist way of seeing. Empiricism clearly leads to a diminished world that is joyless and hollow. The characters in the novel stand in stark contrast as those who realize potential, and the possibilities for growth and transfiguration confront those who reject salvation and end their lives in the failed horror of spiritual emptiness.

Woodcraft is thus a book about possibilities, especially the possibilities for redemption and transcendence. Actions matter and character is fate, but the results of these actions are not always pat. Wisdom is a matter of learning that life, with its deep, sad, and grand mysteries, can never be fully fathomed—that it is both inscrutable and unconquerable. Evil exists. It comes from within and is not imposed from without. The novel is thus a grappling to discern the very nature of life as a constant struggle with the devil "at our elbow." Thus, *Woodcraft* is anti-determinist. Men are not fated, not determined by environment and heredity. Simms even left the resolution of his main plots open to conjecture, but the conjecture alone is enough to undercut rigid determinism (Kibler, "Dory's" 211). What is clear is that at the novel's end a character's treasure of faith is proved true and life affirming, while his foil's reliance on the material proves false and leads to emptiness and a death that is at once physical and spiritual. One of the novel's primary miracles, Dory Bostwick, daughter of a cruel and malignant squatter, "blossoms" in her squalid shack. Man's animal world is still ordered in its larger design by a Providence which allows miracles even for the humblest.

Clearly *Woodcraft* is close in spirit and philosophy to Simms's *Poetry and the Practical* (1854), in which poetry, or the way of seeing that it requires, is the only truly practical endeavor. The novel's main character, Porgy, accepts the mysteries of life, sees the true value of music, poetry, and dance, values the eccentricities of human personality that would prevent easy case-book explanations of human nature, and refuses (like Simms) to allow life to be explained only by uninspired science and the cash nexus or by the pragmatic, empirical, and practical alone. Porgy tells us "The true man does not live by money . . .. There is still better food than that for which I hunger" (*Woodcraft* 235).

On the other hand, Porgy's foil, his utilitarian overseer Millhouse (shades of John Stuart Mill and the mill house of industry) can see no good in allowing slaves to coon hunt or dance or Porgy to entertain poets and guests who cannot pay their way. He would turn out immediately foppish, eccentric Dr. Oakenburg, that "puzzle in a bottle" as Porgy calls him, and poet Geordie Dennison, who is chronicling the late war and its heroes in his verse (Simms, *Sword* 579). Dennison rides with Marion, and who will be there to pass down his exploits and their meaning if not sung by the poet? To summarize the novel in terms of "finance vs. romance," however true the phrase rings, is not the whole story. Although Simms himself famously said that the novel was "probably as good an answer to Mrs. Stowe as has been published" (*Letters* 3: 223), his answer was more philosophical than direct. To treat it simply as a reply to *Uncle Tom's Cabin* is to miss many even more important dimensions and to greatly impoverish the novel.

Porgy's "woodcraft" in the novel has not led to perfection, but he is a tolerant and much wiser man by novel's end. Furthermore, the circumstances of the novel and the plot prove Porgy to be correct in his major assumptions and surmises. His woodcraft has led him a long way; and learning to be less self-indulgent has opened up the larger possibilities of life. He has not gone in circles in the dark like the embittered, demonic Bostwick.

Porgy, the cook for his band of soldiers, now becomes the food provider in peace for those on the plantation who look to him for protection and sustenance. The novel's complex patterns of food imagery thus provide depth of meaning and thematic unity. That Porgy's name derives from a fish—perhaps a sacrificial one suggesting the abiding early Christian symbol ΙΧΘΫΣ, the Ichthus, the Greek word for fish that became the acrostic for Christ, with connotations here of the Christ-fish that fed the multitudes—becomes all the more relevant. Porgy *is* his plantation. His imposing round body is imaged as both host and rice barrel from which his rice plantation community draws its life. The feeding, feasting, and food imagery takes on great importance in delineating both Porgy's character and the novel's themes. So does the imagery of dressing, clothing, and *sans culottism* (324).

As in the ancient Celtic Arthurian legend and Fisher King myth, Porgy's kingdom can be only as healthy as he is. That is another reason that it is crucial that he lift himself out of hedonism, self-pity, and despair—and act manfully. Many are depending upon him. The very existence of the complex little plantation kingdom is at stake. Porgy finally accepts responsibility, imagines himself as the head of a body, with many hands to direct, and understands that this head must be kept soundly functioning. His body servant Tom is a key in that soundness. In a sense, Tom is the cook who feeds the cook (mentally, spiritually, physically), who in turn feeds the plantation. Both *Woodcraft* and *The Cassique of Kiawah* (1859) show that it is through the noble sacrifice of the rare individual that civilization is able to survive at all—even if only by the skin of its teeth.

At the novel's end, the reader is left wondering what will happen to Porgy's plantation community. It seems to be enduring the fortunes of war. Dory may marry Arthur and the plantation world return to harmony. Or maybe Porgy's bachelor world will doom the plantation to a dead end. We should not forget, however, that *The Sword and the Distaff* was preceded in the *Southern Literary Gazette* by *The Golden Christmas* the year before—another comedy of manners set in a Lowcountry plantation community. The setting is 1850, and the fact that the agrarian society is still intact and functioning strongly suggests that *Woodcraft's* chaotic world will finally be survived one way or another through accommodation. In 1850, the plantation community has its own new struggle, with the outcome once again determining whether that community will continue into the future. This time it is the prejudice and pig-headedness of family that might be the end of the plantation. *The Sword and the Distaff,* following on its heels as flash-back to an even more crucial time, might tip the scales into an over-riding optimism premised by the wisdom that the community has been there before and survived. And, after all, survival is triumph enough—indeed is a southern specialty. It is one of Simms's key themes throughout his works. The home and hearth abide. As David Moltke-Hansen makes clear, Simms's 1850 review of Mrs. Ellet's *Women of the Revolution*, declares that it "is from the home that 'spring all the virtues and securities of the nation,' even in the midst of wars and political turmoil" ("Horizons" 12).

But for *Woodcraft*, Porgy's way into the light of responsible action has been the path through the dark tangled wood of the returning veteran, physically and psychologically burned out. At first depressed and at brief moments even suicidal, repairing his ruined plantation lands had seemed too much. Such a treatment thus fully qualifies *Woodcraft* as a "soldier's pay" novel ahead of Stephen Crane, William Faulkner, and Ernest Hemingway. Porgy's complex psychology is only one of several superb, complex characterizations in the work. The others are Bostwick, the Widow Eveleigh, Dory, and Arthur Eveleigh, all very complex and memorable figures.

Porgy stands opposite to Millhouse, Tom to Porgy, Porgy to Bostwick, Millhouse to Dennison and Oakenburg, M'Kewn to Bostwick, Tom to Millhouse, Lance Frampton to Millhouse, Frampton to Porgy, the Widow Griffin to the Widow Eveleigh, but the most important central contrast is of Porgy, surrogate father to Dory, and the Widow Eveleigh and her son Arthur. This double pairing may achieve its resolution at novel's end in classic romance fashion, with the strong likelihood that Dory will marry Arthur and the couple will eventually take possession of both Porgy's and the neighboring Eveleigh lands. All this is left to conjecture however. *Woodcraft* is too sophisticated a book for a pat conclusion. The world it portrays is not assuring a happy ending. What is clear, however, is that, in the end, Dory's and Porgy's treasure of trust and faith are proved true and life-affirming, while M'Kewn's and Bostwick's lust for gold proves false and death-dealing, miring them in their own personal hells in a culture of death. Appropriately, the novel's image patterns associate Dory with the light and Bostwick and M'Kewn with the dark. Dory herself is the gold of genuine treasure. Perhaps her name is a play on the Spanish *D'Or*. The title of Chapter 34, in fact, gets specific by calling her Bostwick's real "Treasure."

It is clear that bachelor Porgy has become Bostwick's replacement in his fatherly protection of Dory. He sees her worth and the "miracle" she is—this flower blossoming in a mud puddle. Although separated by class, she shares much in common with Porgy. They appreciate the non-utilitarian but, more importantly, are both striving for redemption. That search thus becomes a central theme of the novel, one that has universal implications. To treat *Woodcraft* as a social thesis, a probing of history, a critique of the antebellum planter, a close depiction of landscape, a definition of community, a defense of slavery, or a weighing in on various topical issues, while helpful in understanding the great expansive world of the novel, is only to see one or another facet of this work, whose depths are still to be properly plumbed. What elevates the work to greatness is its verisimilitude of complex, engaging character, its believable settings, effective poetic use of imagery and image patterns, and above all its universal themes of redemption and transcendence.

Woodcraft, as Wimsatt shows, is congenial social comedy of manners. Its comic surface has its charms, but the surface belies the true nature beneath, which is anything but humorous and placid. In fact, it is this contrast that often provides the dramatic tension—say, for example, in Simms's attitude toward nature, which can be both a peaceful sanctuary (as for Marion's men), or a place where danger lurks in the form of "varmints," both animal and human—hence, Simms's very complex view of life as a thing of illusions, masks, violent contradictions, and strongest paradoxes. Life can bear its rose among the thorns, but it is more often the twisting path through the dark woods, demanding "woodcraft" at every turn. A man's woodcraft in this light most often involves coming to terms with the world by regarding even its harsher aspects as having ends (a Providential design) that one does not and can never fully comprehend.

Simms uses his tangible, carefully limned, accurate local physical settings to explore the nature of mankind and his world in general and through the ages. From his broad reading and well-developed historical consciousness, Simms learned early that despite shifting social forms and fashions, man's nature is always constant in revealing the same vices, in all times and places. He found these in the society he knew, but just as certainly fully recognized that they were not original with or limited to that society. Simms saw the hypocrisies and weaknesses in his local scene were the same that all flesh is heir to. He was capable of diving below the surface and thus reaches the great universal depths and profundities. He was always fond of saying that in poetry, as in fiction, a writer should find out the depths of feeling within oneself, and then he would know and be able to portray the same in human nature.

In portraying these depths of universal human nature, he presents us with the man God intended, and his opposite, the retort-made, self-made, monomaniacal modern man. The latter loses the whole man as a result of his selfish will to greed, hedonism, and the narrowly utilitarian, thus robbing life of meaning, beauty, and interest, and reducing living to the mechanical routine of going through the dull motions. Man preempts God's place; and the accompanying loss of values reduces him to "the creature he was not made." In this way, man is diminished to the animal, and reality is shrunk to scientific empiricism in a greatly impoverished universe. Such is the trap of determinism and empiricism. In its modernist image patterns of retort-made, obsessive, narcissistic men going in circles in the dark and getting nowhere, placed in the healthy context of whole, self-sacrificing men held within a Providential design, the novel is a bridge from Old America to the New.

Yet another of the novel's strengths is that, despite its length and unlike so many works of its day, the novel has little that is superfluous or extraneous. A case in point is a minor character, Geordie Dennison, who is, after proper consideration, not minor at all. Dennison is the resident poet, and Millhouse rants and raves that he is not providing food or wealth to keep the plantation going. Porgy understands his value, however, and counters that the world must have its "singing birds" as well as poultry (Simms, *Sword* 579). Furthermore, James Cantrell accurately reinforces Davidson's view of Simms as saga-man by discussing his creation of Dennison as the Irish-descended bard with the mission of that central figure's keeping and furthering of the people's story and cultural identity. Davidson writes: "The real strength of Simms is his unselfconscious nearness to what might be called . . . folk tradition, which is pre-literary or pre-bookish . . . . The best fiction of Simms is not a long step away from saga and folk tale" (*Letters* 1: lii). Cantrell writes: "Throughout the Revolutionary War series, Dennison is shown to be the folk poet, the natural bard of both the war and South Carolina and its culture" (90). Simms understood well the mission of the bard, and *Woodcraft*, his humorous mock epic in prose, shows clearly that he deserves Davidson's appellation and accolade. There is a further dimension to consider as well. *Woodcraft* draws heavily on legend, reminiscence, and folk culture. Simms was committed to capturing in print the oral lore that Cleanth Brooks claimed characterized the traditional South as primarily an oral folk culture (332–38). By the mid-nineteenth century, many Europeans were similarly exploring their traditions, myths, and memories with great literary consciousness. The southern writer, as Brooks shows with his comparison of Faulkner to Yeats, was not alone in this. Davidson again hits the mark even more precisely: "As a writer of fiction, Simms belongs to another age—a heroic age . . . . He became what might be called the 'saga-man' of that age" (*Letters* 1: xlv).

The other member of the minor pair of impractical ones for whom Porgy serves as patron is the eccentric Dr. Oakenburg. He cannot be figured out or classified, and that keeps Porgy constantly aware that people cannot be reduced or oversimplified to figure, statistic, or idea. Empirical science is good at recording and quantifying, but not explaining. The thorough-going materialist could never understand Porgy's honoring the riddle and celebrating the mystery. Oakenburg, minor character that he is, is thus, like Dennison, not so minor after all. The abundance of small side-bar touches like these coalesce to contribute to the novel's major strengths to make *Woodcraft* the masterpiece critics have found it.

The novel's reception was favorable from the start. It was not widely reviewed however. Only ten reviews and notices appeared from 1852 to 1854 (Butterworth and Kibler 84–98). Simms blamed his publisher for not disseminating the volume. Many notices were short and non-specific, placing into question whether the reviewer read the volume. The more specific reviews rightly praised Simms's verisimilitude, humor, authentic use of locale, and "actual scenes and circumstances" (qtd. in Butterworth and Kibler 86). Attesting to the work's continued popularity, however, *Woodcraft* was reprinted many times by a number of northern publishers in the late nineteenth century. Several paperback editions have been available for the last half century. The 1854 Redfield Edition is still the standard text, but imperfect owing to copious house-styling.

Woodcraft has continued to elicit favorable response along a spectrum of critical interests. As for its influence on later writers, perhaps the most significant early one is the passage that concerns Dory's reading to her father (*Woodcraft* 222–23). Hayhoe finds a close similarity to Chapter 5 of *Adventures of Huckleberry Finn* (1885), where Huck reads to his father. He notes that "Huck's father and Bostwick are essentially the same type of character—poor whites who drink too much, abandon their families and are criminally involved" (539–40). Charles Frazier's reference to Simms in *Cold Mountain* is the latest. Odds are that *Woodcraft* will continue to find an appreciative audience, as well it should. As Kibler declared in 1990, "It is destined for proper appreciation because it effectively addresses universals" ("Major Fiction" 94–95).

The Yemassee: A Romance of Carolina

DAVID MOLTKE-HANSEN

The Yemassee is historically the best known of the long fictions of William Gilmore Simms. Although a portion of what would become chapter 22 appeared already in the *Southern Literary Gazette* that the twenty-two-year-old Simms edited in 1828–29 (Guilds, *Literary Life* 28–29), he wrote most of the work in the second half of 1834. He did so following publication of his first romance, *Guy Rivers*. His new "Indian tale—a story of an early settlement and of an old tribe in Carolina" (*Letters* 1: 63)—appeared by early April the next year. Stereotyped, it issued from Harper & Brothers of New York. A corrected printing followed almost immediately, because the first sold out so quickly (Holman, *Yemassee* [xxxiii]; *Letters* 2: 389). According to Simms, in his "Advertisement to the Second Edition," this was so even though the initial run "was a remarkably large one—twenty-five hundred copies—twice the number usually put forth, in this country, of similar European publications" ([3]).[1]

Revised further in 1853, *The Yemassee* appeared as one of the first of the twenty volumes in the Redfield edition of Simms's selected writings, published by Justus Starr Redfield, who had begun in the stereotyping business in New York a quarter century before and subsequently issued works by many of Simms's Young America colleagues, such as Edgar Allan Poe and Walt Whitman. *The Yemassee* has been republished perhaps three dozen times in print, as well as numerous times in digital form. In the decades on either side of the Second World War, it was the only Simms book in print aside from his revised and updated *History of South Carolina* (1840). In the century and a half following the Redfield edition, it has received more critical attention than any other Simms work, though more recently *Woodcraft; or, Hawks about the Dovecote: A Story of the South at the Close of the Revolution* (1852–1854) has attracted increasing appreciation and now is often regarded as one of Simms's best historical romances.

Set on the South Carolina frontier, Simms's third book-length fiction treats the Yemassee War of 1715–17, when the Yemassee Indians, with their Spanish and Native American allies, attacked the low country colonial settlements. Scholars have explained the war's origins in part by the mistreatment of Native Americans by unscrupulous traders (Gallay 315–440). Simms, however, writing in the midst of the removal of natives from east of the Mississippi to the newly created Indian Territory in the future Oklahoma, emphasized such motives as the colonists' need for land, the conflict between rival European powers over territory they claimed, and the inevitability of native displacement, given these European-derived ambitions and predations, as well as the attendant power inequalities (Wimsatt, *Major* 33–56; Nakamura 149–63).

Often compared to James Fenimore Cooper's Leatherstocking Tales, Simms's first colonial romance, like later ones—*Vasconselos* (1853) and *The Cassique of Kiawah* (1859)—and numerous short stories in such collections as *The Wigwam and the Cabin* (1845), seems to many critics to render native culture and life in greater depth and with more empathy than Cooper's work showed. John Caldwell Guilds has gone so far as to claim that Simms "wrote more about, thought more about, and almost certainly knew (and cared) more about the American Indian than any other man of letters of the nineteenth century" ("Literary View" xxix). Charles Hudson has added that "Simms had experiences with Indians unmatched by any other man of letters of his time" (xxxviii).

In his introduction to the 1853 edition of the romance, Simms contended that, when he wrote nearly two decades before, "there was little understood, by readers generally, in respect to the character of the red men." Having "seen the red men of the south in their own homes, on frequent occasions," however, Simms "had arrived at conclusions in respect to them, and their habits and moral nature, which seemed to [him] to remove much of that air of mystery which was to disguise most of their ordinary actions." That was why he was able to make "corrections of the vulgar opinions . . . in the body of the [*The Yemassee*]." While he admitted that he had invented the mythology of the Native Americans in his romance, he insisted that his "portraits . . . are true to the Indian as our ancestors knew him at early periods, and as our people, in certain situations, may know him still" (xxviii).

Simms invented more than a mythology. Much of the language and culture, as well as rituals and beliefs presented drew anachronistically on his nineteenth-century experience of the Creek, Cherokee, and Choctaw and on fragments of Indian lore from outside of the lower South. He may even have drawn on Edwin Forrest's dramatic 1831 performance in Charleston of *Metamora, or the Last of the Wampanoags*, a play set in New England but having many of the same themes as Simms would develop in *The Yemassee* (Holman, *Yemassee* xiv). He clearly thought of the natives in pan-Indian terms first, then as members of particular cultural communities. His use of analogy across nations, time, and geography reflects the limits of literary white understanding even among the most knowledgeable.

Later Simms enhanced his knowledge by reading new works of such friends as Henry Rowe Schoolcraft and other early ethnographers (*Views* 1: 102–17). He also continued to read historical sources critically, for instance dismissing as "wild illusions" James Adair's claim, in his *A History of the North American Indians* (1775), that the Indians were descended from the lost tribe of Israel (*Yemassee* [1853],

75). Such added learning, however, did little to change his judgments about the relationship of Native Americans either to whites and blacks or to the forces of history and the consequences of civilization's relentless westward movement and enhancement of European-American domination.

The Work

In treating the Yemassee War, Simms was doing more than reflecting upon Indian Removal in his own day. He understood contemporary issues to have deep roots. These preoccupied him from at least age eighteen, when he first traveled west to Indian country, through to his death in 1870, at age sixty-four. The manifest destiny reflected in the expansion of European (and, later, American) settlement, the competition for empire, the corollary, necessary, yet tragic loss of land, independence, and even people-hood by Native Americans, the educative value of slavery to less culturally advanced, African-descended slaves, the importance of breeding, honor, and the chivalric code, as well as social hierarchy and the progress of civilization—all were elements of the story. The story had epic dimension and purpose.

Writing in 1855, Simms reminded his old New York friend Evert Augustus Duyckinck that "my works are romances, not novels." That is because "[t]hey involve sundry of the elements of heroic poetry. They are imaginative, passionate, metaphysical; they deal chiefly in trying situation, bold characterization, & elevating moral" (*Letters* 3: 388). The romance was to Simms the prose equivalent of the epic. It told the story of a people's early formation and development, as did the national epics that were being celebrated in contemporary Europe. At the same time, romances told of loss, glory, and the high cost of victory.

In contradistinction, the novel, in Simms's view, differs in its "material . . . even more than [its] fabrication," because it is "confined to the felicitous narration of common and daily occurring events, and the grouping and delineation of characters in ordinary conditions of society." Consequently, the domestic novel "is altogether a different sort of composition" (*Yemassee* [1853], xxix). In making this observation in the "Introduction" to the Redfield edition of *The Yemassee,* Simms was elaborating a point he had asserted already in 1835, in the "Advertisement" to the first edition. This made him one of the earliest Americans to reflect on literary realism in its relationship to Romance, "a distinction made notable in the United States by Hawthorne's famous statement in the preface to *The House of Seven Gables*" in 1851 (Guilds, *Yemassee* xvii).

The Yemassee was the first of Simms's four colonial and ante-colonial romances. These four made vivid episodes in the exploration, conquest, and settlement of the Americas. Two—*The Damsel of Darien* (1839) and *Vasconselos* (1853)—treated chapters in the first of what Simms identified as "The Four Periods of American History" (*Views* 1: 75–127). This was when the Spanish conquered the Aztecs and

Incas and explored and lay claim to much of the future South, from Florida to Texas. The epoch lasted for about three-quarters of a century after Columbus first made landfall in the Caribbean in 1492.

In the second period, the British colonized the Atlantic coast of America from Florida to Canada, while competing with the French and Spanish for empire in the interior of the continent and in the Caribbean. South Carolina was established in 1670, in the middle of these two centuries between the first, or "ante-colonial," phase and the American Revolution. Simms's *The Cassique of Kiawah* is set soon after the colony's founding. Two generations later, Carolina was forty-five years old at the beginning of the Yemassee War. Ironically, just three years earlier the Yemassee had helped the colonists defeat the Tuscarora in North Carolina. After the Yemassees' defeat in their turn, the colonists defeated the pirates, such as the famous Blackbeard and Stede Bonnet, who had plagued the coast for two decades.

Simms knew this historical context, thanks in part to his friendship with the Carroll brothers, who, like him, were sons of an immigrant Ulsterman. The Carrolls and he grew up together on the Charleston Neck, just north of the city limits. Later Simms read law with the slightly older Charles Rivers Carroll, to whom he dedicated his first romance and second work of fiction. *Guy Rivers: A Tale of Georgia* treated one of the more immediate causes of Removal—the 1830s gold rush into the southern Appalachian Mountains. Charles and his brother Edward joined Simms in writing the 1833 *Cosmopolitan*, a literary occasional. The third brother, Benjamin Rivers Carroll, compiled and introduced the two-volume *Historical Collections of South Carolina; Embracing Many Rare and Valuable Pamphlets, and Other Documents*. It issued in 1836 from Harper & Brothers of New York, the publisher of *Guy Rivers* and *The Yemassee*, as well as, under a variant company name, Simms's dramatic 1832 poem *Atalantis. A Story of the Sea: In Three Parts*.

The materials in *Historical Collections* no doubt were available to Simms earlier. He also had access to the Charleston Library Society. He saw the Carrolls, not only in Charleston, but at Charles's plantation at Clear Pond in Barnwell District, roughly half-way to Augusta, Georgia. Therefore, Benjamin could share his discoveries, over the three years in the early 1830s, when he searched "most of the principle libraries in the country and . . . all the catalogues of rare books he could meet with" (Carroll 1: ii). The sharing was not just intellectual, but social. Charles's plantation was some fifteen miles from the two Edisto River estates of an English planter, Nash Roach, whose daughter, Chevillette, Simms courted soon after *The Yemassee*'s publication. Possibly they met upon his return to Charleston from New York in the late spring, for the Roaches also had a town home in the port city, where Nash had been a cotton factor (Guilds, *Literary Life* 18–25, 50–53, 69–70; *Letters* 1: xcvii). Or perhaps they met in the summer at Clear Pond, where Augusta, Simms's daughter by his late wife, was visiting with Charles's family and where Simms went in mid-June (*Letters* 1: 69).

In any event, *Historical Collections* includes key texts to which Simms referred in *The Yemassee*—both Dr. George Milligen-Johnston's *A Short Description of the Province of Carolina* (1770) and the Rev. Dr. Alexander Hewatt's two-volume *Historical Account of the Rise and Progress of the Colonies of South Carolina and Georgia* (1776) (*Yemassee* [1835] 1: 9). In addition to providing what Benjamin Carroll judged an "accurate history of the diseases and epidemics prevalent" in Carolina, Milligen-Johnston made striking comments on the importance of protecting Indians as hunters of and guards against run-away, African-descended slaves (1: vii). Simms presumably derived the name of his noble Yemassee chief, Sanutee, from Hewatt, who wrote of Sanute and also Ishiagaska, the great warrior, whom Simms included as well (albeit in a cameo role) (Guilds, *Yemassee* 442). Strengthening this Native American dimension of his *Historical Collections*, Carroll began "with an introductory discourse . . . in which he . . . attempted to describe . . . the country in its first rude and uncultivated state; when its aborigines [were] to be viewed in their true character and condition" (1: ii). Simms shared this ambition for his romance.

Carolina's colonization gave Simms the chance to dramatize the resulting confrontations and intermingling of diverse peoples. These processes led simultaneously to the creation of an emerging culture and the conflict between cultures in the low country. *The Yemassee* tells both stories: European Americans, with their African-descended slaves, are laying the foundations of the world into which Simms will be born almost a century later. There are ethnic, racial, and class, as well as ideological conflicts among elements of the population, but the seeds of the future are being planted, as order and social hierarchy are fitfully established.

At the same time, white encroachment on Yemassee lands forces the natives to decide how to respond to alien and alienating influences. They are divided: some wish to sell out and move; others would rather die than lose their place, either in the world or, more importantly, in relationship to their gods. While illustrating the inevitability of the loss, Simms nevertheless has struck many readers as admiring of and sympathetic to the Native Americans in their dilemma. Other critics see him deploying narrative strategies either to defend slavery or to emasculate sympathy in his "Southern Patriarchal Response" to marginalized and subaltern populations (Weidman; King; Mielke; Shelton).

In structuring the parallel yet intertwined telling of these stories of simultaneous cultural development and conflict, Simms drew on both Sir Walter Scott and *The Iliad*. Scott's Border and Medieval Romances, written in Simms's boyhood, showed Simms how to capture and convey peoples in conflict amid the early development of societies. Scott placed his stories intentionally in liminal zones—for instance, the border country between England and Scotland. Simms followed suit, placing many of his romances in frontier settings, amid warfare, or on the rough, distant edges of the developing South (Holman, *Roots*; Moltke-Hansen, "Horizons"). *The Iliad* taught Simms how to convey sympathy to the side foreordained to lose. Affecting scenes between warriors and their wives, despair at betrayal of pride and their gods, and other moments are straight from the Greek epic and give pathos and desperate nobility to a number of Indian characters, especially Sanutee and his wife, Matiwan.

Other Indian characters are weak, given to drink, unable to see clearly their unfolding fate, or maddened by greed, jealousy, or blood lust. Sanutee joins with Ishiagaska, the war chief, and the high priest Enoree-Mattee to forestall those chiefs who want to sell out to the colonists. These leaders do so by having the totemic tattoos cut from the arms and chests of the would-be sellers; thus, "in a single hour [the socially annihilated] were expatriated men, flying desperately to the forests, homeless, nationless, outcasts from God and man, yet destined to live" (*Yemassee* [1853] 112). Later, Matiwan kills her son Occonestoga rather than have him suffer the same fate—the excision of his social and religious being. She then invites Sanutee to kill her for having impeded tribal justice, but he declines.

In this telling, patriotism—defined as unswerving devotion to one's culture, people, and home—is married to honor to make the noble man—not only a noble savage. It does not matter that patriotism may lead to dispossession and displacement or death. Simms insisted that Native Americans were as capable of this nobility as any people: "the character of the North American Indian exhibited, not merely in common but in large degree," he observed, "all of those moral and human sensibilities, out of which art has usually fashioned her noblest fabrics" (*Views* 1: 145). Given this judgment, Simms believed "there was no better blood than that of Cherokee and Natchez," and that blood "would have been a good infusion into the paler fountain of Quaker and Puritan." This did not happen, because "[o]ur imperfect knowledge of the Indian,—the terror that he inspired,—the constant warfare between his race and our own—have embittered our prejudices, and made us unwilling to see any thing redeeming either in his character or intellect" (*Views* 1: 139).

The patriotism of the colonists confronted that of the Yemassee. Simms saw himself using his writing both to promote this devotion to land and people among his readers, as well as to treat the sentiment as a subject. Simms had patriotic commitment in mind when, for instance, writing the editor of the *Magnolia* in 1841: "The popular mind needs to be awakened, elevated, chastened, nay, goaded and scourged to . . . its duties to patriotism" (*Letters* 1: 219). Armed with this belief, his judgment of the Yemassees' patriotism was admiring but ruthless, for he understood that war is the way history determines where power resides and how society is governed—whose patriotism wins (Moltke-Hansen, "History Failed").

The literary consequence for Simms was less clear, however, as his victors were often less compelling as characters than his losers. Readers have found Sanutee and Matiwan sympathetic figures and Occonestoga at least humanly complex and comprehensible. Part of that humanity stems from his saving from a rattlesnake Bess (Beth) Matthews, daughter of a Puritan minister and the love interest of Gabriel Harrison—aka Charles Craven, Governor of South Carolina. Craven, too, is saved by an Indian—Matiwan—just before he is to suffer ritual torture and death. Where Sanutee bespeaks the nobility and doom of his people, Harrison has a different role. He reflects a triple birthright—as a representative of the value of social hierarchy and breeding, as a leader, builder, and tamer of his infant colony, and as a prefigurement of the colony's future as a cultural and social hearth for the American South. While admirable perhaps, these roles are not exactly heart-warming.

Other characters among the colonists are less ideal models and more personalities, however sketchily rendered. Bess, for instance, is at least vivacious, and she provides a stark contrast to her dour and unyielding, parson father. Sir Edmund Bellinger is well-born, like Craven/Harrison, but is insufferable in his self-conceit and incomprehension. Irishman Teddy Macnamara is vigorous and vehement as he is being tortured and killed in a sacrificial rite. Pirate Richard Chorley is a blackguard with color, if not character. Stolid backwoodsman Wat Grayson is one in a long line of sage white men of the forests, who—in contradistinction to Cooper's Natty Bumpo—works to advance society rather than flee it or lament its encroachment on the wild (Rubin, "Romance"; Nakamura 152, 155). The slave Hector, who turns down Craven/Harrison's offer of freedom, is one of the earliest, print-rendered speakers of Gullah (Guilds, *Yemassee* 414–36; Morris).

Indeed, except the people at the top of the social pyramid, most of the colonists speak dialect, making Simms an early proponent of dialect fiction (K. Holt). In this usage, he was not being merely colorful but trying to convey ethnic, racial, class, and other geo-cultural diversity. He did so impressionistically and anachronistically, perhaps, using what he heard spoken around him as much as what he saw recorded in older texts. One of the most eloquent characters, however, does not speak: the land. Simms is especially evocative of swamps and woods (Kibler, "Naturalist"). In this, as in his rendering of dialects, he sought to be a realist at the same time as a romancer. To the same end, he used historical texts to guide his renderings to the extent they usefully could. For him the romance was not an escape from, but imaginative insight into, the large movements and significant episodes of the past, of life, and of place (S. Frye).

Much of the time, the Indians and colonists carry forward their separate story lines. At key junctures, however, these tales intersect. Sometimes this is privately: thus Occonostoga's shooting of the snake with his bow and arrow as the rattler is about to strike. At other times, it is in meetings among leaders of both sides or in the midst of battle. Colonists dominate the text, commanding roughly sixty percent, but the Indians are at the emotional heart. Their loss is the white future, the future of the South still coming into being through Removal, when the novel first appeared. Before his day, as Simms knew, despite the defeat of the Yemassee, the South had been more red than white and black.

Yet *The Yemassee* looks forward to and justifies not only the progressive shift in the balance of power in the region, but its consequences. The work follows that curve in miniature. At the beginning, the Yemassee's "power extended into the remote interior" as "one of the twenty-eight aboriginal nations among which, at its first settlement by the English, the province of Carolina was divided." There "[a] feeble colony of adventurers from a distant world had taken up its abode alongside of them" (*Yemassee* [1835] 1: 11). Forty-five years later, the deer that the Yemassee hunt have been driven into the swamps by the spread of colonial settlement and the noise of colonial enterprise. Queen Anne also has just died, and King George I is on the throne. The colony is still a rude place, and the colonists are by-and-large the rough-and-ready sorts needed to build society in the wilderness. Yet, by the end, the "tale becomes history. The web of fiction is woven—the romance is nigh over" (*Yemassee* [1835] 2: 229). In the last pages African-descended slaves are clubbing the defeated Indians to death on the battlefield. The inevitable victory of the plantation South is thus prefigured.

The Text

Simms began writing on Native Americans at age eighteen, during his first trip to the Old Southwest in the winter of 1824–25, when he traveled to visit his father and uncle on their frontier plantation in Mississippi. He fastened on Indians as subjects for poetry and fiction for multiple reasons. The interest and knowledge of his father, an Indian fighter under Andrew Jackson, inspired him. Yet long before he got to Mississippi, he was making detailed notes of his encounters with Native Americans and recording incidents he had been told. The Indians were in proximity to their cultural origins and myths, Simms imagined, much as Homer's Greeks or the Vikings of the eddas and sagas (S. Frye 88). That made the Indians appropriate subjects for romances. Further, they were eloquent, with a natural, passionate, and soaring oratory and poetry (*Views* 1: 128–47). Eloquent, too, were the wilds through which Simms trekked. Imbued, by the maternal grandmother with whom he lived in Charleston, with the history of South Carolina and his family there, he reasoned by analogy the relationship of what he was seeing in the Old Southwest to what had happened over the past century and a half in the Carolina low country that he had been exploring since his early youth.

As the boy became a man, these often inchoate ruminations took more definite form (Simms, *Social* 6). Charleston friends, such as the Carrolls and the Simmons brothers, at once shared and fostered some of Simms's literary ambitions but also his reading and connections. It mattered that James W. Simmons was descended from the first English settler in South Carolina and joined Simms for a time in editing and publishing the *Southern Literary Gazette* (*Letters* 1: cxxxvii; Simms, *Charleston Book* 444n). His connections with Lord Byron's circle in London mattered as well.[2] Simms soon was reading and applying what he learned of new poetic approaches and themes from Wordsworth and Coleridge, too, well ahead of Ralph Waldo Emerson and others in the future Transcendentalist circle (Kibler, *Poetry* 13–16; Brennan, *Holy Craft*).

Sir Walter Scott's border ballads melded in Simms's mind with the bardic quality of Scott's tales. As important was Scott's insistence that his romances recorded the development of the English out of the Anglo-Saxons and the Normans, of the Scots out of the Highlanders and the Lowlanders, and of the British out of the Scots and the English. Simms understood, as a result, that peoples' identities emerge and are submerged or rewritten by later developments. This rhythm of identity is an appropriate—indeed, a quintessential—theme for the romance. He knew all this before he sat down to write the bulk of *The Yemassee* in the summer and fall of 1834.

To write out of his native history obliged him to include the history of earlier South Carolina natives—the Yemassee among them—in order to account for their passing from the scene. If he was to use his long fictions to tell of the emergence of southerners out of the peoples and conflicts that had turned a frontier into a civilization, Simms also had to do as Scott did. He needed to show how social order and culture reflected historical developments, as well as perduring moral values, the challenges to them, and art's power and necessity.

The Redfield and Later Editions

When Simms first corrected *The Yemassee*, shortly after its initial printing, he had time to do so only in small ways. Because he was in New York, it was easy to work with the printers to fix little details without having to print a true new edition. In fairly typical fashion, this corrected printing was called the second edition on its title page. In 1853, Simms did more extensive editing. In June of that year he wrote to his oldest New York friend and informal literary agent, James Lawson, about acquiring the copyrights to *The Yemassee* and five other works he had published with Harper & Brothers. He proposed, he said, "to commence publication of a uniform Edition of [his] writing" and was revising *The Yemassee* to this end (*Letters* 3: 236–37). This was the genesis of the Redfield selected edition.

The same day Simms wrote to former South Carolina Governor James Henry Hammond, who also had become a close friend since their first meeting in the late 1830s. He reported that he had "agreed to buy from Harper & Brothers, the Copyrights which [he had] sold them 15 years [before], 6 works, for $1500" and that he had "agreed with another publishing house to try the experiment of a new Edition" that was to "begin with 'The Yemassee' which [he was then] revising" (*Letters* 3: 240). By August, Simms indicated that he was "busy with 3 different volumes in press." In addition to *The Yemassee*, these were *Vasconselos: A Romance of the New World* and *Poems: Descriptive, Dramatic, Legendary and Contemplative* (*Letters* 3: 248). Both the latter titles also almost certainly appeared in 1853.

Although the intention had been to have *The Yemassee* be the first in the Redfield edition, *Poems* probably was. The new *Yemassee* was reviewed on December 3 (*Letters* 3: 261).

With frontispiece and title page illustrations by F.O.C. Darley, who provided illustrations for many of the volumes in the uniform Redfield edition, the "new and revised" *Yemassee* was dedicated, like the original version, "To Professor Samuel Henry Dickson, M.D., of South Carolina." Darley was "regarded as the finest illustrator in the United States" (Greenspan, *George* 227). Like Simms, though eight years older, Dickson attended the College of Charleston. He did so before studying medicine at the University of Pennsylvania. In 1825 he became founding dean of the Medical College of the State of South Carolina in Charleston. He and Simms must have known each other by this time, if not earlier. His *Poems* appeared in 1844 and contains the sole poem still known to some, the one beginning, "I sigh for the land of the cypress and pine." Simms included it in his 1845 anthology of Charlestonians' writings, *The Charleston Book*. Dickson "also was a frequent contributor to the *Southern Literary Messenger* and the *Southern Quarterly Review*. His *Essays on Slavery* appeared in 1845"; among other things, he argued against prohibiting the teaching of slaves to read (Simms, *Charleston Book* 88–89 416n; see also *Letters* 1: ci).

The new dedicatory letter to Dickson indicates that Simms made revisions to *The Yemassee* in order to have the work "more acceptable to the reader." In the process, he realized that the romance's "defects and crudities" had "spoiled and botched . . . much excellent material," that he could to advantage "draw the pen" through "a thousand passages . . ., with the hope to substitute better thoughts, and improved situations, in a more appropriate and graceful style" (iii–iv). Although he made numerous, small deletions, additions, and changes, he did not do the wholesale rewriting that he thought the material justified (Guilds, *Yemassee* 448–62). Rather, he decided he would "economize all his enthusiasm for the new creations of his fancy." Therefore, he only cut "off the more obtrusive excrescences, . . . leaving minor ones to the indifference or the indulgence of the reader" (Simms, *Yemassee* [1853] iv).

The plates for the 1853 edition were used for most subsequent printings of *The Yemassee*, at least until the twentieth century. W. J. Widdleton, occasional partner and successor to the bankrupt Redfield, reprinted the work several times. Later, so did A.C. Armstrong & Son and Lovell, Coryell, also of New York, and Donohue, Henneberry & Co. and Belford, Clarke & Co. of Chicago. At times, more than one reprint issued almost simultaneously. For instance, in 1888, Lovell, Coryell, and Donohue and also Henneberry & Co. both published the work.

In 1898, Newson of New York offered an abridged version "for use of schools." Lyle Spencer edited the first new, full edition in 1911, followed by Alexander Cowie in 1937 and Hugh Holman in 1961. Joseph Ridgely edited the text "for the Modern Reader" in 1964. Guilds, with Caroline Collins, edited the University of Arkansas

Press edition in 1994, including fairly extensive textual apparatus in addition to introductory materials similar to what Cowie, Holman, and Ridgely offered. Dodo Press reprinted a two volume version in 2009, presumably from the 1835 edition. The next year Nabu Press issued a reprint of the edition prepared by Lyle Spencer in 1911. Bibliolife, which offers hand-curated titles from the British Library collections in apps for iPads, is distributing Nabu Press titles, including *The Yemassee*.

The Context

At the time Simms wrote the bulk of *The Yemassee*, he was shifting his focus from poetry, six volumes of which he had published before 1833, to fiction. At least in part, the decision was economic: poetry might earn *le succes d'estime*, but romances sold. This was because prose came before poetry in people's literary tastes, even if poetry preceded prose in the development of literature. For a writer to gain an audience, therefore, he needed to produce prose. His early success in prose encouraged Simms to think that he could make writing a career. *Martin Faber* (1833) and *Guy Rivers* (1834) did remarkably well, both critically and financially. *The Yemassee* did better—indeed, spectacularly by the standards of the day.

Emboldened, Simms gave Harper & Brothers another complete, two-volume romance within six months of the publication of *The Yemassee*. *The Partisan* also did well, despite criticism of its composition. Its importance was not just that it illustrated and carried forward, however awkwardly, Simms's enormous productivity and ambition, but that it began the third of his three series of romances: *Guy Rivers* started the Border series; *The Yemassee* the Colonial (and Ante-Colonial) series; and *The Partisan* the Revolutionary War series. *Martin Faber*, the other separately published tale, was not a full-length romance, but a Gothic novella, another genre to which Simms often recurred as well (Hagstette, "Screams"; Guilds, *Martin*).

The three series have overlapping themes. All deal with the backgrounds and challenges to the nation and the region aborning in the South. All explore the relationship of social hierarchy to socio-cultural progress and those forces that undermine or threaten that progress. All reflect on the demands of leadership and the places of subaltern peoples, so the importance of class, race, and gender in social formation. All ask what determines, defines, and fosters success in the development of a society, culture, and people. Yet the occasions or sites of the three series differ dramatically from one another. In the ante-colonial and colonial romances, America is not yet fully established, and Native Americans are key players. In the Revolutionary romances, the story is of the ideological, political, social, and psychological course and consequences of conflict with the British from the eve of the War of Independence to its immediate aftermath.

Simms was very aware of ethnic, class, and other divisions that determined to a considerable degree who was a Tory and who a Patriot during the War of Independence. Both America and the Americans were still in formation. In the Border

Romances, which take place fifty-plus years later, such divisions still shape the fluid social, cultural, and psychological boundaries between civilization and the wilderness. The protagonists leave behind their models and experience, both of home, the place of cultural production and reproduction, and of ordered society. Either they have internalized and, therefore, are carrying and nursing these legacies, or they are fleeing, denying, and attacking them. In short, though set at different stages in the South's evolution, the three series of romances treat many of the same processes of social conflict and formation. The reason, Simms maintained, is that "[t]he great moral triumph of recent times is the recognition of the race as well as the individual" so that "we now read *human* histories. We now ask after the affections as well as the ceremonies of society" ("Ellet's" 319–20).

By race, in this instance, Simms meant a people, such as Americans were becoming. Or were they? Were they not being split by politics, and did not this split reflect both disparate antecedents and growing social as well as political differences? His characterizations of the Puritan pastor and the cavalier Gov. Craven/Harrison in *The Yemassee* reflect not only literary but political stereotypes. This "racial" divide, like that of the color line, became an ever more contentious issue in the wake of growing attacks on southern slavery by northern abolitionists.

Two-and-a-half years after publication of *The Yemassee*, Simms elaborated his views. He believed in the stage theory of history, articulated variously by Giambattista Vico and the Scottish School in the eighteenth century: all peoples must rise, if rise they will, by predictable stages to civilization (S. Frye 88–89). He also believed blacks and Indians to be at lower stages of development than whites. These stadialist and racialist convictions underlay his judgment, in a review essay ostensibly on an American travel book by an English abolitionist. Simms's "Miss Martineau on Slavery" argues that "[h]e *is a slave only, who is forced into a position below the claims of his intellect*" (653). From that perspective the growing division over the issue between the white North and the white South suggested to Simms that the sections might share a country but were divided between two peoples.

The Yemassee was the first of Simms's long fictions to treat slavery significantly. Nationally, it got more attention than any other during Simms's life. *The Knickerbocker* judged "[n]o modern author understands better the power of contrast, both of scene and human passion, or represents, with more truth to nature, the female heart." The *New York Times* opined that "[h]is savages are different, . . . more true to reality . . . susceptible of the general feelings, passions, weaknesses . . . of human nature . . . ." It added that the romance's large first printing sold out in thirty hours. A notice of the so-called second edition of 1835, also in *The Knickerbocker*, disagreed with the tenor of the *Times*' piece. It both insisted that "[t]he writer, with but little aid from history, has peopled the early forests of the South with creatures of his mind" and concluded that "[a]nachronisms should be scrupulously avoided even in a romance" (qtd. in Butterworth and Kibler 28–29).

In *Graham's*, Edgar Allan Poe was much harsher but also atypical. Positive though he was about Simms as gothicist, he thought Simms "never should have written 'The Partisan,' nor 'The Yemassee,'" because "[h]is genius does not lie in the outward so much as in the inner world" (qtd. in Butterworth and Kibler 50). Of course, the same has been said of Poe. Indeed, writing in 1954, Jay B. Hubbell maintained that Simms deserves "recognition along with Hawthorne and Poe as a forerunner of Henry James and William Faulkner and Robert Penn Warren" as a "psychological novelist of crime and introspection." At the same time, Hubbell disagreed with Poe's assessment of his fellow southerner, suggesting "[p]erhaps the reading public was right in preferring Simms the romancer" (Hubbell 592). He was reacting to Vernon Parrington, who, despite admiration for Simms, famously insisted, in his *Main Currents in American Thought* of 1927–30, that the romancer "was essentially a failed realist" (qtd. in Wimsatt, *Major* 8).

Parrington reacted against, but also was influenced by, William Peterfield Trent, whose 1892 biography of Simms was the first substantive, scholarly study. Impatient with the lingering influence of the overturned order of the old South, Trent argued that Simms was unable to rise to his literary potential in the environment of antebellum Charleston and South Carolina. Giving color to that judgment was the fact that Simms himself sometimes said as much. Moreover, Trent, with his modernist sensibility, was scathing about both the romance tradition and what he judged to be Simms's failures in it. Parrington thought more highly of Simms but also lamented the influence of his literary and social environments.

Such critical perspectives have shaped much of the study and interpretation of Simms. Mary Ann Wimsatt succinctly summarized some of the key instances: "From Parrington the argument passes to Hampton M. Jarrell, whose 1932 Duke University dissertation is entitled 'William Gilmore Simms: Realistic Romancer'; to Edd Winfield Parks, who in *Ante-Bellum Southern Literary Critics* subtitles his chapter on Simms 'Realistic Romanticist'; to Van Wyck Brooks, who states 'it was his realism that kept the work of Simms alive'; and to Clement Eaton, who—in a virtual reprise of Parrington—says 'the popular taste of the period, both North and South, forced [Simms] to compose in the romantic style, but his natural bent was toward realism'" (Wimsatt, *Major* 8–9). Louis Rubin has argued in similar vein. His take was that Simms failed to develop the aesthetic, emotional, and intellectual perspective and posture necessary for effective modern fiction because he was a romancer and defender rather than an ironic, realistic critic of his society.

Rubin's standard of judgment was shaped in substantial part by three divergent sets of concerns. New Criticism was one frame (Roemer and Shaffer 103; Kreyling, *Inventing* 33–55). This southern-born critical perspective, developed by young Agrarians Robert Penn Warren and Cleanth Brooks, among others, drew on formalist principles to investigate how literary texts work and how successfully they do so through their structures, language, and unfolding. Literary modernism framed expectations of literary texts' tone and stance, privileging irony and psychological, as well as sociological distance, complexity, and realism over the romantic nationalist traditions that influenced Scott and Simms. Finally, as a former journalist, Rubin felt compelled to ask environmental questions of the literary texts he considered: how do those texts position themselves vis-à-vis their multiple contexts? Thus his sociological, as well as aesthetic, critique of Simms. Thus, too, his judgment that, by writing from within rather than at odds with his society, Simms was ultimately less successful than his northern contemporaries Melville and Hawthorne (Rubin, "Romance").

Hugh Holman, Rubin's long-time colleague at the University of North Carolina at Chapel Hill, evaluated Simms's literary position and output differently: Simms's "career is a record of a man of minor importance in terms of the intrinsic value today of his voluminous works," Holman observed in 1958, but "of major importance in terms of the degree to which he embodied the attitudes and formalized the assumptions of a region" ("Status" 181). With this reasoning, Holman thought it important to get *The Yemassee*, Simms's most popular work, back in circulation. His analysis also led Holman to adopt a more literary-intellectual historical stance than Rubin and other critics, asking who influenced Simms and how and what Simms sought to portray and accomplish in his writing and why. By this approach, Holman sidestepped the challenge of New Criticism to the sprawling and iterative writer who Simms was (Holman, *Roots*).

Later scholars agree about Simms's historical and cultural importance but in many instances insist that his literary value merits reappraisal. There are three principal lines of argument. Guilds, Simms's literary biographer, was a leading proponent of the contention that Simms is a flawed major writer rather than an occasionally interesting minor one and, therefore, deserves canonical inclusion as well as historical attention. His rationales were several: Simms thought and wrote epically about the relationship of civilization and the wilderness in America on a scale and in ways not equaled by any other "American novelists of the nineteenth century"; similarly, he was unrivalled in his serious attention to Native Americans; further, his flaws are minor and his accomplishments major (Guilds, *Literary Life* 333; Guilds and Hudson); and, finally, he was remarkably prescient in his articulation of an early version of Frederick Jackson Turner's "frontier thesis" (K. Collins "Earlier"). Other scholars—notably James Everett Kibler and Matthew C. Brennan—insist that Simms was more sophisticated and successful, as well as innovative, than all but a few nineteenth-century American poets. Many agree, too, that the romances *Woodcraft* and *The Cassique of Kiawah* and the short-story collection *The Wigwam and the Cabin* rank with the best antebellum American fiction.

Those still inclined to give pride of place to *The Yemassee* make a different case. Wimsatt insisted that Simms needs to be taken on his own terms, as a romancer, not a novelist. In making this argument, she drew on Georg Lukacs's influential 1937 work *The Historical Novel.* There he contended that the historical novel or romance emerged as a distinct genre, developed essentially by Scott, against the backdrop of the cataclysmic events between the the French Revolution and the end of the Napoleonic Wars. Rather than treat history as simply a stage for action, the authors of historical novels asked how history matters in the lives of the individuals—real and imagined—and communities whose stories they told. Created to that end, historical novels became vehicles for romantic nationalism to the emerging bourgeois class. Leading protagonists in the novels elaborated their societies' character and future, while other characters provided verisimilitude to the episodes portrayed.

To this analysis Wimsatt added the archetypal approach of Northrop Frye. She found that Simms naturally gravitated to deep, recurring patterns in literature. Furthermore, Frye helped explain, she believed, how Simms structured his romances using patterned elements (N. Frye, *Anatomy*; *Secular*). Because Simms fundamentally thought historically and archetypally, he did not make the shift from historical to sociological realism as others increasingly did, Lukacs contended, after the failed nationalist revolutions in Europe in 1848 and the rise of the proletariat during the industrial revolution (cf. Holman, *Roots* 79). Hence, to judge Simms by the standards of social realism and the novel, rather than those of the historical romance, is anachronistic and erroneous. Reading the historical romance is a very different experience and requires openness and attention to how the genre works (Wimsatt 33–56).

Adding to this genre criticism is the regionalist reading of Simms. Masahiro Nakamura, translator of *The Yemassee* into Japanese, most fully examines this regionalism. He argues that Simms's historical romances differ from Hawthorne's, despite their many and profound similarities, because Simms wrote out of his southern conservative concern both for his regional setting and for the social order threatened by the instabilities of the frontier, war, politics, and human nature. In his reading, *The Yemassee* is specifically and essentially a reflection of a region, history, and philosophy different from that which informed Hawthorne's work (149–63). Consequently, *The Yemassee* needs to be read as a southern work, not just a historical romance in the tradition of Scott.

Yet the invitation, to read Simms as a rhetor of his society's values, priorities, and culture, is also an invitation to critique him and his writings on those same grounds. In the readings of many of those who accept that invitation, Simms in general and *The Yemassee* in particular conform to historically all-too-typical and morally unacceptable attitudes and assumptions about gender, race, and class. Vincent King makes the point succinctly: "*The Yemassee* suggests that if America is to avoid the horrible bloodletting that characterized the displacement of the American Indian . . . blacks must accept their role as slaves to whites, for it is slavery that secures both their own and the larger community's welfare" (140). African Americans and Native Americans must submit to Hobbesian authority, but whites can assume that the world is ordered for the best—that is for them.

Because "Indian removal was so important to the emerging expression of Southern political power and intellectual culture, as well as to the perpetuation of the Southern economic system," Laura Mielke argued "Simms revises the sentimental impulse of antebellum literature, embracing at the outset not the equalizing impulse of common emotion but the inequality created in the act of sympathy" (51, 53). She quotes Thomas M. Allen, who "emphasizes that Simms's works use sympathy to unite, often in unsettling or even obscure ways, section and nation, diversity and union": "Simms clearly believed that whites could extend sympathetic identification across racial lines," Allen asserts, and then Simms "applied this hierarchical but multiethnic view of North American history, as it played out in the portions of the continent that would become the South, to the problem of fabricating national identity for the US of America in the present and the future." Allen concludes: "It is not necessary to apologize for Simms's own racism in order to acknowledge that his critique of a different form of racialist nationalism [in the North] was quite accurate" (Mielke 53; Allen 504, 506–07).

The positive tone of this assessment is not the norm of such analyses. In exploring "[t]he rhetoric and representation of slavery in *The Yemassee*," Anthony Dyer Hoefer frames the romance "as an attempt to resolve . . . the contradictions that US Indian policy and the legal recognition of chattel slavery pose to a nationalism that celebrates liberty and equality" (118, 128).[31] Bassey Akpan, a Nigerian college student, finds Simms emphasizing in this romance how "the Negro always misuses his freedom. He never grows up but is forever the spineless 'Uncle Tom' . . . who is ever devoted to a romantically benevolent master of the 'superior' race as exists only in Simms' make-believe world" (qtd. in Shelton 77). Bette Weidman observes that, in *The Yemassee*, "even his poor white laborers must learn their places" and that for Simms the proper place for blacks "is servile" and for Indians "dead" (21–22).

To say that the condemnations are anachronistic or ahistorical, as many of the advocates of Simms's literary value have done, has its own considerable risks. It is to insist on historicist rather than moralist criteria of reading. That, however, moves the study of Simms's works from a formalist New Critical to a contextual and genre-based critical engagement. Simms becomes an author stuck in a time, place, and literary movement rather than a transcendent writer speaking to the ages and the human condition.

Most advocates of Simms's literary value insist that Simms is at once historical and universal, not either/or. Although they have not explained and theorized how to warrant simultaneously both localist and universalist readings of Simms, they have an implicit answer: personal, learned experience trumps narrow literary conventions, even that of the romance. Simms meditated on not just historical conditions, but moral truths on the basis of his experience. Morality, unbound from circumstance, becomes totalitarian and dangerous. Simms's attitudes to subaltern populations reflect more than stadialism: they also show empathy and a tragic sense in *The Yemassee* and elsewhere (cf. S. Frye, 85). Consequently, his writing reflects humanity as well as ideology, art as well as history, social responsibility as well as hierarchy, and moral sense as well as manifest destiny.

The issue with this hermeneutic, for many literary scholars and also historians, is that it blends literature's universalist claims with historical relativism: Simms wrote for the ages but as a person of his age and place. He used a genre, as in *The Yemassee*, that had strong cultural salience for only two generations between the Napoleonic War and the revolutions of 1848, a genre that since has become less and less readable to those who refuse to measure Simms's success against the standards and expectations of the genre. This critical history and challenge bring the reader of Simms to several questions: how should I read one of antebellum America's most successful long fictions? With what consequences? To what extent do Simms and *The Yemassee* warrant empathetic and tragic readings? In other words, what are the moral demands of reading Simms in general and *The Yemassee* in particular?

NOTES

1. Holman called the corrected printing a new edition, echoing the language of the title page, but comparison of the texts makes clear that the same plates were used. In preparation of this critical introduction, I did not collate the two versions to see what the changes were. Instead, I have relied on Simms's explanation in the "Advertisement to the Second Edition": there he said that the author could "effect [no] more than a very few of the many corrections which he had meditated in the work."
2. James Everett Kibler writes on this relationship in his and David Moltke-Hansen's *William Gilmore Simms's Selected Reviews on Literature and Civilization*.
3. At the beginning of this essay, Hoefer mistakenly has Simms delivering the oration that he is reviewing—*Americanism in Literature: An Oration before the Phi Kappa and Demosthenian Socieities of the University of Georgia, at Athens, August 8, 1844*. By Alexander B. Meek, of Alabama. Charleston: Burges & James, 1844.

Bibliography

Ackerman, Zeno. *Messing with Romance: American Poetics and Antebellum Southern Fiction*. Frankfurt: Peter Lang, 2012.

Acree, Jill. "The Sorrows of Parson Weems: His Life and Legacy." Diss. Claremont Graduate U, 2007.

Adair, James. *The History of the American Indians*. 1775. Ed. Kathryn E. Holland Braund. Tuscaloosa: U of Alabama P, 2005.

Aiken, David. Introduction. *The Cassique of Kiawah*. By William Gilmore Simms. Gainesville: Magnolia P, 1989. v–xxix.

———. Introduction. *A City Laid Waste: The Capture, Sack, and Destruction of the City of Columbia*. By William Gilmore Simms. Columbia: U of South Carolina P, 2005. 1–46.

———. "The Mock Trial in *The Golden Christmas* and the Theme of Reconciliation." *The Simms Review* 2.1 (1994): 17–20.

———. "Simms's War Poetry: A Battle Cry of Freedom." *The Simms Review* 2.2 (1994): 11–17.

Aiken, Scott D. *Francis Marion: Lessons in Leadership from the Partisan Campaigns of Francis Marion*. Annapolis, MD: Naval Institute P, 2012.

Alfaro, Ricardo J. Preface. *Life and Letters of Vasco Nunez de Balboa*. By Charles L.G. Anderson. Westport, CT: Greenwood P, 1970. 3–13.

Allen, Thomas M. "South of the American Renaissance." *American Literary History* 16.3 (2004): 496–508.

"The American Library." *Blackwood's Edinburgh Review* 62.385 (1847): 574–92.

Anderson, Charles L.G. *Life and Letters of Vasco Nunez de Balboa*. Westport, CT: Greenwood P, 1970.

Anderson, Mary Crow. "The Huguenot in the South Carolina Novel." Diss. U of South Carolina, 1966.

"Astronomical Prizes." *Washington D.C. Daily National Intelligencer* (17 Jan. 1851): 3.

Bakker, Jan. "Simms and the American Apocalypse: *Woodcraft* and *The Cassique of Kiawah*." *Studies in the Novel* 35 (Summer 2003): 149–56.

———. "Simms on the Literary Frontier; or, So Long Miss Ravenel and Hello Captain Porgy: *Woodcraft* is the first 'Realistic' Novel in America." *William Gilmore Simms and the American Frontier*. Ed. John C. Guilds and Caroline Collins. Athens: U of Georgia P, 1997. 64–78.

Barrett, Faith. *To Fight Aloud Is Very Brave: American Poetry and the Civil War*. Amherst: U of Massachusetts P, 2012.

Barrett, John G. *Sherman's March Through the Carolinas*. Chapel Hill: U of North Carolina P, 1956.

Barton, John Cyril. "William Gilmore Simms and the Literary Aesthetics of Crime and Capital Punishment." *Law & Literature* 22.2 (Summer 2010): 220–43.

Bass, Robert D. "*The Autobiography of William J. Grayson*, edited with an Introduction by Robert Duncan." Diss. U of South Carolina, 1933.

———. *Swamp Fox: The Life and Campaigns of General Francis Marion*. London, UK: Alvin Redman, 1959.

Beatty, Richmond Croom. Introduction. *Woodcraft*. By William Gilmore Simms. New York: Norton, 1961. vii–xvi.

Beauchamp, Jereboam O. *The Confession of Jereboam O. Beauchamp. Who was Executed at Frankfort, Ky., on the 7th of July, 1826, for the Murder of Col. Solomon P. Sharp, a Member of the Legislature, and Late Attorney General of Ky*. Bloomfield, KY: Printed for the Publisher, 1826.

Belser, William Gordon. "William Gilmore Simms: Fictionist as Military Historian of the Revolution." Diss. St. John's U, 1977.

Bennett, Charles E. *Settlement of Florida*. Gainesville: U of Florida P, 1968.

Bercovitch, Sacvan, ed. *The Cambridge History of Nineteenth-Century American Poetry, 1800–1910*. Cambridge: Cambridge UP, 1999.

Bernath, Michael T. *Confederate Minds: The Struggle for Intellectual Independence in the Civil War South*. Chapel Hill: U of North Carolina P, 2010.

Blanco, Walter, ed. and trans. *Thucydides: The Peloponnesian War*. New York: W. W. Norton, 1998.

Blease, Coleman L. *Destruction of Property in Columbia, S.C. by Sherman's Army*. 71st Congress, 2nd Session, Senate. Doc. 149. U.S. Government Printing Office, 1930.

Bleiler, E.F. Introduction. *The Castle of Otranto*. By Horace Walpole. Mineola, NY: Dover Publications, 2004. i–xviii.

Bleser, Carol, ed. *The Hammonds of Redcliffe*. New York: Oxford UP, 1981; Columbia: U of South Carolina P, 1997.

———, ed. *Secret and Sacred: The Diaries of James Henry Hammond, a Southern Slaveholder*. New York: Oxford UP, 1988; Columbia: U of South Carolina P, 1997.

Blight, David W. *Race and Reunion: The Civil War in American Memory*. Cambridge: Belknap P of Harvard UP, 2001.

Blythe, Anne M. "William Gilmore Simms's *The Cassique of Kiawah* and the Principles of His Art." *"Long Years of Neglect": The Work and Reputation of William Gilmore Simms*. Ed. John Caldwell Guilds. Fayetteville: U of Arkansas P, 1988. 37–59.

"Books, Magazines, &c. 'War Poetry of the South.'" *Southern Cultivator* 24.11 (Nov. 1866): 273–75.

Boruchoff, David A. "Piety, Patriotism, and Empire: Lessons for England, Spain, and the New World in the Works of Richard Hakluyt." *Renaissance Quarterly* 62.3 (2009): 809–58.

Boucher, Chauncey Samuel. *The Nullification Controversy in South Carolina*. Chicago: U of Chicago P, 1916.

Boyd, Molly. "'The Fall of the House of Usher,' Simms's 'Castle Dismal, ' and *The Scarlet Letter*: Literary Interconnections," *Studies in the Novel* 35.2 (Summer 2003): 231–42.

Braund, Kathryn E. Holland. "A Note on This Edition." *The History of the American Indians*. By James Adair. Tuscaloosa: U of Alabama P, 2005. xi–xiv.

Brennan, Matthew C. *The Poet's Holy Craft: William Gilmore Simms and Romantic Verse Tradition*. Columbia: U of South Carolina P, 2010.

———. "Simms, the Civil War, and the Poetry of Trauma." *William Gilmore Simms's Unfinished Civil War: Consequences for a Southern Man of Letters*. Ed. David Moltke-Hansen. Columbia: U of South Carolina P, 2013. 129–48.

———. "Simms, Hawthorne, and 'The Inutile Pursuit' of 'The Artist of the Beautiful.'" *The Simms Review* 14.2 (2006): 14–21.

Brooke, C.F. Tucker. *The Shakespeare Apocrypha*. Oxford: Clarendon P, 1918.

Brooks, Cleanth. *William Faulkner: Toward Yoknapatawpha and Beyond*. New Haven: Yale UP, 1978.

Brown, Jerome King. "William Gilmore Simms and the American Historical Romance." Diss. U of Kansas, 1978.

Browning, William Shergold. *History of the Huguenots*. London: Whittaker and Co., 1840.

Bruce, Dickson D., Jr. *The Kentucky Tragedy: A Story of Conflict and Change in Antebellum America*. Baton Rouge: Louisiana State UP, 2006.

Bryant, William Cullen. "Simms." *Homes of American Authors; Comprising Anecdotal, Personal and Descriptive Sketches, by Various Authors*. New York: Putnam, 1853. 257–62.

———. Untitled review. *New York Evening Post*. 19 Apr. 1848.

Bush, Lewis M. "Werther on the Alabama Frontier: A Reinterpretation of Simms's *Confession*." *Mississippi Quarterly* 21.2 (Spring 1968): 119–30.

Busick, Sean R. Introduction. *The Cassique of Kiawah*. By William Gilmore Simms. Charleston: History P, 2005. 7–14.

———. Introduction. *The Life of Marion*. By William Gilmore Simms. Charleston, SC: History P, 2007. i–xvi

———. "Simms and Hawthorne on History and Historical Development." *The Simms Review* 19.1–2 (2011): 83–89.

———. "Simms's *War Poetry of the South*: Notes Toward a Reconsideration." *The Simms Review* 17.1–2 (2009): 49–53.

———. *A Sober Desire for History: William Gilmore Simms as Historian*. Columbia: U of South Carolina P, 2005.

Butterworth, Keen and James E. Kibler. *William Gilmore Simms: A Reference Guide*. Boston: G.K. Hall & Co., 1980.

Byron, Lord [George Gordon]. *Childe Harold's Pilgrimage*. *Project Gutenberg*. Web. 15 Oct. 2014.

———. *The Complete Poetical Works*. 5 vols. Ed. Jerome McGann. Oxford: Clarenden P, 1980.

Campbell, Thomas. "Notices of New Works." *London Metropolitan Magazine* (Jan. 1834): 12b.

Cantrell, James P. *How Celtic Culture Invented Southern Literature*. Gretna, LA: Pelican, 2006.

Carroll, Benjamin Rivers, ed. *Historical Collections of South Carolina; Embracing Many Rare and Valuable Pamphlets, and Other Documents*. 2 vols. New York: Harper & Brothers, 1836.

Caseneuve, Pierre de, *et al*. *Dictionnaire Etymologique de la Langue Françoise*. Paris: Chez Briasson, 1750.

Cecil, L. Moffitt. "Simms's Porgy as National Hero." *American Literature* 364 (Jan. 1965): 475–84.

Charlevoix, Pierre François Xavier de. *History and General Description of New France*. Trans. John Gilmary Shea. 1870. 6 vols. Chicago: Loyola UP, [1962].

Child, Francis James, ed. *The English and Scottish Popular Ballads*. 5 vols. 1882–98. New York: Cooper Square Publishers, 1965.

Chudacoff, Howard P. *The Age of the Bachelor: Creating an American Subulture*. Princeton: Princeton UP, 2000.

City Gazette and Commercial Daily Advertiser (19 November 1831).

Cohen, Hennig. "Shakespeare in Charleston on the Eve of the Revolution." *Shakespeare Quarterly* 4.3 (July 1953): 327–30.

Coleridge, Samuel Taylor. *Samuel Taylor Coleridge: The Major Works*. Oxford: Oxford UP, 2009.

Collins, Caroline. "Simms's Concept of Romance and His Realistic Frontier." *William Gilmore Simms and the American Frontier*. Ed. John Caldwell Guilds and Caroline Collins. Athens: U of Georgia P, 1997. 79–94.

———. "Toward a Feminist Reading of Simms." *The Simms Review* 3.1 (1995): 5–13.

Collins, Kevin. Afterword. *The Cassique of Kiawah*. By William Gilmore Simms. Fayetteville: U of Arkansas P, 2003. 531–48.

———. Critical Introduction. *Vasconselos*. By Frank Cooper [William Gilmore Simms]. Columbia: U of South Carolina P, 2012. xxiii–xxxvii.

———. "An Earlier Frontier Thesis: Simms as an Intellectual Precursor to Frederick Jackson Turner." *Studies in the Literary Imagination* 42.1 (2009): 33–58.

———. "Experiments in Realism: Doubling in Simms's *The Cassique of Kiawah*." *Southern Literary Journal* 32 (Spring 2002): 1–13.

———. "Guy Rivers's Self-esteem Deficit and the Psychological Prescience of William Gilmore Simms." *The Simms Review* 7. 2 (1999): 5–10.

Cook, George Allan. "The Beginnings of Porgy." *The South Central Bulletin* 27.4 (Winter 1967): 51–57.

Cowie, Alexander. *The Rise of the American Novel*. New York: American Book Company, 1951.

Current-Garcia, Eugene. "Southern Literary Criticism and the Sectional Dilemma." *Journal of Southern History* 15.3 (1949): 325–41.

Dale, Corinne. "William Gilmore Simms's Porgy as Domestic Hero." *Southern Literary Journal* 13 (Winter 1980): 55–71.

Davidson, Donald. Introduction. *The Letters of William Gilmore Simms*. Ed. Mary C. Simms Oliphant *et al*. 6 vols. Columbia: U of South Carolina P, 1952–2012. xxxi–lviii.

Davidson, James Wood. "William Gilmore Simms, LL.D." *The Living Writers of the South*. James Wood Davidson. Carleton, Publisher, 1869. Reprinted in *Nineteenth-Century Literature Criticism*. Ed. Laurie Lanzen Harris. Vol. 3. Detroit: Gale Research, 1983. *Literature Resource Center*. Web. 13 Jan. 2014.

Davies, Nell Weaver. "New Facts About an Old Story." *Carologue* 15.4 (1999): 16–21.

Davis, David Brion. *Homicide in American Fiction, 1798–1860: A Study in Social Values*. Ithaca, NY: Cornell UP, 1957.

Davis, Richard Beale. *Intellectual Life in Jefferson's Virginia, 1790–1830*. Knoxville: U of Tennessee P, 1972.

Day, Matthew. "Hakluyt, Harvey, Nashe: The Material Text and Early Modern Nationalism." *Studies in Philology* 104.3 (2007): 281–305.

De Leon, T[homas].C[ooper]., ed. *South Songs: From the Lays of Later Days*. New York: Bledock, 1866.

Dean, Paula. "Revisions in the Revolutionary War Novels of William Gilmore Simms." Diss. Auburn U, 1971.

Deen, Floyd H. "A Comparison of Simms's *Richard Hurdis* with its Sources." *Modern Language Notes* 60.6 (1945): 406–08.

———. "The Genesis of *Martin Faber* in *Caleb Williams*." *Modern Language Notes* 59.5 (May 1944): 315–17.

Dentith, Simon. *Bakhtinian Thought: An Introductory Reader*. Critical Studies in Theory and in Practice. New York: Routledge, 1994.

Desment, Christy. "*Confession; or, the Blind Heart*: An Antebellum *Othello*." *Borrowers and Lenders* 1.1 (Spring 2005): 1–24.

Drayton, John. *Memoirs of the American Revolution*. Charleston, 1821.

Dunn, Esther Cloudman. *Shakespeare in America*. New York: Macmillan Co., 1939.

Duyckinck, Evert Augustus. Rev. of *The Cassique of Accabee* and *Father Abbott*. By William Gilmore Simms. *Literary World* 6 (26 Jan. 1850): 80–81.

———. Rev. of *Castle Dismal*. By William Gilmore Simms. *New York Morning News* 1.9 (9 Nov. 1844): 1.

Dye, Renee. "Narrating Social Theory: William Gilmore Simms's *Woodcraft*" *The Simms Review* 4.1 (1996): 23–43.

Eaves, T. C. Duncan. "An Early American Admirer of Keats." *PMLA* 67 (1952): 895–98.

"Editor's Department." *DeBow's Review* 8 (Mar. 1850): 312.

"Editor's Table." *Knickerbocker* 20 (Aug. 1842): 199–200.

"Editor's Table." *Southern Literary Messenger* 37.7 (1 July 1863): 447–48.

"Editorial Bureau." *Magnolia; or, Southern Monthly* 4.5 (May 1842): 312–20.

"Editorial." Rev. of *The Lily and the Totem*. By W. Gilmore Simms. *Sartain's Union Magazine of Literature and Art* 7 (Nov. 1850): 318.

"Editorial." *Sartain's Union Magazine of Literature and Art* 10.5 (May 1852): 432–40.

Evans, R.H., ed. *Hakluyt's Collection of the Early Voyages, Travels, and Discoveries, of the English Nation*. London: R.H. Evans, 1809–1812.

Eyal, Yonatan. *The Young America Movement and the Transformation of the Democratic Party, 1828–1861*. Cambridge: Cambridge UP, 2007.

Fahs, Alice. *The Imagined Civil War: Popular Literature of the North and South, 1861–1865*. Chapel Hill: U of North Carolina P, 2001.

Faust, Drew Gilpin, ed. *The Ideology of Slavery: Proslavery Thought in the Antebellum South, 1830–1860*. Baton Rouge: Louisiana State UP, 1981.

———. *James Henry Hammond and the Old South: A Design for Mastery*. Baton Rouge: Louisiana State UP, 1982.

———. *This Republic of Suffering: Death and the American Civil War*. New York: Alfred A. Knopf, 2008.

———. *A Sacred Circle: The Dilemma of the Intellectual in the Old South, 1840–1860*. Baltimore: Johns Hopkins UP, 1977.

Fellman, Michael. *Citizen Sherman: A Life of William Tecumseh Sherman*. New York: Random House, 1995.

Felton, Cornelius C. "Simms's Stories and Reviews." *North American Review* 63.137 (1846): 357–82.

Ferguson, Stuart. "A Yuletide Celebration in the Old South." *The Wall Street Journal* 246.138 (24 Dec. 2005): 13.

Fiedler, Leslie A. *Love and Death in the American Novel*. 1960. Champaign, IL: Dalkey Archive P, 1997.

Foley, Ehren. "Isaac Nimmons and the Burning of Woodlands: Power, Paternalism, and the Performance of Manhood in William Gilmore Simms's Civil War South." *William Gilmore Simms's Unfinished Civil War: Consequences for a Southern Man of Letters*. Ed. David Moltke-Hansen. Columbia: U of South Carolina P, 2013. 89–111.

———. "William Gilmore Simms and the Unconquered Frontier of Race." *The Simms Review* 20.1–2 (2012): 79–90.

Force, Peter. Papers of Peter Force, Series VII E, Peter Horry Collection, Letter Peter Horry to Mason Lock Weems, February 4 [ca. 1811]. Library of Congress, Washington, DC.

Foster, Gaines M. *Ghosts of the Confederacy: Defeat, the Lost Cause, and the Emergence of the New South, 1865–1913*. New York: Oxford UP, 1987.

Fox-Genovese, Elizabeth and Eugene D. Genovese. "The Divine Sanction of Social Order: Religious Foundations of the Southern Slaveholders' World View. *Journal of the American Academy of Religion* 55.2 (Summer 1987): 211–33.

———. *Fatal Self-Deception: Slaveholding Paternalism in the Old South*. Cambridge and New York: Cambridge UP, 2011.

———. *The Mind of the Master Class: History and Faith in the Southern Slaveholders' Worldview*. Cambridge: Cambridge UP, 2005.

Frazier, Charles. *Cold Mountain*. New York: Grove, 1997.

Freehling, William W. *Prelude to Civil War: The Nullification Controversy in South Carolina, 1816–1836*. New York: Oxford UP, 1965.

"Friendly Notice—Correction." *The Daily Phoenix* (12 Oct. 1865): 2.

Frye, Northrop. *The Anatomy of Criticism*. Princeton: Princeton UP, 1957.

———. *The Secular Scripture A Study of the Structure of Romance*. Cambridge: Harvard UP, 1976.

Frye, Steven. "Simms's *The Yemassee*, American Progressivism and the Dialogue of History." *Southern Quarterly* 35.3 (1997): 83–89.

Gallagher, Gary W. and Alan T. Nolan, eds. *The Myth of the Lost Cause and Civil War History*. Bloomington: Indiana UP, 2000.

Gallay, Alan. *The Indian Trade: The Rise of the English Empire in the American South, 1670–1717*. New Haven: Yale UP, 2002.

Galloway, Patricia. "Commemorative History and Hernando de Soto." *The Hernando de Soto Expedition: History, Historiography, and "Discovery" in the Southeast*. Ed. Patricia Galloway. Lincoln: U of Nebraska P, 1997. 410–35.

Gandhi, Leela. *Postcolonial Theory: A Critical Introduction*. New York: Columbia UP, 1998.

Garden, Alexander. *Anecdotes of the Revolutionary War in America*. Charleston, SC: A.E. Miller, 1822. Reprinted Spartanburg, SC: The Reprint Company, 1972.

Gates, W.B. "William Gilmore Simms and the Kentucky Tragedy." *American Literature* 32.2 (May 1960): 158–66.

Genovese, Eugene D. *The Slaveholders' Dilemma: Freedom and Progress in Southern Conservative Thought, 1820–1860*. Columbia: U of South Carolina P, 1992.

Georgini, Sara. "The Angel and the Animal." *William Gilmore Simms's Unfinished Civil War: Consequences for a Southern Man of Letters*. Ed. David Moltke-Hansen. Columbia: U of South Carolina P, 2013. 212–23.

Gibbes, Robert W. *Documentary History of the American Revolution*. Vol. 1. Columbia, SC: Banner Steam-Power P, 1853.

Gildersleeve, Basil. "A Southerner in the Peloponnesian War." *Atlantic Monthly* (Sep. 1897): 330–43.

Goddu, Teresa A. *Gothic America: Narrative, History, and Nation*. New York: Columbia UP, 1997.

Godey, Louis. Rev. of *Simms's Poems Areytos or Songs and Ballads of the South with Other Poems.* By William Gilmore Simms. *Godey's* LXII (Mar. 1861): 275.

Goldhurst, William. "The New Revenge Tragedy: Comparative Treatments of the Beauchamp Case." *Southern Literary Journal* 22.1 (Fall 1989): 117–27.

Gordon, William. *The History of the Rise, Progress, and Establishment of the Independence of the United States, Volume III*. 1788. Reprinted Freeport, NY: Books for Libraries P, 1969.

Grammer, John M. *Pastoral and Politics in the Old South*. Baton Rouge: Louisiana State UP, 1996.

Grantham, Nancy. "Simms's Frontier: A Collision of Cultures." *William Gilmore Simms and the American Frontier*. Ed. John Caldwell Guilds and Caroline Collins. Athens: U of Georgia P, 1997. 105–17.

Grayson, William J. "Marion." [poem] unsigned. *Russell's Magazine* III IV (1858): 212–18, IV IV (1859): 312–21, V IV (1859): 406–15, VI IV (1859): 505–9.

Greenspan, Ezra. "Evert Duyckinck and the History of Wiley and Putnam's Library of American Books, 1845–1847." *American Literature* 64.4 (1992): 677–93.

———. *George Palmer Putnam: Representative American Publisher*. University Park: Pennsylvania State UP, 2000.

Griffith, Samuel B. *Mao-Tse-Tung on Guerilla Warfare*. Garden City, NY: Double Day, 1978.

Growoll, Adolf. *American Book Clubs: Their Beginnings and History, and a Bibliography of their Publications*. New York: Dodd, Mead and Company, 1897.

Guilds, John Caldwell. "Afterword: Commentary on Each Story." *The Wigwam and the Cabin*. By William Gilmore Simms. Ed. John C. Guilds. Fayetteville: U of Arkansas P, 2000. 381–97.

———. Afterword. *Guy Rivers: A Tale of Georgia*. By William Gilmore Simms. Fayetteville: U of Arkansas P, 1993. 449–73.

———. Introduction and Afterword. *Helen Halsey; or, The Swamp State of Conelachita: A Tale of the Borders*. By William Gilmore Simms. Fayetteville: U of Arkansas P, 1998. xv–xxi, 127–40.

———. Introduction. *The Wigwam and the Cabin*. By William Gilmore Simms. Ed. John C. Guilds. Fayetteville: U of Arkansas P, 2000. xvii–xxviii.

———. Introduction and Apparatus. *The Writings of William Gilmore Simms: Stories and Tales*. Ed. John Caldwell Guilds. Centennial Edition. Columbia: U of South Carolina P, 1974. xi–xxiv, 553–876.

———. "A Literary View." *An Early and Strong Sympathy: The Indian Writings of William Gilmore Simms*. Ed. John C. Guilds and Charles Hudson. Columbia: U of South Carolina P, 2003. xiii–xxxiii.

———. "'Long Years of Neglect': Atonement at Last?" *"Long Years of Neglect": The Work and Reputation of William Gilmore Simms*. Ed. John Caldwell Guilds. Fayetteville: U of Arkansas P, 1988. 3–19.

———, ed. *"Long Years of Neglect": The Work and Reputation of William Gilmore Simms*. Fayetteville: U of Arkansas P, 1988.

———, ed. *Martin Faber: The Story of a Criminal; with "Confessions of a Murderer."* Fayetteville: U of Arkansas P, 2005.

———. *Simms: A Literary Life*. Fayetteville: U of Arkansas P, 1992.

———, ed. *The Simms Reader: Selections from the Writings of William Gilmore Simms*. Charlottesville: U of Virginia P, 2001.

———. "Simms's Use of History: Theory and Practice." *Mississippi Quarterly* 30.4 (1977): 505–11.

———. "William Gilmore Simms and the *Cosmopolitan*," *Georgia Historical Quarterly* 41 (1957): 31–41.

———, ed. *The Yemassee: A Romance of Carolina*. By William Gilmore Simms. 1853. Fayetteville: U of Arkansas P., 1994.

——— and Caroline Collins, eds. *William Gilmore Simms and the American Frontier*. Athens: U of Georgia P, 1997.

——— and Charles Hudson, eds. *An Early and Strong Sympathy: The Indian Writings of William Gilmore Simms*. Columbia: U of South Carolina P, 2003.

Hagstette, Todd. "Private vs. Public Honor in Wartime South Carolina: William Gilmore Simms in Lecture, Letter, and History." *William Gilmore Simms's Unfinished Civil War: Consequences for a Southern Man of Letters*. Ed. David Moltke-Hansen. Columbia: U of South Carolina P, 2013. 48–67.

———. "Screams from the South: The Southern Psycho-gothic Novels of William Gilmore Simms." MA thesis. College of Charleston, 1998.

Hakluyt, Richard, trans. *A Notable Historie Containing Foure Voyages Made by Certayne French Captaynes unto Florida. Written All, Sauing the Last, by Monsieur Laudonnierre*. Evans, *Hakluyt's Collection of the Early Voyages, Travels, and Discoveries, of the English Nation*. 3: 364–419.

———. *Diverse Voyages Touching the Discovery of America* . . . London: Thomas Woodcocke, 1582.

———. *The Principal Navigations, Voyages, Traffiques and Discoueries of the English Nation* London: George Bishop, Ralph Newberie, and Robert Barker, 1599[–1600].

Hale, Sarah J. "Editor's Book Table." *Godey's Lady's Book, and Ladies' American Magazine* 24 (May 1842): 288.

Hammond, James Henry. "Anniversary Oration, of the State Agricultural Society of South Carolina. . . . 25th November, 1841," in *Proceedings of the Agricultural Convention of the State of South Carolina from 1839 to 1845 Inclusive*. Columbia: Summer and Carroll, 1846. 175–92.

———. *Are Working Men Slaves?: The Question Discussed by Senators Hammond, [David C.] Broderick and [Henry] Wilson*. Washington: Buell & Blanchard, 1860.

———. *Cartas del Gobernador Hammond [sobre la esclavitud del Sur, dirigidas a Thomas Clarkson]*. New Orleans, 1845.

———. *Cyclopedia of American Literature: Embracing Personal and Critical Notices of Authors, and Selections from their Writings*. 2 vols. Philadelphia: Wm. Butler & Co., 1875, 2:263–65.

———. *Gov. Hammond's Letters on Southern Slavery: Addressed to Thomas Clarkson, the English Abolitionist*. Charleston: Walker & Burke, 1845.

———. *Letter of His Excellency Governor Hammond to the Free Church of Glasgow, on the Subject of Slavery*. Columbia: A.H. Pemberton, 1844.

———. *Marl. A Letter Addressed to the Agricultural Society of Jefferson County, Georgia*. Augusta: Printed by J. McCafferty, 1846.

———. *The North and the South: A Review of the Lecture on the Same Subject, delivered by Mr. Elwood Fisher, before the Young Men's Mercantile Association, of Cincinnati, Ohio*. Charleston: Printed by James S. Burges, 1849. Reprinted from the *Southern Quarterly Review* July 1849.

———. *An Oration, Delivered at Capt. Lorick's, in Lexington District, S.C. on the Fifth of July, 1830*. Columbia: Printed at the Times & Gazette Office, 1830.

———. *An Oration on the Life, Character and Services of John Caldwell Calhoun: Delivered on the 21st Nov., 1850, in Charleston, S.C. at the Request of the City Council*. Charleston: Walker & James, 1850 and a variant text in *The Carolina Tribute to Calhoun*. Ed. J.P. Thomas. Columbia, SC: Richard L. Bryan, 1857. 283–325.

———. "Overseers." *Carolina Planter* 1.2 (August 1844): 25–30.

———. *The Pro-Slavery Argument: As maintained by the Most Distinguished Writers of the Southern States Containing the Several Essays, on the Subject, of Chancellor Harper, Governor Hammond, Dr. Sim[m]s, and Professor Dew*. Philadelphia: Lippincott, Grambo, & Co., 1853.

———. *The Railroad Mania and a Review of the Bank of the State of South-Carolina: A Series of Essays by Anti-Debt*. Charleston, SC: Burges, James & Paxton, 1848, originally published in the *Charleston Mercury*.

———. *The Regina Coeli: Correspondence between the Hon. James H. Hammond and John H.B. Latrobe* (Baltimore: Printed by J.D. Toy, 1858), 39–47 on the African slave trade originally published in the *Baltimore American*, 20 December 1858.

———. *Remarks of Mr. Hammond, of South Carolina, on the Question of Receiving Petitions for the Abolition of Slavery in the District of Columbia*. Washington, DC: D. Green, [1836].

———. *Selections from the Letters and Speeches of James Henry Hammond*. Ed. Clyde N. Wilson. Columbia, SC: Southern Studies Program, 1978. Reprinted New York: John F. Trow and Co., 1866.

———. *Speech of Hon. James H. Hammond, delivered at Barnwell C[ourt] H[ouse], October 29th, 1858*. Charleston: Walker & Evans, 1858 and Washington [DC]: Henry Polkinghorn, 1858.

———. *Speech of Hon. James H. Hammond, of South Carolina, on the Admission of Kansas, under the Lecompton Constitution. Delivered in the Senate, of the United States, March 4, 1858*. Washington: Lemuel Towers, 1858.

———. *To the People of the South: Senator Hammond and the Tribune*. Charleston: Evans & Cogswell, 1860 by "George Michael Troup."

———. *Two Letters on Slavery in the United States: Addressed to Thomas Clarkson, Esq. by J.H. Hammond*. Columbia: Allen, McCarter, 1845.

Hawthorne, Margaret Rush. "Pierre François Xavier de Charlevoix, S.J.: History and the French Atlantic World in the Short Eighteenth Century, 1682–1761." Diss. U of Kansas, 2007.

Hawthorne, Nathaniel. Rev. of *Views and Reviews in American Literature, History and Fiction*. 1st ser. By William Gilmore Simms. *Salem Advertiser* (2 May 1846).

Hayhoe, George F. Explanatory Notes. *Revolutionary War Novels: Woodcraft*. By William Gilmore Simms. Spartanburg, SC: Reprint Co., 1976.

Hayne, Paul Hamilton. "Ante-Bellum Charleston." *Southern Bivouac* 1 (Oct. 1885): 257–68.

———. "Charlemont; or, The Pride of the Village." *Russell's Magazine* 1.3 (June 1857): 251–55.

———. "The Dramatic Poems of Wm. Gilmore Simms. " *Russell's Magazine* 2.3 (Dec. 1857): 240–59. Reprinted in *Nineteenth-Century Literature Criticism*. Ed. Laurie Lanzen Harris. Vol. 3. Detroit: Gale Research, 1983. *Literature Resource Center*. Web. 13 Jan. 2014.

———. "The Poets, and Poetry of the South." *Russell's Magazine* (Nov. 1857): 152–60.

———. Rev. of *Mellichampe*. By William Gilmore Simms. Charleston *Weekly News* n.s. 4 (6 Apr. 1854): 2.

———. Rev. of *The Partisan*. By William Gilmore Simms. Charleston *Weekly News* n.s. 3 (7 Jan. 1854): 2.

———. Rev. of *Poems*. By William Gilmore Simms. *Charleston Weekly News* (7 Jan. 1854): 3.

[Herbert, Henry William.] Rev. of *Guy Rivers—A Tale of Georgia*. By the author of "Martin Faber," "Atalantis," &c. *American Monthly Magazine* 3 (Jul. 1834): 295–304.

Heriott, Edwin. "Education at the South." *DeBow's Review* 21.6 (1856): 650–59.

Higham, John. "The Changing Loyalties of William Gilmore Simms." *Journal of Southern History* 9.2 (1943): 210–23.

Hirshson, Stanley P. *The White Tecumseh*. New York: John Wiley and Sons, 1997.

"The History of South-Carolina." *Southern Quarterly Review* 4.7 (1843): 247–49.

Hoefer, Anthony Dyer. "'The Slaves That They Are' and the Slaves That They Might Become: Bondage and Liberty in William Gilmore Simms's *The Yemassee*." *MELUS* 34.3 (2009): 115–32.

Hoge, James O. "Byron's Influence on the Poetry of William Gilmore Simms." *Essays in Literature* 2.1 (1975): 87–96.

Hogue, L. Lynn. "The Presentation of Post-Revolutionary Law in *Woodcraft*: Another Perspective on the 'Truth' of Simms." *Mississippi Quarterly* 31 (1978): 201–10.

Holbein, Woodrow L. "Shakespeare in Charleston: 1800–1860." *Shakespeare in the South*. Ed. Philip C. Kolin. Jackson: UP of Mississippi, 1983. 88–111.

Holman, C. Hugh. Introduction. *Views and Reviews in American Literature, History and Fiction*. 1st ser. 1845 [1846]. By William Gilmore Simms. Ed. C. Hugh Holman. Cambridge: Belknap P, 1962.

———. *The Roots of Southern Writing: Essays on the Literature of the American South*. Athens: U of Georgia P, 1972.

———. "Simms and the British Dramatists." *PMLA* 65.4 (June 1950): 129–39.

———. "The Status of Simms." *American Quarterly* 10 (Summer 1958): 181–85.

———. "William Gilmore Simms' Picture of the Revolution as a Civil Conflict." *Journal of Southern History* 15 (Nov. 1949): 441–62.

———, ed. *The Yemassee: A Romance of Carolina*. By William Gilmore Simms. 1853. Boston: Houghton Mifflin Co., 1961.

Holmes, George Frederick. Rev. of *Poems*. By William Gilmore Simms. *Richmond Semi-Weekly Enquirer* (4 Apr. 1854).

Holt, Keri. "Reading Regionalism across the War: Simms and the Literary Imagination of Post-Bellum Literary Magazines." *William Gilmore Simms's Unfinished Civil War: Consequences for a Southern Man of Letters*. Ed. David Moltke-Hansen. Columbia: U of South Carolina P, 2013. 159–82.

Holt, Mack P. *Renaissance and Reformation France, 1500–1648*. New York: Oxford UP, 2002.

Hoobler, Dorothy and Thomas. *Captain John Smith: Jamestown and the Birth of the American Dream*. New Jersey: John Wiley & Sons, 2006.

Hoole, William. "Simms's *Michael Bonham*: A 'Forgotten' Drama of the Texas Revolution." *Southwestern Historical Quarterly* 46 (1942): 255–61.

Horry, Peter. Transcripts of Francis Marion Letters, 1779–1782. 5 vols. Peter Force Papers, Microfilm Series P900013, RW3365. Columbia: South Carolina Department of Archives and History.

——— and Mason L. Weems. *The Life of Marion, a Celebrated Partisan Officer in the Revolutionary War, Against the British and Tories in South Carolina and Georgia*. 1809. Reprinted Philadelphia: Lippincott Company, 1891.

Howard, O. O. *The Autobiography of Oliver Otis Howard*. 2 vols. 1907. Reprinted Harrisburg, PA: The Archive Society, 1997.

Hubbell, Jay B. *The South in American Literature, 1607–1900*. Durham: Duke UP, 1954.

Hudson, Charles. "An Ethnohistorical View." *An Early and Strong Sympathy: The Indian Writings of William Gilmore Simms*. Ed. John C. Guilds and Charles Hudson. Columbia: U of South Carolina P, 2003. xxxiv–li.

Hutchison, Coleman. *Apples & Ashes: Literature, Nationalism, and the Confederate States of America*. Athens: U of Georgia P, 2012.

——— and Elizabeth Renker. "Popular Poetry in Circulation." *U.S. Popular Print Culture 1860–1920*. Ed. Christine Bold. Vol. 6. *The Oxford History of Popular Print Culture*. Ed. Gary Kelly. New York: Oxford UP, 2011. 395–413.

Irving, Washington. *The Companions of Columbus*. *The Works of Washington Irving*. Vol. IV. New York: Putnam, 1881.

James, William Dobein. *A Sketch of the Life of Brig. General Francis Marion, and A History of His Brigade*. 1821. Reprinted Marietta, GA: Continental Book Company, 1948.

Jamison, David Flavel. *Bertrand du Guesclin. His Life and Times, a History of the Fourteenth Century*. London: Trübner & Co., Paternoster Row. Charleston: John Russell, 1864.

Johanyak, Debra. "William Gilmore Simms: Deviant Paradigms of Southern Womanhood?" *Mississippi Quarterly*. 46.4 (1993): 573–88.

John, Richard R. *Spreading the News: The American Postal System from Franklin to Morse*. Cambridge: Harvard UP, 1998.

Johnson, Jason W. "'Dazzling Outlawries of the Imagination': William Gilmore Simms and the 'Americanism' of the Sonnets." *The Simms Review* 14.2 (2006): 5–13.

———. Rev. of *The Poet's Holy Craft: William Gilmore Simms and Romantic Verse Tradition*. By Matthew C. Brennan and *Selected Poems of William Gilmore Simms*, Twentieth Anniversary Edition, ed James Everett Kibler. *The Simms Review* 18.1–2 (2010): 117–25.

Johnson, Paul E. *A Shopkeeper's Millennium: Society and Revivals in Rochester, New York, 1815–1837*. New York: Hill and Wang, 1978.

Justus, James. *Fetching the Old Southwest: Humorous Writing from Longstreet to Twain*. Columbia: U of Missouri P, 2004.

Kammen, Michael. *Selvages & Biases: The Fabric of History in American Culture*. Ithaca, N.Y.: Cornell UP, 1987.

Kaplan, Amy. *Social Construction of American Realism*. Chicago: U of Chicago P, 1988.

Keener, Joseph B. *Shakespeare and Masculinity in Southern Fiction: Faulkner, Simms, Page and Dixon*. New York: Palgrave Macmillan, 2008.

Kelso, William. M. *Jamestown: the Buried Truth*. U of Virginia P, 2008.

Kennedy, John Pendleton. *Horse-Shoe Robinson; A Tale of the Tory Ascendency*. 2 vols. Philadelphia: Carey, Lea and Blanchard, 1835.

Kennett, Lee. *Sherman: A Soldier's Life*. New York: HarperCollins, 2001.

Kibler, James Everett. "Dory's Bible, Acts, and the Devil at Our Elbow," *Studies in the Novel* 35.2 (Summer 2003): 208–18.

———. "The First Simms Letters: 'Letters from the West' (1826)." *Southern Literary Journal* 19 (Spring 1987): 81–91.

———. Introduction. *Selected Poems of William Gilmore Simms*. Athens: U of Georgia P, 1990. xi–xxv.

———. Introduction. *Selected Poems of William Gilmore Simms: Twentieth Anniversary Edition*. Ed. James Everett Kibler. Columbia: U of South Carolina P, 2010. xvii–xxvii.

———. Introduction. *Woodcraft; or, Hawks about the Dovecote*. By William Gilmore Simms. Columbia: U of South Carolina P, 2012. xxiii–xxxvi.

———. "The Major Fiction of William Gilmore Simms." *Mississippi Quarterly* 43 (Winter/Spring 1989–90): 85–95.

———. "On the Pairing of *Woodcraft* and *The Golden Christmas*." *The Simms Review* 2.1 (1994): 13–16.

———. *The Poetry of William Gilmore Simms: An Introduction and Bibliography*. Spartanburg, SC: Reprint Co., 1979.

———. *The Pseudonymous Publications of William Gilmore Simms*. Athens: U of Georgia P, 1976.

———. "Simms' Editorship of the Columbia Phoenix of 1865." *South Carolina Journals and Journalists: Proceedings of the Reynolds Conference, May 17–18, 1974*. Ed. James B. Meriwether. Spartanburg, SC: The Reprint Company for the Southern Studies Program of the University of South Carolina, 1975. 61–75.

———. "Simms as Naturalist: Lowcountry Landscape in His Revolutionary Novels." *Mississippi Quarterly* 31 (Fall 1978): 499–518.

———. "Some Unrecorded English Reviews of W.G. Simms." *Mississippi Quarterly* 47.4 (Fall 1994): 557–66.

———. "The Unpublished Preface to W.G. Simms's Collected Poems." *Studies in Bibliography* 49 (1996): 291–93.

———. "William Gilmore Simms." *Encyclopedia of American Literature*. Ed. Steven R. Serafin. New York: Continuum, 1999. 1039–43.

———. "William Gilmore Simms (17 April 1806–11 June 1870)." *American Magazine Journalists, 1741–1850*. Ed. Sam G. Riley. *Dictionary of Literary Biography* 73. Detroit: Gale Research, 1988. 275–92.

——— and David Moltke-Hansen. "Introduction: The Man of Letters as Critic." *William Gilmore Simms's Selected Reviews on Literature and Civilization*. Columbia: U of South Carolina P, 2014. 1–12.

King, Vincent. "'Foolish Talk 'Bout Freedom': Simms's Vision of America in *The Yemassee*." *Studies in the Novel* 35.2 (2003): 139–48.

Kirk, Russell. "The Moral Imagination." *Literature and Belief* 1 (1981): 137–49.

Kolodny, Annette. "The Unchanging Landscape: The Pastoral Impulse in Simms's Revolutionary War Romances." *Southern Literary Journal* 5.1 (1972), 47–67.

Kong, Lauren L., John J.B. Allen, and Elizabeth L. Glisky. "Interidentity Memory Transfer in Dissociative Identity Disorder." *Journal of Abnormal Psychology*. 117.3 (Aug. 2008): 686–92.

Kreyling, Michael. *Figures of the Hero in Southern Narrative*. Baton Rouge: Louisiana State UP, 1987.

———. *Inventing Southern Literature*. Jackson: UP of Mississippi, 1998.

Laudonniere, René Goulaine de. *A Notable Historie Containing Foure Voyages Made by Certayne French Captaynes unto Florida*. London: Thomas Dawson, 1587.

Lause, Mark A. *Young America: Land, Labor, and the Republican Community*. Champaign: U of Illinois P, 1995.

Lawson, John. *A New Voyage to Carolina*. Ed. Hugh Talmage Lefler. 1709. Chapel Hill: U of North Carolina P, 1967.

Lays of the South: Verses Relative to the War between the Two Sections of the American States. Liverpool, 1864.

LeConte, Emma. *When the World Ended: The Diary of Emma LeConte*. Ed. Earl Shenck Miers. New York: Oxford UP, 1957.

Lederach, John Paul. *The Moral Imagination: The Art and Soul of Building Peace*. New York: Oxford UP, 2005.

Lee, Henry. *Memoirs of the War in the Southern Department of the United States*. Philadelphia, 1812.

Lescarbot, Marc. *Histoire de la Nouvelle-France*. Paris: Chez Iean Millot, 1611.

Levine, Bruce. *Half Slave and Half Free: The Roots of Civil War*. Revised Edition. New York: Hill and Wang, 2005.

"Literariana. American." *The Round Table. A Saturday Review of Politics, Finance, Literature, Society and Art* 4.62 (10 Nov. 1866): 244–45.

"Literary Notices." *Godey's* 53 (July 1856): 84.

"Literary Notices." *Godey's Lady's Book* 64 (May 1852): 406–08.

"Literary Notices." *Godey's Lady's Book and Magazine* 52 (June 1856): 561–65.

"Literary Notices." *Harper's New Monthly Magazine* 4.24 (May 1852): 852–57.

"Literary Notices." Rev. of *The Lily and the Totem*. By William Gilmore Simms. *Harper's New Monthly Magazine* 1 (Oct. 1850): 718.

"Literary Notices: Book Table." *New York Mirror* 16.26 (22 Dec. 1838): 207.

"Literary, Editorial Department, &c." Rev. of *The Lily and the Totem*. By William Gilmore Simms. *De Bow's Review* 9 (Nov. 1850): 574.

"Literature." *Putnam's Monthly; A Magazine of American Literature, Science, and Art* (Feb 1855): 213.

Lloyd-Smith, Allan. *American Gothic Fiction: An Introduction*. New York: Continuum International, 2004.

London, Lawrence F. "Confederate Literature and its Publishers." *Studies in Southern History*. Ed. Joseph Sitterson. Chapel Hill: U of North Carolina P, 1957.

Loomba, Ania. *Colonialism/Postcolonialism*. The New Critical Idiom series. Ed. John Drakakis. New York: Routledge, 1998.

Lorant, Stefan, John White, and Jacques Le Moyne de Morgues. *The New World: The First Pictures of America*. New York: Duell, Sloan, and Pearce, 1965.

Lucas, Marion Brunson. *Sherman and the Burning of Columbia*. 1976. Rpt. Columbia: U of South Carolina P, 2000.

Luce, Dianne C. "John A. Murrell and the Imaginations of Simms and Faulkner." *William Gilmore Simms and the American Frontier*. Ed. John Caldwell Guilds and Caroline Collins. Athens: U of Georgia P, 1997. 237–57.

Lukacs, Georg. *The Historical Novel*. Trans. Hannah Mitchell and Stanley Mitchell. London: Merlin P, 1962. Trans. of *Der historische Roman*, 1937.

Marr, Timothy. Abstract of "Dredging the Swamp Fox: Francis Marion in the Circuits of Cultural Memory." Paper presented at the *Annual Meeting of the American Studies Association*, Philadelphia, 2007.

Marszalek, John F. *Sherman: A Soldier's Passion for Order*. New York: The Free Press, 1993.

Martineau, Harriet. *Society in America*. 2 vols. London: Saunders and Otley, 1837.

Mason, Emily Virginia, ed. *The Southern Poems of the War*. Baltimore: J. Murphy, 1867.

Massey, Gregory D. *John Laurens and the American Revolution*. Columbia: U of South Carolina P, 2000.

Massey, Mary Elizabeth. *Ersatz in the Confederacy*. Columbia: U of South Carolina P, 1952.

Matthiessen, F.O. *American Renaissance: Art and Expression in the Age of Emerson and Whitman*. London and New York: Oxford UP, 1941.

Mayfield, John. "'The Soul of a Man!': William Gilmore Simms and the Myths of Southern Manhood." *Journal of the Early Republic* 15.3 (Fall 1995): 477–500. Reprinted in *Nineteenth-Century Literature Criticism*. Ed. Kathy D. Darrow. Vol. 241. Detroit: Gale, 2011. *Literature Resource Center*. Web. 30 Dec. 2012.

McCardell, John. "Biography and the Southern Mind: William Gilmore Simms." *"Long Years of Neglect": The Work and Reputation of William Gilmore Simms*. Ed. John Caldwell Guilds. Fayetteville: U of Arkansas P, 1988. 202–16.

———. *The Idea of a Southern Nation: Southern Nationalists and Southern Nationalism, 1830–1860*. New York: Norton, 1979.

———. "Trent's Simms: The Making of a Biography," *A Master's Due: Essays in Honor of David Herbert Donald*. Eds. William J. Cooper, Michael F. Holt, and John McCardell. Baton Rouge: Louisiana State UP, 1986. 179–203.

McDavid, Raven I. "*Ivanhoe* and Simms's *Vasconselos*." *Modern Language Notes* 56.4 (April 1941): 294–97.

McHaney, Thomas L. "An Early 19th-Century Literary Agent: James Lawson of New York." *Publications of the Bibliographical Society of America* 64 (Spring 1970): 177–92.

———. "Simms's *Border Beagles*: A Carnival of Frontier Voices." *William Gilmore Simms and the American Frontier*. Ed. John Caldwell Guilds and Caroline Collins. Athens: U of Georgia P, 1997. 95–104.

McManaway, James G. "Shakespeare in the United States." *PMLA* 79.5 (Dec. 1964): 513–18.

McPherson, James M. *Ordeal By Fire: The Civil War and Reconstruction*. New York: Alfred A. Knopf, 1982.

McWhirter, Christian. *Battle Hymns: The Power and Popularity of Music in the Civil War*. Chapel Hill: U of North Carolina P, 2012.

Meitzen, Blocker Dodson. "Francis Marion: His Life as Symbol." MA thesis. Auburn U, 1987.

Meriwether, James B. "The Significance of Simms's First Long Poem." *The Simms Review* 17.1–2 (2009): 13–22.

———. "The Theme of Freedom in *Woodcraft*." *"Long Years of Neglect": The Work and Reputation of William Gilmore Simms*. Ed. John Caldwell Guilds. Fayetteville: U of Arkansas P, 1988. 20–36.

Meriwether, Nicholas G. "'A Scene Which Beggars Art to Portray': Simms and the Writing of the *Sack and Destruction of Columbia, S.C.*" *The Simms Review* 12.1 (2004): 25–37.

———. "Simms's Civil War: History, Healing, and the *Sack and Destruction of Columbia, S.C.*" *Studies in the Literary Imagination* 42.1 (2009): 97–120.

———. "Simms's *The Lily and the Totem*: 'History for the Purposes of Art.'" *"Long Years of Neglect": The Work and Reputation of William Gilmore Simms*. Ed. John Caldwell Guilds. Fayetteville: U of Arkansas P, 1988. 76–105.

———. "An Unfinished Reconstruction: Simms's 'The Brothers of the Coast.'" *William Gilmore Simms's Unfinished Civil War: Consequences for a Southern Man of Letters*. Ed. David Moltke-Hansen. Columbia: U of South Carolina P, 2013. 185–201.

Mielke, Laura L. *Moving Encounters: Sympathy and the Indian Question in Antebellum Literature*. Amherst: U of Massachusetts P, 2008.

Miles, James Warley. "Southern Passages and Pictures." *Southern Literary Messenger* (May 1851): 289–96.

Miller, John D. "The Business of Romanticism: Simms's Political Poetry." *Studies in the Literary Imagination* 42.1 (2009): 141–61.

———. "The Sense of Things to Come: Redefining Gender and Promoting the Lost Cause in *The Sense of the Beautiful*." *William Gilmore Simms's Unfinished Civil War: Consequences for a Southern Man of Letters*. Ed. David Moltke-Hansen. Columbia: U of South Carolina P, 2013. 224–37.

Miller, Lisa Kay. "The Artist as Historian: The Southern Frontier and the Writing of History in the Fiction of William Gilmore Simms, William Faulkner, and Eudora Welty." Diss. U of Missouri, 1987.

Miller, Perry. *The Raven and the Whale: The War of Words and Wits in the Era of Poe and Melville*. New York: Harcourt, Brace and Co., 1956.

Mingura, Corey Don. "'Cash Is Conqueror': The Critique of Capitalism in Simms's 'The Western Emigrants' and 'Sonnet—The Age of Gold.'" *The Simms Review* 17.1–2 (2009): 87–96.

Mintz, Zoe. "Fort Caroline Found? Oldest Fortified Settlement In North America May Be Located In Georgia." *International Business Times*, 21 Feb. 2014. Web. 21 Aug. 2014.

Moltke-Hansen, David. "Between Plantation and Frontier: The South of William Gilmore Simms." *William Gilmore Simms and the American Frontier*. Ed. John Caldwell Guilds and Caroline Collins. Athens: U of Georgia P, 1997. 3–26.

———. "A Critical Revolution and a Revolutionary Critic." *William Gilmore Simms's Selected Reviews on Literature and Civilization*. Ed. James Everett Kibler and David Moltke-Hansen. Columbia: U of South Carolina P, 2014: 197–214.

———. "The Expansion of Intellectual Life: A Prospectus." *Intellectual Life in Antebellum Charleston*. Ed. Michael O'Brien and David Moltke-Hansen. Knoxville: U of Tennessee P 1986. 3–44.

———. "Identity Politics and the Civil War: The Transformation of South Carolina's Public History, 1862–2012." *Historically Speaking* 14.1 (2013): 10–14.

———. Introduction. *Views and Reviews in American Literature, History and Fiction*. By William Gilmore Simms. Columbia: U of South Carolina P, 2013. xxiii–xxxv.

———. Introduction. *The Yemassee: A Romance of Carolina*. Columbia: U of South Carolina P, 2013.

———. "Ordered Progress: The Historical Philosophy of William Gilmore Simms." *"Long Years of Neglect": The Work and Reputation of William Gilmore Simms*. Ed. John Caldwell Guilds. Fayetteville: U of Arkansas P, 1988. 126–47.

———. "Southern Literary Horizons in Young America: Imaginative Development of a Regional Geography." *Studies in the Literary Imagination* 42.1 (2009): 1–31.

———. "When History Failed: William Gilmore Simms's Artistic Negotiation of the Civil War's Consequences." *William Gilmore Simms's Unfinished Civil War: Consequences for a Southern Man of Letters*. Columbia: U of South Carolina P, 2013. 3–31.

———. "Why History Mattered: The Background of Ann Pamela Cunningham's Interest in the Preservation of Mount Vernon," *Furman Studies* n.s. 26 (Dec. 1980): 34–42.

———, ed. *William Gilmore Simms's Unfinished Civil War: Consequences for a Southern Man of Letters*. Columbia: U of South Carolina P, 2013.

Moore, Alexander. "The Swamp Fox in History and Literature." *Carologue* 15.4 (Winter 1999): 14–15.

Moore, Frank, ed. *Rebel Rhymes and Rhapsodies*. New York: G.P. Putnam, 1864.

Moore, Rayburn S. "William Gilmore Simms's *Guy Rivers* and the Frontier." *William Gilmore Simms and the American Frontier*. Eds. John Caldwell Guilds and Caroline Collins. Athens: U of Georgia P, 1997. 55–63.

Moore, Tara Stern. *Christmas in Print*. New York: Palgrave Macmillan, 2009.

Moore-Gilbert, Bart. *Postcolonial Theory: Contexts, Practices, Politics*. London: Verso, 1997.

Morris, J. Allen. "Gullah in the Stories and Novels of William Gilmore Simms." *American Speech* 22.1 (1947): 46–53.

Mosby, Charmaine Allmon. "William Hinkley/Calvert: The Key to *Charlemont* and *Beauchampe*." *Southern Literary Journal* 16.2 (Spring 1984): 21–29.

Moss, William. *Confederate Broadside Poems: An Annotated Descriptive Bibliography Based on the Collection of the Z. Smith Reynolds Library of Wake Forest University*. Westport: Meckler, 1988.

Moultrie, William. *Memoirs of the American Revolution so far as it Related to the States of North and South Carolina*. New York: David Longworth, 1802.

"Mr. Simms's *Norman Maurice*." *The Literary World* 9.242 (20 Sept. 1851): 223–24. Reprinted in *Nineteenth-Century Literature Criticism*. Ed. Laurie Lanzen Harris. Vol. 3. Detroit: Gale Research, 1983. *Literature Resource Center*. Web. 13 Jan. 2014.

Murphy, Andrew. *Shakespeare in Print*. New York: Cambridge UP, 2003.

Murphy, Peter. "Simms's *Vasconselos*: A Multicultural Reading." *Studies in the Novel* 35 (2003): 243–60.

———. "Virtues of Romanticism in Simms's 'Jocaseé. A Cherokee Legend.'" *South Carolina Review* 35.1 (Fall 2002): 40–52.

Nakamura, Masahiro. *Visions of Order in William Gilmore Simms: Southern Conservatism and the Other American Romance*. Columbia: U South Carolina P, 2009.

Nalley, Sarah. "Shakespeare on the Charleston Stage, 1764–1799." *Shakespeare in the South*. Ed. Philip C. Kolin. UP of Mississippi, 1983. 72–87.

Newton, David W. Afterword. *Eutaw: A Sequel to The Forayers, or The Raid of the Dog Days*. 1856. By William Gilmore Simms. Ed. David W. Newton. Fayetteville: U of Arkansas P, 2007. 495–511.

———. "Voices along the Border: Language and the Southern Frontier *in Guy Rivers: A Tale of Georgia*." *William Gilmore Simms and the American Frontier*. Ed. John Caldwell Guilds and Caroline Collins. Athens: U of Georgia P, 1997. 118–44.

———. "Voices from the Enchanted Circle: Simms and the Poetics of the American Renaissance." *Southern Quarterly* 41.2 (2003): 23–36.

Niemi, Carol Superfine Blair. "Toward a Perfect Security: Images of Natural Process in the Revolutionary War Novels of William Gilmore Simms." Diss. U of Georgia, 1982.

Noe, Marcia. "James Hall." *Dictionary of Midwestern Literature, Volume One: The Authors*. Ed. Philip A. Greasley. Bloomington: U of Indiana P, 2001. 233–35.

Nolan, Alan T. "The Anatomy of the Myth." *The Myth of the Lost Cause and Civil War History*. Ed. Gary W. Gallagher and Alan T. Nolan. Bloomington: Indiana UP, 2000. 11–34.

"Notice of Publication." *Charleston Courier* (1 Oct. 1853): 2.

"Notices of New Books." Rev. of *The Lily and the Totem*. By William Gilmore Simms. *Democratic Review* 27 (Oct. 1850): 379.

"Notices of New Books: *War Poetry of the South*." *New Englander and Yale Review* 26.99 (Apr. 1867): 381–86.

"Notices of New Works: The Golden Christmas." *The Southern Literary Messenger* 18.5 (May 1852): 318.

Nudleman, Franny. *John Brown's Body: Slavery, Violence, and the Culture of War*. Chapel Hill: U of North Carolina P, 2004.

O'Brien, Michael. *Conjectures of Order: Intellectual Life and the American South, 1810–1860*. 2 vols. Chapel Hill: U of North Carolina P, 2004.

O'Sullivan, John L. Introduction. *The United States Magazine and Democratic Review* (Oct. 1837): 1–15.

Okker, Patricia. "Gender and Secession in Simms's *Katharine Walton*." *Southern Literary Journal* 29.2 (1997): 17–31.

———. "Serial Politics in William Gilmore Simms's *Woodcraft*." *Periodical Literature in Nineteenth-Century America*. Ed. Kenneth M. Price. Charlottesville: UP of Virginia, 1995. 150–65.

Olesen, Jan. "'Mercyfull Warres Agaynst These Naked People': The Discourse of Violence in the Early Americas." *Canadian Review of American Studies* 39.3 (2009): 253–72.

Osborn, Thomas W. *The Fiery Trail: A Union Officer's Account of Sherman's Last Campaigns*. Ed. Richard Harwell and Philip N. Racine. Knoxville: U of Tennessee P, 1986.

Osterweis, Rollin G. *The Myth of the Lost Cause, 1865–1900*. Hamden, CT: Archon Books, 1973.

Palmer, Phyllis Marynick. Review of *Sherman and the Burning of Columbia*. *Journal of American History* 64.3 (1977): 801–02.

Parks, Edd Winfield. *Southern Poets*. New York: American Book, 1936.

———. "The Three Streams of Southern Humor." *Georgia Review* 9 (Summer 1955): 147–59.

———. *William Gilmore Simms as Literary Critic*. Athens: U of Georgia P, 1961.

Parrington, Vernon L. *Main Currents in American Thought*. 3 vols. New York: Harcourt, Brace and Co., 1927–30.

Patrick, Marietta. "The Serpent in the Garden: Archetypal Patterns in Simms's *Charlemont* and *Beauchampe*. *The Simms Review* 6.1 (1998): 13–23.

Pearce, Colin D. "All Aboard! 'The Philosophy of the Omnibus' and the Problem of Progress in William Gilmore Simms." *The Simms Review* 18.1–2 (2010): 71–91.

———. "The Metaphysical Federalism of William Gilmore Simms." *Studies in the Literary Imagination* 42.1 (2009): 121–39.

Pickett, Albert J. *History of Alabama, and Incidentally of Georgia and Mississippi, from the Earliest Period*. 2 vols. Charleston: Walker and James, 1851.

Poe, Edgar Allan. "Critical Notices." *Broadway Journal* 2.13 (4 Oct. 1845): 190.

———. "Literary Criticism." *Godey's Magazine and Lady's Book* (Jan. 1846): 41–42.

———. Rev. of *Beauchampe, or The Kentucky Tragedy*. By William Gilmore Simms. *Graham's Lady's and Gentleman's Magazine* 20.5 (May 1842): 300–01.

———. Rev. of *Confession; or, The Blind Heart. A Domestic Story*. By William Gilmore Simms. *Graham's Magazine* 19.6 (December 1841): 306.

———. Rev. of *The Kinsmen*. By William Gilmore Simms. *Graham's Magazine* 18 (Mar. 1841): 143

———. Rev. of *The Partisan*. By William Gilmore Simms. *Southern Literary Messenger* 2 (Jan. 1836): 117–21.

———. Rev. of *The Wigwam and the Cabin*. By William Gilmore Simms. *Broadway Journal* 2 (4 Oct. 1845): 190–91.

———. Rev. of *The Wigwam and the Cabin*. By William Gilmore Simms. *Godey's Magazine and Lady's Book* (Jan. 1846): 41–42.

———. "Review of New Books." *The Casket* 15 (Nov. 1839): 283.

Pogue, Lauren. *Francis Marion, the Swamp Fox: The Man and the Myth*. Honor's thesis. U of North Carolina, 2003.

Pollard, E.A. *The Lost Cause: A New Southern History of the War of the Confederates*. New York: E.B. Treat and Co., 1866.

Potter, Claire Bond and Renee C. Romano, eds. *Doing Recent History*. Athens: U of Georgia P, 2012.

Potter, David. *A History of France, 1460–1560*. New York: St. Martin's P, 1995.

The Proslavery Argument: As Maintained by the Most Distinguished Writers of the Southern States: Containing the Several Essays, on the Subject, of Chancellor Harper, Governor Hammond, Dr. Simms, and Professor Dew. Charleston: Walker, Richards, and Co., 1852.

Quinn, Arthur Hobson. *The Literature of the American People: An Historical and Critical Survey*. New York: Appleton-Century-Crofts, Inc., 1951.

Radcliffe, Ann. *The Mysteries of Udolpho*. 1794. *Gutenberg.org*. Project Gutenberg. 28 February 2009. Web. 29 June 2012.

Ramsay, David. *History of South Carolina, From its First Settlement in 1670 to the Year 1808*. Charleston: David Longworth, 1809.

———. *History of the American. Revolution*, vol. 2. Indianapolis: Liberty Fund, Inc., 1990.

———. *History of the Revolution in South Carolina, from a British Province to an Independent State, Volume 2*. Trenton, NJ: Isaac Collins, 1785.

Rankin, Hugh F. *Francis Marion: The Swamp Fox*. New York: Thomas Y. Crowell Company, 1973.

Reed, Glenn M. Introduction. *Martin Faber*. By William Gilmore Simms. Albany, NY: NCUP, 1990. i–xxi.

Regis, Pamela. *Describing Early America: Bartram, Jefferson, Crèvecoeur, and the Influence of Natural History*. Philadelphia: U. of Pennsylvania P. 1999.

Restad, Penne L. *Christmas in America: A History*. New York: Oxford UP, 1995.

Rev. of "Beauchampe or the Kentucky Tragedy." By William Gilmore Simms. *Charleston Mercury* (23 April 1842): 2.

Rev. of *Border Beagles; A Tale of Mississippi*. By William Gilmore Simms. *Burton's Gentlemen's Magazine and American Monthly Review* (Sept. 1840): 156–57.

Rev. of *Border Beagles; A Tale of Mississippi*. By William Gilmore Simms. *Casket* (Oct. 1840): 192.

Rev. of *Border Beagles; A Tale of Mississippi*. By William Gilmore Simms. *The Knickerbocker; or New York Monthly Magazine* (Oct. 1840): 364.

Rev. of *Border Beagles; A Tale of Mississippi*. By William Gilmore Simms. *The New-Yorker* (29 Aug. 1840): 381.

Rev. of "Carl Werner, and Other Tales." *Boston Traveler* (4 Jan. 1839): 3.

Rev. of *Charlemant* [*sic*]; *or, The Pride of the Village*. By William Gilmore Simms. *Graham's American Monthly Magazine of Literature, Art, and Fashion* 48 (May 1856): 467.

Rev. of *The Damsel of Darien*. By William Gilmore Simms. *Knickerbocker* 14 (Nov. 1839): 457–58.

Rev. of *The Damsel of Darien*. By William Gilmore Simms *New York Mirror* 17 (26 Oct. 1839): 143.

Rev. of *Guy Rivers, a Tale of Georgia*, by the author of *Martin Faber*. *Charleston Courier* (19 Jul. 1834): 2.

Rev. of *The Life of the Chevalier Bayard; "The Good Knight," "Sans peur et sans reproche."* By William Gilmore Simms. *The Literary World: A Gazette for Authors, Readers and Publishers* (29 Jan. 1847).

Rev. of *The Life of the Chevalier Bayard; "The Good Knight," "Sans peur et sans reproche."* By William Gilmore Simms. *Holden's Dollar Magazine* 2.3 (March 1848): 182.

Rev. of *The Lily and the Totem*. By William Gilmore Simms. *Holden's Dollar Magazine* 6 (Dec. 1850): 758–59.

Rev. of *The Lily and the Totem*. By William Gilmore Simms. *Literary World* 7 (7 Sep. 1850): 189–90.

Rev. of *Mellichampe*. By William Gilmore Simms. *Knickerbocker* 8 (Dec. 1836): 735–37.

Rev. of *The Partisan*. By William Gilmore Simms. *Knickerbocker* 6 (Dec. 1835): 577.

Rev. of *Richard Hurdis. A Tale of Alabama*. By William Gilmore Simms. *Graham's Magazine* (Nov. 1855): 469.

Rev. of *Richard Hurdis*. By William Gilmore Simms. *Southern Literary Messenger* (Oct. 1855): 639.

Rev. of *Richard Hurdis; or, The Avenger of Blood. A Tale of Alabama*. By William Gilmore Simms. *Knickerbocker* (Oct. 1838): 367–69.

Rev. of *Simms's Poems Areytos or Songs and Ballads of the South with Other Poems*. By William Gilmore Simms. *Charleston Mercury* (22 Dec. 1860).

Rev. of *Simms's Poems Areytos or Songs and Ballads of the South with Other Poems*. By William Gilmore Simms. *Harper's* 22 (Feb. 1861): 411.

Rev. of *Simms's Poems Areytos or Songs and Ballads of the South with Other Poems*. By William Gilmore Simms. *Southern Literary Messenger* 32 (Feb. 1860): 156–59.

Rev. of *A Supplement to the Plays of William Shakespeare*. Ed. William Gilmore Simms. *Graham's Magazine* 33.2 (Aug. 1848): 119.

Rev. of *A Supplement to the Plays of William Shakespeare*. Ed. William Gilmore Simms. *Literary World* 3.63 (15 Apr. 1848): 203.

Rev. of *A Supplement to the Plays of William Shakespeare*. Ed. William Gilmore Simms. *Southern Literary Messenger* 14.5 (May 1848): 333.

Rev. of *War Poetry of the South*. Ed. William Gilmore Simms. *The Land We Love* 2.4 (Feb. 1867): 309.

Rev. of *War Poetry of the South*. Ed. William Gilmore Simms. *The Land We Love* 3.1 (May 1867): 71–74.

Rev. of *War Poetry of the South*. Ed. William Gilmore Simms. *New York Times* (12 Dec. 1866): 2.

Rev. of *War Poetry of the South*. Ed. William Gilmore Simms. *The Old Guard* 5.3 (Mar. 1867): 202–06.

Rev. of *The Wigwam and the Cabin*. By William Gilmore Simms. *New York Evening Mirror* (29 Sep. 1845).

Rev. of *The Wigwam and the Cabin*. By William Gilmore Simms. *New York Mirror* (14 Feb. 1846): 304.

Rev. of *The Wigwam and the Cabin*. By William Gilmore Simms. *New Monthly Magazine* (Dec. 1845).

Rev. of *The Wigwam and the Cabin*. By William Gilmore Simms. *The Harbinger* 2 (14 Mar. 1846): 218.

"Review of the Redfield Edition." *Graham's* (May 1854): 546.

Rhodes, James Ford. "Who Burned Columbia?" *American Historical Review* 7.3 (1902): 485–93.

Richter, Erma. "A Rumpus, to Be Sure: Simms's *Michael Bonham*." *Southern Quarterly* 41.2 (2003): 100–09.

Ridgely, J.V. *William Gilmore Simms*. New York: Twayne Publishers, 1962.

———. "*Woodcraft*: Simms's First Answer to *Uncle Tom's Cabin*." *American Literature* 31.4 (Jan. 1960): 421–33.

Roberts, Leonard. "Beauchamp and Sharp: A Kentucky Tragedy." *Kentucky Folklore Record* 14 (1968): 14–19.

Robertson, James I., Jr. Review of Sherman and the Burning of Columbia. *Military Affairs* 41.4 (Dec. 1977): 217.

Roemer, Kenneth M. and Bethany Shaffer. "Elephant or Chameleon?: Simms & Anthologies." *The Simms Review* 19.1–2 (2011): 100–8.

Rogers, George C., Jr. *Charleston in the Age of the Pinckneys*. Norman: U of Oklahoma P, 1969.

———. *A South Carolina Chronology, 1497–1970*. Columbia: U of South Carolina P, 1973.

Rogers, Jeffery J. "'Art Ready for Battle': William Gilmore Simms and the Civil War." Diss. U of South Carolina, 2004.

———. "The Demands of Citizenship in the Confederate Republic: Simms, Confederate Nationalism, and the Civil War." *William Gilmore Simms's Unfinished Civil War: Consequences for a Southern Man of Letters*. Ed. David Moltke-Hansen. Columbia: U of South Carolina P, 2013. 68–86.

———. Introduction. *The Life of the Chevalier Bayard*. By William Gilmore Simms. Columbia: U of South Carolina P, 2013. xxiii–xxxviii.

Royster, Charles. *The Destructive War: William Tecumseh Sherman, Stonewall Jackson, and the Americans*. New York: Alfred A. Knopf, 1991.

Rubin, Louis D. *The Edge of the Swamp: A Study of Literature and Society of the Old South*. Baton Rouge: Louisiana State UP, 1989.

———. "The Romance of the Colonial Frontier: Simms, Cooper, the Indians, and the Wilderness." *American Letters and the Historical Conciousness: Essays in Honor of Lewis P. Simpson*. Ed. J. Gerald Kennedy and Daniel Mark Fogel. Baton Rouge: Louisiana State UP, 1987. 112–36.

[Ryan, Abram Joseph], ed. *War Lyrics and Songs of the South*. London: Spottiswoode & Co, 1866.

Ryskamp, Charles. "The New England Sources of *The Scarlet Letter*." *The Scarlet Letter*. Ed. Seymour Gross, Sculley Bradley, Richmond Croom Beatty, and E. Hudson Long. New York: W.W. Norton & Company, 1988. 191–204.

Sabine, Lorenzo. *The American Loyalists or Biographical Sketches of Adherents to the British Crown in the War of the Revolution; Alphabetically Arranged; with a Preliminary Historical Essay*. Boston: Charles C. Little and James Brown, 1847.

———. *Biographical Sketches of Loyalists of the American Revolution, with an Historical Essay*. Vol. 1. Boston: Little, Brown and Co, 1864.

Sacks, David Harris. "Richard Hakluyt's Navigations in Time: History, Epic, and Empire." *Modern Language Quarterly* 67.1 (2006): 31–62.

Salley, A.S. Foreword. *Anthology of Poetry and Prose, Original and Selected*. Ed. Gilbert Augustus Selby. Columbia, SC: R.L. Bryan, 1953. xiii–xiv.

———, ed. *Sack and Destruction of the City of Columbia, S.C.* By William Gilmore Simms. Oglethorpe, GA: Oglethorpe UP, 1937.

———. "William Gilmore Simms." *The Letters of William Gilmore Simms*. Ed. Mary C. Simms Oliphant, Alfred Taylor Odell, and T. C. Duncan Eaves. 6 vols. Columbia: U of South Carolina P, 1952. lix–lxxxix.

Salmon, J.H.M. *Society in Crisis: France in the Sixteenth Century*. New York: St. Martin's P, 1975.

Savoy, Eric. "The Rise of American Gothic." *The Cambridge Companion to Gothic Fiction*. Ed. Jerrold E. Hogle. Cambridge: Cambridge UP, 2002. 167–88.

Scheer, George F. "Francis Marion: 'The Elusive Swamp Fox.'" *The American Heritage New Illustrated History of the United States, Volume 3: The American Revolution*. Ed. Robert G. Athearn. New York: Dell Publishing Company. 1963. 261–68.

———. *A Sketch of the Life of Brig. Gen. Francis Marion and a History of His Brigade from Its Rise in June 1780 until Disbanded in December, 1782*. By WIlliam Dobein James. *South Carolina Historical and Genealogical Magazine* 49.4 (1948): 246–48.

Schleck, Julia. "'Plain Broad Narratives of Substantial Facts': Credibility, Narrative, and Hakluyt's *Principall Navigations*." *Renaissance Quarterly* 59.3 (2006): 768–94.

Selby, Julian A. *Memorabilia and Anecdotal Reminiscences of Columbia, South Carolina*. 1905. Reprinted Columbia, SC: R. L. Bryan Co., 1970.

Sexton, Rebecca. "Simms's Use of Food Imagery in *The Golden Christmas*." *The Simms Review* 2.1 (1994): 1–7.

Shaffer, Arthur H. *The Politics of History: Writing the History of the American Revolution, 1783–1815*. Chicago: Precedent Publishing, 1975.

———. *To be an American: David Ramsay and the Making of the American Consciousness*. Columbia: U of South Carolina P, 1991.

Shellabarger, Samuel. *The Chevalier Bayard: A Study in Fading Chivalry*. New York: The Century Company, 1928.

Shelton, Austin J. "African Realistic Commentary on Culture Hierarchy and Racistic Sentimentalism in *The Yemassee*." *Phylon* 25.1 (1964): 72–78.

Shepperson, William G., ed. *War Songs of the South*. Richmond: West and Johnson, 1862.

Sherman, William T. *Memoirs of General William T. Sherman*. 1875. Reprinted Bloomington: Indiana UP, 1957.

Sherzer, Jane. "American Editions of Shakespeare: 1753–1860." *PMLA* 22.4 (1907): 633–96.

Shields, David S. Foreword. *William Gilmore Simms's Unfinished Civil War: Consequences for a Southern Man of Letters*. Ed. David Moltke-Hansen. Columbia: U of South Carolina P, 2013. ix–xix.

Shields, Johanna. "Delusion's Carnival of Death: A Different War Poetry from the South." *William Gilmore Simms's Unfinished Civil War: Consequences for a Southern Man of Letters*. Ed. David Moltke-Hansen. Columbia: U of South Carolina P, 2013. 112–28.

Shillingsburg, Miriam. "The Battered Woman Syndrome in Simms's Fiction." *Studies in the Novel* 35.2 (Summer 2003): 219–30.

———. "The Cub of the Panther: A New Frontier." *William Gilmore Simms and the American Frontier*. Ed. John C. Guilds and Caroline Collins. Athens: U of Georgia P, 1997. 221–36.

———. "Literary Grist: Simms's Trips to Mississippi." *Southern Quarterly* 41.2 (2003): 119–34.

———. "Simms' Benedict Arnold: The Hero as Traitor." *Southern Studies: An Interdisciplinary Journal of the South* 17 (1978): 273–89.

———. "Simms's Failed Lecture Tour of 1856: The Mind of the North." 'Long Years of Neglect': *The Work and Reputation of William Gilmore Simms*. Ed. John Caldwell Guilds. Fayetteville: U of Arkansas P, 1988. 183–201.

———. "West Point Treason in American Drama, 1798–1891." *Educational Theatre Journal*. 30.1 (1978): 73–89.

Shillingsburg, Peter LeRoy. "The Use of Sources in Simms's Biography of Francis Marion." MA thesis. U of South Carolina, 1967.

Simmons, William Hayne. *Notices of East Florida*. 1822. Ed. George E. Buker. Gainesville, U of Florida P, 1973.

Simms, William Gilmore. Advertisement. *The Yemassee*. New York: Harper & Brothers, 1835. v–vii.

———. *Areytos: Or Songs of the South*. Charleston: John Russell, 1846.

———. *The Army Correspondence of Colonel John Laurens in the Years 1777–8, Now First Printed From Original Letters Addressed to his Father Henry Laurens, President of Congress, with a Memoir*. New York: The Bradford Club, 1867.

———. *Atalantis: A Story of the Sea: In Three Parts*. New York: J. & J. Harper, 1832.

———. "Bayard, the Chevalier; 'sans peur et sans reproche." *Southern and Western Monthly Magazine and Review* (Aug. 1845): 75–85 & (Sept. 1845): 193–200.

———. *Beauchampe; or, the Kentucky Tragedy. A Sequel to* Charlemont. New York: Redfield, 1856.

———. *Beauchampe, or the Kentucky Tragedy. A Tale of Passion*. 2 vols. Philadelphia: Lea and Blanchard, 1842.

———. *Benedict Arnold: The Traitor. A Drama, in an Essay*. *Magnolia Weekly* 1 (16 May 1863): 165–67; (23 May 1863): 173–75; (30 May 1863): 186–87; (6 June 1863): 194–95; (13 June 1863): 202–03; (20 June 1863): 210–11; (27 June 1863): 218–19; (4 July 1863): 226–27; (11 July 1863): 234–35; (18 July 1863): 242–43; (25 July 1863): 250–51; (1 Aug. 1863): 258–59.

———. *Border Beagles*. Philadelphia: Carey and Hart, 1840.

———. *Border Beagles; A Tale of Mississippi*. New and rev. ed. New York: Redfield, 1855.

———. "Bulwer's Genius and Writings." *The Magnolia* n.s. 1 (1842): 329–37.

[———]. "Capture, Sack and Destruction of the City of Columbia." *The Columbia Phoenix* (21 Mar. 1865): 1–4; (23 Mar. 1865): 1–3; (25 Mar. 1865): 1–2; (28 Mar. 1865): 2–3; (30 Mar. 1865): 2–3; (1 Apr. 1865): 1–3; (4 Apr. 1865): 1–2; (6 Apr. 1865): 2–3; (8 Apr. 1865): 2–3.

———. *Capture, Sack and Destruction of the City of Columbia: A Collection of Documents*. Ed. Nicholas G. Meriwether. South Caroliniana Library, Columbia, SC, 2003.

———. *Carl Werner, An Imaginative Story; with other Tales of Imagination*. 2 vols. New York: George Adlard, 1838.

———. *The Cassique of Kiawah: A Colonial Romance*. New York: Redfield, 1859.

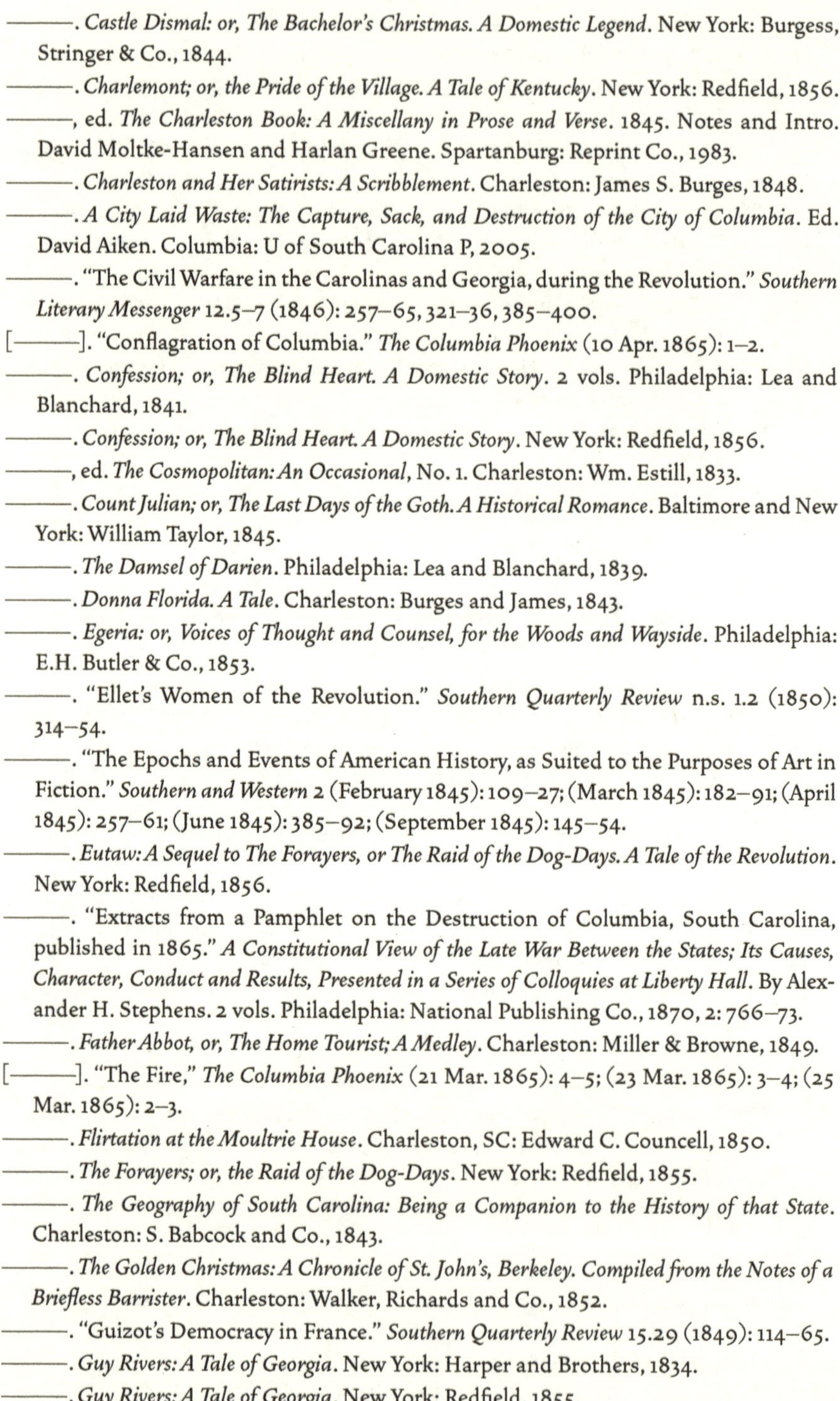

———. *Castle Dismal: or, The Bachelor's Christmas. A Domestic Legend*. New York: Burgess, Stringer & Co., 1844.

———. *Charlemont; or, the Pride of the Village. A Tale of Kentucky*. New York: Redfield, 1856.

———, ed. *The Charleston Book: A Miscellany in Prose and Verse*. 1845. Notes and Intro. David Moltke-Hansen and Harlan Greene. Spartanburg: Reprint Co., 1983.

———. *Charleston and Her Satirists: A Scribblement*. Charleston: James S. Burges, 1848.

———. *A City Laid Waste: The Capture, Sack, and Destruction of the City of Columbia*. Ed. David Aiken. Columbia: U of South Carolina P, 2005.

———. "The Civil Warfare in the Carolinas and Georgia, during the Revolution." *Southern Literary Messenger* 12.5–7 (1846): 257–65, 321–36, 385–400.

[———]. "Conflagration of Columbia." *The Columbia Phoenix* (10 Apr. 1865): 1–2.

———. *Confession; or, The Blind Heart. A Domestic Story*. 2 vols. Philadelphia: Lea and Blanchard, 1841.

———. *Confession; or, The Blind Heart. A Domestic Story*. New York: Redfield, 1856.

———, ed. *The Cosmopolitan: An Occasional*, No. 1. Charleston: Wm. Estill, 1833.

———. *Count Julian; or, The Last Days of the Goth. A Historical Romance*. Baltimore and New York: William Taylor, 1845.

———. *The Damsel of Darien*. Philadelphia: Lea and Blanchard, 1839.

———. *Donna Florida. A Tale*. Charleston: Burges and James, 1843.

———. *Egeria: or, Voices of Thought and Counsel, for the Woods and Wayside*. Philadelphia: E.H. Butler & Co., 1853.

———. "Ellet's Women of the Revolution." *Southern Quarterly Review* n.s. 1.2 (1850): 314–54.

———. "The Epochs and Events of American History, as Suited to the Purposes of Art in Fiction." *Southern and Western* 2 (February 1845): 109–27; (March 1845): 182–91; (April 1845): 257–61; (June 1845): 385–92; (September 1845): 145–54.

———. *Eutaw: A Sequel to The Forayers, or The Raid of the Dog-Days. A Tale of the Revolution*. New York: Redfield, 1856.

———. "Extracts from a Pamphlet on the Destruction of Columbia, South Carolina, published in 1865." *A Constitutional View of the Late War Between the States; Its Causes, Character, Conduct and Results, Presented in a Series of Colloquies at Liberty Hall*. By Alexander H. Stephens. 2 vols. Philadelphia: National Publishing Co., 1870, 2: 766–73.

———. *Father Abbot, or, The Home Tourist; A Medley*. Charleston: Miller & Browne, 1849.

[———]. "The Fire," *The Columbia Phoenix* (21 Mar. 1865): 4–5; (23 Mar. 1865): 3–4; (25 Mar. 1865): 2–3.

———. *Flirtation at the Moultrie House*. Charleston, SC: Edward C. Councell, 1850.

———. *The Forayers; or, the Raid of the Dog-Days*. New York: Redfield, 1855.

———. *The Geography of South Carolina: Being a Companion to the History of that State*. Charleston: S. Babcock and Co., 1843.

———. *The Golden Christmas: A Chronicle of St. John's, Berkeley. Compiled from the Notes of a Briefless Barrister*. Charleston: Walker, Richards and Co., 1852.

———. "Guizot's Democracy in France." *Southern Quarterly Review* 15.29 (1849): 114–65.

———. *Guy Rivers: A Tale of Georgia*. New York: Harper and Brothers, 1834.

———. *Guy Rivers: A Tale of Georgia*. New York: Redfield, 1855.

———. *Helen Halsey; or, The Swamp State of Conelachita. A Tale of the Borders*. New York: Burgess, Stringer & Co., 1845.

———. "History for the Purposes of Art." *Views and Reviews in American Literature, History and Fiction*, First and Second Series. New York: Wiley and Putnam, 1845–6. 20–101.

———. *The History of South Carolina, from Its First European Discovery to Its Erection into a Republic: With a Supplementary Chronicle of Events to the Present Time*. Charleston, SC: S. Babcock and Co., 1840.

———. *The History of South Carolina, from Its First European Discovery to Its Erection into a Republic: With a Supplementary Book, Bringing the Narrative Down to the Present Time*. New York: Redfield, 1860.

———. *The Huguenots in Florida, or, The Lily and the Totem*. 3rd ed. New York: Charles Scribner, 1854.

———. "The Huguenot Settlements in Florida." *Ladies' Companion* I, n.s. (Aug. 1844): 163–69; (Sep. 1844): 228–32.

———. "The Huguenot Settlements in Florida," *Southern and Western* 2 (November 1845): 324–32.

———. *Joscelyn. A Tale of the Revolution*. Columbia: U of South Carolina P, 2013.

———. *Katharine Walton; or, The Rebel of Dorcester*. New York: Redfield, 1854.

———. *The Kinsmen; or, The Black Riders of Congaree. A Tale*. 2 vols. Philadelphia: Lea and Blanchard, 1841.

———. *Lays of the Palmetto: A Tribute to the South Carolina Regiment, in the War with Mexico*. Charleston: John Russell, 1848.

———. *The Letters of William Gilmore Simms*. Ed. Mary C. Simms Oliphant *et al*. 6 vols. Columbia: U of South Carolina P, 1952–2012.

———. *The Life of Captain John Smith. The Founder of Virginia*. New York: A.L. Burt Company, 1902.

———. *The Life of Captain John Smith. The Founder of Virginia*. New York: George F. Cooledge & Brother, 1847.

———. *The Life of the Chevalier Bayard; "The Good Knight," "Sans peur et sans reproche."* New York: Harper & Brothers, 1847.

———. *The Life of Francis Marion*. New York: Henry G. Langley, 1844.

———. *The Life of Nathanael Greene, Major-General in the Army of the Revolution*. George F. Cooledge and Brother, 1849.

———. *The Lily and the Totem, or, the Huguenots in Florida*. New York: Baker and Scribner, 1850.

———. *The Lily and the Totem, or, the Huguenots in Florida*. 2nd printing. New York: Baker and Scribner, 1850.

———. *The Lily and the Totem, or, the Huguenots in Florida*. 4th printing. Charleston, SC: Walker, Evans and Cogswell, 1871.

———. *Marie de Berniere: A Tale of the Crescent City, etc. etc. etc*. Philadelphia: Lippincott, Grambo, and Co., 1853.

———. "Marion" [poem]. *Southern Literary Journal* 3 (Nov. 1836): 192.

———. "Marion-The Carolina Partisan." *Russell's Magazine* I IV (1858):1–16, 113–28.

———. *Martin Faber, the Story of a Criminal; and Other Tales*. New York: Harper & Brothers, 1837.

———. *Martin Faber; The Story of a Criminal*. New York: J. & J. Harper, 1833.

———. *Mellichampe. A Legend of the Santee*. 2 vols. New York: Harper & Brothers, 1836.

———. *Mellichampe: A Legend of the Santee*. New York: Redfield, 1854.

———. *Michael Bonham; or, The Fall of Bexar*. Richmond, VA: John R. Thompson, 1952

———. "Miss Martineau on Slavery." *Southern Literary Messenger* 3 (Nov. 1837): 641–57.

———. *Monody, on the Death of Gen. Charles Cotesworth Pinckney*. Charleston, SC: Gray and Ellis, 1825.

———. *Norman Maurice; or, The Man of the People. An American Dream*. Charleston, SC: Walker and Richards, 1852.

———. *The Partisan: A Romance of the Revolution*. New York: Redfield, 1854.

———. *The Partisan: A Tale of the Revolution*. 2 vols. New York: Harper and Brothers, 1835.

———. *Pelayo: A Story of the Goth*. New York: Harper & Brothers, 1838.

———. "Personal Memorabilia," Charles Carroll Simms Collection, South Caroliniana Library, University of South Carolina.

———. *Poems Descriptive, Dramatic, Legendary and Contemplative*. 2 vols. New York: Redfield, 1853.

———. *Poems Descriptive, Dramatic, Legendary and Contemplative*. 2 vols. 1853. *Romantic Tradition in American Literature*. Ed. Harold Bloom. New York: Arno Press, 1972.

———. *Poetry and the Practical*. Ed. James Everett Kibler. Fayetteville: U of Arkansas P, 1996.

———. "Rawlins' Rookery or the House of Eld and Glamour, A Biography, a Budget, and a 'What Not," Charles Carroll Simms Collection, South Caroliniana Library, University of South Carolina.

———. *The Remains of Maynard Davis Richardson, with a Memoir of His Life. By His Friend*. Charleston: O.A. Roorback. Printed by J.S. Burges, 1833.

———. Rev. of *Julius Caesar*. By William Shakespeare. *Charleston City Gazette* (26–27 Feb. 1830).

———. *Richard Hurdis. A Tale of Alabama*. New York: Redfield, 1855.

———. *Richard Hurdis; or, The Avenger of Blood. A Tale of Alabama*. Philadelphia: E.L. Carey & A. Hart, 1838.

[———]. *Sack and Destruction of the City of Columbia, S.C.* Columbia, SC: Power Press of the Daily Phoenix, 1865.

———. *The Sack and Destruction of Columbia, South Carolina*. 2d ed. Reprinted. Wiggins, MS [Dahlonega, GA]: Crown Rights Book Company, [2000].

———. *The Sack and Destruction of Columbia, South Carolina*. 2d ed. Reprinted. Clearwater, SC: Eastern Digital Resources, [2000].

———. *Sack and Destruction of the City of Columbia, S.C.* Ed. A.S. Salley. 2d. ed. Atlanta: Oglethorpe UP, 1937.

———. *Sack and Destruction of the City of Columbia, S.C.* 2d ed. Reprinted. Freeport, NY: Books for Libraries Press [Ayer Company Publishers], [1971].

———. *The Scout: or, The Black Riders of Congaree*. Rev. ed. of *The Kinsmen*. New York: Redfield, 1854.

———. *Self-Development. An Oration Delivered before the Literary Societies of Oglethorpe University; Georgia; November 10, 1847*. Milledgeville: Thalian Society, 1847.

———. *The Sense of the Beautiful. An Address*. Charleston: Charleston County Agricultural and Horticultural Association, 1870.

———. *Simms's Poems Aerytos or Songs and Ballads of the South with Other Poems*. Charleston: Russell & Jones, 1860.

———. *Slavery in America; Being a Brief Review of Miss Martineau on that Subject*. Richmond: Thomas W. White, 1838.

———. *The Social Principle: The True Source of National Permanence*. Tuscaloosa: The Erosophic Society of the U of Alabama, 1843.

———. *South-Carolina in the Revolutionary War: Being a Reply to Certain Misrepresentations and Mistakes of Recent Writers, in Relation to the Course and Conduct of This State*. Charleston: Walker and Evans, 1853.

———. "South Carolina in the Revolution. The Social Moral." Unpublished lecture. Charles Carroll Simms Collection, South Caroliniana Library, University of South Carolina, Columbia.

———. "South Carolina in the Revolution." *Southern Quarterly Review* (July 1848): 37–77.

———. "The Southern Convention." *Southern Quarterly Review* 2.2 (1850): 191–232.

———. *Southward Ho! A Spell of Sunshine*. New York: Redfield, 1854.

———. *Stories and Tales*. Vol. 5 of *The Writings of William Gilmore Simms*. Ed. John Caldwell Guilds. Centennial Edition. Columbia: U of South Carolina P, 1974.

———, ed. *A Supplement to the Plays of William Shakespeare*. New York: George F. Cooledge & Brother, 1848.

———. *The Sword and the Distaff; or, "Fair, Fat and Forty," A Story of the South at the Close of the Revolution*. Charleston, SC: Walker, Richards, and Co., 1852.

———. "Thoughts on Theatricals." *Southern Patriot* (19–21 Aug. 1846).

[———.] "To the Public." *The City Gazette and Commercial Daily Advertiser* [Charleston, SC] (19 Nov. 1831): 2.

———. *The Tri-Color; or, the Three Days of Blood in Paris. With Some Other Pieces*. London: Wigfall and Davis, Strand, 1830.

———. "Tuckerman's Essays and Essayists." *Southern Quarterly Review* 1.2 (1850): 370–406.

——— [Frank Cooper]. *Vasconselos: A Romance of the New World*. Chicago: Bedford, Clark, 1882.

——— [Frank Cooper]. *Vasconselos. A Romance of the New World*. New York: Redfield, 1853.

———. *Views and Reviews in American Literature, History and Fiction*. 1st ser. New York: Wiley and Putnam, 1845 [1846].

———. *Views and Reviews in American Literature, History and Fiction. 2nd ser*. New York: Wiley and Putnam, 1845 [1847].

———. *Views and Reviews in American Literature, History and Fiction*. First Series. Ed. C. Hugh Holman. Cambridge, MA: The Belknap P of Harvard UP, 1962.

———. *The Vision of Cortes, Cain, and Other Poems*. Charleston, SC: James S. Burges, 1829.

———. *War Poetry of the South*. New York: Richardson, 1866.

———. *The Wigwam and the Cabin*. 1st and *2nd* ser. New York: Wiley and Putnam, 1845 [1846].

———. *The Wigwam and the Cabin*. New and rev. ed. New York: Redfield, 1856.

———. *Woodcraft; or, Hawks about the Dovecote: A Story of the South at the Close of the Revolution*. New York: Redfield, 1854.

———. *The Yemassee. A Romance of Carolina*. 2 vols. New York: Harper and Brothers, 1835.

———. *The Yemassee: A Romance of Carolina*. New and rev. ed. New York: Redfield, 1853.

"Simms's *Father Abbot, &c.*" *The Literary World* 6.156 (26 Jan. 1850): 80–81.

"Simms's Golden Christmas." *The Literary World* 10 (20 Mar. 1852): 206.

Simpson, Lewis P. *The Dispossessed Garden: Pastoral and History in Southern Literature*. Athens: U of Georgia P, 1975.

Smith, Mark M. *Mastered by the Clock: Time, Slavery, and Freedom in the American South*. Chapel Hill: U of North Carolina P, 1997.

Smith, Samuel C. "'That Feel and Touch of the Elbow': Simms and the Whig Interpretation of History." *The Simms Review* 16.1 (2008): 23–31.

Smith, Steven D. "Imagining the Swamp Fox: William Gilmore Simms and the National Memory of Francis Marion." *William Gilmore Simms's Unfinished Civil War: Consequences for a Southern Man of Letters*. Ed. David Moltke-Hansen. Columbia: U of South Carolina P, 2013. 32–47.

———. Introduction. *Traditions of the Swamp Fox: William Boddie's Francis Marion*. By William W. Boddie. Spartanburg, SC: The Reprint Company, 2000. xi–xliv.

"Southern Publications." *DeBow's Review* 13.2 (Aug. 1852): 211.

Speiser, Mathew. "Origins of the Lost Cause: The Continuity of Regional Celebration in the White South, 1850–1872." *Essays in History* 2009. www.essaysinhistory.com/articles/2011/6 (12 Dec. 2013).

Stafford, John. *The Literary Criticism of "Young America": A Study in the Relationship of Politics and Literature, 1837–1850*. Berkeley and Los Angeles: U of California P, 1952.

State Records of North Carolina. Ed. Walter Clark, *The State Records of North Carolina, Volume 14*. Goldsboro, NC: Nash Brothers, 1907.

Stavely, William. *American Military Biography, Containing the Lives and Characters of the Officers of the Revolution*. Philadelphia: William Stavely Publisher, 1831.

Stovall, Rayburn Clifton. *Francis Marion: 1780–1782*. MA thesis. Morehead State U, 1971.

Strauss, Jennifer. "Anthologies and Orthodoxies." *Australian Literary Studies* 13.1 (1987): 87–95.

A Supplement to the Plays of William Shakespeare. Ed. William Gilmore Simms. Advertisement. *Literary World* 3.62 (8 Apr. 1848): 193.

Talbert, Roy Jr. and Meggan A. Farish. *The Journal of Peter Horry South Carolinian*. Columbia: U of South Carolina P, 2012.

Taylor, Jenny Bourne. "Structure of Feeling." *A Dictionary of Cultural and Critical Theory*. Ed. Michael Payne and Jessica Rae Barbera. 2nd ed. Oxford, UK: Wiley-Blackwell, 2010.

Taylor, William R. *Cavalier and Yankee: The Old South and American National Character*. New York: Oxford UP, 1993.

———. *Cavalier and Yankee: The Old South and American National Character*. Cambridge: Harvard UP, 1961.

Thomas, J. Wesley. "German Literature in the Old South." *The American-German Review* 19 (1952): 8–30.

———. "The German Sources of William Gilmore Simms." *Anglo-German and American-German Crosscurrents* 1 (1957): 127–53.

———. "William Gilmore Simms' 'Helen Halsey' as the Source for Friedrich Gerstacker's 'Germelshausen.'" *Monatshefte* 45 (1951): 141–44.

Thompson, G.R. *Poe's Fiction: Romantic Irony in the Gothic Tales*. Madison: U of Wisconsin P, 1973.

Tierney, John J., Jr. *Chasing Ghosts: Unconventional Warfare in American History*. Washington DC: Potomac Books, 2006.

Tocqueville, Alexis de. *Democracy in America*. Vol. 2. New York: Vintage Books, 1945.

Trent, William Peterfield. *William Gilmore Simms*. Boston: Houghton Mifflin, 1892.

Tucker, Robert Cinnamond. "James Henry Hammond, South Carolinian." Diss. U of North Carolina, 1958.

Tuveson, Ernest Lee. *Redeemer Nation: The Idea of America's Millenial Role*. Chicago: U of Chicago P, 1968.

Vandiver, Ernest P., Jr. "Simms's Border Romances and the British Dramatists." *PMLA* 65.4 (June 1950): 346–59.

———. "Simms's Border Romances and Shakespeare." *Shakespeare Quarterly* 5.2 (1954): 129–39.

[Verazzano, John de]. "The Voyage of John de Verazzano a Florentine to the Coast of Florida, Sailing from Thence Northerly to the Latitude of 50. Degrees, Anno 1524." *The Principal Navigations Voyages Traffiques and Discoveries of the English Nation*. By Richard Hakluyt. Vol. 8. 12 vols. Glasgow: James MacLehoge and Sons, 1903–05. 423–38.

Verdier, Antoine du. *La Prosopographie au Description de Personnes Insignes*. Lyon: Antoine Gryphius, 1573.

Vernier, Richard. *The Flower of Chivalry: Bertrand du Guesclin and the Hundred Years War*. Woodbridge, Suffolk, England, UK, 2003.

Wakelyn, Jon L. *The Politics of a Literary Man: William Gilmore Simms*. Westport, CT: Greenwood P, 1973.

Wallace, David Duncan. *South Carolina: A Short History, 1520–1948*. Chapel Hill: U of North Carolina P, 1951.

Wates, Wylma Anne. "Meanderings of a Manuscript: General Peter Horry's Collection of Francis Marion Letters." *South Carolina Historical Magazine* 81.4 (1980): 352–61.

Watson, Charles S. *Antebellum Charleston Dramatists*. Tuscaloosa: U of Alabama P, 1976.

———. "De Soto's Expedition: Contrasting Treatments in Pickett's *History of Alabama* and Simms's *Vasconselos*." *The Alabama Review* 31 (July 1978): 199–208.

———. *From Nationalism to Secessionism: The Changing Fiction of William Gilmore Simms*. Westport, CT: Greenwood P, 1993.

———. Introduction. *Woodcraft*. By William Gilmore Simms. New Haven: New College and UP, 1983. 9–27.

———. "Simms and the American Revolution." *Mississippi Quarterly* 29 (1976): 76–89.

———. "Simms's Answer to *Uncle Tom's Cabin*: Criticism of the South in *Woodcraft*." *Southern Literary Journal* 9.1 (1976): 78–90.

———. "Simms's Use of Shakespearean Characters." *Shakespeare and Southern Writers: A Study in Influence*. Ed. Philip C. Kolin. Jackson: UP of Mississippi, 1985. 13–28.

Weems, Mason Locke. *The Life of Gen. Francis Marion, a Celebrated Partizan Officer in the Revolutionary War, Against the British and Tories, in South-Carolina and Georgia, by Brigadier General P. Horry*. Philadelphia: Mathew Carey, 1809.

Weidman, Bette S. "White Men's Red Man: A Penitential Reading of Four American Novels." *Modern Language Studies* 4.2 (1974): 14–26.

Weir, Robert M. *Colonial South Carolina: A History*. Millwood, NY: KTO P, 1983.

Weller, Jac. "Irregular but Effective: Partisan Warfare and Tactics in the American Revolution Southern Theater." *Military Analysis of the Revolutionary War: An Anthology by the Editors of Military Affairs*. Millwood, NY: KTO P, 1977. 131–44.

Werner, Craig. "The Old South, 1815–1840." *The History of Southern Literature*. Ed. Louis D. Rubin, Jr. *et al*. Baton Rouge: Louisiana State UP, 1985. 81–91.

West, Elliott. "The American Frontier: Romance and Reality." *William Gilmore Simms and the American Frontier*. Ed. John Caldwell Guilds and Caroline Collins. Athens: U Georgia P, 1997. 27–43.

West, James L.W. III. "William Gilmore Simms and the Postwar Literary Marketplace." *The Simms Review* 18.1–2 (2010): 5–14.

Westfall, Alfred Van Rensselaer. *American Shakespeare Criticism*. New York: H.W. Wilson Co., 1939.

Whaley, Grace Wine. "A Note on Simms's Novels." *American Literature* 2.2 (May 1930): 173–74.

White, William B., Jr. *The Ross-Chesnut-Sutton Family of South Carolina*. Franklin, NC: Privately printed, 2002.

Widmer, Edward L. *Young America: The Flowering of Democracy in New York City*. New York: Oxford UP, 1999.

Wiles, A.G.D. "Sir Philip Sidney: The English Huguenot." *Transactions of the Huguenot Society of South Carolina* 45 (1940): 24–37.

Williams, Stanley T. "Spanish Influences on the Fiction of William Gilmore Simms." *Hispanic Review* 21.3 (July 1953): 221–28.

Willis, N.P. "Literature." Rev. of *Southward Ho!. Putnam's Monthly* (Jan. 1855): 213.

Wilson, Clyde N. "Tiger's Meat: William Gilmore Simms and the History of the Revolution." *The Simms Review* 8.2 (2000): 22–31.

Wilson, Daniel H. *General Francis Marion: The Swamp Fox and Marine Corps Warfighting Doctrine*. MA thesis. Marine Corps Command and Staff College, 2001.

Wimsatt, Mary Ann. "The Evolution of Simms's Backwoods Humor." *"Long Years of Neglect": The Work and Reputation of William Gilmore Simms*. Ed. John C. Guilds. Fayetteville: U of Arkansas P, 1988. 148–65.

———. "Frontier Humor and the 'Arkansas Traveler' Motif in *Southward Ho!*" *William Gilmore Simms and the American Frontier*. Ed. John Caldwell Guilds and Caroline Collins. Athens: U of Georgia P, 1997. 147–64.

———. Introduction. *Tales of the South*. By William Gilmore Simms. Ed. Mary Ann Wimsatt. Columbia: U of south Carolina P, 1996.

———. "*Ivanhoe* and Simms's *Pelayo*." *Studies in Scottish Literature* 12.4 (1975): 250–69.

———. *The Major Fiction of William Gilmore Simms: Cultural Traditions and Literary Form*. Baton Rouge: Louisiana State UP, 1989.

———. "Realism and Romance in Simms's Midcentury Fiction." *Southern Literary Journal* 12.2 (1980): 29–48.

———. "Simms and Irving." *Mississippi Quarterly* 20.1 (1966–67): 25–37.

———. "Simms and Southwest Humor." *Studies in American Humor* 3 (Nov. 1979): 118–30.

Wordsworth, William. *William Wordsworth: The Major Works: Including the Prelude*. Oxford: Oxford UP, 2008.

Zagorin, Perez. *Thucydides: An Introduction for the Common Reader*. Princeton: Princeton UP, 2005.

Contributors

MATTHEW C. BRENNAN is the author of *The Poet's Holy Craft: William Gilmore Simms and Romantic Verse Tradition* (U. of South Carolina Press, 2010). He has also edited a special issue on Simms of *Studies in the Literary Imagination* (2009). His previous monographs are *Wordsworth, Turner, and Romantic Landscape* (1987) and *The Gothic Psyche* (1997).

SEAN BUSICK is an associate professor of history at Athens State University in Athens, Alabama. He earned his bachelor's degree from Purdue University and his M.A. and Ph.D. from the University of South Carolina.

KEVIN COLLINS has researched Simms as the Diane C. Blair Fellow for Southern Studies at the University of Arkansas, as the William Gilmore Simms Visiting Research Professor at the University of South Carolina, and at the University of Notre Dame. He has produced fifteen published studies of Simms in university press books and in refereed journals. In 2016, he received the Bernhardt Academic Excellence Award, recognizing him as the outstanding faculty member at Southwestern Oklahoma State University in terms of teaching, scholarship, and service.

BRIAN FENNESSY is a Ph.D. student in the history department at the University of North Carolina at Chapel Hill. His primary field is the nineteenth-century South, and he has previously published "Master of an Interior World: Masculinity, Sensibility, and William Gilmore Simms" in *The Simms Review*.

EHREN FOLEY is staff historian at the South Carolina State Historic Preservation Office. His work on Simms includes contributions to *William Gilmore Simms's Unfinished Civil War* (2012), *William Gilmore Simms's Selected Reviews on Literature and Civilization* (2014), and *The Simms Review*. He received his Ph.D. in history from the University of South Carolina.

TODD HAGSTETTE is an assistant professor of English at the University of South Carolina Aiken, the editor of *The Simms Review*, and the former director of the *Simms Initiatives*. His past work on Simms has focused on the author's Gothic work and on his Civil War writings, including essays on honor and on the burning of Columbia, South Carolina.

COLEMAN HUTCHISON is an associate professor of English at the University of Texas at Austin, where he teaches courses in nineteenth-century U.S. literature and culture. He is the author of *Apples and Ashes: Literature, Nationalism, and the Confederate States of America* (2012), which offers the first literary history of the Civil War South.

JASON W. JOHNSON received a B.A. in English from UNC–Chapel Hill and an M.A. and Ph.D. in English from the University of Mississippi. Johnson is an instructor of English and humanities at Guilford Technical Community College in Jamestown, N.C. Aside from his research in nineteenth-century Anglophone poetry and poetics, Johnson is also a practicing poet.

JAMES EVERETT KIBLER has published or edited seven volumes on Simms, the most recent of which is *William Gilmore Simms's Selected Reviews on Literature and Civilization* (with David Moltke-Hansen). He is the founding editor of *The Simms Review* and a recipient of the Fellowship of Southern Writers Award for Nonfiction for *Our Fathers' Fields*.

SAM LACKEY is a third-year Ph.D. student at the University of South Carolina, where he is studying nineteenth-century American literature with a focus on the development of US crime fiction. He is the secretary-treasurer of the Simms Society, was a research associate with the *Simms Initiatives*, has published multiple essays in *The Simms Review*, and has presented his scholarship at the last three society conferences.

JOHN M. MCCARDELL, JR. is vice-chancellor of the University of the South and president emeritus of Middlebury College. His book *The Idea of a Southern Nation* won the Allan Nevins Prize. A 1971 graduate of Washington and Lee University, he received his Ph.D. in history from Harvard in 1976. He has written numerous essays and reviews on Simms, including "Trent's *Simms*: The Making of a Biography."

NICHOLAS G. MERIWETHER received his A.B. from Princeton and his M.L.I.S. from the University of South Carolina, where he was the first oral historian at the South Caroliniana Library. While there he originated and coauthored the grant that created the *Simms Initiatives*. His work on Simms has appeared in *Studies in the Literary Imagination*, *The Simms Review*, *"Long Years of Neglect": The Work and Reputation of William Gilmore Simms* (1988), and *William Gilmore Simms's Unfinished Civil War* (2013), and he coedited *Pirates and Devils: William Gilmore Simms's Unfinished Postbellum Novels*, published by the University of South Carolina Press in 2015. He is director of the Center for Counterculture Studies in California.

JOHN D. MILLER is an assistant professor of English at Longwood University in Virginia, where he teaches early American and southern literature. He is the author of several articles on antebellum writers and the editor of "'Honorable and Brilliant Labors': The Collected Addresses of William Gilmore Simms," forthcoming from the University of South Carolina Press.

DAVID MOLTKE-HANSEN spent thirty years developing historical collections and programs before turning to full-time writing and editing. Author of fifty-plus essays and editor of nine volumes, primarily on aspects of southern intellectual and cultural history, including Simms, he helped launch the *Simms*

Initiatives at the University of South Carolina and served as founding coeditor of Cambridge Studies on the American South from 2009–2016.

ALEXANDER MOORE is a historian of the American South who specializes in publishing documentary editions of historical texts. He was an editor of *The Papers of John C. Calhoun*, published by the University of South Carolina Press. In 2013 he edited a revised, expanded edition of *The Letters of William Gilmore Simms*.

NAN MORRISON is emerita professor of English at the College of Charleston. Over the span of a thirty-five-year academic career, her teaching and research interests centered on Shakespeare and southern literature.

MICHAEL ODOM is an assistant professor of English at Borough of Manhattan Community College in the City University of New York. He has published articles in the *Southern Literary Journal*, *Flannery O'Connor Review*, and *The Simms Review*.

CAREY M. ROBERTS is the associate dean and chair of history at Liberty University. He serves on the board of the Abbeville Institute and on the editorial board of *Anamnesis: A Journal for the Study of Tradition, Place, and 'Things Divine.'* His most recent work is *Patrick Henry-Onslow Debate: Liberty and Republicanism in American Political Thought*, edited with H. Lee Cheek and Sean R. Busick.

JEFFERY J. ROGERS is professor of history at Gordon State College in Barnesville, Georgia. His scholarly interests center on the early American republic and southern intellectual and cultural history. He has written and lectured widely on the life and work of William Gilmore Simms and is a past president of the William Gilmore Simms Society.

DAVID S. SHIELDS is Carolina Distinguished Professor in the Department of English at the University of South Carolina. He is the author of half a dozen books, countless articles, and several digital projects on various topics related to early American literature, southern studies, photography, and traditional foodways.

W. MATTHEW J. SIMMONS is project coordinator of the Digital U.S. South Initiative of the Institute for Southern Studies at the University of South Carolina. From 2012 to 2014, he worked for USC's *Simms Initiatives*, where he served as assistant director. He is also currently working on a project involving both versions of Simms's account of the burning of Columbia, S.C., in the waning days of the Civil War.

ABIGAIL LUNDELIUS SMITH earned her Ph.D. in English from the University of South Carolina in 2011. Her work focuses on the significance of tables in the literature and material culture of the South. A native of Texas, she was drawn to Simms's dramatic works by *Michael Bonham*, the author's border drama of the Alamo.

STEVEN D. SMITH is the director of the South Carolina Institute of Archaeology and Anthropology, College of Arts and Sciences, University of South Carolina. He has written extensively on Francis Marion, including how our modern memory of Marion has been shaped by William Gilmore Simms.

JILLIAN WEBER is a Ph.D. candidate in nineteenth-century American literature at the University of South Carolina. She worked as a research associate with the *Simms Initiatives*.

Index

Page numbers given in bold type indicate the location of the reproduction of a Simms piece as opposed to discussion or mention of it elsewhere.

www.ingramcontent.com/pod-product-compliance
Lightning Source LLC
LaVergne TN
LVHW050146080826
844660LV00002B/90

* 9 7 8 1 6 1 1 1 7 7 7 2 5 *